JOURNAL FOR THE STUDY OF THE OLD TESTAMENT SUPPLEMENT SERIES
372

Sheffield Academic Press
A Continuum imprint

A Prophet in Debate

The Rhetoric of Persuasion in the Book of Amos

Karl Möller

Journal for the Study of the Old Testament
Supplement Series 372

Copyright © 2003 Sheffield Academic Press
A Continuum imprint

Published by Sheffield Academic Press Ltd
The Tower Building, 11 York Road, London SE1 7NX
370 Lexington Avenue, New York NY 10017-6550

www.continuumbooks.com

British Library Cataloguing-in-Publication Data
A catalogue record for this book is available from the British Library

Typeset by Sheffield Academic Press
Printed on acid-free paper in Great Britain by Bookcraft Ltd, Midsomer Norton, Bath

ISBN 0-8264-6568-4

CONTENTS

LIST OF FIGURES

ACKNOWLEDGMENTS

The writing of this study could not have been done without the support of a number of people, some of whom were more or less directly involved in the project. Others were important to me precisely because they had no part in it and, due to their limited interest in Old Testament prophecy and issues of hermeneutics and interpretation, afforded me some welcome distractions. I should stress, however, that by singling out some, I do not intend to depreciate the contribution and support of those who must remain unnamed.

First, I would like to express my gratitude to Professor Gordon J. Wenham and Professor John Barton, whose generous help and support, together with their great expertise, were of immeasurable value to me. I am also grateful to the University of Gloucestershire and, in particular, the Theology and Religious Studies department for giving me the opportunity to pursue my interest in Amos and for providing some of the necessary funding. My friends and colleagues in the Biblical Studies Seminar deserve special mention because, in many a talk and discussion, they have helped me disentangle my often confused thoughts as well as develop what at first were merely vague hunches and unlikely ideas.

Most of all, however, I would like to thank my wife Maja, who has been a constant source of help, support and encouragement. Her contribution has been vital, especially on those days when I myself, like some of my friends mentioned earlier, had a rather limited interest in Old Testament prophecy and issues of hermeneutics and interpretation. Finally, I must mention our children Tobias and Sarah, who, while not exactly speeding up my work, have made life so much more enjoyable.

Karl Möller
Cheltenham, February 2002

ABBREVIATIONS

AB	Anchor Bible
ABD	D.N. Freedman (ed.), *The Anchor Bible Dictionary* (6 vols.; New York: Doubleday, 1992)
AGJU	Arbeiten zur Geschichte des antiken Judentums und des Urchristentums
AnBib	Analecta biblica
ANET	J.B. Pritchard (ed.), *Ancient Near Eastern Texts Relating to the Old Testament* (Princeton: Princeton University Press, 3rd edn, 1969)
AnOr	Analecta orientalia
AOAT	Alter Orient und Altes Testament
ATANT	Abhandlungen zur Theologie des Alten und Neuen Testaments
ATD	Das Alte Testament Deutsch
ATLA	American Theological Library Association
AUMSR	Andrews University Monograph Studies in Religion
AusBR	*Australian Biblical Review*
AUSS	*Andrews University Seminary Studies*
BARev	*Biblical Archaeology Review*
BASOR	*Bulletin of the American Schools of Oriental Research*
BBB	Bonner biblische Beiträge
BBET	Beiträge zur biblischen Exegese und Theologie
BBR	*Bulletin for Biblical Research*
BDB	F. Brown, S.R. Driver and C.A. Briggs, *A Hebrew and English Lexicon of the Old Testament* (Oxford: Clarendon Press, corr. edn, 1952)
BEATAJ	Beiträge zur Erforschung des Alten Testaments und des Antiken Judentums
BETL	Bibliotheca ephemeridum theologicarum lovaniensium
BEvT	Beiträge zur evangelischen Theologie
BFCT	Beiträge zur Förderung christlicher Theologie
BHH	B. Reike and L. Rost (eds.), *Biblisch-historisches Handwörterbuch* (4 vols.; Göttingen: Vandenhoeck & Ruprecht, 1962–79)
BHS	*Biblia hebraica stuttgartensia*
Bib	*Biblica*

BibInt	*Biblical Interpretation: A Journal of Contemporary Approaches*
BibSem	The Biblical Seminar
BIS	Biblical Interpretation Series
BKAT	Biblischer Kommentar: Altes Testament
BLS	Bible and Literature Series
BN	*Biblische Notizen*
BRT	*The Baptist Review of Theology*
BSac	*Bibliotheca Sacra*
BT	*The Bible Translator*
BTB	*Biblical Theology Bulletin*
BWANT	Beiträge zur Wissenschaft vom Alten und Neuen Testament
BZ NS	*Biblische Zeitschrift*
BZAW	Beihefte zur *ZAW*
CAT	Commentaire de l'Ancien Testament
CBQ	*Catholic Biblical Quarterly*
ConBNT	Coniectanea biblica, New Testament
COT	*Commentary on the Old Testament*
CRBS	*Currents in Research: Biblical Studies*
CTM	*Concordia Theological Monthly*
DCH	D.J.A. Clines (ed.), *The Dictionary of Classical Hebrew* (Sheffield: Sheffield Academic Press, 1993–)
EBib	Etudes bibliques
EdF	Erträge der Forschung
EuroJT	*European Journal of Theology*
EvT	*Evangelische Theologie*
ExpTim	*Expository Times*
FAT	Forschungen zum Alten Testament
FCB	The Feminist Companion to the Bible
FOTL	The Forms of the Old Testament Literature
FRLANT	Forschungen zur Religion und Literatur des Alten und Neuen Testaments
FzB	Forschung zur Bibel
GB	W. Gesenius, *Hebräisches und aramäisches Handwörterbuch über das Alte Testament* (ed. F. Buhl *et al.*; Berlin: Springer-Verlag, 17th edn, 1915)
GBS	Guides to Biblical Scholarship
GK	W. Gesenius, *Hebräische Grammatik* (ed. E. Kautzsch; Leipzig, 28th rev. edn, 1909; repr., Darmstadt: Wissenschaftliche Buchgesellschaft, 1985)
GMD	W. Gesenius, *Hebräisches und aramäisches Handwörterbuch über das Alte Testament* (ed. R. Meyer and W. Donner; Heidelberg: Springer-Verlag, 18th edn, 1987–)
HALAT	L. Koehler *et al.* (eds.), *Hebräisches und aramäisches Lexikon zum Alten Testament* (5 vols.; Leiden: E.J. Brill, 1967–95)

HAR	*Hebrew Annual Review*
HAT	Handbuch zum Alten Testament
HAW	G. Fohrer *et al.* (eds.), *Hebräisches und aramäisches Wörterbuch zum Alten Testament* (Berlin: W. de Gruyter, 2nd rev. edn, 1989)
HBT	*Horizons in Biblical Theology*
HDR	Harvard Dissertations in Religion
HKAT	Handkommentar zum Alten Testament
HSAT	Die heilige Schrift des Alten Testaments
HTR	*Harvard Theological Review*
HUCA	*Hebrew Union College Annual*
IB	*Interpreter's Bible*
ICC	International Critical Commentary
IDB	G.A. Buttrick (ed.), *The Interpreter's Dictionary of the Bible* (4 vols.; Nashville: Abingdon Press, 1962)
IEJ	*Israel Exploration Journal*
Int	*Interpretation*
ISBE	G.W. Bromiley (ed.), *The International Standard Bible Encyclopedia* (4 vols.; Grand Rapids: Eerdmans, rev. edn, 1979–88)
ITC	International Theological Commentary
JAOS	*Journal of the American Oriental Society*
JBL	*Journal of Biblical Literature*
JETh	*Jahrbuch für evangelikale Theologie*
JETS	*Journal of the Evangelical Theological Society*
JM	P. Joüon, *A Grammar of Biblical Hebrew* (trans. and rev. T. Muraoka; SubBib, 14; 2 vols.; Rome: Editrice Pontificio Istituto Biblico, 1991)
JNES	*Journal of Near Eastern Studies*
JOTT	*Journal of Translation and Textlinguistics*
JQRSup	*Jewish Quarterly Review*, Supplements
JSNTSup	*Journal for the Study of the New Testament*, Supplement Series
JSOT	*Journal for the Study of the Old Testament*
JSOTSup	*Journal for the Study of the Old Testament*, Supplement Series
JSS	*Journal of Semitic Studies*
JTS	*Journal of Theological Studies*
KAI	H. Donner and W. Röllig, *Kanaanäische und aramäische Inschriften* (3 vols.; Wiesbaden: Harrassowitz, 1962–64)
KAT	Kommentar zum Alten Testament
KB	L. Koehler and W. Baumgartner (eds.), *Lexicon in Veteris Testamenti libros* (Leiden: E.J. Brill, 2nd edn, 1958)
KD	*Kerygma und Dogma*
KHAT	Kurzer Hand-Kommentar zum Alten Testament
KJV	King James Version

KST	Kohlhammer Studienbücher Theologie
KT	Koren Tenakh
LB	*Linguistica biblica*
LBI	Library of Biblical Interpretation
LCL	Loeb Classical Library
MVAG	Mitteilungen der vorderasiatisch-ägyptischen Gesellschaft
NASB	*New American Standard Bible*
NCB	New Century Bible
NEB	*New English Bible*
NIB	*New Interpreter's Bible*
NIBC	New International Bible Commentary
NICOT	New International Commentary on the Old Testament
NIDOTTE	W.A. VanGemeren (ed.), *New International Dictionary of Old Testament Theology and Exegesis* (5 vols.; Grand Rapids: Zondervan, 1997)
NIV	New International Version
NJPSV	New Jewish Publication Society Version
NovTSup	*Novum Testamentum*, Supplements
NRSV	New Revised Standard Version
NTS	*New Testament Studies*
NZSTR	*Neue Zeitschrift für systematische Theologie und Religionsphilosophie*
OBO	Orbis biblicus et orientalis
OBS	Oxford Bible Series
OPTAT	*Occasional Papers in Translation and Textlinguistics*
OrAnt	*Oriens antiquus*
OTE	*Old Testament Essays*
OTG	Old Testament Guides
OTL	Old Testament Library
OTS	*Oudtestamentische Studiën*
OTWSA	Ou Testamentiese Werkgemeenskap in Suid-Afrika
PAAJR	*Proceedings of the American Academy of Jewish Research*
PSB	*Princeton Seminary Bulletin*
PTMS	Pittsburgh Theological Monograph Series
QJS	*The Quarterly Journal of Speech*
RB	*Revue biblique*
RevExp	*Review and Expositor*
RGG	K. Galling (ed.), *Die Religion in Geschichte und Gegenwart: Handwörterbuch für Theologie und Religionswissenschaft* (Tübingen: J.C.B. Mohr [Paul Siebeck], 3rd edn, 1957)
RhétBib	Rhétorique biblique
SAT	Die Schriften des Alten Testaments
SBL	Society of Biblical Literature
SBLASP	SBL Abstracts and Seminar Papers
SBLDS	SBL Dissertation Series

SBLRBS	SBL Resources for Biblical Study
SBS	Stuttgarter Bibelstudien
SBT	Studies in Biblical Theology
SBTS	Sources for Biblical and Theological Study
ScEs	*Science et esprit*
ScrB	*Scripture Bulletin*
SEÅ	*Svensk exegetisk årsbok*
SHS	Scripture and Hermeneutics Series
SIL	Summer Institute of Linguistics
SJT	*Scottish Journal of Theology*
SOTBT	Studies in Old Testament Biblical Theology
SNTSMS	Society for New Testament Studies Monograph Series
SR	*Studies in Religion/Sciences religieuses*
ST	*Studia theologica*
StSN	Studia Semitica Neerlandica
SubBib	Subsidia biblica
SWBA	The Social World of Biblical Antiquity
TBü	Theologische Bücherei
TDOT	G.J. Botterweck, H. Ringgren and H.-J. Fabry (eds.), *Theological Dictionary of the Old Testament* (Grand Rapids, MI: Eerdmans 1974–)
ThWAT	G.J. Botterweck and H. Ringgren (eds.), *Theologisches Wörterbuch zum Alten Testament* (Stuttgart: W. Kohlhammer, 1970–)
TLZ	*Theologische Literaturzeitung*
TOTC	Tyndale Old Testament Commentaries
TQ	*Theologische Quartalschrift*
TW	Theologische Wissenschaft
TWNT	G. Kittel and G. Friedrich (eds.), *Theologisches Wörterbuch zum Neuen Testament* (11 vols.; Stuttgart, Kohlhammer, 1932–79)
TSK	*Theologische Studien und Kritiken*
TynBul	*Tyndale Bulletin*
TZ	*Theologische Zeitschrift*
UBSHS	United Bible Society Handbook Series
UBSMS	United Bible Society Monograph Series
UF	*Ugarit-Forschungen*
UTB	Uni-Taschenbücher
VT	*Vetus Testamentum*
VTSup	*Vetus Testamentum*, Supplements
WBC	Word Biblical Commentary
WdF	Wege der Forschung
WMANT	Wissenschaftliche Monographien zum Alten und Neuen Testament
WO	*Die Welt des Orients*

WO'C	B.K. Waltke and M. O'Connor, *An Introduction to Biblical Hebrew Syntax* (Winona Lake, IN: Eisenbrauns, 1990)
WSPL	Warwick Studies in Philosophy and Literature
WuD	*Wort und Dienst*
WUNT	Wissenschaftliche Untersuchungen zum Neuen Testament
ZAH	*Zeitschrift für Althebraistik*
ZAW	*Zeitschrift für die alttestamentliche Wissenschaft*
ZDPV	*Zeitschrift des deutschen Palästina-Vereins*
ZTK	*Zeitschrift für Theologie und Kirche*

Part I

READING AMOS—A COMMUNICATION-THEORETICAL APPROACH

Introduction

AMOS AND THE RHETORIC OF PERSUASION

The title of the present study, *A Prophet in Debate*, has been chosen to reflect what I believe we encounter when reading the book of Amos. Indeed, I will argue that this encounter is precisely what those responsible for the book in its final shape were aiming for, as they sought to present to subsequent readers the debate between the prophet Amos and his eighth-century audience.

I was prompted to think of the book in terms of a presentation by the title of Ackroyd's paper, given at the 1977 IOSOT conference and subtitled 'Presentation of a Prophet'.[1] The addition 'in debate' is an essential modification of Ackroyd's title, reflecting the observation that the focus of the book of Amos is not on the prophet himself but on his words of accusation and judgment. These words, it is argued, are best understood not as a random collection of oracles but as a structured 'communication'.

In what follows, I seek to demonstrate that the presentation of the debating prophet is the primary rhetorical means employed by the book's authors or final redactors in order to achieve their communicative aims. Recent years have witnessed an increasing number of structural investigations, demonstrating a coherent structure for all, or at least for parts, of the book. Building upon and developing the insights advanced in these studies,[2] I intend to examine the communicative function of the *book* of Amos. The present study therefore applies a functional approach that proceeds within a communication-theoretical or socio-linguistic paradigm and works primarily along rhetorical-critical lines. My understanding of rhetorical criticism, its interpretative potential and the interpretative tasks it engenders will be outlined below. However, before we embark on these issues, it seems appropriate to utter a word of caution lest its potential be

---

1. The full title is P.R. Ackroyd, 'Isaiah I–XII: Presentation of a Prophet', in *Congress Volume, Göttingen 1977* (VTSup, 29; Leiden: E.J. Brill, 1978), pp. 16-48.
2. See Chapter 1 for further details.

overestimated, as is so often the case when a new interpretative route is advocated.

In his brief introduction to rhetorical criticism, Walton rightly stresses that the approach 'provides *an* interpretative key to texts, but not *the* interpretative key'.[3] Similarly, Stone maintains:

> interpretations sometimes fail to convince not because they make use of a 'bad' method, and not because of their 'bad' use of an otherwise helpful method, but rather because their reliance upon a single method, to the exclusion of questions highlighted by other methods, results in a focus that is too narrow.[4]

The same point has also been made by Barton who asserts:

> much harm has been done in biblical studies by insisting that there is, some-where, a 'correct' method which, if only we could find it, would unlock the mysteries of the text. From the quest for this method flow many evils: for example, the tendency of each newly-discovered method to excommunicate its predecessors...and the tendency to denigrate the 'ordinary' reader as 'non-critical'.[5]

Barton goes on to point out that 'the quest for a correct method is...incapable of succeeding'. This is because 'the pursuit of method assimilates reading a text to the procedures of technology: it tries to process the text, rather than to read it'.[6] I wholeheartedly agree with these sentiments and would like to point out therefore that my promotion of rhetorical criticism should not be understood as suggesting that this is *the* correct method for the interpretation of Amos. However, I do believe it to be a useful tool that allows us to focus on some important aspects that hitherto have been largely neglected.

The second part of this introductory chapter contains my own interpretation of rhetorical criticism, and outlines the methodological steps applied in the present study. Yet before we move on to these issues, I intend to contextualize my approach by comparing it to other interpretative models. By doing this, it is hoped that some of the distinctive features of the interpretative route taken here will come into focus. At the same time, the

---

3. S. Walton, 'Rhetorical Criticism: An Introduction', *Themelios* 21.2 (1996), pp. 4-9 (6; his italics).

4. K. Stone, 'Gender and Homosexuality in Judges 19: Subject—Honor, Object—Shame?', *JSOT* 67 (1995), pp. 87-107 (88).

5. J. Barton, *Reading the Old Testament: Method in Biblical Study* (London: Darton, Longman & Todd, 2nd edn, 1996), p. 5.

6. Barton, *Reading the Old Testament*, p. 5.

comparison is intended to highlight certain aspects that a rhetorical-critical approach has the potential to deal with and that other approaches failed to, or were insufficiently equipped to, address. The subsequent contextualization also includes a brief discussion of issues brought up by the current wave of reader-centred approaches, for example, the value of the author for the process of interpretation, or the issue of intentionality.

However, the focus of the following discussion is on redaction criticism and the reading(s) it has engendered. This is because redaction criticism, despite the enormous variety of interpretative models prevalent today, still is one of the dominant approaches, if not indeed *the* dominant approach, to the study of the Old Testament prophetic books. Another reason for focusing on the differences between (and similarities of) redaction criticism and rhetorical criticism is my sympathy for the former, which is occasioned by the fact that it takes the historicity of the biblical texts seriously. On the other hand, however, much redaction criticism is hampered by what I consider an unwarranted urge to produce ever more complicated (and often highly speculative) accounts of the genesis of the biblical books.

1. *Contextualizing Rhetorical Criticism*

The development of redaction criticism clearly advanced the study of the Old Testament by providing a more 'positive' outlook on the compositional and editorial work of the 'redactors'.[7] Thus, both Steck and Fohrer, for instance, insist that the negative classification of redactional editing as 'secondary' or 'inauthentic' should be abandoned.[8] Positively, the task of redaction criticism has been defined by Steck as follows:

> This approach traces the text's history from its first written form through its expansion, or relatedly commentary, by means of additions. It also traces a text's history through its incorporation into larger complexes all the way up

7. Introductions to the approach can be found in N. Perrin, *What is Redaction Criticism?* (GBS; Philadelphia: Fortress Press, 1970); K. Koch, *Was ist Form-geschichte? Methoden der Bibelexegese* (Neukirchen–Vluyn: Neukirchener Verlag, 3rd edn, 1974), §5; O.H. Steck, *Old Testament Exegesis: A Guide to the Methodology* (trans. J.D. Nogalski; SBLRBS, 39; Atlanta: Scholars Press, 2nd edn, 1998), §6 (cf. also the literature listed on pp. 92-93); G. Fohrer, 'Überlieferungskritik, Kompositions- und Redaktionskritik, Zeit- und Verfasserfrage', in G. Fohrer *et al.*, *Exegese des Alten Testaments*, pp. 119-50 (Fohrer actually differentiates between redaction criticism and composition criticism); and Barton, *Reading the Old Testament*, ch. 4.

8. Steck, *Old Testament Exegesis*, p. 80; and Fohrer, 'Überlieferungskritik', p. 141.

to its final version in the current literary context. This approach thereby *determines the operative historical factors and the intentions of the statements.*[9]

Of particular concern to me at this point is the redaction critics' interest in the historical factors that played a part in the genesis of the text and, most of all, their interest in the intentions of the redactors.[10] According to Barton, redaction critics are interested in 'analysing how the author/editor achieves his effects, *why* he arranges his material as he does, and above all what devices he uses to give unity and coherence to his work'.[11] Because of these concerns, some have pointed to a similarity between redaction criticism and rhetorical criticism. Kennedy, for instance, claims that 'redaction criticism might be viewed as a special form of rhetorical criticism which deals with texts where the hand of a redactor, or editor, can be detected',[12] and Barton notes:

> in a sense, rhetorical criticism is just redaction criticism by another name. But if so it is a distinctive way of looking at the possibilities of redaction criticism, which concentrates on the way the reader is pulled along through the text rather than on the text in its own right. Rhetorical criticism is interested in how writers or redactors do things to readers.[13]

Two observations are crucial at this point. First, Barton rightly observes that rhetorical criticism goes further than redaction criticism in its interest in 'how the reader is pulled along' and, even more importantly, how 'books have persuasive...force with their readers'.[14] Secondly, and this is an in-

---

9.   Steck, *Old Testament Exegesis*, p. 80 (my italics).

10.   Nogalski's translation obscures the fact that Steck had spoken of 'the operative historical factors and intentions' ('die hierin wirksamen geschichtlichen Faktoren und Aussageintentionen'; cf. O.H. Steck, *Exegese des Alten Testaments: Leitfaden der Methodik. Ein Arbeitsbuch für Proseminare, Seminare und Vorlesungen* [Neukirchen–Vluyn: Neukirchener Verlag, 12th edn, 1989], p. 80). That is to say, according to Steck the redaction-historical approach (he prefers this term to 'redaction criticism') is interested in how historical factors as well as *the redactors' intentions* have shaped the genesis of the text. This is implied in the German, which, if spelled out, would read 'die hierin wirksamen geschichtlichen Faktoren und Aussageintentionen [der Redaktoren]', i.e. 'the operative historical factors and intentions of [the redactors, which find expression in] the statements'.

11.   Barton, *Reading the Old Testament*, p. 52 (my italics).

12.   G.A. Kennedy, *New Testament Interpretation through Rhetorical Criticism* (Chapel Hill: University of North Carolina Press, 1984), p. 4.

13.   Barton, *Reading the Old Testament*, p. 200.

14.   Barton, *Reading the Old Testament*, p. 199. Cf. also M. Warner, 'Introduction',

teresting point, Barton also notes that rhetorical criticism 'is a kind of redaction criticism in which the disappearance of the redactor is welcomed'.[15]

Barton's notion of the disappearing redactor is a lucid way of pointing out the dilemma that redaction criticism faces. As Steck emphasized, the necessity of redaction-critical work lies in the texts' contradictory statements that are in need of a (diachronic) explanation.[16] The critic needs to explain how and why these inconsistencies and awkwardnesses came into the text. However, the better the critic succeeds

> in showing that the redactor has, by subtle and delicate artistry, produced a simple and coherent text out of the diverse materials before him; the more also he reduces the evidence on which the existence of those sources was established in the first place.[17]

Furthermore, although Barton thinks that redaction criticism is, in principle, 'a perfectly reasonable approach' that can be illuminating in some instances, he adds:

> *more often than not* it is either unnecessary, because the text is a unity anyway, and we are competent to read it, or unsuccessful, because the inconsistencies that remain, the very inconsistencies that enable us to know the text is a redacted one, are such that we remain in doubt as to how it should be read in its finished form.[18]

in *idem* (ed.), *The Bible as Rhetoric*, pp. 1-25 (4), who points out concerning the redaction-critical undertaking that 'in practice attention is paid less to the editors' persuasive concerns than to their theological preoccupations and the circumstances of the communities in which they lived'. It should be noted furthermore that Barton's portrayal of rhetorical criticism, despite his allusion to the suasive dimension, more or less equates the approach with an interest in aesthetics or stylistics. This is most obvious in his reference to inclusios and chiasms as features that, in his perception, are of prime interest to the rhetorical critic. To be sure, this is an adequate portrayal of rhetorical criticism as it has been practised by most Old Testament rhetorical critics. In the present study, however, the suasive aspect and its implications for the interpretation of the text play a much more prominent role.

15. Barton, *Reading the Old Testament*, p. 203.

16. Steck, *Old Testament Exegesis*, p. 79.

17. Barton, *Reading the Old Testament*, p. 57. Cf. E. Ben Zvi, *A Historical-Critical Study of the Book of Obadiah* (BZAW, 242; Berlin: W. de Gruyter, 1996), p. 7 n. 12, who, in similar vein, points out that 'the more sophisticated these authors/redactors were, and the more they tended to communicate or express more than one perspective on a single issue, or the more that they tended to present a vision that results out of a set of contrasting perspectives, and the more ambiguous they were, then the more hopeless, from a critical point of view, this work of reconstruction becomes'.

18. Barton, *Reading the Old Testament*, p. 58 (my italics).

Sternberg consequently rightly cautions that:

> the task of decomposition calls for the most sensitive response to the arts of composition. How else will one be able to tell deliberate from accidental roughness and identify the marks of disunity in unity throughout a text whose *poesis* covers the tracks of its *genesis*?[19]

Even a cursory glance at the reception history of the book of Amos illustrates how problematic this 'task of decomposition' is. Difficulties already abound when it comes to establishing whether or not a specific text is a unity in the first place. Is the book of Amos a 'rolling corpus' that 'rolled' over a long period of time thereby acquiring, like a snowball rolling downhill, new material on the way?[20] Or, to cite the other extreme, has it been penned by a single author, possibly even Amos himself?[21] Moreover, the crucial question arises as to how, on the basis of which (or whose) criteria that is, a text's condition can be assessed most adequately. Whose impressions are correct? Are those scholars in the right who claim to have stumbled over inconsistencies that call for a diachronic solution? Or are those correct who come up with textual unities that render diachronic explanations unnecessary? The difficulty of deciding this issue is illustrated by Barton's remark, who, while stressing the potential rhetorical criticism has for enabling fresh and illuminating interpretations,[22] nevertheless criticizes its practitioners:

> because they can nearly always 'demonstrate' a rhetorical structure in any given text and so invalidate historical-critical arguments based on its apparent (or evident) formlessness. Thus when rhetorical criticism comes in at the door, critical probing into the text's unity or disunity tends to go out

19. M. Sternberg, *The Poetics of Biblical Narrative: Ideological Literature and the Drama of Reading* (Bloomington: Indiana University Press, 1987), p. 16.

20. The idea of a 'rolling corpus' has been suggested by McKane as a model for the genesis of the book of Jeremiah (cf. W. McKane, *A Critical and Exegetical Commentary on Jeremiah. I. Introduction and Commentary on Jeremiah I–XXV* [ICC; Edinburgh: T. & T. Clark, 1986], pp. xlix-lxxxiii). S.N. Rosenbaum, *Amos of Israel: A New Interpretation* (Macon, GA: Mercer University Press, 1990), p. 72, on the other hand, questions the idea that 'the 'prophetic canon' grew like a snowball rolling downhill, with each successive prophet falling heir to the work and the thought of all the former'.

21. For this view cf., for instance, S.M. Paul, *Amos: A Commentary on the Book of Amos* (Hermeneia; Minneapolis: Fortress Press, 1991), p. 6; and J.H. Hayes, *Amos— The Eighth-Century Prophet: His Times and His Preaching* (Nashville: Abingdon Press, 1988), p. 39.

22. Barton, *Reading the Old Testament*, p. 204.

of the window, the demonstration of its unity being taken as an absolute imperative... The job of the exegete, for most rhetorical critics, is not to ask whether the text hangs together rhetorically, but to show that it does.[23]

Barton concludes that 'the drive behind rhetorical criticism is often an apologetic one: to show that the text makes better sense than historical critics think'.[24]

There is I believe some truth in this contention. Yet Barton's charge that the rhetorical critic's interest often amounts to an apologetic one precisely illustrates the dilemma we are facing. The underlying assumption of Barton's criticism is that the 'traditional' historical-critical findings are correct after all, that the text in question is *not* a unity.[25] This, however, is precisely the disputed issue. It is perhaps preferable therefore to note simply that the recent surge of alternative modes of interpretation (of which rhetorical criticism is only one example) testifies to the fact that an increasing number of scholars now question historical-critical readings.[26] The unease of these scholars with the 'traditional' assumptions (or results)[27] concerning the disunity of the Old Testament books is the result

23. Barton, *Reading the Old Testament*, p. 201.
24. Barton, *Reading the Old Testament*, p. 204.
25. Cf. K. Möller, review of *Reading the Old Testament: Method in Biblical Study* (London: Darton, Longman & Todd, 2nd edn, 1996), by J. Barton, in *EuroJT* 6 (1997), pp. 172-74 (174).
26. See K. Möller, 'Renewing Historical Criticism', in Bartholomew, Greene and Möller (eds.), *Renewing Biblical Interpretation*, pp. 145-71 (150-59) for a summary of philosophical, literary-critical, theological and socio-religious objections to the historical-critical paradigm.
27. When what T. Kuhn, *The Structure of Scientific Revolutions* (Chicago: University of Chicago Press, 2nd edn, 1970), has called a 'paradigm' is firmly in place, it is sometimes difficult to make a clear distinction between assumptions and results. Often the assumptions of one generation become the results the next takes as its starting point. Thus, the text's disunity and inconsistency were frequently simply taken for granted. Indeed, the advance of the discipline of biblical studies was evidently often thought to depend upon producing ever more sophisticated theories concerning the genesis of the biblical books. R. Smend, *Deutsche Alttestamentler in drei Jahrhunderten* (Göttingen: Vandenhoeck & Ruprecht, 1989), for instance, in an otherwise splendid book, tends to regard historical criticism that lacks in radicalness as regressive. N. Lohfink, 'Gab es eine deuteronomistische Bewegung?', in Gross (ed.), *Jeremia und die 'deuteronomistische Bewegung'*, pp. 313-82 (316), on the other hand, criticizes the tendency towards what he calls 'pandeuteronomism'. He mockingly remarks that 'ein anständiger Doktorand [muss] heute irgendwo in der Bibel eine deuteronomistische Hand entdecken. Dann erst gehört er zur Zunft'.

of their own, rather different, readings of the same texts,[28] the aptitude (or inaptitude) of which can be decided only on the basis of the textual evidence itself. The text, as Eco points out, thus needs to serve as the parameter of its interpretations.[29]

At the heart of the matter lies the relationship between synchrony and diachrony and the question of which of the two is to be given priority. While in recent years there has been a tendency for scholars to subscribe to either a diachronic or a synchronic approach,[30] there is now an

Yet there is also the danger of becoming oblivious to marks of disunity as Barr stresses (J. Barr, 'The Synchronic, the Diachronic and the Historical: A Triangular Relationship?', in de Moor [ed.], *Synchronic or Diachronic?*, pp. 1-14 [9]). He parodies the claim that 'the apparent difficulties and inconsistencies, the presence of which has led to the identification of previous versions, are in fact not difficulties or inconsistencies but are highly subtle evidences of the writer's skill and literary talent, qualities which the plodding minds of critical scholars were too lacking in insight to detect'.

However, to revert to Kuhn's model of scientific paradigms, it should be noted that in Old Testament scholarship there is currently no paradigm that can be said to be firmly in place. The discipline is in what Kuhn would call a period of 'crisis'. This is the case, even though, as R. Rendtorff, 'Isaiah 6 in the Framework of the Composition of the Book', in *idem, Canon and Theology*, pp. 170-80 (180), points out: 'some…will not recognize the symptoms of crisis at all, or will not be prepared to recognize them. Instead they will expect that solutions to the problems can be found through an even more rigorous and even more precise application of the old methods.'

28. Sternberg, *Poetics*, p. 7, rightly speaks of 'a reaction against the excesses of historical scholarship'. He also perceptively discerns the danger that this reaction 'overreaches itself and falls short of an adequate countertheory' (p. 8).

29. U. Eco, *Die Grenzen der Interpretation* (trans. G. Memmert; Munich: Deutscher Taschenbuch Verlag, 1995), ch. 1.7.

30. House's claim that 'recently commentators have turned to a more text-oriented approach that accepts that Amos composed most, if not all, of the book that bears his name' (P.R. House, 'Amos and Literary Criticism', *RevExp* 92 [1995], pp. 175-87 [175]), though not without justification, overlooks that much European scholarship, German in particular, resists this trend. As advocates of a text-oriented approach House mentions D. Stuart, *Hosea–Jonah* (WBC, 31; Waco, TX: Word Books, 1987); Hayes, *Amos*; G.V. Smith, *Amos: A Commentary* (LBI; Grand Rapids: Zondervan, 1989); F.I. Andersen and D.N. Freedman, *Amos: A New Translation with Introduction and Commentary* (AB, 24a; New York: Doubleday, 1989); Rosenbaum, *Amos of Israel*; and Paul, *Amos*, a list that can be extended to include the recent commentaries by J.J. Niehaus, 'Amos', in T.E. McComiskey (ed.), *The Minor Prophets: An Exegetical and Expository Commentary*. I. *Hosea, Joel, and Amos* (Grand Rapids: Baker Book House, 1992), pp. 315-494; P. Bovati and R. Meynet, *Le livre du prophète Amos* (RhétBib, 2;

increasing concern to hold these two together. Thus, Rendtorff, for instance, notes that 'an appropriate understanding of...larger compositions often demands an insight into diachronic developments';[31] but at the same time he affirms that it is our task always to interpret the given text.[32] He furthermore observes that, whereas it was often considered a primary task to look for tensions and inconsistencies, now the integrity of the text is the

---

Paris: Cerf, 1994); E. Achtemeier, *Minor Prophets I* (NIBC, 17; Peabody, MA: Hendrickson, 1996); D.E. Gowan, 'The Book of Amos: Introduction, Commentary, and Reflections', in L.E. Keck *et al.* (eds.), *NIB*, VII (Nashville: Abingdon Press, 1996), pp. 337-431; B.C. Birch, *Hosea, Joel, and Amos* (Westminster Bible Companion; Louisville, KY: Westminster/John Knox Press, 1997); and R.J. Coggins, *Joel and Amos* (NCB; Sheffield: Sheffield Academic Press, 2000). However, recent redaction-critical studies by German scholars have come to rather different conclusions about the textual history of Amos. This is evidenced, for instance, in the extensive work of Jeremias (cf. bibliography for details) as well as the studies by G. Fleischer, *Von Menschenverkäufern, Baschankühen und Rechtsverkehrern: Die Sozialkritik des Amosbuches in historisch-kritischer, sozialgeschichtlicher und archäologischer Perspektive* (BBB, 74; Frankfurt: Athenäum, 1989); H. Reimer, *Richtet auf das Recht! Studien zur Botschaft des Amos* (SBS, 149; Stuttgart: Katholisches Bibelwerk, 1992); D.U. Rottzoll, *Studien zur Redaktion und Komposition des Amosbuchs* (BZAW, 243; Berlin: W. de Gruyter, 1996); and A. Schart, *Die Entstehung des Zwölfprophetenbuchs: Neubearbeitungen von Amos im Rahmen schriftenübergreifender Redaktionsprozesse* (BZAW, 260; Berlin: W. de Gruyter, 1998), all of which reckon with a long process of redactional activities. See K. Möller, 'Reconstructing and Interpreting Amos's Literary Prehistory: A Dialogue with Redaction Criticism', in C. Bartholomew *et al.* (eds.), *'Behind' the Text: History and Biblical Interpretation* (SHS, 4; Carlisle: Paternoster Press; Grand Rapids: Zondervan, forthcoming, 2003), for further discussion.

31. R. Rendtorff, 'Between Historical Criticism and Holistic Interpretation: New Trends in Old Testament Exegesis', in *idem, Canon and Theology*, pp. 25-30 (29).

32. Barr recently criticised the anti-historical trend in modern biblical studies, one that is often defended by attributing priority to the final form, i.e. the synchronic rather than the diachronic dimension, of a text (Barr, 'The Synchronic'). The distinction between synchrony and diachrony goes back to F. de Saussure's *Cours de linguistique générale* (Wiesbaden: Otto Harrassowitz, 1967), whose concepts Barr was one of the first to appropriate to the discipline of biblical studies (J. Barr, *The Semantics of Biblical Language* [Oxford: Oxford University Press, 1961]). However, as Barr rightly stresses: 'synchrony in the Saussurean sense...must support a historical approach' since 'historically [a text] meant what it meant synchronically in the relevant biblical time' (Barr, 'The Synchronic', p. 2). 'As soon as one looks at the synchronic state of language in a past time [or a text from a past time, one might add], then one is entering into a historical investigation' (p. 3). On synchrony and diachrony, see the collection of papers in de Moor (ed.), *Synchronic or Diachronic?*

main interest.[33] And even if there are inconsistencies, 'interpreters must face up to the tensions in the text in their interpretation, instead of getting rid of them through analysis, and then expounding their own smoother version'.[34]

A suggestive assessment of the relationship between synchrony and diachrony has been offered by Sternberg in *The Poetics of Biblical Narrative*.[35] Preferring the terms 'source' and 'discourse' to diachrony and synchrony, Sternberg affirms their interpretative value and offers a suggestion as to how interpreters might do justice to both.[36] He stresses that if we are to make sense of a *discourse* in terms of communication, the *sources* too are of fundamental importance. This is because they 'operate as parameters of context: the world they compose becomes a determinant and an indicator of meaning, a guide to the making of sense'.[37] Turning to the practical exegetical consequences, Sternberg underlines the interdependence of the two orientations ('discourse-oriented' and 'source-oriented') and notes that neither can claim priority, not even in a temporal sense, over the other.[38] That is to say, 'Both the interpreter and the historian must perforce combine the two viewpoints throughout, incessantly moving

33. Rendtorff, 'Historical Criticism', p. 28.

34. R. Rendtorff, 'Forty Years On: Four Decades of Old Testament Scholarship as I Have Experienced Them in Heidelberg and Elsewhere', in *idem*, *Canon and Theology*, pp. 207-19 (218).

35. See also the probing remarks by W. Brueggemann, 'Response to James L. Mays, "The Question of Context"', in McCann (ed.), *The Shape and Shaping of the Psalter*, pp. 29-41 (32-33).

36. Sternberg, *Poetics*, pp. 7-23. His terminology is perhaps to be preferred to the expressions 'synchronic' and 'diachronic' because, as Barr, 'The Synchronic', p. 3, has emphasized, an absolute differentiation between the two would require us to 'to take synchronic time as a sort of photographic instant'. This, however, does not make much sense because 'normal use of language allows the language user to command a variety of language states through time' (p. 4). A recent approach that takes this into account, as Barr points out, is the one by Labov and Bailey, who speak of a 'time-incorporating developmental linguistics' (Barr at this point references the articles by P. Mühlhäusler, 'Linguistics: Synchronic', p. 355; and *idem*, 'Language: Variation Theories', in Harré and Lamb [eds.], *Encyclopedic Dictionary of Psychology*, p. 332). Since the notion of a 'time-incorporating developmental linguistics' diminishes the opposition between diachronic and synchronic, Barr prefers to use the terms 'history' and 'literature' (Barr, 'The Synchronic', p. 9), which roughly correspond to Sternberg's 'source' and 'discourse'.

37. Sternberg, *Poetics*, p. 16.

38. Sternberg, *Poetics*, pp. 17-18.

between given discourse and inferred source in an endeavor to work out the best fit, until they reach some firm conclusion'.[39]

Excursus: Reader-Response Theory and the 'Otherness' of the Text
Before we continue with this discussion, it is important at this point to take note of the subjectivity invariably brought to the interpretative process by both the interpreter and the historian. If the recent surge of interpretative models in biblical studies[40] has had one effect, then it is to have alerted us to the 'presence of the reader', so to speak.[41] This is a most welcome development in that, for instance, reader-response theory has challenged 'our naive assumption that our reading is dictated by the text we read' to put it in Barton's words.[42] In similar vein, Wuellner, promoting a rhetorical criticism that embraces reader-response notions, remarks that it 'changes the long-established perception of authors as active and readers as passive or receptive by showing the rationale for readers as active, creative, productive'.[43]

39. Sternberg, *Poetics*, p. 19.
40. These include theories of interpretation, such as reader-response theory (or reception aesthetics, as some prefer to call it), structuralist and narratological criticism, rhetorical criticism, speech act theory, psychoanalytic criticism, semiotics and deconstruction as well as 'ideological criticisms', such as feminist criticism, marxist criticism and liberation hermeneutics. The amount of literature on these is vast but see esp. T. Eagleton, *Literary Theory: An Introduction* (Oxford: Basil Blackwell, 2nd edn, 1996); R. Selden and P. Widdowson, *A Reader's Guide to Contemporary Literary Theory* (New York: Harvester Wheatsheaf, 3rd edn, 1993); A.C. Thiselton, *New Horizons in Hermeneutics: The Theory and Practice of Transforming Biblical Reading* (Grand Rapids: Zondervan, 1992); and The Bible and Culture Collective (G. Aichele *et al.*), *The Postmodern Bible* (New Haven: Yale University Press, 1995).
41. How aware scholars have become of the reader's contribution to the act of interpretation is illustrated by a recent *Semeia* issue devoted to 'autobiographical biblical criticism' (J.C. Anderson and J.L. Staley [eds.], *Taking it Personally: Autobiographical Biblical Criticism* [Semeia, 72; Atlanta: Scholars Press, 1995]).
42. Barton, *Reading the Old Testament*, p. 219. On reader-response theories see E.V. McKnight, *Postmodern Use of the Bible: The Emergence of Reader-Oriented Criticism* (Nashville: Abingdon Press, 1988).
43. W. Wuellner, 'Where Is Rhetorical Criticism Taking Us?', *CBQ* 49 (1987), pp. 448-63 (461). His conception of the approach is a seasonable reminder that rhetorical criticism is by no means a uniform concept but a 'highly fluid and ever-growing interdisciplinary movement whose frontiers have yet to be charted' (thus D.F. Watson, 'Rhetorical Criticism', in *ISBE*, IV, pp. 181-82 [182]). F. Lentricchia, *Criticism and Social Change* (Chicago: University of Chicago Press, 1983), pp. 145-63, for instance, understands it as 'rhetoricopolitical activity'; Eagleton, *Literary Theory*, pp. 179-80, discusses it under the heading 'Political Criticism'; whereas V.K. Robbins, *The Tapestry of Early Christian Discourse: Rhetoric, Society and Ideology* (London: Routledge, 1996), favours a socio-rhetorical perspective (cf. *idem*, *Jesus the Teacher: A Socio-*

Important though this notion is, there is now a strong tendency to overemphasize the creativity of the reader at the expense of other factors pertaining to the interpretative process, such as the author[44] and the text. It is often claimed, for instance, that texts are indeterminate and that the reader consequently has the freedom to deal with them as he or she pleases. Todorov and Frye illustrate this, referring to a derisory remark by the German writer and physicist Lichtenberg (1742–99) on the work of Jakob Boehme. Lichtenberg had maliciously suggested that Boehme's work is like a picnic to which the author brings the words and the reader the meaning. Both Todorov and Frye, however, appropriate what appears to have been a sneer at Boehme, suggesting that it is, in the words of Frye, 'an exact description of all works of literary art without exception'.[45]

However, this Eco rejects. Despite his advocacy of a reader-response approach working with the hypothesis that textual interpretation is potentially unlimited, Eco thinks that 'in the course of the last decades, the rights of the interpreters have been overstressed'.[46] In 1962, Eco published a study, entitled *Opera aperta*,[47] in which he advocated the 'active role of the interpreter in the reading of texts endowed with aesthetic value'.[48] Thirty years on, however, he complains that his readers all too

Rhetorical Interpretation of Mark [repr., Philadelphia: Fortress Press, 1992]; and *idem, New Boundaries in Old Territory: Forms and Social Rhetoric in Mark* [New York: Peter Lang, 1994]).

See also in this context J.D.H. Amador, 'Where Could Rhetorical Criticism (Still) Take Us?', *CRBS* 7 (1999), pp. 195-222, who complains that biblical critics have not even come close to unleashing the potential of Wuellner's 'awesome array of theoretical and methodological insights' put forward in his seminal article 'Where Is Rhetorical Criticism Taking Us?' (p. 195). He urges that much more work by biblical rhetorical critics is needed on genre, social movements, symbolic convergence, sociolinguistics, metaphor, narrative, argumentation theory, feminist critical rhetorics, critical rhetoric and the rhetoric of inquiry, all of which are being pursued in rhetoric and communication departments.

44. According to C.R. Seitz, 'The Changing Face of Old Testament Studies', in *idem, Word without End: The Old Testament as Abiding Theological Witness* (Grand Rapids: Eerdmans, 1998), pp. 75-82 (80), 'it is the lack of a clear and persuasive understanding of the role of "the author" and of intentionality that most troubles Old Testament study at present'.

45. As quoted in E.D. Hirsch, Jr, *Validity in Interpretation* (New Haven: Yale University Press, 1967), p. 1 (cf. also Barton, *Reading the Old Testament*, p. 121). The statement is traced back to Lichtenberg by U. Eco, 'Interpretation and History', in *idem et al., Interpretation and Overinterpretation* (ed. S. Collini; Cambridge: Cambridge University Press, 1992), pp. 23-43 (24), who also refers to T. Todorov, 'Viaggio nella critica americana', *Lettera* 4 (1978), p. 12.

46. Eco, 'Interpretation and History', p. 23.

47. ET: U. Eco, *The Open Work* (trans. A. Cancogni; London: Hutchinson Radius, 1989).

48. Cf. Eco, 'Interpretation and History', p. 23.

readily appropriated the concept of 'openness', 'underestimating the fact that the open-ended reading I was supporting was an activity elicited by (and aiming at interpreting) a work'.[49] The primary regulatory means of the interpretative process, in Eco's view, is the text, which, as we have already noted above, serves as the parameter of its own interpretations. 'The words brought by the author', Eco notes, 'are a rather embarrassing bunch of material evidences that the reader cannot pass over in silence, or in noise'.[50] Eco's view receives support from Ricœur, who notes that the rights of readers are limited in that 'the right of the reader and the right of the text converge in an important struggle that generates the whole dynamic of interpretation'.[51]

I am only too aware that a defence of the claim that the current 'reader centrism' is overdone would require a detailed critique of postmodern (and in particular poststructuralist) theories of interpretation, which is impossible within the confines of the study in hand. Fortunately, however, such a critique is already at our disposal in the form of Thiselton's masterly *New Horizons in Hermeneutics*.[52] His main achievement, in my view, is to have provided a thorough assessment of the philosophical foundations upon which postmodern theories have been built. Thus, he was able to demonstrate that the conclusions drawn by postmodern theorists are not simply the invariable and thus non-negotiable results of the study of language. This claim, though sometimes made, does not stand up to close scrutiny because, as Thiselton has shown, postmodern conceptions rest on a number of philosophical presuppositions, which we may, or may not, embrace.[53] Thus, to cite just one example, Thiselton notes that 'the conclusions which deconstructionists draw *rest not simply on semiotic theory alone, but on an intermixture of semiotics and post-modernist, often neo-Nietzschean, world-view*'.[54]

Instead of following the anti-historical trend in biblical studies that devalues the author and disregards the historical embeddedness of the text, I favour a communication-theoretical approach that affirms the interpretative value of author, text *and* reader. The inclusion of the author, however, should not be understood in terms of a

49. Eco, 'Interpretation and History', p. 23.

50. Eco, 'Interpretation and History', p. 24.

51. P. Ricœur, *Interpretation Theory: Discourse and the Surplus of Meaning* (Fort Worth: Texas Christian University Press, 1976), p. 32.

52. See in particular his discussion of postmodernist theories of textuality (Thiselton, *New Horizons*, ch. 3) as well as 'the hermeneutics of reading in reader-response theories of literary meaning' (ch. 14).

53. In similar vein, Barton, *Reading the Old Testament*, p. 235, notes that while 'some people are not at all *attracted* by postmodernist relativism and self-refutation, but are *convinced* by it', he himself does 'not believe in it for a moment. But as a game, a set of *jeux d'esprit*, a way of having fun with words,' he finds 'it diverting and entertaining'. Barton in this context refers to R. Barthes' *Le plaisir du texte* (Paris: Seuil, 1973), the title of which might be seen as symptomatic for the post-structuralist attitude towards texts. As Barton notes, it could perhaps be translated as *Fun with Texts* or *How to Enjoy Yourself with Texts* (Barton, *Reading the Old Testament*, p. 222).

54. Thiselton, *New Horizons*, p. 92 (Thiselton's italics).

psychologizing approach so strenuously rejected by Wimsatt and Beardsley in 'The Intentional Fallacy'.[55] It would be fallacious, as they have pointed out, to be pre-occupied with the author—his or her circumstances, state of mind, etc.—at the expense of the textual data. Important though this notion is, it does not follow—and Wimsatt and Beardsley did not suggest it would—that we can dispose of the author altogether.[56] This is, first, because the author functions as a regulatory means of textual interpretation by investing the act of interpretation with a historical perspective, one that follows from, and is required by, the author's rootedness in history. The necessity of such a perspective is most obvious on the language level as Eco has shown, referring to Wordsworth's poem 'Daffodils'.[57] To understand the poem, we need to be familiar with the cultural and linguistic background of Wordsworth's time and age.[58] This is most obvious in the line, 'a poet could not but be gay', which, considering the modern connotations for 'gay', is wide open to misinterpretation.[59] In similar vein, Barr notes

55. Their article caused a lively discussion of the issue of intentionality. Wimsatt and Beardsley developed, and to a certain extent reformulated, their original propositions in subsequent publications (cf. W.K. Wimsatt, 'Genesis: A Fallacy Revisisted', in P. Demetz, T. Green and L. Nelson, Jr [eds.], *The Disciplines of Criticism: Essays in Literary Theory, Interpretation, and History* [New Haven: Yale University Press, 1968], pp. 193-225; *idem*, 'Genesis: An Argument Resumed', in *idem*, *Day of the Leopards: Essays in Defense of Poems* [New Haven: Yale University Press, 1976], pp. 11-39; M.C. Beardsley, *Aesthetics: Problems in the Philosophy of Criticism* [New York: Harcourt, Brace & World, 1958]; *idem*, *The Possibility of Criticism* [Detroit: Wayne State University Press, 1970]). Cf. also in this context the earlier debate between Tillyard and Lewis in the 1930s. Tillyard had claimed that the analysis of poetry was about uncovering the author's state of mind (E.M.W. Tillyard, *Milton* [London: Chatto & Windus, 1930]). Lewis, in response, dubbed this the 'personal heresy'. The ensuing debate can be found in E.M.W. Tillyard and C.S. Lewis, *The Personal Heresy: A Controversy* (London: Oxford University Press, pb edn, 1965).

56. Cf. the discussion in Barton, *Reading the Old Testament*, pp. 147-51.

57. For the text of the poem, see T. Hutchinson (ed.), *The Poems of William Wordsworth with Introductions and Notes* (London: Oxford University Press, 1923), p. 187.

58. Cf. Lewis's inaugural lecture as the Professor for Medieval and Renaissance English Literature in the University of Cambridge, in which he wittily defends his conception of the study of literature as a historical one (C.S. Lewis, '*De descriptione temporum*', in *idem*, *Selected Literary Essays* [ed. W. Hooper; Cambridge: Cambridge University Press, 1969], pp. 1-14). He affirms that 'it is my settled conviction that in order to read Old Western literature [in Lewis's terms this is Western European literature from its Greek or pre-Greek beginnings down to, roughly, Victorian times] aright you must suspend most of the responses and unlearn most of the habits you have acquired in reading modern literature' (Lewis, '*De descriptione temporum*', p. 13).

59. Cf. U. Eco, 'Between Author and Text', in *idem et al.*, *Interpretation and Overinterpretation*, pp. 67-88 (68).

that 'even fully contemporary synchronic description is dependent at many points on diachronic information', and that 'part of the success of those who exclude diachronic information has come about because they already knew that same information'.[60] On the other hand, however, it is also true that, as Ben Zvi criticizes, reader-centred approaches often do not 'consider the world of biblical societies in their own terms'.[61]

Secondly, a communication-theoretical (or socio-linguistic) approach will want to affirm that texts are means of communication—that by penning a text someone intended to communicate something.[62] Even considering that we have no access to the author, and that communication via texts is different from oral communication in which the speaker (or 'author') is physically present, this does not force us to abandon the concept of intentionality altogether. Eco in this context helpfully brings into play the intention of the text (*intentio operis*), which is an intention that is embedded in the text. This may be different from the actual intention(s) of the author—as it would be if he or she did not, or did only partially, succeed in communicating his or her thoughts—but it is the only intention 'available' to us. In addition, modern literary critics are right to point out that there is not just one single intention. In fact, this is rather obvious once we consider our own intentions in saying or doing something. These may be, and often are, manifold, sometimes even conflicting—and this without taking into consideration all our subconscious intentions. It is not at all surprising, then, that a reader should uncover intentions that are embedded in the text but that the author had been unaware of, and may even claim not to have intended.

Eco therefore correctly underlines, and welcomes, the fact that the number of possible interpretations is unlimited. However, he also points out that not all of them are equally successful (it is for the text to judge, as said earlier).[63] This, together with the points made in the previous paragraph, has important repercussions for textual interpretation. First, *the* perfect interpretation is unattainable.[64] Secondly, however, this

60. Barr, 'The Synchronic', p. 7. He speaks of a 'fully contemporary [i.e. ahistorical] synchronic description' in order to distinguish between the understanding of 'synchronic' as evidenced in many recent writings and that of de Saussure, which is not an ahistorical one.

61. E. Ben Zvi, *A Historical-Critical Study of the Book of Zephaniah* (BZAW, 198; Berlin: W. de Gruyter, 1991), p. 4.

62. Cf. Eco, *Grenzen*, p. 21, for a refutation of the idea that an intersubjective communicatable meaning does not exist.

63. Cf. Eco, *Grenzen*, ch. 1.7. On p. 51, Eco refers to J.H. Miller, *Thomas Hardy: Distance and Desire* (Cambridge, MA: Belknap/Harvard University Press, 1970), p. ix, who too rejects the idea that 'all readings are equally valid or of equal value. Some readings are certainly wrong. Of the valid interpretations all have limitations... Some approaches reach more deeply into the structure of the text than others.'

64. A detailed explication of this statement would lead us deeply into metaphysical territory, which I do not intend to, and do not have the space to, enter. Readers are referred instead to U. Eco's delightful *The Search for the Perfect Language* (trans. J. Fentress; London: Fontana, 1997), in which he narrates the story of how people

is not to say that we are therefore free to do with texts whatever our whimsy prompts us to. Or, in a way we are of course free to do just that, but then, to use Eco's distinction, we *use* the text rather than interpret it.[65] Thus, to conclude this line of thought, the 'presence of the author', albeit a theoretical and remote one,[66] functions as a regulatory means of textual interpretation also by requiring us to take into account the notion of 'intention'. Both, the text's rootedness in history as well as the intention embedded in the text, have consequences for the act of interpretation in that they restrict the freedom of the reader.

Let me end this excursus on 'reader centrism' by pointing out that in putting the reader at centre-stage, we have indeed much to lose. Reader-centred approaches, as Ben Zvi notes, tend to 'negate the relevancy of any human culture that differs from the culture of the reader'.[67] Thus, they replace the perspective an ancient text has the potential to offer—indeed does offer if we let it—with a contemporary one. This 'reader centrism' fits in rather well with the general anti-historical and individualistic trend of modern culture.[68] Whether this is an improvement is, however, debatable, to say the least. I believe that Lewis is right in stressing that 'to study the past does… liberate us from the present, from the idols of our own market-place'.[69] Or perhaps it would be better to say that it has the potential to do so, a potential that we, however, as readers, have the power to suppress. Yet, if texts are part of a process of communication, which I take them to be, then Thiselton is right to call for 'attentive respect'. A text, he notes, deserves '*respect for the otherness of the Other as Other*'.[70] This respect Thiselton characterizes in terms of the New Testament concept of ἀγάπη and notes,

throughout the centuries attempted to rediscover the perfect (unambiguous) language spoken in the Garden of Eden. Notice should also be taken of the insight of mediaeval interpreters, such as Wyclif, who discussed the reader's resistance to texts (in particular *the* Text) within a hamartiological context (see D.L. Jeffrey, *People of the Book: Christian Identity and Literary Culture* [Grand Rapids: Eerdmans, 1996], ch. 6, 'Authorial Intent and the Willful Reader').

65. Cf. U. Eco, *Lector in fabula: Die Mitarbeit der Interpretation in erzählenden Texten* (Munich: Deutscher Taschenbuch Verlag, 1990), ch. 3.4 (pp. 72-74); *idem*, *Grenzen*, ch. 1.5 (pp. 47-48).

66. The paradoxical notion of a 'remote presence' seems to describe the involvement of the author rather well. See also in this context Husserl's judgment that an author's intentions can never be present to the reader but can only be 'appresented' by her (J.K.A. Smith, *The Fall of Interpretation: Philosophical Foundations for a Creational Hermeneutic* [Downers Grove, IL: InterVarsity Press, 2000], p. 215 n. 50).

67. Ben Zvi, *Zephaniah*, p. 4.

68. The anti-historical trend of modern culture has been stressed by Barr, 'Synchronic', p. 2.

69. Lewis, '*De descriptione temporum*', p. 12.

70. A.C. Thiselton, *Interpreting God and the Postmodern Self: On Meaning, Manipulation and Promise* (Edinburgh: T. & T. Clark, 1995), p. 51 (Thiselton's italics).

with Schleiermacher, that 'all understanding, including the interpretation of texts, involves stepping "out of one's own frame of mind"'.[71] What is thus called for is *'creative regard for the Other...a love prompted by will, not by prior "likemindedness"'*.[72]

This then brings us back to our starting point, namely the crucial role the interpreter's assumptions about the text's condition play for his or her reading of that text. A look at the practice and development of biblical criticism over the centuries confirms this. The assumptions an exegete starts off with not only determine his or her working hypothesis but also condition which methodological approach will be applied and what interpretative goals will be pursued. They even influence the outcome of the reading in that diachronic approaches *tend to* yield composite texts while synchronic ones *tend to* produce textual unities.

Since any interpretation is bound to be subjective, it is all the more important to 'say what reading we are guilty of', to use Althusser's phraseology.[73] I should point out therefore that the starting point of the present study is the assumption, or as I would prefer to call it, 'initial impression', that the book of Amos is a unity featuring a coherent 'argument'. It is not, I believe and intend to demonstrate, simply an anthology of Amosian 'aphorisms' gathered and assembled for archival purposes. Nor do I believe it likely for the book to have evolved over a lengthy period of time, a period spanning several centuries. Having said that, however, it needs to be pointed out that it is not in my intention to deny redactional activity in general or to reject redaction criticism per se.[74]

71. Thiselton, *Interpreting God*, p. 51, quoting F.D.E. Schleiermacher, *Hermeneutics: The Handwritten Manuscripts* (ed. H. Kimmerle; Missoula, MT: Scholars Press, 1977), pp. 42, 109.

72. Thiselton, *Interpreting God*, p. 51 (Thiselton's italics). See also my discussion of this issue in Möller, 'Renewing Historical Criticism', pp. 163-65; as well as F.W. Dobbs-Allsopp, 'Rethinking Historical Criticism', *BibInt* 7 (1999), pp. 235-71, who rejects an ahistorical approach on the basis of pragmatic, ethical and salvific considerations.

73. L. Althusser, 'From *Capital* to Marx's Philosophy', in *idem* and E. Balibar, *Reading Capital* (trans. B. Brewster; New York: Verso, 1970), pp. 11-39 (14).

74. As R.E. Clements, 'The Prophet and His Editors', in D.J.A. Clines, S.E. Fowl and S.E. Porter (eds.), *The Bible in Three Dimensions: Essays in Celebration of Forty Years of Biblical Studies in the University of Sheffield* (JSOTSup, 87; Sheffield: JSOT Press, 1990), pp. 203-20 (205), has rightly stressed, the collection, preservation and editing of originally oral prophetic oracles or speeches in literary works is in itself secondary and thus 'redactional' (cf. also *idem*, 'Prophecy as Literature: A Re-

Indeed, considering not only the obvious redactional traces in Amos 1.1 and 7.10-17 but also the compository character of the larger sections of the book, its unity is best seen as the result of some sort of redactional operation.

However, the focus of the present study is on the text as a means of rhetorical persuasion rather than on its history. To repeat, the book *is* a collection of prophetic oracles (and perhaps one or two longer speeches) but—and in this I differ from many redaction critics—this collection, I will argue, was compiled comparatively shortly after the time of Amos. It was compiled, I should add, in order to address what in the terminology of rhetorical criticism is called a specific 'rhetorical problem'. In addition, I shall also argue that those who compiled the book arranged the prophetic oracles in a way that resulted in a coherent 'argument' or 'presentation', in which Amos appears as leading a debate with his eighth-century audience. This presentation of the debating prophet serves as the rhetorical means by which the redactors, compilers, or authors of the book addressed the rhetorical problem they were facing. Thus, what is rejected here as unconvincing, at least as far as the book of Amos is concerned, is the 'snowball approach' mentioned earlier.[75] My belief that the book in its final form originated relatively shortly after the end of Amos's ministry I have already stated. It should be added that I also think that the oracles and visions collected in the book (incl. Amos 9.7-15) make perfect sense when read against the historical context of eighth-century Israel. How, I shall outline in Chapter 2.[76]

Some, I am sure, will want to criticize my approach for ignoring widely accepted redaction-critical results, such as the conclusion that the book underwent a deuteronomistic redaction, that the hymnic sections are late additions, etc. These issues, too, will be discussed in Chapter 2 but I

appraisal', in D.G. Miller [ed.], *The Hermeneutical Quest. Essays in Honor of J.L. Mays for his 65th Birthday* [PTMS, 4; Allison Park: Pickwick Press, 1986], pp. 56-76).

75. See in this context E.W. Conrad, 'The End of Prophecy and the Appearance of Angels/Messengers in the Book of the Twelve', *JSOT* 73 (1997), pp. 65-79 (66), who points out that even where a complex redaction history is likely, we do not 'have the necessary data to trace the diachronic development of [a prophetic] book through time as many redaction critics attempt to do' (cf. also *idem*, 'Prophet, Redactor and Audience: Reforming the Notion of Isaiah's Formation', in R.F. Melugin and M.A. Sweeney [eds.], *New Visions of Isaiah* [JSOTSup, 214; Sheffield: Sheffield Academic Press, 1996], pp. 306-26).

76. In fact, all the issues brought up in this paragraph will be discussed in more detail in that chapter.

should point out at this point that such a criticism would not, in fact, be altogether mistaken. That is to say, because of my impressions concerning the unity of Amos and my dissatisfaction with redaction-critical proposals, I suggest setting them aside for the time being and starting again from scratch. A similar route has been taken by Wright in *Jesus and the Victory of God* in which he rejects the claim that the judgment oracles found in the Gospels do not originate with Jesus. Wright urges his readers to 'wait and see', as it were, to suspend their preconceived ideas about Jesus until his case has been fully presented. Only then will it be possible to judge whether all the pieces of the mosaic fall into place or whether we are left with some that do not fit.[77] Mason, too, argues along similar lines in his attempt to reaffirm, against Van Seters,[78] that the Pentateuchal J source should be dated early, that is in the period of the united Davidic monarchy. Mason stresses that 'it is the material which forms its contents which must speak for themselves, and in the light of that we must each form our opinion of what interests it may best be seen to be serving'.[79]

To conclude, I, too, would like to ask readers to suspend all judgements about the genesis of the book of Amos until the rhetorical reading I am about to propose has been completely set out. As Sternberg rightly emphasizes, 'hypotheses about source stand or fall on the cogency of the analysis of discourse'.[80] I have to leave it to the reader therefore to judge the success, or lack thereof, of the interpretation presented in the study in hand. However, for deciding this issue, the following questions are, I believe, crucial: (1) Is the reading suggested here a cogent one? (2) Does it render the proposal of a complex redactional process spanning several centuries unnecessary?[81] Does it perhaps even make it unlikely? (3) Is the

77. Cf. N.T. Wright, *Jesus and the Victory of God* (Christian Origins and the Question of God, 2; London: SPCK, 1996), p. 184.

78. J. Van Seters, *Abraham in History and Tradition* (New Haven: Yale University Press, 1975).

79. R. Mason, *Propaganda and Subversion in the Old Testament* (London: SPCK, 1997), p. 26; cf. also p. 38: 'all we can do is observe what is there and try as far as we can to see "who is saying what to whom".'

80. Sternberg, *Poetics*, p. 17.

81. Cf. Barton's remarkable comment mentioned earlier that redaction-critical operations are more often than not either unnecessary or unsuccessful (Barton, *Reading the Old Testament*, p. 58). In the case of Amos, I believe them to be largely unnecessary (see also the discussion in K. Möller, 'Words of [In-]evitable Certitude? Reflections on the Interpretation of Prophetic Oracles of Judgement', in Bartholomew, Greene and Möller [eds.], *After Pentecost*, pp. 352-86 [360-64]).

'initial impression' that the material of the book makes sense when read against an eighth-century background confirmed by my reading? That is to say, did I successfully demonstrate that the presentation of Amos's debate with his audience fits the proposed rhetorical situation? (4) What (and whose) interests is the material in its entirety best seen to be serving, to revert to Mason's terminology?

This then brings us to the second part of this introductory chapter, which is devoted to an outline of rhetorical criticism, as it is understood and practised in the study in hand.

2. *Definition and Procedural Outline of Rhetorical Criticism*

The twentieth century has seen a remarkable number of studies on the book of Amos. As is to be expected, the primary emphasis of most of them is on historical questions, such as the 'historical Amos', the genesis of the book, the socio-historical background of the prophet's time, etc. In recent decades, however, interest has shifted to literary issues so that we are now well equipped also with literary studies. It is interesting to note, however, that most of these focus primarily on structural issues. This is not necessarily inappropriate but it is striking that for many the investigation of structure seems to have become an end in itself,[82] which, in my view, *is* inappropriate. In contrast, the methodological approach advocated here is a functional one—one that investigates the text with the aim to uncover the role its various literary and structural devices play in the communicative process.

After what I said about the lack of attention towards the functional aspect of textual features, it comes as no surprise that rhetorical investigations of the book of Amos have, until fairly recently, been extremely rare, indeed, almost non-existent. The third edition of van der Wal's extensive bibliography (1986) lists approximately 1,600 titles, 21 of which are subsumed under the heading 'Compositie'.[83] A section comprising rhetorical studies does not even feature. Thompson's recent annotated bibliography (1997), enumerating some 1,800 titles, presents a similar picture. His subject index includes the term 'rhetoric' but lists no more

---

82. See Chapter 1 for a discussion of recent structural investigations of the book of Amos.

83. A. van der Wal, *Amos: A Classified Bibliography* (Applicatio, 3; Amsterdam: Free University Press, 3rd edn, 1986), pp. 45-47.

than four works under that label.[84] Of these, only the 1959 dissertation by Lewis comes in some respects close to the aims pursued in the present analysis. Ironically, Thompson's compilation includes a small number of works that should have been identified as rhetorical investigations but are not.[85] Even so, the fact remains that the text's suasive dimension is still very much neglected, as many exegetes are preoccupied with structural and stylistic issues.[86]

84. H.O. Thompson, *The Book of Amos: An Annotated Bibliography* (ATLA Bibliographies, 42; Lanham, MD: Scarecrow Press, 1997), p. 431. The studies listed are T.W. Chambers, 'The Literary Character of Amos', *The Old Testament Student* 3.1 (1883), pp. 2-6 (which argues that Amos displays a polished rhetorical style); R.L. Lewis, 'The Persuasive Style and Appeals of the Minor Prophets Amos, Hosea, and Micah' (dissertation, University of Michigan, 1959); J.L. Crenshaw, 'The Influence of the Wise upon Amos: The "Doxologies of Amos" and Job 5_{9-16}; 9_{5-10}', *ZAW* 79 (1967), pp. 42-52 (which seems to have been listed under this rubric only because Crenshaw happens to mention rhetorical questions); and J. Barton, 'History and Rhetoric in the Prophets', in Warner (ed.), *Bible as Rhetoric*, pp. 51-64 (who argues that the prophets used rhetorical tricks to justify God's judgmental dealings with Israel and Judah).

85. These include Y. Gitay, 'A Study of Amos's Art of Speech: A Rhetorical Analysis of Amos 3.1-15', *CBQ* 42 (1980), pp. 293-309; S.M. Paul, 'Amos 3.3-8: The Irresistible Sequence of Cause and Effect', *HAR* 7 (1983), pp. 203-20; and N.J. Tromp, 'Amos V 1-17. Towards a Stylistic and Rhetorical Analysis', in A.S. van der Woude (ed.), *Prophets, Worship and Theodicy: Studies in Prophetism, Biblical Theology and Structural and Rhetorical Analysis, and the Place of Music in Worship* (OTS, 23; Leiden: E.J. Brill, 1984), pp. 56-84.

86. A striking example is the recent commentary by Bovati and Meynet, *Le livre du prophète Amos*, p. 19, who contrast 'l'analyse rhétorique' (i.e. rhetorical-critical analysis in the terms of Wuellner's 'Where Is Rhetorical Criticism Taking Us?') with 'la recherche d'une logique hébraïque', the latter being understood as an attempt to 'chercher à découvrir la logique qui a présidé à l'organisation des textes'. This 'logique hébraïque', according to their analysis, apparently expresses itself first and foremost in 'compositions concentriques'. Cf. also R. Meynet, *Rhetorical Analysis: An Introduction to Biblical Rhetoric* (JSOTSup, 256; Sheffield: Sheffield Academic Press, 1998), for a detailed account of their methodological approach. In that work, Meynet employs the term 'rhetorical analysis' to refer to his approach but interestingly remarks that it is also called in French 'analyse structurelle' (Meynet, *Rhetorical Analysis*, p. 19).

However, for a recent discussion of Amos's rhetoric of persuasion, in which the prophet's rhetorical task is understood as bringing his audience under the divine judgment, see now ch. 5 in D. Patrick, *The Rhetoric of Revelation in the Hebrew Bible* (Overtures to Biblical Theology; Philadelphia: Fortress Press, 1999), pp. 119-61. Cf. also Möller, 'Words of (In-)evitable Certitude?', for a critique of Patrick's interpretation.

The discipline of rhetorical criticism is on the agenda of Old Testament studies largely because of Muilenburg's often referred to 1968 presidential address to the Society of Biblical Literature. It was published a year later in *JBL*, under the title 'Form Criticism and Beyond'. As the title indicates, Muilenburg and his followers developed rhetorical criticism primarily as a means to overcome the shortcomings of form criticism. Muilenburg complained, for instance, that 'there has been a proclivity among scholars …to lay such stress upon the typical and representative that the individual, personal, and unique features of the particular pericope are all but lost to view'.[87] He consequently urged his colleagues to pay more attention to authorial accomplishment and personal creativity as expressed in the unique stylistic or aesthetic qualities of a particular text. The perception of literature that found expression in Muilenburg's conceptions thus led to an increased interest in structural patterns and literary devices such as inclusios, chiasms, parallelism, refrains, repetition, rhetorical questions, and so on.[88]

The year that saw the publication of Muilenburg's programmatic article (1969) witnessed also the publication of Perelman and Olbrechts-Tyteca's *The New Rhetoric: A Treatise on Argumentation*.[89] Whereas the Muilen-

87. J. Muilenburg, 'Form Criticism and Beyond', *JBL* 88 (1969), pp. 1-18 (5). Cf. also in this context R.F. Melugin, 'The Typical Versus the Unique Among the Hebrew Prophets', in McGaughy (ed.), *SBLASP* 108.2, pp. 331-41.

88. Muilenburg, 'Form Criticism', pp. 8-18. Many scholars responded to Muilenburg's call and produced a substantial quantity of rhetorical-critical investigations along the lines proposed by him. See, for instance, the articles in J.J. Jackson and M. Kessler (eds.), *Rhetorical Criticism: Essays in Honor of James Muilenburg* (PTMS, 1; Pittsburgh: Pickwick Press, 1974); and D.J.A. Clines, D.M. Gunn and A.J. Hauser (eds.), *Art and Meaning: Rhetoric in Biblical Literature* (JSOTSup, 19; Sheffield: JSOT Press, 1982). For assessments of Muilenburg's achievements and programmatic interactions with his proposal cf. Melugin, 'The Typical'; B.W. Anderson, 'The New Frontier of Rhetorical Criticism. A Tribute to James Muilenburg', in Jackson and Kessler (eds.), *Rhetorical Criticism*, pp. ix-xviii; M. Kessler, 'A Methodological Setting for Rhetorical Criticism', in Clines, Gunn and Hauser (eds.), *Art and Meaning*, pp. 1-19; *idem*, 'An Introduction to Rhetorical Criticism of the Bible: Prolegomena', *Semitics* 7 (1980), pp. 1-27; R.J. Clifford, 'Rhetorical Criticism in the Exegesis of Hebrew Poetry', in P.J. Achtemeier (ed.), *SBLSP* 19 (Missoula, MT: Scholars Press, 1980), pp. 17-28; and R.F. Melugin, 'Muilenburg, Form Criticism, and Theological Exegesis', in M.J. Buss (ed.), *Encounter with the Text: Form and History in the Hebrew Bible* (Semeia Supplements, 8; Philadelphia: Fortress Press; Missoula, MT: Scholars Press, 1979), pp. 91-100.

89. C. Perelman and L. Olbrechts-Tyteca, *The New Rhetoric: A Treatise on*

burg School, as it came to be known, focused on stylistics,[90] Perelman and Olbrechts-Tyteca were interested primarily in rhetoric as argumentation, thus reverting to its classical Aristotelian conception. Their work soon became one of the most influential textbooks of rhetorical criticism, but in Old Testament studies the approach of the Muilenburg School dominated the scene for some time to come.[91] In 1987, in another article that has become a classic, Wuellner criticized Muilenburg's definition of rhetorical criticism, which he considered indistinguishable from literary criticism, as 'rhetoric restrained'.[92] Wuellner even speaks of 'the Babylonian captivity of rhetoric reduced to stylistics'[93] and 'the ghetto of an estheticizing preoccupation with biblical stylistics'.[94] In similar vein, Kennedy rejected the approach, calling it 'letteraturizzazione'.[95] On the other hand, Wuellner

Argumentation (trans. J. Wilkinson and P. Weaver; Notre Dame: University of Notre Dame Press, 1969). The original French edition appeared 1958 under the title *La nouvelle rhétorique: traité de l'argumentation*.

90. T.B. Dozeman, 'Old Testament Rhetorical Criticism', in *ABD*, V, pp. 712-15 (714), stresses that, despite all the similarities, there are important differences that distinguish the Muilenburg School from their mentor. Thus, whereas Muilenburg understood his approach as a supplement to form criticism, many of his followers were influenced more by the literary movement known as 'New Criticism'. D.M. Howard, Jr, 'Rhetorical Criticism in Old Testament Studies', *BBR* 4 (1994), pp. 87-104 (90), on the other hand, finds close parallels to Prague School structuralism. However that may be, it is clear that many abandoned any interest in authorial intention and focused on a text's synchronic dimension, thus giving up the traditional historical interest of form criticism. Cf. in this context D. Greenwood, 'Rhetorical Criticism and Formgeschichte: Some Methodological Considerations', *JBL* 89 (1970), pp. 418-26; Anderson, 'New Frontier'; Kessler, 'Methodological Setting'; I.M. Kikawada, 'Some Proposals for the Definition of Rhetorical Criticism', *Semitics* 5 (1977), pp. 67-91; Melugin, 'Muilenburg'; P. Trible, *God and the Rhetoric of Sexuality* (London: SCM Press, 1992); and *idem*, *Rhetorical Criticism: Context, Method, and the Book of Jonah* (GBS; Philadelphia: Fortress Press, 1994), who share Muilenburg's concerns to varying degrees.

91. In New Testament Studies, Kennedy's influence effected a different development, which led scholars to take the text's suasive dimension into account much earlier than their Old Testament colleagues.

92. Wuellner, 'Rhetorical Criticism', p. 453; the term is Genette's; cf. G. Genette, 'Rhetoric Restrained', in *idem*, *Figures of Literary Discourse* (trans. A. Sheridan; New York: Columbia University Press, 1982), pp. 103-26.

93. Wuellner, 'Rhetorical Criticism', p. 457.

94. Wuellner, 'Rhetorical Criticism', p. 462.

95. Kennedy, *New Testament Interpretation*, p. 3; cf. also Y. Gitay, 'Rhetorical Criticism', in S.L. McKenzie and S.R. Haynes (eds.), *To Each Its Own Meaning: An Introduction to Biblical Criticisms and Their Application* (London: Geoffrey Chap-

embraced the alternative conception advanced by Perelman and Olbrechts-Tyteca as 'rhetoric revaluated'[96] or 'rhetoric reinvented'.[97] Similarly, Bakhtin welcomes the renaissance of rhetorical criticism because it promotes 'rhetoric to all its ancient rights'.[98] It has become customary to label the two orientations initiated by Muilenburg, on the one hand, and Perelman and Olbrechts-Tyteca, on the other, respectively as the 'art of composition' and the 'art of persuasion',[99] terms that identify the different foci aptly.[100]

a. *Rhetoric—the 'Art of Persuasion'*

Earlier on, I referred to the approach applied in the present study as a communication-theoretical or socio-linguistic one, in which literature is understood as communication. Wuellner stresses that this is charac-

man, 1993), pp. 135-49 (136); and L. Eslinger, *House of God or House of David: The Rhetoric of 2 Samuel 7* (JSOTSup, 164; Sheffield: JSOT Press, 1994), pp. 4-5, who follow the lead of rhetorical critics such as Kennedy and Wuellner.

96. Wuellner, 'Rhetorical Criticism', p. 453, the term being taken from B. Vickers (ed.), *Rhetoric Revalued* (Medieval & Renaissance Texts and Studies, 19; Binghamton, NY: Center for Medieval & Renaissance Studies, 1982).

97. Wuellner, 'Rhetorical Criticism', p. 453; cf. Eagleton, *Literary Theory*, p. 183, who proposed to 'reinvent rhetoric'.

98. M. Bakhtin, *The Dialogic Imagination: Four Essays* (ed. M. Holquist; trans. C. Holquist and M. Holquist; University of Texas Press Slavic Series, 1; Austin: University of Texas Press, 1981), p. 267.

99. Cf., for instance, Trible, *Rhetorical Criticism*, pp. 32, 41.

100. The development of these two foci has historical reasons, which cannot be dealt with in this context. However, useful accounts of the historical development of rhetoric can be found, for instance, in Kennedy's works (cf. G.A. Kennedy, *The Art of Persuasion in Greece* [Princeton: Princeton University Press, 1963]; *idem, The Art of Rhetoric in the Roman World 300 B.C.–A.D. 300* [Princeton: Princeton University Press, 1972]; *idem, Classical Rhetoric and Its Christian and Secular Tradition from Ancient to Modern Times* [Chapel Hill: University of North Carolina Press, 1980]; *idem, Greek Rhetoric under Christian Emperors* [Princeton: Princeton University Press, 1983]; and *idem, A New History of Classical Rhetoric: An Extensive Revision and Abridgment of* The Art of Persuasion in Greece, The Art of Rhetoric in the Roman World *and* Greek Rhetoric under Christian Emperors *with Additional Discussion of Late Latin Rhetoric* [Princeton: Princeton University Press, 1994]). See also E.P.J. Corbett, *Classical Rhetoric for the Modern Student* (New York: Oxford University Press, 3rd edn, 1990), part V; M. Fuhrmann, *Die antike Rhetorik: Eine Einführung* (Zürich: Artemis & Winkler, 4th edn, 1995), part I; G. Ueding, *Klassische Rhetorik* (Munich: Beck, 2nd edn, 1996), and the works listed in Corbett, *Classical Rhetoric*, pp. 582-85.

teristic for the new rhetoric, which 'approaches all literature...as *social discourse*'.[101] This definition, as I have already pointed out, recaptures the classical Aristotelian understanding, concerning which Eagleton notes that it

> saw speaking and writing not merely as textual objects, to be aesthetically contemplated or endlessly deconstructed, but as forms of *activity* inseparable from the wider social relations between writers and readers, orators and audiences, and as largely unintelligible outside the social purposes and conditions in which they were embedded.[102]

However, neither the notion of communication, which is a rather general conception comprising all kinds of communicative action, nor that of persuasion, which, although narrower, still is too imprecise, provide sufficiently nuanced concepts for what specifically is in view here. For that, we have to turn to Bitzer who introduced the concept of 'rhetorical situation' as distinct from 'persuasive situation'. A 'persuasive situation... exists', according to Bitzer, '*whenever* an audience can be changed in belief or action by means of speech.'[103] A 'rhetorical situation', on the other hand, is a specific situation that determines and controls the rhetorical utterance it occasions.[104] It is characterized, moreover, by an 'exigency which amount[s] to *an imperative stimulus*'[105] and which the rhetorical discourse is designed to address with the aim of modifying it. Rhetoric, thus defined, therefore 'is a mode of altering reality...by the creation of discourse which changes reality through the mediation of thought and action.'[106]

Such an understanding of rhetoric fits the prophetic mode well. It is a commonplace that the prophets were public speakers who, as Brenner puts

101. Wuellner, 'Rhetorical Criticism', pp. 462-63 (his italics).

102. Eagleton, *Literary Theory*, p. 179 (his italics).

103. L.F. Bitzer, 'The Rhetorical Situation', in W.R. Fisher (ed.), *Rhetoric: A Tradition in Transition. In Honor of Donald C. Bryant* (East Lansing, MI: Michigan State University Press, 1974), pp. 247-60 (249; my italics).

104. See Bitzer, 'Rhetorical Situation', p. 249; cf. also pp. 250-52. I shall continue to use the terms 'persuasion' and 'art of persuasion', however, despite their lack of precision. Both are well-established expressions in the field of rhetorical criticism and have the advantage of conveying to the biblical scholar more meaningful connotations than the rather elementary designations 'rhetoric' and 'rhetorical'. Readers should bear in mind, however, that in the present study the 'art of persuasion' is understood as being occasioned by and directed at a specific rhetorical situation.

105. Bitzer, 'Rhetorical Situation', p. 251 (my italics).

106. Bitzer, 'Rhetorical Situation', p. 250.

it, 'appeal[ed] to addressees in order to gain influence over them'.[107] How-ever, in addition to the modification of this rather general view made in the previous paragraph, it needs to be stressed that I am not concerned here with the prophets' original speeches. I am interested rather in the written legacy of these figures as found in the Old Testament prophetic books, which, like the New Testament epistolary literature, suggest themselves as promising objects for a rhetorical-critical approach that focuses on persuasive intent.[108] Having said that, however, the question arises as to whether the notion of rhetoric as a reaction to a specific historical exigency can be applied to books, which, after all, are rather different in nature from public speeches. This question can be answered in the affirmative because, as Eagleton emphasizes:

> rhetoric, which was the received form of critical analysis all the way from ancient society to the eighteenth century, examined the way discourses are constructed in order to achieve certain effects. It was not worried about whether its objects of enquiry were speaking or writing, poetry or philosophy, fiction or historiography: its horizon was nothing less than the field of discursive practices in society as a whole, and its particular interest lay in grasping such practices as forms of power and performance.[109]

107. A. Brenner, 'Preface', in *idem* (ed.), *A Feminist Companion to The Latter Prophets*, pp. 13-19 (18). See A. Kuenen, *De Profeten en de Profetie onder Israël: Historisch-dogmatische studie* (2 vols.; Leiden: Engels, 1875), II, p. 81, who refuted the earlier concept that saw the prophets as fortune-tellers by stressing that 'es war ihnen nicht darum zu tun, mitzuteilen, was geschehen wird, sondern um sich zu bemühen, was geschehen muß' (cited in M.J. Mulder, 'Kuenen und der "ethische Monotheismus" der Propheten des 8. Jahrhunderts v. Chr.', in P.B. Dirksen and A. van der Kooij [eds.], *Abraham Kuenen [1828–1891]: His Major Contributions to the Study of the Old Testament. A Collection of Old Testament Studies Published on the Occasion of the Centenary of Abraham Kuenen's Death [10 December 1991]* [OTS, 29; Leiden: E.J. Brill, 1993], pp. 65-90 [77]).

108. Rhetorical-critical studies of prophetic books that move beyond a mere stylistic interest include Y. Gitay, *Prophecy and Persuasion: A Study of Isaiah 40–48* (Forum theologiae linguisticae, 14; Bonn: Linguistica Biblica, 1981); *idem*, 'Reflections on the Study of the Prophetic Discourse: The Question of Isaiah 1.2-20', *VT* 33 (1983), pp. 207-21; *idem, Isaiah and His Audience: The Structure and Meaning of Isaiah 1–12* (StSN, 30; Assen: Van Gorcum, 1991); R.J. Clifford, *Fair Spoken and Persuading: An Interpretation of Second Isaiah* (New York: Paulist Press, 1984); B. Wiklander, *Prophecy as Literature: A Text-Linguistic and Rhetorical Approach to Isaiah 2–4* (ConBOT, 22; Malmö: C.W.K. Gleerup, 1984); C.S. Shaw, *The Speeches of Micah: A Rhetorical-Historical Analysis* (JSOTSup, 145; Sheffield: JSOT Press, 1993); and T. Renz, *The Rhetorical Function of the Book of Ezekiel* (VTSup, 76; Leiden: E.J. Brill, 1999).

109. Eagleton, *Literary Theory*, p. 179.

It should also be noted that in the case of ancient texts the difference between oral and written communications anyway was rather slight compared to our modern culture. 'Written communications', as Walton notes, 'had a quality of orality because reading aloud was the norm in antiquity'.[110] Aristotle, for instance, discusses written discourse (τὸ γεγραμμένον) in *Rhet.* 3.5.6, which, according to Walton, 'suggests that the boundary between written and oral communication was seen as porous'.[111] It is not surprising therefore that the same analytical tools were used for examining both speeches and literary works.

However, the practice of subjecting literature to rhetorical-critical investigation continued, even when, in much later times, the reading habits had changed. Indeed, as Abrams points out, the 'pragmatic orientation'[112] has been the major player in literary criticism 'from the time of Horace through the eighteenth century'.[113] It was then replaced as the dominant model by expressive theories connected with, and occasioned by, the romanticist movement. Currently, notwithstanding the strong appeal of post-structuralist theories of interpretation, there is renewed interest among literary critics in pragmatic theory, which is sometimes redefined along postmodern lines. A scholar associated with the reintroduction of rhetoric to literary studies is Booth,[114] who is interested in 'the technique

110. Walton, 'Rhetorical Criticism', p. 6.

111. Walton, 'Rhetorical Criticism', p. 6. We shall return to the issue of orality and its effects upon the production of literature in the next chapter.

112. Rhetorical criticism is 'pragmatic' because of its interest in the use of utterances (spoken or written) as means to an end.

113. See M.H. Abrams, 'Orientation of Critical Theories', in D. Lodge (ed.), *20th Century Criticism: A Reader* (London: Longman, 1972), pp. 1-26 (11-16). For an appropriation of Abrams's model to the field of biblical criticism cf. J. Barton, 'Classifying Biblical Criticism', *JSOT* 29 (1984), pp. 19-35.

114. See esp. W.C. Booth, *The Rhetoric of Fiction* (Harmondsworth: Penguin Books, 2nd edn, 1983); but also *idem, A Rhetoric of Irony* (Chicago: University of Chicago Press, 1974); *idem,* 'The Rhetoric of Fiction and the Poetics of Fiction', *Novel: A Forum on Fiction* 1 (1968), pp. 105-17; and *idem,* 'Rhetorical Critics Old and New', in L. Lerner (ed.), *Deconstructing Literature* (Oxford: Basil Blackwell, 1983), pp. 123-41. Cf. further E.P.J. Corbett, *Rhetorical Analyses of Literary Works* (New York: Oxford University Press, 1969); N. Frye, 'Rhetorical Criticism: Theory of Genres', in *idem, Anatomy of Criticism: Four Essays* (Harmondsworth: Penguin Books, 1990), pp. 241-337; and *idem, The Great Code: The Bible and Literature* (San Diego: Harcourt Brace Jovanovich, 1983), pp. 27-29. Frye, however, is not so much interested in a communication perspective reckoning with authorial intention as in the literary/rhetorical effect of devices such as myth, metaphor, typology, etc.

of fiction, "viewed as the art of communication with readers," the art of "imposing fictional worlds" on readers'.[115] He regards the rhetorical-critical enterprise as a 'study of *use*, of purposes pursued, targets hit or missed, practices illuminated for the sake not of pure knowledge but of further (and improved) practice'.[116] In Old Testament studies, critics like Alter and Sternberg built persuasive rhetoric into their approach called biblical poetics.[117] Alter, for instance, notes:

> it is the exception in any culture for literary invention to be a purely aesthetic activity. Writers put together words in a certain pleasing order partly because the order pleases but also, very often, because the order helps them refine meanings, make meanings more memorable, more satisfyingly complex, so that what is well wrought in language can more powerfully engage the world of events, values, human and divine ends.[118]

These are, however, rather general remarks so that Wuellner is right to point out that Alter's approach is practically indistinguishable from literary criticism.[119] Sternberg, on the other hand, in *The Poetics of Biblical Narrative*, advances a great deal further along the path towards more comprehensive consideration of rhetorical-critical concerns.[120] Even more expressly rhetorical approaches to Hebrew narrative are Eslinger's *House of God or House of David*[121] and *The Persuasive Appeal of the Chronicler* by Duke.[122]

---

115. Booth, *Rhetoric of Fiction*, p. 419.

116. Booth, *Rhetoric of Fiction*, p. 441 (his italics).

117. Cf. R. Alter, *The Art of Biblical Narrative* (New York: Basic Books, 1981); (see also *idem*, *The Art of Biblical Poetry* [New York: Basic Books, 1985]; and *idem*, *The World of Biblical Literature* [London: SPCK, 1992]); and Sternberg, *Poetics*.

118. R. Alter, 'Introduction to the Old Testament', in *idem* and F. Kermode (eds.), *The Literary Guide to the Bible* (London: Fontana, 1987), pp. 11-35 (15).

119. Wuellner, 'Rhetorical Criticism', p. 452. He also, for the same reasons, criticizes the approach of L. Alonso Schökel, *The Inspired Word: Scripture in the Light of Language and Literature* (New York: Herder & Herder, 1965). For the latter writer's latest formulation of his approach, see L. Alonso Schökel, with J.M. Bravo, *A Manual of Hermeneutics* (ed. B.W.R. Pearson; trans. L.M. Rosa; BibSem, 54; Sheffield: Sheffield Academic Press, 1998).

120. This tendency is reflected, for instance, in the chapter headings of chs. 12 and 13 of *Poetics*, which are entitled respectively 'The Art of Persuasion' and 'Ideology, Rhetoric, Poetics'.

121. Eslinger, *House of God*, pp. 7-9, however, studies rhetoric within the context of the story world as opposed to the social context provided by the interaction between authors and their audience.

122. R.K. Duke, *The Persuasive Appeal of the Chronicler: A Rhetorical Analysis*

In the light of the stress placed on the historical, as reflected in the importance attributed to the rhetorical situation that occasioned the discourse under investigation, one final comment is necessary. It needs to be pointed out that this conception does not necessarily degrade the texts in question to 'mere' historical documents, sources, that is to say, with little or no use for us today. In fact, Alter, in his discussion of 'prophecy and poetry', notes that the prophetic books display what he calls 'the archetypifying force of vocative poetry'.[123] He points out that the poetic language of most biblical prophecies 'tends to lift the utterances to a second power of signification, aligning statements that are addressed to a concrete historical situation with an archetypal horizon'.[124] With regard to Isa. 1.2-10, Alter thus remarks that:

> a set of messages framed for a particular audience of the eighth century BCE is not just the transcription of a historical document but continues to speak age after age, inviting members of otherwise very different societies to read themselves into the text.[125]

Even Bitzer, who, as we have seen, is interested primarily in the specific historical situation that occasions a rhetorical utterance, is aware of such a phenomenon. However, whereas Alter regards the 'archetypifying force' as an effect of poetic language, Bitzer notes that some rhetorical situations persist, thus allowing the existence of 'a body of truly *rhetorical literature*'.[126] Some texts, he explains, 'exist as rhetorical responses *for us* precisely because they speak to situations which persist—which are in some measure universal'.[127]

(JSOTSup, 88; BLS, 25; Sheffield Academic Press, 1990). Cf. also T.A. Lenchak, *'Choose Life!' A Rhetorical-Critical Investigation of Deuteronomy 28,69–30,20* (AnBib, 129; Rome: Editrice Pontificio Istituto Biblico, 1993), for a detailed rhetorical-critical analysis of Deut. 28.69–30.20 that makes extensive use of ancient and modern textbooks of rhetoric; and see J.W. Watts, *Reading Law: The Rhetorical Shaping of the Pentateuch* (BibSem, 59; Sheffield: Sheffield Academic Press, 1999), who argues that conventions of oral rhetoric were adapted to shape the literary form and contents of the Pentateuch. As regards Old Testament wisdom, C.G. Bartholomew, *Reading Ecclesiastes: Old Testament Exegesis and Hermeneutical Theory* (AnBib, 139; Rome: Editrice Pontificio Istituto Biblico, 1998), pp. 212-26, calls for a 'communication model' to be applied to the study of Ecclesiastes.

123. Alter, *Art of Biblical Poetry*, p. 146.
124. Alter, *Art of Biblical Poetry*, p. 146.
125. Alter, *Art of Biblical Poetry*, p. 146.
126. Bitzer, 'Rhetorical Situation', p. 259 (his italics).
127. Bitzer, 'Rhetorical Situation', p. 259 (his italics).

Having noted some essential concerns of rhetorical criticism, we are now in a position to consider the practical side of the subject, which I shall turn to presently by outlining five steps of rhetorical-critical analysis. However, before we come to that, a few comments on what I would regard as in many ways closely related interpretative models seem pertinent at this point. The approaches in question are discourse analysis, on the one hand, and speech act theory, on the other, both of which have provided me with important stimuli for my analysis of the book of Amos at various points.

Discourse Analysis. Brown and Yule describe their approach of discourse analysis as being concerned with 'what people using language are doing'.[128] This interest is shared by Green who speaks of a focus on 'language in use' and emphasizes the need for a definition that is wide enough to accommodate linguistic as well as paralinguistic features.[129] With such a wide definition being applied, the approach is 'a potentially fruitful way for navigating between apparently competing modes of interpretation that focus on either the history behind the text, the world of the text, or the reading community in front of the text'.[130] Noting that discourse analysis has often been confined to the practice of text-linguistics, Green argues for a multilevel analysis that regards texts as '*cultural products* providing witness to a (past) discourse' *and* as '*partners* in a new discourse situation'.[131] 'Every engaged reading', he notes, 'is…participation in a communicative event whereby we join in the generation of meaning and are shaped in the give and take of active discourse'.[132] Discourse analysis, therefore, 'is interested in *how* language-in-use invites such participation and formation'.[133] I have quoted Green at some length in order to demonstrate the similarities of his interpretative perspective with several of my concerns expressed earlier.

Especially the focus on communication with its 'give and take of active discourse' is of importance, as it emphasizes both the author's interest in

128. G. Brown and G. Yule, *Discourse Analysis* (Cambridge Textbooks in Linguistics; Cambridge: Cambridge University Press, 1983), p. 26.

129. J.B. Green, 'Discourse Analysis and New Testament Interpretation', in *idem* (ed.), *Hearing the New Testament*, pp. 175-96 (175).

130. Green, 'Discourse Analysis', p. 175.

131. Green, 'Discourse Analysis', pp. 176-77 (his italics).

132. Green, 'Discourse Analysis', p. 177.

133. Green, 'Discourse Analysis', p. 177.

getting a message across *and* the active participation of readers in the
communicative process. The former has been placed at the centre of rhetorical-critical interest by Bitzer, as we have seen above. However, it is
given much attention also by advocates of discourse analysis such as Green
or Callow, who promotes what he calls a 'semantically or cognitively ori-
ented theory'. This 'stresses the communicative situation:[134] the author is
passing a message on to his or her readers and the meaning that the author
desires to communicate determines the form in which the message is
cast'.[135] It is important therefore to ask with Wendland, 'what was the
author seeking to *do*...how did he intend the message to *affect* his
receptors—what *impact* did he want his carefully selected 'modes of
discourse' to have upon them, e.g. narration, reflection, invocation, inter-
rogation, rebuke, warning...?'[136] Wendland calls this an interest in 'the
cognitive-emotive principle of *relevance*'.[137]

  These are only a few randomly chosen examples of statements by discourse analysts emphasizing the need to take into account the author's
communicative intent.[138] They clearly demonstrate a close affinity with
rhetorical-critical concerns. This is particularly evident in Wendland's
stated interest in 'how the biblical poet *sought to move his audience*
through the verbal artistry of his text to experience either a conversion or a
confirmation with regard to their thinking and behavior concerning
Yahweh'.[139] In speaking of the poet's desire to 'move' his audience,
Wendland even takes up what we shall see to be one of the technical terms
of rhetorical-critical analysis. It comes as no surprise therefore that, as

---

  134. The term 'communicative situation' is interesting, as it in some ways resembles
the 'rhetorical situation' rhetorical criticism is interested in. Green at other points
speaks of a 'discourse situation', the relationship of a text to its 'co-text, intertext, and
context', and an ongoing social interaction in which (textual) utterances are embedded
(cf. Green, 'Discourse Analysis', pp. 180, 183-84).

  135. J. Callow, 'Units and Flow in the Song of Songs 1.2–2.6', in Bergen (ed.),
Biblical Hebrew, pp. 462-88 (462).

  136. E.R. Wendland, 'The Discourse Analysis of Hebrew Poetry: A Procedural
Outline', in *idem* (ed.), *Discourse Perspectives on Hebrew Poetry in the Scriptures*
(UBSMS, 7; Reading: United Bible Societies, 1994), pp. 1-27 (18).

  137. Wendland, 'Discourse Analysis', p. 18.

  138. Cf. also E. Talstra, 'Text Grammar and Biblical Hebrew: The Viewpoint of
Wolfgang Schneider', *JOTT* 5 (1992), pp. 269-97 (269), who remarks that 'language
should not be studied as a means of the purely personal expression but as a means of
communication'.

  139. Wendland, 'Discourse Analysis', p. 20 (my italics).

Wuellner notes, there is a great variety of rhetorical criticisms that are based on models of modern linguistics or semiotics.[140]

Having illustrated how discourse analysis and rhetorical criticism converge in their interest in the author's communicative intent, I should point out that both are marked also by their attention to the active participation of readers in the process of communication. Again, this has been stressed by Green referring approvingly to Eco's views on the multiplicity of possible readings.[141] Green understands the process of communication engendered by a text as 'discourse *event*, the temporal moment when a text is realized or actualized'.[142] However, Green, too, notes that meaning is textually constrained. Discourse analysis, therefore, like the version of rhetorical criticism advocated in the study in hand, seeks 'to account both for textual constraints on meaning and for the ongoing interplay of text and readers'.[143]

Speech Act Theory. This study is influenced also in some respects by what has come to be known as speech act theory, developed by Austin, Grice, Searle and others.[144] As Selden and Widdowson put it:

---

140. Cf. the works listed by Wuellner, 'Rhetorical Criticism', p. 454. Major studies on prophetic books that combine linguistic/semiotic and rhetorical interests include C. Hardmeier, *Texttheorie und biblische Exegese: Zur rhetorischen Funktion der Trauermetaphorik in der Prophetie* (BEvT, 79; Munich: Chr. Kaiser Verlag, 1978); and Wiklander, *Prophecy*. For a useful bibliography on semantics, discourse analysis, historical/comparative linguistics, etc., which also contains some references to works that apply discourse analysis to the study of the prophetic literature, see W.R. Bodine (ed.), *Linguistics and Biblical Hebrew* (Winona Lake, IN: Eisenbrauns, 1992), pp. 279-305. See also P. Cotterell, 'Linguistics, Meaning, Semantics, and Discourse Analysis', in *NIDOTTE*, I, pp. 134-60.

141. Green, 'Discourse Analysis', p. 178.

142. Green, 'Discourse Analysis', p. 179 (his italics).

143. Green, 'Discourse Analysis', p. 179.

144. Cf. J.L. Austin, *How to Do Things With Words* (Oxford: Clarendon Press, 2nd edn, 1975); J.R. Searle, *Speech Acts: An Essay in the Philosophy of Language* (Cambridge: Cambridge University Press, 1969); *idem, Expression and Meaning: Studies in the Theory of Speech Acts* (Cambridge: Cambridge University Press, 1979); H.P. Grice, 'Logic and Conversation', in P. Cole and J.L. Morgan (eds.), *Syntax and Semantics*. III. *Speech-Acts* (New York: Academic Press, 1975), pp. 41-58; *idem*, 'Utterance-Meaning, Sentence-Meaning, and Word-Meaning', in J.R. Searle (ed.), *The Philosophy of Language* (London: Oxford University Press, 1971), pp. 54-70.

Austin's theory of 'speech acts' was developed to supersede the old logical-
positivist view of language which assumed that the only meaningful
statements are those which describe a state of affairs in the world.[145]

Austin distinguished between 'constatives' (descriptive statements) and
'performatives' (statements that 'get something done').[146] Based on this
general distinction, Austin in a second step differentiated between three
kinds of performative statements: the 'locutionary' act, the 'illocutionary'
act and the 'perlocutionary' act.[147] Whereas the first is defined as 'the performance of an act *of* saying something', an illocution is 'the performance
of an act *in* saying something' and a perlocution is 'the performance of an
act *by* saying something'. This differentiation becomes meaningful when
we look at one of Austin's many instructive examples in which he notes
that we can, for instance, 'distinguish the locutionary act 'he *said* that…'
from the illocutionary act 'he *argued* that…' and the perlocutionary act
'he *convinced* me that…'[148]

Especially the distinction between different kinds of speech acts, or
rather different aspects of a speech act, between 'locution', 'illocution'
and 'perlocution',[149] is a useful conception in that it provides us with well-
defined concepts that allow further refinement of my functional approach
to the book of Amos. To mention just one example, the above distinction
helps us differentiate between what a prophet said (e.g. בא הקץ אל־עמי
ישראל לא־אסיף עוד עבור לו; Amos 8.2), what he was doing in making

145. Selden and Widdowson, *Reader's Guide*, p. 148; cf. M.H. Abrams, *A Glossary of Literary Terms* (Fort Worth, TX: Harcourt Brace College, 6th edn, 1993), p. 277.
146. The general distinction between constatives and performatives is made in the first lecture (cf. Austin, *How to Do Things With Words*, pp. 1-11). Lectures 2-4 deal with what Austin called 'infelicities', reflecting his basic distinction between con-statives, which can be true or false, and performatives, which are either 'happy' or 'unhappy' (cf. pp. 12-52). In lectures 5-7, Austin then discusses criteria for distin-guishing performatives from constatives (pp. 53-93).
147. For the basic distinction see lecture 8 (pp. 94-107). The subsequent lectures (9-10, pp. 108-31) follow this up by providing criteria for distinguishing 'illocutions' from 'perlocutions'.
148. Austin, *How to Do Things With Words*, p. 102 (my italics).
149. It should be noted furthermore that Austin ends his study by suggesting a list of various illocutionary forces an utterance might have. His list includes 'verdictives' (statements that give a verdict), 'exercitives' (statements that exercise powers, rights, or influence), 'commissives' (statements that commit one to doing something), 'be-habitives' (statements that have to do with attitudes and social behaviour), and 'expositives' (statements that are expository) (cf. Austin, *How to Do Things With Words*, pp. 147-63).

that statement (depending on how the illocutionary force of this particular statement is construed, issuing a threat or announcing Yahweh's immutable decree) and what the effects of that speech act were (or might have been). I will return to this issue at a later stage but it should be noted that the application of speech act theory can help us overcome one particular weakness often encountered in traditional historical-critical exegesis.[150] As

150. For programmatic statements on the use of speech act theory in biblical studies cf. the articles in H.C. White (ed.), *Speech Act Theory and Biblical Criticism* (Semeia, 41; Atlanta: Scholars Press, 1988), esp. H.C. White, 'Introduction: Speech Act Theory and Literary Criticism', pp. 1-24; M. Hancher, 'Performative Utterances, the Word of God, and the Death of the Author', pp. 27-40; H.C. White, 'The Value of Speech Act Theory for Old Testament Hermeneutics', pp. 41-63; D. Patte, 'Speech Act Theory and Biblical Exegesis', pp. 85-102; and M.J. Buss, 'Potential and Actual Interactions Between Speech Act Theory and Biblical Studies', pp. 125-34. See also J.G. du Plessis, 'Speech Act Theory and New Testament Interpretation with Special Reference to G.N. Leech's Pragmatic Principles', in P.J. Hartin and J.H. Petzer (eds.), *Text and Interpretation: New Approaches in the Criticism of the New Testament* (Leiden: E.J. Brill, 1991), pp. 129-42; and A. Wagner, *Sprechakte und Sprechaktanalyse im Alten Testament: Untersuchungen im biblischen Hebräisch an der Nahtstelle zwischen Handlungsebene und Grammatik* (BZAW, 253; Berlin: W. de Gruyter, 1997).

The theory has been applied to a number of effects. N. Wolterstorff, *Divine Discourse: Philosophical Reflections on the Claim that God Speaks* (Cambridge: Cambridge University Press, 1995), for instance, used it to develop a hermeneutic in which Scripture is defined as divine speech (cf. A.C. Thiselton, 'Speech-Act Theory and the Claim that God Speaks: Nicholas Wolterstorff's *Divine Discourse*', *SJT* 50 [1997], pp. 97-110; R. Swinburne, 'Review of Nicholas Wolterstorff's *Divine Discourse*', *Philosophy* 71 [1996], pp. 465-68; M. Westphal, 'Theology as Talking About a God Who Talks: Review of Nicholas Wolterstorff's *Divine Discourse*', *Modern Theology* 13 [1997], pp. 525-36; and M.P. Levine, 'Review of Nicholas Wolterstorff's *Divine Discourse*', *Mind* 106 [1997], pp. 359-63, for reviews of that work). See also K.J. Vanhoozer, 'God's Mighty Speech-Acts: The Doctrine of Scripture Today', in P.E. Satterthwaite and D.F. Wright (eds.), *A Pathway into the Holy Scripture* (Grand Rapids: Eerdmans, 1994), pp. 143-81; *idem, Is There a Meaning in This Text? The Bible, the Reader, and the Morality of Literary Knowledge* (Grand Rapids: Zondervan, 1998); and *idem,* 'From Speech Acts to Scripture Acts: The Covenant of Discourse and the Discourse of the Covenant', in Bartholomew, Greene and Möller (eds.), *After Pentecost*, pp. 1-49, who applied speech act theory in his proposals for an author-oriented biblical hermeneutics.

Directly relevant to Old Testament studies are H.C. White, *Narration and Discourse in the Book of Genesis* (Cambridge: Cambridge University Press, 1991); N. Lohfink, 'Bund als Vertrag im Deuteronomium', *ZAW* 107 (1995), pp. 215-39; D.K. Berry, *The Psalms and Their Readers: Interpretive Strategies for Psalm 18* (JSOTSup, 153; Sheffield: JSOT Press, 1993), pp. 119-30; S.B. Reid, 'Psalm 50: Prophetic Speech and

I have argued elsewhere, traditional interpretation of Amos is often characterised by a striking literalism.[151] That is to say, exegetes frequently look only at the 'surface grammar' of the texts in question, failing to consider the *function* of the statements they contain. Sometimes diachronic answers are then sought for questions that would never have arisen in the first place had exegetes abandoned what Selden and Widdowson have called the 'old logical-positivist view of language'[152] in favour of a functional approach.

As already indicated, my exegesis of Amos will illustrate, at a couple of places, how the application of speech act theory can help us elucidate the function and possible effects of Amos's rhetoric. At this point, however, we need to move on to the next step, which is to provide an outline of the methodological procedures applied in the study in hand.

God's Performative Utterances', in *idem* (ed.), *Prophets and Paradigms: Essays in Honor of Gene M. Tucker* (JSOTSup, 229; Sheffield: Sheffield Academic Press, 1996), pp. 217-30; W. Houston, 'What Did the Prophets Think They Were Doing? Speech Acts and Prophetic Discourse in the Old Testament', in Gordon (ed.), *'The Place Is Too Small for Us'*, pp. 133-53; T. Eagleton, 'J.L. Austin and the Book of Jonah', in R.M. Schwartz (ed.), *The Book and the Text: The Bible and Literary Theory* (Oxford: Basil Blackwell, 1990), pp. 231-36; Patrick, *Rhetoric of Revelation*; and Möller, 'Words of (In-)evitable Certitude'.

See also the following works in the area of New Testament studies: T. Aurelio, *Disclosures in den Gleichnissen Jesu: Eine Anwendung der Disclosure-Theorie von I.T. Ramsey, der modernen Metaphorik und der Sprechakte auf die Gleichnisse Jesu* (Regensburger Studien zur Theologie, 8; Frankfurt: Peter Lang, 1977); A.C. Thiselton, 'The Parables as Language-Event: Some Comments on Fuchs's Hermeneutics in the Light of Linguistic Philosophy', *SJT* 23 (1970), pp. 437-68; *idem*, 'The Supposed Power of Words in the Biblical Writings', *JTS* 25 (1974), pp. 283-99; *idem*, 'Christology in Luke, Speech-Act Theory and the Problem of Dualism in Christology after Kant', in J.B. Green and M. Turner (eds.), *Jesus of Nazareth: Lord and Christ* (Grand Rapids: Eerdmans, 1994), pp. 453-72; J.E. Botha, *Jesus and the Samaritan Woman: A Speech-Act Reading of John 4.1-42* (NovTSup, 65; Leiden: E.J. Brill, 1991); D. Neufeld, *Reconceiving Texts as Speech Acts: An Analysis of 1 John* (BIS, 7; Leiden: E.J. Brill, 1994); and W.R. Baker, *Personal Speech-Ethics in the Epistle of James* (WUNT, 2.68; Tübingen: J.C.B. Mohr, 1995).

151. Cf. K. Möller, 'Rehabilitation eines Propheten: Die Botschaft des Amos aus rhetorischer Perspektive unter besonderer Berücksichtigung von Am. 9,7-15', *EuroJT* 6 (1997), pp. 41-55; *idem*, 'Words of (In-)evitable Certitude'.

152. Selden and Widdowson, *Reader's Guide*, p. 148, as quoted above.

b. *Five Steps of Rhetorical-Critical Analysis*

Surveying various types of rhetorical criticism, Black has argued that Kennedy's definition is the most useful one for practical criticism because it exhibits a very comprehensive understanding of rhetoric. It is capable therefore of aiding even the concerns of scholars who pursue aims very different from those at the fore in Kennedy's approach. More importantly, it comprises an articulated procedure, a methodology, and thus moves beyond a mere interpretative perspective.[153] For these reasons, his model has been very influential, especially in New Testament studies, but it begins to exert an increasing influence also on the study of the Old Testament. Based on ancient textbooks of rhetoric, Kennedy proposed a rhetorical-critical analysis that proceeds in five steps. These have been followed by many, although sometimes slight modifications have been made. In what follows, I present my own version of these five steps, which takes into account some of the suggested modifications.[154]

1. To start with, the critic needs to identify the *rhetorical unit(s)* in the text. These have been defined by Wuellner as 'argumentative units affecting the reader's reasoning or...imagination'.[155] Characteristic for the concept of rhetorical units is that it can be applied to sections of varying length and complexity. Thus, starting with the smallest, in the book of Amos these would include metaphors, hymns, short oracles, etc. On the next level, we find combinations of small units as, for instance, in the series of oracles against the nations (Amos 1.3–2.16). This combination of small rhetorical or argumentative units results in discourses that feature arguments that are different from or exceed those of the individual units. These larger discourses, of which the book of Amos according to my analysis contains ten,[156] therefore need to be investigated in their own right. Finally, the largest rhetorical unit we are concerned with is the book as a whole.[157]

---

153. C.C. Black, 'Rhetorical Criticism and Biblical Interpretation', *ExpTim* 100 (1988–89), pp. 252-58 (256-57).

154. The steps of rhetorical-critical analysis are outlined in Kennedy, *New Testament Interpretation*, pp. 33-38; Wuellner, 'Rhetorical Criticism', pp. 455-60; Bible and Culture Collective, *Postmodern Bible*, pp. 150-56; Black, 'Rhetorical Criticism and Biblical Interpretation', pp. 254-55; and Walton, 'Rhetorical Criticism', p. 5.

155. Wuellner, 'Rhetorical Criticism', p. 455; cf. Bible and Culture Collective, *Postmodern Bible*, p. 150.

156. These are Amos 1.1-2; 1.3–2.16; 3.1-15; 4.1-13; 5.1-17; 5.18-27; 6.1-14; 7.1–8.3; 8.4-14 and 9.1-15.

157. The investigation could be extended, of course, to consider the Book of the

2. The next tasks then consist in identifying the *rhetorical situation* that occasioned the utterance (i.e., the book of Amos in our case) and in determining the *rhetorical problem* the author felt compelled to address. I have already referred to Bitzer's definition of the rhetorical situation as the specific condition or situation that prompts a specific oral or textual utterance. This utterance would not exist without the exigency that caused it, which is why Bitzer stresses that 'it is the situation which calls the discourse into existence'.[158] More precisely, he defines this situation 'as a natural context of persons, events, objects, relations, and an exigency which strongly invites utterance'.[159] The exigency, however, Bitzer continues, 'can be completely or partially removed if discourse, introduced into the situation, can so constrain human decision or action as to bring about the significant modification of the exigency'.[160] This is necessary because 'any *exigency* is an imperfection marked by urgency; it is a defect, an obstacle, something waiting to be done, a thing which is other than it should be'.[161]

Lausberg points out that the rhetorical situation determines the rhetorical choices made by the rhetorician or author; for instance, which rhetorical genre(s) and what strategy to use.[162] But how can we establish what the rhetorical situation was? Wuellner notes that traditionally there are three possible procedures.[163] (1) by looking at the *status* of the utterance, its basic issue,[164] (2) by investigating its underlying *topoi*,[165] or

Twelve or even the canon of the Old or of both Testaments.

158. Bitzer, 'Rhetorical Situation', p. 248; on the concept of 'rhetorical situation' see also A. Brinton, 'Situation in the Theory of Rhetoric', *Philosophy & Rhetoric* 14 (1981), pp. 234-48.

159. Bitzer, 'Rhetorical Situation', p. 251.

160. Bitzer, 'Rhetorical Situation', p. 252.

161. Bitzer, 'Rhetorical Situation', p. 252 (his italics).

162. H. Lausberg, *Elemente der literarischen Rhetorik* (Munich: Hueber, 8th edn, 1984), pp. 21-23.

163. Wuellner, 'Rhetorical Criticism', p. 456.

164. Cf. also H. Lausberg, *Handbuch der literarischen Rhetorik: Eine Grundlegung der Literaturwissenschaft* (2 vols.; Munich: Hueber, 1960), §§79-138; and Kennedy, *New Testament Interpretation*, pp. 18-19.

165. Concerning this issue, which I am not going to pursue, see W. Wuellner, 'Toposforschung und Torainterpretation bei Paulus und Jesus', *NTS* 24 (1978), pp. 463-83; J.C. Brunt, 'More on the Topos as a New Testament Form', *JBL* 104 (1985), pp. 495-500; and F. Siegert, *Argumentation bei Paulus gezeigt an Röm 9-11* (WUNT, 34; Tübingen: J.C.B. Mohr [Paul Siebeck], 1985), pp. 35-38, 199-206.

(3) by considering its *rhetorical genre*. These issues are interconnected, however, as becomes clear in the following statement by the authors of the Bible and Culture Collective:

> The preeminent concern for rhetorical critics is the relation of the choice of a rhetorical genre to the specific rhetorical situation, to the basic issue (status or *stasis*) of the argument. The chosen genre, in its specificity rather than its typicality, becomes part of the rhetorical situation and must be a major factor in the delineation of that situation.[166]

3. This then brings us to the next step, namely the investigation of the *rhetorical genre*. Rhetorical critics traditionally distinguish a triad of possible genres, which are specified using the different reactions that are demanded of the audience as criteria.[167] *Judicial* rhetoric (*genus iudiciale*) asks hearers or readers to judge past events. In *deliberative* rhetoric (*genus deliberativum*), the audience is invited to make 'a *deliberative* assessment of actions that would be expedient or beneficial for future performance'.[168] *Epideictic* rhetoric (*genus demonstrativum*), finally, treats the audience as spectators pursuing the aim of reinforcing certain beliefs and values.[169] Epideictic rhetoric is often regarded as being either laudatory or polemical but Perelman and Olbrechts-Tyteca made a strong case for viewing it as primarily educational in nature.[170] Kennedy charts the positive and negative forms for each of these categories: for judicial rhetoric, these would be prosecution and defence, for deliberative rhetoric, exhortation and dissuasion, and in the case of epideictic rhetoric, encomium and invective.[171]

It needs to be stressed, however, that due to my interest in how the authors or editors of the book addressed the particular rhetorical problem they were facing, I am concerned primarily with the specific manifestation

166. Bible and Culture Collective, *Postmodern Bible*, p. 152.

167. Cf. Kennedy, *New Testament Interpretation*, pp. 19, 36-37; Black, 'Rhetorical Criticism and Biblical Interpretation', p. 254; Walton, 'Rhetorical Criticism', p. 4; and Gitay, *Isaiah*, p. 7.

168. Black, 'Rhetorical Criticism and Biblical Interpretation', p. 254.

169. Ueding, *Klassische Rhetorik*, p. 55, notes that under the influence of Christianity a fourth genre emerged, that of the spiritual speech or sermon (*genus praedicandi*).

170. Perelman and Olbrechts-Tyteca, *New Rhetoric*, pp. 47-54; cf. Bible and Culture Collective, *Postmodern Bible*, p. 156. Lausberg, *Handbuch*; *idem*, *Elemente*, has been criticized precisely for his restriction of epideictic rhetoric to laudatory purposes (cf. Wuellner, 'Rhetorical Criticism', p. 452 n. 25 and the literature cited there).

171. Kennedy, *New Testament Interpretation*, p. 20; cf. Walton, 'Rhetorical Criticism', p. 4.

and application of rhetorical genres rather than their typical features. We need to reckon, furthermore, with the possibility that a rhetorician might have utilized a hybrid, a mixture of various genres.[172] This is particularly likely in the case of a larger rhetorical unit such as the book of Amos. Thus, although in Amos the judicial genre appears to predominate,[173] there are also examples where the prophet's rhetoric is best described as deliberative and, in a few cases, perhaps, as epideictic.

However, applying concepts developed by speech act theorists, I am going to argue that despite the predominant use of judicial rhetoric, the overall *strategy* is best described as deliberative, not judicial. Contra Kennedy, according to whom the dominant genre 'reflects the author's major purpose',[174] I would contend that, at least in the case of Amos, it reflects the *rhetorical strategy* rather than the main purpose of those responsible for the book.[175] Thus, while most of Amos's oracles appear to be of a judicial nature,[176] the aim in uttering them and, more importantly for our purposes, in presenting them in the book that bears his name may have been, indeed I believe was, a deliberative one. The distinction made here between the employment of a certain genre and the resultant effects, it should be noted, reflects the classic speech-act-theoretical differentiation between *illocution* and *perlocution* mentioned above.

172. Kennedy, *New Testament Interpretation*, p. 19; and Walton, 'Rhetorical Criticism', p. 7; cf. also Bible and Culture Collective, *Postmodern Bible*, pp. 152-54; and Wuellner, 'Rhetorical Criticism', p. 459, for Paul's use of mixed genres in 1 Corinthians.

173. Cf. Kennedy, *New Testament Interpretation*, p. 19, who notes that 'a discourse usually has one dominant species'.

174. Kennedy, *New Testament Interpretation*, p. 19.

175. It would be interesting to follow this up because I suspect that this could be true in general, i.e. that a text's dominant genre is indicative of its principal rhetorical strategy rather than its major purpose. This anyway is one context in which speech act theory usefully complements rhetorical-critical analysis. See Möller, 'Words of (In-)evitable Certitude', for further discussion.

176. Westermann, finding the roots of the prophetic judgment speech in Israelite legal practice, strongly argued that judgment oracles are best understood as what we might call a judge's final verdict (C. Westermann, *Basic Forms of Prophetic Speech* [trans. H.C. White; Cambridge: Lutterworth, new edn, 1991]). However, as Tucker has pointed out in his foreword to the reprinted English edition of Westermann's work (pp. ix-xvi [xiii]), this has not remained uncontested, as, for instance, Koch has denied 'both a judicial background and a legal pattern in the speeches'. For Koch's own understanding of the prophetic judgment speech see Koch, *Formgeschichte*, pp. 251-54.

4. In the last paragraph, I already trespassed upon the territory of the next step of rhetorical-critical enquiry, namely the analysis of the *rhetorical strategy and style* employed by the rhetorician. In classical rhetorical terms, the critic needs to pay attention to the aspects of invention (*inventio*, εὕρεσις), structure (*dispositio*, τάξις) and style (*elocutio*, λέξις).[177] The guiding concern of the investigation is to establish 'how the rhetorical choices made (the *invention*) create a particular organization (*disposition*) of the argument, and how this organization generates specific stylistic techniques'.[178]

First, *inventio*, in this conception, includes 'the discovery of material suitable to the occasion'[179] (*materia*), the determination of the issue at stake (*status*) and the selection of techniques suitable to support the position of the rhetorician. The latter was helped by a list of categories containing a host of argumentative techniques, the so-called *topoi*.[180] Integral to Aristotle's system of rhetoric are the 'proofs', concerning which he distinguished between inartificial and artificial ones. In the present study, I am interested primarily in the latter, which comprise *ethos, pathos* and *logos*.[181] These correspond respectively to the moral character of the rhetorician (τὸ ἦθος τοῦ λέγοντος), his ability of 'putting the hearer into a certain frame of mind' (τὸ τὸν ἀκροατὴν διαθεῖναί πως) and the speech itself (αὐτός ὁ λόγος).[182] Commenting on these concepts, Wuellner notes that 'rhetorical criticism makes us more fully aware of the *whole* range of appeals embraced and provoked by rhetoric: not only the

---

177. These reflect the first three of the five aspects of the practice of rhetoric, the final two being concerned with memorization (*memoria*, μνήμη) and delivery (*pronunciatio/actio*, ὑπόκρισις); Fuhrmann, *Die antike Rhetorik*, pp. 77-80.

178. Bible and Culture Collective, *Postmodern Bible*, p. 154.

179. Trible, *Rhetorical Criticism*, p. 8.

180. See Ueding, *Klassische Rhetorik*, pp. 55-56; Ø. Andersen, *Im Garten der Rhetorik: Die Kunst der Rede in der Antike* (trans. B. Mannsperger and I. Tveide; Darmstadt: Wissenschaftliche Buchgesellschaft, 2001), pp. 156-62; and B.L. Mack, *Rhetoric and the New Testament* (GBS; Minneapolis: Fortress Press, 1990), p. 32.

181. On the basis of these concepts, Cicero distinguished three *officia oratoris*: to teach (*docere*), to please (*delectare*) and to move (*movere*). Each of these has its appropriate style; i.e. the 'plain' style is best for instruction, the 'intermediate' style for giving pleasure and the 'grand' style for rousing the audience's emotions (Cicero, *Orator* 69).

182. These concepts are outlined in Aristotle, *Rhet.* 1.2.3-6. Aristotle thought *ethos* to be the most effective means of persuasion (*Rhet.* 1.2.4). See Möller, 'Rehabilitation', pp. 49-50, for an appropriation of the concept of *ethos* for the reading of Amos.

rational and cognitive dimensions, but also the emotive and imaginative ones'.[183] However, rhetoricians do not necessarily employ the whole range but usually favour one of these appeals. Depending on whether a rhetorician is predisposed to using *ethos* and *logos* or prefers *pathos*, scholars distinguish between 'convincing' and 'persuasive' strategies.[184]

Secondly, interest in a text's *dispositio*, its structure or the organization of its argument, goes beyond the mere delineation of its rhetorical units referred to as the first step of rhetorical-critical enquiry. The focus at this point is on the persuasive effect of the textual units. To uncover this effect, the critic asks whether and how these units work together to achieve some unified purpose, or indeed fail to do so.[185] Thirdly, yet another important factor of suasive discourse is what rhetorical critics call *elocutio*, the style of a text. Rhetorical criticism regards stylistic features not as mere embellishments of an oral or written utterance but recognizes that a rhetorician utilizes them in order to amplify certain parts of his or her discourse. Stylistic features are a potent means for achieving the desired effect(s);[186] and the critic—being interested in the rhetorical nature of the utterance, not its poetic nature—seeks to elucidate their role for the argumentative development of the rhetorical discourse.

5. Finally, the critic needs to evaluate the *rhetorical effectiveness* of the discourse in question. Here, the leading question is whether, or to what degree, the utterance is a fitting response to the exigency that occasioned it. This question can be addressed by asking whether the rhetorical utterance successfully modified the exigency, or whether it had the potential of doing so. This distinction is necessary since the actual rhetorical effectiveness of an utterance evidently does not depend on internal factors (such as its genre, disposition, etc.) alone. And given that in the case of an

183. Wuellner, 'Rhetorical Criticism', p. 461 (his italics). This has been stressed also by D. Ehninger, 'A Synoptic View of Systems of Western Rhetoric', *QJS* 61 (1975), pp. 448-53.

184. Wuellner, 'Rhetorical Criticism', p. 457; Perelman and Olbrechts-Tyteca, *New Rhetoric*, pp. 26-31; and C. Perelman, *The Realm of Rhetoric* (trans. W. Kluback; Notre Dame: University of Notre Dame Press, 1982), p. 15.

185. Kennedy, *New Testament Interpretation*, p. 37.

186. Cf. Kennedy, *New Testament Interpretation*, p. 37. Detailed lists of figures of speech, and illustrations of how they work, can be found in W. Bühlmann and K. Scherer, *Stilfiguren der Bibel: Ein kleines Nachschlagewerk* (Fribourg: Schweizerisches Katholisches Bibelwerk, 1973); and E.W. Bullinger, *Figures of Speech Used in the Bible Explained and Illustrated* (London: Eyre & Spottiswoode, 1898; repr., Grand Rapids: Baker Book House, 1968).

ancient text, such as the book of Amos, we mostly lack the evidence to evaluate the discourse's actual effectiveness, it is the second part of the question—whether the utterance had the potential of modifying the exigency—that needs to be our primary focus.

Before I end this introductory chapter by addressing some criticisms put forward against the rhetorical-critical approach, let me underline that the steps of rhetorical-critical analysis outlined above should be seen as a circular process.[187] Thus, for instance, insight into the disposition of the text may lead to a better grasp of its genre, which will then influence the critic's understanding of the rhetorical situation, and so on.

3. *Rhetorical Criticism and the Study of Amos*

Rhetorical criticism has been criticized on various grounds. I have already discussed Barton's reservations concerning its potential apologetic thrust. I have also already dealt with the question of whether the rhetorical-critical system is applicable to written discourse, to which Eagleton has given an affirmative answer. At this point then, we need to ask whether the method is applicable, more specifically, to a prophetic book that does not belong to the realm of 'Old Western literature', to use Lewis's words.[188] That is to say, is it not anachronistic to subject a prophetic book such as Amos to the system of classical Graeco-Roman rhetoric? After all, neither Amos nor the editors of the book were familiar with Aristotle's system of rhetoric, let alone those of his successors. Thus, in their crafting of spoken or written discourse, they, obviously, were not guided by the conventions of classical rhetoricians.

However, for our approach to be valid, these are not absolute preconditions. Aristotle and his successors, after all, did not *invent* rhetorical discourse. As noted earlier, whoever is prompted by the 'imperative stimulus' of a 'rhetorical situation' to address the exigency of that situation is making a rhetorical utterance, regardless of whether or not he or she is familiar with ancient rhetoric. Aristotle and others merely investigated rhetorical utterances and then developed a concept of rhetoric that was based partly on their observations and partly on philosophical ideas and concepts. To be sure, the emerging system of rhetoric did influence later generations of

187. Cf. Kennedy, *New Testament Interpretation*, p. 33.
188. Cf. Lewis, *'De descriptione temporum'*, p. 12. As already noted, Lewis uses this term to refer to Western European literature from its Greek or pre-Greek beginnings down to, roughly, Victorian times.

rhetoricians, who would attempt to construct their rhetorical discourses according to the guidelines provided by the classical theorists of rhetoric. However, even before the time of Aristotle there existed what Kennedy befittingly called 'natural' or 'pre-conceptual' rhetoric.[189] Furthermore, Classen, considering the possible sources of Paul's rhetorical skills, stresses that, in addition to rhetorical theory, there are other factors that come into play. These, according to Classen, are conscious imitation of written or spoken practice,[190] unconscious borrowing from the practice of others, and a natural gift for effective speaking or writing.[191] Classen's observations have been noted here because they help to explain the existence of what I would regard as unmistakable 'rhetorical qualities' in Amos. These can be investigated and assessed using classical rhetorical theory, which, as Kennedy maintains, is a helpful tool because of its highly developed con-ceptualization.[192] In fact, the use of 'anachronistic' conceptual tools is the norm in the study of any ancient literature. For instance, recourse to modern linguistics is generally thought appropriate for the study of biblical Hebrew despite the evident possibility that the authors of the texts under considera-tion may not have been aware of the insights associated with that discipline.

However, when investigating a book that was not composed according to the system of classical rhetoric, it is important to resist what Black has called the 'disquieting tendency to press oracles or letters into elaborate rhetorical schemes of organization'.[193] To avoid that fallacy, I have been careful to apply the rhetorical-critical conceptuality outlined above somewhat loosely.[194] More important than the precise rhetorical classifica-tion of every single speech form is the general awareness that the book of Amos *is* a rhetorical utterance that addresses a specific rhetorical problem. Such awareness is, I believe, urgently needed as it provides a corrective to the pitfalls of redaction criticism alluded to earlier.

189. Kennedy, *Classical Rhetoric*, pp. 9-15.

190. For this aspect see also Kennedy, *New Testament Interpretation*, p. 11.

191. C.J. Classen, 'St Paul's Epistles and Ancient Greek and Roman Rhetoric', in S.E. Porter and T.H. Olbricht (eds.), *Rhetoric and the New Testament: Essays from the 1992 Heidelberg Conference* (JSNTSup, 90; Sheffield: JSOT Press, 1993), pp. 265-91 (269).

192. Kennedy, *New Testament Interpretation*, pp. 10-11. Cf. Classen, 'St Paul's Epistles', p. 268, who maintains that 'rhetoric provides a system for the interpretation of all texts (as well as of oral utterances and even of other forms of communication)'.

193. Black, 'Rhetorical Criticism and Biblical Interpretation', p. 255.

194. Cf. Eslinger, *House of God*, p. 6, who too urges reticence in this respect.

Moreover, Kennedy rightly stressed that 'if rhetorical criticism is to be valid, it must be practised with some awareness of the traditions of Jewish speech'.[195] This, too, needs to be taken into account if ever the approach is to make a serviceable contribution to the study of the Old Testament in general and the prophetic books in particular. In this context, form-critical findings about prophetic speech forms make an important contribution in helping us understand prophetic rhetoric in the context of ancient Israelite speech and culture.[196] After what has been said so far, it will be apparent, however, that caution is needed in the application of form criticism. Most of all, we must resist what has been called the tyranny of the analytical category of genre, with its reductionistic and simplistic tendencies.[197] As we have already seen, this can be achieved only by taking into account both the typical *and* the unique. More importantly, however, form criticism is best employed alongside rhetorical criticism providing, as it does, the kind of information the latter requires.

In an article, entitled 'Old Testament Form Criticism Reconsidered', in which he reconceptualizes the form-critical approach, Knierim stresses:

> interpreting Old Testament literature and language ought to be within a context in which both appear as manifestations of communication, born by a will to communicate and functioning within such communication; that is, they include the horizon of understanding and expectation of readers and listeners and, having a historical dimension, are subject to the changing horizons of communication.[198]

Interestingly, Knierim reformulates the approach in a way that renders it quite similar to rhetorical criticism as understood in the present study (i.e., as different from the Muilenburg approach). Note especially his demand that form criticism 'would have to ask what, in a given text, constituted the communication event between writer and readers, between speaker and

195. Kennedy, *New Testament Interpretation*, p. 12. R. Majercik, 'Rhetoric and Oratory in the Greco-Roman World', in *ABD*, V, pp. 710-12 (711), sees as one characteristic of Jewish traditions of speech that 'the object is to persuade through divine authority rather than modes of rational proof'.

196. Useful succinct definitions of prophetic forms or genres can be found in M.A. Sweeney, *Isaiah 1–39 with an Introduction to Prophetic Literature* (FOTL, 16; Grand Rapids: Eerdmans, 1996), pp. 512-47.

197. Cf. Brueggemann, 'Response', pp. 34-35.

198. R.P. Knierim, 'Old Testament Form Criticism Reconsidered', *Int* 27 (1973), pp. 435-68 (467).

listener in a typical way'.[199] Knierim is also aware of the possibility that 'a text is governed by factors beyond those asked for by the form-critical method, for example, by a thematic concern or a motif'.[200] This, I believe, is not only occasionally the case, as Knierim expects, but seems to be the norm. I do agree, however, with his further expectation that

> by being subservient to those factors that dominate texts rather than by dominating texts through its own methodological system, form criticism will, probably with some kind of new face, continue to have its unique role in the concert of the exegetical disciplines.[201]

Having thus specified 'what reading I am guilty of', I now proceed to apply the approach outlined above to the book of Amos, starting with the first step of rhetorical-critical enquiry, the investigation of its rhetorical structure.

199. Knierim, 'Old Testament Form Criticism', p. 468. As regards the notion of 'a typical way', it should be noted that Knierim continues by pointing out that 'the communication event in a text *may* be constituted by the typicality of a genre understood in a certain way or it may function through some other typicality *or it may be governed by none whatsoever*' (italics added).
200. Knierim, 'Old Testament Form Criticism', p. 468.
201. Knierim, 'Old Testament Form Criticism', p. 468.

Chapter 1

RHETORICAL STRUCTURE

'The prophetic books…clearly represent the work of craftsmen and rhetoricians who sought to influence not only by the content of the message but also by the literary form into which they molded it.' Thus recently Gordon,[1] who also notes that whereas in the past scholars have been interested primarily in the anatomy of texts, 'attention is gradually expanding to include the *rhetorical intent* behind the structures' as well.[2] This development marks a significant advance over against earlier scholarly views on the arrangement of prophetic books. Von Rad, for instance, thought:

> the prophetic corpus lies before us in what are, to some extent, very shapeless collections of traditional material, arranged with almost no regard for content or chronological order, and apparently quite unaware of the laws with which we are familiar in the development of European literature.[3]

As von Rad notes, Luther reacted similarly when he complained that the prophets 'have a queer way of talking, like people who, instead of proceeding in an orderly manner, ramble off from one thing to the next, so that you cannot make head or tail of them or see what they are getting at'.[4] Or consider the following words by Coote, who asserted that 'Amos has too little story, too little train of thought, and too little internal coherence

---

1. R.P. Gordon (ed.), *'The Place Is Too Small for Us': The Israelite Prophets in Recent Scholarship* (SBTS, 5; Winona Lake, IN: Eisenbrauns, 1995), p. 107.
2. Gordon (ed.), *'The Place Is Too Small For Us'*, p. 108 (emphasis added).
3. G. von Rad, *Old Testament Theology* (trans. D.M.G. Stalker; 2 vols.; Edinburgh: Oliver & Boyd, 1962–65), II, p. 33.
4. Von Rad, *Old Testament Theology*, II, p. 33 n. 1. Luther's actual words, as quoted by von Rad, were, 'Sie (die Propheten) haben eine seltsame Weise zu reden, als die keine Ordnung halten, sondern das Hundert ins Tausend werfen, daß man sie nicht fassen noch sich drein schicken mag' (G. von Rad, *Theologie des Alten Testaments* [2 vols.; Munich: Chr. Kaiser Verlag, 10th edn, 1992–93], II, p. 41).

to hold interest for more than a few verses or, at most, a chapter'.[5] Even Dorsey, who himself contributed to the study of the final form of Amos, notices a 'mild disorder' in some sections. At the same time, however, he affirms that 'the reader cannot help noticing an orderliness in [other] parts of the book, particularly in such highly structured sections as 1, 3–2,16; 3, 3-8; 4,6-12; and 7,1-9'.[6]

What are we to make of such views? Dorsey's observations especially deserve further scrutiny. Is it true that there is a mixture of 'mild disorder' and 'highly structured sections', and if it is, what are the implications? Like most prophetic books, Amos features a complex array of structural devices and literary forms. But how are these used? Is it possible to discern any underlying pattern? Is there a structure that can legitimately be called 'rhetorical', and if so, what does it look like? These questions are important because if Gordon is right in stressing that the prophetic books seek to influence readers also by their literary form or structure, we need to understand that structure in order to trace their persuasive aims.[7] According to Callow:

> the progression of the author's thought is best seen in the light of his own grouping of his material. As the author moves towards his *communicative goal*, he does not do so in an undifferentiated string of clauses. The clauses will be grouped and that grouping will be controlled by the author's purpose in writing...[8]

5.   R.B. Coote, *Amos among the Prophets: Composition and Theology* (Philadelphia: Fortress Press, 1981), p. 1.

6.   D.A. Dorsey, 'Literary Architecture and Aural Structuring Techniques in Amos', *Bib* 73 (1992), pp. 305-30 (305). According to E.R. Wendland, 'The "Word of the Lord" and the Organization of Amos: A Dramatic Message of Conflict and Crisis in the Confrontation Between the Prophet and the People of Yahweh', *OPTAT* 2.4 (1988), pp. 1-51 (1), Amos is one of the most clearly constructed prophetic books.

7.   Cf. Bovati and Meynet, *Le livre du prophète Amos*, p. 10: 'Parmi les nombreuses opérations nécessaires au travail exégétique, l'étude de la structuration littéraire non seulement des petites unités, mais davantage encore des ensembles, depuis la "séquence" qui regroupe plusieurs péricopes, jusqu'au livre dans sa totalité, est essentielle pour comprendre et interpréter le message.'

8.   Callow, 'Units and Flow', p. 464 (my italics); cf. M.A. Sweeney, 'Formation and Form in the Prophetic Literature', in Mays, Petersen and Richards (eds.), *Old Testament Interpretation*, pp. 113-26 (116), who notes that 'the structure or arrangement of the book reveals the final redactor's overall perspectives and conceptualization of the prophet's message in that the sequence of texts within the final form of the book points to those aspects of the prophetic message that the redactor wishes to emphasize'. According to H. van Dyke Parunak, 'Some Axioms for Literary Architecture', *Semitics*

Similarly, Childs affirms that:

> *the final form of the text performs a crucial hermeneutical function* in establishing the peculiar profile of a passage. Its shaping establishes an order in highlighting certain features and subordinating others, in drawing elements to the foreground, and in pushing others to the background.[9]

1. *Parameters for Structural Investigation*

Recent years have witnessed an increased interest in the structure of prophetic books. And yet the survey of recent works on Amos, which forms the second part of this chapter, has left me with the impression that many structural investigations lack theoretical and methodological rigour. In particular, the current fascination with chiasms raises many questions. Before we go on to look at individual proposals, it is therefore necessary to consider whether (and how) the structure of a prophetic book can be charted with any measure of certainty. In keeping with the functional approach advocated in the Introduction, I would suggest, for instance, that any structural investigation must consider not only a text's structure per se, but also what purpose it is meant to be serving. It also needs to be taken into account that if a structure (or indeed a text) is intended to serve a particular purpose, it is crucial that the audience be able to grasp its structure without too much difficulty.

Thus, in this section dealing with parameters for structural investigation, I will attempt to determine the structural markers that are intended to guide readers or hearers in their perception of the book of Amos. Moreover, for any structure to be rhetorically effective, it needs to accentuate rather than run counter to the content of the text it governs. Secondly, therefore, we need to consider the interrelation of form and content, structure and message.

a. *Recognizability*
As already indicated, structural markers simply will not work if they are not easily perceivable by the hearer or reader. If a text is to function as a

8 (1983), pp. 1-16 (5-6), the biblical writers wrote in paragraphs or thought units. More than 70 years ago, J. Boehmer, 'Amos nach Gedankengang und Grundgedanken', *Nieuwe Theologische Studien* 10 (1927), pp. 1-7, anticipated this idea, attempting a thematic outline of Amos based on thought units, but his proposal is not very convincing.

9.   B.S. Childs, 'The Canonical Shape of the Prophetic Literature', *Int* 32 (1978), pp. 46-55 (48; my italics).

means of persuasion, i.e. if it is to have rhetorical impact, and if its structure is to guide the audience's understanding, it follows that its structural markers must be readily discernible. However, this then leaves us with the question of which kind of structural markers an audience can be expected to discern without too much difficulty, and which kind it would most likely not be able to pick up. To answer these questions, let us consider briefly ancient reading practices in particular as well as the nature of the reading act[10] in general, as both these factors have a direct impact on the recognisability of structural markers.

Reading Practices Ancient and Modern.
1. *Reading, literacy and orality in antiquity.* The importance of investigating ancient reading practices has been stressed by Ben Zvi, who notes:

> since it is *only* through reading that the communicative message of the text may emerge, it is absolutely imperative to address the process of reading itself, and to critically advance the most likely reconstruction of how the 'original' communities of readers could have read and understood the text.[11]

Müller, investigating the reading practices of Graeco-Roman antiquity and ancient Judaism, highlights two major differences between the reading act in ancient times and our own reading practices: While we read silently and to ourselves, in antiquity reading most often was a social event, and it was at almost all times done aloud (this even applied when someone was reading to herself).[12]

---

10. This phrase mirrors the title of one of Iser's works; cf. W. Iser, *Der Akt des Lesens: Theorie ästhetischer Wirkung* (UTB, 636; Munich: Fink, 3rd edn, 1990).

11. Ben Zvi, *Obadiah*, pp. 3-4.

12. P. Müller, *'Verstehst du auch, was du liest?' Lesen und Verstehen im Neuen Testament* (Darmstadt: Wissenschaftliche Buchgesellschaft, 1994), esp. ch. 3. In the New Testament, in Acts 8.30, we read about Philip *hearing* the Ethiopian eunuch reading from the prophet Isaiah. Also some of Müller's examples from the Graeco-Roman world are instructive:

(a) Public reading: In *Phaidon*, Plato has Socrates saying ἀκούσας μέν ποτε ἐκ βιβλίου τινός (Plato, *Phaid.* 97b), and in *Theaitetos*, Eukleides and Terpsion speak of a slave-boy (described as ὁ παῖς ἀναγνώσεται), who is commanded to read to them (λαβὲ τὸ βιβλίον καὶ λέγε; Plato, *Theait.* 143b, c). The slave is thus a *lector*, an ἀναγνώστης. At other times, however, the *lectio* ('reading') was less welcome, as Martial's sarcastic rebuke of an unknown poet indicates: 'Do you wish to know why it is, Ligurinus, that nobody is glad to meet you, that, wherever you go, there is flight and a vast solitude around you? You are too much of a poet. This is a very dangerous fault.

While our knowledge of reading practices in Old Testament times unfortunately is rather limited, what we do know confirms Müller's conclusions. In the first place, the Hebrew verb used to refer to the process of reading is קרא, the most common meaning of which is 'to call'. And although Müller is correct to note that it does not occur very often in the sense of 'reading'[13] there are, nevertheless, some important passages where it refers to the reading of written sources to an audience.[14] In the Septuagint, the term is translated as ἀναγινώσκω (see Jer. 2.2; 3.12; 7.2, 27; 19.2), which is used also in the New Testament with the meaning 'to read' or 'to read to someone'.[15] Based on his findings, Müller notes that the term depicts reading 'within a context of proclamation and [public]

A tigress roused by the theft of her cubs is not feared so much, nor yet a viper burnt by the midday sun, nor yet a vicious scorpion. For I ask you, who would endure such trials? You read to me as I stand, you read to me as I sit, you read to me as I run, you read to me as I shit. I flee to the baths: you boom in my ear. I head for the pool: I'm not allowed to swim. I hurry to dinner: you stop me in my tracks. I arrive at dinner: you drive me away as I eat. Tired out, I take a nap: you rouse me as I lie. Do you care to see how much damage you do? A just man, upright and innocent, you are feared' (Martial, *Epigr.* 3.44).

(b) Private reading: Pliny (*Epist.* 1.9) affirms that he talks to himself and to his books: *mecum tantum et cum libellis loquor*, and Augustine speaks in his *Confessions* about a most unusual observation, namely that he often met Ambrose reading silently to himself. That this is indeed very unusual is confirmed by Augustine going to great lengths to assure the reader that Ambrose must surely have had good reasons for this practice (Augustine, *Conf.* 6.3). According to Parunak, 'Some Axioms', pp. 2-3, this is the earliest clear reference to silent reading.

13. Müller, *'Verstehst du auch, was du liest?'*, p. 33.

14. Cf. Exod. 24.3-7; Deut. 31.9-11; Josh. 8.30-35; 2 Kgs 23.2-3 || 2 Chron. 34.30-31; Jer. 36.6-10 and Neh. 8–9. For a brief discussion of texts that refer to public readings of the Torah see J.W. Watts, 'Public Readings and Pentateuchal Law', *VT* 45 (1995), pp. 540-57 (540-42). Of particular importance is his observation that these readings could be quite extensive. Cf. J.W. Watts, 'Rhetorical Strategy in the Composition of the Pentateuch', *JSOT* 68 (1995), pp. 3-22 (3): 'The Hebrew Bible rarely depicts the reading of books or documents, but when it does, it usually portrays public readings of entire law codes.'

15. R. Bultmann, 'ἀναγινώσκω, ἀνάγνωσις', in *TWNT*, I, p. 347, points out that in the New Testament the words ἀναγινώσκω and ἀνάγνωσις are most often used to indicate a public reading from the Old Testament (Mk 2.25 par.; 12.10 par.; Mt. 12.5; Acts 8.28; 13.15; 2 Cor. 3.14; Gal. 4.21; 1 Tim. 4.13; cf. Josephus, *Ant.* 4.209; 10.267; and Philo, *Rer. Div. Her.* 253). Cf. also W. Bauer, *Griechisch-deutsches Wörterbuch zu den Schriften des Neuen Testaments und der frühchristlichen Literatur* (ed. K. Aland and B. Aland; Berlin: W. de Gruyter, 6th rev. edn, 1988), sub. ἀναγι(γ)νώσκω.

address', and that 'it belongs to a process of communication, which emanates from God and which addresses people through his words laid down in the Scriptures'.[16]

Another phrase used to express the idea of reading is הגה (see Josh. 1.8 and Ps. 1.2). Sarna, commenting on Ps. 1.2, is adamant that הגה 'carries a decidedly oral nuance', and that in Ps. 1 it should not be translated as 'to meditate'.[17] Thus, whereas קרא speaks of the public reading in front of an audience, הגה can denote the audible murmuring of the Law.[18] According to Sarna, the individual of Ps. 1.2 'studies a sacred text which is the object of intense focus and concentration; and the method of study is reading aloud, rote learning, and constant oral repetition.'[19] These, Sarna claims, 'formed the standard pattern of teaching and learning in the ancient world, neareastern and classical'.[20] He supports his claim by referring to the practices of ancient Egyptian schools. Thus, he mentions an instruction from the ninth or tenth Dynasty (22nd–21st centuries BCE), which is addressed to King Merikare and which speaks of a schoolmate as someone

16. Müller, *'Verstehst du auch, was du liest?'*, pp. 35-36.

17. N.M. Sarna, *On the Book of Psalms: Exploring the Prayers of Ancient Israel* (New York: Schocken Books, 1995), p. 38. He notes that the verb also features in the Balaam inscription from Deir 'Alla where it has the meaning 'say, speak' (cf. J. Hoftijzer, [ed.], *Aramaic Texts from Deir 'Alla* [Documenta et monumenta orients antiqui, 19; Leiden: E.J. Brill, 1976], p. 173). Sarna also directs our attention to CD 10.6; 13.2; 14.6-7 (*sic*; the last passage should be CD 14.7-8) where we find the phrase ספר ההגי, 'the book of the *hgw* (study)'. This phrase Sarna takes as pointing to the fact that the Torah 'was invariably recited aloud' (Sarna, *Book of Psalms*, p. 222 n. 82). In rabbinical Judaism, the learning of Scripture by heart, which was achieved by repeatedly reciting texts aloud, was an important part of Jewish education (cf. S. Safrai, 'Education and the Study of the Torah', in *idem* and M. Stern [eds.], *The Jewish People in the First Century: Historical Geography, Political History, Social, Cultural and Religious Life and Institutions* [Compendia rerum Iudaicarum ad Novum Testamentum, Section 1; 2 vols.; Assen: Van Gorcum, 1974–76], II, pp. 945-70; R. Riesner, *Jesus als Lehrer: Eine Untersuchung zum Ursprung der Evangelien-Überlieferung* [WUNT, 2.7; Tübingen: J.C.B. Mohr (Paul Siebeck), 3rd edn, 1988], *passim*; and Müller, *'Verstehst du auch, was du liest?'*, pp. 38-39; see also *'Erub.* 53b-54a).

18. A. Negoiță and H. Ringgren, 'הִגָּיוֹן, הָגוּת, הֶגֶה, הָגָה', in *TDOT*, III, pp. 321-24 (323). Although the term is not a common word for speaking, it does occur in the Psalms to indicate the giving of praise (cf. Pss. 35.28; 71.24), as J. Herrmann, 'Das Gebet im AT', in *TWNT*, II, pp. 782-99 (784), remarks.

19. Sarna, *Book of Psalms*, p. 38.

20. Sarna, *Book of Psalms*, p. 38.

'with whom one "chanted the writings" in class'.[21] Another Egyptian text, this time from the twentieth Dynasty (c. 1185–1069 BCE), advises a schoolboy to 'write with your hand, read with your mouth'.[22]

Given this evidence, it seems reasonable to conclude that people in Old Testament times would have been likely to read aloud.[23] If they read at all that is. Most would not have been able to read or, even if they were, would not have had easy access to books.[24] Public reading, therefore, was the only means by which to teach the 'common' people 'the law and the prophets'.[25] However, as the example of the individual in Ps. 1.2 illustrates, in Israel as well as in ancient Graeco-Roman culture, to read aloud

21. Sarna, *Book of Psalms*, p. 39 (cf. *ANET*, p. 145).

22. Sarna, *Book of Psalms*, p. 39 (cf. M. Lichtheim [ed.], *Ancient Egyptian Literature: A Book of Readings* [3 vols.; Berkeley: University of California Press, 1973–80], II, p. 168).

23. Indeed, as again Sarna emphasizes, 'Eli's reaction to Hannah's silent praying, in 1 Sam. 1.12-14, shows that audible prayer was the rule' (Sarna, *Book of Psalms*, p. 222 n. 84).

24. Cf. Y. Gitay, 'Deutero-Isaiah: Oral or Written?', *JBL* 99 (1980), pp. 185-97 (191): 'copies of written material in the pre-printing period were limited in number for physical reasons'. He adds that 'the appearance of the elements of speech in written material has to be understood in light of the limited knowledge of reading which was restricted to professionals' (p. 194). See also Ben Zvi, *Obadiah*, p. 5, who notes that 'the reading of the ['popular' public] would proceed through the intermediary function of the [educated elite]'. He furthermore claims that, for instance, Gen. 18.23-32 'was composed within a social group of trained sages and teachers who had in mind two different audiences', i.e. themselves and 'common' people (E. Ben Zvi, 'The Dialogue between Abraham and Yhwh in Gen. 18.23-32: A Historical-Critical Analysis', *JSOT* 53 [1992], pp. 27-46 [44]).

25. In later times, readings from Old Testament passages were an important part of the worship in the synagogue, as can be seen from Lk. 4.16-20; Acts 13.15; 15.21. See Josephus (*Apion* 2.17; *Ant.* 16.43) and Philo (*Hypoth.* 7.12-13), who also mention public hearings of the law. Müller, *'Verstehst du auch, was du liest?'*, pp. 53-54, highlights the importance that was attributed to the reading of Scripture: 'Während sich der intensive Umgang mit Literatur bei Griechen und Römern überwiegend als Privileg der gesellschaftlich führenden Schicht erweist, bekommt das Lesen der biblischen Schriften in Schule und Gottesdienst einen anderen Stellenwert. Angefangen von der öffentlichen Lesung des Gesetzes durch Esra hat das Lesen der Schriften eine Bedeutung für das ganze Volk. Es wird nicht als Privileg weniger verstanden, sondern als Aufgabe für alle'. Interestingly, J. Jeremias, ' "Zwei Jahre vor dem Erdbeben" (Am 1,1)', in *idem*, *Hosea und Amos*, pp. 183-97 (197), notes that the editors of Amos aimed their work at a readership that was capable of 'reading' the book of Amos as whole and of relating its individual parts to one another.

was the norm even when people read for themselves. A possible reason for this has been pointed out by Müller, noting that the ancient scrolls did not offer many reading aids. Instead, reading was rendered more difficult by, among other reasons, the *scriptio continua*. Thus, Müller concludes, we need to think of the practice of reading aloud also in terms of a reading aid.[26]

A similar point has been made by Parunak, who has pointed out that the ancient Hebrew writers had no such things at their disposal as italics, underlining, parentheses, footnotes, chapter headings, and so on.[27] Indeed, even a cursory glance at old manuscripts makes us aware of the difficulties involved in reading a text that lacks all the visual signs that facilitate the reading of modern books. However, Parunak rightly stresses that 'where we use signals specially tailored to the printed page, [ancient authors or rhetoricians] employ *a system of indicators that can function in either oral or written presentations*'.[28] It is therefore to be expected that ancient writers (who knew that their writings would be read out loud) would use indicators that could be detected in *listening* to such a presentation.

This is confirmed by the data as we have it, not only in the Pentateuch but in the prophetic literature as well. Concerning the former, Watts re-

---

26. Müller, *'Verstehst du auch, was du liest?'*, p. 22 ('führte das laute Lesen zur besseren Erfassung des Geschriebenen, Sinnabschnitte konnten auf diese Weise leichter verstanden werden, *die Verlautlichung diente als Lesehilfe*'; emphasis added); cf. also p. 52; and see F.F. Bruce, *The Acts of the Apostles* (Leicester: Apollos, 3rd edn, 1990), p. 226. Aristotle, for instance, once complained that Heraclitus is difficult to punctuate, and that there are a number of problems concerning the accents and the division of words (*Rhet.* 3.5.6; cf. Müller, *'Verstehst du auch, was du liest?'*, p. 18). See also A. Manguel, *A History of Reading* (London: Flamingo, 1996), p. 48, who remarks that 'the ancient writing on scrolls...served the purposes of someone accustomed to reading aloud, someone who would allow the ear to disentangle what to the eye seemed a continuous string of signs'. He notes furthermore that 'Augustine, like Cicero before him, would have had to practise a text before reading it out loud, since sight-reading was in his day an unusual skill and often led to errors of interpretation. The fourth-century grammarian Servius criticized his colleague Donat for reading, in Virgil's *Aeneid*, the words *collectam ex Ilio pubem* ("a people gathered from Troy") instead of *collectam exilio pubem* ("a people gathered for exile"). Such mistakes were common when reading a continuous text.'

27. H. van Dyke Parunak, 'Oral Typesetting: Some Uses of Biblical Structure', *Bib* 62 (1981), pp. 153-68.

28. Parunak, 'Oral Typesetting', p. 154 (my italics); cf. Gitay, 'Deutero-Isaiah', p. 191; and Dorsey, 'Literary Architecture', p. 329, who speaks of 'aurally-oriented structuring techniques'.

marks that 'Israel's tradition of reading law in public...gave shape to literary conventions and genres...which governed the combination of law and narrative in the Pentateuch'.[29] This resulted in the 'rhetoric of a literary genre shaped by oral conventions'.[30] The same applies to the prophetic books as well. In fact, early form critics, in investigating the oral background of prophetic speech forms, were interested as much in oral conventions as in the forms' literary genres, thus testifying to the shaping of the prophetic books by oral conventions. However, since the prophetic books are more than just collections of originally oral traditions, it seems reasonable to conclude that in composing the prophetic writings, the oral indicators were deliberately retained, as the books were meant to be read out loud.[31] Gitay is therefore right to point out that:

> whether the prophecies were originally written, or were delivered orally and written down a short time after they were delivered, or even were written a long period after their oral delivery, in each of these potential cases, the speaker or writer designed his material to be heard; he tried to appeal through the ear.[32]

Indeed, he goes on to say that 'written and oral media functioned similarly',[33] which has a number of implications for the structural analysis of a

29. Watts, 'Rhetorical Strategy', p. 4.

30. Watts, 'Rhetorical Strategy', p. 21; cf. *idem*, 'Public Readings', p. 557, where he remarks that the forms established in the originally oral context 'remained unchanged long after public reading had become a rarity and perhaps an anachronism'. This appears to be a sensible conclusion but it might well be asked whether in Old Testament times public readings ever became an anachronism.

31. Thus Riesner, *Jesus als Lehrer*, p. 285. See also Gitay's observations on Deutero-Isaiah (Gitay, 'Deutero-Isaiah', pp. 185-97) and those by Watts, 'Public Readings', p. 543, on the Pentateuch. Watts, for instance, claims 'that much of Pentateuchal law was written or at least edited with such public readings in mind'.

32. Gitay, 'Deutero-Isaiah', p. 194. For similar conclusions cf. Wendland, 'Discourse Analysis', p. 2; and L. Alonso Schökel, *A Manual of Hebrew Poetics* (SubBib, 11; Rome: Editrice Pontificio Istituto Biblico, 1988), p. 20, who notes that 'whether it was written or not, it was meant for oral recitation, in public'. In this context it is also interesting to note Preuss's claim that the '"Aufmerksamkeitsruf" [שמעו את הדבר] oft weniger der mündlichen Rede als der schriftlichen Redaktion der Prophetenbücher zu entstammen scheint' (H.D. Preuss, *Theologie des Alten Testaments* [2 vols.; Stuttgart: W. Kohlhammer, 1991–92], II, p. 83; cf. P.K.D. Neumann, *Hört das Wort Jahwäs. Ein Beitrag zur Komposition alttestamentlicher Schriften* [Hamburg: Stiftung Europa-Kolleg, 1975]). If this were correct (I am not entirely convinced), it would confirm that the prophetic books were composed for oral recitation.

33. Gitay, 'Deutero-Isaiah', p. 194.

book such as Amos, as we shall see. However, let me just say at this point that Alonso Schökel, in my view, has struck the right note in voicing his regret that 'scholars of the Old Testament generally have a habit of 'seeing' the biblical text, without listening to it'.[34] Yet if this is so, it raises the question what 'listening to the text' would mean for the analysis of the structure of Amos in general, and the quest for recognizable structural markers in particular. But before we move on to investigate recent structural investigations of the book of Amos in the light of these observations, we need to broaden our perspective and come to an understanding of the reading act in general.

2. *The reading act.* While I am not concerned here with a general theory of reception, which could easily become a detour of the most momentous proportions, it is necessary to consider briefly one particular aspect of the reading act. This is the 'temporary' character of reading, to which reader-response critics have alerted us, and on which Fish comments with great clarity in *Is There a Text in This Class?*. He notes, for instance, that:

> literature is a kinetic art, but the physical form it assumes prevents us from seeing its essential nature, even though we so experience it. The availability of a book to the hand, its presence on a shelf, its listing in a library catalogue—all of these encourage us to think of it as a stationary object. Somehow when we put a book down, we forget that while we were reading, *it* was moving (pages turning, lines receding into the past) and forget too that *we* were moving with it...[35]

Accordingly, Fish speaks 'of the developing responses of the reader in relation to the words as they succeed one another in time...'[36] and 'of the *temporal* flow of the reading experience',[37] and comments that 'it is assumed that the reader responds in terms of that flow and not to the whole utterance'.[38] In similar vein, Green stresses that:

34. Alonso Schökel, *Manual of Hebrew Poetics*, p. 20.

35. S. Fish, *Is There a Text in This Class? The Authority of Interpretive Communities* (Cambridge, MA: Harvard University Press, 1980), p. 43 (his italics); cf. R.M. Fowler, 'Who Is "The Reader" in Reader Response Criticism?', in House (ed.), *Beyond Form Criticism*, pp. 376-94 (391).

36. Fish, *Text*, p. 26.

37. Fish, *Text*, p. 27 (his italics).

38. Fish, *Text*, p. 27; cf. Ben Zvi, *Obadiah*, p. 4: 'Competent readers...begin to read a text by first developing a scheme about what the text is about, by deciding on the grounds of the text along with the inferences made on the basis of their general knowledge what is the genre of the text and its main characteristics, and then by constantly developing and testing their hypotheses.'

a text's *immediate (or local) co-text*, that is, the immediately preceding material, is often of paramount importance in shaping how a text is received. This is because of memory limitations: As reading or listening progresses, comprehension of past utterances becomes more and more summary.[39]

If this is true of the reading of (modern) books, how much more then does it apply to the act of *hearing* literature that is being read out loud. While in the former instance, the reader can turn back to previous pages to make sure she understood them properly, the hearer lacks the possibility of 're-hearing'. Spoken language is 'one-dimensional', as Parunak has pointed out, as it follows a linear order.[40] Kennedy too speaks of a speech being 'linear and cumulative', and notes that 'any context in it can only be perceived in contrast to what has gone before, especially what has immediately gone before'.[41]

To summarize, our consideration of reading practices has resulted in two findings that have to be taken into account in the subsequent examination of the structure of Amos. First, in Old Testament times an author or editor was likely to write or edit literature for being read out loud publicly to an audience. This, in turn, will have determined the way in which he employed structural devices as well as which devices to use in the first place. Secondly, the temporal character of reading (and especially hearing) suggests that rhetorical signals can only function properly if they can be detected in passing. They were, as Kennedy rightly notes, 'intended to have an impact on first hearing'.[42]

Which Signals Are Recognizable? In what follows, we will look at a variety of proposals concerning the structure of Amos. These work, with varying degrees of success, with different kinds of structural signals, thus prompting the question as to which of these structural devices are likely to be the most reliable guides to the book's structure. Applying the criteria advanced in the preceding discussion, two questions need to be asked. First, which signals was an 'original' hearer[43] most likely to pick up?

---

39. Green, 'Discourse Analysis', p. 184.
40. Parunak, 'Some Axioms', p. 4.
41. Kennedy, *New Testament Interpretation*, p. 5.
42. Kennedy, *New Testament Interpretation*, p. 6.
43. In this context, an 'original' hearer would be someone who heard a reading of the book (or parts thereof), and not a member of Amos's original audience.

And secondly, which signals will an 'ordinary' reader[44] of our own time recognize?

Despite the danger of oversimplifying matters, it seems helpful in this context to distinguish between two types of markers or structural devices. On the one hand, there are what may be called *rhetorico-literary markers*, which are easily recognizable and can function therefore both in an oral and a literary context. They include introductory and closing formulas,[45] series consisting of similar components (sometimes including a refrain), rhetorically highlighted features such as hymnic doxologies, and so on. Inclusios and chiasms may also function in such a way,[46] provided they do not extend over too large a section, in which case it might be difficult (or indeed impossible) for an audience to detect them. On the other hand, scholars have often turned their attention to what I would consider *complex literary designs*. These include extensive palistrophic structures, inclusios encompassing large sections of a text, and other similar devices.[47]

In the study in hand, the focus is on rhetorico-literary markers, which, from a rhetorical point of view, deserve our special attention, as they are more easily perceived by an audience, and thus are more likely to guide an audience's understanding of a text than complex literary designs.

---

44. An 'ordinary' reader is defined in contrast to a 'critic'. He is supposed 'simply' to read the text and thereby, as Fish puts it, experience its temporal character. This distinction between the 'reader' and the 'critic' has been made, for instance, by Fowler, 'Reader', pp. 379-81, 383. Although it is desirable to become a 'discerning reader' or a 'critical reader' (P. Ricœur, *The Symbolism of Evil* [Boston: Beacon Press, 1967], p. 351, actually prefers a 'post-critical reader'), the effectiveness of a text as a means of persuasion is dependent on it being comprehensible by a 'reader' who, as Fowler (p. 383) remarks, 'will tend to take the reading experience to be an encounter with the discourse of a real author directed to him/herself as a real reader'.

45. P.R. Noble, 'The Literary Structure of Amos: A Thematic Analysis', *JBL* 114 (1995), pp. 209-26 (209), claims that such formal criteria 'have been given much greater prominence than they merit', a view for which he gives no reasons.

46. Cf. Riesner, *Jesus als Lehrer*, p. 285; and J.R. Lundblom, *Jeremiah: A Study in Ancient Hebrew Rhetoric* (SBLDS, 18; Missoula: Scholars Press, 1975), pp. 16-19 and *passim*, according to whom these two devices are the controlling structures for the whole book of Jeremiah. See also Parunak, 'Some Axioms', pp. 6-10.

47. Cf., for instance, R.H. O'Connell, *Concentricity and Continuity: The Literary Structure of Isaiah* (JSOTSup, 188; Sheffield: Sheffield Academic Press, 1994), pp. 23-29, who detects what he calls 'complex frameworking in Isaiah'; and W.A. Smalley, 'Recursion Patterns and the Sectioning of Amos', *BT* 30 (1979), pp. 118-27, who refers to 'larger recursion patterns' in Amos.

b. *Subservience to the Text's Message*

Effective communication also requires *the interrelation of form and content*, of structure and message.[48] This has been emphasized by Wendland, who directs our attention to the dangers that inhere in any structural investigation. He complains that 'the pursuit of form, or structure, seems almost to become an end in itself, and the results bear little or no relation to the content of the biblical text as it is overtly presented to the reader.'[49] He therefore demands that '*the structures*...revealed by a linguistic/literary investigation *must be related* in some significant way *to the communication of the prophet's message*, especially his major themes and emphases'.[50] Wendland thus shares my concern to produce a structural outline that does not bend the data in order to fit a preconceived theory, but is flexible enough to describe the given data as we have it. In line with these theoretical reflections, Wendland offers a helpful criterion for structural investigations, noting that 'the greater the number of formal and semantic elements of recursion that happen to coincide in the formation of a supposed pattern of discourse, the more reliable, or established, that particular structure would consequently be from an organizational standpoint'.[51] Thus, an ideal case would see the coincidence of a number of structural devices *as well as* a correspondence of form and content.

However, this is not always the case. In fact, there are cases where either form and content seem to contradict each other, or where there are

---

48. Cf. Aristotle's concept of the four causes that are operative in any teleological process (which the writing of a book for communicative purposes surely is). These include the *causa efficiens* (in the case of a literary work this is the author, who pens the book), the *causa finalis* (the reason for writing), the *causa formalis* (a specific plan, i.e. the book's structure) and the *causa materialis* (the words that make up a literary work, the material). Of these, the latter two are of particular importance in the present context. For a brief recapitulation of Aristotle's four causes see P. Kunzmann, F.-P. Burkard and F. Wiedmann, *dtv-Atlas zur Philosophie: Tafeln und Texte* (Munich: Deutscher Taschenbuch Verlag, 3rd edn, 1993), p. 49.

49. Wendland, 'Word', p. 2. This has also been emphasized by H. Gese, 'Komposition bei Amos', in J.A. Emerton (ed.), *Congress Volume, Vienna 1980* (VTSup, 32; Leiden: E.J. Brill, 1981), pp. 74-95 (74), who pointedly speaks of the 'Gefahr, daß bloß formale Beobachtungen gesammelt werden, ohne den unmittelbaren Zusammenhang mit der inhaltlichen Bedeutung herauszustellen'.

50. Wendland, 'Word', p. 5 (emphasis added). For this principle see also M.V. Fox, 'The Rhetoric of Ezekiel's Vision of the Valley of the Bones', in Gordon (ed.), *'The Place Is Too Small for Us'*, pp. 176-90 (178-79).

51. Wendland, 'Word', p. 5.

structural ambiguities, in that different structural markers seem to point in different directions. Thus, we may find that indicators marking a structural division coincide with features performing the role of what Finley and Payton have called 'markers of connectivity'.[52] The effect of this is that while a textual break is signalled, it is at the same time levelled down in some respects. An example of this technique, which structures a discourse without being too disruptive, can be found in Amos 4.1-3, where the introductory phrase שמעו הדבר הזה introduces a new prophetic discourse, the content of which, however, exhibits unmistakable links with what precedes.[53]

2. *Structural Outlines for Amos: An Evaluation*

Having established some general criteria for structural investigations, we will now look at the main proposals for the structure of Amos. This review will confirm the need for reliable and appropriate criteria, as many structural investigations suffer from the lack of sound theoretical and methodological principles. Yet I also intend to build on the insights of previous scholarship, which will provide the starting point for my own investigation of the structure of Amos.

a. *Reconsidering 'Words' and 'Visions'*
The most popular—and most general—structural approach is to divide the book into three (sometimes four) parts: Amos 1–2 (the introduction), 3–6

---

52. T.J. Finley and G. Payton, 'A Discourse Analysis of Isaiah 7–12', *JOTT* 6 (1993), pp. 317-35 (331). Structural markers either divide or unify a text, or they emphasize certain parts of it. Depending on whether they have a dividing or a unifying function, they are used 'disjunctively' or 'conjunctively' (cf. Wendland, 'Discourse Analysis', pp. 13-14, who lists a number of examples for both categories). In this context, see also Parunak's comments on 'similarity' in 'Some Axioms', pp. 4-10, and the discussion of 'repetition' and 'variation' in the Pentateuch by Watts, 'Public Readings', pp. 545-57. Concerning the former, Watts remarks that 'regardless of its origins, repetition must be acceptable to the text's first audience or else it would not be preserved. The function of repetition thus requires literary description, but this does not preclude finding the origins of repetition in the diachronic development of the text' (p. 546 n. 18)'. As regards 'variation', he notes that 'developmental hypotheses...leave half the question unanswered: though they account for the origins of the contradictions, they do not explain why such differences were acceptable to the earliest hearers and readers of the Pentateuch' (p. 549).

53. To be sure, there are also links with the subsequent material in Amos 4.

(often called the 'words') and 7–9 (the 'visions'). Sometimes the final verses of Amos 9, the (postexilic) 'appendix', are considered a separate part.[54] This outline provides a helpful starting point, but due to its rather general nature, it is not sufficient for a detailed analysis of the book. Even more importantly, however, the classification into 'words' and 'visions' is not entirely appropriate in that Amos 7–9 contains some 'non-visionary' material as well (8.4-14). Faced with this problem, some scholars have succumbed to the urge to rearrange the text to make it fit their theory rather than revise their preconceived ideas.

A good example of this practice can be found in Sellin's Old Testament Introduction. He thinks of Amos 7–9 as five visions featuring an inserted historical episode (7.10-17), fragments of judgment speeches[55] (8.4-14) and an appended promise (9.8b-15).[56] Sellin is thus well aware of the 'non-visionary' material in Amos 7–9, but he is also quick to claim that the judgment oracles in 8.4-14 must have been misplaced arguing that, originally, they must have been part of Amos 3–6.[57] Concerning the supposedly 'intrusive' narrative in 7.10-17, a great number of solutions have been suggested, which trace its origin to different places in the book.[58] Finally, those who regard the salvation oracle in Amos 9 as an appendix avoid at least the difficulty of having to subsume it under 'the visions'. Overall, however, one is inclined to agree with Childs, that, given the variety of material to be found in Amos 7–9, 'the editorial shaping established no theological significance between Amos' words and his visions'.[59]

To summarize, the suggested threefold structure is a helpful starting point in that it aptly distinguishes between the book's introduction, middle part and concluding section, all of which have particular rhetorical functions, as I shall argue below. However, the labelling of the second and third sections as 'words' and 'visions' is less helpful (and also partly inaccurate), and the tendency to rewrite the text by transfering certain parts

---

54. This outline has been offered by virtually all modern commentaries on Amos.

55. Sellin actually speaks of 'penitential speeches' ('Bußreden'; E. Sellin, *Einleitung in das Alte Testament* [Leipzig: Quelle & Meyer, 2nd rev. edn, 1914], p. 104).

56. Sellin, *Einleitung*, p. 104.

57. Sellin, *Einleitung*, p. 104.

58. For a brief overview cf. R. Gordis, 'The Composition and Structure of Amos', in *idem, Poets, Prophets and Sages: Essays in Biblical Interpretation* (Bloomington: Indiana University Press, 1971), pp. 217-29 (217-18).

59. B.S. Childs, *Introduction to the Old Testament as Scripture* (Philadelphia: Fortress Press, 1979), p. 404.

to their supposed original locations is to be treated with caution, speculative as it is.

b. *The Function of the Hymn Fragments*
In the past, most scholars investigating the hymn fragments (4.13; 5.8-9; 9.5-6) focused on their origin. In recent years, however, interest has shifted to the question of how the passages now function in their present contexts. Whether one considers them as parts of an ancient doxology or as (post)exilic additions, the question remains as to why they have been placed in their present locations. Also, what is their function within the book as a whole? Do they serve a structural purpose, or do we have to define their task in other terms?

A structural function has been proposed by Koch who, in his discussion, includes Amos 1.2 as a fourth hymn fragment. According to Koch, the hymnic piece in 1.2 introduces the first part of the book (Amos 1–2) while those in 4.13 and 9.5-6, which are more extensive than the one in 5.8, close major sections (i.e., Amos 3–4 and 5.1–9.6, respectively). The shorter fragment in 5.8, on the other hand, concludes only a sub-section.[60] Koch rightly stresses that the hymns need to be understood in the context of the entire book. Yet his understanding of the structural role of 5.8 is unsatisfactory, as it distorts the unity of 5.1-17, which he divides into two parts, vv. 1-8 and vv. (7) 9-17. Koch's analysis also does not account for the major break at 7.1, the existence of which has been acknowledged by almost all commentators. In fact, the subsequent discussion of the book's macrostructure will make it clear that Koch's proposals concerning the functional role of 4.13 and 9.5-6 are unsatisfactory as well.[61]

But how then is the role of the hymn fragments best described? As some studies have shown, an answer to this question can be found by paying

---

60. K. Koch, 'Die Rolle der hymnischen Abschnitte in der Komposition des Amos-Buches', *ZAW* 86 (1974), pp. 504-37 (535). H.-P. Mathys, *Dichter und Beter: Theologen aus spätalttestamentlicher Zeit* (OBO, 132; Freiburg: Universitätsverlag, 1994), p. 112, agrees with Koch concerning the first and third hymns but rules out a structural function for the one in Amos 5 (he does not discuss 1.2). For a critique of Koch's view cf. A. van der Wal, 'The Structure of Amos', *JSOT* 26 (1983), pp. 107-13 (108); and R.F. Melugin, 'The Formation of Amos: An Analysis of Exegetical Method', in Achtemeier (ed.), *SBLASP* 114.1, pp. 369-91 (376).

61. Cf. J.L. Mays, *Amos: A Commentary* (OTL; Philadelphia: Westminster Press, 1969), p. 84, who notes that 'the hymns do not mark or conclude any discernible collections'. According to A.G. Auld, *Amos* (OTG; Sheffield: JSOT Press, 1986), p. 58, on the other hand, the hymnic pieces in 4.13 and 9.5-6 'are simply pious conclusions'.

close attention to the contexts, in which they appear. This may seem rather obvious but it needs to be stressed because earlier scholarship tended to view them as extraneous elements. Horst, for instance, was adamant that the fragments are not tied up with their contexts but are quite isolated.[62] However, by paying close attention to the surrounding material, Marks perceptively noticed that the hymn fragments are 'introduced into the collection at moments of exceptional severity, as though to solemnize the words of divine judgment'.[63] If this is correct, the hymn fragments are best regarded as indicators of climax or local highlighting rather than as major structuring devices.

If we extend the discussion to include Amos 1.2 (for which there are good reasons),[64] the first 'solemnization' of the divine judgment, to use Marks's concept, occurs right at the outset of the book. This extraordinary opening statement inaugurates its gloomy mood, using image-laden and highly emotive language. The second hymn fragment (4.13) in fact does function as a marker of closure, but not in the way envisaged by Koch. According to my analysis, its structural significance is of a more local nature in that is closes the discourse of Amos 4. Yet its real significance seems to lie in its climactic role, as it causes that passage to end on a rather ominous note. This capacity clearly applies also to the fragments in 5.8-9 and 9.5-6, both of which occur at the centre of their respective discourses and thus have no structural significance. Like the one in 4.13, they underline who it is that Israel will have to face when the divine judgement is finally unleashed. Thus, as Marks has rightly observed, all the hymnic pieces highlight this judgment by stressing the awesome power and might of the judge.[65]

McComiskey points to yet another function in regarding the hymn fragments as a kind of 'refrain', a device which according to him is 'integral to Amos' literary style'.[66] Occurring, as they do, at the outset of the book

62. F. Horst, 'Die Doxologien im Amosbuch', *ZAW* 47 (1929), pp. 45-54 (45): they are 'in ihrer Umgebung nach vorn und rückwärts isoliert'.

63. H. Marks, 'The Twelve Prophets', in Alter and Kermode (eds.), *The Literary Guide to the Bible*, pp. 207-33 (218); cf. Stuart, *Hosea–Jonah*, pp. 286-87.

64. See the discussion in Koch, 'Rolle', pp. 530-34; and cf. Wendland, 'Word', p. 38; and J. Jeremias, 'Amos 3–6: From the Oral Word to the Text', in G.M. Tucker, D.L. Peterson and R.R. Wilson (eds.), *Canon, Theology, and Old Testament Interpretation: Essays in Honor of Brevard S. Childs* (Philadelphia: Fortress Press, 1988), pp. 217-29 (219), who also regard Amos 1.2 as a hymn fragment.

65. Cf. Chapter 2 for further discussion.

66. T.E. McComiskey, 'The Hymnic Elements of the Prophecy of Amos: A Study

(1.2), in the middle part (4.13; 5.8-9) and towards the end (9.5-6), they add
to the coherence of the entire work. Yet they do not govern the macrostructural arrangement in that they do not mark the beginning or closure of
major sections.

c. *Inclusios and Chiasms*
Another area that has attracted considerable attention is the investigation
of 'inclusios' and 'chiasms'.[67] Research has shown the Old Testament
to contain a remarkable number of these devices, which has lead Alter to
speak of a 'general fondness of ancient Hebrew writers of all genres for
so-called envelope structures'.[68] While this may be the case, it seems to
me that the Hebrew writers' fondness is matched, not infrequently, by an
even more pronounced partiality towards these devices on the part of the

of Form-Critical Methodology', *JETS* 30 (1987), pp. 139-57 (156).
    67. For extensive lists of chiastic structures in the Old Testament cf. A. di Marco,
'Der Chiasmus in der Bibel: Ein Beitrag zur strukturellen Stilistik', *LB* 36 (1975),
pp. 21-97; and *LB* 37 (1976), pp. 49-68; and J.W. Welch (ed.), *Chiasmus in Antiquity:
Structures, Analyses, Exegesis* (Hildesheim: Gerstenberg, 1981). Di Marco traces the
interest in chiasms back to the discipline of classical rhetoric and notes that it was
Bengel who in 1742 introduced the term 'chiasm' to the field of biblical exegesis.
    It would, in fact, be more precise to speak of a 'chiasm' (or 'chiasmus') only when
referring to an A–B=B'–A' structure (cf. Abrams, *Glossary*, pp. 183-84), which is why
Wendland, 'Word', p. 7, distinguishes a chiasm from a 'tripartite A–B–A' ring
construction', on the one hand, and an 'introversion', which may expand to any length,
on the other (cf. Wendland, 'Discourse Analysis', p. 12). In the present investigation,
however, in line with common practice, the term 'chiasm' is used for any concentric
structure. Cf., for instance, G. Wanke, 'Sprachliche Analyse', in Fohrer *et al.*, *Exegese
des Alten Testaments*, pp. 58-83 (72), who defines a 'chiasm' as a 'Kreuzstellung von
wenigstens vier Wörtern, Wortgruppen oder Sätzen' (my italics).
    On the whole issue see also M. Weiss, 'Wege der neuen Dichtungswissenschaft in
ihrer Anwendung auf die Psalmenforschung: Methodologische Bemerkungen, dargelegt am Beispiel von Psalm XLVI', in P.H.A. Neumann (ed.), *Zur neueren Psalmenforschung* (WdF, 192; Darmstadt: Wissenschaftliche Buchgesellschaft, 1976), pp. 400-
51, esp. 425-28; F.I. Andersen, *The Sentence in Biblical Hebrew* (Janua Linguarum,
Series Practica, 231; The Hague: Mouton, 1974), ch. 9; Lundblom, *Jeremiah*, ch. 3;
A.R. Ceresko, 'The A:B::B:A Word Pattern in Hebrew and Northwest Semitic, with
Special Reference to the Book of Job', *UF* 7 (1975), pp. 73-88; *idem*, 'The Chiastic
Word Pattern in Hebrew', *CBQ* 38 (1976), pp. 303-11; *idem*, 'The Function of
Chiasmus in Hebrew Poetry', *CBQ* 40 (1978), pp. 1-10.
    68. R. Alter, 'The Characteristics of Ancient Hebrew Poetry', in *idem* and
Kermode (eds.), *Literary Guide to the Bible*, pp. 611-24 (621).

investigating scholar.[69] That is to say that some of the chiastic structures that have been proposed appear to be rather forced. And it is for this reason that we need to contemplate controls for the discernment of inclusios and chiasms. However, this will only be possible once we have gained some general ideas about their function, and it is to this that we now turn.

We have already seen that ancient writers were bound to use rhetorical signals to mark breaks or peaks since these had to be recognizable in an oral context. It is in this context that Parunak views the function of concentric arrangements. In a study that is concerned with what he calls 'oral typesetting',[70] Parunak remarks that a chiasm 'signals its own conclusion'.[71] This view is confirmed by Berlin, noting that inclusios 'provide cohesion and unity for the text' they frame.[72] At the same time, a concentric arrangement, being of course a figure of repetition, emphasizes certain elements precisely by repeating them.[73] In addition, it is often assumed that, in the case of an 'odd' chiasm, the stress falls on the unique centre item.[74] Thus, according to Wendland:

> an important topical element...is frequently located in the center of two or more pairs of corresponding enclosing units, thus highlighting the thematic peak, emotive climax, and/or structural turning point of the entire discourse.[75]

---

69. See J.A. Emerton, 'An Examination of Some Attempts to Defend the Unity of the Flood Narrative in Genesis', *VT* 37 (1987), pp. 401-20; and *VT* 38 (1988), pp. 1-21 (20-21), who notes, rather laconically, that 'the search for examples of chiasmus has become fashionable'.

70. The term has also been adopted by Wendland, 'Discourse Analysis', p. 12, who speaks of an 'oral-aural "typesetting" process'.

71. Parunak, 'Oral Typesetting', p. 156.

72. A. Berlin, *The Dynamics of Biblical Parallelism* (Bloomington: Indiana University Press, 1985), p. 132.

73. According to some, yet another function of inclusios is to mark secondary material, such as editorial additions (cf. H.M. Wiener, *The Composition of Judges II 11 to 1 Kings II 46* [Leipzig: J.C. Hinrichs, 1929]; and C. Kuhl, '"Die Wiederaufnahme"—ein literarkritisches Prinzip?', *ZAW* 64 [1952], pp. 1-11). Moreover, Parunak, 'Oral Typesetting', p. 160, notes that 'an inclusio...is often used (whether by the author or by a later editor) to set off material that is peripheral to the course of the argument'. Examples of this technique can be found in 2 Chron. 2.1-17 (compare this with the parallel account in 1 Kgs 5.16-25); and 2 Chron. 6.12-13 (which Parunak describes as a kind of 'footnote'; cf. p. 161).

74. Parunak, 'Oral Typesetting', p. 165 (n. 24).

75. Wendland, 'Discourse Analysis', p. 12; cf. also the following articles in Welch

A good example for this is the hymn fragment in Amos 5.8-9, which is at the centre of the chiastic unit 5.1-17. However, some scholars have rightly urged us to be cautious not to generalize this idea. Clines, for instance, warns that 'it would be unwise in our present state of knowledge about Hebrew poetry to conclude that the centre of the strophic structure is also the centre of the thought of the poem'.[76] With this issue remaining un-resolved, one can at least conclude that concentric structures are markers of unity and cohesion, and that, as figures of repetition, they also serve as focusing or highlighting devices.

Having considered the function of inclusios and chiasms in brief, we now turn to the question of how to detect them. While in the case of a chiasm, it is essential for its corresponding parts (A and A', B and B', etc.) to share sufficient similarities to be considered parallel, the recognition of an inclusio is often beset with difficulties. According to Berlin, an inclusio is a device 'in which the first and last lines of a text contain the same words or phrases'. This she regards as a specific form of parallelism.[77] However, while at first this appears to be a perfectly reasonable definition, I very much doubt that it is of much practical value. It means, in effect, that for two verses to function as an inclusio, all that may be required is for them to share the same word. If this were true, how could we then distinguish between a genuine inclusio and a 'simple' repetition? Let me illustrate the problem that I envisage by giving a specific example. Some scholars argue that Amos 1.2–3.8 is a self-contained unit because of the inclusio provided by the use of שאג in 1.2 and 3.8.[78] Yet, as I shall argue

---

(ed.), *Chiasmus*: Y.T. Radday, 'Chiasmus in Hebrew Biblical Narrative', pp. 50-117 (51); W.G.E. Watson, 'Chiastic Patterns in Biblical Hebrew Poetry', pp. 118-68 (146); and J.W. Welch, 'Introduction', pp. 9-16 (10).

76. D.J.A. Clines, *Ezra, Nehemiah, and Esther* (NCB; Grand Rapids: Eerdmans, 1984), p. 193; cf. also M.J. Boda, 'Chiasmus in Ubiquity: Symmetrical Mirages in Nehemiah 9', *JSOT* 71 (1996), pp. 55-70 (58).

77. Berlin, *Dynamics*, p. 3. She adds that inclusios are the kind of parallelism, in which 'the greatest distance between parallel parts is found' (p. 132).

78. Thus van der Wal, 'Structure of Amos', p. 108; di Marco, 'Chiasmus', *LB* 36, p. 93; J. Jeremias, 'Amos 3–6: Beobachtungen zur Entstehungsgeschichte eines Prophetenbuches', *ZAW* 100, Sup. (1988), pp. 123-38 (132); Noble, 'Literary Struc-ture', p. 218; and A. Condamin, *Poèmes de la Bible: Avec une introduction sur la strophique hébraïque* (Paris: Beauchesne, 1933), pp. 59-71. Van der Wal shows quite a remarkable predilection for inclusios, and suggests that Amos 3.9–4.3 should be regarded as one unit framed by the term אמרון. Yet, as he remarks, 'in order for this inclusio to become apparant [*sic*], a change of the text is necessary in Am. 4.3'

below (in line with most commentators), there are more compelling reasons for regarding Amos 1.3–2.16 as the first major unit and hence Amos 3 as a discourse on its own.[79] However, if this is correct, it follows that the recurrence of שאג in 3.8 does not signal an inclusio but needs to be taken as a 'simple' instance of repetition, albeit possibly a significant one.

Be that as it may, the example clearly demonstrates that criteria are needed that allow us to distinguish inclusios from repetitions. Without intending to go into an extensive discussion, I would like to pick up on a point made earlier, namely that structural analyses receive confirmation by claiming the support of coinciding structural markers. That is to say, ideally an inclusio should agree with other formal markers demarcating the boundaries of the passage in question. For an illustration of this, let us consider Amos 3, a discourse that is framed by the term פקד, which functions as an inclusio, occurring as it does in vv. 2 and 14 (the second and penultimate verses of the passage). This judgment receives support by the fact that the boundaries of the discourse are marked also by the introductory formulas in 3.1 and 4.1. It is confirmed furthermore by the observation that Amos 3 functions as a rhetorically self-contained unit. As such, it opens with an initial declaration (vv. 1-2), which is followed by an argumentation (vv. 3-8), a provocative confirmation (vv. 9-11), an ironic intensification (v. 12) and a concluding reaffirmation of the initial decla-

('Structure of Amos', p. 109). So to achieve the desired inclusio he has to 'emend' הארמונה to ההרמונה. Van der Wal seeks to justify this by pointing out that ארמון, which occurs frequently in Amos 1–2, is missing in the Israel strophe. In his opinion, 'the whole passage Am. 3.9-4.3 replaces the use of this formulation regarding Israel' (p. 110). However, there is no need for an occurrence of ארמון in 4.3 (cf. the criticisms by T.J. Finley, *Joel, Amos, Obadiah* [Wycliffe Exegetical Commentary; Chicago: Moody Press, 1990], p. 117 n. 28; and Wendland, 'Word', p. 43), as the term occurs not only in Amos 1–2 but also in 3.9-11. Indeed, its appearance in those verses, while not being an inclusio, links the entire discourse Amos 3.1-15 with the preceding oracles in Amos 1–2.

79. C.F. Kraft, 'Some Further Observations Concerning the Strophic Structure of Hebrew Poetry', in E.C. Hobbs (ed.), *A Stubborn Faith: Papers on Old Testament and Related Subjects. Presented to Honor William Andrew Irwin* (Dallas: Southern Methodist University Press, 1956), pp. 62-89 (67), therefore rightly speaks of an 'arbitrary conclusion of the poem at 3.8'. This is confirmed, for instance, by the introductory phrase שמעו את־הדבר הזה, which indicates that the major break occurs at 3.1 and not, as van der Wal has suggested, after 3.8. As Wendland, 'Word', p. 42, notes, van der Wal's 'suggestion obscures the importance of what would seem to be an even more pronounced break in the discourse, namely, the one occurring at 3.1'.

ration (vv. 13-15).[80] It should also be noted that the prominent position of
פקד, denoting a '(hostile) visit' (in order to punish),[81] accords well with
the thematic thrust of the passage, which highlights the divine judgment
(which is referred to at the outset and the end of Amos 3).

This then takes us to the related issue of chiasms. Because of a recent
tendency in Amos studies to regard large parts of the book as chiastic
arrangements, this needs to be discussed in some detail. Although in
theory a chiasm should be more or less unequivocally identifiable, in practice this is clearly not the case. Problems arise once, as is increasingly the
case, large-scale chiasms are identified, in which not only certain lines but
entire paragraphs are regarded as parallel.[82] This need not be a problem,
but a review of the relevant literature on Amos indicates that the larger the
chiasms get, the lesser the requirements for what can count as parallel
sections in a palistrophic structure tend to become.

The quest for chiasms in Amos takes its lead from the work of de Waard
and Tromp, who argued convincingly that Amos 5.1-17 displays the
following concentric arrangement:[83]

A   Amos's lamentation over fallen Israel (vv. 1-3)
  B   Exhortation to seek Yahweh (vv. 4-6)
    C   Condemnation of injustice (v. 7)
      D   Hymn depicting Yahweh's destructive power (vv. 8-9)
    C'   Condemnation of injustice (vv. 10-13)
  B'   Exhortation to seek good (vv. 14-15)
A'   The people's wailing and lamentation (vv. 16-17)[84]

Figure 1. *The Chiastic Arrangement of Amos 5.1-17*

---

80.   See Chapter 4 for detailed discussion.

81.   In German, the positive and negative connotations of פקד can be expressed by
the simple exchange of a prefix: '*be*suchen' (positive) and '*heim*suchen' (negative).

82.   Berlin, *Dynamics*, in contrast, examines morphologic, syntactic, lexical, semantic and phonological parallelisms on a smaller scale, i.e. within subsequent lines in
poetic passages. She notes that 'attempts to define parallelism by limiting it to one
form or another have failed' (p. 129), and defines the phenomenon as 'a matter of
intertwining a number of linguistic equivalences and contrasts' (p. 130).

83.   J. de Waard, 'The Chiastic Structure of Amos v 1-17', *VT* 27 (1977), pp. 170-
77; and Tromp, 'Amos V 1-17', pp. 56-84. See also D.W. Wicke, 'Two Perspectives
(Amos 5.1-17)', *CurTM* 13 (1986), pp. 89-96; Dorsey, 'Literary Architecture',
pp. 312-14; and Wendland, 'Word', pp. 14-16.

84.   This is my own outline, which is based, however, on the work of de Waard,
Tromp and others.

The importance of de Waard and Tromp's studies can hardly be overestimated in that they inaugurated a shift in attitude towards this central passage, the supposed disorderliness of which has long puzzled scholars. However, in the present context, what needs to be stressed is that the chiasm discovered by de Waard and Tromp coincides with one of the major units of the book. As such, it is opened by the introductory phrase שמעו את־הדבר הזה in 5.1 and ends in v. 17, with the subsequent section 5.18–6.14 containing two woe oracles. The boundaries of the chiasm, that is to say, are therefore confirmed by further textual signals demarcating the outer limits of the discourse.

Building on the work of de Waard and Tromp, others have attempted to extend the limits of the chiasm in 5.1-17. For instance, Lust proposed that it embraces the whole of 4.1–6.7.[85] Wendland and Noble go one step further in extending it to comprise almost the entire middle section of Amos 3.9–6.14,[86] and Bovati and Meynet even regard the whole of Amos 3–6 as a concentric structure.[87] They, in turn, are outdone by the suggestions by Smalley, Dorsey and Rottzoll, according to whom the entire book is arranged chiastically.[88] While a detailed discussion of these proposals is impossible within the confines of the present study, some general comments are pertinent at this point. Thus, it needs to be said that, with the exclusion of the groundbreaking work of de Waard and Tromp on Amos 5, there are a number of recurring problems that beset most of them. First,

---

85. J. Lust, 'Remarks on the Redaction of Amos V 4-6, 14-15', in B. Albrektson *et al.* (eds.), *Remembering All the Way...: A Collection of Old Testament Studies Published on the Occasion of the Fortieth Anniversary of the Oudtestamentisch Werkgezelschap in Nederland* (OTS, 21; Leiden: E.J. Brill, 1981), pp. 129-54 (cf. esp. his diagram on p. 154).

86. Wendland, 'Word', p. 19; and Noble, 'Literary Structure', p. 211.

87. Bovati and Meynet, *Le livre du prophète Amos*, p. 102, cf. p. 249. They show a remarkable predilection for concentric structures, which they discover in almost every section of the book. A chiastic arrangement for all of Amos 3–6 had already been proposed in 1978 by S. Bergler, *Die hymnischen Passagen und die Mitte des Amosbuches: Ein Forschungsbericht* (Magisterschrift, Tübingen, 1978), pp. 228-29.

88. Smalley, 'Recursion Patterns', pp. 122-27 (cf. also J. de Waard and W.A. Smalley, *A Handbook on the Book of Amos* [UBSHS; New York: United Bible Societies, 1979], pp. 189-95, a rigorous critique of which can be found in Wendland, 'Word', pp. 44-48); Dorsey, 'Literary Architecture', pp. 325-29; and Rottzoll, *Studien*, pp. 1-7 (cf. esp. the diagram on p. 3). However, their proposals differ considerably. Rottzoll, for instance, in good historical-critical fashion, is quick to identify material that does not fit into the supposed chiastic structure (i.e. Amos 7.[9]10-17; 8.[3]4-14; 9.7-15) as later additions (p. 5).

there is a tendency to suggest rather obscure breaks between sections. Secondly, superficial relations between supposedly parallel parts are sometimes exaggerated by endowing them with quite ingenious descriptions or headings. And thirdly, some scholars are guilty of propounding rather selective readings of (some of) the passages in question.[89]

First, while de Waard and Tromp delimited their analyses to a self-contained rhetorical unit (5.1-17), Lust, Wendland and Noble, in order to arrive at parallel sections, need to advocate rather unconvincing section breaks. Lust's analysis, for instance, requires us to regard 6.8-14 as self-contained (for compatibility reasons, the section needs to open with a divine oath), a solution that seems not very plausible.[90] Wendland and Noble, on the other hand, want us to regard Amos 3.9 as the opening verse of the extensive section 3.9–6.14. Again, this is not likely since the verse shows no signs of functioning as a major structural marker. In fact, the 'traditional' contention that Amos 3–6 is one of the major parts of the book is much more accurate and helpful than these recent proposals. This has been recognized by Bovati and Meynet, who, therefore, suggest that the chiasm at the centre of Amos covers the whole of this middle section. However, this again is not compelling, as it requires them to regard Amos 3.1-8 and 6.8-14 as parallel units,[91] a view that is hardly defensible, given the differences in subject matter. This observation leads us to the second problem, namely the fact that the parallels between supposedly corresponding parts are often based on what amounts to little more than superficial resemblances.

To illustrate this, let us look briefly at Amos 3 and the various parallels that have been suggested by different exegetes.[92] Bovati and Meynet, for

89. A detailed list of 'errors in the rhetorical analysis of chiasmus' has recently been compiled by Boda, 'Chiasmus', pp. 56-58. He distinguishes between 'errors in symmetry', 'errors in subjectivity', 'errors in probability' and 'errors in purpose'.

90. Indeed, it is more appropriate to regard all the oaths (i.e. 4.2; 6.8; 8.7) as linked not only to what follows but also to what precedes them.

91. Bovati and Meynet, *Le livre du prophète Amos*, pp. 255-57.

92. It needs to be pointed out that this is only one example chosen, more or less, at random. Thus, we might equally well ask whether 1.1-2a can in fact be seen as corresponding to 9.7-15 (as suggested by Smalley, 'Recursion Patterns', p. 122); or whether 4.6-12 parallels 5.18-20 (thus Noble, 'Literary Structure', pp. 212-13). In Noble's view, to recognize that these two sections complement each other 'enables us both to identify this encounter [i.e. the one in 4.12] as the Day of Yahweh and to understand that Day more fully in the context of the first five strophes of D [i.e. 4.6-12].' One wonders, however, whether this criterion of 'complementation' justifies

instance, regard 3.1-8 and 6.8-14 as parallel, which they classify as 'A Trap for the Sons of Israel' (3.1-8) and 'The Poison of the House of Israel' (6.8-14).[93] However, as already noted above, even a cursory glance at the passages reveals their thematic and structural differences. Wendland, on the other hand, compares 6.8-11 to 3.13-15 and 6.12-14 to 3.9-12. The first pair he designates as 'testimony against the "house(s) of Jacob"' (3.13-15 || 6.8-11), while the second he transcribes respectively as 'an enemy will oppress oppressive Israel' (3.9-12) and 'a nation will oppress unrighteous Israel' (6.12-14).[94] This too is unsatisfactory. While 3.13-15 do indeed speak about a testimony against the people, this is not the case in 6.8-11. Moreover, the headings given to 3.9-12 and 6.12-14 are rather general, thus suggesting a higher degree of parallelism than is actually present. Yet another correlation has been suggested by Dorsey, who relates the whole of Amos 3 to 7.1–8.3. He classifies Amos 3 as 'Coming destruction of Israel, Including Bethel's Cult Center: Prophet's Responsibility to Prophesy Because of Yahweh's Revelation', while Amos 7.1–8.3 is summarized as 'Visions of Coming Judgment, Amos at the Cult Center of Bethel and His Responsibility to Prophesy Because of Yahweh's Call'.[95] A somewhat similar analysis has been propounded by Smalley, who compares 3.3–4.3 ('the prophet's role and commission') with 7.1–8.3 ('the prophet's experiences: visions' and 'the prophet's role and commission').[96] Again, in both cases, the ingenious headings suggest closer parallels than are to be found in the text.

All the proposals mentioned in the previous paragraph tend to over-em-

Noble's decision of seeing the two units as parallel parts in a chiastic arrangement.

Similarly, Noble compares 4.4-5 (C) with 5.21-27 (C') and notes that 'viewed in the light of C', then, C depicts a religious busyness that is vigorously pursued for its own sake, without reference to the ethical requirements that Yahweh himself regards as primary' (p. 212). This is an apt summary of 4.4-5 but to arrive at that understanding it is by no means necessary to read these verses in the light of 5.21-27. In fact, the contrasting arrangement of 4.4-5 and 4.1-3, which is more readily perceived by the book's readers or hearers, leads to the same insight. Thus, to conclude, Noble's contention that 'literary criteria, such as palistrophic structuring and inclusios, have often been employed too loosely and impressionistically' (p. 209) characterises his own methodological procedures only too well.

93. Bovati and Meynet, *Le livre du prophète Amos*, p. 102.

94. Wendland, 'Word', p. 19.

95. Dorsey, 'Literary Architecture', pp. 327-28.

96. Smalley, 'Recursion Patterns', p. 122; cf. the criticisms by Wendland, 'Word', p. 46.

phasize the actual correspondences between respective parts. In addition, if any problems are encountered, these are often glossed over by devising rather general, and sometimes plainly misleading, section headings. Noble, however, avoids some of these difficulties by proposing the following scheme for the outer sections of Amos 3.9–6.14:

A. Introductory oracles (3.9-15)
    x. Israel vis-à-vis the foreign nations (3.9-11)
    y. An image of ruin (3.12)
    z. The devastation of Israel (3.13-15)
A'. Concluding oracles (6.2, 8-14)
    x'. Israel vis-à-vis the foreign nations (6.2, 8)
    y'. An image of ruin (6.9-10)
    z'. The devastation of Israel (6.11-14).[97]

Figure 2. *The Parallel Arrangement of Amos 3.9-15 and 6.2, 8-14 according to Noble*

The remaining inner part (4.1–6.7) Noble regards as an ordinary chiasm. However, as I have already pointed out, his analysis is no more convincing than the ones mentioned above.[98] In addition, in order to arrive at the suggested outline for the outer parts of Amos 3.9–6.14, Noble has to rearrange the text. That is to say, 6.2 needs to be transferred after vv. 3-7 and combined with v. 8 in order to have the motif 'Israel vis-à-vis the foreign nations' in the desired place.[99]

My final reservation with the current preoccupation with chiasms is related to the previous one. Often the parallelism of certain parts can only be argued by focusing on selective themes, images, words, etc. This is most obvious in Dorsey's study; having outlined a chiastic pattern for all of Amos, he provides a list of correspondences. He tracks nine concurrences for Amos 1–2 and 8.4–9.15, three for Amos 3 and 7.1–8.3, and seven for Amos 4 and 5.18–6.14. To concentrate on one example, according to Dorsey, Amos 1–2 and 8.4–9.15 share the following similarities:

- condemnation of the wealthy: sevenfold listing of sins;
- ואביון בעבור נעלים (2.6; cf. 8.6);
- השאפים (2.7; cf. 8.4);
- inescapability of judgement, with sevenfold presentation (2.14-16; cf. 9.1-4);
- לא־ימלט and נוס (2.15, 16; cf. 9.1);

97. Noble, 'Literary Structure', p. 211.
98. See n. 92 above.
99. See Noble, 'Literary Structure', pp. 211, 217.

- Israel's delivery out of Egypt (2.10; cf. 9.7);
- the Philistines;
- Edom;
- Yahweh will exile Aram to Kir (1.5; cf. 9.7);
- ראֹשׁ הכרמל (1.2; cf. 9.3);
- figures of drinking wine, planting and uprooting, the sword, etc.[100]

While this list looks quite impressive, it does not support the conclusion that Amos 1–2 and 8.4–9.15 form the book's concentric outer frame. To be sure, these agreements should not be ignored. Indeed, they indicate that many of the issues, themes and motives brought up at the outset are re-visited in the final part of Amos. This is an important observation and confirms my contention that we are dealing with a literary work that is more than a mere anthology of prophetic oracles. However, while at first glance Dorsey's list might suggest a close correspondence between the two sections in question, what it does not display are the significant thematic and structural differences. Thus, it is rather telling that the oracles against foreign nations (the bulk of Amos 1–2) are hardly represented (most of the examples having been taken from the Israel strophe). Telling though this is, however, the omission is not all that surprising, given that it is difficult to find corresponding emphases in Amos 8.4–9.15.

To summarize, I entirely concur with Smalley's judgment, who, as one of the advocates of a large-scale chiastic structure for all of Amos, could actually bring himself to admit that it 'doesn't all fit neatly', and that 'some people may not find it convincing'.[101] More importantly, however, he does hit the nail on the head, when he concedes that his analysis 'would not help...less sophisticated readers'.[102] And although his is by far the most complicated of all the analyses considered, his judgment applies to the others as well. This, I believe, warrants for Emerton's advice to be reiterated, who suggests:

> it would help the progress of Old Testament study if those who believe that they have found instances [of chiasmus] were to be self-critical and strict in their methods and to subject their theories to vigorous testing before seeking to publish them.[103]

As already indicated above, I would suggest that the credibility of any proposed chiastic arrangement depends, first and foremost, on its percepti-

---

100. Dorsey, 'Literary Architecture', pp. 327-29.
101. Smalley, 'Recursion Patterns', p. 122.
102. Smalley, 'Recursion Patterns', p. 125.
103. Emerton, 'Examination', pp. 20-21.

bility, and that, in an oral setting, a chiasm is most likely to be perceptible when its boundaries coincide with other formal or rhetorical markers. Secondly, the perceptibility of a chiasm is also facilitated when its corresponding parts share a high degree of similarity. This, it should be noted, is a particular requirement for its outer parts. Wendland is therefore right to affirm that any (portion of a) text that is regarded as a self-contained unit 'must have recognizable borders that can be precisely defined and defended—at whatever level in the compositional hierarchy it happens to lie'.[104] Amos 5.1-17 is a good example for a text that meets these requirements. Its outer boundaries coincide with additional rhetorical markers, namely, the introductory phrase in v. 1 and the words...הוי המתאוים in v. 18, which open the subsequent woe oracle. In addition, both outer segments (vv. 1-3, 16-17) are easily identifiable as laments. Similarly, the correspondence of the second and penultimate sections (vv. 4-6, 14-15) is also readily apparent, as these are the only exhortations in the whole of Amos. Finally, it needs to be stressed that the more extensive the chiasm becomes, the less recognizable it will be, and that this basically rules out the use of large-scale chiastic structures in an oral context.

d. *Indicators of Aperture and Closure*

The use of introductory markers (roughly equivalent to the employment of headings in modern publications) or of signals that demarcate the ending of a section are also possible means for indicating breaks in a text. In the case of the prophetic books it is, first of all (but not exclusively), the speech formulas that suggest themselves as possible structural markers, even though their role should not be limited to a structural one.[105] Thus, if the assumptions that Amos is shaped by oral conventions and that it has been composed for public readings are correct, one needs to ask whether the retention of the speech formulas is in any way significant. That is to say, have they simply been preserved as part of the oral traditions, or have they been consciously employed by the authors or editors? And if the latter is the case, to what effect have they been used?

Speech or Quotation Formulas and Other Structural Markers. Studies of the structural function of prophetic speech formulas and other structurally relevant words or phrases have been undertaken mainly from a discourse-

---

104. Wendland, 'Discourse Analysis', p. 7.
105. For instance, they also stress the divine origin of the prophetic message (cf. Wendland, 'Word', pp. 26-29).

linguistic perspective. Although there is as yet no detailed study available that investigates the use of these devices in Amos, Wendland in particular considers them important for any attempt to understand the organization of the book.[106] A detailed analysis of the function of every relevant word or phrase is, of course, impossible within the confines of this study, but I intend to give at least a tentative list of words and phrases that may be of structural significance. Particular attention will be paid to the formulas אמר יהוה and נאם יהוה, which feature repeatedly in the book of Amos and have often been understood as assuming structural roles.

An attempt to determine the distinctive function of a variety of speech formulas in Jeremiah has been made by Parunak, who notes that they (1) make it possible for us to identify the individual oracles and sometimes provide information about their original settings; (2) enable us to analyse the *internal structure of individual oracles*; and (3) provide a means of *connecting different oracles* with one another, thereby helping us to identify the message of the prophetic book.[107]

Based on an examination of the use of these speech formulas, Parunak proposes a 'disjunctive cline'—that is, a hierarchy—in which each formula has its specific place in that it may introduce a paragraph, a section, a division, or the book as a whole.[108] While this is not the place to evaluate Parunak's proposal, other studies have shown that it is notoriously difficult to establish a cline that can be applied to the prophetic books in general. Thus, it may well be that each book has its own distinctive cline, or that, in some cases, no cline can be established at all.[109]

Because of these difficulties, I am not going to propose a 'disjunctive cline' for Amos. However, I aim to show that it is possible, on a general level at least, to distinguish between macro-structural markers (which introduce major sections) and subordinate ones. The following words and

106. Wendland, 'Word', p. 2.
107. H. van Dyke Parunak, 'Some Discourse Functions of Prophetic Quotation Formulas in Jeremiah', in Bergen (ed.), *Biblical Hebrew*, pp. 489-519 (492).
108. For Jeremiah this cline includes (in ranking order): הדבר אשר (...) אל/על/, כה אמר יהוה, שמע דבר־יהוה, ויאמר יהוה (אלי), דבר־יהוה (...) ויהי/היה, ביד ירמיהו and נאם יהוה (Parunak, 'Discourse Functions', p. 513). The formula היה הדבר הזה (...) מאת יהוה, which occurs only three times, is not included in this scheme.
109. Cf. Finley and Payton, 'Discourse Analysis', pp. 317-35, who, looking at Isa. 7–12, list 18 words or phrases, many of which function on more than one level (thus, a particular marker may introduce an episode, a paragraph or a sub-paragraph). In the end, they acknowledge that 'the relative ranks are not conclusive but only suggestive' (p. 329).

phrases deserve special attention in this context: זאת, כה אמר יהוה
אמר יהוה, כה הראני (אדני יהוה) והנה, הוי, שמעו (את־)הדבר הזה/שמעו,
הנה יהוה, נאם, ואנכי and אנכי/וגם־אני/כי, לכן, הנה, the temporal markers
ביום ההוא, and הנה ימים באים, rhetorical questions, imperatives, as well as
extended divine names or titles. Their specific function and possible location in a structural hierarchy will be discussed in the context of the
subsequent structural analysis of the book. At this point, I focus on the
phrases נאם יהוה and אמר יהוה, asking whether they have any significant
structural role to play.

Parunak, in his analysis of Jeremiah, comes to the conclusion that the
formula נאם יהוה 'is disjunctively the weakest' and serves mainly as a
focusing device.[110] He therefore defines it as 'a highly local highlighting
of a clause or phrase that merits the recipient's special attention'.[111] As
such, it can occur at various points in a paragraph (it frequently appears at
the end but often also towards the beginning or indeed somewhere in the
middle).[112]

In Amos, the phrase נאם יהוה occurs towards the closure of a major
section only in 2.16; 3.15; 6.14 and 8.3; and only in the first two instances
does it literally close the sections in question. I will come back to these
cases in a moment. At this point, however, it needs to be stressed that, as
far as its use in Amos is concerned, the phrase often complements (or is
complemented by) other rhetorical markers. These include rhetorical questions (2.11; 9.7), a divine oath (6.8)[113] and the temporal markers ביום ההוא

---

110. Parunak, 'Discourse Functions', p. 514. For a detailed discussion of the formula
cf. pp. 508-12, where he interacts with F.S. North, 'The Expression "the Oracle of
Yahweh" as an Aid to Critical Analysis', *JBL* 71 (1952); R. Rendtorff, 'Zum Gebrauch
der Formel *ne'um jahwe* im Jeremiabuch', *ZAW* 66 (1954), pp. 27-37; and F. Baumgärtel, 'Die Formel *ne'um jahwe*', *ZAW* 73 (1961), pp. 277-90.

111. Parunak, 'Discourse Functions', p. 511.

112. See also S.A. Meier, *Speaking of Speaking: Marking Direct Discourse in the
Hebrew Bible* (VTSup, 46; Leiden: E.J. Brill, 1992), p. 226.

113. In 6.8, the formula נאם יהוה is absent from the LXX so some prefer to delete it
(cf. Mays, *Amos*, p. 117; and Meier, *Speaking*, p. 228 n. 3). According to H.W. Wolff,
Joel and Amos: A Commentary on the Books of the Prophets Joel and Amos (ed. S.D.
McBride, Jr; trans. W. Janzen, S.D. McBride, Jr and C.A. Muenchow; Hermeneia;
Philadelphia: Fortress Press, 1977), p. 279; and W. Rudolph, *Joel, Amos, Obadja, Jona*
(KAT, 13.2; Gütersloh: Gütersloher Verlagshaus Gerd Mohn, 1971), p. 218, it may
have belonged—in its shorter form, i.e. without אלהי צבאות—after v. 7 (both assume
the phrase to be a closing formula). However, in the text as it stands, it clearly
functions as a marker of emphasis, being reinforced, in this particular instance, by the

(8.3, 9) and הנה ימים באים (8.11; 9.13). Clear signals of emphasis are also to be found in 3.13 (cf. the attenuated divine name אדני יהוה אלהי הצבאות), where the phrase addresses imaginary witnesses, in 6.14, which concludes the second woe oracle and is introduced by כי הנני, and in 9.12, where the announcement that Israel will possess the remnant of Edom is underlined by the words נאם־יהוה עשה זאת.

A similar use can be demonstrated for 3.10 and 9.8, where the phrase is not accompanied by other rhetorical markers. Yet in these instances, it is used in conjunction with what are clearly important statements. Thus, in 3.10 it stresses that the Israelites do not know how to do right, and in 9.8 it underlines the declaration that the destruction of the house of Jacob will not be all-inclusive. Especially the four occurrences of נאם יהוה in Amos 9 (vv. 7, 8, 12, 13) are a good illustration of its use as a local highlighting device. Andersen and Freedman oddly claim that in 9.7-15 'the placement of the oracle formula *n'm yhwh* (*'šh z't*) as a marker at the end of units or between units is the key to the organization of the material'.[114] However, this is clearly not the case, as the uneven distribution of the phrase indicates.[115] Indeed, the major break of the section at the beginning of v. 11 is not marked by a נאם יהוה formula at all. Again, the best explanation for the repeated use of the formula in this section therefore seems to be that it provides rhetorical emphasis.

Yet there are a few cases, where (at least at first sight) the phrase appears to be of structural significance. Its use is particularly prominent in Amos 4, where it closes the initial judgment oracle (vv. 1-3) as well as the mock exhortation to perform cultic activities in vv. 4-5. It also concludes each of the five strophes that accuse Israel for not having returned to their God despite his previous judgments (vv. 6-11). However, in the light of its use in other parts of the book, it seems preferable to regard the words נאם יהוה as a focusing device even in these cases. As such, it stresses the drastic punishment notion in vv. 2-3 and highlights the words כי כן אהבתם בני ישראל in v. 5. Meier rejects a structural significance also for vv. 6-11, where נאם־יהוה appears together with the refrain ולא־שבתם עדי, thus stressing the Israelites' unwillingness to return to their God. As Meier notes:

> the uniformity of form and content in Am 4.6-11, with explicit syntactic bonds (e.g. וגם in v. 7), underscore that each unit closed by נאם יהוה cannot meaningfully stand alone. If נאם יהוה were absent entirely from 4.6-11,

highly emotive words מתאב אנכי את־גאון יעקב וארמנתיו שנאתי.

114. Andersen and Freedman, *Amos*, p. 906.
115. Cf. Meier, *Speaking*, p. 310 (n. 1).

there would be no justification for identifying five distinct oracles in these six verses.[116]

Accordingly, he concludes that 'one cannot use it as a means of structuring a text without other formal controls'.[117] This is confirmed by the fact that in those four cases where the phrase does occur at the end of a major section (2.16; 3.15; 6.14 and 8.3), the section breaks are reinforced by introductory phrases in subsequent verses.

Thus, Parunak's conclusions about the use of נאם יהוה in Jeremiah are applicable also to the book of Amos. This has been confirmed by Meier, who regards the formula as an 'oratorical device' with no macrostructural function.[118] As such, it will have alerted Amos's original audience to key points in his message. Indeed, it will have performed a similar function also in the context of a public reading of the book.

This then brings us to the phrase אמר יהוה,[119] which differs from the former formula in that it always occurs in ultimate position. On three occasions, it closes a major section, and in the remaining six cases, it occurs at the end of a smaller paragraph. Yet, this notwithstanding, it too appears to be mainly a focusing device. As such, it highlights Yahweh's passing through Israel's midst (5.17), the people's exile beyond Damascus (5.27) and God's planting of the people upon their land (9.15). In the latter two cases, the stress provided by the words אמר יהוה is reinforced by the use of attenuated divine names. The function of אמר יהוה as a means of local highlighting is also evident at the end of the first two visions, where the formula accentuates the words לא תהיה (7.3, 6). The picture is similar in the oracles against the nations, where אמר יהוה occurs only in the strophes dealing with Aram, Philistia, Ammon and Moab (1.5, 8, 15; 2.3). This is

116. Meier, *Speaking*, p. 309.

117. Meier, *Speaking*, pp. 309-10.

118. Meier, *Speaking*, p. 297. It should also be noted that Meier has taken issue with the claim that 'נאם is the strongest word denoting prophetic utterance and especially marks its divine character', to put it in Harper's words (see W.R. Harper, *A Critical and Exegetical Commentary on Amos and Hosea* [ICC; Edinburgh: T. & T. Clark, 1905], p. 59; and also H. Eising, 'נאם', in *ThWAT*, V, pp. 119-23). As Meier, *Speaking*, pp. 311-13, has pointed out, נאם can in fact also refer to the speech of humans (i.e. that of Balaam [Num. 24.3, 15], David [2 Sam. 23.1] or Agur [Prov. 30.1]), which thus makes it 'precarious to insist that the word refers specifically to divine speech' (Meier, *Speaking*, p. 312). Indeed, neither Tg nor LXX distinguish between אמר יהוה and נאם יהוה, with the former rendering both as אמר while LXX translates them as λέγει.

119. At this point, I am not concerned with the introductory formula כה אמר יהוה, which will be dealt with in the subsequent investigation of Amos's macro structure.

interesting because these strophes differ from the others in that they feature an extended punishment section.[120] It is precisely this notion of punishment, on which the strophes end, that is highlighted by means of the אמר יהוה formula. On the basis of these observations, it seems reasonable to conclude that the divine speech formula אמר יהוה serves to emphasize what immediately precedes it.[121]

Let me then end this section by stressing that any investigation of formulas and other recurring phrases needs to pay close attention to the textual contexts in which they occur. Only thus will it be possible to establish whether they assume a structural role or function as local indicators of emphasis. In the case of the divine speech formulas נאם יהוה and אמר יהוה, my examination has led me to conclude that both function as local markers of emphasis[122] and therefore are not reliable guides to the structural arrangement of the book of Amos.

The Distribution and Function of the Divine Names. Scholars have long been puzzled by the unusual use of (at times quite elaborate) divine names in Amos. Sometimes these are regarded as late additions.[123] Yet it is not the redaction-critical question that I am concerned about at this point but whether these names can be shown to serve a particular function in the book. Pursuing a similar question, Koch has devoted special attention to the use of the divine epithet צבאות. Commenting on the phrase נאם־אדני יהוה אלהי הצבאות in 3.13, Koch believes that its extraordinary length is designed to mark the subsequent statement in 3.14-15 as the summary of all the announcements of doom directed at Samaria found in Amos 3. He also notes that the same phrase (albeit without אדני) also marks a concluding oracle in 6.14 and concludes that the צבאות predications featuring נאם are used in the same way as the phrase יהוה אלהי־צבאותשמו at the end of the hymns in 4.13; 5.8 and 9.6[124] or at the end of a collection of oracles, as in 5.27.[125]

120. See Chapter 3 for further comments.
121. See Meier, *Speaking*, pp. 226-27.
122. Already Rudolph, *Joel, Amos, Obadja, Jona*, p. 119, noted that no qualitative difference between the two can be demonstrated. Wolff, *Joel and Amos*, p. 143, on the other hand, thought that the phrase נאם יהוה provided what he described as 'ceremonial emphasis'.
123. Cf., e.g., Wolff, *Joel and Amos, passim*.
124. In 5.8 and 9.6, where the MT has only יהוה שמו, Koch adopts the LXX reading, which has κύριος ὁ θεὸς ὁ παντοκράτωρ ὄνομα αὐτῷ.
125. Koch, 'Rolle', p. 529, cf. p. 535.

Although this at first appears to be a promising route for further investigation, Koch's proposal has been rightly criticized. Dempster, in an article investigating the use and distribution of the divine names in the book
of Amos, demonstrated that neither the צבאות predications nor the doxologies can be said always to mark the closure of a passage.[126] Yet Dempster
maintains that the divine names and titles are 'carefully arranged throughout the text'[127] and, what is more, that 'the book is essentially structured
around the various names and designations of God'.[128]

According to Dempster, the book can be divided into the following
sections: 1.3–2.16; 3.1-15; 4.1-13; 5.1-17; 5.18-27; 6.1-14; 7.1–9.6 and
9.7-15. He notes that in the first section (1.[2]3–2.16), with the sole
exception of 1.8 (where we find אדני יהוה), the simple יהוה is used and
claims that 'the fact that there is a fourteen-fold repetition of the name
[יהוה] alone after its introduction in the title is probably not accidental in a
text where the number of completion and totality is stressed'.[129] In the next
part (Amos 3) the two forms יהוה and אדני יהוה alternate.[130] What is striking here is the lengthened form אדני יהוה אלהי הצבאות in 3.13, which
'occurs before the climactic announcement of judgement'.[131] The picture
is similar in Amos 4 where, again, we encounter יהוה and אדני יהוה forms,
and where the elongated form יהוה אלהי־צבאות is used to mark a climax
(v. 13). In 5.1-17, the most remarkable feature is the accumulation of
יהוה אלהי צבאות (אדני) forms in vv. 14-16, that is, towards the closure
(and climax?) of the discourse. Dempster thinks that 'as if to sustain the
drama, the name is repeated (15). Finally, the drama reaches its peak in
5.16 when the lengthened form is elongated further in "staircase-like"
fashion.' This pattern Dempster regards as an 'appellative overkill'.[132]

In 5.18-27, we find the simple יהוה (three times), followed by the long

126. S. Dempster, 'The Lord is His Name: A Study of the Distribution of the Names
and Titles of God in the Book of Amos', *RB* 98 (1991), pp. 170-89 (172; cf. n. 11).

127. Dempster, 'Lord', p. 170. A similar point has been made by Tromp, 'Amos V
1-17', pp. 56-85, concerning the use of the divine names in Amos 5.1-17. See also
Andersen and Freedman, *Amos*, pp. 617-18, 718, who too have devoted some attention
to patterns in the distribution of the divine names.

128. Dempster, 'Lord', p. 174.

129. Dempster, 'Lord', p. 177.

130. The alternating pattern is as follows: יהוה (twice, in vv. 1, 6), אדני יהוה (twice,
in vv. 7, 8), יהוה (v. 10), אדני יהוה (v. 11), יהוה (v. 12), אדני יהוה אלהי הצבאות (v. 13)
and יהוה (v. 15).

131. Dempster, 'Lord', p. 178.

132. Dempster, 'Lord', p. 180.

form יהוה אלהי־צבאות at the end of the discourse (cf. v. 27). In 6.1-14, however, the usage of the names differs from that in the preceding parts in that the longer form יהוה אלהי(ה)צבאות occurs twice. Thus, while it again closes the section (v. 14), it also features in v. 8, where it accompanies a divine oath. The following, according to Dempster's analysis rather long, section (7.1–9.6) contains the short form יהוה as well as the compound אדני יהוה. However, it also features the only three occurrences of an unaccompanied אדני form (cf. 7.7, 8; 9.1)[133] as well as the elongated אדני יהוה הצבאות in 9.5, that is, towards the climactic closure of the passage. Finally, the epilogue in 9.7-15 ends with the unique and more intimate form יהוה אלהיך. This, as Dempster points out, is 'highly appropriate to its context, the only one in the text in which there is no longer any alienation and distance between God and His people.'[134] Concluding his analysis, Dempster stresses that:

> the major units of the core of the book, with their focus at the end of each on the announcement of a name of God, *together build to a climax throughout the book* in which there is the *seventh* announcement: יהוה שמו. This declaration is thus the theme of the book.[135]

Dempster's results concerning the use of section-ending divine name formulas in what he calls the 'core of the book' (Amos 3.1–9.6) are summarized in the following figure.

Phrase	No.	Passage
אדני יהוה אלהי הצבאות	1	3.13
יהוה אלהי־צבאות[136] (שמו)	2	4.13
יהוה אלהי צבאות אדני	3	5.16
יהוה אלהי־צבאות[136] (שמו)	4	5.27
יהוה אלהי הצבאות	5	6.14
אדני יהוה הצבאות	6	9.5
יהוה שמו	7	9.6

Figure 3. *Section-Ending Divine Name Formulas
in Amos 3.1–9.6 according to Dempster*

133. These occur in the third and fifth visions, both of which have a prominent role to play. The third vision marks the turning point of the series in ruling out any further relenting on Yahweh's part. In the fifth vision, which ends the series, the final judgment is brought under way (cf. Dempster, 'Lord', p. 182).

134. Dempster, 'Lord', p. 182.

135. Dempster, 'Lord', p. 184 (Dempster's italics).

136. I have included שמו for reasons that will become clear in my subsequent evaluation of Dempster's analysis.

Dempster's analysis offers many valuable insights and rightly underlines that the use of different divine names and titles is not accidental.[137] Thus, he is right, I believe, to stress that 'the usage of the names and titles of God in Amos is not the haphazard work of a redactor or glossator with a pleonastic style'.[138] And yet it needs to be said that Dempster's investigation is not altogether convincing. First, the occurrence of a prolonged divine title in itself is not a reliable structural guide. This can be seen in that Amos 1.3–2.16 does not contain any such phrase, which indicates that the closure of major sections need not be marked by an elaborate divine name formula. In addition, the occurrence of יהוה אלהי צבאות in 6.8 indicates that these formulas may occur also in the middle of a prophetic discourse.[139] Thus, rather than viewing them as structural markers, it seems preferable to regard them as another example of rhetorical highlighting.

This then takes us to Dempster's conclusions concerning the phrase יהוה שמו, which, for similar reasons, are also unsatisfactory. In particular, one wonders why he attributes so much weight to its occurrence in 9.5-6. After all, the phrase appears also in 4.13; 5.8, 27 where, according to Dempster's analysis, it does not seem to be of major importance.[140] Indeed in two of these passages we find the longer form יהוה אלהי־צבאות שמו (4.13; 5.27), which stands out even more. Another open question, related to the former, is why Dempster regards the expression יהוה שמו as the theme of the book. Again, I would contend that its actual function and significance need to be ascertained by investigating all five occurrences in their respective contexts. This reveals that the phrase features in each of the book's hymn fragments (4.13; 5.8; 9.6) and that it accompanies one of the announcements of exile (5.27). This usage suggests that, like the אמר יהוה and נאם יהוה formulas, and like the elongated divine names, the words יהוה שמו are employed for rhetorical reasons. They draw attention to the identity of the one Israel will have to face in the impending judgment.

e. *Patterns of Numerical Sequence*
Limburg and O'Connell, in their attempts to discover criteria for outlining the structure of Amos, rely mainly on so-called 'patterns of numerical

---

137. Cf. in this context T.L. Thompson, 'How Yahweh Became God: Exodus 3 and 6 and the Heart of the Pentateuch', *JSOT* 68 (1995), pp. 57-74 (68). He notes that the 'play on the divine names', i.e. the alternation of יהוה and אלהים (as well as the use of אל שדי), in the Pentateuch 'is part of the narrative's signification'.

138. Dempster, 'Lord', p. 184.

139. Cf. Dempster, 'Lord', p. 181.

140. Dempster, 'Lord', p. 184 n. 36.

sequence'. These are defined by Roth as 'x/x+1' sequences.[141] Noting that they play an important part in the book of Amos, Limburg and O'Connell reason that they may have been employed for structural purposes.

Heptads and Seven-plus-one Series. Limburg, in a 1987 article, concentrates on so-called 'heptads' (i.e., series consisting of seven components) as well as seven-plus-one series.[142] He begins by investigating the divine speech formulas, which, according to his findings, occur in clusters of seven constituents. Having identified Amos 1.1-2 as the book's introduction, which is followed by the oracles against the nations (OAN)[143] in 1.3–2.16, he then delineates the next three units on the basis of the introductory formula 'hear this word' (3.1; 4.1; 5.1). As Limburg points out, in each of the first three major sections (i.e., 1.3–2.16; 3.1-15; 4.1-13), there are either seven divine speech formulas or even two times seven, as in 1.3–2.16, where we have eight introductory אמר formulas (1.3, 6, 9, 11, 13; 2.1, 4, 6), four concluding אמר formulas (1.5, 8, 15; 2.3)[144] and two נאם formulas (2.11, 16), thus amounting to a total of fourteen.[145] In Amos 3, there are two introductory אמר formulas (vv. 11, 12), three נאם formulas (vv. 10, 13, 15) and the doubly introduced divine saying in v. 1, where we find a דבר formula followed by לאמר. In this case, the total amounts to seven.[146] The same number is found in Amos 4, where all the occurrences are נאם formulas (vv. 3, 5, 6, 8, 9, 10, 11).

In order to detect the end of the next unit beginning in 5.1, Limburg

---

141. W.M.W. Roth, 'The Numerical Sequence x/x+1 in the Old Testament', *VT* 12 (1962), pp. 300-11; cf. also *idem*, *Numerical Sayings in the Old Testament: A Form-Critical Study* (VTSup, 13; Leiden: E.J. Brill, 1965). For an extensive 'chronological bibliography of the ascending numerical pair' cf. R.H. O'Connell, 'Telescoping N+1 Patterns in the Book of Amos', *VT* 46 (1996), pp. 56-73 (71-73).

142. J. Limburg, 'Sevenfold Structures in the Book of Amos', *JBL* 106 (1987), pp. 217-22.

143. In the present study, the term 'oracles against the nations' as well as the acronym 'OAN' represent the literary unit Amos 1.3–2.16, including the Israel oracle in 2.6-16.

144. Not three, as Limburg erringly remarks.

145. According to Limburg, the lack of a concluding divine speech formula in the Tyre, Edom and Judah strophes may be due to the fact that 'the editor was striving for seven or a multiple of seven divine speech formulas in each section of the book' (Limburg, 'Sevenfold Structures', p. 222).

146. Limburg does not count the words אדני יהוה דבר in 3.8, which are not part of the framework of direct speech (Limburg, 'Sevenfold Structures', p. 217 n. 2).

then counts another seven divine speech formulas, thus arriving at 6.14. 'This division', he remarks, 'fits well with the content, since the series of vision reports begins with 7.1.'[147] In this case, the section features three initial אמר formulas (5.3, 4, 16), two concluding אמר formulas (5.17, 27) and two נאם formulas (6.8, 14). In using the same method of counting speech formulas, Limburg, in a next step, finds the end of the vision report series in 8.3. It in turn contains six אמר formulas (7.3, 6, 8, 15, 17, 8.2) and one נאם formula (8.3). And, as Limburg notes, the delineation again 'fits well with the contents, since 7.1-8.3 contains four vision reports and the narrative section in 7.10-17'.[148] The phrase 'hear this' (8.4), which resembles the introductory formula 'hear this word' in 3.1; 4.1 and 5.1, then introduces the final part of the book, in which we encounter six נאם formulas (8.9, 11; 9.7, 8, 12, 13) and one אמר formula (9.15). Summarizing his findings, Limburg concludes that all the divine speech formulas amount to 'a grand-total of forty-nine, or seven times seven'. Moreover, 'if we count the introduction in 1.1-2 as the first section, then the book falls into seven parts'.[149]

Limburg's results look very impressive but, as is so often the case, the data does not fit quite as neatly, as he would make us believe. First, one wonders why Limburg does not count ויאמר in 9.1, the subject of which is אדני. It may be that he disregards it because it is not immediately followed or preceded by a divine name or title. But this is also the case as far as לאמר in 3.1 is concerned. Or maybe ויאמר is left out because the following divine words are addressed to Amos, whereas in the other instances they introduce oracles addressed to the people of Israel? However, if that were the case, we would have difficulties accounting for the divine speech formulas in the vision report series, all of which address the prophet. This, in turn, takes us to another problem. In 7.8 as well as in 8.2, we have two divine speech formulas each but in both cases Limburg only counts one. Does he not include the ones that introduce questions directed at the prophet, or are only those taken into account that include the divine name יהוה (i.e., the first in 7.8 and the second in 8.2)?

In the second part of his article, Limburg discusses further groupings of seven or seven-plus-one items, arriving at quite an impressive number.[150]

---

147. Limburg, 'Sevenfold Structures', p. 218.
148. Limburg, 'Sevenfold Structures', p. 218.
149. Limburg, 'Sevenfold Structures', p. 218.
150. Limburg, 'Sevenfold Structures', pp. 219-21.

Dorsey adds even further examples[151] so that, on the basis of their combined findings, we end up with the following list:

- seven oracles against foreign nations (1.3–2.5), followed by a climactic oracle against Israel (2.6-16);
- seven transgressions (2.6-8);
- seven consequences of the divine punishment and seven classes of military that will not escape (2.14-16);
- seven rhetorical questions, followed by a climactic statement (3.3-8);
- seven verbal clauses describing Yahweh's punishment (3.14-15);
- seven imperatives, followed by a punch line (4.4-5);
- seven first person verbs with כֶם suffix forms, followed by a climax (4.6-12);
- seven verbs of exhortation (5.4-6a);
- seven verbs in the hymn fragment 5.8-9;
- seven bicola depicting Israel's condemnation (5.10-13);
- seven verbs of exhortation or promise (5.14-15);
- seven things that Yahweh abhors, followed by an indication of what he desires (5.21-24);
- seven participles/woes (6.1-6);
- seven things that the people do, followed by what they ought to do instead (6.4-6);
- seven accusations against the merchants (8.4-8);
- seven punishing acts, followed by a climactic statement (9.1-4);
- seven lines featuring the construction מְשֹם...אִם (9.2a-4a);
- seven good things that Yahweh will do for Israel in the future (9.11-15);
- and seven third person plural verbs depicting Israel's future life (9.14-15).

---

151. Dorsey, 'Literary Architecture', p. 324. Heptads play an important part in the Old Testament as well as in ancient Near Eastern texts. See J. Hehn, *Siebenzahl und Sabbat bei den Babyloniern und im Alten Testament: Eine religionsgeschichtliche Studie* (Leipziger semitistische Studien, 2.5; Leipzig: J.C. Hinrichs, 1907); *idem*, 'Zur Bedeutung der Siebenzahl', in K. Budde (ed.), *Vom Alten Testament. Karl Marti zum siebzigsten Geburtstage* (BZAW, 41; Giessen: Alfred Töpelmann, 1925), pp. 128-36; M.H. Pope, 'Seven, Seventh, Seventy', in *IDB*, IV, pp. 294-95; A.S. Kapelrud, 'The Number Seven in Ugaritic Texts', *VT* 18 (1968), pp. 494-99; R. Gordis, 'The Heptads as an Element of Biblical and Rabbinic Style', *JBL* 62 (1943), pp. 17-26; J.M. Sasson, 'A Genealogical "Convention" in Biblical Chronography?', *ZAW* 90 (1978), pp. 171-85; C.J. Labuschagne, 'The Pattern of the Divine Speech Formulas in the Pentateuch: The Key to Its Literary Structure', *VT* 32 (1982), pp. 268-96; G. Braulik, 'Zur Funktion von Siebenergruppierungen im Endtext des Deuteronomiums', in F.V. Reiterer (ed.), *Ein Gott, eine Offenbarung: Beiträge zur biblischen Exegese, Theologie und Spiritualität. Festschrift für Notker Füglister OSB zum 60. Geburtstag* (Würzburg: Echter Verlag, 1991), pp. 37-50; G.J. Wenham, *Numbers* (OTG; Sheffield: Sheffield Academic Press, 1997), pp. 24-25; and *idem*, *Genesis 1–15* (WBC, 1; Dallas: Word Books, 1987), pp. 6-7, 96.

This list does, of course, raise the question of the function of these series, which, it should be noted, occur on all levels of Amos's structural hierarchy. While some of the examples may well be accidental, the consistent use of heptads throughout the book suggests that, on the whole, they have been put to deliberate use. Without intending to enter into a detailed discussion, I should like to point out that I would regard them as a rhetorical device that underlines a particular issue, such as the scandalous behaviour of the merchants in 8.4-8. In the specific case of the seven-plus-one series, on the other hand, the stress is on the eighth climactic statement, as can be seen in the OAN, where seven oracles against foreign nations are followed by the climactic condemnation of Israel, the prophet's real target. In some cases, the eighth element forms a contrast with the preceding ones, as in 6.4-6, where an account of what the people do is followed by a statement that sets out what they ought to do instead.

Telescoping N+1 Patterns. O'Connell, in his article 'Telescoping N+1 Patterns in the Book of Amos', pursues an interest similar to that of Limburg. Yet he focuses more broadly both on seven-plus-one series as well as on occurrences of three-plus-one items.[152] His main theses are that the arrangement of Amos is based on such N+1 groupings and that the final (+1) component deviates from the pattern established in the preceding parts, thus contributing an element of surprise. Even more importantly, according to O'Connell, the final component serves as a transition to the following N+1 groupings, which is why he speaks of 'telescoping N+1 patterns'.

The first series is to be found in 1.3–2.16, a passage that contains eight instances of the ascending numerical parallelism (על־שלשה פשעי... ועל־ארבעה). The transitional element (2.6-16) focuses on Israel, which from now on becomes the prophet's exclusive target. The next part, Amos 3–6, according to O'Connell, contains three judgment oracles (3.1–5.17) followed by a double woe oracle (5.18–6.14). O'Connell goes to great lengths to argue that the two woe oracles in 5.18-27 and 6.1-14 ought to be seen as the +1 element, which in this case would complete a three-plus-one series. However, at this point he runs into problems. First, this is the only instance where the final component is not introduced by the same formulaic introduction that opens the preceding constituents (in 5.18, הוי is used rather than the expected שמעו). Secondly, as already noted, in

---

152. In theory, N could, of course, signify any number but as far as the book of Amos is concerned, O'Connell detects only 3+1 and 7+1 series.

5.18–6.14 we have two woe oracles so that the series might just as well be seen as a 3+2 pattern. Concerning the divergent introduction, O'Connell reasons that this is part of the surprise, which sometimes characterizes the final part, before asserting that 'the change from judgement oracle to woe oracle does not represent a change of disposition'[153] anyway. As far as the second problem is concerned, O'Connell argues that woe oracles are often arranged as doublets or quadruplets, and that the two in Amos may therefore form a single rhetorical entity. This double woe oracle would then function as the next telescoping device by focusing on the disastrous outcome of the יום יהוה, thus providing a negative connotation that is sustained in the subsequent sections.

According to O'Connell, the next major section is Amos 7.1–8.2. In this case, another 3+1 series, the final component (8.1-2) is set off from the preceding ones not by being constructed differently but by the inclusion of the 'tension-building' narrative inset in 7.10-17. In line with his general argument, O'Connell regards Amos 8.1-2 as the transitional element, noting that 'it is the very brevity of this threat, anticipating that judgement is about to fall immediately upon Israel, that issues in the succeeding series of eschatological oracles (in viii 3-ix 15).'[154] Turning to the final part, Amos 8.3–9.15, O'Connell points out that it contains four eschatological oracles, the first three of which are 'juxtaposed and separated from the last by the formal interruption of the prophetic vision of ix 1-10',[155] thus creating another 3+1 series. In this case, each component is introduced by a temporal formula (either ביום ההוא or הנה ימים באים), and the element of surprise consists in the fact that Amos 9.11-15 promises restoration, thus departing from the austere message that characterizes the rest of the book.

I share O'Connell's belief that there is a progression of thought in the book of Amos but remain unconvinced by his proposal of a telescoping N+1 pattern. O'Connell's theory works well enough for the first major section, the final component of which clearly functions as a transition that brings the sin and judgment of Israel, the prophet's actual target, into focus. Difficulties arise in the case of the other sections, however. To begin with, the construal of Amos 3–6 and 7.1–8.2 as two 3+1 series seems somewhat forced. O'Connell's analysis of the final section (8.3–9.15) is even less convincing. Although some redaction critics regard Amos 8.3-14 as a later

153. O'Connell, 'Telescoping N+1 Patterns', p. 64.
154. O'Connell, 'Telescoping N+1 Patterns', p. 69.
155. O'Connell, 'Telescoping N+1 Patterns', pp. 61-62.

addition,[156] in the text as it now stands, the structural break clearly occurs after 8.3 (cf. the introductory phrase שמעוּ־זאת).[157] O'Connell, by contrast, regards 8.3 as an opening statement due to the temporal marker ביום ההוא, which in his view introduces each part of this last section of the book. However, this judgment ignores the fact that in Amos 8.3 the words ביום ההוא occur in non-initial position and are closely linked to the preceding statements. They are part of what de Vries has called 'a dramatically epitomizing conclusion'.[158]

This alone is sufficient to invalidate O'Connell's proposal, which stands or falls with the temporal formulas. That is to say, if the final section were to begin in 8.4, there would be no three-plus-one series introduced by temporal formulas, as envisaged by O'Connell. However, there are yet further problems. For instance, why does the phrase ביום ההוא introduce a new section in 8.3, where it occurs in a non-initial position, and in 8.9, where it is preceded by והיה, but not in 8.13, where it is initial? Similarly, why are the words הנה ימים באים considered introductory in 8.11 but not in 9.13?[159] Finally, it is also somewhat unsatisfactory to think of 9.1-10 as a mere inset, given that this is a relatively lengthy section, which includes a variety of material, and which, in significant ways, develops some of the book's most important themes.

f. *Conclusions*

Having seen the strengths and weaknesses of the proposals discussed above, it appears that what is needed is an 'integrative approach' to the structure of Amos, which is flexible enough to account for the data in all its complexity. As such, it needs to investigate how *all* the structural devices, of which there could be a large variety, and the content of the passages in question contribute to the text's rhetorical structure. As Weiss has pointed out, it is important to understand how the formal elements of,

156. Cf. e.g. H.G.M. Williamson, 'The Prophet and the Plumb-Line: A Redaction-Critical Study of Amos vii', in A.S. van der Woude (ed.), *In Quest of the Past: Studies on Israelite Religion, Literature and Prophetism* (OTS, 26; Leiden: E.J. Brill, 1990), pp. 101-21 (118).

157. Almost all modern commentators treat 8.4-14 as a separate section.

158. S.J. de Vries, *Yesterday, Today and Tomorrow: Time and History in the Old Testament* (London: SPCK, 1975), p. 319.

159. O'Connell's observation ('Telescoping N+1 Patterns', p. 62) that the temporal formulas in 8.11, 13; 9.11, 13 are arranged chiastically, while correct, does not answer this question.

for instance, a poetical structure work, and how they all work together.[160] In addition, we must attempt to resist any urge of subjecting the text to a particular theory, especially if that requires it to be tailored in order to make it fit the theory.[161]

Before we then proceed to investigate the macrostructure of Amos, let me summarize the findings of this review. First, the general proposal of a three- or four-partite structure consisting of an introduction, 'the words', 'the visions' (and an appendix) has proved to be a helpful starting point. Secondly, the hymn fragments do not appear to function as structural markers but seem to have been employed to accentuate the announcements of judgment, which they accompany. Thirdly, concentric structures, such as inclusios and chiasms, do have structural significance (but also require a fair amount of *phronesis*, 'good judgment', on the part of the investigating scholar). In addition, as a means of repetition, inclusios and chiasms are also used to signal rhetorical emphasis. Fourthly, the same applies to recurring phrases and formulas, which at the same time can, but do not necessarily, function as structural markers. Fifthly, and finally, yet another means of highlighting is provided by heptads and seven-plus-one series. These either stress a particular point by elaborating on it (heptads) or by providing a climactic conclusion (seven-plus-one series).

3. *The Macrostructure of Amos*

In what follows, I am going to argue that, in addition to a historical superscription in 1.1 and a motto in 1.2, the book of Amos consists of nine major units. The first of these is the introductory series of oracles against the nations in 1.3–2.16, which is followed by three sections in 3.1-15; 4.1-13 and 5.1-17, all of which are introduced by שִׁמְעוּ. Two elaborate woe

---

160. M. Weiss, 'Die Methode der "Total-Interpretation": Von der Notwendigkeit der Struktur-Analyse für das Verständnis der biblischen Dichtung', in *Congress Volume, Uppsala 1971* (VTSup, 22; Leiden: E.J. Brill, 1972), pp. 88-112 (93). However, against Weiss, 'Methode', p. 102, it needs to be stressed that even by paying careful attention to all the relevant signals, we will not be able to uncover the 'real meaning' ('wahren Sinn') of a text (cf. the discussion in the Introduction).

161. Cf. D.A. Dawson, *Text-Linguistics and Biblical Hebrew* (JSOTSup, 177; Sheffield: Sheffield Academic Press, 1994), p. 16, who notes that 'too many people engaged in analysis of this language [i.e. Classical Hebrew] come to it with inflexible theories and/or ideologies, which they are unwilling to re-examine in the light of the data. Radical restructuring of the text is, for some, only a starting point in their protection of theory or ideology: difficulties in the text lead to rewriting the text.'

oracles ensue in 5.18-27 and 6.1-14, which in turn lead to the vision-cum-narrative series in 7.1–8.3, another 'שמעו section' in 8.4-14 and the book's dramatic conclusion in 9.1-15.

Concerning the introductory section there is widespread agreement that it extends to 2.16.[162] The strophic arrangement of the eight oracles that make up this initial part is a clear pointer to the passage's structural unity. And although the final Israel strophe deviates from the established pattern in some respects, it is nevertheless clearly connected to the previous strophes, which it brings to a climactic close. The occurrence of a major break after 2.16 is confirmed also by the introductory words in 3.1, שמעו את־הדבר הזה אשר דבר יהוה עליכם בני ישראל.[163] As noted above, Amos 3–6, termed 'the words', have often been regarded as one of the book's main sections. However, a close look at these chapters shows that they themselves consist of five parts, featuring two distinct types of discourses, which are introduced in different ways. Thus, whereas 3.1-15; 4.1-13 and 5.1-17 are opened by the words שמעו(את) הדבר הזה, the following parts, 5.18-27 and 6.1-14, are introduced by the prophetic exclamation הוי.

While Amos 5.1-17 is today regarded as a self-contained unit by most scholars,[164] the demarcation of the preceding parts is disputed. Thus, while I would argue for structural breaks to occur after 2.16 and 3.15, some have detected major divisions after 3.8 and 4.3.[165] Yet the division of this part

---

162. This view has been challenged by some, who suggest that the break occurs after 3.2 (cf. K. Budde, 'Zu Text und Auslegung des Buches Amos', *JBL* 43 [1924], pp. 46-131; and *JBL* 44 [1925], pp. 63-122 [esp. *JBL* 43, pp. 75-76]; and Smalley, 'Recursion Patterns', pp. 122-23). However, Wolff, *Joel and Amos*, p. 175, rightly rejects this, noting that 'as a conclusion to 2.6-9 and 13-16, the announcement of punishment in 3.2 would...read as a pale generalization' (cf. also Hayes, *Amos*, p. 122; and Andersen and Freedman, *Amos*, p. 378).

163. Cf. Dempster, 'Lord', p. 175; Finley, *Joel, Amos, Obadiah*, p. 180; and Wolff, *Joel and Amos*, p. 175.

164. This conclusion has been reached because of its chiastic arrangement (see above). However, some have suggested to insert either הוי or הה at the beginning of 5.7 (cf. Gordis, 'Composition and Structure', p. 225 n. 3; van der Wal, 'Structure of Amos', pp. 110-11; and Rudolph, *Joel, Amos, Obadja, Jona*, pp. 194-95; see also Elliger's *fortasse lege* הֹ(הַ) יֹ(וֹ)ה in *BHS ad loc.*). According to Gordis, Amos 5–6 thus falls into four parts (5.1-6, 7-17, 18-27; 6.1-14), each of which opens with the exclamation 'woe'. However, the proposed emendation in 5.7 has been criticized by Jeremias, 'Amos 3-6: Oral Word', p. 228 ns. 4, 9, as an 'arbitrary conjecture' necessitated by the fact that the 'text [was] erroneously viewed as disordered'.

165. Thus, for instance, Smith, *Amos*; Reimer, *Recht*; and M.D. Carroll R., *Contexts*

of the book into 3.1-15 and 4.1-13 is to be preferred for a number of reasons.[166] First, the introductory שמעו phrase in 4.1, which parallels the ones in 3.1 and 5.1, indicates the beginning of a major unit. Secondly, as I shall argue in my subsequent discussion of Amos 3, the use of פקד in vv. 2, 14 creates a framing inclusio, which, together with the introductory phrases in 3.1 and 4.1, demarcates the boundaries of that passage. Thirdly, vv. 14-15 are correctly described by Andersen and Freedman as depicting 'a summation of the national disaster'.[167] As such, they are the concluding culmination of the prophetic discourse in Amos 3. And fourthly, Amos 3.9 and 4.4 contain no clear signals that would mark them out as introductions to large prophetic discourses. That is to say, there is nothing in these verses that would prompt the reader to pause or expect the commencement of a new macrostructural section.

To anticipate the outcome of my analysis, it appears that all major discourses in the book are introduced or controlled by specific structural markers. Thus, the first major unit in Amos 1.3–2.16 is governed by the recurring phrase כה אמר יהוה, which opens each of the eight strophes. The call to listen, שמעו, introduces a discourse in 3.1; 4.1; 5.1 and 8.4, while הוי performs a similar role in 5.18 and 6.1. In 7.1–8.3, the words כה הראני אמר יהוה function in a way similar to the כה אדני יהוה phrase in 1.3–2.16

---

for *Amos: Prophetic Poetics in Latin American Perspective* (JSOTSup, 132; Sheffield: JSOT Press, 1992).

166. Amos 3.1-15 is regarded as a self-contained prophetic discourse by Gordis, 'Composition and Structure', p. 217; Gitay, 'Study', p. 294; Limburg, 'Sevenfold Structures', p. 217; Dorsey, 'Literary Architecture', pp. 308-11; Melugin, 'Formation', pp. 376-77; Wendland, 'Word', pp. 11-12; K. Koch *et al.*, *Amos untersucht mit den Methoden einer strukturalen Formgeschichte* (AOAT, 30; 3 vols.; Kevelaer: Butzon & Bercker, 1976), II, pp. 107-108; Finley, *Joel, Amos, Obadiah*, p. 177; D.A. Hubbard, *Joel and Amos: An Introduction and Commentary* (TOTC; Leicester: InterVarsity Press, 1989), p. 121; and Niehaus, 'Amos', p. 328.

Those who view Amos 4.1-13 as one of the book's major sections include Gordis, 'Composition and Structure', p. 217; Dorsey, 'Literary Architecture', pp. 311-12; Wendland, 'Word', p. 13; Finley, *Joel, Amos, Obadiah*, p. 198; Hubbard, *Joel and Amos*, p. 121; and Niehaus, 'Amos', p. 328. Sweeney, 'Formation', p. 119, on the other hand, regards the whole of Amos 3–4 as one unit, and J. Jeremias, *The Book of Amos: A Commentary* (trans. D.W. Stott; OTL; Louisville, KY: Westminster/John Knox Press, 1998) distinguishes between Amos 3–4, 'the divine speech', and Amos 5–6, 'the prophetic speech' (see also Jeremias, 'Amos 3-6: Beobachtungen', p. 131; and *idem*, 'Amos 3-6: Oral Word', p. 221).

167. Andersen and Freedman, *Amos*, p. 370.

in that they open each of the four visions,[168] and the final section is introduced by ראיתי את־אדני (9.1), an expression that resembles the introductory phrase כה הראני אדני יהוה. Against this analysis, it is sometimes
argued that the שמעו phrase in 4.1 differs from the ones in 3.1 and 5.1, and
that it therefore does not mark the beginning of a major discourse.[169] As
far as the second part of this claim is concerned, I believe that, despite the
structural differences, there are nevertheless strong reasons for regarding
all three cases as functionally equivalent.[170] And while it is true that there
are structural differences between the שמעו phrase in 4.1 and the ones in
3.1 and 5.1 (cf. Figure 4), this requires some further comments.

Let me begin with the structure of the שמעו phrases. They all open with
the (2nd masc. pl.) imperative 'hear', which is followed by references to
what is to be heard and to who is to hear.[171] However, whereas the expressions in 3.1 and 5.1 resemble one another in that in both cases further
information about the object is given in an אשר phrase, only 3.1 and 4.1
contain a detailed subject description (SD). In 3.1 this description consists
of the phrase על כל־המשפחה אשר העליתי מארץ מצרים, which is linked to
the preceding words through the repetition of על (cf. עליכם), while in 4.1
the subject is described in more detail in the subsequent lines with the help
of three feminine participles (הרצצות, העשקות and האמרת). Thus while
the expressions in 3.1 and 5.1 share the אשר phrase, which distinguishes
them from 4.1, the detailed subject descriptions in 3.1 and 4.1 set those
two phrases apart from the one in 5.1.

+ SD	בני ישראל	שמעו את־הדבר הזה אשר דבר יהוה עליכם	3.1
+ SD	פרות הבשן אשר בהר ש'	שמעו הדבר הזה	4.1
	על יכם קינה בית ישראל	שמעו את־הדבר הזה אשר אנכי נשא	5.1

Figure 4. *The Introductory Addresses in Amos 3, 4 and 5*

168. The narrative in 7.10-17 is, for obvious reasons, not opened by the words
כה הראני אדני יהוה.

169. See e.g. Sweeney, 'Formation', p. 119; Jeremias, *Book of Amos*, p. 57 n. 11;
idem, 'Amos 3–6: Beobachtungen', p. 131; Smith, *Amos*, p. 127 (cf. n. 93) and
E. Zenger, 'Das Zwölfprophetenbuch', in *idem et al.* (eds.), *Einleitung in das Alte
Testament*, pp. 369-436 (388).

170. Thus also Andersen and Freedman, *Amos*, p. 414.

171. See Parunak, 'Discourse Functions', p. 499, who notes concerning the use of
'hear the word of the LORD' in Jeremiah that 'when the addressee of the oracle is to be
marked explicitly in the text of the oracle…the paragraph begins with "Hear the word
of the LORD"' (cf. also p. 507). According to his analysis, the formula is a stronger
disjunction than כה אמר יהוה.

In order for me to substantiate my claim that all three phrases function as introductory markers that open major prophetic discourses, we will need to look at the use of שמע in the book of Amos generally. Of its ten occurrences, seven are of particular interest in this context, as they occur in initial position, which makes it more likely for them to function as structural markers.[172] In six cases, a qal imperative is used (שמעו in 3.1, 13; 4.1; 5.1; 8.4 and שמע in 7.16), while the remaining example features the hiphil השמיעו (3.9).

The repeated occurrence of שמע in Amos 3–4 has led some scholars to regard 3.9–4.3 as a self-contained unit, in which every sub-section would then be introduced by a שמע formula.[173] This conclusion is weakened, however, by the observation that v. 12, which is introduced by כה אמר יהוה and taken by most commentators as a separate sub-unit, lacks such a שמע formula. Even more damaging is the fact that this construal does not take into account the rhetorical function of the formulas in question. When this is taken into account, it becomes clear that only the formulas in 3.1; 4.1; 5.1 and 8.4 are directed at the people of Israel.[174] In 3.9 (where the hiphil is used), the prophet commands an unknown messenger to proclaim a message to the strongholds of Ashdod and Egypt. Yet from a rhetorical point of view, the qal formula in 3.13 is even more striking. At first glance it looks as if its use is comparable to the other occurrences of שמעו but the immediate context rules this out, as it becomes clear that it too is not directed at Israel but at the witnesses summoned earlier.

This leaves us with the phrase ועתה שמע דבר־יהוה in 7.16, which in many ways comes closest in usage to the שמעו phrases in 3.1; 4.1; 5.1 and 8.4. However, the prophet here addresses the priest Amaziah and, as the context indicates, the opening phrase clearly does not introduce a major section but sets up the following oracle directed against the priest. Yet like the שמעו phrases, it is meant to focus the recipient's attention on what follows, thus performing a similar rhetorical function (albeit on a more microstructural level). To conclude this excursus on the use of שמע in the book of Amos, it has become clear that only the formulas in 3.1; 4.1; 5.1 and 8.4, which are directed at the Israelites, serve as introductory markers in that they now also address the audience of the book, who are thereby called upon to 'hear this word' that Amos is about to proclaim.[175]

---

172. The remaining three cases are: השמיעו in 4.5, אשמע in 5.23 and לשמע in 8.11.
173. Cf., e.g., Smith, *Amos*, pp. 8, 117.
174. This has been overlooked by Paul, *Amos*, p. 128.
175. Jeremias's objection that the vocative in 4.1 aims at a limited group within the

Those who deny that the שמעו phrase in 4.1 functions as an introductory marker usually regard 4.1-3 as the conclusion of the 'Samaria cycle' in 3.9–4.3. Jeremias gives the following reasons in support of this theory.[176] First, the root עשק, which occurs in 3.9 and 4.1, functions as an inclusio, tying the whole section together.[177] Secondly, the threatened deportation in 4.3 surpasses the announcements of judgment in 3.11, 15, thus providing closure to the entire passage. Thirdly, the cult-critical statement in 4.4-5, which is closely linked to the subsequent 'liturgy of disasters' in vv. 6-13, is not resumed until later in Amos 5. Most importantly, all the words in 3.9–4.3 are directed against the inhabitants of Samaria, which is thus the unifying theme of the section.[178]

While this is an impressive list of arguments, none of these points are decisive. First, while the root עשק does feature in 3.9-11 and 4.1-3, it does not necessarily follow that it functions as an inclusio. Whether this is the case can only be decided once the boundaries of the section have been de-

---

nation (Jeremias, *Book of Amos*, p. 57 n. 11) does not preclude the possibility that the initial verses of Amos 4 serve as an introduction to the entire discourse. Singling out a particular group at the beginning of a speech can be a very effective rhetorical means. On the other hand, the jumbled gender forms in 4.1-3 may even indicate that the address פרות הבשן was intended to refer to male upper-class members as well. See the discussion in Chapter 5.1 below for further elaboration.

176. Jeremias, *Book of Amos*, p. 57.

177. See also Rudolph, *Joel, Amos, Obadja, Jona*, p. 166, who argues that in 4.1-3 the reproofs of the exploitation of the poor (3.9-10) and of excessive luxury (3.12b, 15) are combined.

178. See also Jeremias, 'Amos 3–6: Beobachtungen', p. 130; *idem*, 'Amos 3–6: Oral Word', p. 224; Wolff, *Joel and Amos*, p. 205; R.S. Cripps, *A Critical and Exegetical Commentary on the Book of Amos* (London: SPCK, 1929), p. 165; and Reimer, *Recht*, p. 93.

Further reasons for regarding 3.9–4.3 as a unity have been proposed by Stuart, *Hosea–Jonah*, p. 329, who claims that each of the four oracles describes a related aspect of Samaria's degenerate wealthy style, concludes with a Pentateuchal covenant curse, quotes Yahweh and refers overtly to his being quoted, assumes the coming defeat of the capital by a foreign enemy, speaks about Samaria's complacent lifestyle in an ironic or mocking tone, and is composed in parallelistic prose. However, most of these points apply to many other oracles as well and are therefore not just characteristic for the ones in 3.9–4.3. Stuart himself, for instance, has made a case for Amos's message to be dependent, to a significant degree, upon Pentateuchal covenant curses and blessings, and it can easily be shown that there are many oracles that quote Yahweh or display an ironic or mocking tone. In the end, Stuart's arguments amount to not much more than that all the oracles in 3.9–4.3 are levelled against Samaria.

marcated. That is to say, if there are no other reasons for regarding Amos 3.9–4.3 as a self-contained unit, the recurrence of עשׁק in 4.1-3 needs to be understood not as an inclusio but as an example of repetition. Secondly, it is also true that the punishment theme reaches a new height with Amos talking about exile. Yet this is again surpassed later on by the ominous reference to the meeting with God that Israel is to prepare itself for (4.12-13). Thus, all one can say regarding this issue is that throughout Amos 2–4 there is an intensification of the punishment notion.

Thirdly, Jeremias's observation that the criticism of the cult, which surfaces in 4.4-5, is not pursued until later in Amos 5 is again correct. Yet I am not entirely sure what Jeremias is implying at this point, as he surely does not want us to connect Amos 4.4-13 with 5.1-17, whose chiastic structure he affirms.[179] In fact, the discourse in Amos 5.1-17 supports my conclusions containing, as it does, a combination of cult-critical and socio-critical remarks (cf. vv. 4-6, 7, 10-15), which is precisely what we find in Amos 4.1-13 as well. Or to put it differently, the fact that we have cult-critical notions both in 4.4-5 and 5.4-5 does not mean that these belong, necessarily, to the same discourse, nor indeed does it mean that 4.4-5 cannot belong to the same discourse as 4.1-3 with its focus on social injustice.

Finally, as regards Jeremias's fourth point that all the oracles in Amos 3.9–4.3 focus on Samaria, this does not do full justice to the text, as it ignores part of the data. To be sure, Samaria does figure prominently in the oracles in question. In 3.9 foreign witnesses are commanded to assemble on Mount Samaria, in 3.12 a total devouring of the people of Samaria is announced, and in 4.1 the 'cows of Bashan' are said to be located on Mount Samaria. However, it should not be overlooked that 3.14 also mentions the destruction of the altars at Bethel, thus reflecting an interest in 'the king's sanctuary', as it is called in 7.13, an interest that resurfaces in 4.4-5. Thus, rather than to conclude that the references to Samaria in Amos 3.9–4.3 necessitate structural breaks at 3.9 and 4.4, it could equally well be said that both discourses, Amos 3.1-15 and 4.1-13, are concerned with Samaria and Bethel, just as we find that the two themes of cultic and social offences are interwoven throughout the book of Amos.

In fact, Jeremias does recognize the structural significance of both the שׁמעו phrases and the inclusio created by the use of פקד in 3.2, 14, but

179. See J. Jeremias, 'Tod und Leben in Amos 5,1-17', in *idem, Hosea und Amos*, pp. 214-30; and *idem, Book of Amos*, pp. 81-97.

attempts to invalidate this by means of familiar redaction-critical operations. In his own words:

> the late addendum of an admonitory saying in 3.13f., with its double
> emphasis on the verb 'punish' in v. 14, created a framing inclusio to 3.2,
> now causing 4.1 to sound like a new beginning, something also prompted
> by the chapter division (which actually derives only from the Middle Ages).
> Originally, however, the summons 'hear this word...' in 4.1 did not, like 3.1
> and 5.1, introduce larger collections, but rather only the subunit 4.1-3.[180]

While it is certainly possible that, originally, some of the structural
markers either were not present or did not function in the way they do now
(simply because they were not yet part of the same text), it is the structure
of the text as we now have it that I seek to elucidate. And in this text it
appears that the שמעו phrases and the inclusio in 3.2, 14 both are of
structural significance.

However, at this point, I would like to come back to the intensification
of the punishment notion in Amos 2–4 (Jeremias's second point), which is
an interesting rhetorical feature. The initial threat of punishment (2.6, 13-
16) is picked up and developed in 3.2, at the outset of the second prophetic
discourse, where it is stressed that Israel will be punished precisely
because (על־כן) God has known only them. The judgment theme also
closes the second part, spelling out the implications of God's intervention
in more detail (3.11-12, 14-15). In Amos 4 we have a similar picture in
that this discourse too is opened and closed by references to the divine
punishment. As has been observed by Jeremias, the declaration that this
will include exile (4.2-3) adds further austerity but it, in turn, is surpassed
by the ominous notion of an impending meeting with the deity in 4.12-13.
This punishment theme could be pursued through the rest of the book
(note, for instance, the redefinition of the יום יהוה concept in 5.18-20 and
the depiction of Yahweh's relentless pursuit of his people in 9.1-4) but it
should just be noted in passing that this is a good example of the book's
'developing argument', which I will discuss in more detail in the following chapter.

To sum up the discussion, I would conclude that the שמעו phrases in
3.1; 4.1 and 5.1 do introduce the first three discourses in Amos 3–6, a
section often labelled 'the words', as we saw earlier. Yet it should also be
pointed out that for both the sub-units in 3.1-2 and 4.1-3 it is fair to say

---

180. Jeremias, *Book of Amos*, p. 57.

that they contain 'evidence of structural links in both directions'.[181] These 'structural ambiguities', which have led some scholars to connect 3.1-2 to the OAN in 1.3–2.16 and 4.1-3 to the so-called 'Samaria cycle' in Amos 3.9-15, allow the two sections to function as transitional elements linking the ensuing discourses to the preceding ones.

This then takes us to 5.18-27 and 6.1-14, the only two units in Amos that are introduced by the exclamation הוי (cf. 5.18; 6.1). The boundaries of the entire section 5.18–6.14 are marked also by external signs. The function of הוי as an opening marker in 5.18 is thus confirmed by the fact that the chiasm of the preceding pericope extends to 5.17. The end of the section, on the other hand, is signalled by the commencement of the vision report series in 7.1. Finally, as far as the internal division of 5.18–6.14 is concerned, the recurrence of הוי in 6.1 clearly signals the beginning of the second extended woe oracle.[182] It should also be noted that the two woe oracles[183] are very appropriate at this point in the book. Following the divine announcement that there will be wailing and lamentation (cf. הו-הו in 5.16-17) because of God's passing through Israel's midst, they function as what could be called 'variations on a theme', namely that of mourning.

If there is a section in Amos that can legitimately be labelled 'visions' then it is probably best to confine it to 7.1–8.3,[184] although even this part, in the Amaziah narrative in 7.10-17, contains 'non-visionary' material. From a structural point of view, the narrative, at first glance, seems to interrupt the vision series. However, in the next chapter, I shall attempt to demonstrate that, as far as its rhetorical function is concerned, it actually serves the development of the overall argument rather well, and that it is well placed in its present context. Despite its different structural make-up, it is also well integrated into the vision series, linked as it is to the third vision by the repetition of the remark that Jeroboam shall die by the sword (cf. 7.9, 11).

Finally, it should be noted that there is an overall consistency in the section 7.1–8.3, with the visions conforming to a pattern that resembles the

181. Thus Wendland, 'Word', p. 12.

182. However, Sweeney, 'Formation', p. 120, prefers to view the whole of Amos 5–6 as one unit rather than breaking it up into three parts (i.e. 5.1-17, 18-27; 6.1-14). Dorsey, 'Literary Architecture', pp. 314-17, on the other hand, regards 5.18–6.14 as one large chiasm.

183. For an extensive discussion of הוי and the prophetic woe oracle in general see Hardmeier, *Texttheorie*.

184. Cf. Dorsey, 'Literary Architecture', pp. 317-20.

strophic arrangement of 1.3–2.16. In both cases, a specific introductory formula is used to introduce each sub-section. In 1.3–2.16 this is the expression כה אמר יהוה,[185] while in 7.1–8.3 the words (אדני יהוה) והנה mark the beginning of each vision. Thus, unlike the discourses in Amos 3–6, the present unit is not opened by a single introductory marker but consists of a series of similar components, each of which is introduced by what might be called a 'chain marker'.

The following section (8.4-14) is often considered to be a conglomerate of a variety of judgment oracles and, as we have already seen above, is sometimes thought to be out of place in its present context. From a rhetorical point of view, the latter judgment seems rather rash even though the observation that the text includes various short judgment oracles is correct. As far as its structural make-up is concerned, I have already suggested that the introductory words שמעו־זאת resemble the שמעו phrases in 3.1; 4.1 and 5.1 and that they therefore appear to mark the beginning of a new major discourse.[186] A comparison of 8.4-7 and 4.1-2 lends further support to this conclusion. In both cases, the שמעו phrase is followed by participles that provide additional information about the addressees of the judgment speeches.[187] Both pericopes, furthermore, address the oppression of the weak and powerless (compare דל ים and אביונים in 4.1 with אביון and עניי־ארץ[188] in 8.4). Interestingly, in both cases a quote then follows, which exposes the unacceptable behaviour of those responsible for the social injustice. In 4.1 it is but a brief utterance introduced by another participle (האמרת) while in 8.5 לאמר is employed and the quote is much more extensive (cf. vv. 5-6). This, however, does not yet exhaust the similarities, as the quotes are accompanied by divine oaths, which, in both cases, are introduced by the phrase נשבע (אדני) יהוה ב'. Thus we arrive at quite a number of thematic, grammatical and linguistic correspondences, which buttress the conclusion that the two pericopes can be compared also in terms of their function, that is, that they can be seen as introducing larger prophetic discourses.

Yet if the words שמעו־זאת in 8.4 introduce a new section, where then does it end? Several possibilities suggest themselves in that the phrases והיה ביום ההוא in 8.9, הנה ימים באים in 8.11 and ביום ההוא in 8.13 could

185. The words אדני יהוה do not occur in 7.7.
186. For this view see also Dorsey, 'Literary Architecture', p. 320.
187. However, 4.1 differs from 8.4 in that the epithet פרות הבשן and the relative clause אשר בהר שמרון have no equivalents in the latter passage.
188. This reading adopts the Qere.

all conceivably introduce a new discourse. In the first two cases, the addition of the oracle formula נאם אדני יהוה makes this even more likely but a close look reveals that actually none of the above phrases functions in such a way. Thus, the words והיה ביום ההוא in 8.9 connect the declarations in vv. 9-10 with the divine oath in vv. 7-8 and the charges made in vv. 4-6. Similarly, ביום ההוא in 8.13 refers back to the statements in vv. 11-12, making it clear that all the announcements of judgment relate to the same time. The remaining case, the phrase הנה ימים באים in 8.11, however, is slightly more complex, and in order to establish its function, it will be necessary to consider briefly how הנה is used in the book of Amos in general.

This investigation can be limited to those cases where הנה is unmodified and occurs in initial position (as, for instance, in 8.11) since these are the only instances, in which הנה can be supposed to serve as an introductory marker.[189] This leaves us with four examples (2.13; 8.11; 9.8, 13), the first of which, we have already implicitly decided, is not a major introductory marker. To be sure, הנה in 2.13 does introduce a section (2.13-16), but this is only a sub-unit of the Israel strophe in 2.6-16, which in turn is part of the OAN in 1.3–2.16. Similarly, in 9.8 הנה clearly does not indicate a break. It follows the rhetorical questions in v. 7, which stress that Israel no longer enjoys a special status. The exodus, that is to say, should not be understood as being indicative of Yahweh's special favour, given that even the Philistines and Aramaeans could boast about comparable experiences. הנה, in this context, directs the attention of the hearer or reader to the implications of this astonishing claim, namely that Yahweh will indeed judge his people and wipe the sinful kingdom of Israel off the face of the earth. The remaining two examples in 8.11 and 9.13 resemble one another in that in both cases הנה is followed by the words ימים באים נאם (אדני) יהוה. Again, in 9.13 הנה does not mark a major break although it does introduce a sub-section of the salvation oracle in 9.11-15. Thus, in the light of these findings, according to which הנה in three out of four cases introduces a sub-section, it seems reasonable to assume that it performs a similar function also in 8.11.

To be sure, 8.4-14 is normally treated as a single, if not necessarily

---

189. In Amos the term הנה occurs 13 times. In addition to the unmodified cases, we find כי־הנה (4.2, 13; 6.11; 9.9) and והנה (7.1 [twice], 4, 7; 8.1). Whereas כי־הנה clearly performs a connective function, והנה occurs solely in the vision reports in order to specify what it is that Amos saw.

coherent, unit by most commentators.[190] However, as there is no closing marker at the end of v. 14, one would have to infer that the words ראיתי את־אדני in 9.1 indicate the beginning of the book's final discourse in Amos 9.1-15.[191] This is confirmed by two observations. On the one hand, the resulting two discourses in 8.4-14 and 9.1-15 exhibit a similar structural arrangement. In both cases, the final parts are introduced by the expression הנה ימים באים נאם (אדני) יהוה (8.11; 9.13). Likewise, the penultimate parts correspond to one another in that each is opened by the words (והיה) ביום ההוא (8.9; 9.11). Secondly, it should also be noted that the words ראיתי את־אדני in 9.1 resemble the phrase (אדני יהוה) והנה כה הראני, which introduces each of the visions in Amos 7–8.

Those who prefer to connect the vision in Amos 9.1-4 with the previous ones argue that it constitutes the climax to the whole series. However, as Hayes has shown, there are a number of structural differences between 9.1 and the visions in Amos 7–8 in that Amos 'sees' rather than 'being shown', there is 'no symbolic component [that] serves as an interpretive key' and 'no verbal exchange takes place between God and the prophet'. Hayes therefore concludes that 'even should the prophet's reference to seeing Yahweh and the altar be considered a vision report, it hardly constitutes the climactic vision in a series of five.'[192] This is a judicious assessment but I would not want to deny the climactic character of 9.1 per se, thus following Sweeney, who regards this verse as the climax not specifically of the vision report series but of the book as a whole.[193] In fact, it would be better to say that it is the pinnacle of its judgment message, given that this is not where the book ends. In any case, for our purposes it is important to note that the vision in 9.1 is not closely linked to the preceding ones and that it therefore may well introduce a new discourse.

In contrast to this proposal, Wendland, like many others, takes the whole of Amos 7.1–9.10 as one major unit, entitled 'Five visions of Israel's ruin',[194] which is followed by the concluding salvation oracle (9.11-15).

---

190. Dorsey, 'Literary Architecture', pp. 320-23, however, regards the whole of 8.4–9.15 as one unit, which, according to his view, possibly forms a sevenfold chiasm.

191. For the use of ראיתי to introduce a vision in Zech. 1.8 and 4.2 cf. D.J. Clark, 'Vision and Oracle in Zechariah 1–6', in Bergen (ed.), *Biblical Hebrew*, pp. 529-60 (552). In comparison to its use in Zechariah, we may note that the phrase is even more clearly marked in Amos 9.1, where it occurs in initial position.

192. Hayes, *Amos*, p. 216; cf. also Dorsey, 'Literary Architecture', p. 319 n. 28.

193. Sweeney, 'Formation', p. 121.

194. Wendland, 'Word', pp. 19-25, who proposes the following outline:

However, this analysis does not accord well with his professed intention to focus on the 'speech formulas as a means of introducing the process of demarcating the prophet's message and its organization'.[195] For instance, Wendland's analysis does not account for the discourse opening markers in 8.4 and 9.1. Even more crucially, however, Wendland fails to explain why, according to his outline, the phrase ביום ההוא opens a new section in 9.11 but not in 8.13. It appears, therefore, that his conclusions are based on thematic considerations rather than the distribution of the speech formulas. And although this, in itself, is not necessarily inadequate, in this particular case, the transitional character of 9.8-10 seems to support my conclusion that vv. 11-15 do not form a major section on their own.[196]

The macrostructure of the book of Amos can thus be outlined as follows: The heading and motto in 1.1-2 lead up to the introductory series of OAN in 1.3–2.16. This, in turn, is followed by three 'שמעו sections' (3.1-15; 4.1-13; 5.1-17), two extended woe oracles (5.18-27; 6.1-14) and the vision report series in 7.1–8.3, which includes the Amaziah narrative in 7.10-17. The ensuing penultimate part (8.4-14) then resumes the 'שמעו sections', while the introduction to the final discourse (9.1-15), ראיתי את־אדני, alludes to the visions in Amos 7–8. Together, the last two discourses draw the message of the book to a close, as is indicated, for instance, by the prominent use of the 'futuristic transitions'[197] ביום ההוא and הנה ימים באים (cf. 8.9, 11, 13; 9.11, 13). Providing, as they do, a sense of finality, these

Vision one: locusts (7.1-3)
Vision two: fire (7.4-6)
Vision three: plumb line (7.7-9)
    Comment one: a dramatization of the vision's message (7.10-17)
Vision four: basket of ripe fruit (8.1-3)
    Comment two: an oracle of judgment on the day of the Lord (8.4-14)
Vision five: the Lord by the altar (9.1-4)
    Comment three: a word in praise of Yahweh's power and a final word of judgment upon Israel (9.5-10)
        1. Doxology (9.5-6)
        2. Judgment oracle (9.7-10)

195. Wendland, 'Word', p. 2.
196. They may, of course, be regarded as an appendix for redaction-critical reasons but in the text as it stands they are closely connected to the preceding material by means of the transition in 9.8-10.
197. For this term see S.J. de Vries, *From Old Revelation to New: A Tradition-Historical and Redaction-Critical Study of Temporal Transitions in Prophetic Prediction* (Grand Rapids: Eerdmans, 1995), *passim*.

formulas are aptly employed in the book's closing sections.

To conclude, let me also summarize my findings concerning the use of structural markers. To begin with, it appears that the book's structural arrangement is governed mainly by introductory markers, which fall into two categories. On the one hand, there are those that occur only once at the outset of the discourse they introduce. These include the שמעו formulas in 3.1; 4.1 and 5.1, the exclamation הוי in 5.18 and 6.1 and the words ראיתי את־אדני in 9.1. On the other hand, there are two sections, the OAN in Amos 1.3–2.16 and the vision reports in 7.1–8.3, where no such major introductory markers occur. Instead, we find that these passages are composed as series of similar components, each of which is introduced by what I have called 'chain markers'. In 1.3–2.16, this role is assumed by the phrase כה אמר יהוה, which introduces each of the eight strophes. In 7.1–8.3, on the other hand, it is the phrase כה הראני (אדני יהוה) והנה that performs this function, although it does not, for obvious reasons, introduce the Amaziah narrative in 7.10-17. This then leaves us with the following picture as illustrated in the table below.

Passage	Introductory Marker
1.1-2	
1.3–2.16	כה אמר יהוה as 'chain marker'
3.1-15	שמעו את־הדבר הזה
4.1-13	שמעו הדבר הזה
5.1-17	שמעו את־הדבר הזה
5.18-27	הוי
6.1-14	הוי
7.1–8.3	כה הראני (אדני יהוה) והנה as 'chain marker'
8.4-14	שמעו־זאת
9.1-15	ראיתי את־אדני

Figure 5. *Major Introductory Markers in Amos*[198]

Closing markers, on the other hand, are not employed with the same consistency. Nor are the ones that do occur necessarily macrostructural signals. For instance, the discourses in 1.3–2.16 and 3.1-15 are both closed

198. Bovati and Meynet, *Le livre du prophète Amos*, p. 16, referring to L. Alonso Schökel and J.L. Sicre Diaz, *Profetas: Introducciones y comentario*. II. *Ezequiel, Doce Profetas Menores, Daniel, Baruc, Carta de Jeremías* (Nueva Biblia Española; Madrid: Ediciones Cristiandad, 2nd edn, 1980), p. 957, present a similar list without sharing my conclusions concerning the structural significance of these phrases.

by the words נאם־יהוה, a phrase that, as we saw earlier, does not function as a reliable structural guide. The same applies to the formula אמר יהוה, which concludes the discourses in 5.1-17; 5.18-27 and 9.1-15. Amos 4, in turn, is closed by a hymn fragment but this being the only example of these passages functioning in such a way, it is clear that they too do not perform a structural role. In Amos 6 and 7.1–8.3 there are no closing markers, at least none that occur in ultimate position. In both cases, the phrase נאם־יהוה appears towards the end of the sections, where it functions, as the above discussion has shown, as a local marker of emphasis. Finally, the end of the discourse in 8.4-14 does not appear to be marked at all.

Chapter 2

RHETORICAL SITUATION AND STRATEGY

Having analysed the book of Amos in terms of its structure, we now turn to the next steps of the rhetorical-critical inquiry. In the present chapter, I will maintain a 'landscape perspective' that looks at the book in its entirety and seeks to elucidate the rhetorical situation that occasioned its compilation, the rhetorical problem that is being addressed and the rhetorical strategy that has been chosen to tackle this problem or exigency. These general observations are then followed, in the subsequent chapters, by more detailed investigations of the rhetoric of Amos 1–4. I will seek to demonstrate in particular how a rhetorical-critical reading approaches prophetic discourses that, in some cases, fall into a number of short oracles, which are often thought to be unconnected. Throughout, my primary concern will be to uncover how the rhetoric of persuasion (or one might say, the argument) unfolds.

1. *Rhetorical Situation and Problem*

The first issue to be examined is the book's *rhetorical situation*, the circumstances that led to its compilation. I will also, in this context, comment on the specific problem that the book is designed to address. Yet before we turn to this, it is necessary to consider briefly the nature of the book. This, in turn, will be followed by some remarks on its date, which, for obvious reasons, is a determinative factor for the reconstruction of the rhetorical situation.

a. *The Nature of the Book*

In *The Speeches of Micah*, a work that pursues interests similar to the ones at the fore in the present study, Shaw has emphasized the importance of establishing the rhetorical situation that gave rise to the prophetic discourse. He notes that that discourse 'presupposes a complex matrix of factors to which it is responding and which must, to some extent, be reflected in the discourse itself'.[1] He furthermore advances the view that 'the prophets did not speak in short, self-contained sayings, but delivered discourses which attempted to persuade the hearers of a particular conviction or to take a specific course of action'.[2] Shaw then sets out to 'attempt to gain insight into the historical setting presupposed by each discourse in the book of Micah'.[3] This interest in uncovering the historical setting for *each* discourse reflects Shaw's belief that the book contains the actual discourses (or *speeches*) delivered by the prophet Micah.

I do not, at this point, intend to discuss Shaw's reading of Micah, yet I would like to stress that his approach would not work for the book of Amos, which by and large does not seem to preserve the prophet's 'original' speeches. To be sure, a section such as the OAN in Amos 1.3–2.15 could conceivably comprise an example of an 'original' prophetic speech preserved in the book. It is, after all, likely that Amos would have delivered oracles such as these serially, given that they do not make much sense when taken individually.[4] Yet the fact remains that, on the whole, the book appears to be an edited collection of prophetic oracles (and visions).

A look at the visions-cum-narrative series Amos 7.1–8.3 should confirm this. Again, it might just be possible that 7.1-9; 8.1-3 preserve one of Amos's 'original' speeches. Yet, even if that were the case, the insertion of the narrative in 7.10-17 now interrupts that 'original sequence'[5] and, more importantly, adds an element that cannot be classified as a prophetic speech. Thus, even if the position of the narrative were to reflect the actual course of events, as some have suggested,[6] the text as it stands, in

1. Shaw, *Speeches of Micah*, p. 22.
2. Shaw, *Speeches of Micah*, p. 19.
3. Shaw, *Speeches of Micah*, p. 22.
4. See Chapter 3 for further discussion.
5. For particularly illuminating analyses of the narrative's function in the present literary context cf. L. Eslinger, 'The Education of Amos', *HAR* 11 (1987), pp. 35-57; and D.N. Freedman, 'Confrontations in the Book of Amos', *PSB* 11 (1990), pp. 240-52.
6. This seems rather unlikely, however, as it contains a number of shifts in scene. In 7.1-9, we witness Amos relating his visions before being informed in vv. 10-11 about Amaziah's dispatch to the king. When the priest finally commands the prophet to leave the country (vv. 12-13), it is apparently presupposed that the king had agreed with his official that 'the land cannot bear Amos's words'. E.B. Pusey, *The Minor Prophets with a Commentary Explanatory and Practical, and Introductions to the*

including the narrative, does not just reproduce Amos's speeches. The insertion of the narrative clearly shows that the book's compilers were not interested simply in preserving the prophet's utterances for later generations of readers. Their concern was to 'present' these utterances in a certain way, to 'capture', as it were, Amos's debate with his audience. Mostly throughout the book, the audience's contribution to this debate is implied, as we shall see in the subsequent discussion of the book's rhetorical strategy. Yet in 7.10-17, we find the reaction of one of the audience's more prominent members reported, the effect of which will also be discussed in what follows.

Consideration of the dispute between Gitay and Dempster about the nature of Amos 3 will provide further illustration of why I believe Shaw's approach to be impracticable in the case of Amos. In 'A Study of Amos's Art of Speech', Gitay argued that Amos 3 should be seen as one rhetorical unit. He insisted that 'if we isolate the separate units of the pericope, it is clear that these units in themselves do not constitute complete statements'.[7] However, Dempster rightly contended that 'although Gitay presents a strong case, the text bears the signs of being carefully edited collections of different oracles'.[8] To combine their respective insights, it would appear that Amos is more likely to have made 'speeches' rather than to have uttered merely small poetic oracles, as Gunkel and his followers believed.[9] However, it would also seem that the book does not preserve these 'speeches' (contra Gitay) but contains a mixture of edited collections of oracles (taken perhaps from different speeches) as well as abstracts or summaries of prophetic discourses.[10] For this reason, I will

Several Books. II. *Amos* (London: James Nisbet, 1906), p. 294, on the other hand, takes the text's silence about Jeroboam's reaction to mean that the king 'apparently took no account of the false priest's message'. Yet whatever we make of this, it is difficult to imagine that the two encounters between Amaziah and Amos as well as the priest's audience with King Jeroboam should have happened between the reciting of the third and fourth vision.

7.   Gitay, 'Study', p. 294; cf. H. Lubsczyk, *Der Auszug Israels aus Ägypten: Seine theologische Bedeutung in prophetischer und priesterlicher Überlieferung* (Erfurter Theologische Studien, 11; Leipzig: St. Benno, 1963), pp. 42-48, who also speaks of a 'kerygmatische Einheit'.

8.   Dempster, 'Lord', p. 179.

9.   See esp. H. Gunkel, 'The Prophets as Writers and Poets' (trans. J.L. Schaaf), in D.L. Petersen (ed.), *Prophecy in Israel: Search for an Identity* (Issues in Religion and Theology, 10; Philadelphia: Fortress Press, 1987), pp. 22-73.

10.   Thus already Lewis, 'Persuasive Style'.

focus on the rhetorical situation of the book as a whole rather than the elusive rhetorical situations of the individual discourses.

It should also be noted in this context that some scholars have argued that the book of Amos consists of one single speech delivered by the prophet on a single occasion. Thus, according to Rosenbaum, the book comprises one 'twenty-minute harangue' after which the prophet had to leave the country.[11] Noting that the whole book 'could be spoken, aloud, in less than twenty minutes', Rosenbaum thinks of it as 'a piece that was delivered in a fit of passion',[12] as 'the brief outpouring of one man's soul'.[13] A similar proposal had been made earlier by Morgenstern who even attempted to date Amos's prophecy to a specific day, New Year's Day 751 BCE.[14] Such an approach is unconvincing, however, because many of the book's literary features are unlikely to have their origin in 'a fit of passion'. The frequent heptads, for instance, the existence of which Rosenbaum acknowledges,[15] reflect a more sophisticated process of formation. Furthermore, what was said above on the Amaziah narrative also precludes an interpretation along the lines suggested by Rosenbaum and Morgenstern.

b. *The Date of Compilation*
Before I move on to outline the book's rhetorical situation, some remarks on its date of compilation are required, as this has major repercussions for the delineation of its rhetorical situation. Many redaction critics believe the book, in its final form, to be a product of (late) postexilic times. According to this view, it comprises a number of redactional layers attesting to successive adaptations and updates of the prophetic message. These adaptations, it is suggested, relate Amos's prophecies to the times of the respective redactors and reflect their specific theological concerns.

In recent years, however, an increasing number of scholars have begun to express their dissatisfaction with the genetic theories propounded by

---

11. Rosenbaum, *Amos of Israel*, p. 100.

12. Rosenbaum, *Amos of Israel*, p. 76.

13. Rosenbaum, *Amos of Israel*, p. 82.

14. J. Morgenstern, 'Amos Studies II: The Sin of Uzziah, the Festival of Jeroboam and the Date of Amos', *HUCA* 12/13 (1937–38), pp. 1-53. Unlike Rosenbaum, however, Morgenstern arrived at this single sermon only by means of extensive deletions and rearrangements (cf. J. Morgenstern, *Amos Studies. I. Parts I, II, and III* [Cincinnati: Hebrew Union College, 1942]).

15. Rosenbaum, *Amos of Israel*, pp. 76-77.

redaction critics. While the 'dissidents' do not necessarily doubt the legitimacy of redaction criticism as such, many feel that its adherents have played their hand far too confidently and have come up with questionable results. Questions were raised, for instance, as to whether it is at all possible to engage in such minute reconstruction of the formation of the book as is often attempted.[16] Doubting this, many would now regard the theories that have been advanced as too speculative to be of immediate interpretative value.[17] Hence, some have abandoned the diachronic pursuit altogether, favouring synchronic approaches instead. Others have subjected redaction-critical arguments to a penetrating examination and found them wanting. Paul, for instance, concludes that 'almost all of the arguments for later interpolations and redactions, including a Deuteronomistic one, are shown to be based on fragile foundations and inconclusive evidence'.[18] According to him, therefore, 'the book in its entirety (with one or two

16. Cf. Melugin, 'Formation', p. 375; and J. Bright, 'A New View of Amos', *Int* 25 (1971), pp. 355-58 (357), who rightly asks whether 'in so small a book as Amos…we have a broad enough field of evidence to entitle us to say that this stylistic trait, this line of thought, this formal characteristic, could not have been employed by the prophet, but must be assigned to some later stratum of the tradition'. Bright's remark, it should be remembered, was made as early as 1971 in a review of Wolff's commentary, which was to become so influential in later years.

   Wolff, *Joel and Amos*, pp. 106-13 (followed to a large extent by Mays, *Amos*, pp. 12-14; J.A. Soggin, *The Prophet Amos: A Translation and Commentary* [trans. J. Bowden; London: SCM Press, 1987], pp. 17-18; and J. Vermeylen, *Du prophète Isaïe à l'apocalyptique. Isaïe, I–XXXV, miroir d'un demi-millénaire d'expérience religieuse en Israël*, II [EBib; Paris: J. Gabalda, 1978], pp. 519-69) distinguished 6 textual layers while others posited even more. For instance, S. Jozaki, 'The Secondary Passages of the Book of Amos', *Kwansei Gakuin University Annual Studies* 4 (1956), pp. 25-100, found 8 strata and Rottzoll, *Studien*, pp. 285-90, even arrived at a total of 12, thus providing a striking example of what Sternberg has called an 'incredible abuse…of frenzied digging into the Bible's genesis, so senseless as to elicit either laughter or tears' (Sternberg, *Poetics*, p. 13).

17.   There is a clear tendency in recent works to concentrate on what Landy has called the 'aesthetic wholeness of the text' rather than its 'hypothetical evolution' (F. Landy, 'Vision and Poetic Speech in Amos', *HAR* 11 [1987], pp. 223-46 [223]). Cf., e.g., the commentaries by Andersen and Freedman, *Amos*; Smith, *Amos*; Finley, *Joel, Amos, Obadiah*; Paul, *Amos*; Bovati and Meynet, *Le livre du prophète Amos*; Gowan, 'Book of Amos'; Achtemeier, *Minor Prophets I*; Birch, *Hosea, Joel, and Amos*; Coggins, *Joel and Amos*; and M.A. Sweeney, *The Twelve Prophets. I. Hosea, Joel, Amos, Obadiah, Jonah* (Berit Olam; Collegeville, MN: Michael Glazier, 2000), as well as most of the structural investigations mentioned in the previous chapter.

18.   Paul, *Amos*, p. 6.

minor exceptions) can be reclaimed for its rightful author, the prophet Amos'.[19] While this seems to overstate the case (the book nowhere claims to be written by Amos), I am inclined to follow those who believe that it was transmitted into writing not long after the end of Amos's ministry.[20]

Referring to Sternberg's thoughtful comments on the mutually corrective relationship of source and discourse, I have already argued for the need of a fresh analysis of the discourse, which can then serve as the starting point for renewed diachronic inquiry.[21] This claim receives further support if Paul and other recent commentators are right in their evaluation of the 'traditional' redaction-critical proposals. However, it needs to be emphasized that the stress placed on the text's synchronic dimension does not render the present interpretation ahistorical. In fact, a rhetorical-critical approach as advocated in this study cannot ignore the synchronic dimension because of its intrinsic interest in the rhetorical situation. And as this is determined by the discourse's historical setting, it requires careful consideration of the text's synchronic dimension.[22] Yet because of my expressed dissatisfaction with redaction-critical explanations of the book's formation prevalent today, I propose to reconsider the discourse, setting aside redaction-critical results for the moment. It is indeed important, I

19. Paul, *Amos*, p. 6.

20. Thus many of the commentaries listed in n. 18 above. Recently Sweeney, 'Formation', pp. 124-25, contended that the latest additions (with the possible exception of the Judah oracle in 2.4-5) had been added by the time of King Josiah of Judah (639–609 BCE), thus proposing a pre-exilic date for the book of Amos. This period he regards as the most probable rhetorical setting, suggesting that the object of the book of Amos is to support Josiah's religious reforms. On the question of whether there was a cultic reform initiated by Josiah cf. recently H. Niehr, 'Die Reform des Joschija. Methodische, historische und religionsgeschichtliche Aspekte', in Gross (ed.), *Jeremia und die 'deuteronomistische Bewegung'*, pp. 33-55 ('no, there wasn't') and, in the same volume, C. Uehlinger, 'Gab es eine joschijanische Kultreform?', pp. 57-89 ('yes, there was').

21. See the discussion in the Introduction.

22. Thus, hypothetical historical reconstruction of some sort cannot be avoided. Responding to the increased interest in the function of the Psalter as a whole and the role of individual psalms in their present literary setting, Murphy has rightly stressed that this shift in interest does not result in a more 'objective' approach. According to him, 'hypothetical historical reconstruction is as inescapable in contextual interpretation as it is in the usual historical criticism that is applied to the Psalter' (R.E. Murphy, 'Reflections on Contextual Interpretation of the Psalms', in McCann [ed.], *The Shape and Shaping of the Psalter*, pp. 21-28 [21]).

believe, to rethink what interests the book in its entirety may best be seen to be serving, to use once more Mason's words.[23] This, after all, is what characterizes a rhetorical-critical approach in the first place.

Readers are asked, therefore, to judge whether the reading suggested here is a cogent one. This involves, first of all, asking whether it is co-herent, whether it deals adequately with the textual data in its entirety. Secondly, for this reading to be persuasive it also needs to fit the suggested rhetorical situation—it needs to be historically credible. Provided it fulfils these two requirements, the question can then be asked whether the sometimes rather complicated evolutionary theories of the book's forma-tion are still required and plausible.[24]

However, before I proceed to sketch the rhetorical situation, a few comments on some key passages that are often considered late additions seem pertinent. Recently, Jeremias has reaffirmed the view that the book underwent a number of redactional adaptations and revisions spanning several centuries.[25] He claims that 'the older book of Amos underwent its most incisive alteration after the fall of Jerusalem in the sixth century B.C.E.'.[26] Jeremias's reconstruction of this later period of the text's history is determined by three factors. Following standard redaction-critical practice, Jeremias detects deuteronomistic additions,[27] augmentations characterised by a 'hymnic diction',[28] and a post-exilic discussion of how Amos's uncompromising message can be related to the old traditions of salvation (Amos 9.7-10). The latter is followed by the even later salvation oracle promising a new Davidic kingdom (9.11-15).[29] Thus, according to this view, the book of Amos received its present shape in the late post-exilic era, a period often 'understood as being the formative epoch to

23. Cf. Mason, *Propaganda and Subversion*, p. 26.

24. See Jeremias, *Book of Amos*, p. 5, who claims that 'Amos' message...can be recovered only through complicated, and in many instances only hypothetical, reconstruction'.

25. Jeremias, *Book of Amos*, pp. 5-9.

26. Jeremias, *Book of Amos*, p. 7.

27. Jeremias, *Book of Amos*, p. 8. These are 1.9-12; 2.4-5, 7b, 9, 10-12; 3.1b, 7, 13-14; 5.6, 25, 26; 8.11-14. For the deuteronomistic redaction of Amos cf. esp. W.H. Schmidt, 'Die deuteronomistische Redaktion des Amosbuches: Zu den theologischen Unterschieden zwischen dem Prophetenwort und seinem Sammler', *ZAW* 77 (1965), pp. 168-93.

28. These hymnic pieces are 1.2; 4.13; 5.8-9 and 9.5-6. According to Jeremias, they originated in the 'exilic services of penance' (Jeremias, *Book of Amos*, p. 8).

29. Jeremias, *Book of Amos*, p. 9.

which the Old Testament owes its present configuration, not merely formally but in its theological shaping too'.[30]

Fundamental for the proposal of a deuteronomistic redaction of the book of Amos was Schmidt's influential article, 'Die deuteronomistische Redaktion des Amosbuches'. Schmidt's arguments met with widespread acceptance and, for instance, Wolff's magisterial commentary is strongly indebted to his analysis.[31] This, perhaps more than anything else, almost institutionalized Schmidt's conclusions. Yet, in recent years they have been called into question, for instance, by Lohfink who passionately disapproves of what he calls 'pan-deuteronomistic tendencies' in Old Testament circles.[32] Investigating Schmidt's arguments concerning the exodus formula in Amos 2.10, the transitional formula in 3.1 and the Judah oracle in 2.4-5, Lohfink found none of them convincing.[33] Especially Lohfink's refutation of the deuteronomistic redaction of Amos 2.4-5 is of crucial importance[34] because, as he correctly notes:

> the stone, which one should by no means be able to pull out of the evidential structure supporting the deuteronomistic redaction of the book of Amos, without everything collapsing, is the Judah oracle... Only if there really are deuteronomistic additions in Amos 1–2 can one...even begin to think about a deuteronomistic redaction for the entire book of Amos.[35]

Similarly, Rottzoll noted that the language of Amos 2.4-5 does not support the claim for it being of deuteronomistic origin.[36] However, according to him, this does not mean that the book of Amos did not undergo a deuteronomistic redaction. In fact, in his view there were two. First, an initial deuteronomistic revision took place during the exile, which was followed by a 'priestly-deuteronomistic redaction' in the middle of the fifth century.[37] Recognition of the problems pertaining to the 'traditional'

---

30. R. Rendtorff, 'The Importance of the Canon for a Theology of the Old Testament', in *idem, Canon and Theology*, pp. 46-56 (52-53).

31. See Wolff, *Joel and Amos*, pp. 112-13 and *passim*.

32. Lohfink, 'Bewegung', pp. 316-17.

33. Lohfink, 'Bewegung', pp. 325-33.

34. For further details see the discussion in Chapter 3. Lohfink's discussion of Amos 2.4-5 was taken up by Bons who confirmed his findings (cf. E. Bons, 'Das Denotat von כזביהם "ihre Lügen" im Judaspruch Am 2,4-5', *ZAW* 108 [1996], pp. 201-13).

35. Lohfink, 'Bewegung', p. 329.

36. Cf. Rottzoll, *Studien*, pp. 23-30.

37. For a summary of his findings see Rottzoll, *Studien*, pp. 287-89. The first

position advanced by Schmidt thus leads Rottzoll to introduce conjectures that are even more complicated. Yet if one intends to go down this route, it is doubtful whether even Rottzoll's model is sophisticated enough to account for all the data. In Amos 2.4-5, for instance, Rottzoll traces elements that, instead of being deuteronomistic, are found regularly in the prophetic and poetic literature. Yet others, according to his analysis, are characteristic for the Chronicler's history, are 'post-deuteronomistic' or '(proto-)chronistic', or indeed feature in the Holiness Code and the book of Ezekiel.[38]

On the whole, these recent studies therefore illustrate that, as far as the book of Amos is concerned, the evidence for a deuteronomistic redaction is rather meagre to say the least.[39] Yet instead of reverting to increasingly complex evolutionary theories, I would like to repeat my suggestion that we first reconsider what interests the passages previously considered deuteronomistic are in fact serving. It is with this in mind that I shall attempt to explain them against their present literary cotext *and* suggested historical context (rhetorical situation), inviting readers to judge for themselves the success (or lack thereof) of this exercise.

This then takes us to the hymnic material in Amos 4.13; 5.8-9; 9.5-6, passages that are characterized by their distinct vocabulary and theology.[40] Two principal views have been put forward concerning their date. They are regarded either as (post)exilic editorial additions[41] or as early hymnic

---

deuteronomistic redaction (responsible for 1.1bβγ; 2.10-11, 12b; 3.1b [except לאמר] and 5.25-26) is the fifth in Rottzoll's 12 layer scheme, with the priestly-deuterono-mistic redaction (2.4-5, 7bβ, 8aβ, bβ; 3.7; 7.9 [16-17]) representing the seventh layer. The latter, according to Rottzoll, is characterized by language similar to that of the deuteronomist while at the same time featuring vocabulary that is untypical for the deuteronomist but is at home in the priestly literature.

38. Rottzoll, *Studien*, pp. 23-27. His analysis of the similarities between the deuter-onomistic history, the Holiness Code and the book of Ezekiel and their significance for the redaction of Amos (pp. 27-30), therefore, does not, in my view, successfully take into account all the linguistic data in Amos 2.4-5.

39. For further discussion see the exegesis of Amos 2.4-5, 9-12 and 3.7 in Chapters 3 and 4 and the literature cited there.

40. Sometimes Amos 1.2 is regarded as yet another hymn fragment as, for instance, by Koch, 'Rolle'; and Jeremias, *Book of Amos*, p. 8.

41. Thus Horst, 'Doxologien'; G. von Rad, 'Gerichtsdoxologie', in Bernhardt (ed.), *Schalom*, pp. 28-37; J.L. Crenshaw, *Hymnic Affirmation of Divine Justice: The Doxologies of Amos and Related Texts in the Old Testament* (SBLDS, 24; Missoula, MT: Scholars Press, 1975); W. Berg, *Die sogenannten Hymnenfragmente im Amos-buch* (Europäische Hochschulschriften, 23.45; Bern: Herbert Lang, 1974), p. 319;

material that has been reworked and incorporated into the book by Amos or the earliest tradents of the book.[42] Jeremias, an advocate of the former view, thinks of the hymn fragments as major adaptations of Amos's message. In an article, entitled 'Das Proprium der alttestamentlichen Prophetie', he comments on the function of such adaptations, noting that the original situation of the oral word becomes a kind of model by being transmitted into writing. It now conveys general insights about God's dealings with Israel that are applicable to new historical situations. Yet for this to work, the prophets' words need to be 'translated', actualised and adapted so as to render them suitable to changed historical circumstances.[43]

As regards the hymnic passages in Amos, Jeremias and others have argued that they are best understood as what has been called 'doxologies of judgement'.[44] According to this conception, their liturgical *Sitze im Leben* are the exilic 'services of penance' in which they served as doxologies acknowledging that Yahweh's judgment of his people was justified. Horst comments that the people had heard, out of the prophet's mouth, their past sins. Now they had to accept the divine judgment, that is to say, they had to recite a doxology, retrospectively affirming the validity of the catastrophe of the exile and praising the deity's mighty judgmental power. The doxologies in the book of Amos therefore invest the gloomy threats of the prophet with a beam of light.[45]

This interpretation I find rather unconvincing. While it is certainly possible to imagine a setting like the one proposed by Horst and others, I find no indications in the book that would prompt us to do so. What evidence is there to suggest that certain parts of the book need to be read as liturgical responses to the prophetic message of judgment? If this is how the redactors intended these passages to be read, then it has to be said

Wolff, *Joel and Amos, passim*; Jeremias, *Book of Amos*, p. 8; *idem*, 'Amos 3–6: Beobachtungen', to name but a few.

42. Thus, for instance, J.D.W. Watts, 'An Old Hymn Preserved in the Book of Amos', *JNES* 15 (1956), pp. 33-39; *idem*, *Vision and Prophecy in Amos* (Macon, GA: Mercer University Press, new edn, 1997), pp. 9-27; Mays, *Amos*, p. 84; E. Hammershaimb, *The Book of Amos: A Commentary* (Oxford: Basil Blackwell, 1970), p. 133; Rudolph, *Joel, Amos, Obadja, Jona*, pp. 181-83; Stuart, *Hosea–Jonah*, p. 286; Hayes, *Amos*, p. 150; Andersen and Freedman, *Amos, passim*. McComiskey, 'Hymnic Elements', thinks they were penned by Amos himself.

43. J. Jeremias, 'Das Proprium der alttestamentlichen Prophetie', in *idem*, *Hosea und Amos*, pp. 20-33 [31].

44. To my knowledge the first to advance this view was Horst, 'Doxologien'.

45. Horst, 'Doxologien', pp. 53-54.

that they did not succeed in making this clear to an unsuspecting readership. For a start, as they now stand, the hymn fragments are clearly presented as Amos's own words. Secondly, Jeremias's claim that they 'praise God's creative power for the sake of enticing Israel, with the help [of] Amos' own words, to turn anew to God'[46] is not supported by the textual evidence. It might perhaps just be possible to read 4.13 in this way;[47] in the case of 5.8-9 and 9.5-6, however, this is simply not a viable option.

Jeremias's comments on 5.8-9 are particularly instructive in this context. Noting the verbal similarities in vv. 7-8 (Israel turns [הפך] justice to wormwood; Yahweh turns [הפך] darkness into the morning), he rightly stresses that these similarities carry an ominous connotation in the judgmental context in which they are found. 'Yahweh, who so sovereignly governs day and night, can 'overturn' Israel's fate in an instant'.[48] However, since the positive statement והפך לבקר צלמות precedes the words ויום לילה החשיך, Jeremias claims that 'the text wants primarily to encourage those who are in despair…to seek Yahweh anew…and only secondarily does it threaten destruction'.[49] This interpretation is unlikely, given the subsequent lines. It is preferable to understand v. 8aβ as simply describing the power of Yahweh, which manifests itself in his authority over day and night. Likewise, the preceding line, 'the one who made the Pleiades and Orion' (8aα), highlights the deity's cosmic might. The rest of the hymn then stresses the destructive potential of Yahweh's power (vv. 8b-9), which is its predominant theme.

In an attempt to defend his doxological interpretation, Jeremias has suggested that v. 9 was added by a later redactor with the intention of stressing Yahweh's destructive power.[50] That is to say, at first, the text did not contain any part of the hymn, but only Amos's message of judgment. Then somebody inserted the 'nice bit', the praise of the creator (8aα), in order to encourage the desperate exiles and help them come to terms with their past. This, in turn, occasioned another redactor, apparently thinking

46. Jeremias, *Book of Amos*, p. 8.
47. See, however, my interpretation of Amos 4.13 in Chapter 5.
48. Jeremias, *Book of Amos*, p. 91. Of all the hymn fragments, this one was once thought to be the most disruptive but is now recognized by many as the centre of the chiasm in Amos 5.1-17 (cf. the works listed in Chapter 1, n. 83). Its placement therefore is not accidental and, as Jeremias rightly notes, effectively contrasts Israel's acts with those of Yahweh.
49. Jeremias, *Book of Amos*, p. 91.
50. Jeremias, *Book of Amos*, p. 91.

the text was now too reassuring, to tighten things up again, which he did by inserting another gloomy bit (v. 9). Inventive though this interpretation is, it is hardly convincing.[51] Not only does it envisage quite complex and highly conjectural redactional scenarios; it also generates more difficulties than it solves.

Against those advocating a doxological interpretation, I want to stress that Amos 4.13; 5.8-9 and 9.5-6 are best understood as lending special force to Amos's message of judgment stressing, as they do, Yahweh's destructive power.[52] The first hymn fragment, following the ominous announcement that Israel is to meet its God, is the most ambiguous one in that in 4.13 the judgmental notion is not yet as clear as in the subsequent passages. Yet, even here, the second line, עשׂה שׁחר עיפה ודרך על־במתי ארץ, does not sound too comforting. The implications of judgment are much more obvious, however, in 5.8-9 and 9.5-6, with their allusions to the Flood and their explicit talk of destruction and mourning. The tone of the hymn fragments thus gets ever more threatening as we move from one to the next. A comparison of Amos 5.8-9 and 9.5-6 confirms this. Both contain allusions to the Flood, the expression יהוה שׁמו as well as phrases depicting Yahweh's power as creator and majestic ruler in the heavens (5.8a; 9.6a). At the same time, however, Amos 9.5-6 goes well beyond the second hymn in outlining the scope of the divine judgment. Whereas Amos 5.8-9 speaks of Yahweh's destruction coming upon the עז and the מבצר, apparently denoting 'the military machine',[53] Amos 9.5-6 envisages a divine intervention on a more cosmic scale, causing כל־יושבי הארץ to mourn. This observation fits in well with the conception of the book as presenting a debate between the prophet Amos and his audience. In his

---

51. Jeremias's proposal is not helped by v. 8b (obviously an allusion to the Flood), which indicates, as he freely admits, that already the older hymn stressed Yahweh's destructive power (Jeremias, *Book of Amos*, p. 91).

52. J.A. Thompson, 'The 'Response' in Biblical and Non-Biblical Literature with Particular Reference to the Hebrew Prophets', in E.W. Conrad and E.G. Newing (eds.), *Perspectives on Language and Text: Essays and Poems in Honor of Francis I. Andersen's Sixtieth Birthday July 28, 1985* (Winona Lake, IN: Eisenbrauns, 1987), pp. 255-68, comparing these hymns to the chorus in Greek tragedy and the chorus responses in Händel's *Messiah*, understands them as antiphonal responses. That is to say, the prophet, having perceived Yahweh's words, reacts to them by contributing a hymnic response or credal affirmation. This is not far off the mark but as Amos is talking to the Israelites and not to Yahweh, it would be better to say that he backs up God's words by stressing the deity's mighty power.

53. Cf. Carroll R., *Contexts*, p. 231.

struggle to convince the people that divine judgment will befall them, Amos is presented as having employed increasingly drastic images of the deity and his actions.

To sum up, Amos 4.13; 5.8-9 and 9.5-6 do stand out, when compared to the rest of the book, by their hymnic diction. Yet these passages do not function as doxologies praising the creator. On the contrary, they affirm and indeed exacerbate Amos's message of judgment. It is therefore preferable, in my opinion, to regard them as fragments of an ancient hymn employed by the prophet in order to drive home his point.[54] This, it should be noted, is completely in line with Amos's general practice of quoting religious traditions and beliefs only to subvert them.[55]

Finally, before moving on to outline the book's rhetorical situation, we need to consider briefly the epilogue in Amos 9. Ever since Wellhausen's famous comment, describing the passage as 'roses and lavender instead of blood and iron',[56] Amos 9.11-15 has been regarded by many not only as a later addition to but also as a distortion of Amos's message. Smend, for instance, even speaks of treason, implicating that whoever was responsible for these insertions has betrayed Amos and his objectives.[57] Kraus is therefore correct to say that the suggested deletion of the salvation oracle is primarily an 'ideenkritische' operation.[58] Both Wellhausen's and Smend's

54. For a discussion of the linguistic evidence countering the claim that the language requires a late date cf. the works listed in n. 42 above.

55. See also the discussion of the hymn fragments in K. Möller, '"Hear this Word against You": A Fresh Look at the Arrangement and the Rhetorical Strategy of the Book of Amos', *VT* 50 (2000), pp. 499-518 (512-15).

56. J. Wellhausen, *Die kleinen Propheten übersetzt und erklärt* (Berlin: W. de Gruyter, 4th edn, 1963), p. 96.

57. R. Smend, 'Das Nein des Amos', *EvT* 23 (1963), pp. 404-23 [423], referring not only to Amos 9.11-15 but to all those passages that attempt to 'build bridges where Amos...saw only a cleft' ('Brücken zu schlagen da, wo Amos...nur die Kluft sah'; Smend here quotes A. Weiser, *Die Profetie des Amos* [BZAW, 53; Giessen: Alfred Töpelmann, 1929], p. 324).

58. H.-J. Kraus, *Geschichte der historisch-kritischen Erforschung des Alten Testaments* (Neukirchen–Vluyn: Neukirchener Verlag, 4th edn, 1988), p. 282. To be sure, the passage has been assigned a late date also because of historical and linguistic reasons. These cannot be discussed in the present context but for an extensive review of the linguistic evidence cf. Paul, *Amos*, pp. 282-95; on the historical data see Hayes, *Amos*, pp. 218-28.

Some claim that there is a scholarly consensus that regards Amos 9.11-15 as secondary (cf. Zenger, 'Zwölfprophetenbuch', p. 392; T. Collins, *The Mantle of Elijah: The Redaction Criticism of the Prophetical Books* [BibSem, 20; Sheffield: JSOT Press,

comments on the passage illustrate this quite clearly. The former thinks that Amos cannot suddenly say that he didn't mean it badly and that it will still all turn out fine,[59] and the latter, as we have already seen, speaks of treason. Thus, according to Nägele, the decisive question is whether it is even thinkable that Amos could have uttered words of salvation.[60] Simi-

1993], p. 70). This, however, obscures the fact that there have always been a great number of dissidents including, for instance, C. von Orelli, *Die zwölf kleinen Propheten* (Kurzgefasster Kommentar zu den heiligen Schriften Alten und Neuen Testamentes sowie zu den Apokryphen, A.5.2; Munich: Beck, 2nd edn, 1896), p. 60; V. Maag, *Text, Wortschatz und Begriffswelt des Buches Amos* (Leiden: E.J. Brill, 1951), pp. 247-49; E. Rohland, 'Die Bedeutung der Erwählungstraditionen Israels für die Eschatologie der alttestamentlichen Propheten' (dissertation, University of Heidelberg, 1956), pp. 230ff.; G.J. Botterweck, 'Zur Authentizität des Buches Amos', *BZ* NS 2 (1958), pp. 176-89 [188-89]; Watts, *Vision and Prophecy*, pp. 6-7, 83; Hammershaimb, *Book of Amos*, ad loc.; von Rad, *Old Testament Theology*, II, p. 138; H. Graf Reventlow, *Das Amt des Propheten bei Amos* (FRLANT, 80; Göttingen: Vandenhoeck & Ruprecht, 1962), p. 92; R. Fey, *Amos und Jesaja: Abhängigkeit und Eigenständigkeit des Jesaja* (WMANT, 12; Neukirchen–Vluyn: Neukirchener Verlag, 1963), pp. 54-56; J. Mauchline, 'Implicit Signs of a Persistent Belief in the Davidic Empire', *VT* 20 (1970), pp. 287-303; S. Wagner, 'Überlegungen zur Frage nach den Beziehungen des Propheten Amos zum Südreich', *TLZ* 96 (1971), pp. 653-70 [661-63] (who claims [pp. 661, 669 n. 18] that Alt advocated the same view in his lectures given 1950–51 in Leipzig); H.N. Richardson, '*skt* (Amos 9.11): "Booth" or "Succoth"?', *JBL* 92 (1973), pp. 375-81; Rudolph, *Joel, Amos, Obadja, Jona*, pp. 278-87 (esp. 285-86); G.F. Hasel, *The Remnant: The History and Theology of the Remnant Idea from Genesis to Isaiah* (AUMSR, 5; Berrien Springs: Andrews University Press, 3rd edn, 1980), pp. 209-15; G.H. Davies, 'Amos—The Prophet of Re-Union', *ExpTim* 92 (1980–81), pp. 196-200; M.E. Polley, *Amos and the Davidic Empire: A Socio-Historical Approach* (New York: Oxford University Press, 1989), pp. 70-74, 173-75; Stuart, *Hosea–Jonah*, p. 397; Hayes, *Amos*, pp. 220-28; Andersen and Freedman, *Amos*, ad loc.; Smith, *Amos*, pp. 277-80; Paul, *Amos*, pp. 288-95; Rosenbaum, *Amos of Israel*, pp. 73-75. In addition to these, G.F. Hasel, 'The Alleged "No" of Amos and Amos' Eschatology', *AUSS* 29 (1991), pp. 3-18 (15-16), lists many more (cf. also *idem*, *Remnant*, pp. 207-208 n. 300). Rudolph, *Joel, Amos, Obadja, Jona*, p. 285, provides a fair assessment of the debate when he notes that 'der Streit um die Echtheit des Amosschlusses wogt schon ein gutes Jahrhundert hin und her. In der Wellhausenschen Ära war die Unechterklärung Trumpf, und die Andersdenkenden wurden vielfach als rückständig bemitleidet... Das hat sich seither geändert, man wird sagen können, daß sich das Für und Wider heute annähernd die Waage hält.'

   59. Wellhausen, *Die kleinen Propheten*, p. 96.

   60. S. Nägele, *Laubhütte Davids und Wolkensohn: Eine auslegungsgeschichtliche Studie zu Amos 9,11 in der jüdischen und christlichen Exegese* (AGJU, 24; Leiden: E.J. Brill, 1995), p. 172.

larly, Hayes urges us to ask 'whether or not the optimistic material is consistent with the remainder of the prophet's preaching and reflects the rhetorical and historical horizons of the total proclamation',[61] thus directing our attention to the key issues.

In an article entitled 'Rehabilitation eines Propheten', I have already argued that there is no contradiction between the epilogue and the rest of the book. Nor does the salvation oracle in 9.11-15 soften or even jeopardize the prophet's message of judgment. Indeed, the claim for the epilogue to be inconsistent with the rest of the book reflects a strikingly literalistic (and thus inappropriate) approach to the prophetic text.[62] That is to say, before we can decide whether certain statements are at odds with others, it is important to consider their precise function. Employing insights advanced by speech act theorists as well as concepts provided by rhetorical criticism, I re-examined Amos's message and then reviewed the rhetorical function of Amos 9.7-15 in the light of my findings.[63] This has led me to conclude that the epilogue not only is a suitable ending to the book but also reflects the rhetorical horizon of Amos's total proclamation, to use Hayes's terminology. It is not possible, in this context, to repeat the whole argument, but a brief recapitulation of the main results can be found in the subsequent outline of the debate between Amos and his audience as captured in the book (section 2c below).

I want to end this section by restating my conviction that the book of Amos in its final form is not a product of the postexilic era. To repeat, I am not attempting to establish Amosian authorship, nor is it for apologetic reasons that I advocate an early date. With many recent exegetes, I simply believe that not only can the book be read against an eighth-century background but also that doing so actually minimizes the problems of interpretation. This is most certainly the case as far as the hymnic sections are concerned. However, the primary concern of the present study is to review the 'discourse', in the light of which the questions pertaining to the 'source' can then be readdressed. The latter is not possible within the confines of this study whereas to the former we now turn in the ensuing discussion of the book's rhetorical situation and strategy.

61. Hayes, *Amos*, p. 220.
62. Möller, 'Rehabilitation'. Readers are referred to that article for a full discussion of what Hayes has called the prophet's 'rhetorical horizon'. On the historical horizon see esp. the commentaries by Rudolph and Hayes *ad loc.*
63. Möller, 'Rehabilitation', pp. 46-52. See also now Möller, 'Words of (In-)evitable Certitude', for a discussion of the function of Amos's oracles of judgment employing speech act theory, rhetorical criticism and theories of metaphor.

c. *The Rhetorical Situation and the Problem Addressed*

According to 7.12-13, Amos was told by Amaziah, the priest of Bethel, to leave the country and prophesy in Judah instead. Shortly after his ministry, his message of judgment found its grim fulfilment in the catastrophe of 722 BCE, which caused the northern kingdom of Israel to cease to exist. The words of Amos, however, lived on having been preserved by tradents south of the border. The first parameter that defines the book's rhetorical situation (in contrast to that of the original oral oracles) therefore is its Judaean (and possibly Jerusalemite)[64] setting. The second parameter, as I have just argued, is its relatively early date sometime after the end of Amos's ministry but before 587 BCE. While I tend towards an early rather than a late date within this period, all I want to stress at this point is the book's pre-exilic setting.

I also want to draw attention in this context to Ben Zvi's investigation of Obadiah where he introduced the term 'past-fulfilment perspective',[65] which is a useful concept to apply here as it helps us understand a key element of Amos's function in a post-Israel Judaean setting. In a time when Amos's successors were struggling to convince the Judaeans that Yahweh would judge *them* too if they did not alter their conduct, the book of Amos fittingly addresses that 'rhetorical problem' by presenting a precedent, as it were.[66] It shows Amos struggling and, regrettably, failing in his struggle to convince the Israelites that judgment will befall them. Yet the presentation of that struggle is a powerful rhetorical device especially when one looks at it from a past-fulfilment perspective. That is to say, the people of Judah knew that Amos had been proved right by history; Israel had indeed gone into exile as he had threatened, and the northern kingdom had truly come to an end. It should also be noted that the book's rhetorical impact must have been all the more powerful given Amos's sporadic allusions to Judah. Knowing that the prophet had been right in what he had said about the fate of their brothers and sisters in the

---

64. Thus Sweeney, 'Formation', pp. 122-23, who reaches this conclusion because of Amos 1.2 with its emphasis that Yahweh roars from Zion. See also Stuart, *Hosea–Jonah*, p. 288, who states that 'it was in Judah that the book was probably preserved as well as read most, after the fall of Samaria in 722'.

65. Ben Zvi, *Obadiah*, p. 39.

66. In this sense Amos was a 'Vorläufer' (precursor) of the Deuteronomists as H.-H. Krause, 'Der Gerichtsprophet Amos, ein Vorläufer des Deuteronomisten', *ZAW* 50 (1932), pp. 221-39 (239), suggested long ago. See also 2 Kgs 17.7-41 (esp. vv. 13-14).

north must have made the Judaeans rather uneasy when confronted with an oracle like 2.4-5.[67]

On the basis of these considerations, the period 722–587 BCE, which witnessed repeated waves of prophetic ministry,[68] suggests itself as a candidate for the book's rhetorical situation. Moreover, Sweeney has rightly stressed that its argument would have been well received in particular during the reigns of the Judaean kings Ahaz (735–715 BCE), Hezekiah (715–687/6 BCE) and Josiah (640–609 BCE).[69]

2. *Rhetorical Strategy*

Having looked at the book's rhetorical units, its rhetorical situation and the specific problem addressed, we can now examine its overall rhetorical strategy. The primary focus will be on the means by which the audience is induced to agree with the speaker or writer or, as in our case, those responsible for the final edition of the book of Amos. As noted in the introduction, an investigation of the rhetorical strategy needs to deal with the aspects of invention (*inventio*), structure (*dispositio*) and style (*elocutio*). At this point though, I am going to focus on the general suasive means, concentrating on *inventio* and *dispositio*. The discussion of stylistic features I reserve for the examination of the rhetoric of Amos 1–4 presented in subsequent chapters.

a. *Introductory Observations*
As expressed earlier, I am concerned primarily with the rhetorical strategy of the *book*, not the one employed by the prophet Amos in his public appearances. Thus, I intend to explain to what effects and purposes Amos's oracles have been collected and arranged in the way we now have them. It should be noted, however, that in presenting the prophet's oracles, the book to a certain extent also reveals Amos's own rhetorical strategy. This is, of course, to be expected in a book that captures the debate between the prophet and his audience. That is to say, by reproducing Amos's words—his sharp and often ironic indictments, his unsettling rhetorical questions, and so on—the book offers us a glimpse into the

---

67. On the authorship of the Judah oracle see the discussion in Chapter 3.

68. On this period's prophetic activities see esp. K. Koch, *The Prophets*. I. *The Assyrian Period* (trans. M. Kohl; London: SCM Press, 1982); and J. Blenkinsopp, *A History of Prophecy in Israel* (Philadelphia: Westminster Press, 1983), ch. 3.

69. Sweeney, *Twelve Prophets*, p. 195.

prophet's ministry. Even more important for my concerns, however, is the fact that the presentation of Amos's rhetorical strategy is actually part of that of the book. More than that, this presentation is, as I shall seek to demonstrate, the primary suasive means by which the book's compilers attempted to affect their readership.

In recent years, the subjectivity of the interpreter has come into sharper focus as being an integral part of the interpretative process. If this is true in general, it needs to be taken into account in this context in particular since the sketching of the overall rhetorical strategy clearly involves subjective impressions. Already Kennedy emphasized that 'criticism...*can be* a creative act'.[70] He was criticized, however, precisely for this 'can be' by the Bible and Culture Collective whose members objected to his 'missing ...awareness that the power of the text includes the reader as part of the text'.[71] Still, it is important to stress that while the power of the text includes the contribution of the reader, the latter is only one factor in the interpretative process. Thus, as Eco has emphasized, a distinction can and should be made between a reader's *use* of a text, on the one hand, and his or her *interpretation*, on the other.[72]

In addition, although even then the number of possible interpretations is infinite, it does not follow that all of them are equally convincing or appropriate. Eco is therefore right to point out that the text itself functions as the parameter of its own interpretations. He elaborates that readers begin with a supposition about the *intentio operis*, which then needs to be confirmed by the text as an organic whole. And while in principle it is possible to come up with an infinite number of suppositions, these need to be shown to be congruent with the text.[73]

In the above discussion of the rhetorical situation, I have argued that many redaction-critical interpretations of the text's function are unconvincing. In particular, I have criticized the view that the book's hymnic sections function as 'doxologies of judgment'. This, I would contend, is not supported by the text as an organic whole, to put it in Eco's words. In what follows, therefore I propose a different reading for these and other sections, one that gives predominance to the *textual cotext* rather than a

---

70. Kennedy, *New Testament Interpretation*, p. 38 (my italics).

71. Bible and Culture Collective, *Postmodern Bible*, p. 163.

72. Cf. Eco, *Lector*, pp. 72-74; *idem*, *Grenzen*, pp. 47-48; and see my discussion in the Introduction.

73. Eco, *Grenzen*, p. 49.

reconstructed *historical context*.[74] I shall first outline in slightly more detail what I believe to be the principal rhetorical strategy before developing my proposal by offering a concise interpretation of the book of Amos in the light of that strategy.

b. *Presenting a Prophet in Debate*

I have already indicated what I believe to be the book's primary rhetorical strategy by suggesting that in reproducing the prophet's oracles and arranging them in a certain way, the text presents Amos as leading a debate with his eighth-century audience. Reading the book consecutively, one gets the impression of a prophet struggling, and indeed failing, to persuade his addressees that they stand condemned in the eyes of Yahweh. Because of the people's horrible social wrongdoings together with a misplaced complacency, Amos argues, the deity is no longer willing to tolerate their behaviour but is about to punish them severely. This portrayal of the debating prophet I understand to be the primary suasive means employed by the redactors to achieve their own persuasive aims. The book is thus best understood as an attempt to persuade its hearers or readers to learn from the failure of the prophet's audience to respond appropriately to his message. The recipients are induced, therefore, not to repeat the stubborn attitude and self-assured behaviour of Amos's original addressees. To achieve this rhetorical aim, those responsible for the book use the debate they are presenting in the context of their own debate with their audience. This construal of the book's function is similar to du Plessis's understanding of the parables, advanced on the basis of concepts drawn from speech act theory, according to which:

> the primary function of the parables in the narrative world of the gospels is to establish Jesus, as the narrator of the parables, in an authoritative position towards his addressees... *The gospels report the relationship between Jesus and his addressees in order that the recipients of the gospels may enter into the same dependent relationship with Jesus...*[75]

The notion of a debating prophet is, of course, not a novelty. Form critics, for instance, have long recognized the existence of a prophetic speech

74. In saying that, I do not intend to play off one against the other (see the discussion of the relationship between 'source' and 'discourse' in the Introduction).

75. J.G. du Plessis, 'Clarity and Obscurity: A Study in Textual Communication of the Relation between Sender, Parable, and Receiver in the Synoptic Gospels' (D.Theol. dissertation, University of Stellenbosch, 1985), p. 5 (my italics); the quote is from Thiselton, *New Horizons*, p. 289.

form called 'disputation speech'. Graffy in his investigation of this speech form remarks that already 'Gunkel maintains that differences of opinion between the prophets and others are the key to understanding many ideas of the prophets, even when a dispute is not presented explicitly'.[76] Similarly, Wolff in his extensive article 'Das Zitat im Prophetenspruch' described prophetic quotes as a kind of 'contradicting proclamation';[77] and Begrich, investigating the disputation speeches in Deutero-Isaiah, regarded them 'as a *literary imitation* of the controversies experienced by the prophet'.[78] Even more interesting is Begrich's observation that in the context of a discussion between a prophet and his hearers one often finds rhetorical questions and hymnic material. This was emphasized also by von Waldow, as again Graffy notes. 'Like Begrich, von Waldow points out the frequent use of rhetorical questions to gain the people's assent... Like Begrich, he notes the use of well-known hymnic material to ensure agreement'.[79] Like Begrich and von Waldow, I too believe that the hymnic sections are best understood in a confrontational rather than a doxological setting.

As already mentioned, the notion of a debating prophet is not a new one. My claim, however, that the book of Amos captures, represents or imitates the debate between Amos and his original audience and utilizes it as a rhetorical means of persuasion is different from traditional readings of that book. What is more, it offers a new answer to the problem of the book's arrangement, an area where there is still considerable disagreement among scholars as Sweeney notes.[80] Some are unable to detect any underlying principles at all. According to Mays, 'there is no demonstrable scheme to

76. A. Graffy, *A Prophet Confronts His People: The Disputation Speech in the Prophets* (AnBib, 104; Rome: Biblical Institute Press, 1984), p. 4, referring to Gunkel, 'Prophets'.

77. H.W. Wolff, 'Das Zitat im Prophetenspruch: Eine Studie zur prophetischen Verkündigungsweise', in *idem, Gesammelte Studien*, pp. 36-129 (94-95): 'Verkündigung im kontradiktorischen Sinne'; cf. also Wolff, *Joel and Amos*, p. 99, 'even the disputations which certainly derive from Amos himself are exclusively bent on effecting the assent of the hearers to the prophetic message of calamity'.

78. This was noted by Graffy, *Prophet*, p. 6, who refers to J. Begrich, *Studien zu Deuterojesaja* (BWANT, 4.25; Stuttgart: W. Kohlhammer, 1938), pp. 42-47 (my italics).

79. Graffy, *Prophet*, p. 8; cf. H.-E. von Waldow, *Anlass und Hintergrund der Verkündigung des Deuterojesaja* (Bonn, 1953), pp. 28-36.

80. Sweeney, 'Formation', p. 118.

the arrangement, historical, geographical, or thematic'.[81] In similar vein, Stuart maintains that 'it is not possible to infer either a strictly chronological or a strictly thematic ordering for most of the oracles'.[82] On the other hand, however, many recent redaction-critical studies have stressed that the prophetic books in general are to be understood as what Zenger calls 'methodical compositions'.[83] Similarly, Koch speaks of a redaction that does not just rework the text by adding glosses but consciously structures and shapes the prophetic inheritance.[84] This view has led to an increased interest in structural features, with chiasms and inclusios being especially popular.[85] Often, however, the investigation of structure has become an end in itself, with the question of the function of the detected structures being neglected.

Yet all this notwithstanding, Mays and Stuart are right to maintain that the arrangement of Amos is not historical, geographical, thematic or chronological. A better way forward is Hayes's conclusion that 'the material in the book is best understood in terms of large rhetorical units rather than in terms of a multiplicity of small isolated units'.[86] This confirms my own observations outlined in the previous chapter. Building on Hayes's insight, I want to suggest at this point that these large rhetorical units are arranged furthermore in a way that results in what I have called the 'presentation of a prophet in debate'.[87] The arrangement of the book is thus best described as being a rhetorical one, as being motivated by rhetorical interests.[88] It is important to note that the introductory phrases, which I found to be major

81. Mays, *Amos*, p. 14.

82. Stuart, *Hosea–Jonah*, p. 287.

83. E. Zenger, 'Eigenart und Bedeutung der Prophetie Israels', in *idem et al.* (eds.), *Einleitung in das Alte Testament*, pp. 293-303 (297): 'planvolle Kompositionen'.

84. Koch, 'Rolle', p. 535.

85. See the previous chapter for a review of this trend.

86. Hayes, *Amos*, p. 39.

87. This comes close to Darr's view that a 'sophisticated, sequential reading... promises to shed new light on elements of narrativity present in the final arrangement of originally discrete poetic units' (K.P. Darr, 'Literary Perspectives on Prophetic Literature', in Mays, Petersen and Richards [eds.], *Old Testament Interpretation*, pp. 127-43 [142]).

88. It is strange that not even Gibson in his recent book considers this to be an option (see J.C.L. Gibson, *Language and Imagery in the Old Testament* [London: SPCK, 1998]). Despite his interest in rhetoric, when it comes to the arrangement of Amos, he simply echoes the familiar 'we don't know' (after having considered subject matter, date or a mixture of both as possible options).

structural markers, play a crucial role in this context. Not only do speech formulas like שמעו את־הדבר הזה 'present' Amos as attempting to gain the attention of his eighth-century audience. They also directly address *the book's hearers or readers*, thus performing an important rhetorical function on the level of the book as well.

Having emphasized the importance of the book's arrangement and stressed that it results in the much referred to debate, I now proceed to offer a succinct outline of the presentation of that debate as found in the book. Particular attention will be paid to the seams of the book, to the way in which different oracles or collections of oracles have been joined together.

c. *The Debate as it Unfolds throughout the Book*[89]

The book opens with a superscription providing the historical framework in which the subsequent material is to be understood (1.1) followed by a motto that introduces the ominous tone of Amos's stern message (1.2). The prophet is then portrayed as initiating what at first does not appear to be a debate. In denouncing the dreadful practices of Israel's neighbours and threatening them with divine judgment (1.3–2.5), Amos seems to be firmly on the side of his audience who, regarding these matters, would not have found it difficult to agree with him. This, however, soon changes in that Amos suddenly starts to accuse the Israelites themselves. He even goes on to threaten them with a divine judgment similar to that of the other nations (2.6-16). With this, the debate begins. Having related the divine accusations, Amos quotes Yahweh who justifies the impending judgment by reporting his past salvific deeds on Israel's behalf (vv. 9-11). However, these met with intolerable reactions on the part of the people (v. 12) so that, because of these reactions and the wrongdoings condemned earlier, Yahweh is now going to punish them (vv. 13-16).

When Amos then moves on to bring up the issue of Israel's election (3.2) he gives it an entirely new twist, stressing that rather than affording special privileges it leads to an increased accountability. Amos here appears to be reacting to an objection by the people who, considering themselves as Yahweh's elect, deny that the deity would ever punish them. This Amos disputes. Using rhetorical questions (vv. 3-8), he stresses that he has no choice but to proclaim his terrible message because 'the Sovereign LORD has spoken'. From the perspective of the Aristotelian

---

89. As the following chapters offer an extensive analysis of Amos 1–4, that passage will not be discussed in detail at this point.

category of *ethos*, this passage seeks to establish the prophet's moral character by pointing out that Yahweh forced him to perform his unpleasant ministry.[90] Amos, it becomes clear, is not someone who enjoys all this judgment talk; he simply has no other choice but to do what he must. Amos 3.9-10 then offers the corroborative evidence of two witnesses, ironically provided by Ashdod and Egypt, two nations that themselves must have been regarded by Amos's audience as well versed in the practices they accuse Israel of. Finally, the judgment section proper (vv. 11-15) underlines that Yahweh is indeed going to punish his people and that there will be no refuge anymore as the horns of the altar are cut off (v.14).

Having ended the previous discourse on a note of judgment stressing the punishment of the ruling elite, Amos is next presented as singling out a group of upper-class women as an illustration of the lifestyle Yahweh denounces (4.1-3). The deity now even swears that they will be punished for their outrageous behaviour (v. 2). All their sacrifices and tithes, numerous and fastidious though they may be, will not prevent the judgment (vv. 4-5). They only add to the sins of those who are ruthless in their dealings with the poor and needy. The debate then continues with Yahweh enumerating previous judgments inflicted upon his people with the intention of bringing about their return (שׁוּב) and restoring their relationship with him (vv. 6-11). Yet failing to respond, the people are called upon to prepare themselves for a meeting with their God (v. 12), the prospective terror of which is underlined by the hymn fragment stressing the awesome power of the one they are going to meet (v. 13).

The drama increases when Amos suddenly laments Israel's fall. This, it first appears, is the inevitable consequence of Israel's meeting with Yahweh (Amos 5.1-3). But is it inevitable? In contrasting the lamentation with an exhortation to seek God and live (vv. 4-6), the audience are given yet another opportunity to avoid this fate. As O'Rourke Boyle notes:

> the paranetic passage in which Amos extends a slim, dramatic hope after the announcement of the death-sentence is not arbitrarily but deliberately situated. It provides rationale for the remainder of the prophetic sayings and within the dramatic unity of the book it creates a suspense which is only resolved by the final words (ix 8) and the editorial commentary upon them (ix 9-15).[91]

90. See Kennedy, *New Testament Interpretation*, p. 36, who notes that rhetoricians might have to face an audience's prejudices against them or an unwillingness to perceive them as possessing the authority necessary for their claims.

91. M. O'Rourke Boyle, 'The Covenant Lawsuit of the Prophet Amos: iii 1–iv 13',

Amos 5.7-13, which is at the centre of the chiastic arrangement (5.1-17), highlights the existing crisis between Yahweh and Israel. God's people who pervert justice (vv. 7, 10, 12), commit social crimes (v. 11) and live a complacent life (v. 11) are to face Yahweh, the creator, whose awesome destructive powers are once again singled out in another hymn fragment (vv. 8-9). This contrast between Yahweh and his people provides a powerful prelude to a further exhortation (vv. 14-15), which takes up the negative portrayal of the people, admonishing them to seek good instead of evil. In actual terms, this means that they are to establish justice instead of turning it to wormwood (cf. v. 7). If they do, Yahweh may be merciful towards the שארית יוסף (v. 15). Yet the concluding prediction suggests otherwise. Forecasting the people's wailing in response to the divine passing-through-their-midst, it clearly anticipates a negative outcome (vv. 16-17).[92]

The subsequent sections Amos 5.18-27 and 6.1-14 are fitting sequels to the preceding lament in that both are extended woe oracles. Again, the transition deserves special attention as it, once more, gives the impression of Amos reacting to an implied response by his addressees. Amos's references to a divine theophany (4.12; 5.17)[93] apparently caused the people to resort to the tradition of the יום יהוה,[94] which they understood to refer to a time when the deity would intervene to deliver them from whatever calamity might befall them. Yahweh was, after all, a God who was with

---

VT 21 (1971), pp. 338-62 (362).

92. Yahweh's passing through the midst of Israel is referred to by עבר, thus echoing Exod. 11.4-5; 12.12, 23. As the Lord passed through Egypt to strike down their firstborn, so he will now pass through the midst of his own people. Cf. Paul, *Amos*, p. 180; C. van Leeuwen, 'The Prophecy of the *Yōm YHWH* in Amos V 18-20', in A.S. van der Woude (ed.), *Language and Meaning: Studies in Hebrew Language and Biblical Exegesis* (OTS, 19; Leiden: E.J. Brill, 1974), pp. 113-34 (132); and G.V. Smith, 'Continuity and Discontinuity in Amos' Use of Tradition', *JETS* 34 (1991), pp. 33-42 (38).

93. J.L. Crenshaw, 'Amos and the Theophanic Tradition', *ZAW* (1968), pp. 203-15 (211), stresses that the so-called 'doxologies' in 4.13 and 5.8-9 'are saturated with theophanic language and theology' and are therefore appropriately placed in their present contexts.

94. The association of the יום יהוה with the theophany alluded to in 5.17 has been emphasized by, among others, Crenshaw, 'Amos', p. 206; M. Weiss, 'The Origin of the "Day of the Lord"—Reconsidered', *HUCA* 37 (1966), pp. 29-60 (38-39); and Smith, *Amos*, pp. 180, 184.

them—or so they thought (5.14).[95] Amos, however, having questioned that notion by making Yahweh's beneficial presence with his people dependent upon their life-style, now even turns the יום יהוה tradition against his audience (vv. 18-20). That day, he insists, would do Israel no good, as it would bring only further terror. The following section (vv. 21-27) then specifies the reasons for Amos's negative interpretation of the יום יהוה as well as setting out the consequences that that day will have.[96] Empty cultic rituals going hand in hand with a lack of concern for justice are said to result in the people's exile. And with that, Amos repeats a threat voiced earlier on against the upper-class women (4.3), now applying it indiscriminately to all the people.

In the second extended woe oracle (6.1-14), Amos again rebukes the people's complacency and contemptuous lifestyle, which slights 'the ruin of Joseph' (vv. 1-7). Somewhat surprisingly, he includes the Judaean leadership in his accusation. This reference to the שׁאננים בציון (6.1) seems somewhat out of place in its present context, as indeed most scholars have noted. Yet, lacking a convincing solution,[97] I follow those who accept the

---

95. According to Crenshaw, 'Amos', p. 208, 'the phrase "With us is God" is the people's misunderstanding of the real nature of the theophany...'

96. Cf. Stuart, *Hosea–Jonah*, p. 353; J.L. Berquist, 'Dangerous Waters of Justice and Righteousness: Amos 5.18-27', *BTB* 23 (1993), pp. 54-63 (58); and J. Gray, 'The Day of Yahweh in Cultic Experience and Eschatological Prospect', *SEÅ* 39 (1974), pp. 5-37 (24). Hubbard, *Joel and Amos*, p. 180, points to a further connection between 5.18-20 and vv. 21-27, noting that it 'was in public worship, probably at Bethel (5.5-6; 7.13), that the wrong conception of the Day of the Lord was perpetuated'. See also M. Weinfeld, 'The Day of the Lord: Aspirations for the Kingdom of God in the Bible and Jewish Liturgy', in S. Japhet (ed.), *Studies in the Bible* (Scripta hierosolymitana, 31; Jerusalem: Magnes Press, 1986), pp. 341-72 (366), according to whom 'the belief in a future redeeming revelation lies at the heart of the Day of the Lord prophecies, and is expressed in the prayers of the people'. Others, however, deny the links between the יום יהוה passage and vv. 21-27 (cf. G. von Rad, 'The Origin of the Concept of the Day of Yahweh', *JSS* 4 [1959], pp. 97-108 [105]; Rudolph, *Joel, Amos, Obadja, Jona*, pp. 201-202; and Wolff, *Joel and Amos*, p. 254).

97. According to G. Fohrer, 'Zion-Jerusalem im Alten Testament', in *TWNT*, VII, pp. 292-318 (294), ציון in Amos 6.1 is a technical term indicating the (elevated) position of the capital and thus, in the case of the northern kingdom, refers to its 'Zion', the mountain of Samaria. Rosenbaum, *Amos of Israel*, pp. 33-34, 90-91 (following J.P. Peters, *The Psalms as Liturgies* [New York: Macmillan, 1922], p. 210) understands the term to denote the place that 'tradition associates with God's primary dwelling'.

W. von Soden, 'Zu einigen Ortsbenennungen bei Amos und Micha', *ZAH* 3 (1990), pp. 214-20 (214-16), on the other hand, emends ציון to עיון (cf. 1 Kgs 15.20 || 2 Chron.

text as it stands.[98] The problem is not so much that it would have been unlikely for the prophet to accuse Judah as well as Israel[99] but that, from a

16.4; 2 Kgs 15.29), which is graphically the best emendation that has been suggested as שׂ and עׂ are easily confused (for others see Budde, 'Text und Auslegung', pp. 122-23; Maag, *Text*, pp. 37, 205; Rudolph, *Joel, Amos, Obadja, Jona*, p. 215; H.L. Ginsberg, *The Israelian Heritage of Judaism* [New York: Jewish Theological Seminary, 1982], p. 31; and those listed in Rottzoll, *Studien*, pp. 153-54). However, why עָיוֹן should have been singled out in this context is more difficult to explain, especially as צִיּוֹן and הַר שֹׁמְרוֹן make for a much better pair.

Weiser, *Profetie*, p. 230, takes yet another route in reinterpreting שַׁאֲנָן, which he translates as 'being proud of' and understands as referring to the Israelites' proud reference to an earlier victory over Judah. Similarly, the LXX attempts to solve the problem by rendering שַׁאֲנָן as 'to despise' (cf. τοῖς ἐξουθενοῦσιν Σιων).

Others regard צִיּוֹן as a gloss inserted by a Judaean redactor or as a deuteronomistic addition (thus H.E.W. Fosbroke, 'The Book of Amos: Introduction and Exegesis', in G.A. Buttrick *et al.* (eds.), *IB*, VI [New York: Abingdon Press, 1956], pp. 761-853 [822-23]; V. Maag, 'Amos', in *RGG*, I, pp. 328-31 [331]; Polley, *Amos*, pp. 94-95; and A. Deissler, *Zwölf Propheten*. I. *Hosea, Joël, Amos* [Neue Echter Bibel, 4; Würzburg: Echter Verlag, 3rd edn, 1992], p. 119). However, Rudolph, *Joel, Amos, Obadja, Jona*, p. 215; Finley, *Joel, Amos, Obadiah*, p. 259; Gowan, 'Book of Amos', p. 399; and Jeremias, *Book of Amos*, p. 107 n. 1, rightly note that its deletion would distort the balanced metrical arrangement.

Wolff, *Joel and Amos*, pp. 270-71 (followed by L. Markert, *Struktur und Bezeichnung des Scheltworts: Eine gattungskritische Studie anhand des Amosbuches* [BZAW, 140; Berlin: W. de Gruyter, 1977], pp. 164-65; Hardmeier, *Texttheorie*, p. 238 n. 164; Fleischer, *Von Menschenverkäufern*, p. 226; and Reimer, *Recht*, p. 137) bypasses the problem by deleting v. 1aα as well as the equally troublesome 1bα, a solution that does away with the difficulties rather too easily.

98. Cf. S. Oettli, *Amos und Hosea: Zwei Zeugen gegen die Anwendung der Evolutionstheorie auf die Religion Israels* (BFCT, 5.4; Gütersloh: Bertelsmann, 1901), p. 72; Wellhausen, *Die kleinen Propheten*, pp. 84-85; Harper, *Commentary*, p. 143; B. Duhm, 'Anmerkungen zu den zwölf Propheten', *ZAW* 31 (1911), pp. 1-43, 81-110, 161-204 (11); H. Gressmann, *Die älteste Geschichtsschreibung und Prophetie Israels (von Samuel bis Amos und Hosea)* (SAT, 2.1; Göttingen: Vandenhoeck & Ruprecht, 2nd edn, 1921), p. 350; Cripps, *Commentary*, p. 202; Gordis, 'Composition and Structure', p. 244; T.H. Robinson, 'Hosea bis Micha', in *idem* and F. Horst, *Die Zwölf Kleinen Propheten* (HAT, 1.14; Tübingen: J.C.B. Mohr [Paul Siebeck], 2nd edn, 1954), pp. 1-152 (94); S. Amsler, 'Amos', in E. Jacob, C.-A. Keller and S. Amsler, *Osée, Joël, Amos, Abdias, Jonas* (CAT, 11a; Neuchâtel: Delachaux & Niestlé, 1965), pp. 157-247 (217); Mays, *Amos*, pp. 114-15; Stuart, *Hosea–Jonah*, p. 358; Hayes, *Amos*, pp. 182-83; Andersen and Freedman, *Amos*, pp. 110-11; Smith, *Amos*, pp. 199-200; Finley, *Joel, Amos, Obadiah*, pp. 259-60; and Paul, *Amos*, p. 200.

99. Thus with Robinson, 'Hosea bis Micha', p. 94; Hayes, *Amos*, pp. 182-83; and

rhetorical or argumentative point of view, the reference to Judah appears to interrupt what up to this point has been an unswerving focus on Israel.

Hayes and Finley have suggested interpreting 6.1 along the same lines as the Judah oracle in 2.4-5. Hayes notes that the reference to Zion 'illustrates the prophet's rhetorical skill. Beginning with reference to someone other than his immediate audience, it functions to engage and disarm the hearers'.[100] However, this interpretation only works when the oracle in 6.1-7 is read individually. On the level of the book, the debate is in full swing at this point, the audience is, or should be, engaged, and the Judah reference thus needs to be explained differently. I would suggest that it is best understood in terms of Aristotle's concept of *ethos*, thus taking it as another attempt at establishing the prophet's character and integrity. Amos, as his own words confirm, is not just a Judaean nationalist who simply pours scorn and contempt on the apostate northerners. Far from it, he makes it clear that he rejects the complacency of the Judaean leaders just as readily as that of their Israelite counterparts.

This, then, may explain the function of the Zion reference in the debate between Amos and his audience as presented in the book. However, the reference to Judah also has a very important function in the debate that, by means of the book, transpires between its compilers and their audience. For those who know that history has proved Amos right in his announcements of impending judgment upon Israel, the words הוֹי שַׁאֲנַנִּים בְּצִיּוֹן become all the more ominous alluding, as they do, to the possibility that there might be yet more woe in store.

It has been noted frequently that in Amos 6.1-7 the prophet appears to be reacting to objections voiced by the audience against his message of judgement. Weiser, for instance, comments that, having become complacent because of their military successes under Jeroboam II, the people will have attempted to refute Amos's message of doom more than once.[101] Yet Amos unmasks the hubris and pretension of those he sarcastically refers to as נְקֻבֵי רֵאשִׁית הַגּוֹיִם (v. 1).[102] Battering his audience with a series of rhetorical questions, he makes it clear that Israel and Judah are no

---

Finley, *Joel, Amos, Obadiah*, pp. 259-60.

100. Hayes, *Amos*, p. 182; cf. Finley, *Joel, Amos, Obadiah*, p. 260.

101. A. Weiser, *Das Buch der zwölf kleinen Propheten*. I. *Die Propheten Hosea, Joel, Amos, Obadja, Jona, Micha* (ATD, 24; Göttingen: Vandenhoeck & Ruprecht, 8th edn, 1985), p. 175.

102. Amos 6.1 (esp. bβ) poses a number of difficulties. See the commentaries for attempts to solve them.

stronger than Calneh, Hamath and Gath, all of whom had suffered military defeat despite their assumed strength.[103] The ruling classes' attempt to thrust off and push away the יום רע (v. 3; cf. יום יהוה in 5.18, 20 and יום מר in 8.10) therefore only testifies to their self-delusion, and their excessive decadence and complacency pictured in vv. 4-6[104] becomes all the more

---

103. Many commentators take v. 2 to refer to the campaigns of Tiglath-Pileser III in 738 BCE (cf. recently Jeremias, *Book of Amos*, pp. 114-15). Yet Paul, *Amos*, p. 203, points out that at that time Tiglath-Pileser III intervened also in the politics of Israel. Hence, he asks: 'What effect...would such a historical comparison have upon the people precisely at this time? For all intents and purposes, they were already no better off than these other defeated kingdoms. The threatened analogy simply would not be relevant or meaningful. Why should they fear that the same fate would overtake them as the others, if they were already experiencing the Assyrian onslaught?' Paul concludes that the reference must precede the western campaigns of Tiglath-Pileser III, being perhaps an allusion to the campaigns of Shalmaneser III some one hundred years before the time of Amos.

104. Amos's portrayal of the people's luxurious and decadent lifestyle intensifies as one moves through the book, with 6.4-6 being the most extensive and graphic passage. Cf. S.D. Snyman, 'Amos 6.1-7 as an Intensification of Amos 3.9-11', *In die Skriflig* 28 (1994), pp. 213-22.

H.M. Barstad, *The Religious Polemics of Amos: Studies in the Preaching of Am 2,7B-8; 4,1-13; 5,1-27; 6,4-7; 8,14* (VTSup, 34; Leiden: E.J. Brill, 1984), p. 141, referring to recent archaeological and ancient Near Eastern research, which has shown Amos 6.4-6 to depict a *marzeaḥ* banquet (cf. מרזח סרוחים in v. 7), has argued that 'the banquet is condemned for its connections with non-Yahwistic deities rather than for its immorality'. Earlier on, Eissfeldt had denied this link and proposed a root רזחI, 'to shout, scream', for Jer. 16.5 and Amos 6.7 (the term denoting the *marzeaḥ* banquet being derived from רזחII, 'to assemble'; cf. O. Eissfeldt, 'Etymologische und archäologische Erklärung alttestamentlicher Wörter', *OrAnt* 5 [1966], pp. 166-71). Eissfeldt's distinction was embraced, for instance, by Wolff, *Joel and Amos*, p. 277; and Rudolph, *Joel, Amos, Obadja, Jona*, p. 218, but has since been abandoned, as most scholars are now agreed that Amos 6.4-6 depicts a *marzeaḥ* banquet.

Having said that, however, Barstad's conclusion about Amos primarily renouncing non-Yahwistic practices finds no support in the text. As Carroll R., *Contexts*, p. 260; and Jeremias, *Book of Amos*, p. 112, have noted, the cultic character of these feasts, while certainly implied by the term מרזח, is not stressed in Amos 6. The meals are condemned rather because of the complacency they excite and the decadence by which they are characterized.

The amount of literature on the *marzeaḥ* banquet is immense, but see especially M.H. Pope, 'A Divine Banquet at Ugarit', in J.M. Efird (ed.), *The Use of the Old Testament in the New and Other Essays: Studies in Honor of William Franklin Stinespring* (Durham, NC: Duke University Press, 1972), pp. 170-203; D.B. Bryan, 'Texts Relating to the *Marzeaḥ*: A Study of an Ancient Semitic Institution' (unpub.

inappropriate. Indeed, all these feasts will soon end, Amos warns, when Israel's leaders will lead their people into exile (עתה יגלו בראש גלים, v. 7).

The following verses (vv. 8-14) again illustrate how Amos is struggling to get his message across, failing to convince the Israelites that Yahweh is going to punish them and that the impending judgment will be of the utmost severity (vv. 8-11, 14). Neither can he make it clear to them that their pride and complacency are not only unfounded but, what is worse, are abhorred by the deity (vv. 8, 13). To add to this, his audience apparently does not perceive that the injustice they commit is not only unbefitting but also profoundly irrational and unnatural (v. 12). Again, the impression is given that Amos does all he possibly can to convince his audience of their dangerous situation. He informs them about Yahweh's renewed oath to bring about their destruction (v. 8; cf. 4.2)[105] before zooming in on the consequences of the impending tragedy in a short macabre prose inset (vv. 9-10). Reverting to further rhetorical questions, he highlights the stupidity of the people's behaviour (v. 12) and once again quotes their own words in order to demonstrate the foolishness of their thinking (v. 13).

This brings us to the visions in 7.1–8.3, which until fairly recently have been studied primarily from a historical perspective. Thus, scholars would ask, for instance, whether they marked Amos's call to the prophetic ministry or whether they occurred at a later stage of his career. Recently, however, exegetes have begun to pay more attention to their literary setting. Yet, while this new focus has clearly advanced our understanding of the visions-cum-narrative series, the use of rhetorical categories and concepts can shed further light on their rhetorical function challenging, as it does, some frequently expressed views.

To illustrate this, let us consider the following comments by Jeremias who notes that the visions'

---

diss., The Johns Hopkins University Press, Baltimore, 1973); J.C. Greenfield, 'The *Marzeaḥ* as a Social Institution', *Acta antiqua academiae scientarum hungaricae* 22 (1974), pp. 451-55; H.-J. Fabry, 'מַרְזֵחַ', in *ThWAT*, V, pp. 11-16; O. Loretz, 'Ugaritisch-biblisch *mrzḥ*: "Kultmahl, Kultverein" in Jer 16,5 und Am 6,7', in L. Ruppert, P. Weimar and E. Zenger (eds.), *Künder des Wortes: Beiträge zur Theologie der Propheten. Josef Schreiner zum 60. Geburtstag* (Würzburg: Echter Verlag, 1982), pp. 87-93; P.J. King, 'The *Marzeaḥ* Amos Denounces', *BARev* 15.4 (1988), pp. 34-44; idem, *Amos, Hosea, Micah—An Archaeological Commentary* (Philadelphia: Westminster Press, 1988), ch. 6; Barstad, *Religious Polemics*, ch. 5; and H.L. Bosman, 'מַרְזֵחַ', in *NIDOTTE*, II, pp. 1102-1103.

105. The introductory phrase נשבע אדני יהוה בנפשו נאם־יהוה אלהי צבאות stresses Yahweh's determination.

intention is to show Amos' readers how he changed from the messenger of divine patience to the messenger of relentless divine judgment; put differently, they serve to legitimize the prophetic message of judgment against Israel. They attest how little Amos actually wanted to be the kind of messenger of disaster these visions forced him to become, and how he struggled to the maximum against this new determination of his function.[106]

Especially the second part of the quote deserves closer attention.[107] Without being aware of it, Jeremias here utilizes the Aristotelian category of *ethos*, which once again proves to be helpful in this context. By relating his attempts to avert the divine judgment (7.2, 5), Amos makes it clear that he by no means desires the punishment he has been ordered to proclaim. Not only that, he even tried to dissuade Yahweh from its execution. This portrayal of the prophet is best understood as another attempt to establish his moral character, to let him appear as someone who cares for the people he so vigorously condemns for their actions.[108] As far as the placement of the vision-cycle at this point in the book is concerned, Jeremias incisively notes that its

> position at the end of the book [can most likely be explained by the fact] that according to the logic of the book itself, Israel's enormous sin must first be presented (in chaps. 2–6) before Yahweh's inaccessibility to prophetic intercession and thus Amos' own new function become comprehensible.[109]

Far from being out of place in its present context, the Amaziah narrative in Amos 7.10-17 too has a crucial role to play in the presentation of the

106. Jeremias, *Book of Amos*, p. 126.

107. The view that the visions serve to legitimize the message of judgment, although frequently stated, is less satisfactory. In the visions, the judgment is never actually legitimized (its legitimization occurs in the multiple sections dealing with Israel's guilt); Yahweh's decision to bring it about is simply stated. Yet, as we shall see, some kind of legitimizing, or better confirmative, function is exercised by the Amaziah narrative in Amos 7.10-17.

108. J.E. Goldingay, 'The Logic of Intercession', *Theology* 101 (1998), pp. 262-70 (264), notes that 'Amos instinctively asks for the suspending of the very judgements he announces'. 'We meet with a prophet who simply takes for granted that his job is to confront God when given pictures of calamity, to query whether judgement really should be implemented'. Amos may, or may not, have taken this for granted. Following the debate between him and his audience, readers or hearers of the book certainly cannot but be surprised to learn about this aspect of his personality, which the preceding litany of judgment speeches did not prepare them for.

109. Jeremias, *Book of Amos*, p. 126.

debating prophet. This was clearly seen by Eslinger who offers an interesting interpretation of the passage. Eslinger notes that:

> proceeding through this balanced intricacy of interwoven visions that revolve around the pivotal intervention of Amaziah, the reader, like Amos himself, gains an education through the vehicle of this literary creation on the necessity of judgment. But only when Amaziah's intervention is left to stand where the author of the book put it is the reader able to see the education of Amos.[110]

Eslinger is right in noting the narrative's important role. He also correctly affirms that vv. 10-17 are not an intrusive inset but are well placed in their present context. I disagree with him, however, when it comes to analysing their function. According to Eslinger, Amaziah's intervention 'educates' Amos, which is to say, it convinces him that Yahweh's verdict in 7.9 is justified. 'Amaziah's interruption is the turning point in Amos' perception of the judgments foretold by the visions'.[111] Amos, therefore, finally sides with Yahweh and refrains from further intercession on Israel's behalf. Thus, Eslinger claims, 'Amaziah's intrusion literally shoves aside Amos' intercession'.[112]

Against this line of interpretation, I would contend that it is Yahweh's assertion לא־אוסיף עוד עבור לו in 7.8, not the intervention of the priest, that forecloses further intercession by Amos. Scholars have correctly drawn attention to the fact that the third and fourth visions are structurally different from visions one and two. In the first pair, on seeing Yahweh's destructive actions, Amos bursts out with his pleas for forgiveness (סלח־נא; 7.2) or simply restraint (חדל־נא; 7.5). In the third vision, however, Yahweh asks the prophet to describe what he sees. So what does Amos see? He perceives Yahweh standing on a חומת אנך with an אנך in his hand (v. 7). Whatever the precise meaning of these phrases,[113] what is most significant is that, contrary to the first two visions, Amos is not confronted with a picture of devastation. As yet, there is, therefore, no reason for him to intervene. And by the time another intervention would have been called for—once Amos has understood the implications of the vision—his intercession has already been precluded in that Yahweh, before spelling out the punishment (v. 9), declared that he would not be prevailed upon to

---

110. Eslinger, 'Education', p. 55.
111. Eslinger, 'Education', p. 45.
112. Eslinger, 'Education', p. 45.
113. See M. Weigl, 'Eine "unendliche Geschichte": אנך (Am 7,7-8)', *Bib* 76 (1995), pp. 343-87, for a detailed discussion and review of the scholarly literature.

spare Israel again (לֹא־אוֹסִיף עוֹד עֲבוֹר לוֹ). Thus, Amos does get an education, but it is Yahweh who does the educating, not the priest.

Why then has the Amaziah narrative been included at this point? What is its function within the overall 'presentation'? Earlier on, I have already pointed out that I do not believe the text to imply that Amaziah interrupted Amos precisely at the time when he was relating the visions.[114] In addition to what I said then, it is hard to imagine that, after what Amos had said about the priest's fate (v. 17), Amaziah would have allowed the prophet to proceed with the account of his visionary experiences (8.1-3). Just as we do not know at what time in his ministry Amos had the visions, so we also do not know precisely when the clash with Amaziah occurred. Just as the visions, with their emphasis on Amos's attempts to avert the divine judgment, serve the rhetorical purpose of establishing the prophet's moral character, so also the inclusion of the Amaziah incident is rhetorically motivated.

Yet already before the priest intervenes, the reader learns that, however sympathetic Amos may be towards the Israelites, in the end he cannot succeed in his course because Yahweh is determined not to spare his people any longer (7.8-9). What purpose then does the Amaziah narrative serve at this point? The priest's blatant refusal to take Amos's words as a divine message (compare כִּי־כֹה אָמַר עָמוֹס in 7.11 with וַיֹּאמֶר יְהוָה in v. 8) illustrates the problem Amos is facing. It confirms that the people simply are not prepared to accept his message of divine punishment. Amaziah's reaction is the most flagrant example of this disbelief.[115] Furthermore, with

---

114. See n. 6 above. Of course, Amaziah's actions are a reaction—even if most likely not an immediate one—to the words of Yahweh reported in 7.9. As it is never expressly said that Amos actually reported his visions, Eslinger, 'Education', p. 44, thinks that 'Amaziah has unwittingly stumbled onto part of the explanation of the vision that Yhwh had just given to Amos'. Regarding this as 'dramatic irony', Eslinger adds that 'the reader too shares Amos' appreciation of the dramatic irony because the narrator has privileged him with a covert audition of Amos' vision and Yhwh's explanation of it'. However, against this view, it needs to be maintained that the introductory phrase (כֹּה הִרְאַנִי אֲדֹנָי יְהוָה) (7.1, 4, 7; 8.1) clearly suggests that Amos did relate his visionary experience. This in turn supports the traditional interpretation that the priest reacted against Yahweh's words in 7.9.

115. It should be noted in this context that J. Applegate, 'Narrative Patterns for the Communication of Commissioned Speech in the Prophets: A Three-Scene Model', in G.J. Brooke and J.-D. Kaestli (eds.), *Narrativity in Biblical and Related Texts. La narrativité dans la Bible et les textes apparentés* (BETL, 149; Leuven: Leuven University Press, 2000), pp. 69-88, has recently underlined that responses to prophets are a significant part of prophetic narratives.

the priest's actions the debate between Amos and his audience intensifies. Whereas up to this point, the people either simply ignored the prophet's warnings or else contradicted them, Amaziah now takes measures to prevent Amos from continuing with his subversive ministry. For a Judaean readership who know the fate of the northern kingdom, the narrative is a stern warning that, even if they attempted to prevent the prophetic voice from being heard in their day, Yahweh would in the end prevail.[116]

This then takes us to Amos 8.4-14, another passage that is often thought to be out of place in its present context since it is so clearly reminiscent of the first half of the book. For this reason, various transpositions have been proposed.[117] Again, this is unnecessary, reflecting, as it does, the desire for too neat and tidy a solution as well as a misapprehension of the book's rhetorical structure. In order to understand the presence of further prophetic indictments (e.g. 8.4-6) at this point in Amos's debate with his

---

116. On Amos 7.10-17 cf. also Möller, 'Hear this Word', pp. 515-17. For other interpretations see L. Rost, 'Zu Amos 7,10-17', in *Festgabe für Theodor Zahn* (Leipzig: Deichert, 1928), pp. 229-36; Gordis, 'Composition and Structure'; G.M. Tucker, 'Prophetic Authenticity: A Form-Critical Study of Amos 7.10-17', *Int* 27 (1973), pp. 423-34; Z. Zevit, 'A Misunderstanding at Bethel: Amos vii 12-17', *VT* 25 (1975), pp. 781-90; P.R. Ackroyd, 'A Judgment Narrative Between Kings and Chronicles? An Approach to Amos 7.9-17', in Coats and Long (eds.), *Canon and Authority*, pp. 71-87; A.J. Bjørndalen, 'Erwägungen zur Zukunft des Amazja und Israels nach der Überlieferung Amos 7,10-17', in R. Albertz *et al.* (eds.), *Werden und Wirken des Alten Testaments. Festschrift für Claus Westermann zum 70. Geburtstag* (Göttingen: Vandenhoeck & Ruprecht, 1980), pp. 236-51; G. Pfeifer, 'Die Ausweisung eines lästigen Ausländers: Amos 7 10-17', *ZAW* 96 (1984), pp. 112-18; H. Utzschneider, 'Die Amazjaerzählung (Am 7,10-17) zwischen Literatur und Historie', *BN* 41 (1988), pp. 76-101; H.J. Stoebe, 'Noch einmal zu Amos vii 10-17', *VT* 39 (1989), pp. 341-54; Williamson, 'Prophet'; G. Sauer, 'Am 7, 10-17 und mesopotamischer Briefstil', in J.J. Adler (ed.), *Haim M.I. Gevaryahu Memorial Volume* (Jerusalem: World Jewish Bible Center, 1990), pp. 119-28; R.E. Clements, 'Amos and the Politics of Israel', in Garrone and Israel (eds.), *Storia e Tradizioni di Israele*, pp. 49-64; and F.O. García-Treto, 'A Reader-Response Approach to Prophetic Conflict: The Case of Amos 7.10-17', in J.C. Exum and D.J.A. Clines (eds.), *The New Literary Criticism and the Hebrew Bible* (JSOTSup, 143; Sheffield: JSOT Press, 1993), pp. 114-24.

117. Especially many of those who believe the vision series to include 9.1-4 find it difficult to make sense of 8.4-14 in its present context. Cf., e.g., M. Löhr, *Untersuchungen zum Buche Amos* (BZAW, 4; Giessen: Rickert, 1901), *ad loc.*; Sellin, *Einleitung*, p. 104; O. Eissfeldt, *The Old Testament: An Introduction* (trans. P.R. Ackroyd; New York: Harper & Row, 1965), p. 399; Weiser, *Buch der zwölf kleinen Propheten*, p. 194; Rudolph, *Joel, Amos, Obadja, Jona*, p. 101; and Soggin, *Prophet Amos, ad loc.*

audience, it is important to realize that the present passage opens the final part of the book. Its function is perhaps more easily appreciated when seen in the context of the whole argument, which is why I prelude the discussion of Amos 8.4-14 with a succinct recapitulation of the debate up to this point.

The OAN in Amos 1–2 started the debate off by accusing God's people of committing offences that were just as bad as, if not worse than, the ones their neighbours were guilty of. This initial accusation is then developed and defended in Amos 3–6 with its constant alternation between prophetic accusations and announcements of punishment. Throughout this middle section, the tension of the debate intensifies, as Amos's employment of theophany and יום יהוה motifs, dirges and woe oracles illustrates. An initial ominous hint of a meeting with Yahweh (4.12) leads to the manifest threat of the deity's passing through Israel's midst (obviously an allusion to Exod. 12.12), an event that will result in dire consequences (5.17). Indeed, as Amos points out, *this* is the long-awaited יום יהוה, and it will be rather different from what the people were expecting (5.18-20). Similarly, the lament taken up by Amos to mourn the fall of בתולת ישראל (5.1-2) foreshadows the people's own future wailing and mourning (5.16-17). It is more than appropriate therefore that the book's middle section is brought to a close by two extended woe oracles (5.18-27; 6.1-14).

Up to this point, Amos is presented as arguing his case. This is suggested by the frequent references to Israel's offences, which aim to convince his audience of their guilt (cf. 5.7, 10-12, 21-26; 6.1-6, 12-13). The picture changes somewhat in the visions-cum-narrative series 7.1–8.3, one purpose of which appears to be to reassure readers or hearers that this prophet is neither a maniac nor a Judaean nationalist who wants to see the Israelites perish. Yet as Yahweh is resolved to spare his people no longer, Amos's intercession is fated to be unsuccessful. Having just learned about Yahweh's resolution, the following Amaziah incident illustrates one of the key problems Amos is facing, namely, the stubbornness of his audience. Eslinger is therefore right to suggest that the narrative educates readers who now learn more about the extent of the people's obstinacy. This highlighting of the people's unwillingness to respond to the prophetic message is thus best understood as an attempt to persuade readers that Yahweh's decision to punish his people is justified.

Amos 8.4-14 then resumes the discussion proper by bringing up, once more, the predominant issue of social injustice (vv. 4-6). For one last time Amos majors on the incredible misbehaviour of the wealthy before moving on to a long liturgy of judgment, which clearly is the dominant topic in Amos 8.7–9.10. This extensive judgment section is introduced by a divine oath that deserves special comment. Whereas earlier on in the book, Yahweh is said to have sworn by his holiness (cf. בקדשו in 4.2) or by himself (cf. בנפשו in 6.8), he now swears by the pride or arrogance of Jacob (בגאון יעקב; 8.7). The fact that Yahweh swears by his people's arrogance is highly sarcastic suggesting, as it does, that as an 'unalterable given' it can even be used to back up a divine oath.[118] Once more, Yahweh's awful cosmic power (v. 9) is conjured up before Amos then zooms in on Israel's punishment (vv. 10-14). Again, the theme of mourning appears just as the 'in that day' language (characteristic of Amos 8–9) connects to the יום יהוה motif in 5.18-20. Most significant, however, in this section is the announcement of a famine, viz. one of hearing the דברי יהוה (8.11-13). This is poetic judgment par excellence: those who do not want to hear Yahweh's word mediated by Amos will one day hunger and thirst for it, but in vain. Their search for the life-sustaining word of Yahweh is described in vivid colours, but it will be a futile attempt: they will not find it (לא ימצאו; 8.12).

In Amos 9, the divine judgment culminates in a climax. To top his previous images of disaster, Amos now pictures the deity as actively ordering the destruction of the temple (9.1). When it falls, it brings down the people with it. Some may be able to make an initial escape, but to no avail. Whether they flee to ראש הכרמל, השמים, שאול, or קרקע הים, Yahweh will track them down eventually (vv. 2-3). Indeed, he is no longer content with his people's exile, being determined to extinguish them (v. 4). Once more, the announcement of judgment is followed by a hymn fragment drawing attention to the awesome power and might of the one Israel will have to face (vv. 5-6). Following upon vv. 2-4, it stresses that nobody can escape from the judgement of a God who has the power to let

---

118. Thus Wellhausen, *Die kleinen Propheten*, p. 93; Fey, *Amos und Jesaja*, p. 37; Wolff, *Joel and Amos*, p. 328; and Rudolph, *Joel, Amos, Obadja, Jona*, p. 264. The phrase גאון יעקב also occurs in 6.8 where it clearly refers to 'the arrogance of Jacob'. Yet it could also be translated 'the pride of Jacob', in which case it could be a predicate of Yahweh (cf. נצח ישראל in 1 Sam. 15.29 and בגאון שם יהוה אלהיו in Mic. 5.3 and see K. Marti, *Das Dodekapropheton erklärt* [KHAT, 13; Tübingen: J.C.B. Mohr, 1904], p. 217; and Pusey, *Minor Prophets*, p. 307). However, the fact that the phrase גאון יעקב is not otherwise know as an epithet of Yahweh (in Ps. 47.5 it refers to the land of Israel while in Nah. 2.3 it also cannot refer to Yahweh), together with its use in Amos 6.8, suggests that it is best understood as a reference to Israel's arrogance.

the whole earth melt and pour the waters of the sea out upon the earth. This is all the more terrifying as Yahweh has made it clear that he will not spare his people any longer.

Indeed, Israel now even seems to have lost its special status (vv. 7-8). While earlier on Amos acknowledged a special relationship between Yahweh and his people (2.9-11; 3.2), he now flatly denies any uniqueness on Israel's part (9.7). Sometimes utterances such as this are overinterpreted as indicating that Amos altogether rejected the exodus tradition. Yet it needs to be borne in mind that the book of Amos is a kind of *Streitschrift* ('polemical treatise') and that verses like Amos 9.7 are to be understood in a highly polemical context. With the rhetorical questions in v. 7, the discussion continues; and again, it is implied that Amos's audience objected to his message of judgment, referring to the exodus, which they believed to have established their special status as Yahweh's chosen people.

Amos challenges this, concluding that the החטאה הממלכה, the sinful *kingdom* of Israel, will be wiped out (v. 8). The well-known and oft-quoted words בא הקץ אל־עמי ישראל ('the end has come upon my people Israel') in 8.2 are to be understood against this background. They do not signify the complete annihilation of all the people but indicate that Israel as a national entity is under threat. This is not to downplay the severity of the prophet's message because, as Amos goes on to explicate, כל חטאי עמי will be extinguished (9.9-10). Given the impression one gets of Amos's audience, this must include a large share of the populace; and yet it is significant that a distinction is being made between חטאים and 'non-חטאים' as it were.

It has of course been claimed that Amos did not make such a distinction. Proponents of this view stress that the notion surfaces only here in Amos 9, claiming that the book in general leaves one with rather different impressions of Amos's views and concerns, and that the concept of the people's sifting therefore must go back to subsequent editors.[119] Yet while

---

119. Cf., e.g., U. Kellermann, 'Der Amosschluss als Stimme deuteronomistischer Heilshoffnung', *EvT* 29 (1969), pp. 169-83; P. Weimar, 'Der Schluss des Amos-Buches: Ein Beitrag zur Redaktionsgeschichte des Amos-Buches', *BN* 16 (1981), pp. 60-100; Jeremias, *Book of Amos*, pp. 162-66; Rottzoll, *Studien*, pp. 270-76; and K. Koenen, *Heil den Gerechten—Unheil den Sündern! Ein Beitrag zur Theologie der Prophetenbücher* (BZAW, 229; Berlin: W. de Gruyter, 1994), pp. 9-18.

The distinction between the righteous and the wicked is thought to be a typical postexilic concept. Yet it should be noted that Amos 9.8-10 does not envisage or presuppose a paradigmatic contrast between the righteous and the wicked (the term צדק does not occur). The point of v. 10 is that *all* sinners are going to perish (כל חטאי עמי—the stress being on כל) and that those who believe they will be all right are

Amos does employ generalizations, his message clearly implies a distinction between culprits and victims. Indeed, he *identifies* both. Moreover, it always needs to be borne in mind that his words originated in a context of controversy and polemics, which makes it notoriously difficult for us to reconstruct his true 'theological' beliefs and convictions. Amos's talk of Israel's end in 8.2 is a case in point. Is this indicative of his conviction that Yahweh will eliminate his people? Is it not more likely that such a remark calls for a rhetorical interpretation? After all, it might be a bit of an exaggeration, employed with the aim of stirring up the audience. But then again, there could be more than just a kernel of truth in it. Whatever we make of these options, we also need to come to a decision about the *interpretative significance* of 8.2. Is it to be taken as the hermeneutical key that controls our reading (and compels us to dispense with those passages that don't fit)? Or do the implications of 8.2 have to be ascertained in view of the book as a whole, including Amos 9.8-10?

To answer these questions, I am going to propose an interpretation that may not be as neat and tidy as some others but seeks to do justice to the book of Amos in its entirety. Thus, I would maintain that the implications of the words בא הקץ אל־עמי ישראל need to be established in the light of their context, including Amos 9.8-10, which makes it clear that it is the הממלכה החטאה and כל חטאי עמי that are doomed. This, it should be stressed, seems to me to be in perfect agreement with the book as a whole. As already noted, all those passages that renounce the luxurious and oppressive lifestyle of the upper classes imply a distinction between culprits and victims (cf. esp. Amos 6.6). Yet the threatened destruction of the *kingdom* of Israel suggests that, in one sense at least, Amos's talk of Israel's end needs to be taken literally. At the same time, however, the polemical context does require a rhetorical interpretation. That is to say, throughout the book one needs to reckon with the presence of exaggerations designed to

---

to be counted among them. *They* are the החטאים. Rudolph, *Joel, Amos, Obadja, Jona*, pp. 277-78, is therefore right to point out that given Amos's message as a whole and especially his distinction between culprits and victims, it is unlikely that he could not have moved beyond the primitive concept of collective responsibility. It seems absurd to assume that Amos (J.F.A. Sawyer, *Prophecy and the Prophets of the Old Testament* [OBS; Oxford: Oxford University Press, 1987], p. 112, stresses that he 'was no country bumpkin') should condemn the abuse of the powerless only to go on to consign both culprits *and* victims to an undiscriminating divine judgment. It should also be noted that the words 'I will not utterly destroy the house of *Jacob*' in v. 8 connect well with Amos's questions in 7.2, 5 (i.e. 'how can *Jacob* stand?').

make a particular point or shatter the audience's perception of reality. Weiser has quite rightly stressed that:

> the oratorical is...always pointed, one-sided, contemplated and formulated with a specific aim in mind so that certain aspects and consequences, which are not in the line of this aim, are not taken into account by the author.[120]

It is also necessary in this context to consider the intention or aim of Amos's judgment speeches. The general issue of the intention of prophetic judgment speeches has caused an ongoing debate in which two principal positions have been advocated.[121] According to many, they serve to explain why Yahweh is going to judge, or has judged, his people. Envisaged as a response to the problem of theodicy, the oracles are thus understood as an attempt to justify the divine act of punishment.[122] Others, on the other

---

120. Weiser, *Profetie*, p. 110.

121. For a detailed discussion and research review cf. esp. Fleischer, *Von Menschen-verkäufern*, ch. 6; see also J.M. Schmidt, 'Ausgangspunkt und Ziel prophetischer Verkündigung im 8. Jahrhundert', *Verkündigung und Forschung* (Beihefte zu *EvT*, 22; Gütersloh: Chr. Kaiser Verlag, 1977), pp. 65-82; Hasel, *Remnant*, pp. 173-76; A.V. Hunter, *Seek the Lord! A Study of the Meaning and Function of the Exhortations in Amos, Hosea, Isaiah, Micah, and Zephaniah* (Baltimore: St. Mary's Seminary & University, 1982), pp. 7-38; R. Martin-Achard, *Amos: L'homme, le message, l'influ-ence* (Publications de la Faculté de Théologie de l'Université de Genève, 7; Geneva: Labor et Fides, 1984), pp. 143-59; and L. Markert and G. Wanke; 'Die Propheten-interpretation: Anfragen und Überlegungen', *KD* 22 (1976), pp. 191-220.

122. Thus J. Wellhausen, *Israelitische und jüdische Geschichte* (Berlin: W. de Gruyter, 9th edn, 1958), p. 107; Weiser, *Profetie*, pp. 310-11; H.W. Wolff, 'Die Begründungen der prophetischen Heils- und Unheilssprüche', in *idem, Gesammelte Studien*, pp. 9-35; *idem, Die Stunde des Amos: Prophetie und Protest* (Munich: Chr. Kaiser Verlag, 1986), pp. 23-30; *idem*, 'Die eigentliche Botschaft der klassischen Propheten', in *idem, Studien zur Prophetie*, pp. 39-49; *idem*, 'Einführung in die klassische Prophetie', in *idem, Studien zur Prophetie*, pp. 9-24; *idem*, 'Endzeitvorstel-lungen und Orientierungskrise in der alttestamentlichen Prophetie', in *idem, Studien zur Prophetie*, pp. 65-78; W.H. Schmidt, 'Die prophetische "Grundgewissheit": Erwägungen zur Einheit prophetischer Verkündigung', in Neumann (ed.), *Das Prophetenverständnis*, pp. 537-64; *idem, Zukunftsgewissheit und Gegenwartskritik: Grundzüge prophetischer Verkündigung* (Biblische Studien, 64; Neukirchen–Vluyn: Neukirchener Verlag, 1973); *idem, Alttestamentlicher Glaube in seiner Geschichte* (Neukirchener Studienbücher, 6; Neukirchen–Vluyn: Neukirchener Verlag, 6th edn, 1987), pp. 272-96; H.-J. Kraus, 'Die prophetische Botschaft gegen das soziale Unrecht Israels', *EvT* 15 (1955), pp. 295-307; Smend, 'Das Nein des Amos'; O.H. Steck, 'Die Gesellschaftskritik der Propheten', in W. Lohff and B. Lohse (eds.), *Christentum und Gesellschaft* (Göttingen: Vandenhoeck & Ruprecht, 1969), pp. 46-62; M. Krause, *Das*

hand, contend that the judgment speeches were designed to warn the audience and, if possible, cause them to repent.[123] However, as I have argued elsewhere, this very polarization of regarding Amos either as a preacher of unconditional doom (almost in the manner of Stella Gibbons's Amos in her 1932 novel *Cold Comfort Farm*)[124] or as being interested solely in effecting repentance appears to be far too simplistic.[125] A more nuanced proposal is called for and has been suggested recently by Eagleton and Houston.[126] Applying insights advanced by speech act theorists, Eagleton and Houston considered the effect *unconditional* announcements of judgment had on their audiences, noting that these could be, and sometimes were in fact, taken as warnings.[127] Thus, Eagleton notes:

Verhältnis von sozialer Kritik und kommender Katastrophe in den Unheilsprophezeiungen des Amos (Hamburg, 1972); G. Warmuth, *Das Mahnwort: Seine Bedeutung für die Verkündigung der vorexilischen Propheten Amos, Hosea, Micha, Jesaja und Jeremia* (BBET, 1; Frankfurt: Peter Lang, 1976); A.J. Bjørndalen, 'Jahwe in den Zukunftsaussagen des Amos', in J. Jeremias and L. Perlitt (eds.), *Die Botschaft und die Boten. Festschrift für Hans Walter Wolff zum 70. Geburtstag* (Neukirchen–Vluyn: Neukirchener Verlag, 1981), pp. 181-202 (200-202); and H.J. Zobel, 'Prophet in Israel und Juda: Das Prophetenverständnis des Amos und Hosea', *ZTK* 82 (1985), pp. 281-99.

123. See G. Fohrer, 'Bemerkungen zum neueren Verständnis der Propheten', in Neumann (ed.), *Das Prophetenverständnis*, pp. 475-92; Amsler, 'Amos', pp. 321-27; H.D. Preuss, *Jahweglaube und Zukunftserwartung* (BWANT, 87; Stuttgart: W. Kohlhammer, 1968), p. 159 and *passim*; G. Wanke, 'Zu Grundlagen und Absicht prophetischer Sozialkritik', *KD* 18 (1972), pp. 2-17; O. Keel, 'Rechttun oder Annahme des drohenden Gerichts? Erwägungen zu Amos, dem frühen Jesaja und Micha', *BZ* NS 21 (1977), pp. 200-18; W. Kornfeld, 'Die Gesellschafts- und Kultkritik alttestamentlicher Propheten', in R. Schulte (ed.), *Leiturgia—Koinonia—Diakonia. FS Kardinal F. König* (Wien: Herder, 1980), pp. 181-200; C. Hardmeier, 'Die judäische Unheilsprophetie: Antwort auf einen Gesellschafts- und Normenwandel im Israel des 8. Jahrhunderts vor Christus', *Der altsprachliche Unterricht* 26 (1983), pp. 20-44; A. Schenker, 'Gerichtsverkündigung und Verblendung bei den vorexilischen Propheten', *RB* 93 (1986), pp. 563-80; A. Deissler, *Dann wirst du Gott erkennen: Die Grundbotschaft der Propheten* (Freiburg: Herder, 1987), p. 27 and *passim*; J.M. Berridge, 'Zur Intention der Botschaft des Amos: Exegetische Überlegungen zu Am. 5', *TZ* 32 (1976), pp. 321-40; and Hasel, *Remnant*, p. 187 and *passim*.

124. See S. Gibbons, *Cold Comfort Farm* (Harmondsworth: Penguin Books, 1938), pp. 85-86.

125. See Möller, 'Rehabilitation', pp. 46-52.

126. See Eagleton, 'J.L. Austin'; and Houston, 'Prophets'.

127. See 2 Sam. 12.1-25 (esp. vv. 13-14, 22) and Jon. 3.4-9. In this context, reference should be made also to Lohfink, 'Bund', p. 221, who notes that a speech act is

in the terms of J.L. Austin's *How to Do Things with Words*, prophetic utterances of Jonah's sort are 'constative' (descriptive of some real or possible state of affairs) only in what one might call their surface grammar; as far as their 'deep structure' goes they actually belong to Austin's class of 'performatives', linguistic acts which get something done. What they get done is to produce a state of affairs in which the state of affairs they describe won't be the case. Effective declarations of imminent catastrophe cancel themselves out, containing as they do a contradiction between what they say and what they do.[128]

As Houston observes, 'the question whether the intention of judgement prophecy is to condemn absolutely or to awaken repentance is transcended'.[129] This is because 'the possibilities of inexorable doom and of mercy evoked by repentance were always implicit in the use of the genre of the oracle of doom'.[130] Similarly, Steiner notes that the prophet's

> enunciation of the future makes that future alterable. If man repents and changes his conduct, God can bend the arc of time out of foreseen shape...
> The force, the axiomatic certainty of the prophet's prediction lies precisely in the possibility that the prediction will go unfulfilled. From Amos to Isaiah, the true prophet 'does not announce an immutable decree. He speaks into the power of decision lying in the moment...'.[131]

Steiner here quotes Buber[132] who was criticized by Smend, objecting to Buber's view that prophets, even when uttering an unconditional announcement of judgment, aimed or might have aimed at repentance.[133] This view, according to Smend, cannot be demonstrated from Amos's words.[134] However, speech act theory with its distinction between *locution* ('the performance of an act *of* saying something'), *illocution* ('the performance of an act *in* saying something') and *perlocution* ('the performance of an

defined not only by words and syntax but also by social, situational and textual circumstances.

128. Eagleton, 'J.L. Austin', p. 233.

129. Houston, 'Prophets', p. 187.

130. Houston, 'Prophets', p. 186.

131. G. Steiner, *After Babel: Aspects of Language and Translation* (Oxford: Oxford University Press, 3rd edn, 1998), p. 154.

132. The quote is from M. Buber, *The Prophetic Faith* (trans. C. Witton-Davies; New York: Macmillan, 1949), p. 103.

133. Buber contended further that 'behind every prediction of disaster there stands a concealed alternative' (*Prophetic Faith*, p. 134). This, too, is quoted approvingly by Steiner, *After Babel*, p. 154.

134. Smend, 'Das Nein des Amos', p. 416.

act *by* saying something')[135] invalidates Smend's criticism. Its application to prophetic speech suggests that when prophets utter unconditional announcements of judgment (*locution*), these can (indeed, may even have been intended to) function as warnings (*illocution*), which can (and may have been intended to) result in the audience's repentance (*perlocution*).[136]

Yet all this notwithstanding, the question that remains is why Amos did not urge the people to repent if that is what he wanted them to do. The answer to this is, I believe, quite simple. Following the debate between Amos and his audience, one gets the strong impression that the people simply would not have seen any need for repentance. As Huffmon rightly notes, 'Amos addresses an audience that in its own sight is pious and faithful'.[137] All his rhetoric therefore aims (indeed, must aim) at convincing his hearers of the magnitude of their guilt as well as the fact that Yahweh is going to punish them. As long as the people do not grasp these facts, any talk of repentance would be a futile exercise. Bitzer refers to problems such as this as rhetorical 'constraints', noting that these are:

> made up of persons, events, objects, and relations which are part of the [rhetorical] situation because they have the power to constrain decision and action needed to modify the exigency. Standard sources of constraint include beliefs, attitudes, documents, facts, traditions, images, interests, motives and the like...[138]

Finally, the suggestion that Amos did not announce the people's annihilation necessitates some comments on passages, such as Amos 9.1-4, that appear to stress the totality of the divine punishment. First, it needs to be emphasized that these passages are to be understood in the light of the indictments interspersed throughout the book. They indicate that it is the ones charged with economic exploitation, pride and complacency, the

---

135. Cf. the discussion in the Introduction above.

136. For more extensive discussion see now Möller, 'Words of (In-)evitable Certitude', pp. 365-71.

137. H.B. Huffmon, 'The Social Role of Amos' Message', in *idem*, F.A. Spina *et al.* (eds.), *The Quest for the Kingdom of God: Studies in Honor of George E. Mendenhall* (Winona Lake, IN: Eisenbrauns, 1983), pp. 109-16 (110). He adds: 'Amos assumes that the hearers of the oracles understand themselves as God's chosen community (...3.2), as connected with the Exodus, Wilderness and Settlement traditions (2.9-10...), as taking part in the Yahwistic cult at traditional religious centers such as Bethel and Gilgal (4.4-5; 5.5), and as confidently looking forward to the Day of the Lord (5.18)'.

138. Bitzer, 'Rhetorical Situation', p. 254.

חטאי עמי in other words, that are the targets of the judgment to come. Secondly, Amos 9.1-4 in particular primarily emphasizes the *ineluctability* of the divine judgment, not its totality. The passage makes it clear, therefore, that when Yahweh fixes his eyes on his people (9.4), there will be no escape.

Before we then turn to the concluding oracle of salvation in Amos 9.11-15, it should be noted that v. 10 once again discloses the delusive self-assurance so characteristic of Amos's audience. The words חטאי עמי האמרים לא־תגיש ותקדים בעדינו הרעה are an apt summarizing description of the attitude of the prophet's audience. And as such, they are of importance for the interpretation of the book as a whole. Any interpretation, either knowingly or unconsciously, operates with some kind of hermeneutical key. Wolff and many following in his wake found this key in Amos 8.2, a passage that prompted them to regard Amos as a preacher of unconditional and unlimited doom. However, this understanding, in turn, led to sections that were incongruous with this view to be ascribed to subsequent editors bent on adapting the prophet's message for later generations.

Over against this line of interpretation, I would contend that a statement like the one in 9.10 provides a more suitable hermeneutical key than Amos 8.2. And if v. 10 were taken to be inauthentic, a judgment that in the light of the conclusions reached above seems both unnecessary and unconvincing, the whole thrust of the debate as presented by the book of Amos in its entirety confirms its point. I therefore want to suggest that one of the hermeneutical keys to the book is the perception that Amos is portrayed as arguing a case against a people who find it hard to respond appropriately. However, this perception, in turn, calls for a rhetorical-critical reading that reckons with overstatements, deliberate provocations and so on. One of the main advantages of such a reading is that it can account for all the data and thus does not require major textual surgery. And, it should be noted, it makes perfect sense in the light of the rhetorical (or historical) situation outlined above.

This then takes us to the salvation oracle in Amos 9.11-15. Contra Wellhausen and his followers, it needs to be pointed out that this passage does not mitigate, let alone negate, the message of judgment.[139] Indeed, the preceding verses, Amos 9.1-10, had just unmistakably underlined the severity and ineluctability of the divine punishment, at the same time making it clear, however, that Yahweh's intervention will not lead to the

---

139. Cf. Wellhausen, *Die kleinen Propheten*, p. 96.

people's total annihilation. If, as I have argued above, this is implied also by those passages that are generally assumed to be Amosian (the distinction between culprits and victims so crucial for the prophet's message would seem to suggest that it is), there would be no contradiction between 9.11-15 and the rest of the book. True, the salvation oracle does sound a strikingly different note when compared to the announcements of judgment prevalent throughout the book. And yet, there is no discord, as its message makes perfect sense in the light of the rhetorical horizon of Amos's message as a whole.[140] The חטאי עמי will perish (according to the book, they clearly account for a major part of the population) but there is a glimmer of hope for some.

This notion of hope, when understood in terms of persuasive rhetoric, fulfils a dual function. It encourages those who are not to be counted among the חטאי עמי by pointing beyond the divine judgment to a time when Israel's fortunes will be restored. But, at the same time, it is also an attempt to motivate the audience to change their lifestyle, indicating what they would have to gain by not being part of the חטאי עמי. Thus while all the announcements of judgment provide 'negative motivation' (by warning the addressees *not* to do something), the salvation oracle in 9.11-15 offers 'positive motivation'.[141] It does that mainly by appealing to the

---

140. A detailed investigation of Amos 9.11-15 is not possible within the confines of this study. Readers are referred therefore to Rudolph, *Joel, Amos, Obadja, Jona*, pp. 278-87, whose interpretation I largely follow. He stresses, first, that the סכת דויד הנפלת in v. 11 refers to the divided kingdom, which will be rebuilt כימי עולם, i.e. as in the time of David and Solomon. Secondly, he takes the phrase יירשו את־שארית אדום (v. 12) to indicate territorial possession, with שארית suggesting that some parts of Edom were already under Israelite control when the announcement was made. This, Rudolph notes, was the case in Amos's time when Elath was 'restored to Judah' (cf. 2 Kgs 14.22). Not long afterwards, however, the Edomites were able to recover Elath (cf. 2 Kgs 16.6). This Rudolph, *Joel, Amos, Obadja, Jona*, p. 282, sees as important evidence for the passage's authenticity because in exilic and postexilic times up to the period of the Maccabees and Hasmonaeans there was no other political constellation that would allow us to assume any part of Edom to be under Judaean control. Indeed, Rudolph concludes that 'unsere Exegese nichts ergeben hat, was gegen Amos spräche, daß im Gegenteil "der Rest Edoms" (V. 12) eindeutig für Amos entscheidet, und da sich zugleich die Einheitlichkeit des ganzen Abschnitts herausgestellt hat, läßt sich für ihn mit guten Gründen eben wegen V. 12 die Echtheit verfechten' (*Joel, Amos, Obadja, Jona*, p. 285).

141. Cf. Watts, 'Rhetorical Strategy', pp. 12-14, who employs the concept of motivation in his investigation of the rhetorical function of the Pentateuchal blessings and curses. Deut. 30.15 combines positive and negative motivation, asking the people

audience's emotions, thus falling within the Aristotelian category of *pathos*. As Walton notes, a 'speaker may face hostility from the audience and need to overcome it, especially in the exordium and the epilogue'.[142]

In our specific case, this works on two levels. Amos himself, in his own context, could only achieve his aims by having something positive to offer in addition to all the judgment talk, which however had to be the main focus, given the people's extraordinary complacency. On the level of the book as it has come down to us, Amos 9.11-15 clearly serves as the final attempt at inducing the readership to react favourably to the message conveyed by means of the presentation of Amos's debate with his eighth-century audience.[143] It is also interesting to note, in this context, that the book closes with the words אמר יהוה אלהיך, the only time in Amos that יהוה אלהיך, 'Yahweh, *your* God', speaks to the people. This too seems to be motivated by rhetorical purposes in that it clearly reinforces the emotional impact of the book's ending, thus playing its part in the attempt to elicit a positive response from the readership.

d. *Concluding Remarks on the Arrangement and Rhetorical Strategy*
One of the key aspects of the analysis offered above is the suggestion that Amos is presented by the book as interacting with his audience. Sometimes this is made explicit, as in 2.12; 4.1; 6.13; 7.10, 11, 16; 8.5, 14 and 9.10 where the people's reactions, beliefs, suppositions and so on are quoted. Hoffman has pointed out that in these cases, 'popular cliché[s] [frequently serve] as a basis for a dispute'.[144] Even more interesting, however, is the observation by Carroll R. who notes that 'whenever others beside the prophet speak in this textual world they condemn themselves with their own words. Those who break into the steady condemnatory oracles of Yahweh only confirm their perversity and empty pretensions'.[145]

Yet, at other times the audience's reaction is 'merely' implied as, for example, in Amos 3.2. This has been seen by Vollmer who notes that the historical motives in 3.2 and 9.7 originated in the prophet's discussion with his audience. They are answers to objections voiced by Amos's hearers, seeking to invalidate his message of judgment by appealing to

---

to choose between את־החיים ואת־הטוב ואת־המות ואת־הרע.

142. Walton, 'Rhetorical Criticism', p. 5.

143. Cf. Möller, 'Rehabilitation', pp. 50-51, for further comments.

144. Y. Hoffman, 'A North Israelite Typological Myth and a Judaean Historical Tradition: The Exodus in Hosea and Amos', *VT* 39 (1989), pp. 169-82 (180).

145. Carroll R., *Contexts*, p. 202.

Yahweh's historical acts on Israel's behalf.[146] As we saw earlier, the presence of this dialogical dimension is not all that surprising given that the prophets' ministry was, by its very nature, quite confrontational.

What needs to be stressed at this point, however, is that the arrangement of the book of Amos results in some kind of 'dramaesque' development or 'narrativity'. Watts and House have suggested respectively that books such as Isaiah and Zephaniah be read as 'prophetic dramas'.[147] To be sure, their approach is beset with a number of difficulties. For instance, Watts's division of the text into different speeches assigned to various characters (such as a herald, Yahweh, the Heavens and the Earth, the people of Jerusalem, the prophet, etc.) is, as he himself admits, quite imaginative, lacking any clearly defined criteria.[148]

146. J. Vollmer, *Geschichtliche Rückblicke und Motive in der Prophetie des Amos, Hosea und Jesaja* (BZAW, 119; Berlin: W. de Gruyter, 1971), p. 20.

147. See J.D.W. Watts, *Isaiah 1–33* (WBC, 24; Waco, TX: Word Books, 1985), esp. pp. xliv-liv; *idem*, *Isaiah 34–66* (WBC, 25; Waco, TX: Word Books, 1987); and P.R. House, *Zephaniah: A Prophetic Drama* (BLS, 16; Sheffield: Almond Press, 1988). Cf. also *idem*, *The Unity of the Twelve* (JSOTSup, 97; BLS, 27; Sheffield: Almond Press, 1990).

148. In addition, it should be noted that Watts, having to explain the lack of signs of dramatic presentation in the texts, relies on what are rather speculative historical considerations. Arguing that in ancient Israel drama originated in the cult (he refers to Exod. 7.16; Gen. 14.18-21; Exod. 12.1; 1 Kgs 8 as well as the Psalms), Watts goes on to describe its development as follows: 'Prophecy, having already established a vehicle of protest and of change, now moved beyond the individual figure to literary (and dramatic) forums. Wisdom (the schools) moved in to fill the vacuum. Village festival lore moved into the center of the people's consciousness (the Festal Scrolls). Not bound to either cult or king, literature (including drama) could look critically at life and history and could ask questions beyond those allowed in the cult. The Deuteronomic History, Jeremiah, and Ezekiel belong here.

This era also produced a second wave of prophetic drama and literature to help gain perspective on the Exile. This included Isaiah and the Book of the Twelve Prophets. It brought Wisdom to the fore in Proverbs and Job, which probed the meaning of guilt and spoke of the way ahead' (*Isaiah 1–33*, p. xlvii).

Watts also speaks of a third (Deuteronomy) and a fourth wave (Chronicles, the Zion-Psalms, and Ezra–Nehemiah) but the most peculiar part of his theory is his explanation of the lack of signs of dramatic presentation in the biblical texts. He surmises that 'in Athens, Socrates accused the theater of having destroyed his credibility, but a reforming and moralistic city put the philosopher to death instead of judging the theater. In Jerusalem, at close to the same time, Ezra was incensed at the profligacy of the city and ordered reforms that sealed the people off from surrounding cultures and effectively suppressed the thriving literary (and dramatic) movement.

Yet this criticism notwithstanding, there often is, certainly in the book of Amos, some kind of what I have called 'dramaesque development' by which I mean a progressive interaction of the book's *dramatis personae* (e.g., Amos and his audience). Thus, for instance, by joining a judgment oracle condemning Israel (2.13-16) to a passage that refutes or reinterprets one of the people's cherished traditions (3.1-2), the editors have captured the dialogical dimension of Amos's interaction with his audience. More than that, the very juxtaposition of these passages now reproduces the dialogue in the book, resulting in a kind of 'narrativity', which I contend not to be accidental. Indeed, this 'narrativity' is an integral part of the book's persuasive rhetoric, presenting as it does the debate between the prophet and his audience.

What Wolff once said about the rhetorical questions in Amos 3.3-8 therefore appears to be true for the book of Amos in general. Noting that rhetorical questions stir up 'the emotions through the self-evident lack of necessity for such an interrogative formulation', Wolff went on to say that in the text as it now stands, 'the reader can still perceive the atmosphere of passionate controversy'.[149] 'By being drawn into the flow of the argument, the reader—just as the first hearer—is to be convinced that it was Yahweh's own speaking which irresistibly compelled Amos to issue his terrifying proclamation'.[150] Throughout the book, this drawing in of the reader into the debate between Amos and his audience is intended to induce readers to contemplate the behaviour of Amos's original audience as well as its outcome. Readers are presented with a choice, as it were: to act as the original audience and suffer the consequences (consider the past-fulfilment perspective mentioned earlier) or to let themselves be warned not to repeat the mistakes of Amos's addressees.

However, this reading raises the question of whether it is legitimate to interpret the textual arrangement along the lines suggested above. Or would that be an overinterpretation? This is precisely the charge Davies has levelled against Wolff's reading of Hosea. Davies notes that according to Wolff the 'kerygmatic units' in Hosea 'were the record of particular appearances of the prophet (*Auftrittsskizzen*), the later sayings often being

---

Some of the best of its products have survived, *shorn of almost all signs of their dramatic presentation*. In stodgy literary clothes they have lost some of their power and brilliance...' (*Isaiah 1–33*, p. xlviii; italics mine).

149. Wolff, *Joel and Amos*, p. 183 (the statement about the force of rhetorical questions is a quote from Lausberg's *Elemente der literarischen Rhetorik*).

150. Wolff, *Joel and Amos*, p. 184.

his responses to objections raised by his audience which the tradition did not preserve'.[151] Being unconvinced, Davies comments that:

> this is an interesting theory, with some support in the text, and if it is correct it presents us with some very vivid evidence of the cut-and-thrust of a prophet in debate with his audience. But the facts which it is designed to explain can just as well be explained by envisaging a process whereby utterances on similar subjects were strung together as a convenient way of giving some order to the collections.[152]

The issue at stake is whether the redactors actually intended to present these 'Auftrittsskizzen' or, in our case, the debate I reckon to have detected in the book of Amos. As far as Hosea is concerned, Davies prefers to see its arrangement simply as an attempt to achieve an ordered collection of oracles. In the case of Amos, however, we have already seen that no thematic or chronological arrangement can be demonstrated. Yet, the structural and literary features discussed in the previous chapter clearly indicate that whoever was responsible for the book was interested in presenting a well-structured work. So where, then, does that leave us? Is it likely that the authors or editors intended the book to be read as the presentation of a debate between Amos and his audience? Or am I making too much of joints and seams that are nothing but the accidental outcome of the material's compilation into a book?

151. G.I. Davies, *Hosea* (OTG; Sheffield: JSOT Press, 1993), p. 103; cf. H.W. Wolff, *Dodekapropheton. I. Hosea* (BKAT, 14.1; Neukirchen–Vluyn: Neukirchener Verlag, 4th edn, 1990), pp. xxiii-xxvii. For additional comments on his concept of 'Auftrittsskizzen', see H.W. Wolff, 'Haggai literarhistorisch untersucht', in *idem*, *Studien zur Prophetie*, pp. 129-42, where he refers to W.A.M. Beuken, *Haggai–Sacharja 1–8: Studien zur Überlieferungsgeschichte der frühnachexilischen Prophetie* (StSN, 10; Assen: Van Gorcum, 1967), pp. 204-205, 335.

The concept of 'Auftrittsskizzen' is not without problems. See, e.g., E. Bons, *Das Buch Hosea* (Neuer Stuttgarter Kommentar: Altes Testament, 23.1; Stuttgart: Katholisches Bibelwerk, 1996), p. 17, who rightly notes that 'Eingewandt wurde allerdings gegen die Theorie der "Auftrittsskizzen", daß sie eine Redesituation postuliert, in die sie die oft wenig zusammenhängend erscheinenden hoseanischen Sprüche einbettet. Der Kommentator verfaßt somit eine Art Biographie des Propheten, in die er dessen so disparat überlieferten Aussagen einordnet.' This, to repeat the point made earlier in my discussion of Shaw's reading of Micah, is not what I am envisaging. The larger prophetic discourses found in the book of Amos are better understood as a secondary development in its transmission history. They do not (normally) reproduce Amos's original speeches but consist of a collection of editorially arranged oracles. For fuller discussion see Möller, 'Hear this Word', pp. 499-500, 507-509.

152. Davies, *Hosea*, p. 103.

In order to answer these questions, we must distinguish between the intention of the real author and that of the text or its implied author. In the introduction, I have argued for a communication-theoretical framework of interpretation in which the author's intention matters as *one* side of the hermeneutical triangle (consisting of author, text and reader). Yet, as the real author's actual intention cannot be ascertained, all we can attempt to do is to look in the text for the intention of its implied author. As this is inscribed in the text, it is often called the intention of the text (*intentio operis*). Eco stresses its importance for evaluating conflicting interpretations, noting that 'between the unattainable intention of the author and the arguable intention of the reader there is the transparent intention of the text, which disproves an untenable interpretation'.[153]

However, one of the means by which to trace the *intentio operis* is precisely the text's arrangement or structure. Eco illustrates this with a fascinating example. Commenting on the reception of his novel *Il nome della rosa*, Eco looks at the interpretation of two passages dealing with the theme of 'haste'. Since these appear in close proximity, readers have naturally interpreted one reference in the light of the other despite the fact that Eco, as the 'real author', claims not to have intended any specific relationship between the two.[154] Yet, Eco acknowledges the validity of interpretations that relate the two passages to one another, noting that the text as it stands creates its own meaning connections (intertextuality). He admits finding it difficult to make sense of the conflict between the two passages in question, yet understands that it does have a meaning (or even many meanings) even though these were not intended.[155]

In similar vein, Brown and Yule note that readers are always going to attempt to make sense of a text as it stands. 'The natural effort of hearers and readers alike is to attribute relevance and coherence to the text they encounter until they are forced not to'.[156] Thus, whether or not the dialogical dimension in the book of Amos is intentional (in the sense of it having

---

153. Eco, 'Author and Text', p. 78.

154. Eco, 'Author and Text', p. 74; cf. also *idem, Nachschrift zum 'Namen der Rose'* (trans. B. Kroeber; Munich: Deutscher Taschenbuch Verlag, 8th edn, 1987), pp. 12-13. Eco interestingly points out that one of the passages was not part of the original manuscript but was inserted later on in order to create a literary bridge. Indeed, Eco furthermore notes that, when inserting the second passage, he was completely unaware of the thematic correspondence with the first (Eco, 'Author and Text', p. 74).

155. Eco, *Nachschrift*, pp. 13-14.

156. Brown and Yule, *Discourse Analysis*, p. 66.

been intended by the book's real authors), we, as readers, cannot but rely on the text. And it is on its basis that all interpretations, including this one, must be judged.

Thus far, I have discussed the rhetorical structure of the book of Amos, its rhetorical situation and the specific problem that occasioned its compilation. I have also looked at the rhetorical strategy and have outlined the debate between Amos and his audience presented in the book. Up to this point, that is to say, the focus has been on the rhetoric of the book as a whole. However, in order to illustrate the exegetical implications and relevance of the approach applied in the present study, I will now take a closer look at Amos 1–4. In addition to general exegetical and structural issues, the focus will be on the individual units' rhetorical function. This will help us understand the development of the 'argument', as we follow the debate up to the point where Amos voices his ominous warning that Israel must prepare itself for a meeting with Yahweh (4.12-13). It would, of course, have been desirable to offer a detailed investigation of the book as a whole but due to space limitations, it has become necessary to concentrate on the first three major rhetorical units: the OAN in Amos 1–2 as well as the following two discourses in Amos 3.1-15 and 4.1-13.[157]

157. For an application of the approach adopted here to the book of Amos as a whole see my forthcoming commentary in the Two Horizons Old Testament Commentary Series published by Eerdmans.

Part II
THE RHETORIC OF AMOS 1–4

Chapter 3

Amos 1–2

When compared to the other Old Testament prophetic books, Amos stands out because of its unique introduction consisting of a series of oracles against foreign nations. Not surprisingly, therefore, scholars have devoted much thought to the reasons for this peculiarity. Although some find these still elusive,[1] there is now widespread agreement that the answer has to be sought along rhetorical lines. Amos 1.3–2.16, whatever its textual history, needs to be read as a whole, its rhetorical impact depending heavily on such a reading strategy. This observation is highly significant for the present study since the very existence of a large rhetorical unit like Amos 1–2 makes the quest for similarly extensive sections in Amos plausible. However, before we turn to the investigation of the structure and rhetorical function of the OAN, we need to take a close look at the book's prologue in vv. 1-2. Setting the scene for all that follows, it too performs an important rhetorical function.

1. *Amos 1.1-2*

The prologue consists of a historical superscription (v. 1) and what is often called the book's motto (v. 2). While the superscription briefly introduces the prophet Amos[2] and puts the דברי עמוס in the context of a particular

1.   V. Fritz, 'Die Fremdvölkersprüche des Amos', *VT* 37 (1987), pp. 26-38 (26), for instance, finds the positioning of this pericope incomprehensible (cf. also p. 38; and *idem*, 'Amosbuch, Amos-Schule und historischer Amos', in *idem*, Pohlmann and Schmitt [eds.], *Prophet und Prophetenbuch*, pp. 29-43 [34]).
2.   Studies on Amos's origin, social background and occupation include K. Budde, 'Die Überschrift des Buches Amos und des Propheten Heimat', in G.A. Kohut (ed.), *Semitic Studies in Memory of Rev. Dr. Alexander Kohut* (Berlin: Calvary, 1897), pp. 106-10; H. Schmidt, 'Die Herkunft des Propheten Amos', in K. Marti (ed.), *Beiträge zur alttestamentlichen Wissenschaft: Karl Budde zum siebzigsten Geburtstag* (BZAW, 34; Giessen: Alfred Töpelmann, 1920), pp. 158-71; M. Bič, 'Der Prophet Amos—ein

period in Israel's history,[3] the motto, portraying Yahweh as a roaring lion whose roar causes great anxiety, introduces the book's rather gloomy mood.

a. *Exegetical Observations and Structure*

The structure of Amos 1.1 is fairly complex (cf. Figure 4 below), include-ing two relative sentences introduced by אשר together with two further temporal expressions (a double בימי phrase and the words שנתים לפני הרעש). This observation, together with the fact that the prophecy is

Haepatoskopos?', *VT* 1 (1951), pp. 293-96; A. Murtonen, 'The Prophet Amos—A Hepatoscoper?', *VT* 2 (1952), pp. 170-71; A.S. Kapelrud, *Central Ideas in Amos* (Oslo: Aschehoug, 1956), pp. 5-7; H.J. Stoebe, 'Der Prophet Amos und sein bürgerlicher Beruf', *WuD* 5 (1957), pp. 160-81; S. Segert, 'Zur Bedeutung des Wortes *nōqēd*', in B. Hartmann *et al.* (eds.), *Hebräische Wortforschung: Festschrift zum 80. Geburtstag von Walter Baumgartner* (VTSup, 16; Leiden: E.J. Brill, 1967), pp. 279-83; T. Yamashita, 'Noqed', in L.R. Fisher (ed.), *Ras Shamra Parallels: The Texts from Ugarit and the Hebrew Bible*, II (AnOr, 50; Rome: Pontifical Biblical Institute, 1975), pp. 63-64; T.J. Wright, 'Did Amos Inspect Livers?', *AusBR* 23 (1975), pp. 3-11; S. Speier, 'Bemerkungen zu Amos', *VT* 3 (1953), pp. 305-10; Wagner, 'Überlegungen'; C.D. Isbell, 'A Note on Amos 1.1', *JNES* 36 (1977), pp. 213-14; M. Dietrich and O. Loretz, 'Die ugaritische Berufsgruppe der *NQDM* und das Amt des *RB NQDM*', *UF* 9 (1977), pp. 336-37; Koch, *Prophets*, p. 70; P.C. Craigie, 'Amos the *nōqēd* in the Light of Ugaritic', *SR* 11 (1982), pp. 29-33; H. Weippert, 'Amos: Seine Bilder und ihr Millieu', in *idem*, Seybold and Weippert, *Beiträge zur prophetischen Bildsprache*, pp. 1-29 (1-5); Rosenbaum, *Amos of Israel*, chs. 3-4; *idem*, 'Northern Amos Revisited: Two Philological Suggestions', *Hebrew Studies* 18 (1977), pp. 132-48; G.F. Hasel, *Under-standing the Book of Amos: Basic Issues in Current Interpretations* (Grand Rapids: Baker Book House, 1991), chs. 2, 4; I. Cornelius, 'נקד', in *NIDOTTE*, III, p. 151; P.D.F. Strijdom, 'What Tekoa Did to Amos', *OTE* 9 (1996), pp. 273-93; R.W. Byargeon, 'Amos: The Man and His Times', *Southwestern Journal of Theology* 38.1 (1995), pp. 4-10.

3.   On Amos's historical context see F. Dijkema, 'Le fond des prophéties d'Amos', in *OTS*, 2 (Leiden: E.J. Brill, 1943), pp. 18-34; Morgenstern, 'Amos Studies II'; T.J. Meek, 'The Accusative of Time in Amos 1.1', *JAOS* 61 (1941), pp. 63-64, 190-91; S. Cohen, 'The Political Background of the Words of Amos', *HUCA* 36 (1965), pp. 153-60; M. Haran, 'The Rise and Decline of the Empire of Jeroboam ben Joash', *VT* 17 (1967), pp. 266-97; J.A. Soggin, 'Das Erdbeben von Amos 1 1 und die Chronologie der Könige Ussia und Jotham von Juda', *ZAW* 82 (1970), pp. 117-21; M. Schwantes, *Das Land kann seine Worte nicht ertragen: Meditationen zu Amos* (trans. I. Kayser; Munich: Chr. Kaiser Verlag, 1991), ch. 1; Rosenbaum, *Amos of Israel*, ch. 2; J.A. Burger, 'Amos: A Historical-geographical View', *Journal for Semitics* 4 (1992), pp. 130-50; and C. Levin, 'Amos und Jerobeam I.', *VT* 45 (1995), pp. 307-17.

referred to by the phrases דבר *and* חזה, has led to a number of theories concerning the redaction history of Amos 1.1 in particular and the book of Amos in general.[4] Often the two terms are taken to refer to distinctive collections of prophetic material within the book of Amos, identified respectively as the 'words' (Amos 3–6) and visions (Amos 7–9).[5]

However, already Jepsen has argued that חזה, when used for a נביא, functions as a technical term for the receipt of divine revelation in general or the divine *word* in particular.[6] Jepsen even claims that 'visual manifestation...plays no role, or at most a minor one'.[7] This usage is confirmed by Mic. 1.1, another prophetic superscription, which reads דבר־יהוה אשר היה אל־מיכה...אשר־חזה. Since the book of Micah contains no visions, Wolff rightly notes that in this context, being used of the 'word of Yahweh', a collection of sayings, חזה does not denote a specifically visionary experience but, more generally, the reception of a revelation.[8] Such an

---

4.   Cf. Weiser, *Buch der zwölf kleinen Propheten*, p. 131; *idem, Profetie*, pp. 252-56; Wolff, *Joel and Amos*, pp. 117-21; Jeremias, *Book of Amos*, pp. 11-13; *idem*, 'Zwei Jahre', p. 186; H.F. Fuhs, 'Amos 1,1: Erwägungen zur Tradition und Redaktion des Amosbuches', in H.-J. Fabry (ed.), *Bausteine biblischer Theologie: Festgabe für G. Johannes Botterweck zum 60. Geburtstag dargebracht von seinen Schülern* (BBB, 50; Cologne: Peter Hanstein: 1977), pp. 271-89 (281); and recently Rottzoll, *Studien*, pp. 8-16.

5.   Cf. R. Smend, *Die Entstehung des Alten Testaments* (TW, 1; Stuttgart: W. Kohlhammer, 2nd rev. edn, 1978), p. 173; Fosbroke, 'Book of Amos', p. 778; Amsler, 'Amos', p. 167; Polley, *Amos*, p. 5; and Jeremias, *Book of Amos*, p. 12. For an evaluation of this proposal, see the section entitled 'Reconsidering "Words" and "Visions"' in Chapter 1.

6.   A. Jepsen, 'מַחֲזֶה, מְחֱזֶה, חִזָּיוֹן, חָזוּת, חֲזוּת, חָזוֹן, חֹזֶה, חָזָה', in *TDOT*, IV, pp. 280-90 (283-84). According to Ben Zvi, *Obadiah*, p. 12 n. 11, at least seventy-five per cent of the occurrences of the root חזה/י in the Old Testament are in the context of prophecy.

7.   Jepsen, 'חָזָה', p. 284; against Wolff, *Joel and Amos*, p. 124, who believes that חזה 'refers to the reception of visions'. D.L. Petersen, *The Roles of Israel's Prophets* (JSOTSup, 17; Sheffield: JSOT Press, 1981), p. 86, oddly claims that according to Jepsen the significant aspect of the root חזה is the visual mode of revelation.

8.   H.W. Wolff, *Dodekapropheton. IV. Micha* (BKAT, 14.4; Neukirchen–Vluyn: Neukirchener Verlag, 1982), p. 6, who interestingly references Isa. 2.1 and Amos 1.1 in this context. On the aural dimension of חזה cf. further J. Calvin, *A Commentary on the Twelve Minor Prophets. II. Joel, Amos and Obadiah* (trans. J. Owen; Calvin Translation Society, 1846; repr., Edinburgh: Banner of Truth Trust, 1986 [1846]), p. 148; Stuart, *Hosea–Jonah*, p. 298; Weiser, *Buch der zwölf kleinen Propheten*, p. 234; Ben Zvi, *Obadiah*, p. 12; *HALAT* sub חָזוֹן 2.; and Tg, where חזה in Amos 1.1 is rendered as 'prophesied'.

interpretation of חזה is most appropriate also in the case of Amos 1.1, which therefore does not point to a distinction between two prophetic 'modes', that is, words and visions.[9] Nor does it hint at the book's twofold structure.

Turning to the complex syntax of v. 1, it needs to be stressed that the second אשר is best seen as parallel to the first one so that both are modifying עמוס.[10] The alternative option, according to which the second אשר refers to דברי, unnecessarily complicates the grammatical construction,[11] also leaving us with the problematic statement that Amos saw the words of Amos.[12] If, on the other hand, both relative clauses are taken to modify עמוס, the verse would say that the book contains the words of Amos *who saw*, i.e. who functioned as an agent of divine revelation.

The following two temporal expressions then specify when it was that Amos 'saw' the words concerning Israel, namely during the prosperous and peaceful[13] period of the kings Uzziah of Judah and Jeroboam ben Joash of Israel (c. 780–740 BCE)[14] or, more precisely, 'two years before the

9. Against van der Wal, 'Structure of Amos', p. 108.

10. Against LXX (λόγοι...οὓς εἶδεν; the Greek translators even relate the first relative sentence to דברי, rendering it λόγοι...οἳ ἐγένοντο), Vg (*verba Amos...quae vidit*), NRSV, KJV, NIV, NASB and most exegetes. The view advocated here is shared by Weiser, *Buch der zwölf kleinen Propheten*, p. 131; Maag, *Text*, p. 2; Rudolph, *Joel, Amos, Obadja, Jona*, p. 110 (he lists further proponents); Andersen and Freedman, *Amos*, pp. 188-89; Bovati and Meynet, *Le livre du prophète Amos*, p. 26; Rottzoll, *Studien*, p. 12; and Fuhs, 'Amos 1,1', pp. 277-78, who is probably right to suggest that the prevalent translation is influenced by the superscriptions in Isa. 2.1 (הדבר אשר חזה); Mic. 1.1 (...דבר־יהוה) and Hab. 1.1 (...המשא).

11. It is considered awkward, for instance, by Fosbroke, 'Book of Amos', p. 777; J. Theis, 'Der Prophet Amos', in J. Lippl and J. Theis, *Die zwölf kleinen Propheten. 1. Osee, Joel, Amos, Abdias, Jonas, Michäas* (HSAT, 8.3.1; Bonn: Peter Hanstein, 1937), pp. 107-37 (113); and Wolff, *Joel and Amos*, p. 117.

12. One would rather have expected the prophet to 'see' the words of Yahweh as, for instance, in Mic. 1.1. See Wolff, *Joel and Amos*, p. 118; Rudolph, *Joel, Amos, Obadja, Jona*, p. 110; and Andersen and Freedman, *Amos*, p. 189.

13. Cf. Calvin, *Minor Prophets*, pp. 149-50; Harper, *Commentary*, pp. 5-6; Robinson, 'Hosea bis Micha', p. 75; Weiser, *Buch der zwölf kleinen Propheten*, p. 131; J.-L. Vesco, 'Amos de Teqoa, défenseur de l'homme', *RB* 87 (1980), pp. 481-513; King, *Amos, Hosea, Micah*, p. 22; and Bovati and Meynet, *Le livre du prophète Amos*, p. 32.

14. Sometimes this synchronistic dating is seen as the mark of a deuteronomistic redactor; cf. Mays, *Amos*, p. 18; Schmidt, 'Die deuteronomistic Redaktion', p. 170;

earthquake'.[15] Referred to as הרעש, the quake is apparently supposed to be well known by the book's hearers or readers,[16] indicating that, given the frequency of earthquakes in Israel,[17] it must have been an extremely violent and unparalleled one.

Finally, it should be noted that the verse, despite its syntactical complexity, does not contain any contradictory information.[18] Its structure can be outlined as follows.

G.M. Tucker, 'Prophetic Superscriptions and the Growth of a Canon', in Coats and Long (eds.), *Canon and Authority*, pp. 56-70 (60, 69); cf. *idem, Form Criticism of the Old Testament* (GBS; Philadelphia: Fortress Press, 1971), pp. 71-72.

15. This probably indicates that Amos's public appearance was confined to the short period of less than one year (Wolff, *Joel and Amos*, p. 124; Rudolph, *Joel, Amos, Obadja, Jona*, pp. 114-15; Jeremias, *Book of Amos*, p. 13; and G. Pfeifer, *Die Theologie des Propheten Amos* [Frankfurt: Peter Lang, 1995], p. 24), though some understand the phrase in a durative sense, 'during two years...' (e.g., Bovati and Meynet, *Le livre du prophète Amos*, p. 27).

16. It is also referred to in Zech. 14.4-5 and Josephus, *Ant.* 9.222-227.

17. Cf. D.H. Kallner-Amiran, 'A Revised Earthquake Catalogue of Palestine', *IEJ* 1 (1950–51), pp. 223-46; and *IEJ* 2 (1952), pp. 48-65; and J. Milgrom, 'Did Isaiah Prophesy during the Reign of Uzziah?', *VT* 14 (1964), pp. 178-82. The earthquake in Amos 1.1 is often identified as the one attested at stratum VI of Hazor for which a date of 760 BCE has been suggested (Y. Yadin *et al., Hazor II: An Account of the Second Season of Excavations, 1956* [Jerusalem: Magnes Press, 1960], pp. 24-37; followed by Soggin, 'Erdbeben'; Wolff, *Joel and Amos*, p. 124; Mays, *Amos*, p. 20; Paul, *Amos*, p. 35; Smith, *Amos*, pp. 25-26; Gowan, 'Book of Amos', p. 352; and D.K. Ogden, 'The Earthquake Motif in the Book of Amos', in K.-D. Schunck and M. Augustin [eds.], *Goldene Äpfel in silbernen Schalen. Collected Communications to the XIIIth Congress of the International Organization for the Study of the Old Testament, Leuven 1989* [BEATAJ, 20; Frankfurt: Peter Lang, 1992], pp. 69-80 [69-72]). However, Y. Yadin, 'Hazor', in M. Avi-Yonah (ed.), *Encyclopedia of Archaeological Excavations in the Holy Land*, II (London: Oxford University Press, 1976), pp. 474-95 (485, 495), later on corrected his proposal, suggesting a much broader time-frame, i.e., the first half of the century (Blenkinsopp, *History of Prophecy*, pp. 127-28 n. 31, reasons that the more precise date given earlier was itself based on the supposed date of Amos's ministry rather than on archaeological data). Others maintain that even the identification of the earthquake in Amos 1.1 as the one attested at Hazor remains tentative (Rudolph, *Joel, Amos, Obadja, Jona*, p. 114; and Jeremias, *Book of Amos*, p. 13).

18. Contra Fuhs, 'Amos 1,1', p. 274, who thinks that the words שנתים לפני הרעש and the two בימי phrases conflict with one another. However, while the reference to the earthquake narrows down the period of Amos's ministry, it does not contradict the information given in the בימי phrases.

דברי עמוס
אשר־היה בנקדים[19] מתקוע
אשר חזה על־ישראל

בימי עזיה מלך־יהודה
ובימי ירבעם בן־יואש מלך ישראל
שנתים לפני הרעש

Figure 6. *The Structure of Amos 1.1*

The motto in v. 2 is introduced by ויאמר, a phrase that is part of the book's 'narrative frame' surfacing only here and in Amos 7,[20] where the Amaziah encounter is told using *wayyiqtol* forms. However, ויאמר in Amos 1.2 introduces not only the short utterance in 1.2 but the entire book as Amos's speech.[21]

ויאמר	1.2
וישלח אמציה	7.10
ויאמר אמציה	7.12
ויען עמוס	7.14

Figure 7. *The 'Narrative-Frame' of Amos*

19. מתקוע defines the origin of the נקדים (C.F. Keil, *The Minor Prophets* [COT, 10; Edinburgh: T. & T. Clark, 1866–91; repr., Peabody, MA: Hendrickson, 1996], p. 157; Harper, *Commentary*, p. 3; H. Guthe, 'Der Prophet Amos', in E. Kautzsch and A. Bertholet [eds.], *Die Heilige Schrift des Alten Testaments*, II [Tübingen, 4th edn, 1923; repr., Hildesheim: Georg Olms, 1971], pp. 30-47 [31]; S. Terrien, 'Amos and Wisdom', in B.W. Anderson and W. Harrelson [eds.], *Israel's Prophetic Heritage: Essays in Honor of James Muilenburg* [New York: Harper, 1962], pp. 108-15 [114 n. 13]; I. Willi-Plein, *Vorformen der Schriftexegese innerhalb des Alten Testaments: Untersuchungen zum literarischen Werden der auf Amos, Hosea und Micha zurückgehenden Bücher im hebräischen Zwölfprophetenbuch* [BZAW, 123; Berlin: W. de Gruyter, 1971], p. 15; and Stuart, *Hosea–Jonah*, p. 296) rather than modifying עמוס (Schmidt, 'Die deuteronomisticsche Redaktion', p. 170; Wolff, *Joel and Amos*, p. 117; Rudolph, *Joel, Amos, Obadja, Jona*, pp. 109-10; and Fuhs, 'Amos 1,1', p. 275). For partitive מן ('from') cf. GK §119v; JM §133e; WO'C §11.2.11b; see also Andersen and Freedman, *Amos*, pp. 186-87.

20. A.W. Park, *The Book of Amos as Composed and Read in Antiquity* (Studies in Biblical Literature, 37; New York: Peter Lang, 2001), pp. 47-48, is on the right track in presenting all of Amos 1.3–9.15 as the 'Editorial Presentation of the Prophetic Account of YHWH's Speech'. Proper consideration of the book's narrative frame, however, would require the inclusion 1.2 in this editorial presentation as well as paying attention to the 'narrator's' comments in 7.10-17. Park rightly identifies this passage as a 'prophetic story' presented as a third person report but wrongly includes it in the editorial presentation of the prophet's account of Yahweh's speech.

21. Meier, *Speaking*, pp. 228-29, notes that this phenomenon is unique within the prophetic canon.

Most exegetes interpret v. 2 in the context of Israel's theophanic tradition.[22] According to this understanding, Yahweh's roaring manifests itself in a thunderstorm (v. 2a).[23] This interpretation, however, is open to discussion, as I shall demonstrate by looking at the terms שָׁאַג and נתן קול in 2a. The theophanic interpretation of Amos 1.2 is based, among other reasons,[24] on the latter phrase, which—when combined with Yahweh as its

22. Cf. Weiser, *Buch der zwölf kleinen Propheten*, pp. 131-32; Wagner, 'Über-legungen', p. 660; J.J. Niehaus, *God at Sinai: Covenant and Theophany in the Bible and Ancient Near East* (SOTBT; Carlisle: Paternoster Press, 1995), p. 309; Crenshaw, 'Amos', p. 211; B. Kedar-Kopfstein, 'קוֹל', in *ThWAT*, VI, pp. 1237-52 (1249). For a distinction between 'theophanies' and 'epiphanies', cf. C. Westermann, *Lob und Klage in den Psalmen* (Göttingen: Vandenhoeck & Ruprecht, 1977), pp. 69-76; F. Schnuten-haus, 'Das Kommen und Erscheinen Gottes im Alten Testament', *ZAW* 76 (1964), pp. 1-22 (2); and J. Jeremias, *Theophanie: Die Geschichte einer alttestamentlichen Gattung* (WMANT, 10; Neukirchen–Vluyn: Neukirchener Verlag, 2nd edn, 1977).

23. Wellhausen, *Die kleinen Propheten*, p. 67; W. Nowack, *Die kleinen Propheten übersetzt und erklärt* (HKAT, 3.4; Göttingen: Vandenhoeck & Ruprecht, 2nd edn, 1903), p. 128; Budde, 'Text und Auslegung', pp. 51-53; Gressmann, *Geschichts-schreibung*, p. 331; C. van Leeuwen, 'Amos 1.2, Épigraphe du livre entier ou intro-duction aux oracles des chapitres 1–2?', in M. Boertien (ed.), *Verkenningen in een Stromgebied. Proeven von oudtestamentisch Onderzoek. Festschrift M.A. Beek* (Amster-dam: Theologisch Instituut, 1974), pp. 93-101; Niehaus, *God*, p. 309. A. Bertholet, 'Zu Amos 1.2', in *Theologische Festschrift. G. Nathanael Bonwetsch zu seinem 70. Geburtstag* (Leipzig: Deichert, 1918), pp. 1-12, believed that this thunderstorm marked Amos's call to prophesy; but cf. Weiser, *Profetie*, pp. 79-85.

Others think of an earthquake (J. Morgenstern, 'Amos Studies I', *HUCA* 11 [1936], pp. 19-140 [137 n. 144]; Weiser, *Profetie*, p. 84) or an easterly wind (Guthe, 'Der Prophet Amos', p. 31), or they understand the text as referring to the divine voice, word, wrath, or self-revelation (J. Lindblom, *Die literarische Gattung der propheti-schen Literatur* [Uppsala Universitetsårskrift Theologi, 1; Uppsala: Lundquist, 1924], pp. 70-71; *idem, Prophecy in Ancient Israel* [Oxford: Basil Blackwell, 1962], p. 116; I.P. Seierstad, 'Erlebnis und Gehorsam beim Propheten Amos', *ZAW* 52 [1934], pp. 22-41 [25]; Maag, *Text*, p. 197; and A. Bentzen, 'The Ritual Background of Amos 1,2-2,16', in P.A.H. de Boer [ed.], *OTS*, 8[Leiden: E.J. Brill, 1950], pp. 85-99 [95-96]). For a detailed discussion cf. M. Weiss, 'Methodologisches über die Behandlung der Metapher dargelegt an Am. 1,2', *TZ* 23 (1967), pp. 1-25 (6-15); and *idem, The Bible from Within: The Method of Total Interpretation* (Jerusalem: Magnes Press, 1984), pp. 196-207.

24. Formal characteristics have also played a role (cf. the works mentioned in n. 23) but Wolff, *Joel and Amos*, pp. 118-19, while supporting the 'theophanic inter-pretation', notes that formally Amos 1.2 differs considerably from other theophanies. Cf. also Pfeifer, *Theologie*, p. 127; Smith, *Amos*, p. 18; and Hayes, *Amos*, p. 63, who

subject—in the majority of Old Testament passages indicates thunder.[25] However, as this is not always the case,[26] its precise connotation has to be determined on the basis of the context in which it is used. In the case of Amos 1.2, it is the combination of נתן קול with שאג that deserves special attention. This collocation, with Yahweh as subject, also appears in the parallel passages Jer. 25.30 and Joel 4.16. While the former contains no obvious allusions to a thunderstorm, the focus being on the mighty voice of Yahweh instead (cf. the accumulation of expressions denoting a loud voice: הידד)...יענה, שאג ישאג, יתן קולו, ישאג),[27] this is clearly different in Joel 4.16. There the dramatic account of the nation's judgment in the valley of Jehoshaphat (vv. 9-14) together with the description of cosmic upheaval (v. 15) makes a theophanic interpretation of v. 16 entirely feasible.

Yet, Amos 1.2 is best understood as portraying Yahweh as a roaring lion.[28] As we have seen, נתן קול appears to have the same meaning also in Jer. 25.30. Further confirmation is supplied by two references in which the combination of שאג and נתן קול is actually used in connection with lions (i.e., Jer. 2.15 and Amos 3.4). These passages demonstrate that both expressions, שאג and נתן קול, *can* signify the roaring of a lion. In addition, Amos 3.8—where Yahweh's speech is compared to a lion's roar—obviously refers back to Amos 1.2.[29] Finally, reference should be made to

stresses that in genuine theophanic texts, the deity *comes* from some locale in order to intervene in a certain situation, which is not the case here.

25. Cf. Exod. 9.23; 1 Sam. 12.17-18; 2 Sam. 22.14; Pss. 18.14; 46.7; 68.34. The same applies to numerous ANE occurrences many of which refer to a storm-god who reveals himself primarily in the sound of thunder (cf. Jeremias, *Theophanie*, pp. 73-90; and F.M. Cross, *Canaanite Myth and Hebrew Epic: Essays in the History of the Religion of Israel* [Cambridge, MA: Harvard University Press, 1973], pp. 148-56).

26. Cf. 2 Chron. 24.9; Prov. 1.20; 2.3; 8.1; Jer. 4.16; 22.20; 48.34 and Lam. 2.7, where the phrase simply indicates a loud voice or sound.

27. McKane, *Commentary*, p. 648, understands נתן קול as an 'utterance of threats'; cf. also R.K. Harrison, *Jeremiah and Lamentations: An Introduction and Commentary* (TOTC; Leicester: InterVarsity Press, 1973), pp. 126-27; against F. Nötscher, *Das Buch Jeremias übersetzt und erklärt* (HSAT, 7.2; Bonn: Peter Hanstein, 1934), pp. 193-94; and J.A. Thompson, *The Book of Jeremiah* (NICOT; Grand Rapids: Eerdmans, 1980), pp. 518-19. While it could be argued that the accumulation of metaphors might include a reference to thunder as well, the sequence שאג ישאג, יתן קולו, ישאג, i.e., the framing of נתן קול by two occurrences of שאג, makes this unlikely.

28. Thus also Maag, *Text*, pp. 195-97.

29. Cf. Andersen and Freedman, *Amos*, pp. 225-26; and P.C. Craigie, *The Twelve Prophets*. I. *Hosea, Joel, Amos, Obadiah, and Jonah* (Edinburgh: Saint Andrew Press,

the Middle Assyrian 'Fable of the Fox' where the dog, a disputant against
the fox and the wolf, describes his own strength in the following terms:
'My strength is overpowering, I am the claw of the Zû-bird, a very lion...
At my terrible bellow the mountains and the rivers dry up [*e-ta-na-ab-ba-
la-a*; cf. אבל in Amos 1.2].'[30] This passage, which is clearly not a
theophany, indicates that the drying up of mountains, pastures and rivers
should be understood as symbolizing the fear caused by the roar of
Yahweh or, in the case of the fable, the dog.[31]

The interpretation of Amos 1.2 is further aggravated in that the relationship between the two halves of the verse is not easy to define.[32] However,
Weiss has rightly emphasized that we should not expect a clear logical
relationship between them. He notes that 'it is methodologically unsound
to argue against the unity of our verse or against the understanding of the
tenor of its metaphors on the grounds that there is a logical discrepancy
between the two parts of the verse'.[33] Reflecting on the nature of metaphors in general, he points out that metaphors are 'demiurgic tools' the
function of which is to supply analogies and correspondences.[34] Using
poetic language, the text paints a picture of the effects the powerful voice
of Yahweh is going to have. Weiss comments: 'True, in the world of
nature, roaring only leads to fright, trembling and flight but in the world,
which forms itself in the soul, developing in and by means of a linguistic
construction, roaring can even lead to drought.'[35]

Another interesting feature of Amos 1.2a is the use of the terms מציון
and מירושלם, which appear in prominent position, thus emphasizing the

1984), p. 126.

30. Quoted from W.G. Lambert, *Babylonian Wisdom Literature* (Oxford: Clarendon Press, 1960), pp. 192-93 (= Vorderasiatisches Museum Berlin, Vorderasiat. Abt.
Tontafeln 13836 lines 16, 18).

31. Cf. Weiss, 'Methodologisches', p. 14. For the use of lion imagery to portray a
divine judgment cf. A. Benson, '"From the Mouth of the Lion": The Messianism of
Amos', *CBQ* 19 (1957), pp. 199-212 (199-200); and W.E. Staples, 'Epic Motifs in
Amos', *JNES* 25 (1966), pp. 106-12 (109).

32. Hence, some have concluded that it contains two originally independent
elements; thus Budde, 'Text und Auslegung', p. 53 (cf. *idem*, 'Amos 1 2', *ZAW* 30
[1910], pp. 37-41); and H. Gressmann, *Der Ursprung der israelitisch-jüdischen
Eschatologie* (FRLANT, 6; Göttingen: Vandenhoeck & Ruprecht, 1905), p. 23.

33. Weiss, *Bible*, p. 202.

34. Weiss, *Bible*, p. 202; cf. *idem*, 'Methodologisches', p. 11.

35. Weiss, 'Methodologisches', p. 19.

locale from which Yahweh's roar goes forth.[36] Whether the verse is an integral part of Amos's original message[37]—perhaps an utterance that, having been considered an apt condensation of his message, was placed at the head of the book containing his words[38]—or has been added by a later Judaean, possibly deuteronomistic, redactor,[39] Blenkinsopp rightly notes that it 'has the effect of deriving the divine judgment...from the Jerusalem temple as its ultimate source'.[40]

But what exactly are the consequences of Yahweh's roar; 'do [the pastures] dry up, or is it that they mourn?'[41] Sometimes a root אבל[II], 'drying up', is assumed.[42] Yet this is not listed in the older lexica, and its existence is now again questioned by many.[43] Clines notes that the main reason

36. Cf. Polley, *Amos*, p. 110.

37. Duhm, 'Anmerkungen', p. 1; Seierstad, 'Erlebnis und Gehorsam', p. 25; Robinson, 'Hosea bis Micha', p. 75; Botterweck, 'Authentizität', pp. 177-78; H. Gottlieb, 'Amos und Jerusalem', *VT* 17 (1967), pp. 430-63 (452); Wagner, 'Überlegungen', pp. 659-61; Rudolph, *Joel, Amos, Obadja, Jona*, p. 117 n. 37; Pfeifer, *Theologie*, p. 25; and Achtemeier, *Minor Prophets I*, p. 176.

38. Cf. Andersen and Freedman, *Amos*, p. 222. R.E. Clements, *Prophecy and Covenant* (SBT, 43; London: SCM Press, 1965), p. 43 n. 1, points out that 'no absolute ground for denying [the verse] to Amos exists'.

39. Cf. Harper, *Commentary*, pp. 9-10; Weiser, *Profetie*, pp. 85, 265; Wolff, *Joel and Amos*, pp. 121-22; M.L. Barré, 'Amos', in R.E. Brown, J.A. Fitzmyer and R.E. Murphy (eds.), *The New Jerome Bible Commentary* (London: Geoffrey Chapman, 1989), pp. 209-16 (210); and Jeremias, *Book of Amos*, p. 13.

40. Blenkinsopp, *History of Prophecy*, pp. 88-89.

41. M.D. Carroll R., 'God and His People in the Nations' History: A Contextualised Reading of Amos 1-2', *TynBul* 47 (1996), pp. 39-70 (58). Weiss, 'Methodologisches', p. 7 n. 28, notes that most interpreters understand 2b as depicting a drought. Others have thought of a devastation or dereliction (Duhm, 'Anmerkungen', p. 1; E. Sellin, *Das Zwölfprophetenbuch*. I. *Hosea–Micha* [KAT, 12.1; Leipzig: Deichert, 3rd edn, 1929], *ad loc.*) or have understood the text allegorically (Kapelrud, *Central Ideas*, p. 19; cf. Tg). For a detailed account of these proposals, cf. Weiss, 'Methodologisches', pp. 16-23

42. Its existence was proposed by G.R. Driver, 'Confused Hebrew Roots', in B. Schindler and A. Marmorstein (eds.), *Occident and Orient, Being Studies in Semitic Philology and Literature, Jewish History and Philosophy and Folklore in the Widest Sense, in Honour of Haham Dr. M. Gaster's 80th Birthday* (London: Taylor's Foreign Press, 1936), pp. 73-82 (73-75), and accepted by KB; *HALAT*; GMD; Maag, *Text*, p. 117; and R.E. Hayden, 'אבל', in *NIDOTTE*, I, p. 248; cf. also NEB, NIV, NRSV.

43. Cf. GB; BDB; *HAW*; F. Stolz, 'אבל', in E. Jenni and C. Westermann (eds.), *Theological Lexicon of the Old Testament*, I (Peabody, MA: Hendrickson, 1997), pp. 21-23 (21); A. Baumann, 'אָבַל, אָבֵל, אֵבֶל', in *TDOT*, I, pp. 44-48; A. Oliver, 'אבל', in *NIDOTTE*, I, pp. 243-48 (244); and esp. recently D.J.A. Clines, 'Was There an *'bl* II

behind the proposal for אבלII was that scholars found it odd for inanimate objects to be portrayed as mourning.[44] But since the textual data does not support the existence of a homonym אבלII, we are required to take the verb to indicate 'mourning'. On the other hand, in the present context אבל is followed by יבש, a root that clearly indicates 'being or becoming dry'.[45] Interestingly, however, יבש can also be used metaphorically to signify distress or even death.[46] Thus, the two lines complement one another other in that the first evokes the notion of mourning, which fits very well with the lion imagery in the preceding line, while the second specifies its outward manifestation, the drying up or withering.[47] This being so, both verbs could go with the נאות הרעים as well as ראש הכרמל, thus reinforcing each other. On the other hand, the present order might be significant in that the mourning or withering of the top of Carmel is even more surprising and staggering than the mourning or withering of the shepherds' pastures.[48] Thus while the predicate of the second line interprets the idea of the first line,[49] in the case of the subjects, the second line adds what has been called 'heightening or intensification'.[50] Amos 1.2, therefore, is a good illustration of parallelism being dynamic rather than static,[51] of being an instance of 'A, and what's more, B', to employ Kugel's words.[52]

"Be Dry" in Classical Hebrew?', *VT* 42 (1992), pp. 1-10; and *DCH*. See also J. Scharbert, *Der Schmerz im Alten Testament* (BBB, 8; Bonn: Peter Hanstein, 1955), pp. 47-58; E. Kutsch, '"Trauerbräuche" und "Selbstminderungsriten" im Alten Testament', *Theologische Studien* 78 (1965), pp. 23-42; R. Bultmann, 'πένθος, πενθέω', in *TWNT*, VI, pp. 40-43 (41-42); Koch, 'Rolle', p. 532 n. 104; Jeremias, *Book of Amos*, p. 11 n. 1; LXX, KJV, NASB and KT.

44. Clines, '*'bl* II'.

45. See H.D. Preuss, 'יָבֵשׁ, יָבְשָׁה, יַבֶּשֶׁת', in *TDOT*, V, pp. 373-79; and R.E. Hayden, 'יבשׁ', in *NIDOTTE*, II, pp. 393-94.

46. Cf. Ps. 22.16; Job 14.11-12; Ezek. 37.11. The combination of both verbs occurs also in Jer. 12.4; 23.10.

47. Cf. Clines, '*'bl* II', p. 9.

48. The mountainous region of Carmel was famous for its abundant vegetation; M.J. Mulder, 'כַּרְמֶל', in *TDOT*, VII, pp. 325-36 (330); cf. *idem*, 'Carmel', in van der Toorn, Becking and van der Horst (eds.), *Dictionary of Deities and Demons in the Bible*, pp. 182-85; and see Isa. 35.2; Jer. 50.19 and Nah. 1.4. According to Harper, *Commentary*, p. 11, 'the greatest calamity imaginable would be the withering of Carmel'.

49. Alter, *Art of Biblical Poetry*, p. 19, more vividly speaks of 'dramatization'.

50. Alter, *Art of Biblical Poetry*, p. 19.

51. Cf. again Alter, *Art of Biblical Poetry*, pp. 10-11, who cites Shklovsky ('The purpose of parallelism...is to transfer the usual perception of an object into the sphere

b. *Rhetorical Function*

'The beginning of a novel is a threshold, separating the real world we inhabit from the world the novelist has imagined. It should therefore, as the phrase goes, "draw us in".'[53] Although the book of Amos differs considerably from a novel, the requirement of 'drawing the reader or hearer in', here voiced by Lodge, is a prerequisite for the opening of rhetorical discourse as well. The writer or editor of Amos was obviously aware of this, as can be seen especially from Amos 1.2. Here the 'drawing in effect' is achieved by utilising powerful poetic language that is both highly pictographic[54] and ambiguous. In addition, the opening section also provides readers with important information. Both, the facts and the 'emotive appeal', are intended to shape and guide our interpretation of the text.[55] As Callow notes:

> it is to be expected that an author would use the opening words to orient the reader/hearer to what is to follow, to give them some clues as to what to expect, and hence to enable them to bring to the front of their minds relevant frames and concepts within which the author's work is to be understood.[56]

And as far as readers are concerned, Ben Zvi has pointed out that:

> it is expected that after reading the opening sentence or paragraph of a book...(re)readers would attempt to develop a working model of what the book is about, and, of course, about its basic genre. Needless to say, even a

of a new perception' [p. 10]; cf. V. Shklovsky, 'Art as Technique', in L.T. Lemon and M.J. Reis [eds.], *Russian Formalist Criticism: Four Essays* [Lincoln: University of Nebraska Press, 1965], pp. 3-24 [21]), noting that already J.G. Herder, *Vom Geist der ebräischen Poesie: Eine Einleitung für die Liebhaber derselben, und der ältesten Geschichte des menschlichen Geistes* (2 vols.; Dessau, 1782–83) questioned Lowth's influential 'static' parallelism theory (cf. R. Lowth, *Lectures on the Sacred Poetry of the Hebrews* [London: Tegg, 1835]). This had already been pointed out before by Kraus, *Geschichte*, p. 119.

52. J. Kugel, *The Idea of Biblical Poetry: Parallelism and Its History* (New Haven: Yale University Press, 1981), p. 58.

53. D. Lodge, 'Beginning', in *idem, The Art of Fiction*, pp. 3-8 (5).

54. Andersen and Freedman, *Amos*, p. 228, speak of a 'balance and synthesis between the realistic and the mythic'.

55. Cf. Davies, *Hosea*, p. 106. Jeremias, *Book of Amos*, p. 13, calls Amos 1.2 an 'initial aid to understanding' (the German edition has 'Lesehilfe' ['reading aid']; J. Jeremias, *Der Prophet Amos* [ATD, 24.2; Göttingen: Vandenhoeck & Ruprecht, 1995], p. 3).

56. Callow, 'Units and Flow', pp. 475-76.

tentative decision concerning the theme and genre of the text strongly
influences the following reading.[57]

At the outset of our encounter with the book of Amos, we are first of all
informed in v. 1 that what we are about to read are the דברי עמוס. We are
not given many details about this Amos, however, except that he was
among the נקדים from Tekoa, that he functioned as an agent of divine
revelation and that he appeared in public during a certain period of Israel's
history.

The claim that Amos received divine revelation is arguably the most
important point, inviting readers or hearers to regard the prophet's words
as authorized by Yahweh. Fuhs rightly notes that the phrase עמוס אשר חזה
legitimizes the prophet 'as a spokesman, called and authorised by Yahweh'.[58] It functions as a 'Legitimationsausweis' (a certificate of legitimization).[59] From a rhetorical point of view, this grounding of 'the authority
and legitimacy of [Amos's] message...on God'[60] is of great consequence
for the reading of the subsequent material. Ben Zvi, noting the predominant association of the root חזה/י with prophecy, is therefore correct
to highlight that 'on another level, the title claims that a prophetic book is
"prophecy".[61] Accordingly, it suggests that the communal reading and

57. Ben Zvi, *Obadiah*, p. 37.
58. Fuhs, 'Amos 1,1', p. 284; cf. Ben Zvi, *Obadiah*, p. 12, who notes that 'naming
a vision is tantamount to a claim for the legitimacy and social authority of the vision'.
59. Usually, it is the call narratives that are classified as 'Legitimationsausweis' or
'Legitimationsurkunde'; cf. J. Jeremias, 'Grundtendenzen gegenwärtiger Prophetenforschung', in *idem*, *Hosea und Amos*, 1-19 (14-15).
60. Thus Ben Zvi, *Obadiah*, p. 38, commenting on חזון in Obad. 1; cf. Finley, *Joel,
Amos, Obadiah*, p. 126; and Bovati and Meynet, *Le livre du prophète Amos*, p. 31.
61. There is an ongoing debate on the nature of prophecy and whether the so-called
writing prophets were actually prophets; cf. the articles in *JSOT* 27 (1983) by A.G.
Auld, 'Prophets through the Looking Glass: Between Writings and Moses', pp. 3-23;
R.P. Carroll, 'Poets not Prophets: A Response to "Prophets through the Looking Glass"
', pp. 25-31; H.G.M. Williamson, 'A Response to A.G. Auld', pp. 33-39; and A.G.
Auld, 'Prophets through the Looking Glass: A Response to Robert Carroll and Hugh
Williamson', pp. 41-44; and in *JSOT* 48 (1990) by T.W. Overholt, 'Prophecy in His-
tory: The Social Reality of Intermediation', pp. 3-29; A.G. Auld, 'Prophecy in Books:
A Rejoinder', pp. 31-32; R.P. Carroll, 'Whose Prophet? Whose History? Whose Social
Reality? Troubling the Interpretative Community Again: Notes towards a Response to
T.W. Overholt's Critique', pp. 33-49; and T.W. Overholt, ' "It is Difficult to Read" ',
pp. 51-54.
See also J. Jarick, 'Prophets and Losses: Some Themes in Recent Study of the
Prophets', *ExpTim* 107 (1995–96), pp. 75-77, for a brief summary of that debate; and

learning of this book is akin to receiving prophecy, to get acquainted with YHWH's message.'[62] One can, of course, reject such a textual claim, but the fact remains that the text itself urges its readers or hearers to read the book of Amos as the 'words that Amos saw', that he received as divine revelation.[63]

Given such an authoritative claim, it is interesting to note that the only personal information about Amos is that he 'was among the shepherds of Tekoa'.[64] And it is only later in the book that the prophet himself explains the significance of this detail. In his famous encounter with Amaziah, he points out that he is/was[65] not a prophet nor does/did he belong to a prophetic school but he is/was a בוקר and a בולס שקמים. Yet, Yahweh took him from following the flock and commanded him to prophesy (הנבא; Amos 7.14-15). In contrast to these more detailed explanations, the superscription merely informs us that Amos was one of the shepherds from Tekoa who, nonetheless, became the agent of divine revelation. The text thus accents the prophet's lay background.[66]

Amos 1.1 also sets out the historical framework in which the book is to be understood. Its material is said to relate to the eighth century BCE, or to

B. Vawter, 'Were the Prophets *nābî's*?', *Bib* 66 (1985), pp. 206-19; R.P. Carroll, 'Night Without Vision: Micah and the Prophets', in F. García Martínez, A. Hilhorst and C.J. Labuschagne (eds.), *The Scriptures and the Scrolls: Studies in Honour of A.S. van der Woude on the Occasion of his 65th Birthday* (VTSup, 49; Leiden: E.J. Brill, 1992), pp. 74-84; H.M. Barstad, 'No Prophets? Recent Developments in Biblical Prophetic Research and Ancient Near Eastern Prophecy', *JSOT* 57 (1993), pp. 39-60; and M.S. Odell, 'The Prophets and the End of Hosea', in Watts and House (eds.), *Forming Prophetic Literature*, pp. 158-70; for further developments.

62. Ben Zvi, *Obadiah*, p. 38 (cf. also p. 12).

63. On the authoritative claim of the biblical literature in general cf. K. Stendahl, 'The Bible as a Classic and the Bible as Holy Scripture', in House (ed.), *Beyond Form Criticism*, pp. 39-46. P. Ricœur, 'Toward a Hermeneutic of the Idea of Revelation', *HTR* 70 (1977), pp. 1-37 (3), differentiating prophetic, narrative, prescriptive and wisdom discourse, notes that only prophetic discourse claims this kind of authority of being 'pronounced in the name of [God]'.

64. Some have remarked that Amos's style betrays his former career as a shepherd or farmer; cf. Keil, *Minor Prophets*, p. 159; and Weippert, 'Amos'.

65. Amos 7.14 has generated an extensive debate about Amos's understanding of his own status and the nature of Israelite prophecy in general. One important question is whether the nominal clauses should be understood as present or as past tense. For a detailed review of the debate cf. Å. Viberg, 'Amos 7.14: A Case of Subtle Irony', *TynBul* 47 (1996), pp. 91-114.

66. Finley, *Joel, Amos, Obadiah*, p. 125.

be more precise, to the time of King Uzziah of Judah and King Jeroboam ben Joash of Israel. This is an important point that has not always received the attention it deserves. However, Darr commenting on the book of Isaiah, has justly emphasized that 'text's invitation to read Isaiah as what it purports to be—the vision that the eighth-century prophet saw'.[67] A similar point has been made by Rendtorff, noting that 'the books themselves always give the historical framework in which they are to be read and understood'.[68] Childs, *too*, concurs with this stance when he criticizes Wolff because his 'historical interpretation of the redactional layers of Amos has the effect of reading the biblical text from a perspective which often runs counter to that demanded by the literature itself'.[69]

These remarks clearly call for an approach that takes the text's synchronic dimension seriously, acknowledging, for instance, the interpretative value of the prophetic superscriptions. Concerning the latter, Ben Zvi has correctly stressed that they represent the author's point of view and that, for that reason, they should be taken into account.[70] Yet, this still leaves us with a number of possible approaches, as Ben Zvi himself demonstrates. For the superscriptions could be taken literally as indicating that the book of Amos contains the actual words the prophet spoke. Or the oracles included in the book could be regarded as representing Amos's message in *essentia*; or again the superscription might just 'provide the literary hero who holds together otherwise diverse traditions'.[71] Hence, Rendtorff is correct to stress that the employment of synchronic methods does not cause the diachronic questions to disappear.[72]

How important these diachronic questions are, becomes clear when we consider Carroll's lament, voiced in an article discussing the interpretation of Jeremiah, that 'the colophon [i.e., Jer. 1.1-3] is an inflection of the tradition which has given rise to so many misreadings of the book'.[73] Which route, then, shall we take? Are we to accept the text's invitation to

67. Darr, 'Literary Perspectives', p. 141.

68. Rendtorff, 'Old Testament Theology: Some Ideas for a New Approach', in *idem, Canon and Theology*, pp. 1-16 (11).

69. Childs, *Introduction*, p. 408.

70. Ben Zvi, *Zephaniah*, p. 11.

71. For these possibilities see Ben Zvi, *Zephaniah*, p. 11.

72. Rendtorff, 'Historical Criticism', p. 28.

73. R.P. Carroll, 'Arguing About Jeremiah: Recent Studies and the Nature of a Prophetic Book', in J.A. Emerton (ed.), *Congress Volume, Leuven 1989* (VTSup, 43; Leiden: E.J. Brill, 1991), pp. 222-35 (230; italics added).

read the *entire* book of Amos against an eighth-century background, as Darr has suggested for Isaiah? Or would that be to misread the text, as Carroll claims has been the outcome in the case of Jeremiah? As has been pointed out already, I see no reason not to take the superscription Amos 1.1 seriously, that is, not to read the book's material against an eighth-century background. It is interesting to note in this context that an early eighth-century perspective has been maintained throughout the book. This can be seen in that, for instance, Assyria is never referred to by name, nor is the chaotic situation in Israel following the death of Jeroboam II reflected in any way.[74] Rofé calls such an assertion an *argumentum e silentio*, pointing to its limited value. Yet his own conclusion, that 'the interpolators and editors […] took care not to betray their time or place',[75] surely is a much more convoluted argument compared to the simple observation that the book of Amos does not mention Assyria.

To continue with the analysis of the superscription's rhetorical function, it is significant that the Judaean king Uzziah is mentioned first, a fact that appears to point to a Judaean readership.[76] These readers, as has already been noted above, I would locate historically after the fall of the northern kingdom but before the exile of Judah.[77] However, the text provides yet another interesting piece of information by situating Amos's ministry two years before the earthquake (הרעש). The rhetorical effect of this statement has been aptly described by Jeremias, noting that it forces readers to relate the threats of an earthquake that are interspersed throughout the book back to the earthquake that happened only two years after Amos's ministry. The reference to the earthquake therefore confirms and highlights the accuracy of the prophet's words.[78]

However, for a Judaean readership after the collapse of the northern kingdom in 722 BCE,[79] not only this earthquake but most of Amos's

74. See Blenkinsopp, *History of Prophecy*, p. 93; and Andersen and Freedman, *Amos*, p. 192.

75. A. Rofé, *Introduction to the Prophetic Literature* (trans. J.H. Seeligmann; BibSem, 21; Sheffield: Sheffield Academic Press, 1997), p. 34.

76. See Jeremias, 'Zwei Jahre', p. 185; and Stuart, *Hosea–Jonah*, pp. 297, 299.

77. See the discussion of the book's rhetorical situation in Chapter 2.

78. Jeremias, 'Zwei Jahre', p. 187; cf. Rudolph, *Joel, Amos, Obadja, Jona*, p. 110; and D.N. Freedman and A. Welch, 'Amos's Earthquake and Israelite Prophecy', in Coogan (ed.), *Scripture and Other Artifacts*, pp. 188-98.

79. The reference to *the* earthquake clearly indicates an early date for this remark as many have noted. But that still leaves the issue of the book's redaction history undecided since the superscription could have introduced originally a smaller book. Cf.

announcements (including, most significantly, the proclamation of exile) were already history. Thus while early readers would be likely to see the book's references to an earthquake they knew about as proof that Amos had been right about that quake, Judaean readers who had witnessed the exile of the northern state would have found even further proof for the reliability of Amos's words. Ben Zvi calls this a 'past-fulfilment' perspective, noting that it 'clearly strengthens the case for the fulfillment of the still unfulfilled section[s]'.[80] In the case of the readers I am envisaging here, this would include the salvation oracle in Amos 9. More to the point, however, this 'past-fulfilment perspective' carries an implicit warning that the same fate might be in store for the southern kingdom if they replicate the attitude of Amos's original hearers.

Having discussed the hermeneutical implications of Amos 1.1 in some detail, we now turn to the rhetorical effects of the motto in v. 2.[81] We have already seen that it, together with the bulk of the material, is presented as the prophet's words. The implications of this are highlighted by Ben Zvi, noting that 'direct (quoted) speech connotes objectivity, a sense that the words are reported exactly as spoken, and even more so, that the readers are—as it were—at the scene, listening to the envoy'.[82] Direct speech thus 'dramatizes' the discourse, as Wendland remarks,[83] and thereby 'draws the reader in' who is about to meet the prophet Amos delivering his stern message.

That it is going to be a stern message already becomes clear at this point, as v. 2 right at the outset introduces the book's gloomy mood.[84] Moreover, as Lindblom rightly notes, the verse seems to be 'placed here in order to prepare and evoke the appropriate emotional response to all the

the contrasting views in Jeremias, *Book of Amos*, p. 13; *idem*, 'Zwei Jahre', pp. 187-95; Wolff, *Joel and Amos*, p. 120; Rudolph, *Joel, Amos, Obadja, Jona*, p. 115; and Andersen and Freedman, *Amos*, p. 195.

80. Ben Zvi, *Obadiah*, p. 39.

81. Scholars disagree about the relationship between v. 2 and its context (see Weiss, 'Methodologisches', pp. 5-6; and Paul, *Amos*, p. 36 n. 39). In my view, v. 2 is best seen as a sub-unit of the book's prologue, which consists of the superscription in v. 1 and the motto in v. 2. It is, after all, closely linked to the preceding verse by means of ויאמר the referent of which is עמוס in v. 1 (see Keil, *Minor Prophets*, p. 163).

82. Ben Zvi, *Obadiah*, p. 36 n. 110.

83. Wendland, 'Discourse Analysis', p. 4.

84. Cf. J. Dines, 'Reading the Book of Amos', *ScrB* 16 (1986), pp. 26-32 (27); Weiser, *Buch der zwölf kleinen Propheten*, p. 132; and Niehaus, 'Amos', p. 338, who calls it 'a terrible introduction'.

oracles which follow'.[85] The metaphor depicting Yahweh as a lion indicates that there is danger looming at the horizon.[86] But it is not yet apparent
what the exact implications of Yahweh's roar are going to be. Does it
indicate that the deity is going to attack somebody? And if so, who will be
his target?[87] Or is his voice the prime referent so that the verse would hint
at what the words concerning Israel (עַל־יִשְׂרָאֵל) will be like? This un-
resolved ambiguity creates tension and suspense as the reader or hearer
wonders how Yahweh is going to act.[88] In any case, the negative connotations, which are evoked here, are reinforced by the illustration of the
devastating effects of Yahweh's action in the next line.[89] Baumann notes
that the use of אבל in this context, with reference to nature or vegetation,
emphasizes the totality of the judgment: 'even nature participates in the
humiliation, the "diminution" of the people struck with the calamity'.[90]

85. Lindblom, *Prophecy*, p. 116. I do not agree, however, with his cultic interpretation (pp. 116-17).

86. Van Leeuwen, 'Amos 1.2', p. 94; and Rudolph, *Joel, Amos, Obadja, Jona*,
p. 115, draw attention to the fact that the very first word Amos is said to have uttered
is the divine name יהוה.

87. Seen in the context of the Book of the Twelve as a whole, this question
becomes even more interesting. Amos 1.2a parallels Joel 4.16a. In both cases,
Yahweh's roar causes devastating effects. However, in Joel the image is followed by
the reassuring announcement that Yahweh will protect his people. This, in turn, is
followed by an oracle of salvation. Reading Joel and Amos consecutively, one cannot
but wonder, therefore, whether Amos is going to repeat Joel's reassuring message, an
idea that momentarily receives support by the subsequent oracles against foreign
nations in Amos 1.3–2.5. Yet, once the reader is confronted with the Israel oracle in
2.6-16, this notion turns out to be misconceived.

88. For a detailed discussion of the concept of ambiguity see Sternberg, *Poetics*, ch.
6, 'Gaps, Ambiguity and the Reading Process', and *passim*. See also D.M. Gunn and
D.N. Fewell, *Narrative in the Hebrew Bible* (OBS; Oxford: Oxford University Press,
1993), pp. 155-58 (a section termed 'Multivalence, ambiguity, and metaphor') and
passim.

89. Van Leeuwen, 'Amos 1.2', p. 99, comments: 'Il n'est, pourtant, pas impossible
qu'Amos ait déjà fait une allusion voilée au vrai dessein de son message dans sa description des effets de la théophanie en 1.2b' (cf. p. 100). See also Keil, *Minor Prophets*,
p. 164; Harper, *Commentary*, p. 9; von Orelli, *Die zwölf kleinen Propheten*, p. 61;
Cripps, *Commentary*, p. 115; J.J. Owens, 'Exegetical Studies in the Book of Amos',
RevExp 63 (1966), pp. 429-40 (429); and J.P. Hyatt, 'Amos', in M. Black and H.H.
Rowley (eds.), *Peake's Commentary on the Bible* (London: Nelson, 1962), pp. 617-25
(617), who all understand 1.2 as containing the message of the book in a nutshell.

90. Baumann, 'אָבַל', p. 47. The notion of 'diminution' has been suggested by

2. *Amos 1.3–2.16*

Having discussed the book's superscription, we now turn to the series of oracles against foreign nations (and Israel) in 1.3–2.16. As my main concern is the development of the argument throughout the book, it will not be necessary to deal with the individual strophes in detail. This is because, as has long been recognized, their rhetorical effect is due primarily to their structural arrangement, which will, therefore, be the chief focus in the subsequent investigation.

a. *Structural Arrangement*

The passage Amos 1.3–2.16 features a strophic arrangement in which all parts are built according to a comparatively regular pattern. Yet, while some elements recur in each strophe, there is also a principle of alternation at work in the series. It is therefore possible to distinguish between two types of strophes (cf. Figure 8). Pattern A is characterized by an elaboration on the nation's punishment and an additional (concluding) divine speech formula. The oracles against Aram (Damascus), Philistia (Gaza), Ammon and Moab are arranged according to this model. Pattern B (exemplified in the strophes dealing with Tyre, Edom, Judah and Israel), on the other hand, has an extended guilt section but lacks the elaboration on the punishment as well as the concluding divine speech formula.

(a)	A	B	divine speech formula (כה אמר יהוה)
(b)	A	B	formulaic reference to the nation's guilt (על־שלשה פשעי...ועל־ארבעה לא אשיבנו)
(c)	A	B	exemplary reference to a specific guilt (introduced by על)
(d)		B	elaborate guilt section
(e)	A	B	formulaic announcement of punishment (ושלחתי אש בבית...ואכלה ארמנות...)[91]

Kutsch, 'Trauerbräuche', pp. 23-42, who proposed that the root אבל not only entails the idea of being diminished by some catastrophe but also of 'self-diminution' as it describes the outward behaviour rather than the inner feelings of the mourner (cf. Maag, *Text*, pp. 115-16; and esp. H. Jahnow, *Das hebräische Leichenlied im Rahmen der Völkerdichtung* [BZAW, 36; Giessen: Alfred Töpelmann, 1923]).

91. A deviation from this formula occurs in 1.14 where והצתי is used instead of ושלחתי. Yet, there is no need for an 'emendation' because, as D.N. Freedman, 'Deliberate Deviation from an Established Pattern of Repetition in Hebrew Poetry as a Rhetorical Device', in *Proceedings of the Ninth World Congress of Jewish Studies.*

(f)	A		elaborate punishment section
(g)	A		concluding divine speech formula (אמר יהוה)[92]

Figure 8. *The Internal Structure of the OAN*[93]

The arrangement alternates between the two patterns described above to the effect that two strophes of the A-pattern are followed by two of the B-type, and so on. This results in three pairs of oracles dealing with foreign nations proper (AA/BB/AA) followed by the climactic strophes concerning Judah and Israel (BB*), as illustrated in Figure 9.

1.	A		Aram
2.	A		Philistia
3.		B	Tyre
4.		B	Edom
5.	A		Ammon
6.	A		Moab
7.		B	Judah
8.		B*	Israel

Figure 9. *The Alternating Arrangement (Pairing) of the OAN*[94]

The final strophe concerning Israel presents a case on its own. Parts (a) to (c) resemble those of the previous strophes while part (d), although being introduced by על like all the others, varies greatly in length, thus highlighting Israel's sin. Thereafter, the pattern breaks down completely. First, the formulaic announcement of punishment (e) is not repeated at all. Although the strophe does refer to the divine judgment, it seems to avoid replicating the vocabulary employed in the previous oracles. Interestingly, the judgment (f) is outlined in rather vague terms, the formulaic terminology of the preceding strophes having been abandoned entirely, and leaves open the question of what its precise nature is going to be. What vv. 13-16

Division A: The Period of the Bible (Jerusalem: World Union of Jewish Studies, 1986), pp. 45-52 (46), has pointed out, editors would have been more likely to substitute the repeated ושלחתי for the unusual והצתי than to introduce an irregularity. S. Segert, 'A Controlling Device for Copying Stereotype Passages? (Amos i 3–ii 8, vi 1-6)', *VT* 34 (1984), pp. 481-82, suggests that the deviation might reflect an attempt to guarantee correct copying.

92. Amos 1.8 has the extended formula אמר אדני יהוה, which appears to be a purely stylistic variation.

93. Andersen and Freedman, *Amos*, pp. 211-13, discuss this at length, offering their findings in tabular form.

94. See again Andersen and Freedman, *Amos*, pp. 203-206, for further structural observations; and see Park, *Book of Amos*, pp. 71-73, for a minute structural analysis.

are stressing instead, is the ineluctability of the divine intervention, an important feature that I will come back to later on.

A further deviation from the previous strophes occurs in vv. 9-11, which speak of Yahweh's salvific deeds on Israel's behalf, thereby introducing an entirely novel element. These verses are embedded within a section that lists Israel's manifold sins so that, by way of contrasting the people's behaviour with the divine acts, the inappropriateness of the former comes into sharp focus. Finally, as concerns (g), the Israel strophe features the oracle formula יהוה־נאם instead of the divine speech formula אמר יהוה found in the A-pattern. In fact, the phrase נאם־יהוה, the main function of which is to provide a 'highly local highlighting',[95] occurs twice (cf. vv. 11, 16). In v. 11, it accompanies a rhetorical question and the two devices concur in stressing the contrast between Yahweh's actions and those of the people.

> I destroyed…,
> I brought up…,
> and I raised…;
> 　　is it not so, O people of Israel?
> 　　*says the Lord*;
> 　　but you made…
> 　　and you commanded…!

Figure 10. *Local Highlighting in Amos 2.11*

The oracle formula also features at the end of v. 16 where it concludes and highlights the description of the judgment's ineluctability. The subsequent figure outlines the structure of the Israel oracle, at the same time displaying the main indicators of rhetorical emphasis.

Elaboration of Israel's guilt (vv. 6-8)

↔　*contrasted with Yahweh's acts on behalf of his people (vv. 9-11)*
　　…ואנכי (twice: vv. 9, 10)
　　divine confirmation (v. 11c): האף אין־זאת בני ישראל נאם יהוה
　　　　　　　　　　　　(i.e., rhetorical question + divine speech formula)

guilt resumed (v. 12)

→　*punishment: vague, ineluctability stressed (vv. 13-16)*
　　…הנה אנכי (v. 13)
　　divine confirmation (v. 16c): נאם יהוה

Figure 11. *The Rhetorical Structure of Amos 2.6-16*

95. See the discussion of speech and quotation formulas in Chapter 1.

b. *Rhetorical Emphases in and the Rhetorical Function of the OAN*
The objective of the following analysis of Amos 1.3–2.16 is to probe into its 'rhetorical design' in order to expose its rhetorical emphases as well as the overall rhetorical effect of this extensive section.[96] It is important, in this context, to direct our attention, first, to the various recurring formulas, as these contribute significantly to the passage's rhetorical effect. In addition to this, I will also discuss a number of general issues, which are of fundamental importance for the interpretation of Amos in general.

The Divine Speech Formula
To begin with, each oracle is introduced by the divine speech formula כה אמר יהוה, which stresses that what Amos has to say about the nations' 'crime and punishment' has to be seen ultimately as Yahweh's word. The emphasis of the divine origin of the prophetic message is designed to lend authority to all the statements that follow. Frye aptly called this an expression of the biblical 'voice of authority'.[97] However, Meier recently called into question the designation of the phrase...כה אמר as 'messenger formula'.[98] Investigating its use in the Old Testament and the ancient Near East, Meier concluded (1) that the phrase does not indicate messenger speech[99] and (2) that it is an optional feature that is not employed with any regularity in many early writing prophets,[100] so that (3) 'one may confidently argue that there is no perception of the prophet as messenger, for

96. Few sections have received as much attention as the OAN. For a concise summary of the main issues under debate see Hasel, *Understanding*, ch. 5, who lists most of the literature for 1967–89 (pp. 58-59 n. 3). Since then, the steady flow of articles on Amos 1–2 has never ceased.

97. Frye, *Great Code*, p. 212.

98. Meier, *Speaking*, pp. 273-98. That understanding had been advanced esp. by Lindblom, *Gattung*; L. Köhler, *Deuterojesaja (Jes 40–55) stilkritisch untersucht* (BZAW, 37; Giessen: Alfred Töpelmann, 1923), pp. 102-109; and Westermann, *Basic Forms*, pp. 98-128. Before Meier, doubts concerning the validity of the messenger concept had already been expressed by R. Rendtorff, 'Botenformel und Botenspruch', *ZAW* 74 (1962), pp. 165-77, and others (cf. Meier, *Speaking*, pp. 277-78). That scholars were working with an inappropriate definition became apparent particularly in H. Wildberger, *Jahwewort und prophetische Rede bei Jeremia* (Theologische Dissertationen, 2; Zürich: Zwingli-Verlag, 1942), p. 73, who felt compelled to conclude that 26 times in Jeremiah the 'messenger formula' is used incorrectly (cf. the critiques in Rendtorff, 'Botenformel und Botenspruch', p. 166 n. 7; and Meier, *Speaking*, p. 283).

99. Meier, *Speaking*, p. 278.

100. Meier, *Speaking*, p. 289.

God's voice is rarely identified'.[101] Meier, therefore, prefers to speak of a 'citation formula', which is much broader, thus fitting the diversity of the data better.[102]

Meier's analysis contains a number of incisive insights yet is marred in that he occasionally overstates his case. For instance, he draws too sharp a line between the 'desire to point to the words of God as distinct from man' evidenced by the sixth-century prophets and the implied absence of this interest in the earlier prophetic books.[103] To appropriate Meier's in many ways convincing results for the reading of Amos, some cautionary remarks are therefore pertinent. First, the phrase כה אמר יהוה is far from being rare in the book of Amos. Secondly, the divine origin of the prophet's words is highlighted also by means of various other phrases,[104] which indicates that it appears to have been an important concern to Amos and/or those responsible for the book.[105]

Moreover, I do not share Meier's expectation that 'once the citation dimension of the phrase...כה אמר is recognized, the debate over the significance of the verb tense in *kôh 'āmar yhwh* (present? past? perfect?) may recede'.[106] In particular, I do not agree with his verdict that 'the verb

101. Meier, *Speaking*, p. 289. Meier also notes that the term מלאך is never applied to the early writing prophets (p. 288).

102. Cf. Amos 7.10-11 where the words כה אמר עמוס do not refer to a messenger. Meier, *Speaking*, p. 290 n. 3, notes that the broader function of...כה אמר as a citation formula has already been acknowledged by Wolff, 'Zitat', p. 38; Westermann, *Basic Forms*, p. 58; and A.J. Bjørndalen, 'Zu den Zeitstufen der Zitatformel...כה אמר im Botenverkehr', *ZAW* 86 (1974), pp. 393-403 (393); but that that insight was over-shadowed by the messenger metaphor.

103. Cf. Meier, *Speaking*, pp. 289-90.

104. See the discussions of the use and distribution of speech and quotation formulas as well as references to the divine name in Chapter 1.

105. Meier, *Speaking*, p. 228, is aware of this. He notes that: 'Amos represents a curious mixture of a number of conventions in different parts of the book that show a high priority for marking explicitly God's voice.' This clearly stands regardless of his assertion that 'other parts of the book show a contrary reticence to be explicit as to who is speaking, even when it is clear that it is often God within some of these sections (3.2-9; 5.6-15, 18-26; 6.1-7)'.

106. For that discussion see esp. Bjørndalen, 'Zeitstufen'; but also W. Zimmerli, *Ezechiel* (BKAT, 13.1, 2; 2 vols.; Neukirchen–Vluyn: Neukirchener Verlag, 2nd edn, 1979), I, p. 73; *idem, Grundriss der alttestamentlichen Theologie* (TW, 3.1; Stuttgart: W. Kohlhammer, 6th edn, 1989), p. 87; von Rad, *Old Testament Theology*, II, pp. 36-37; Rendtorff, 'Botenformel und Botenspruch', p. 167 n. 8; and Wolff, *Joel and Amos*, p. 137.

must be translated as past'.[107] While the formula does refer to words that have been spoken in the past, it may still be rendered in the present tense since the citation represents the *continuously* valid view of the person quoted. Thus, Bjørndalen argues for a present tense translation even in the case of כה אמר עמוס in Amos 7.11 because the phrase introduces a 'timeless statement of facts' ('*zeitlose* Tatsachenfeststellung').[108] What Meier calls the 'over-theologizing of the verb tense when applied to God's speech'[109] is therefore not precluded by his definition of the phrase כה אמר יהוה as 'citation formula'. It may well be that the writing prophets did not conceive of themselves as Yahweh's messengers in a technical sense. Yet, the fact remains that Amos goes to great lengths to underline that he is, in one way or another, acting on Yahweh's behalf since he was taken from behind the flock and commanded to הנבא (7.15; cf. 3.8).[110]

It is, therefore, surely legitimate to conclude that the book portrays Amos as claiming divine authority for his message. And in that sense, the phrase here named 'divine speech formula' functions as a 'legitimization formula', even though it is not a 'messenger formula'.[111] Finally, when talking about a 'citation formula', one has to be careful not to apply twentieth-century notions about citations (this trap Meier certainly does not fall into). In using the words כה אמר יהוה, Amos is not indicating that he is repeating verbally the very words of Yahweh. In fact, the diversity of contexts in which the phrase...כה אמר appears in the Old Testament suggests that there was no general concern to distinguish formally between citations and paraphrases of somebody else's words.[112]

107. Meier, *Speaking*, p. 290.

108. Bjørndalen, 'Zeitstufen', p. 398. In fact, Meier himself, when quoting secondary literature, often employs the present tense to the same effect.

109. Meier, *Speaking*, p. 291.

110. Compare the 'call narratives', which also serve to authenticate the prophet. See N. Habel, 'The Form and Significance of the Call Narratives', *ZAW* 77 (1965), pp. 297-323; W. Richter, *Die sogenannten vorprophetischen Berufungsberichte* (FRLANT, 101; Göttingen: Vandenhoeck & Ruprecht, 1970); and Zimmerli, *Ezechiel*, I, pp. 16-21.

111. Hayes, *Amos*, p. 69, classifies prophetic speech as 'assertive, authoritative address' and prefers to call phrases like כה אמר יהוה 'attribution formulas' rather than 'messenger formulas'.

112. Cf. Rendtorff, 'Botenformel und Botenspruch', pp. 168-69; and M. Fishbane, *Biblical Interpretation in Ancient Israel* (Oxford: Clarendon Press, 1985), *passim*, who has shown that the Old Testament writers often handled the *traditum* rather freely.

The Statement Declaring the Irrevocability of the Divine Judgment
Another recurring feature, the formulaic expression לֹא אֲשִׁיבֶנּוּ, stresses
that God's decree to punish the nations is settled. There has been some
debate about the proper understanding of the suffix of אֲשִׁיבֶנּוּ. In my view,
it is best interpreted in a cataphoric sense as referring either to the subsequent announcement of punishment[113] or, more likely, to the punishment
itself.[114] The ambiguity of the suffix also adds an element of mystery and

113. Thus Wolff, *Joel and Amos*, p. 128; Mays, *Amos*, p. 24; P. Höffken, *Unter-suchungen zu den Begründungselementen der Völkerorakel des Alten Testaments* (Bonn, 1977), p. 52; and J. Barton, *Amos's Oracles against the Nations: A Study of Amos 1.3–2.5* (SOTSMS, 6; Cambridge: Cambridge University Press, 1980), p. 18.

114. Cf. Wellhausen, *Die kleinen Propheten*, p. 68; Sellin, *Zwölfprophetenbuch*, p. 203; G.H. Jones, 'An Examination of Some Leading Motifs in the Prophetic Oracles Against Foreign Nations' (dissertation, University of Wales at Bangor, 1970), pp. 165-66; Gese, 'Komposition', p. 89; T.E. McComiskey, 'Amos', in F.E. Gaebelein *et al.* (eds.), *The Expositor's Bible Commentary*. VII. *Daniel–Minor Prophets* (Grand Rapids: Zondervan, 1985), pp. 267-331 (283); Finley, *Joel, Amos, Obadiah*, p. 136; and Paul, *Amos*, pp. 46-47.

Other proposals include the following:

(a)   The suffix refers back to the voice of Yahweh in v. 2 (thus Hayes, *Amos*, p. 71; *idem*, 'Amos's Oracles Against the Nations [1.2-2.16]', *RevExp* 92 [1995], pp. 153-67 [155]).

However, this has been criticized by McComiskey, 'Amos', p. 283; and P.R. Noble, ' "I Will Not Bring 'It' Back" (Amos 1.3): A Deliberately Ambiguous Oracle?', *ExpTim* 106 (1994–95), pp. 105-109 (106-107).

(b)   It stands for the individual nation, which is no longer tolerated by Yahweh as a vassal (J. Morgenstern, 'Amos Studies IV: The Addresses of Amos—Text and Commentary', *HUCA* 32 [1961], pp. 295-350 [314]; M.L. Barré, 'The Meaning of *l' 'šybnw* in Amos 1.3–2.6', *JBL* 105 [1986], pp. 611-31 [622]; Stuart, *Hosea–Jonah*, pp. 303-305; and A.R. Ceresko, 'Janus Parallelism in Amos's "Oracles Against the Nations" [Amos 1.3–2.16]', *JBL* 113 [1994], pp. 485-90).

This view has been refuted by Finley, *Joel, Amos, Obadiah*, p. 140; and esp. P.R. Noble, 'Israel among the Nations', *HBT* 15 (1993), pp. 56-82.

(c)   The suffix refers to the wrath of Yahweh (cf. Harper, *Commentary*, p. 16; R.P. Knierim, ' "I Will Not Cause It to Return" in Amos 1 and 2', in Coats and Long [eds.], *Canon and Authority*, pp. 163-75 [170]; and Coote, *Amos*, pp. 115-16).

For a refutation of this view see Barré, 'Meaning', p. 613; Gese, 'Kompo-sition', p. 89; and Noble, ' "I Will Not Bring 'It' Back" ', pp. 105-106.

For further suggestions see H.W. Hogg, 'The Starting Point of the Religious Message

suspense, as Amos's audience grapples with the implications of this introductory phrase.[115]

However, this interpretation has been challenged by Noble, stressing that 'after the first oracle in the series has made [the] identification' of -*ennû* with the subsequent punishment, 'there is no more "mystery" and "tension" in "it" '.[116] Noble suggests instead that the suffix is 'genuinely ambiguous'. In his view, it refers to the judgment subsequently announced and the future restoration of the nations envisaged in the salvation oracle 9.11-15, which, as he believes, does not exclude the foreign nations from the depicted reversal of fortunes.[117] This interpretation maintains that not only is the suffix ambiguous, but so is the preposition על, which can be understood in a *causative* sense ('*because of* three transgressions...the nations will be punished') or in an *adversative* (or *concessive*) sense ('*despite* three transgressions...they will be restored').

Noble's proposal is hardly convincing, however. First, although an *adversative* or *concessive* rendering of על cannot be ruled out,[118] its *causative* use outweighs those options by far.[119] Secondly, a reference to the restoration depicted in 9.11-15 is rather unlikely given the textual distance separating the use of the suffix in Amos 1–2 from its supposed referent in Amos 9.[120] In addition, I am not convinced that Amos 9 envisages a restoration of the nations in the first place. Thirdly, and most importantly, Noble's well-taken observation that the first oracle effectively ends the

of Amos', in P.S. Allen and J. de M. Johnson (eds.), *Transactions of the Third International Congress for the History of Religions*, I (Oxford: Clarendon Press, 1908), pp. 325-27; R. Gordis, 'Some Hitherto Unrecognized Meanings of the Verb *Shub*', *JBL* 52 (1933), pp. 153-62 (159); *idem*, 'Studies in the Book of Amos', *PAAJR* 46–47 (1979–80), pp. 201-46 (202-203); A. Neher, *Amos: Contribution à l'étude du prophètisme* (Paris: Vrin, 1950); D.N. Freedman, 'The Burning Bush', *Bib* 50 (1969), p. 246; Maag, *Text*, p. 247; and Barstad, *Religious Polemics*, pp. 12-13. For an evaluation of these, cf. the comments by Paul, *Amos*, pp. 46-47; and Barton, *Amos's Oracles against the Nations*, p. 18.

115. Cf. Rudolph, *Joel, Amos, Obadja, Jona*, p. 130; Paul, *Amos*, p. 47; McComiskey, 'Amos', p. 283; and Carroll R., 'God', p. 59.

116. Noble, ' "I Will Not Bring 'It' Back" ', p. 108.

117. Noble, ' "I Will Not Bring 'It' Back" ', pp. 108-109.

118. See JM §171e; GK §160c; WO'C 36.2.2b (#17).

119. JM §§133-34; 170h; GK §§119dd; 158c; WO'C 36.2.2b (#14); 38.4a.

120. Noble, ' "I Will Not Bring 'It' Back" ', p. 109, is, of course, well aware of this problem but claims that 'it is by no means implausible to think that an ambiguity that was "left hanging" in the opening section should be resolved in the final chapter'. This is certainly *possible* but is it *likely* given that we are talking about a simple suffix?

sense of mystery by bringing out the implications of -*ennû* also precludes his own interpretation. From now on, that is to say, the audience knows Yahweh's punishment to be the referent of the suffix.

But, asks Noble, why did Amos not say 'I will not revoke the punishment' throughout if that was what he meant? For a start, that would have precluded the suspense desired at the outset of his speech. Secondly, even the continued use of לא אשׁיבנו is best explained in rhetorical terms and that despite the fact that it is clear, after the initial strophe, that Amos is talking about judgment. The effect of the indeterminate 'it' is to leave it open what precisely 'it' is that will not be revoked in the case of Gaza, Tyre, Edom and so on. Of course, we also must not forget the highly formulaic character of the OAN, which provides yet another explanation as to why the expression is not dropped after the first strophe.

The 'Graded Numerical Sequence'
The statement declaring the irrevocability of the divine judgment is preceded by another formulaic expression, namely the phrase...על־שׁלשׁה ועל־ארבעה. It has been labelled respectively as 'numerical saying', 'graded numerical sequence', 'staircase formula' or 'ascending numerical pair'.[121] While it is clear that it states the reason for Yahweh's decree to punish the nations, scholars disagree in their assessment of the meaning (and *Sitz im Leben*) of the numerical sequence x/x+1. Wolff, accepting Terrien's suggestion that its background is to be seen in the Old Testament wisdom literature,[122] concluded that Amos had four specific crimes in mind while mentioning only the fourth and most repulsive one.[123] However, Wolff's

---

121. For an extensive bibliography, see O'Connell, 'Telescoping N+1 Patterns', pp. 71-73.

122. H.W. Wolff, *Amos' geistige Heimat* (WMANT, 18; Neukirchen–Vluyn: Neukirchener Verlag, 1964), pp. 24-30; cf. Terrien, 'Amos and Wisdom', p. 109; further B.B. Margulis, 'Studies in the Oracles Against the Nations' (dissertation, Brandeis University, Waltham, MA, 1966), pp. 245, 250; J. Lindblom, 'Wisdom in the Old Testament Prophets', in M. Noth and D.W. Thomas (eds.), *Wisdom in Israel and in the Ancient Near East: Presented to Prof. H.H. Rowley by the Society for Old Testament Study* (VTSup, 3; Leiden: E.J. Brill, 1955), pp. 192-204 (esp. 202-203); *idem*, *Prophecy*, p. 240; and G. von Rad, *Weisheit in Israel* (Gütersloh: Gütersloher Verlagshaus Gerd Mohn, new edn, 1992), pp. 53-56 (also *idem*, *Old Testament Theology*, I, p. 425).

123. Wolff, *Amos' geistige Heimat*, p. 29; see also M. Haran, 'The Graded Numerical Sequence and Phenomenon of "Automatism" in Biblical Poetry', in *Congress Volume, Uppsala 1971* (VTSup, 22; Leiden: E.J. Brill, 1972), pp. 238-67 (260, 266-67); B. Gosse, 'Le recueil d'oracles contre les nations du livre d'Amos et l'"histoire

approach has been criticised precisely because Amos does not list four items, which is what one would have expected in the light of the wisdom texts where all items represented by the numbers are listed.[124] Because of this, as well as for other reasons, many scholars remain unconvinced of the proposed links between Amos and what Wolff had called *Sippenweisheit*.[125]

According to Crenshaw, the use of numerical pairs is the strongest argument in Wolff's case,[126] but even this does not prove Amos's depen-

deutéronomique" ', *VT* 38 (1988), pp. 22-40 (24); Mays, *Amos*, pp. 23-24; and P.P. Jenson, 'אַרְבַּע', in *NIDOTTE*, I, pp. 495-97 (496). A somewhat similar interpretation has been offered by the rabbis, according to whom a sin could be forgiven three times but not a fourth time (cf. *Yom.* 86b; *Sanh.* 7a; thus also B.K. Soper, 'For Three Transgressions and for Four: A New Interpretation of Amos 1.3, etc.', *ExpTim* 71 [1959–60], pp. 86-87). Terrien, 'Amos and Wisdom', p. 110, however, understood the formula as 'an implication of indefiniteness', thus adopting the approach of the scholars mentioned in n. 130 below.

124. Cf. Fritz, 'Fremdvölkersprüche', p. 28; Andersen and Freedman, *Amos*, p. 230; R.B. Chisholm, Jr., ' "For Three Sins…Even For Four": The Numerical Sayings of Amos', *BSac* 147 (1990), pp. 188-97 (195); Soper, 'For Three Transgressions'; Rudolph, *Joel, Amos, Obadja, Jona*, pp. 128-29'; and M. Weiss, 'The Pattern of Numerical Sequence in Amos 1–2: A Re-Examination', *JBL* 86 (1967), pp. 416-23 (417-19). In the case of a 'graded numerical sequence' x/x+1, it is the x+1 phrase that determines how many items are enumerated.

125. Wolff, *Amos' geistige Heimat*; cf. the criticism in R.N. Whybray, 'Prophecy and Wisdom', in R.J. Coggins, A. Phillips and M. Knibb (eds.), *Israel's Prophetic Tradition: Essays in Honour of Peter R. Ackroyd* (Cambridge: Cambridge University Press, 1982), pp. 181-99 (188-89); *idem*, *The Intellectual Tradition in the Old Testament* (BZAW, 135; Berlin: W. de Gruyter, 1974), p. 119. On the relationship between prophecy and wisdom, cf. J. Fichtner, 'Jesaja unter den Weisen', *TLZ* 74 (1949), pp. 75-80; H.-J. Hermisson, *Studien zur israelitischen Spruchweisheit* (WMANT, 28; Neukirchen–Vluyn: Neukirchener Verlag, 1968); J.W. Whedbee, *Isaiah and Wisdom* (Nashville: Abingdon Press, 1971); Whybray, 'Prophecy and Wisdom'; H. Graf Reventlow, *Hauptprobleme der alttestamentlichen Theologie im 20. Jahrhundert* (EdF, 173; Darmstadt: Wissenschaftliche Buchgesellschaft, 1982), p. 202; R.C. van Leeuwen, 'The Sage in the Prophetic Literature', in J.G. Gammie and L.G. Perdue (eds.), *The Sage in Israel and the Ancient Near East* (Winona Lake, IN: Eisenbrauns, 1990), pp. 295-306; and with special emphasis on Amos, Crenshaw, 'Influence'; H.H. Schmid, 'Amos: Zur Frage nach der "geistigen Heimat" des Propheten', *WuD* 10 (1969), pp. 85-103; G.H. Wittenberg, 'A Fresh Look at Amos and Wisdom', *OTE* 4 (1991), pp. 7-18; and recently J.A. Soggin, 'Amos and Wisdom', in J. Day, R.P. Gordon and H.G.M. Williamson (eds.), *Wisdom in Ancient Israel: Essays in Honor of J.A. Emerton* (Cambridge: Cambridge University Press, 1995), pp. 119-23.

126. Crenshaw 'Influence', p. 49.

dency on wisdom because, as Roth has demonstrated, numerical pairs are by no means confined to wisdom texts.[127] Hardmeier, utilizing Roth's findings, thus argued convincingly that the use of the 'graded numerical sequence' in Amos 1–2 should be seen not as stereotypical wisdom language, which opens the door to tradition-historical conclusions about Amos's 'geistige Heimat', but rather as a rhetorically motivated borrowing, which precludes any such conclusions.[128] The main significance of Roth's findings for the purposes of this investigation lies exactly in his demonstration that numerical sayings were widely used and would thus have been well known to Amos's audience.[129] However, before I am going to elaborate on this, let us look briefly at some further suggestions concerning Amos's use of the numerical pair that are prevalent in the scholarly literature.

Some have stressed that the formula cannot be taken literally as indicating a precise number, but should be understood rather as denoting an indefinite total of crimes.[130] While this is true in many cases, this interpretation does not fit Amos 1–2 either because if an indefinite number were in view, no specific case should have been referred to.[131] Yet another route has been taken by Weiss, suggesting that an interpretation of the formula in Amos 1–2 ought to proceed from the evidence of the eighth strophe where seven crimes, three *plus* four, are listed.[132] He concludes that 'seven transgressions...signify the whole, the full sin', and that 'judgment is pronounced on each nation because of its complete sin'.[133]

The strength of Weiss's proposal lies not least in the fact that the number seven appears to be of great importance in the book of Amos.[134] According to his investigation, then, the Israel oracle is climactic in that it

127. Roth, 'Numerical Sequence'; and *idem, Numerical Sayings*.
128. Hardmeier, *Texttheorie*, pp. 293-300.
129. See Roth, *Numerical Sayings*, p. 19; and Whybray, *Intellectual Tradition*, p. 119, who notes that these 'forms of speech...were current among the common people'.
130. Thus Keil, *Minor Prophets*, p. 164; Sellin, *Zwölfprophetenbuch*, p. 202; Robinson, 'Hosea bis Micha', p. 75; Stuart, *Hosea–Jonah*, p. 310; Finley, *Joel, Amos, Obadiah*, p. 138; and McComiskey, 'Amos', p. 282.
131. See esp. Roth, *Numerical Sayings*, p. 63 n. 3.
132. Others, however, have arrived at a total of four crimes (see p. 185).
133. Weiss, 'Pattern of Numerical Sequence', p. 420; followed by Rudolph, *Joel, Amos, Obadja, Jona*, p. 129.
134. Cf. the list of 7 and 7+1 items in Amos in Chapter 1 above; see further Gordis, 'Composition and Structure', p. 219; Weiss, 'Pattern of Numerical Sequence', p. 420; and Limburg, 'Sevenfold Structures'.

not only hints at the fullness and totality of the nation's sins but also spells them out in unprecedented detail. However, the problem with this suggestion is that Weiss is not able to provide any further examples of the 'graded numerical sequence' where its rhetorical impact depends on the numbers of the two parts of the parallelism being added up (i.e., $x/x+1 = x+x+1$), a problem which he himself admits.[135] His pleading to understand the phrase as a hendiadys, which he calls an *ad hoc* interpretation that fits the *ad hoc* creation by Amos,[136] does not solve the problem either because Amos's audience was much more likely to understand the formula in the 'traditional way', as indicating four crimes in this instance.[137]

The most complex and sophisticated rhetorical analysis has been offered by Chisholm who, like Hardmeier, presumes that Amos purposefully adapted the 'graded numerical sequence' for his own rhetorical purposes.[138] Before evaluating his proposal, however, let me first return briefly to the interpretation offered by Wolff. While proven wrong in his analysis of the phrase's *Sitz im Leben*, Wolff was right to suspect a specific reason for Amos's deviation from the general custom according to which the x+1 phrase determined the number of items listed. Yet, although Wolff's conclusion that the one crime that has been listed probably was the most repulsive one is a sensible proposal, it is worth postponing such a conclusion for a moment.

It should be noted, first, that Amos's use of the device may have had a bewildering effect not only on modern scholars. Being a deviation from normal usage, it will most likely have puzzled the prophet's original audience as well.[139] And taking into account the 'temporal flow' of speeches—that is the fact that in the process of hearing, the expectations and conclusions of the audience are permanently subject to revision—we are now in a position to refine Wolff's ideas as follows. When Amos employed the 'graded numerical sequence' 3–4 followed by a reference to only one crime in the opening strophes, his audience must have been surprised by this deviation from the expected pattern. Indeed, they may even have conjectured, just as Wolff did, that the crime that is mentioned

135. Weiss, 'Pattern of Numerical Sequence', p. 421.
136. Weiss, 'Pattern of Numerical Sequence', pp. 421-23.
137. For a detailed critique of Weiss's proposal, see Paul, *Amos*, pp. 27-30.
138. Cf. Chisholm, 'For Three Sins…', p. 196; Hardmeier, *Texttheorie*, pp. 295-96; and also Barton, *Amos's Oracles against the Nations*, p. 15, who speaks of 'Amos as an innovator'.
139. Cf. Hardmeier, *Texttheorie*, p. 299.

is so severe as to compensate, as it were, for the listing of the other transgressions. Yet, whether this was in fact their conjecture is of no consequence. All that matters is that Amos's deviation from the norm[140] initiated a mental process of surprise and conjecture.

It is at this point that Chisholm's contribution comes in. Chisholm correctly observed that already before the Israel strophe we have two cases—the oracles against Edom (1.10-11) and Judah (2.4-5)—that elaborate on the nations' guilt.[141] The Edom strophe, depending on how it is construed, either lists four crimes or focuses on one transgression in detail.[142] Whichever view one prefers, it is in any case rhetorically marked. Hence, Chisholm suggests that this may have been taken as a marker of conclusion by Amos's audience,[143] which is possible for several reasons. First, the more elaborate treatment of Edom's guilt in itself suggests a climax. Secondly, Edom being Israel's 'arch enemy', it would not have been surprising to find this nation's crimes singled out as particularly severe and numerous. Thirdly, if 1.11 were taken to list four crimes, the number would match the x+1 element in the 'graded numerical saying'. Indeed, it would also match the audience's expectations, thereby contributing to the idea that this must be the goal of the entire series. Interestingly, as Chisholm comments, 'the 3/4 pattern of the introductory saying would be mirrored in the structure of the speech as a whole'.[144] However, the series does not end here but continues until Amos eventually turns to Judah, the seventh nation to be accused and threatened with the divine punishment. Chisholm notes that

140. Hardmeier, *Texttheorie*, p. 299, speaks of a 'Normverletzung'.

141. Chisholm, 'For Three Sins…', p. 192.

142. Cf. Amos 1.11b:

על־רדפו בחרב אחיו   ושחת רחמיו
ויטרף לעד אפו   ועברתו שמרה נצח

Chisholm, 'For Three Sins…', pp. 191-94, distinguishes between a formal counting of crimes and a conceptual one. While in the former case all the verbal phrases are simply added up, the latter takes into account features such as purpose clauses (להסגיר in 1.6 and למען הרחיב in 1.13), explanatory statements (ולא זכרו in 1.9) parallelism (1.11) etc., thus arriving at a smaller number of crimes.

143. Chisholm, 'For Three Sins…', p. 196.

144. Chisholm, 'For Three Sins…', p. 196. It is also interesting to note that exactly at this point there is a 'missing link' in the so-called 'concatenous pattern' suggested by Paul, *Amos*, pp. 13-15; and *idem*, 'Amos 1.3–2.3: A Concatenous Literary Pattern', *JBL* 90 (1971), pp. 397-403. As Carroll R., 'God', p. 61, has pointed out, the reason for this might be to alert hearers or readers to pause at the Edom oracle.

Amos's Israelite audience would have delighted in this and expected the speech to conclude here, probably with another fourfold list of crimes like that of Edom. Their expectations were almost realized, but instead of capping off the list of Judah's sins with a fourth charge (the list includes only three formal accusatory statements), Amos delivered a brief announcement of judgment (2.5) and then surprisingly turned to Israel. Israel was the worst rebel of all...[145]

Whatever the number of crimes listed in the Israel strophe—four (thus confirming to the x+1 pattern)[146] or seven (i.e., x+x+1, a rhetorical device created *ad hoc* by Amos)[147]—the final oracle clearly functions as the climax of the whole series. This, in turn, means that the OAN in Amos 1–2 contain two pseudo-climaxes before ending on another unexpected note. And the unusual use Amos makes of the 'graded numerical saying' is an important part of the text's rhetorical strategy, evoking anticipation, suspension, surprise and even shock.

The Nations' פְּשָׁעִים

The reason for the divine punishment is regularly given as the respective nation's פְּשָׁעִים. According to Seebass, פֶּשַׁע is a general term designating a variety of offences, which are particularly repulsive.[148] This definition fits Amos 1–2 well, where the term in the first six strophes refers to brutal and disgusting war crimes,[149] such as the subjugation of Gilead by extremely brutal means (1.3),[150] the deportation of people and slave trading (1.6,[151]

145. Chisholm, 'For Three Sins...', p. 197.

146. Pusey, *Minor Prophets*, p. 121; Gese, 'Komposition', pp. 89-90; D.L. Christensen, 'The Prosodic Structure of Amos 1–2', *HTR* 67 (1974), pp. 427-36 (436); *idem*, *Transformations of the War Oracle in Old Testament Prophecy: Studies in the Oracles against the Nations* (HDR, 3; Missoula: Scholars Press, 1975), pp. 66, 71; M. Köckert, 'Das Gesetz und die Propheten in Amos 1–2', in J. Hausmann and H.-J. Zobel (eds.), *Alttestamentlicher Glaube und Biblische Theologie. Festschrift für Horst Dietrich Preuss zum 65. Geburtstag* (Stuttgart: W. Kohlhammer, 1992), pp. 145-54 (146); and O'Connell, 'Telescoping N+1 Patterns', p. 60.

147. Weiss, 'Pattern of Numerical Sequence'; Rudolph, *Joel, Amos, Obadja, Jona*, p. 140; W. Dietrich, 'JHWH, Israel und die Völker beim Propheten Amos', *TZ* 48 (1992), pp. 315-28 (315); and Hayes, 'Amos's Oracles Against the Nations', p. 163.

148. In H. Ringgren and H. Seebass, 'פֶּשַׁע, פָּשַׁע', in *ThWAT*, VI, pp. 791-810 (799).

149. Cf. R.P. Knierim, *Die Hauptbegriffe für Sünde im Alten Testament* (Gütersloh: Gütersloher Verlagshaus Gerd Mohn, 1965), p. 178; and Wolff, *Joel and Amos*, p. 173.

150. On the guilt of Damascus, see Vesco, 'Amos de Teqoa', p. 487; P.T. Crocker, 'History and Archaeology in the Oracles of Amos', *Buried History: A Quarterly Newsletter of the Australian Institute of Archaeology* 23 (1987), pp. 7-15 (8); Andersen

9),[152] the murder of allies (1.11),[153] the shocking cruelty against pregnant women (1.13)[154] and the burning of the bones of the king of Edom (2.1).[155]

It should be noted at this point that the 'B strophes' dealing with Tyre, Edom and Judah are often seen as secondary[156] (1) because of form-criti-

and Freedman, *Amos*, pp. 237-39; Wolff, *Joel and Amos*, p. 154; Kapelrud, *Central Ideas*, p. 22; and K.H. Singer, *Die Metalle Gold, Silber, Bronze und Eisen im Alten Testament und ihre Symbolik* (FzB, 43; Würzburg: Echter Verlag, 1980), p. 186, who understand the allegation metaphorically. Keil, *Minor Prophets*, pp. 164-65; and G. Pfeifer, 'Denkformenanalyse als exegetische Methode, erläutert an Amos 1 $_{2}$–2 $_{16}$', *ZAW* 88 (1976), pp. 56-71 (60); on the other hand, opt for a literal interpretation.

151. On the severity of these charges see L.M. Muntingh, 'Political and International Relations of Israel's Neighbouring Peoples According to the Oracles of Amos', in *Studies on the Books of Hosea and Amos* (OTWSA, 7/8; Potchefstroom: Pro Rege-Pers Beperk, 1966), pp. 134-42 (139). Birch, *Hosea, Joel, and Amos*, p. 182, compares the crime of the Philistines to what we would call 'ethnic cleansing'.

152. On the Tyre strophe see H. Cazelles, 'L'arrière-plan historique d'Amos 1,9-10', in Shinan (ed.), *Proceedings of the Sixth World Congress of Jewish Studies*, I, pp. 71-76.

153. The terms אחיו and רחמיו identify the Israelites as Edom's brothers and allies; cf. M. Fishbane, 'The Treaty-Background of Amos 1.11 and Related Matters', *JBL* 89 (1970), pp. 313-18; *idem*, 'Additional Remarks on *rhmyw* (Amos 1.11)', *JBL* 91 (1972), pp. 391-93; M.L. Barré, 'Amos 1.11 Reconsidered', *CBQ* 47 (1985), pp. 420-27; Andersen and Freedman, *Amos*, pp. 264-67; and R. Gordis, 'Edom, Israel and Amos—An Unrecognized Source for Edomite History', in A.I. Katsh and L. Lemoy (eds.), *Essays on the Occasion of the Seventieth Anniversary of the Dropsie University* (Philadelphia: Dropsie University, 1979), pp. 109-32 (131); but see also R.B. Coote, 'Amos 1.11: *rhmyw*', *JBL* 90 (1971), pp. 206-208; and H. Simian-Yofre and U. Dahmen, 'רחם, רחמים, רחום, רחמני, רחמני', in *ThWAT*, VII, pp. 460-77 (471).

154. Höffken, *Untersuchungen*, pp. 108-109, points out that the motive ('to enlarge their territory') indicates that this particular crime stands *pars pro toto* for all the crimes committed.

155. R.W. Klein, *1 Samuel* (WBC, 10; Waco, TX: Word Books, 1983), p. 290, notes that 'burning was used in certain forms of capital punishment' (Gen. 38.3; Lev. 20.14; 21.9; Josh. 7.25). It was considered a particularly disgraceful practice (2 Kgs 23.16, 20). Normally, even the corpses of foes were treated with respect, as Jehu's demand that Jezebel be buried demonstrates (2 Kgs 9.34). The addition of לשיד even heightens the offence (Wolff, *Joel and Amos*, pp. 162-63; Andersen and Freedman, *Amos*, p. 288), stressing 'the completeness of the destruction' (J.N. Oswalt, *The Book of Isaiah: Chapters 1–39* [NICOT; Grand Rapids: Eerdmans, 1986], p. 598).

156. Schmidt, 'Die deuteronomistische Redaktion', pp. 174-78; Wolff, *Joel and Amos*, pp. 139-41; Fleischer, *Von Menschenverkäufern*, p. 19; G. Pfeifer, 'Über den Unterschied zwischen Schriftstellern des zwanzigsten Jahrhunderts nach und des ersten Jahrtausends vor Christus. Zur Entstehung des Amosbuches', *VT* 41 (1991), pp. 123-27

cal assumptions that do not allow for the textual variations found in Amos 1–2; (2) because of their vocabulary, which is thought to reflect deuteronomistic influences; and (3) because of historical considerations. While I do not intend to enter into a detailed discussion of these issues, it needs to be stressed that I am not convinced of the inauthenticity of the strophes in question. First, the rigid form-critical assumptions that do not allow for stylistic variations are too arbitrary to be convincing. Secondly, recent works have shown the analysis of Schmidt, who in his influential 1965 article, 'Die deuteronomistische Redaktion des Amosbuches', argued for a number of deuteronomistic additions in Amos, to be badly flawed.[157] Finally, the authenticity of the disputed strophes is also by no means precluded by historical observations.[158]

(126); Köckert, 'Gesetz'; and J.T. Strong, 'Tyre's Isolationist Policies in the Early Sixth Century BCE: Evidence from the Prophets', *VT* 47 (1997), pp. 207-19. Dietrich, 'JHWH', pp. 316-17, adds to these the Gaza strophe; Jeremias, 'Zur Entstehung der Völkersprüche im Amosbuch', in *idem, Hosea und Amos*, pp. 172-82; *idem, Book of Amos*, p. 25, believes that only the Damascus and Ammon strophes originate with Amos; and Fritz, 'Fremdvölkersprüche', p. 38; and H.M. Niemann, 'Theologie in geographischem Gewand: Zum Wachstumsprozess der Völkerspruchsammlung Amos 1-2', in *idem*, M. Augustin and W.H. Schmidt (eds.), *Nachdenken über Israel, Bibel und Theologie: Festschrift für Klaus-Dietrich Schunck zu seinem 65. Geburtstag* (BEATAJ, 37; Frankfurt: Peter Lang, 1994), pp. 177-96 (191 n. 18), consider the entire passage a *vaticinium ex eventu*.

For a critique of the latter view, see G. Pfeifer, 'Die Fremdvölkersprüche des Amos—Spätere *vaticinia ex eventu*?', *VT* 38 (1988), pp. 230-33; and Jeremias, 'Entstehung', pp. 177-81. The 'traditional view' (that the Tyre, Edom and Judah strophes are secondary additions) has been criticized by Botterweck, 'Authentizität', pp. 178-81; Hayes, *Amos*, pp. 52-55; *idem*, 'The Oracles against the Nations in the Old Testament: Their Usage and Theological Importance' (Th.D. dissertation, Princeton Theological Seminary, 1964), pp. 177, 180; Paul, *Amos*, pp. 16-27; *idem*, 'A Literary Reinvestigation of the Authenticity of the Oracles Against the Nations of Amos', in Doré, Grelot and Carrez (eds.), *De la Tôrah au Messie*, pp. 189-204; Rudolph, *Joel, Amos, Obadja, Jona*, pp. 119-22; and *idem*, 'Die angefochtenen Völkersprüche in Amos 1 und 2', in Bernhardt (ed.), *Schalom*, pp. 45-49. Christensen, 'Prosodic Structure', on the other hand, relentlessly trims down all the strophes to make them fit his, no doubt highly aesthetic, ideas of prosody.

157. Cf. in particular Bons, 'Denotat'; and Lohfink, 'Bewegung'. For further discussion see nn. 182, 184 below.

158. Studies of the historical allusions in the OAN include J.R. Bartlett, 'The Brotherhood of Edom', *JSOT* 4 (1977), pp. 2-27 (10-16); Barton, *Amos's Oracles against the Nations*, ch. 4; Gordis, 'Edom'; M. Haran, 'Observations on the Historical Background of Amos 1.2–2.6', *IEJ* 18 (1968), pp. 201-12; *idem*, 'Rise and Decline',

However, to return to the indictments in Amos 1.3–2.3, we need to consider briefly the grounds on which Amos censures Israel's neighbours, as these are of fundamental importance for an appreciation of the rhetorical strategy that underlies Amos 1–2 as a whole. As some have pointed out, in condemning the crimes of foreign nations, Amos appeals to a 'common ethos', or in the words of Barton, 'an ethos which he thought ought to be common'. Discussing the basis of Amos's condemnations in detail, Barton argues for the existence of an 'international customary law', which Amos had been able to build his argument on.[159] Alternative proposals, rejected by Barton, include: (1) the nationalistic interpretation according to which Amos is simply agitating against Israel's enemies;[160] (2) the 'Davidic Empire theory', which stresses that Israel's neighbours were subject to Yahweh's laws because they once had been, and in Amos's view still were, vassals of Israel (and thus also of Yahweh);[161] (3)

pp. 272-78; P. Höffken, 'Eine Bemerkung zum 'Haus Hasaels' in Amos 1 4', *ZAW* 94 (1982), pp. 413-15; A. Malamat, 'Amos 1.5 in the Light of the Til Barsip Inscriptions', *BASOR* 129 (1953), pp. 25-26; H.-P. Müller, 'Phönizien und Juda in exilisch-nachexilischer Zeit', *WO* 6.2 (1971), pp. 189-204; Muntingh, 'Political and International Relations'; J. Priest, 'The Covenant of Brothers', *JBL* 84 (1965), pp. 400-406; K.N. Schoville, 'A Note on the Oracles of Amos Against Gaza, Tyre, and Edom', in *Studies on Prophecy. A Collection of Twelve Papers* (VTSup, 26; Leiden: E.J. Brill, 1974), pp. 55-63; *idem*, 'The Sins of Aram in Amos 1', in Shinan (ed.), *Proceedings of the Sixth World Congress of Jewish Studies*, I, pp. 363-75; and J.A. Soggin, 'Amos VI.13-14 und I.3 auf dem Hintergrund der Beziehungen zwischen Israel und Damaskus im 9. und 8. Jahrhundert', in H. Goedicke (ed.), *Near Eastern Studies in Honor of W.F. Albright* (Baltimore: Johns Hopkins University Press, 1971), pp. 433-41. See also Hayes, *Amos, ad loc.*, whose views on the historical background of the OAN I follow.

159. Barton, *Amos's Oracles against the Nations*, ch. 6; see also Hayes, *Amos*, pp. 58-59; *idem*, *Oracles against the Nations*, pp. 187-88; C.J.H. Wright, *Living as the People of God: The Relevance of Old Testament Ethics* (Leicester: InterVarsity Press, 1983), p. 124; and S. Amsler, 'Amos et les droits de l'homme', in Doré, Grelot and Carrez (eds.), *De la Tôrah au Messie*, pp. 181-87.

160. This has been advocated by C.H. Toy, 'The Judgment of Foreign Peoples in Amos i. 3–ii. 3', *JBL* 25 (1906), pp. 25-28; Haran, 'Rise and Decline', pp. 273-74; and E. Würthwein, 'Amos-Studien', *ZAW* 62 (1950), pp. 10-52 (35-40).

161. Thus E. Beaucamp, 'Amos 1–2: Le pèsha' d'Israel et celui des Nations', *ScEs* 21 (1969), pp. 435-41 (esp. 439-40); Christensen, *Transformations*, pp. 71-72; Barré, 'Meaning'; Mauchline, 'Implicit Signs', esp. p. 289; Polley, *Amos, passim*. Barton, *Amos's Oracles against the Nations*, pp. 39-40, discusses the first two views under the same heading, 'Nationalism and Covenant', but focuses more on the former. For another detailed discussion—and rejection—of the 'Davidic Empire theory' cf. Noble, 'Israel', pp. 56-62.

the idea that Israel's covenantal obligations apply, by way of logical extension, also to the nations;[162] and (4) the proposal of a universal law, often seen as deriving from the prophets' 'ethical monotheism'.[163]

Challenging these theories, Barton emphasizes that 'the principles at stake in [the OAN] are essentially part of conventional morality…rather than actual laws supposed to be issued by [Yahweh] for all the nations of the world to observe'.[164] Yet, these conclusions too have been questioned recently. While agreeing that Amos is dealing with crimes that 'should have been recognised as evil…by their perpetrators', Noble objects to Barton's interpretation, especially rejecting 'its implicit anthropocentrism'. As he points out, in Barton's explanation 'mankind is given the primary role in developing moral norms, whereas God has a reflexive role of recognising (where appropriate) the rightness of what man has formulated'. According to Noble, who holds that 'Amos' thought …moves in precisely the opposite direction', nothing could be further from the truth.[165]

Noble himself, therefore, prefers the universal law theory supported by Lindblom who contends that the nations are condemned because 'they have offended against the holy will of Yahweh, which is valid for all peoples'.[166] This view had been rejected by Barton, claiming that we have no reason to think that Yahweh ever revealed his law to the nations. It would thus be unjust of him to punish them 'for breaking an edict they were unaware of'.[167] However, as Noble points out, there is no need for a *revelatio specialis*[168] because the crimes for which the foreign nations are condemned 'are particularly extreme instances of wrongdoing which all right-minded men ought to recognise as wrong'.[169] Thus Barton and Noble

162. F.C. Fensham, 'Common Trends in Curses of the Near Eastern Treaties and *Kudurru*-Inscriptions Compared with Maledictions of Amos and Isaiah', *ZAW* 75 (1963), pp. 155-75 (173).

163. Thus, for instance, K. Cramer, *Amos: Versuch einer theologischen Interpretation* (BWANT, 51; Stuttgart: W. Kohlhammer, 1930), pp. 156-74; Kapelrud, *Central Ideas*, pp. 26-29; Vesco, 'Amos de Teqoa', pp. 486-87; and E. Carpenter and M.A. Grisani, 'פֶּשַׁע', in *NIDOTTE*, III, pp. 706-10 (708).

164. Barton, *Amos's Oracles against the Nations*, p. 44.

165. Noble, 'Israel', pp. 63-64.

166. Lindblom, *Prophecy*, p. 335.

167. Barton, *Amos's Oracles against the Nations*, p. 43.

168. Introducing the concepts of *revelatio specialis* and *revelatio generalis sive naturalis* may help us get a clearer picture of the differences that separate Noble and Barton.

169. Noble, 'Israel', p. 64 (his emphasis); cf. also Deissler, *Zwölf Propheten*, p. 102; and Smith, *Amos*, p. 33.

agree that Amos's indictments do not require a *revelatio specialis* but disagree on whether they presuppose, rather generally, a 'conventional morality' (Barton) or, more specifically, a *revelatio generalis sive naturalis* (Noble). As I do not intend to embark on a detailed discussion of this issue,[170] I should just point out that Noble's rejection of Barton's interpretation as too anthropocentric for an Israelite prophet appears to me to strike the right note. From a rhetorical perspective, however, what is important to note at this point is that Amos accuses the nations of actions, which everyone should have been able to identify as particularly inhuman and detestable crimes.

It should also be noted that, although both rhetorically and theologically the primary focus of the OAN is on the Israel strophe,[171] Amos does portray Yahweh as a judge also of the foreign nations—a judge who does not tolerate their crimes and cruelties. Indeed, this underlying theological principle is very important if the rhetoric is to work at all. This has been rightly underlined by Hayes, stressing that:

> if, in speaking on the other nations, Amos could convince his Israelite audience that Yahweh was in charge, had condemned their atrocities, and would bring punishment upon them, then he was in a better position to convince his hearers that Yahweh has also judged and would bring judgment on Israel.[172]

In fact, Weiser, one of the pioneers of a rhetorical interpretation of the OAN,[173] was criticized by Würthwein, claiming that a rhetorical interpretation along the lines of Weiser's proposal does not do justice to the ancient Hebrew world where words were thought to be dynamic and energetic.[174] Würthwein based his view on Procksch's contention that 'each דבר is filled with power, which can manifest itself in manifold energies'.[175] Yet this view, working with a questionable understanding of

---

170. For a general discussion of *revelatio specialis* and *revelatio generalis sive naturalis* cf. H.G. Pöhlmann, *Abriss der Dogmatik: Ein Kompendium* (Gütersloh: Gütersloher Verlagshaus Gerd Mohn, 5th edn, 1990), pp. 50-59, 202-205.

171. This will be demonstrated in more detail in the subsequent discussion.

172. Hayes, 'Amos's Oracles Against the Nations', p. 166; cf. Barton, *Amos's Oracles against the Nations*, pp. 3-4. Against Weiser, *Profetie*, pp. 100-16; and J.B. Geyer, 'Mythology and Culture in the Oracles Against the Nations', *VT* 36 (1986), pp. 129-45 (135), who view the individual oracles as having 'little significance in themselves'.

173. See Weiser, *Profetie*, pp. 100-16.

174. Würthwein, 'Amos-Studien', p. 37, speaks of a 'wirkungsmächtiges Wort'.

175. O. Procksch, '"Wort Gottes" im AT', in *TWNT*, IV, pp. 89-100 (90).

language,[176] unnecessarily drives a wedge between rhetoric and theology.[177] Indeed, the theological significance of the OAN does not depend on the דבר being filled with power[178] but is due to nothing other than the authority of Yahweh, who, after all, is the one announcing the impending punishment.

To return to the rhetorical effect of the OAN; scholars have rightly pointed out that from an Israelite perspective the condemnation of the surrounding nations, who time and again inflicted pain and suffering on the people, must have been much appreciated.[179] Amos thus apparently makes use of his audience's nationalistic feelings but, as already noted above, his charges against Israel's neighbours do not appear to have been motivated by such sentiments on his part. This is confirmed in particular by the Moab strophe, which does not deal with offences perpetrated

176. Thiselton, 'Power', p. 283, rightly criticizes the mistaken semantic conceptions of this understanding (pp. 289-90; cf. Barr, *Semantics*), noting that it generalizes a principle that applies only to words uttered by a deity (or sometimes an authoritative person like a king or prophet) (pp. 290-93). Appropriating insights advanced by linguists and speech act theorists, Thiselton also points out that when words 'do things', this is not due to an inherent magical power but to social conventions (pp. 293-96; cf. de Saussure, *Cours de linguistique générale*; J. Lyons, *Introduction to Theoretical Linguistics* [Cambridge: Cambridge University Press, 1968]; S. Ullmann, *Semantics: An Introduction to the Science of Meaning* [Oxford: Basil Blackwell, 1962]; Austin, *How to Do Things With Words*; Searle, *Speech Acts*; *idem*, *Expression and Meaning*; and see also Thiselton, *New Horizons, passim*; and *idem*, 'Parables'). Thus according to Thiselton, Procksch and von Rad wrongly polarized the discussion around the two views of language being either *dynamic* or *dianoetic* (Thiselton, 'Power', pp. 296-98).

177. Thus with S. Lehming, 'Erwägungen zu Amos', *ZTK* 55 (1958), pp. 145-69 (158); but against Würthwein, 'Amos-Studien', p. 37.

178. Against L. Dürr, *Die Wertung des göttlichen Wortes im Alten Testament und im antiken Orient. Zugleich ein Beitrag zur Vorgeschichte des neutestamentlichen Logosbegriffes* (MVAG, 42.1; Leipzig: J.C. Hinrichs, 1938). A similar dynamic view of the spoken word has been advocated, among others, by E. Jacob, *Theology of the Old Testament* (trans. A.W. Heathcote and P.J. Allcock; London: Hodder & Stoughton, 1958), pp. 127-34; W. Zimmerli, 'Wort Gottes im AT', in *RGG*, VI, pp. 1809-12; O. Grether, *Name und Wort Gottes im Alten Testament* (BZAW, 64; Giessen: Alfred Töpelmann, 1934), pp. 103-107; W. Eichrodt, *Theologie des Alten Testaments* (2 vols.; Stuttgart: Klotz, 1962–64), II, pp. 40-48; O. Schilling, 'Das Wort Gottes im AT', *Erfurter Theologische Studien* 12 (1962), pp. 7-26; and von Rad, *Old Testament Theology*, II, pp. 80-98 (referring to E. Cassirer, *Philosophie der symbolischen Formen* [4 vols.; Darmstadt: Wissenschaftliche Buchgesellschaft, new edn, 1994]).

179. Paul, 'Literary Reinvestigation', p. 197.

against Israel.[180] However, two points need to be underlined here. First, Amos's audience will have thought it quite appropriate that Yahweh should punish their neighbours for their brutal deeds. Secondly, most strophes do speak of crimes committed against Israel and thereby trigger a process of 'self-identification', a consciousness of having been violated by one's enemies.[181] This, it is hardly necessary to point out, obviously contributes greatly to the passage's rhetorical effect.

When Amos then moves on to Judah, his audience's enjoyment of the speech must have reached new heights. What is interesting, however, is that Judah's guilt—while being equated with that of the nations by being termed פֶּשַׁע—is portrayed in different terms. Amos accuses Israel's southern relatives of a wholesale rejection of the divine law and a willingness to be deceived by the teaching of false prophets.[182] Whatever the terms תורה and חקים allude to in this context—a so-called 'prophetic

---

180. Cf. Barton, *Amos's Oracles against the Nations*, pp. 9, 21; and N.K. Gottwald, *All the Kingdoms of the Earth: Israelite Prophecy and International Relations in the Ancient Near East* (New York: Harper & Row, 1964), pp. 109-10; against Würthwein, 'Amos-Studien', p. 36 n. 51.

181. Cf. Carroll R., 'God', pp. 63-64.

182. Traditionally, v. 4c has been seen as a reference to idol worship (G.A. Smith, *The Book of the Twelve Prophets Commonly Called the Minor*. I. *Amos, Hosea and Micah. With an Introduction and a Sketch of Prophecy in Early Israel* [Expositor's Bible; London: Hodder & Stoughton, 1908], p. 135; von Orelli, *Die zwölf kleinen Propheten*, p. 63; Nowack, *Die kleinen Propheten*, p. 133; Robinson, 'Hosea bis Micha', p. 76; Wolff, *Joel and Amos*, p. 133; Mays, *Amos*, p. 41; Deissler, *Zwölf Propheten*, p. 98; R. Mosis, 'כֹּזָב, כָּזָב, אָכְזָב, כְּדָבָה, כָּזִבִי, אַכְזִיב, כֹּזִיב, כֹּזֵבָא, in *TDOT*, VII, pp. 104-21 [114]; E. Carpenter and M.A. Grisani, 'כֹזֵב', in *NIDOTTE*, II, pp. 619-21 [620]; for other interpretations, see G. Pfeifer, ' "Ich bin in tiefe Wasser geraten, und die Flut will mich ersäufen" [Psalm lxix 3]—Anregungen und Vorschläge zur Aufarbeitung wissenschaftlicher Sekundärliteratur', *VT* 37 [1987], pp. 327-39 [337-38]).

However, this view has been challenged recently by Bons, 'Denotat'. First, he notes that כֹּזָב nowhere else refers to idols (p. 201). Secondly, תעה hi. is generally used with humans as subject, not gods (pp. 209-10). Thirdly, both terms are used in particular in connection with false prophets (p. 210). Fourthly, the idiom הלךְ אחרי, although often used as a technical term for the worship of foreign gods (p. 209), does not always denote idolatry. It can also signify an attitude that Bons describes as 'sich [z. B. in der Erwartung eines Vorteils] an jemanden halten' (p. 211). He notes furthermore that there is some indication that כֹזביהם refers to humans, very probably to false prophets (pp. 211-13). Cf. also Lohfink, 'Bewegung', pp. 331-32; and Andersen and Freedman, *Amos*, pp. 301-305.

torah' or Yahweh's commands in a more general sense[183]—they do not require the existence of the book of Deuteronomy. Indeed, the entire accusation is most likely not of deuteronomistic origin, as Bons and Lohfink have shown recently.[184]

Some have argued that the charge against Judah, couched in somewhat formulaic language, is colourless and anti-climactic. However, this conclusion results from a misconceived understanding of formulaic language, as has been shown by Niditch in her study *Oral World and Written Word*.

---

183. For the former option cf. Bons, 'Denotat', p. 208; for the latter view see Rudolph, 'Völkersprüche', p. 48; and Niemann, 'Theologie', p. 185. See also the excursus in S.R. Driver, *The Books of Joel and Amos with Introduction and Notes* (Cambridge: Cambridge University Press, 1897), pp. 230-31.

184. Bons, 'Denotat'; and Lohfink, 'Bewegung', pp. 329-33. Schmidt, 'Redaktion', found the following characteristics of deuteronomistic language in Amos 2.4-5: שָׁמֹר חֻקֵּי יהוה, מָאַס אֶת־תּוֹרַת יהוה, the parallelism of תּוֹרָה and חֹק, הֹלֵךְ אַחֲרֵי with foreign gods as object and the combination of the rejection of Yahweh's laws and the following of foreign gods. However, reviewing the Old Testament evidence, Lohfink has recently concluded that none of these is specifically deuteronomistic. Schmidt's analysis has been criticized also by Wagner, 'Überlegungen', p. 666; Rudolph, *Joel, Amos, Obadja, Jona*, pp. 120-21; *idem*, 'Völkersprüche', pp. 48-49; Blenkinsopp, *History of Prophecy*, p. 89; Hayes, *Amos*, pp. 102-104; C. van Leeuwen, *Amos* (De Prediking van het Oude Testament; Nijkerk: Callenbach, 1985), p. 76; Andersen and Freedman, *Amos*, pp. 295-306; Paul, *Amos*, pp. 20-23; *idem*, 'Literary Reinvestigation', pp. 193-94; and Smith, *Amos*, pp. 76-79.

For a research review cf. Martin-Achard, *Amos*, pp. 128-29; and for an extensive bibliography see Pfeifer, 'Ich bin in tiefe Wasser geraten', pp. 332-35. Some scholars now warn against the danger of what has been labelled 'pandeuteronomism' (cf. Lohfink, 'Bewegung'; G. Braulik, 'Die Theorien über das Deuteronomistische Geschichtswerk ["DtrG"]', in Zenger *et al.* [eds.], *Einleitung in das Alte Testament*, pp. 127-31 [131]; J. Day, 'Pre-Deuteronomic Allusions to the Covenant in Hosea and Psalm lxxviii', *VT* 36 [1986], pp. 1-12 [1]; and C. Brekelmans, 'Deuteronomistic Influence in Isaiah 1–12', in J. Vermeylen [ed.], *Le livre d'Isaïe: Les oracles et leurs relectures, unité et complexité de l'ouvrage* [BETL, 81; Leuven: Leuven University Press, 1989], pp. 167-76 [176]). This warning is surely appropriate given Ringgren's claim to 'know at least one scholar who is prepared to write off the entire book, with the exception of two or three verses, as a Deuteronomistic composition' (H. Ringgren, 'Israelite Prophecy: Fact or Fiction?', in J.A. Emerton [ed.], *Congress Volume, Jerusalem 1986* [VTSup, 40; Leiden: E.J. Brill, 1988], pp. 204-10 [204]). Recently Rottzoll, *Studien*, pp. 23-30, also rejected the attribution of 2.4-5 to a deuteronomistic redactor but, noting some similarities with the holiness code in Lev. 17–26 and the book of Ezekiel, advocated a 'priestly-deuteronomistic redaction' instead.

Basing her argument on Foley's work *Immanent Art*, she notes that a formula is:

> a signifier rich in inherent cultural meanings...a template of the tradition and an indicator of worldview. Formulas bring the larger tradition to bear on the passage, allowing a few words to evoke a wider and deeper range of settings, events, characters, emotions, and meanings than the immediate textual context of the phrase might suggest.[185]

Thus, although the reference to the Torah in Amos 2.4 is correctly classified as being formulaic, this does in no way diminish its impact. Similarly misconceived is Wellhausen's understanding of the passage's rhetoric, who complained that the insertion of the Judah strophe lessens the impact of the flash of lightning shortly to strike Israel.[186] Apart from the fact that an exclusion of Judah might easily have been interpreted as favouritism,[187] the strophe actually heightens the rhetorical impact of the series in that it misleads the prophet's audience to assume that with the condemnation of their southern relatives the climax had already been reached.

To appreciate the clever organization and rhetorical power of the OAN, let us return to their arrangement. First, the general effect of dealing with all these *foreign* nations in such an elaborate *tour de force* must have been to 'lull the audience into a false sense of security'.[188] We have already seen that this strategy involves two pseudo-climaxes in the Edom and Judah oracles but, in addition to that, two further observations can be made. First, the oracles proceed in staircase fashion from foreign nations proper to blood relatives in general,[189] the sister nation Judah in particular and, finally, Israel as the ultimate target (see Figure 12).

185. S. Niditch, *Oral World and Written Word: Ancient Israelite Literature* (Library of Ancient Israel; Louisville, KY: Westminster/John Knox Press, 1996), p. 11; cf. J.M. Foley, *Immanent Art: From Structure to Meaning in Traditional Oral Epic* (Bloomington: Indiana University Press, 1991).

186. Wellhausen, *Die kleinen Propheten*, p. 71; cf. also Nowack, *Die kleinen Propheten*, p. 133.

187. Bons, 'Denotat', p. 203; Rudolph, 'Völkersprüche', p. 48; and Wagner, 'Überlegungen', p. 668.

188. Thus J. Barton, *Isaiah 1–39* (OTG; Sheffield: Sheffield Academic Press, 1995), p. 84. Carroll R., 'God', p. 60, notes that the repetitious formulaic language together with the concatenous pattern observed by Paul, 'Amos 1.3–2.3', have the effect of 'pulling forward' the hearer or reader to the next strophe.

189. For this differentiation, see Theis, 'Der Prophet Amos', p. 114; and Chisholm, 'For Three Sins...', p. 188.

A   Condemnation of foreign nations

    1.   Aram   (1.3-5)
    2.   Philistia   (1.6-8)
    3.   Tyre   (1.9-10)

B   Condemnation of blood relatives

    4.   Edom   (1.11-12)
    5.   Ammon   (1.13-15)
    6.   Moab   (2.1-3)

C   Supposedly climactic condemnation of the sister nation

    7.   Judah   (2.4-5)

D   Climactic condemnation of Israel

    8.   Israel   (2.6-16)

Figure 12. *The Rhetorical Structure of the OAN*[190]

Secondly, the series is also arranged geographically according to a pattern that is, slowly but steadily, closing in on Israel. As some have noted, the oracles alternate between nations that border on Israel and those that are neighbouring Judah; and as they alternate they move progressively closer to Israel and Judah's common border. The geographical orientation thus moves from the northeast (Aram) to the southwest (Philistia), the northwest (Phoenicia), the southeast (Edom, Ammon, Moab) and finally to Judah and Israel (Figure 13).[191]

---

190. Bovati and Meynet, *Le livre du prophète Amos*, p. 38, proposed a chiastic structure (A: 1.3–2.3, B: 2.4-5, A': 2.6-16), the outer parts of which form further chiasms. Thus section A (1.3–2.3) is defined as A (1.3-8), B (1.9-12), A' (1.13–2.3) (p. 39) and A' (2.6-16) as A (2.6a), B (2.6b-8), C (2.9-10), D (2.11-12), C' (2.13), B' (2.14-16a), A' (2.16b) (p. 73). However, J.L. McLaughlin, review of *Le livre du prophète Amos* (RhétBib, 2; Paris: Cerf, 1994), by P. Bovati and R. Meynet, in *Bib* 77 (1996), pp. 114-17, has rightly noted that the proposal of the major chiasm distorts the passage's rhetoric by making the Judah oracle the core element instead of regarding it as 'a building block in an argument culminating in the final sequence'.

191. A.E. Steinmann, 'The Order of Amos's Oracles Against the Nations: 1.3–2.16', *JBL* 111 (1992), pp. 683-89 (687); Hayes, 'Amos's Oracles Against the Nations', pp. 153-54; Birch, *Hosea, Joel, and Amos*, p. 181; Niemann, 'Theologie', pp. 187-88; and Eslinger, 'Education', p. 36.

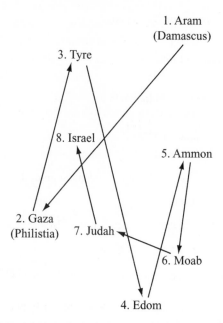

Figure 13. *The Geographical Arrangement of the OAN*[192]

Other geographical arrangement theories were proposed previously by Marti and Bentzen, neither of which carried its point, even though Bentzen's ideas were quite influential for a while.[193]

---

192. P.C. Beentjes, 'Oracles Against the Nations: A Central Issue in the "Latter Prophets"', *Bijdragen, tijdschrift voor filosofie en theologie* 50 (1989), pp. 203-209 (204), finds a similar order in the OAN in Ezek. 25–32; and E. Zenger, *A God of Vengeance? Understanding the Psalms of Divine Wrath* (trans. L.M. Maloney; Louisville, KY: Westminster/John Knox Press, 1996), p. 43, detects a geographical pattern of encirclement in Ps. 83.7-8.

193. K. Marti, 'Zur Komposition von Amos 1₃–2₃', in W. Frankenberg and F. Küchler (eds.), *Abhandlungen zur semitischen Religionskunde und Sprachwissenschaft: Wolf Wilhelm Graf von Baudissin zum 26. September 1917 überreicht von Freunden und Schülern* (BZAW, 33; Giessen: Alfred Töpelmann, 1918), pp. 323-30 (326-27), thought the order was determined by the conquest route of the Assyrians, but his theory could accommodate only the oracles against Aram, Ammon, Moab and Israel.

Bentzen, 'Ritual Background' (followed by Kapelrud, *Central Ideas*, pp. 17-33; Beaucamp, 'Amos 1–2', pp. 438-39; A. van Selms, 'Amos' Geographic Horizon', in *Studies on the Books of Hosea and Amos* [OTWSA, 7/8; Potchefstroom: Pro Rege-Pers Beperk, 1966], pp. 166-69 [166]; G. Fohrer, 'Prophetie und Magie', *ZAW* 78 [1966], pp. 25-47 [40ff.]; *idem*, 'Bemerkungen', p. 479; J.H. Hayes, 'The Usage of Oracles

Combining the two analyses outlined above, I would suggest that the rhetoric works in two ways. First, the movement from strangers to blood relatives and then on to Judah and Israel brings the divine judgment closer and closer to the people's own sphere. Secondly, the rhetorical effect of the geographical order is 'to throw a kind of geographical noose around Israel and thus to make the climactic accusation against her even more devastatingly powerful'.[194] In a similar vein, Jemielity notes:

> this series works like a progressively chilling, ironic thriller in which the ultimate and principal victim, disarmingly satisfied and rendered complacent by the misfortune of others, comes slowly and fearfully to realize that she has been witnessing an irresistible movement towards her own destruction. Amos moves geographically from the farthest peripheries of the northern kingdom in Damascus and Gaza, Tyre and Edom, to the very eastern and southern borders of the kingdom—Ammon, Moab, and Judah—until, ironically, only Israel is left, to receive not words of encouragement but rather the longest of the oracles of doom.[195]

Some scholars, however, are not convinced that the series reflects a deliberate geographical arrangement since the one outlined above is not as neat as it might have been. Perhaps, then, the audience would not have been alert to this geographical movement? It is difficult to decide this one way or another, yet even if Amos's hearers were unaware of the tightening geographical noose, the passage's rhetoric would still have been extremely powerful. Good captures its force well, pointing out:

> we can imagine the xenophobic listeners nodding in happy agreement as the prophet's doom moves across one enemy after another, the very piling up

against Foreign Nations in Ancient Israel', *JBL* 87 [1968], pp. 81-92; and Gottwald, *Kingdoms*, pp. 103-112), proposed that the arrangement was based on the pattern of the Egyptian execration texts. This has been criticized, however, by M. Weiss, 'The Pattern of the "Execration Texts" in the Prophetic Literature', *IEJ* 19 (1969), pp. 150-57; Fey, *Amos und Jesaja*, p. 46; Wolff, *Joel and Amos*, pp. 145-47; and Barton, *Amos's Oracles against the Nations*, pp. 12-14.

Wolff, *Joel and Amos*, p. 147, also refuted Reventlow's relation of the OAN to a ritual cursing at a covenant festival (cf. Reventlow, *Amt*, pp. 73-75; and E. Würthwein, 'Der Ursprung der prophetischen Gerichtsrede', in Neumann [ed.], *Das Prophetenverständnis*, pp. 361-79). For a discussion of various proposals concerning their *Sitz im Leben*, see Barton, *Amos's Oracles against the Nations*, ch. 2.

194. Wright, *Living as the People of God*, p. 123; cf. J.D. Nogalski, 'A Teaching Outline for Amos', *RevExp* 92 (1995), pp. 147-51 (147), who speaks of an 'encircling'.

195. T. Jemielity, *Satire and the Hebrew Prophets* (Literary Currents in Biblical Interpretation; Louisville, KY: Westminster/John Knox Press, 1992), p. 91.

of oracles lulling them to a doze until suddenly, with that characteristic
prophetic shock, they are jerked awake with 'For three transgressions of—
Israel, or for four...' *The oracles are so adroitly arranged as to appear
haphazard*, satisfying the hearers' desire for destruction on their enemies,
while all the time the doom circles closer and closer. The irony lies in the
shock of the climax, which is surely not intended to be noticed until too
late.[196]

However the minutiae of the oracles' arrangement are interpreted, once
the by now familiar words 'for three sins and for four of...' resound again
followed by the mention of Israel itself, it is clear that the real climax has
been reached. And it is no less obvious that the entire piece is contrived in
a masterly fashion, designed to achieve what has been called a 'rhetoric of
entrapment'.[197]

Before we then turn to the rhetoric of the Israel oracle, it should be
noted that Israel's equation with the surrounding nations must have been
regarded by Amos's audience as extremely impudent. As Wolff notes, to
include Israel in the list of peoples ripe for judgment was quite simply
scandalous.[198] 'Amos boldly does so for the first time, and more than once
(9.7; cf. 6.2).'[199] In a similar vein, Stuart notes that '*Israel*, being the most
guilty of the group, *has become in effect a foreign nation to Yahweh*',[200]
and according to Carroll R., 'Israel is enmeshed within several entwining
webs of structural devices that make it part of this world of nations and
their history'.[201]

The equation is achieved by employing the same introductory formula
as in the preceding strophes, including the catchword פשע. This in effect
means that the social injustice against the poor and needy, of which Israel

196. E.M. Good, *Irony in the Old Testament* (BLS; Sheffield: Almond Press, 2nd
edn, 1981), p. 34 (emphasis added).

197. Alter, *Art of Biblical Poetry*, p. 144; cf. also K.J. Dell, 'The Misuse of Forms in
Amos', *VT* 45 (1995), pp. 45-61 (54-55). Similar examples of entrapment are to be
found in 2 Sam. 12.1-14; 1 Kgs 20.35-43 and Amos 3.1-8.

198. The English translation uses the term 'unprecedented' (Wolff, *Joel and Amos*,
p. 148) yet the term 'unerhört' (as found in H.W. Wolff, *Dodekapropheton. II. Joel und
Amos* [BKAT, 14.2; Neukirchen–Vluyn: Neukirchener Verlag, 3rd edn, 1985], p. 180) is
better translated as 'scandalous' or 'outrageous'.

199. Wolff, *Joel and Amos*, p. 148; cf. Eichrodt, *Theologie*, II, p. 114; Gese, 'Komposition', p. 93; and J. Jeremias, 'Völkersprüche und Visionsberichte im Amosbuch',
in Fritz, Pohlmann and Schmitt (eds.), *Prophet und Prophetenbuch*, pp. 82-97 (90).

200. Stuart, *Hosea–Jonah*, p. 309 (my italics).

201. Carroll R., 'God', p. 63.

is guilty, is placed on a par with the shocking war crimes committed by its neighbours. Amos thus 'transfer[s] as it were the horror to commonplace everyday misdemeanours which people may have regretted but would mostly shrug off as the kind of thing that just happens in an imperfect world'.[202] Sometimes this is seen as a rhetorical trick used in an attempt to justify Yahweh's judgment as well as to provide an answer to the burning question of theodicy, which arose in consequence of the nation's exile.[203] However, Noble rightly rejects the notion of a rhetorical trick because:

> if Amos' attempt to persuade us that sharp practices in the marketplace are every bit as reprehensible as ripping open pregnant women is really just a rhetorical trick that masks the difference in content behind the similarity of form, then, once we recognise the trick, we will no longer be persuaded— and quite rightly too, for our moral sense protests that there really is a massive difference of degree between such things. But with this Amos' theodicy collapses...[204]

It therefore seems best to take the prophet's words at face value. Indeed, the fierceness of Amos's accusations against Israel, illustrated by the often highly emotive language,[205] confirms that, in his view, the offences of God's people were just as bad as, or perhaps even worse than, the crimes committed by the foreign nations. The Israelites wronged, after all, their fellow citizens.[206] A similar point is made in Amos 3.9-11 where two former oppressors of Israel (representing *inter*-national crimes) are called to witness the oppression found *within* Israel. Commenting on Amos 1–2,

---

202. Barton, *Amos's Oracles against the Nations*, p. 48; cf. T.H. McAlpine, 'The Word Against the Nations', *Studia biblica et theologica* 5.1 (1975), pp. 3-14 (5).

203. Cf. Barton, 'History and Rhetoric', pp. 60-61; and H.-P. Müller, 'Ein Paradigma zur Theorie der alttestamentlichen Wissenschaft: Amos, seine Epigonen und Interpreten', *NZSTR* 33 (1991), pp. 112-38 (113-17), who compares the use of the sociocritical indictments to the thought model of the *usus elenchticus legis*. Indeed, Fritz, 'Amosbuch', regards almost the entire book as a '*vaticinium ex eventu*...um das eingetroffene Unheil als gerechtes Handeln Jahwes zu deuten' (p. 41).

204. Noble, 'Israel', p. 66.

205. Cf. esp. למען חלל and השאפים על־עפר־ארץ בראש דלים ודרך ענוים יטו in v. 7 as well as ועל־בגדים חבלים יטו אצל כל־מזבח in v. 8; see also 3.9-10; 4.1; 5.7, 10-13; 6.1-6, 12 and 8.4-6.

206. Similarly Weiser, *Profetie*, p. 105; J. Jeremias, 'The Interrelationship Between Amos and Hosea', in Watts and House (eds.), *Forming Prophetic Literature*, pp. 171-86 (183); and Deissler, *Zwölf Propheten*, p. 102. Whether the text is taken as an attempt to answer the question of theodicy or as an endeavour to alert the audience to the seriousness of their wrongdoings depends on how one dates it.

Marks thus rightly notes that 'the cited atrocities of the nations...are only preliminaries to the more severe transgressions against social justice perpetrated in Israel'.[207]

Having turned to Israel itself, Amos makes it unmistakably clear where his main emphasis lies. The list enumerating the people's sins (2.6-8) is much longer than in any of the preceding oracles. As regards the content of the accusations, Amos's principal focus is on social offences.[208] While it is beyond the scope of the present investigation to engage in a minute discussion of the socio-economic issues involved in the interpretation of Amos in general, or to present a detailed exegesis of the passage in question, some brief comments are required at this point. It is often affirmed that throughout the book, Amos accuses *all* Israel and accordingly threatens the whole people with a comprehensive divine judgment.[209] This view, however, fails to pay sufficient attention to the actual referents of Amos's accusations as well as to the fact that the prophet's charges imply a distinction between culprits and victims. The neglect of these two aspects, in turn, results in questionable conclusions, as is illustrated by Schmidt's complaint that Amos:

207. Marks, 'Twelve Prophets', p. 222; cf. also Smith, *Book of the Twelve Prophets*, pp. 122-23, who speaks of 'the atrocities of Barbarism' on the one hand and 'the sins of Civilisation' on the other.

208. There appear to be cultic overtones as well, however, which it is not necessary to delete (contra Elliger, *BHS, ad loc.*; Vollmer, *Geschichtliche Rückblicke und Motive*, pp. 21-22; and Dietrich, 'JHWH', pp. 321-24) since Amos frequently portrays the social and cultic spheres as interwoven dimensions of Israel's life (see Carroll R., *Contexts*, ch. 5; *idem*, 'The Prophetic Text and the Literature of Dissent in Latin America: Amos, García Márquez, and Cabrera Infante Dismantle Militarism', *BibInt* 4 [1996], pp. 76-100).

209. Cf. Smend, 'Das Nein des Amos'; Wolff, *Joel and Amos*, pp. 102-104 and *passim*; *idem, Stunde des Amos*, pp. 23-38; *idem*, 'Das unwiderstehliche Wort: Amos und das verschuldete Ende', in *idem, Prophetische Alternativen: Entdeckungen des Neuen im Alten Testament* (Munich: Chr. Kaiser Verlag, 1982), pp. 9-23; J. Jeremias, *Kultprophetie und Gerichtsverkündigung in der späten Königszeit Israels* (WMANT, 35; Neukirchen–Vluyn: Neukirchener Verlag, 1970), p. 151; Schmidt, 'Prophetische "Grundgewissheit"'; *idem*, ' "Suchet den Herrn, so werdet ihr leben." Exegetische Notizen zum Thema "Gott suchen" in der Prophetie', in J. Bergman, K. Drynjeff and H. Ringgren (eds.), *Ex Orbe Religionum. Studia Geo Widengren XXIV mense Apr. MCMLXXII quo die lustra tredecim feliciter explevit oblata ab collegis, discipulis, amicis, collegae magistro amico congratulantibus*, I (Studies in the History of Religions, 21; Leiden: E.J. Brill, 1972), pp. 127-40; *idem, Zukunftsgewissheit*; and Schmid, 'Amos', p. 97.

threatens the end of the people of God yet in the main substantiates this announcement of the future by appealing to the oppression, which the rich practice against the poor, even though the facts of the matter only suffice as a motive for the punishment of the high society [cf. Amos 4.1-2] but not for a threat of doom against everyone [5.2 *et al.*].[210]

The problem besetting this line of interpretation has been adroitly expressed by Crüsemann, who once complained about the radicalization of Amos's message, achieved by means of literary-critical and theological operations, which has turned the prophet into the messenger of a God who murders entire nations and who therefore may safely be regarded as theologically outdated.[211] Finally, the view that Amos announces the end of all Israel is characterized all too often by a patent literalism, which does not take into account the rhetoric of Amos's message in particular, let alone the functional aspect of literary and/or oral discourse in general.[212]

Instead of attempting to solve the many questions involved in the interpretation of Amos 2.6-8,[213] however, I shall merely set out the issues

210. Schmidt, 'Prophetische "Grundgewissheit"', p. 546.

211. F. Crüsemann, 'Vorwort', in Schwantes, *Das Land kann seine Worte nicht ertragen*, pp. 8-11 (10).

212. Cf. Möller, 'Rehabilitation'; and *idem*, 'Words of (In-)evitable Certitude'.

213. Extensive discussions can be found in Fleischer, *Von Menschenverkäufern*, pp. 47-79; and Reimer, *Recht*, pp. 31-50; but cf. also R. Bach, 'Gottesrecht und weltliches Recht in der Verkündigung des Propheten Amos', in W. Schneemelcher (ed.), *Festschrift für Günther Dehn* (Neukirchen–Vluyn: Erziehungsverein, 1957), pp. 23-34 (28-33); M.A. Beek, 'The Religious Background of Amos 2.6-8', in *OTS*, 5 (Leiden: E.J. Brill, 1948), pp. 132-41; Barstad, *Religious Polemics,* ch. 2; B. Lang, 'Sklaven und Unfreie im Buch Amos (ii 6, viii 6)', *VT* 31 (1981), pp. 482-88; *idem, Monotheism and the Prophetic Minority: An Essay in Biblical History and Sociology* (The Social World of Biblical Antiquity, 1; Sheffield: Almond Press, 1983), *passim*; J.A. Dearman, *Property Rights in the Eighth-Century Prophets: The Conflict and Its Background* (SBLDS, 106; Atlanta: Scholars Press, 1988), pp. 19-25; Dietrich, 'JHWH', pp. 320-24; D.R. Hillers, 'Palmyrene Aramaic Inscriptions and the Old Testament, especially Amos 2.8', *ZAH* 8 (1995), pp. 55-62; as well as the commentaries *ad loc*.

For a general discussion of the referents of Amos's social criticism, see Fleischer, *Von Menschenverkäufern*, ch. 3.2, who summarizes and evaluates the proposals by M. Noth, 'Das Krongut der israelitischen Könige und seine Verwaltung', *ZDPV* 50 (1927), pp. 211-44; H. Donner, 'Die soziale Botschaft der Propheten im Lichte der Gesellschaftsordnung in Israel', in Neumann (ed.), *Das Prophetenverständnis*, pp. 493-514; S. Timm, *Die Dynastie Omri: Quellen und Untersuchungen zur Geschichte Israels im 9. Jahrhundert vor Christus* (FRLANT, 124; Göttingen: Vandenhoeck & Ruprecht, 1982); C. Schäfer-Lichtenberger, *Stadt und Eidgenossenschaft im Alten*

at stake, an apt discussion of which is possible only in the context of an analysis of Amos's message as a whole.[214] First, how are we to define the culprits mentioned in vv. 6-8? Do they belong to the higher stratum of society,[215] or is a broader definition indicated?[216] How significant is the

Testament: Eine Auseinandersetzung mit Max Webers Studie 'Das antike Judentum' (BZAW, 156; Berlin: W. de Gruyter, 1983); M. Clauss, Gesellschaft und Staat in Juda und Israel (Eichstätter Hochschulreden, 48; Munich: Minerva, 1985); U. Rüterswörden, Die Beamten der israelitischen Königszeit: Eine Studie zu śr und vergleichbaren Begriffen (BWANT, 117; Stuttgart: W. Kohlhammer, 1985); and M. Fendler, 'Zur Sozialkritik des Amos: Versuch einer wirtschafts- und sozialgeschichtlichen Interpretation alttestamentlicher Texte', EvT 33 (1973), pp. 32-53.

See also the annotated bibliography by J.E. Sanderson, 'War, Peace, and Justice in the Hebrew Bible: A Representative Bibliography', in G. von Rad, Holy War in Ancient Israel (ed. and trans. M.J. Dawn; Grand Rapids: Eerdmans, 1991), pp. 135-66, which lists works on 'Political Power and Modes of Government in the Hebrew Bible' (pp. 149-58) and 'Violence, Peace, and Justice in the Hebrew Bible' (pp. 158-64).

214. As stated elsewhere ('Rehabilitation', pp. 53-54 n. 30), I favour the approach of Carroll R., who rejects any simplistic solution that turns Amos into a champion of the poor and is then forced to disregard all passages that do not fit the concept. Comparing the complex cultural (esp. cultic/religious) and socio-economic factors surfacing in Amos's textual world with those at work in modern Latin American countries, Carroll R. stresses that the prophet's message 'cannot be reduced to a neat liberation paradigm' ('God', p. 68). Even if those arguing for a narrow definition of the culprits in 2.6-8 are correct, the book as a whole paints a much more complex picture. It portrays a society characterized by social injustice, a nationalistic cult serving the people's self-satisfaction as well as a utopian militarism, all of which are censured by the prophet. See Carroll R., Contexts, ch. 2 for a discussion of sociological studies of Old Testament texts and ch. 5 for his reading of Amos 3–6; see also his articles 'God'; 'Prophetic Text'; and 'Reflecting on War and Utopia in the Book of Amos: The Relevance of a Literary Reading of the Prophetic Text for Central America', in idem, D.J.A. Clines and P.R. Davies (eds.), The Bible in Human Society: Essays in Honour of John Rogerson (JSOTSup, 200; Sheffield: Sheffield Academic Press, 1995), pp. 105-21.

215. Cf. Donner, 'Botschaft'; K. Koch, 'Die Entstehung der sozialen Kritik bei den Propheten', in Wolff (ed.), Probleme biblischer Theologie, pp. 236-57; Lang, 'Sklaven und Unfreie'; idem, Monotheism, passim; Dearman, Property Rights, pp. 19-25; Fleischer, Von Menschenverkäufern, pp. 47-79; and Reimer, Recht, pp. 31-50.

216. Fendler, 'Sozialkritik'; Huffmon, 'Social Role'; I. Jaruzelska, 'Social Structure in the Kingdom of Israel in the Eighth Century B.C. as Reflected in the Book of Amos', Folia orientalia 29 (1992–93), pp. 91-117; idem, Amos and the Officialdom in the Kingdom of Israel: The Socio-economic Position of the Officials in the Light of the Biblical, the Epigraphic and Archaeological Evidence (Uniwersytet im. Adama Mickiewicza w Poznaniu, Seria Socjologie, 25; Poznań: Adam Mickiewicz University

distinction between victims and culprits? Does it imply a non-inclusive understanding of the prophet's charges in that some people were simply victims,[217] so not guilty themselves, and thus not in view in the prophet's announcements of judgment? How, on the other hand, are we to understand the general reference to יִשְׂרָאֵל in v. 6? Does this indicate that the entire people are in view, as is so often assumed? Or do the specific cases listed in vv. 6-8 require the term יִשְׂרָאֵל to be defined much more narrowly? Are these specific culprits, after all, the real reason for Amos's harangue? Or could they just be representatives of a society that as a whole disregards Yahweh's standards? What light do vv. 9-12 shed on the interpretation of vv. 6-8, and how comprehensive is the punishment announced in vv. 13-16?

I will attempt to offer some answers to these questions in what follows. What needs to be stressed here, however, is that the prophet's charges must have been well justified if ever he was to convince his hearers of his position. Thus, Israelite society must have been thoroughly permeated by the kind of social injustice referred to. Secondly, the general reference to יִשְׂרָאֵל in v. 6 clearly opens up the possibility that not only those guilty of the wrongdoings listed in vv. 6-8 but also the populace at large are in view here. And as Amos subsequently expands his critique of Israelite society to include its wrong perception and performance of the cult, the list of the guilty extends well beyond the culprits of 2.6-8. But what, then, is the rhetorical function of this section? Rather than reducing the options to the question as to whether Amos aimed at leading his audience to repent of their lifestyle or whether he simply announced Israel's end, one should also consider the possibility that he first had to convince the people of how short

Press, 1998); Smith, *Amos*, p. 72; and E.F. Campbell, 'Archaeological Reflections on Amos's Targets', in Coogan (ed.), *Scripture and Other Artifacts*, pp. 32-52, who because of archaeological evidence at Shechem infers that cheating in trade and a comfortable lifestyle at the expense of others were not restricted to the higher classes.

217. On the victims, see Fleischer, *Von Menschenverkäufern*, ch. 3.1; M. Schwantes, *Das Recht der Armen* (BBET, 4; Frankfurt: Peter Lang, 1977), esp. pp. 87-99; Koch, 'Entstehung', pp. 242-49; T. Giles, '*Dal* and *'ebyon*: The Poor and the Needy in the Book of Amos', *BRT* 1 (1991), pp. 12-20; see also the lexical entries by B. Johnson, 'צָדַק, צֶדֶק, צְדָקָה, צַדִּיק', in *ThWAT*, VI, pp. 898-924; D.J. Reimer, 'צדק', in *NIDOTTE*, III, pp. 744-69; G.J. Botterweck, 'אֶבְיוֹן', in *TDOT*, I, pp. 27-41; W.R. Domeris, 'אֶבְיוֹן', in *NIDOTTE*, I, pp. 228-32; H.-J. Fabry, 'דַּל, דָּלַל, דָּלָה, דַּל', in *TDOT*, III, pp. 208-30 (esp. 222-23); M.D. Carroll R., 'דלל', in *NIDOTTE*, I, pp. 951-54; E.S. Gerstenberger, 'עָנָו, עָנִי, תַּעֲנִית, עֹנֶה, עֲנֻוֹת, עֲנָוָה, עָנָה II, עָנָה', in *ThWAT*, VI, pp. 247-70; and W.J. Dumbrell, 'עָנִי', in *NIDOTTE*, III, pp. 454-64.

they fell of Yahweh's standards.[218] As the ensuing discussion between Amos and his audience indicates, this was not an easy task given the people's heavy reliance on religious traditions and military and economic successes. Perhaps the drastic language in passages like 3.9-10; 4.1-5 and 5.21-23 is best explained in this context, namely, as an attempt to overcome the people's ill-founded yet deeply rooted self-assurance.

Proceeding then to the next sub-section in vv. 9-12, one notices that the structural pattern exhibited by the previous strophes is here expanded. This serves to underline the inappropriateness of the people's behaviour, which is contrasted with Yahweh's past acts of salvation (2.9-10) as well as his attempts to guide his people by raising up prophets and nazirites (v. 11).[219] This is followed by a statement charging the people with the rejection of these divine representatives (v. 12).[220] The conflict between Yahweh and

218. This is in some respects close to the 'repentance theory', but it is not the same. By defining the prophet's objective as an attempt to correct the audience's perceptions of reality, criticisms like that by Smend against the 'repentance theory' are foreclosed (cf. the discussion in Chapter 2). To say that Amos had to convince the people of their guilt, while at the same time rebutting their misconceived theological convictions, explains why he did not focus on calling his audience to repentance. As their reactions captured in the book of Amos amply testify, they simply would have seen no need for that.

219. There is no need to take the reference to the prophets as a retrospective acknowledgment of the prophecy of doom (against Köckert, 'Gesetz', p. 148 and Schmidt, 'Die deuteronomistische Redaktion', pp. 181-82). It is just as easily understood as referring to the 'line of [named and unnamed] prophetic messengers following Moses' (Paul, *Amos*, p. 92; cf. J. Rieger, *Die Bedeutung der Geschichte für die Verkündigung des Amos und Hosea* [Giessen: Alfred Töpelmann, 1929], p. 11; and Rudolph, *Joel, Amos, Obadja, Jona*, p. 146).

220. Amos 2.9-12 (or parts thereof) have sometimes been attributed to deuteronomistic editors (cf. Schmidt, 'Die deuteronomistische Redaktion', pp. 178-83; Reimer, *Recht*, pp. 29-30 [n. 5]; Dietrich, 'JHWH', pp. 320-21; and Köckert, 'Gesetz', pp. 147-52). This has been questioned, however, by Krause, *Verhältnis*, pp. 71-88; T.R. Hobbs, 'Amos 3 $_{1b}$ and 2 $_{10}$', *ZAW* 81 (1969), pp. 384-87; and Lohfink, 'Bewegung', pp. 325-27. The latter two have called into question the supposed deuteronomistic origin of the Exodus formula as it appears here and in 3.1, pointing out that Amos uses the 'pre-deuteronomistic' עלה (cf. Rudolph, *Joel, Amos, Obadja, Jona*, p. 146 n. 21; and Paul, *Amos*, p. 90) rather than the 'deuteronomistic' יצא. On the two formulas, cf. P. Humbert, 'Dieu fait sortir', *TZ* 18 (1962), pp. 357-61; J.N.M. Wijngaards, *The Formulas of the Deuteronomic Creed* (Tilburg: Reijnen, 1963); *idem*, 'הוציא and העלה: A Twofold Approach to the Exodus', *VT* 15 (1965), pp. 91-102; W. Gross, 'Die Herausführungsformel: Zum Verhältnis von Formel und Syntax', *ZAW* 86 (1974), pp. 425-53 (443); and B.S. Childs, 'Deuteronomic Formulae of the Exodus Tradition', *VT* 17 (1967), pp. 30-39.

his people is accentuated by the double use of an emphatic ואנכי[221] (vv. 9, 10). The rhetorical impact of this 'expansion' is heightened further by the interesting grammatical phenomenon of repeated shifts in person (i.e., Yahweh is referred to in the first as well as the third person and Israel is either addressed directly, employing second person pronouns, or spoken about using the third person).

In the past, scholars have often been tempted to purge the texts of such 'unevennesses'. However, given the frequency of these phenomena in the Old Testament and the ancient Near Eastern literatures, there are now an increasing number of exegetes who, instead of finding fault with the ancient authors or detecting evidence for editorial work (which only shifts the blame to someone else), prefer to look into the possible reasons for these grammatical inconsistencies. Thus, Goldingay in an article on Isa. 42.18-25 suggested that so-called 'unevennesses' in the Hebrew text 'may seem such because of mistaken expectations on our part'.[222] He also maintained that phenomena such as the combination of singular and plural, finite verb and infinite, second and third person verb or first and third person verb etc., serve to make a point. As he points out:

> different rhetorical effects are achieved by each form of speech—for instance, distancing which encourages open thinking, or confrontation which encourages self-examination, or identification which encourages openness by forswearing a criticism such as aspires to lofty transcendence.[223]

Bearing these observations in mind, let us then probe into the effects of the grammatical shifts found in Amos 2.6-10. First, it should be noted that up to the end of v. 9, Yahweh is not addressing Israel but is talking *about* them. This only changes in v. 10 where Yahweh suddenly begins to speak *to* his people ('I brought *you* up', העליתי אתכם). Seen in the light of the overall argument and rhetoric of the OAN, the following picture emerges. In 1.3–2.5 Yahweh is portrayed as speaking *about* Israel's surrounding nations, interrupted only by Amos's use of the introductory and closing formulas כה אמר יהוה and אמר יהוה. When, finally, Israel itself becomes the target of the divine harangue, the fact that Israel, just like the foreign nations, is also spoken about in the third person creates the impression of Yahweh distancing himself from his people by reducing them to the same status as their neighbours.

221. Cf. GK §135a.
222. J.E. Goldingay, 'Isaiah 42.18-25', *JSOT* 67 (1995), pp. 43-65 (46).
223. Goldingay, 'Isaiah 42.18-25', p. 48.

At the same time, Yahweh talks about himself in the first person
(וְאָנֹכִי הִשְׁמַדְתִּי) thus expressing his personal involvement. This is stressed
particularly in the phrase 'so that my holy name is profaned' in 2.7b.
However, there is one notable exception to this first person discourse—the
construct בֵּית אֱלֹהֵיהֶם in v. 8, which is used instead of the expected
בֵּיתִי.[224] In the light of the reasons for grammatical inconsistencies suggested by Goldingay, this appears to be an example of deliberate distancing by Yahweh. It achieves an ironic effect in that Israel's God is
portrayed as talking about his people who, he says, desecrate the temple
of—who they believe to be—*their* god.[225] However, as Amos emphasizes
repeatedly throughout the book, this belief is fundamentally and
dangerously mistaken: Yahweh is not *their* god; he is not a deity that is
easily manipulated by cultic rituals replacing obedience to his demands
(e.g. of social justice).

From v. 9 onwards, Yahweh relates his saving acts on Israel's behalf.
And it needs to be remembered that Israel is still spoken *about* as if it were
just another foreign nation: Yahweh destroyed the Amorites 'before them'
(מִפְּנֵיהֶם). However, in v. 10 the narrational perspective suddenly changes
when Yahweh addresses his people in a very personal way, reminding
them that 'I brought *you* up out of Egypt'. The rhetorical effect of this
grammatical shift is best understood in the light of the Aristotelian concept
of *pathos*. According to Aristotle, 'the orator persuades by means of his
hearers, when they are roused to emotion by his speech, for the judgments
we deliver are not the same when we are influenced by joy or sorrow, love
or hate'.[226] This idea of rousing the audience's emotions helpfully
elucidates the shift in 2.9-10 from talking *about* the Israelites to speaking
to them.[227] In relating the exodus, the guidance in the desert and the

---

224. See also אֶת־תּוֹרַת יְהוָה in 2.4 and the comments by Rudolph, *Joel, Amos,
Obadja, Jona*, p. 121; and Hayes, *Amos*, p. 102.

225. Finley, *Joel, Amos, Obadiah*, p. 162, suggests that the phrase 'might get across
Amos's desire to disassociate himself from [the people's] practices'.

226. *Rhet.* 1.2.5: διὰ δὲ τῶν ἀκροατῶν, ὅταν εἰς πάθος ὑπὸ τοῦ λόγου
προαχθῶσιν· οὐ γὰρ ὁμοίως ἀποδίδομεν τὰς κρίσεις λυπούμενοι καὶ χαίροντες
ἢ φιλοῦντες καὶ μισοῦντες. Ueding, *Klassische Rhetorik*, p. 44, points out that this
'rhetorical psychagogy' received particular attention in Cicero's *De Oratore* (i.e.
2.178, a passage that well illustrates the interdependence of the two concepts of *ethos*
and *pathos*).

227. B.K. Smith, 'Amos, Obadiah', in *idem* and F.S. Page, *Amos, Obadiah, Jonah*
(New American Commentary, 19b; Broadman & Holman, 1995), pp. 23-201 (66),
notes that the shift 'heightens the direct and personal nature of the appeal'.

raising up of prophets and nazirites as something '*I* did for *you*', Yahweh appeals to the people's cherished memories of the 'golden past'. These divine acts, however, the Israelites mistook to guarantee that the future would be bright too.

We may note in passing that some interpreters were puzzled by the 'wrong order' of the narration of Israel's history in vv. 9-11 and have taken this, as one might have guessed, as indicative of intrusive editorial work.[228] However, Hoffman rightly maintains that the premise 'that chronological order is the only possible structure in such a prophetic address' is an unnecessary one.[229] He adds that the progress of thought here is circular, proceeding from Yahweh's destruction of the Amorites, which is related to the inheritance of the land, to the exodus and then back again to the possession of the land. This, Hoffman concludes, is due to the nature of the passage in question, which 'is not a pure historiographical review, but a sharp polemic using historiographical motifs'.[230] Mays adds that the unusual order 'emphasizes that Israel's existence in the land of the Amorites is the result of Yahweh's work',[231] the effectiveness of which is underlined in that Yahweh affirms he has 'destroyed [the Amorite's] fruit above, and his roots beneath' (ואשמיד פריו ממעל ושרשיו מתחת).[232] Regrettably, however, this self-portrayal of Yahweh as a deity who caringly attended to his weak people stands in sharp contrast to Israel's current treatment of their own weak members of society.[233] This being the case, the affirmation of Yahweh's total destruction of the strong and powerful

228. Cf. e.g. Weiser, *Profetie*, p. 95; and Wolff, *Joel and Amos*, pp. 169-70.

229. Hoffman, 'North Israelite Typological Myth', p. 178.

230. Hoffman, 'North Israelite Typological Myth', p. 178. Rudolph, *Joel, Amos, Obadja, Jona*, p. 146, also opposes both a rearrangement of the verses as well as the deletion of v. 10; and Amsler, 'Amos', p. 182 n. 1, notes that 'un glossateur aurait certainement respecté l'ordre chronologique'.

231. Mays, *Amos*, p. 50; cf. Hayes, *Amos*, p. 114. J.G. Strydom, 'Sosiale geregtigheid by die profeet Amos: Die landsbelofte as vertrekpunt', *Hervormde Teologiese Studies* 52 (1996), pp. 431-48, stresses the importance of the land promise as the basis for Amos's social criticism.

232. See Isa. 37.31 and a curse in the Phoenician *'Ešmun 'azar* inscription, which reads אל יכן לם שרש למט ופר למעל (*KAI* §14.11-12; see also H.L. Ginsberg, ' "Roots Below and Fruit Above" and Related Matters', in D.W. Thomas and W.D. McHardy [eds.], *Hebrew and Semitic Studies: Presented to Godfrey Rolles Driver in Celebration of his Seventieth Birthday, 20 August 1962* [Oxford: Clarendon Press, 1963], pp. 72-76).

233. Deissler, *Zwölf Propheten*, p. 100; cf. Wolff, *Joel and Amos*, p. 168.

(the Amorites) in order to help and protect the weak (the Israelites) implies that there is a dangerous threat looming over his own people who themselves have now become oppressors of the weak and disadvantaged.[234]

Yet the crisis in the relationship between Yahweh and Israel is even graver, inasmuch as his people went so far as to thwart Yahweh's attempts to guide them by the prophets and nazirites he had appointed (vv. 11-12). This charge interestingly anticipates the reaction of Amos's audience to his own message. As Carroll R. remarks, 'the difficulty at 2.11-12 that God's people do not often listen to his words is reconfirmed in the following chapters'.[235] The ensuing rhetorical question in v. 11b then urges the audience to acknowledge Yahweh's claims made in vv. 9-11.[236] Amos thus leads his hearers to confirm that there is indeed a discrepancy between Yahweh's actions on their behalf and their own behaviour, which includes not only the merciless exploitation of the weak and defenceless but also the deliberate attempt to corrupt Yahweh's servants and prevent them from performing their duty.

The Punishment Formula

Having focused on the series' overall arrangement and the prolonged guilt section of the Israel oracle, let us now turn to the fifth formulaic expression, the punishment formula...וְשִׁלַּחְתִּי אֵשׁ בְּבֵית...וְאָכְלָה אַרְמְנוֹת,[237] which is followed by a statement outlining the details of the divine punishment. The fact that the judgment sections (as well as the parts charting the nations' wrongdoings) are not entirely formulaic but reflect the respective nation's circumstances underlines that the introductory oracles, while being employed primarily as a rhetorical preparation for the final blow against Israel, are themselves of theological significance as well. Yahweh, Amos strongly affirms, is as disgusted by the crimes of Israel's neighbours as are his hearers or readers; and he will therefore deal with them accordingly.

Most significantly, however, the punishment formula is missing from the Israel strophe. Precisely at the point when one would expect to en-

---

234. Cf. Jeremias, *Book of Amos*, pp. 38-39; and Niehaus, 'Amos', p. 368.

235. Carroll R., 'God', pp. 67-68, who lists examples of this 'reconfirmation'.

236. Cf. Rudolph, *Joel, Amos, Obadja, Jona*, p. 147. The question is rhetorically marked in that the question marker הַ is followed by אַף (cf. GB sub אַף[I]; *HALAT* sub אַף[I] 5.) and the entire phrase ends with a local marker of emphasis, i.e., the oracle formula נְאֻם־יְהוָה (cf. the discussion in Chapter 1 and P.R. Noble, 'The Function of *n'm Yhwh* in Amos', *ZAW* 108 [1996], pp. 623-26 [624 n. 3]).

237. Or וְהִצַּתִּי, as in 1.14.

counter the words ואכלה ארמנות...בבית אש ושלחתי, Yahweh relates his past beneficent dealings with his people. And when he finally comes to announce the punishment that is to befall Israel, the formulaic introductory phrase is dropped in favour of...הנה אנכי. This construction again highlights the crisis between the deity and Israel ('*You* made...drink wine [ותשקו], and commanded...[צויתם]. So, *I*...').[238] In addition, the ensuing account of the punishment differs considerably from those of the preceding strophes. Not only is it much more detailed, what is particularly striking is that it focuses not so much on the nature of the punishment as on its ineluctability. This is stressed by means of one of the book's many heptads listing various members of the military who will find it impossible to resist it (cf. vv. 14-16). Thus, neither will Yahweh revoke his judgment (לא אשיבנו), nor will anybody, regardless of strength or swiftness, be able to withstand it or flee from it.

The nature of the punishment is not easy to determine because the meaning of מעיק and העיק is unclear. There is not even agreement about the root the terms are derived from.[239] These difficulties notwithstanding, most commentators believe that v. 13 refers to an earthquake,[240] while others maintain that vv. 14-16 clearly suggest a battle context for the entire section.[241] However, this is not necessarily the case as the connection between

238. אנכי might even be considered a 'Leitmotif' in vv. 9-13. Yahweh, who destroyed the Amorites, brought Israel up out of Egypt etc., will now מעיק them (cf. Mays, *Amos*, p. 53; and Jeremias, *Book of Amos*, p. 43).

239. There has not been a lack of proposals, however. See Weiser, *Profetie*, p. 97; H. Gese, 'Kleine Beiträge zum Verständnis des Amosbuches', *VT* 12 (1962), pp. 417-38 (417-24); H.-P. Müller, 'Die Wurzeln *'yq, y'q* und *'wq*', *VT* 21 (1971), pp. 556-64; J.A. Arieti, 'The Vocabulary of Septuagint Amos', *JBL* 93 (1974), pp. 338-47 (344-45); and H.N. Richardson, 'Amos 2.13-16: Its Structure and Function in the Book', in Achtemeier (ed.), *SBLASP* 114.1, pp. 361-67 (362); as well as the commentaries *ad loc.*

240. Von Orelli, *Die zwölf kleinen Propheten*, p. 64; Weiser, *Buch der zwölf kleinen Propheten*, p. 143; Wolff, *Joel and Amos*, p. 171; Mays, *Amos*, p. 54; Rudolph, *Joel, Amos, Obadja, Jona*, pp. 148-49; Markert, *Struktur und Bezeichnung*, p. 81; Deissler, *Zwölf Propheten*, p. 101; Fleischer, *Von Menschenverkäufern*, pp. 21-22; Smith, *Amos*, pp. 90-91; Jeremias, *Book of Amos*, p. 43; and Gowan, 'Book of Amos', p. 366.

241. Keil, *Minor Prophets*, p. 173; Harper, *Commentary*, p. 61; C.L. Feinberg, *The Minor Prophets* (repr. of *The Major Messages of the Minor Prophets* [5 vols., 1948–52]; Chicago: Moody Press, 1990), pp. 93-94; Hayes, *Amos*, p. 119; R.B. Chisholm, Jr, *Interpreting the Minor Prophets* (Grand Rapids: Zondervan, 1990), p. 83; and Birch, *Hosea, Joel, and Amos*, p. 188. For other interpretations see, e.g., Paul, *Amos*, pp. 94-95; and Reimer, *Recht*, pp. 50-51.

v. 13 and vv. 14-16 could be ironic. Thus, while Israel trusts in its army (cf. 6.13), Yahweh threatens them with a major quake that renders the קל (ברגליו), the חזק, those who rely on their כח, the גבור, the תפש הקשת, the רכב הסוס, and the אמיץ לבו בגבורים alike utterly helpless. The nature of the punishment therefore needs to be determined primarily on the basis of v. 13. And while the precise meaning of מעיק and תעיק is difficult to ascertain, the likening of Yahweh's action to something a cart full of sheaves does, might indicate that an earthquake is in view here. From a rhetorical point of view, however, the most interesting comment on the image of v. 13 comes from Ryken, who notes that Amos inverts 'the idealized associations of pastoral literature. A cart full of sheaves is supposed to be an image of abundance, a pastoral version of the good life, yet here it becomes an image of torture.'[242]

Some regard the textual arrangement of vv. 14-16 as awkward, suggesting the deletion of some lines.[243] A more convincing way of dealing with these textual problems has been suggested by Rendtorff, arguing that the stichos 15b is misplaced due to a scribal error and that it should be transferred to follow 14a.[244] This solution is quite intriguing as it results in a logical order in that the first bistichos then deals with the swift (קל, קל ברגליו), the second one with the strong (גבור, חזק), and the final one with those who are armed (רכב הסוס, תפש הקשת).[245] In addition, each bistichos would then end on the refrain (לא ימלט נפשו) (cf. Figure 14).[246] Given Amos's frequent use of formulaic language and strophic arrangements, this reconstruction has a lot to commend itself.

242. L. Ryken, 'Amos', in *idem* and T. Longman III (eds.), *A Complete Literary Guide to the Bible* (Grand Rapids: Zondervan, 1993), pp. 337-47 (344).

243. Thus Elliger in *BHS ad loc.*; Wolff, *Joel and Amos*, pp. 134-35; Dietrich, 'JHWH', p. 325; and Jeremias, *Book of Amos*, pp. 43-44.

244. Rendtorff speaks of lines 14aα and 15aβ whereas I prefer to refer to them as stichoi 14a and 15b. Thus, there are three stichoi each in vv. 14-15 or, according to Rendtorff's counting, one and a half lines each.

245. According to Reimer, *Recht*, p. 52, both the תפש הקשת and the רכב הסוס were part of the crew of the war chariot (he refers to Zech. 9.10 as well as to M.L. Henry, 'Pferd', in *BHH*, III, pp. 1438-39; S. Mowinckel, 'Drive and/or Ride in O.T.', *VT* 12 [1962], pp. 278-99; A.E. Rüthi, 'Reiter/Reiterei', in *BHH*, III, pp. 1584-85; and R. Bach, '...Der, der Bogen zerbricht, Spiesse zerschlägt und Wagen mit Feuer verbrennt', in Wolff [ed.], *Probleme biblischer Theologie*, pp. 13-26).

246. R. Rendtorff, 'Zu Amos 2 14-16', *ZAW* 85 (1973), pp. 226-27.

ואבד מנוס מקל   וקל ברגליו לא ימלט
וחזק לא־יאמץ כחו   וגבור   לא־ימלט נפשו
ותפש הקשת לא יעמד   ורכב הסוס לא ימלט נפשו

Figure 14. *Rendtorff's Reconstruction of Amos 2.14-15*

Richardson, on the other hand, has argued for the text to be retained as it
stands. He agrees, however, that the stichoi 14a and 15b together
constitute a bistichos, which, as he points out, is arranged chiastically (cf.
Figure 15).

14a   ואבד מנוס מקל

15b   וקל ברגליו לא ימלט

Figure 15. *The Chiasm in Amos 2.14a, 15b*

He stresses that, while he too felt tempted to relocate 15b, he considers the
present arrangement 'a very skillful interlocking'[247] (see col. 1 below).
Yet, as he points out, if 15b followed 14c, the order of the interlocking
stichoi would be of a 'more common type' (col. 2). Rendtorff, by contrast
and as already noted, transferred 15b to follow 14a (col. 3).

	MT		Richardson		Rendtorff
14a	A—	14a	A—	14a	A ⌐
14b	B ⌐	14b	B ⌐	15b	A'⌐
14c	B'⌐	14c	B'⌐	14b	B ⌐
15a	⌐C	15b	A'—	14c	B'⌐
15b	A'⌐	15a	C ⌐	15a	C ⌐
15c	⌐C'	15c	C'⌐	15c	C'⌐

Figure 16. *The Order of the* Bistichoi *in Amos 2.14-15*

In the end, however, Richardson does not succumb to the temptation to
rearrange the text, regarding its arrangement as 'more striking, very skillful and quite unusual'.[248] He also points out that 'one would be hard
pressed to find an explanation as to how the change came about'.[249] His
second point is well taken since Rendtorff has to conjecture that a copyist
erroneously omitted the stichos 15b but added it in the margins. Another
copyist then reinserted it back into the text, putting it in the wrong

247. Richardson, 'Amos 2.13-16', p. 363.
248. Richardson, 'Amos 2.13-16', p. 363.
249. Richardson, 'Amos 2.13-16', p. 364.

place.[250] While this is no more than a conjecture, I am inclined to follow Rendtorff's analysis for a number of reasons.[251] First, it causes the bistichos constituted by vv. 14a, 15b to stand together, thus bringing the chiasm to the fore.[252] Secondly, the strophic result displays a logical order of thought, at the same time causing the refrain (נפשׁו) לֹא יְמַלֵּט to come to stand at the end of the 'strophes', which in turn results in a patterned arrangement not unlike those found elsewhere in the book (i.e., 1.3–2.5; 3.3-6; 4.6-11; 7.1-9; 8.1-3).

In keeping with the view that Amos announces Israel's end, it is often maintained that the notion of an all-encompassing judgment is present also in vv. 13-16.[253] This, however, cannot be deduced with certainty.[254] While the text does make it quite clear that no one has the ability to resist Yahweh's punishment or flee from it, it does not say that Israel's God is going to destroy his entire people. Yet it needs to be stressed that the focus on the military in vv. 13-16 cannot be taken as proof that others will be excluded from the judgement to come.[255] As already noted above, the point of vv. 14-16 is not to define who the objects of Yahweh's punishment are going to be but rather to stress its ineluctability.[256] And it should

250. Rendtorff, 'Zu Amos 2 $_{14-16}$', p. 227.

251. It has been accepted also by Reimer, *Recht*, p. 51, but was rejected by Paul, *Amos*, p. 95 n. 507.

252. However, D.T. Tsumura, '"Inserted Bicolon", the AXYB Pattern, in Amos i 5 and Psalm ix 7', *VT* 38 (1988), pp. 234-36, has alerted us to the phenomenon of an 'inserted bicolon' in Amos 1.5, resulting in what he calls the 'distant parallelism' of A ‖ B.

וּשְׁבַרְתִּי בְּרִיחַ דַּמֶּשֶׂק	A
וְהִכְרַתִּי יוֹשֵׁב מִבִּקְעַת־אָוֶן	X
וְתוֹמֵךְ שֵׁבֶט מִבֵּית עֶדֶן	Y
וְגָלוּ עַם־אֲרָם קִירָה	B

253. Cf. Wolff, *Joel and Amos*, p. 103; Vollmer, *Geschichtliche Rückblicke und Motive*, p. 26; and Jeremias, *Book of Amos*, pp. 34, 43-44.

254. Thus with Reimer, *Recht*, pp. 53-58, who takes issue with Wolff because of his failure to pay sufficient attention to the actual referents of Amos's charges and declarations of punishment. Reimer further argues that the preceding strophes do not indicate the total destruction of the foreign nations either (pp. 61-64).

255. Against Reimer, *Recht*, pp. 53-58, 65.

256. This interpretation avoids the problem of vv. 6-8 being incongruous with vv. 14-16, which is exactly the difficulty that, for instance, Reimer is facing. As he himself notes, his interpretation implies that '*in der Israelstrophe eine deutliche Unstimmigkeit zwischen Angeklagten und Bedrohten besteht. In der Strafansage wird dem Militär ein Desaster angekündigt. Nach meinen Analysen der in V. 6b-8 aufgelisteten Vergehen*

come as no surprise that, in order to convey this idea, Amos refers to the strongest, bravest, swiftest and best armed, i.e. the military. If these cannot escape or withstand the divine intervention, nobody can.

Considering the rhetoric of the Israel oracle as a whole, therefore, a picture of ambiguity and uncertainty emerges. On the one hand, the general reference to יִשְׂרָאֵל in v. 6 together with the relation of the people's 'salvation history' in vv. 9-11 points to an inclusive understanding suggesting that the northern kingdom as a whole is in view. The juxtaposition of the people's treatment of the prophets and nazirites (see the general 'you' in v. 12) and of Yahweh's punishment (again the 'you' in v. 13 appears to include all and sundry) has the same effect. Furthermore, the allusion to Yahweh's total destruction of the Amorites (v. 9) underlines the enormity of the threat by suggesting that a similar experience might be in store for his own people.

On the other hand, however, vv. 6-8 clearly distinguish between culprits and victims[257] by singling out certain members of society, who are said to be responsible for the wrongdoings Yahweh condemns. Should it not follow, then, that the punishment is to befall only the culprits[258] rather than everyone, including even the צַדִּיק of v. 6? Since vv. 13-16 do not explicitly state otherwise, a restrictive understanding of the scope of the judgment is certainly possible. Yet, there is no way of telling at this point which interpretation is correct. This, I submit, is precisely the effect the text is meant to have, as it leaves hearers or readers in the dark about its exact implications, thus creating the suspense that is guaranteed to hold the audience's interest.[259] Indeed, what more could we desire from a rhetorically well-designed introduction?

---

konnte jedoch eine Verantwortung des Militärs *allein* nicht erwiesen werden' (Reimer, *Recht*, p. 55; his italics). Reimer attempts to solve this problem by affirming that what is under attack here as well as in the preceding strophes is the mechanism of the state (p. 63). Krause, *Verhältnis*, p. 139, on the other hand, postulates that those referred to in vv. 6-8 and 14-16 are 'wenn nicht identisch, so doch in der sozialen Stellung und in der Intention gleich...nämlich möglichst viel Bodenbesitz für das Krongut zu erwerben'.

257. Cf. Reimer, *Recht*, p. 55.

258. Reimer favours this interpretation, suggesting that we equate יִשְׂרָאֵל in v. 6 with the culprits responsible for the wrongdoings listed in vv. 6-8 (*Recht*, p. 55).

259. As D. Lodge, 'Suspense', in *idem, The Art of Fiction*, pp. 13-16 (14), notes, one holds 'the interest of an audience by raising questions in their minds, and delaying the answers'.

The Concluding Divine Speech Formula
To return once more to the recurring devices of Amos 1.3–2.16, the one that yet needs to be mentioned is the concluding divine speech formula אָמַר יְהוָה, which is used only in the strophes modelled on the A pattern. As I have already discussed its significance elsewhere,[260] it should suffice for me to repeat that it functions as a 'local marker of emphasis'. As such, it is used in the OAN to accentuate the prolonged judgment sections of the A strophes. However, the Israel oracle, an adaptation of the A pattern, once more deviates from the established model in featuring the oracle formula נְאֻם־יְהוָה instead of the expected אָמַר יְהוָה. And while the oracle formula appears to be employed to roughly the same effect,[261] it may perhaps be possible to see it as possessing slightly more nuanced force. This would be more than appropriate in Amos 2.16, following as it does the vivid portrayal of Yahweh's irresistible punishment.

Conclusions and Final Observations. The OAN in 1.3–2.16 clearly serve as the book's introduction, the function of which comes into sharper focus once the following observations, advanced in the course of the above investigation, are taken into account:

1. The OAN's 'rhetoric of entrapment' takes the hearers by surprise and aims at putting them on a par with their heathen neighbours. It promotes a novel perspective on Israel's internal affairs (in particular the social injustice characterizing the nations socio-economic life) as well as on the people's relationship with their God. To employ Brueggemann's concept of imagination,[262] Amos instigates his audience's imagination by raising

260. See the discussion in Chapter 1.
261. Noble, 'Function', p. 623, has suggested that it is equivalent to 'And mark my words!' I remain unpersuaded, however, of his conclusion that the judgment section in 2.14-16 applies to all the oracles in Amos 1–2 and that the function of נְאֻם־יְהוָה is to hint at precisely that (Noble, 'Function', p. 625; see also Andersen and Freedman, *Amos*, pp. 215, 239).
262. I should stress that Brueggemann's interpretative concepts of imagination (W. Brueggemann, *The Prophetic Imagination* [Philadelphia: Fortress Press, 1978] and *Hopeful Imagination: Prophetic Voices in Exile* [Philadelphia: Fortress Press, 1986]), of a 'counterworld' (*Texts under Negotiation: The Bible and Postmodern Imagination* [Philadelphia: Fortress Press, 1993], ch. 2), the 'destabilising presence' of a prophet ('The Prophet as a Destabilizing Presence', in *idem*, *A Social Reading of the Old Testament: Prophetic Approaches to Israel's Communal Life* [ed. P.D. Miller; Minneapolis: Fortress Press, 1994], pp. 221-44) and a 'countertestimony' (*Theology of*

the possibility that in Yahweh's perception they are thought of as being no better, indeed, perhaps even worse than all those foreign nations.

2. The equation of Israel's domestic infringements with their neighbours' war crimes is obviously provocative and contentious. As such, it carries both the chance of evoking a positive shock that might lead to change as well as the danger of being rejected forthwith. What the introductory passage clearly does, however, is to trigger a dialogue or debate between the prophet and his audience, whose interpretation of their theological traditions Amos rejects.

3. The ambiguity surrounding the referents of Amos's charges and threats adds to the rhetorical power of the introduction. Having been left in the dark about some of the implications of the prophet's message, the audience is forced to 'stay tuned', as it were, in order not to miss the resolution to their questions.

All this contributes to the effect of 'drawing the hearer or reader in', to revert once again to Lodge's phrase cited above. As concerns the 'rhetoric of entrapment', however, it should be noted that this description recapitulates the OAN's rhetorical effect from the point of view of the text's internal audience, namely, Israelites living in the eighth century BCE. However, given that the compilation and reception history of the *book* of Amos need to be understood against a Judaean background, it is also necessary to consider the impact of this opening section on a Judaean readership.

In saying this, I am not implying, of course, that the preceding discussion of the text's *internal* perspective is obsolete. Far from it, as the book addresses its hearers or readers by *presenting* the prophet Amos debating with his eighth-century Israelite audience, it is important to unravel the 'poetics' of that presentation.[263] Its primary effect, I would suggest, is to transfer readers to the scene, as it were, enabling them to follow and participate in the debate. The text's main rhetorical effect thus arises out of the reader's encounter with the debating prophet.

the Old Testament: Testimony, Dispute, Advocacy [Philadelphia: Fortress Press, 1997], Part II) have helpfully spurred my own imagination.

263.   A. Berlin, *Poetics and Interpretation of Biblical Narrative* (Winona Lake, IN: Eisenbrauns, 1994), p. 15, defines poetics as 'an inductive science that seeks to abstract the general principles of literature from many different manifestations of those principles as they occur in actual literary texts'. However, Carroll R., *Contexts*, p. 155, referring to Sternberg, *Poetics*, rightly regards the goal as 'more than the grasp of formal textual mechanics'. In his view, the aim must be 'to move beyond mere aesthetics to what Sternberg calls the "ideology" of the text, which seeks not just to entertain, but to persuade'.

However, when considering the text's function for a Judaean audience, what needs to be stressed in particular is that its rhetorical situation is post 722 BCE. Thus, readers of the book approached it with a 'past-fulfilment perspective', knowing that Amos's threats of exile had come true. Read with that knowledge, the presentation of Amos's futile attempts to convince his Israelite audience of the danger they were in becomes even more powerful. Indeed, the book now effectively urges its Judaean readers not to repeat the mistakes of the prophet's original audience lest they suffer the same fate. The Judah oracle in 2.4-5 increases the text's impact even further by indicating that Amos, who, after all, had been right about Israel, had Judah on his list as well. If, as I think likely, the references to Judah originated with Amos, they may have been one reason for keeping the 'Amos tradition' alive long after the prophet had disappeared from the scene.

Chapter 4

AMOS 3

Due to form-critical considerations, Amos 3 has often been thought to consist of five small units (i.e., vv. 1-2, 3-8, 9-11, 12 and 13-15).[1] However, recent commentators have criticized the division of the passage 'into a series of supposedly self-contained sayings or oracles', noting that it 'leaves them without meaningful contexts'.[2] Despite these welcome developments, the form-critical outline of Amos 3 is a good starting point for the present investigation. Indeed, as will become clear in what follows, the outline as such is actually confirmed by my findings.[3] Yet, my concern is not with these small parts but with the rhetorical structure and function of the prophetic discourse in Amos 3.1-15 as a whole. Advocating the passage's structural unity, Dorsey has suggested that it consists of a seven-part chiasm (see Figure 17 below).[4]

> A   Yahweh will punish Israel for their sins (vv. 1-2)
>   introduced by שׁמעו; key word: פקד
>   B   Coming disaster, declared by the prophets (vv. 3-8)
>   theme: lion (אריה) and its prey
>   C   Foreign people called to gather on the mountains of Samaria (v. 9)
>   key word: ארמנות
>   D   Condemnation:
>   Israel does not know how to do right (v. 10)
>   C' Israel's fortresses and strongholds will be destroyed (v. 11)
>   key word: ארמנות

1.   Cf. Stuart, *Hosea–Jonah*, pp. 321, 324, 329; Melugin, 'Formation', pp. 377-79 (following Koch *et al.*, *Amos*); Wolff, *Joel and Amos*, pp. 175, 181, 191-92, 197, 200; and Andersen and Freedman, *Amos*, p. 369.

2.   Thus, for instance, Hayes, *Amos*, p. 122.

3.   According to Melugin, 'Formation', pp. 378-79, Amos 3 consists of the following parts: 3.1-2 prophetic oracle of judgement; 3.3-8 disputation; 3.9-11 oracle of doom; 3.12 proclamation of the future; 3.13-15 proclamation of disaster.

4.   Dorsey, 'Literary Architecture', pp. 310-11.

    B' Near-total disaster coming (v. 12)
        theme: lion (אֲרִי) and its prey
  A' Yahweh will punish Israel for their iniquities (vv. 13-15)
      introduced by שִׁמְעוּ; key word: פָּקַד

Figure 17. Amos 3 as a Seven-Part Chiasm (Dorsey)

Interestingly, this outline is in accordance with form-critical findings in that the units of the seven-part chiasm correspond to those detected by form critics. The only difference is vv. 9-11, which form critics treat as one unit but which Dorsey breaks up into three parts. While I am sceptical about the suggested chiastic arrangement, Dorsey helpfully recognizes some important key words, which lend unity to the passage as a whole. In the following examination, I am going to focus on the structure and rhetoric of Amos 3, attempting to show both the passage's internal structural and rhetorical design as well as its contribution to the rhetoric of the book of Amos in general.

1. *Amos 3.1-2, 13-15*

a. *Exegetical Observations and Structure*

To begin with the outer parts of the proposed chiasm (i.e., A [vv. 1-2][5] and A' [vv. 13-15]), it is evident that both announce Israel's punishment. Each opens with a call to listen introduced by שִׁמְעוּ and followed by the announcement of punishment proper, which uses the verb פָּקַד to refer to the impending judgment.[6] Yet, as one would expect from a concentric structure, there are also differences because, as Wendland has pointed out:

> recursion is not exact, but there is a progressive augmentation of the main constituent notions occurring at the same time, both to maintain interest and to highlight the main elements of the author's theme line. Thus, despite the correspondences which may be present, the ending of the discourse is not

---

    5.   Various deletions have been suggested for these verses, for which cf. G. Pfeifer, 'Amos und Deuterojesaja denkformenanalytisch verglichen', *ZAW* 93 (1981), pp. 439-43 (440). Following Schmidt, 'Die deuteronomistische Redaktion', p. 173, many have attributed the passage to deuteronomistic redactors, but see Lohfink, 'Bewegung', pp. 327-28, for a rejection of this view.

    6.   פָּקַד appears once in the first part (v. 2) and twice in the second (v. 14). The inclusio provided by the use of this verb is all the more remarkable given that פָּקַד is used nowhere else in the book of Amos. Cf. Gitay, 'Study', p. 295; Andersen and Freedman, *Amos*, pp. 377, 382; Paul, *Amos*, pp. 102, 108; and Hubbard, *Joel and Amos*, p. 153, who notes that 'the twice used verb *punish* (v. 14; Heb. *pqd*) harks back to the general announcement of 3.2 and is a clue to the unity of the chapter'.

really the same as its beginning, either cognitively or emotively, because it has been subtly, and often substantially, modified and refined by what has been presented between them.[7]

In both parts, the initial call to listen features an additional element (cf. Figure 18). In vv. 1-2, the focus is on the addressee, namely, the Israelites whom alone Yahweh has delivered out of Egypt. This theme carries on into the speech of Yahweh introduced by לֵאמֹר, which begins with the affirmation that the Israelites are the only ones he has known of all the families of the earth. This is highlighted by the prominent position of רק אתכם at the beginning of the sentence,[8] the use of ידע, which underlines the close relationship between Yahweh and his chosen people,[9] as well as the phrase כל משפחות האדמה, which reflects Yahweh's covenant with the patriarchs (Gen. 12.3; cf. Gen. 28.14).[10]

The closing unit (vv. 13-15) also opens with the call שמעו but as Yahweh's speech unfolds, one suddenly realizes that he is not speaking to the Israelites. Instead, Israel's God is addressing the witnesses of vv. 9-11 who are requested to hear and testify against (עוד hi. + ב) his own people.[11] The focus then shifts to Yahweh himself, to the one who is threatening to bring about the punishment. Underlining his authority, he is

7.   Wendland, 'Word', pp. 6-7.
8.   GK §142-43; Cripps, *Commentary*, p. 151; Paul, *Amos*, p. 101; and Smith, *Amos*, p. 105, all rightly note that the occurrence of רק אתכם at the beginning of the sentence constitutes a reversal of the expected word order, lending special emphasis to the notion of Israel's exceptional status.
9.   Wolff, *Joel and Amos*, pp. 176-77; and Rudolph, *Joel, Amos, Obadja, Jona*, p. 153. H. Wildberger, *Jahwes Eigentumsvolk: Eine Studie zur Traditionsgeschichte und Theologie des Erwählungsgedankens* (ATANT, 37; Stuttgart: Zwingli, 1960), p. 108, notes that while ידע is not a technical term for the election of Israel, in combination with רק אתכם it clearly indicates their 'Sonderstellung'. A. Böckler, *Gott als Vater im Alten Testament: Traditionsgeschichtliche Untersuchungen zur Entstehung und Entwicklung eines Gottesbildes* (Gütersloh: Gütersloher Verlagshaus, 2000), pp. 136-37, concludes that while, with God as subject, ידע usually connotes the divine care for human beings, it can also mean 'to elect'.
10.   Cf. Cripps, *Commentary*, p. 151; and Finley, *Joel, Amos, Obadiah*, p. 181. The use of משפחה in vv. 1 and 2 connects the prophet's introductory words with those of the deity.
11.   Thus with Cripps, *Commentary*, p. 162; Finley, *Joel, Amos, Obadiah*, p. 192; and Hubbard, *Joel and Amos*, p. 153, but against Harper, *Commentary*, p. 82; and Wolff, *Joel and Amos*, p. 200, who claims that in v. 13 'other foreigners, who are already present in Samaria, are addressed' and that 'witnesses of the punishment are [now] added to the witnesses of the guilt'.

referred to as אדני יהוה אלהי הצבאות. As Dempster has pointed out, the lengthened name, which is an exclusively Amosian feature, has a unique discourse function in its specific context.[12] And commenting on its function in Amos 3.13, Dempster reasons that 'it is no accident that such a lengthening occurs before the climactic announcement of judgment'.[13] Indeed, the pronouncement of judgment in Amos 3.13-15 is framed by references to the word of Yahweh (cf. נאם־יהוה in 3.15), thus confirming that the evocation of divine authority is fundamental the prophet's rhetoric.

The second element found in both parts (vv. 1-2, 13-15) is the announcement of punishment proper. Yet, there are again noteworthy differences between the two parts. In the first, the announcement is very short. Yahweh only so much as declares that he is going to punish Israel for all their iniquities (כל־עונתיכם) *because* (על־כן) he has known only them of all the families of the earth, a statement that paradoxically turns 'the history of salvation into a history of judgment'.[14] It should also be noted that Amos here for the third time employs the term כל, stressing that *all* Israel [the whole family], known by Yahweh of *all* the families of the earth, will now be punished for *all* their iniquities.[15] And, shedding light on Amos's skilful rhetoric, Hubbard perceptively comments that 'it is not until *iniquities* are mentioned at the end of the verse' that the implications of פקד are understood 'since *punish* (Heb. *pqd*) means literally "to visit" whether with weal or woe'.[16]

The second unit (vv. 13-15) has an extensive punishment section stressing that Yahweh is going to punish Israel for their transgressions (פשע). This punishment, the prophet underlines, will include the luxurious houses owned by the oppressors (v. 15;[17] note the *Leitmotiv* בית in vv. 13-15[18]) as

---

12. Dempster, 'Lord', pp. 185-86.

13. Dempster, 'Lord', p. 178.

14. Thus R. Martin-Achard, 'The End of the People of God: A Commentary on the Book of Amos', in *idem* and S.P. Re'emi, *God's People in Crisis: A Commentary on the Book of Amos and a Commentary on the Book of Lamentations* (ITC; Edinburgh: Handsel Press, 1984), pp. 1-71 (28). H. McKeating, *The Books of Amos, Hosea and Micah* (Cambridge Bible Commentary; Cambridge: Cambridge University Press, 1971), p. 26, remarks that the announcement in v. 2 'is virtually a summary of Amos' entire message'.

15. See Paul, *Amos*, p. 102.

16. Hubbard, *Joel and Amos*, p. 148 (his italics); cf. also Smith, *Amos*, p. 106.

17. McKeating, *Books of Amos, Hosea and Micah*, p. 31, somewhat precariously speculates that Amos, whom he describes as a semi-nomad, 'displays the contempt that

well as the altars at Bethel (v. 14). The cutting off of the horns of the altar, which makes it impossible for an offender to grasp them and thus gain sanctuary (cf. Exod. 21.13-14; 1 Kgs 1.50; 2.28), reaffirms the ineluctability of the punishment already stressed in 2.14-16. As Paul notes, 'the destruction of the altar and its horns...symbolizes the end of the sanctuary, immunity, and expiation for the people'.[19] Most shocking, however, is the notion that it is Yahweh himself who will bring about the end of Israel's cultic existence. From a rhetorical perspective, the reference to the destruction of the horns of the altar aptly contributes to Amos's challenge of his audience's complacency believing, as they did, that Yahweh was not going to punish them.[20]

Another important difference between the two announcements of punishment is that in v. 2 Yahweh addresses the Israelites directly while vv. 13-15 take up the courtroom motif from vv. 9-11,[21] which results in the deity

such men feel for settled life'. Concerning the winter and summer houses, cf. S.M. Paul, 'Amos iii 15—Winter and Summer Mansions', *VT* 28 (1978), pp. 358-60.

18. Cf. Stuart, *Hosea–Jonah*, p. 332.

19. Paul, *Amos*, p. 124; cf. also Rudolph, *Joel, Amos, Obadja, Jona*, p. 166; Hubbard, *Joel and Amos*, p. 153; and G. Pfeifer, 'Das Ja des Amos', *VT* 39 (1989), pp. 497-503 (499).

20. Cf. Gitay, 'Study', p. 301.

21. It is possible to regard all of vv. 9-15 as one courtroom motif featuring an extended punishment section (vv. 11-15). The only verse that does not sit comfortably in such a setting is v. 12, which is an ironic comment on the likelihood of Israel's rescue. O'Rourke Boyle, 'Covenant Lawsuit', p. 342, on the other hand, regards all of Amos 3–4 as one covenant lawsuit comprising the following parts: (1) Call to witnesses to hear and testify (3.1–4.3); (2) Introductory statement of the case (4.4-5); (3) Recital of the plaintiff's benevolent acts and indictment (4.6-11); (4) Sentence and warning (4.12); (5) Recognition (4.13).

Yet, O'Rourke Boyle's proposal does not stand up to close scrutiny. To mention only one weakness, I fail to see how Amos 3.1–4.3 as a whole can be classified as a 'call to witnesses to hear and testify'. What, after all, have vv. 3-8 got to do with a summons of witnesses? With regard to vv. 1-2, O'Rourke Boyle proposes that 'the prophet arraigns Israel to testify against itself' ('Covenant Lawsuit', p. 344). Yet, vv. 1-2 do not say anything about witnessing. And commenting on v. 7, O'Rourke Boyle even adds the prophet to her list of witnesses.

Rather than attempting to make the text fit any narrowly conceived notions of genre, it is preferable to recognize that Amos 3 contains a combination of rhetorical features, such as rhetorical questions (vv. 3-8), a courtroom motif (vv. 9-11), an ironic illustration (v. 12) and another allusion to the preceding courtroom motif (vv. 13-15). Indeed, the passage is none the poorer for it, as the assortment of literary forms will not have failed to surprise and shock its audience.

speaking to the foreign witnesses about his chosen people. The following
figure displays the corresponding elements in both sections (the call to
listen, the announcement of punishment) as well as the differences
between the two parts. Concerning the internal structure of vv. 13-15, it is
also important to note that it features one of Amos's characteristic heptads,
in this instance consisting of seven verbs depicting Israel's coming
destruction.[22]

b. *Rhetorical Function*

Having discussed the similarities and differences between the two sections, we are now in a position to move on to an investigation of their
rhetorical function. Two issues, in particular, call for our attention. The
first concerns their arrangement at the beginning and end of the discourse,
thus forming an inclusio for Amos 3 as a whole. Secondly, some further
comments on the rhetorical function of the differences between the two
parts are pertinent.

As regards the first point, the arrangement quite clearly leads to the
punishment theme receiving particular attention. The fact that the discourse both opens and closes on a note of judgment[23] makes it reasonable
to conclude that its primary aim is to convince the Israelites that Yahweh
has indeed resolved to punish them for their sins. As Martin-Achard notes,
'God's "visit"…evoked at the beginning just as at the end of this collection (3.2, 14) signifies in a concrete way a catastrophe without precedent
for the northern kingdom'.[24]

Yet, the differences between the two parts are equally significant. Designed to major on the divine punishment to come, the discourse opens
with the paradoxical notion that Yahweh will punish Israel precisely

22. Cf. Dorsey, 'Literary Architecture', p. 311. I have underlined the repeated
words שמעו and פקד and indicated the heptadic series of verbs by numbering them. In
addition, the letters (a) to (c) point to the threefold use of כל in vv. 1-2.

23. The introductory character of vv. 1-2 has also been noted by Hayes, *Amos*, p.
123, who points out that 'the "iniquities" (a term occurring only here in Amos) are not
defined in verse 2, indicating that 3.1-2 should not be treated as an independent, self-
contained saying'. Cf. also Gitay, 'Study', p. 295; and Wolff, *Joel and Amos*, pp. 177-
78, who states that 'in contrast to all the other oracles of Amos, the threat of punishment here is not concrete… Equally unusual is the fact that the summarizing concept
"all your transgressions" takes the place of a list of specific crimes. It is precisely these
peculiarities, however, which enable this oracle of Amos to function so well as the
introduction to a collection of oracles.'

24. Martin-Achard, 'End', p. 32.

1   שִׁמְעוּ אֶת־הַדָּבָר הַזֶּה אֲשֶׁר דִּבֶּר יְהוָה עֲלֵיכֶם בְּנֵי יִשְׂרָאֵל
על כל־המשפחה[a] אשר העליתי מארץ מצרים לאמר

2   רק אתכם ידעתי מכל משפחות האדמה על־כן[c] אפקד עליכם את כל־עונתיכם[b]

13   שמעו והעידו בבית יעקב נאם־אדני יהוה אלהי הצבאות

14   כי ביום פקדי[1] פשעי־ישראל עליו ופקדתי על־מזבחות בית־אל[2]
ונגדעו[3] קרנות המזבח ונפלו[4] לארץ
והכיתי בית־החרף[5] על־בית הקיץ[6]

15   ואבדו[7] בתי השן וספו בתים רבים
נאם־יהוה

Figure 18. *The Relationship between Amos 3.1-2 and 13-15*

because he has known only them of all the families of the earth. According to Stuart, 'reminders of the exodus deliverance serve as reminders of Israel's covenantal relationship to Yahweh'.[25] More importantly, however, Gitay has stressed that from a 'rhetorical perspective the unexpected turn functions as a tool for arousing curiosity and attracting attention'.[26] As the audience is drawn in by the prophet's unusual conclusion, they come to realize that it is their very privileges that guarantee their punishment.[27] On a more mundane level, Andersen and Freedman are right to conclude that 'the first two verses summarize the case against Israel'.[28]

However, as this introductory statement all but invites opposition, Amos apparently feels compelled to explain that his message is nothing other than the very word of Yahweh (vv. 3-8) and that the punishment is well-deserved (vv. 9-10). At the end of the discourse (vv. 14-15), the punishment theme is picked up again and developed at greater length. This, together with its prominent position and the emphasis placed on the fact that it is the 'Lord GOD, the God of hosts' who is announcing the punishment and who is going to carry it out (cf. vv. 13, 15), results in what Cripps has called an 'effective climax'.[29] And it is a climax that unflinchingly confronts the audience with the implications of Yahweh's resolve to punish: not only the mansions of the well-to-do but Israel's refuge too will crumble in the face of the divine intervention. The rhetorical connection of vv. 9-11, v. 12 and vv. 13-15 has been recognized also by Wolff whose perceptive comments I quote at some length:

> That it is impending destruction which this rare form of oracle prepares the witnesses to observe makes even more probable a close spatial as well as temporal connection with the two preceding oracles (3.9-11, 12). This explains the absence of the demonstration of guilt—it was already given in 3.9b-10. The punishment depicted here, namely the destruction of the buildings, corresponds to the guilt which was demonstrated above in conjunction with the 'strongholds.' And yet, one should not read vv 13-15 as a direct continuation of 3.9-11. Not only does the messenger speech in 3.11 conclude a well-rounded oracle, but it is highly probable that 3.12 also belongs to the presuppositions of our new oracle.[30]

25. Stuart, *Hosea–Jonah*, p. 321.

26. Gitay, 'Study', p. 300.

27. Finley, *Joel, Amos, Obadiah*, p. 179; and Pfeifer, 'Amos und Deuterojesaja', p. 442.

28. Andersen and Freedman, *Amos*, p. 371.

29. Cripps, *Commentary*, p. 165.

30. Wolff, *Joel and Amos*, p. 200.

Not much needs to be added at this point except to say that, ironically, at the end of the chapter, Yahweh is not addressing the Israelites any more. Instead, foreigners (those of vv. 9-11) are commanded to hear and testify against Israel that their God is indeed going to intervene and punish his chosen people (v. 13).

2. *Amos 3.3-8*

a. *Exegetical Observations and Structure*

According to Dorsey, vv. 3-8 parallel v. 12, with the two parts representing B and B' of the proposed chiasm. To be sure, they both speak about 'a lion and its prey', as Dorsey rightly notes, but his suggested headings ('Coming disaster, declared by the prophets' and 'Near-total disaster coming') and the implied links between the two sections are far less persuasive, as the subsequent analysis will reveal.

The internal structure and logic of Amos 3.3-8 have received much attention. Yet, its function in the wider textual context has often been neglected. To add to this deficiency, many of the studies of this little pericope are marred by dispensing too quickly with vv. 3 and 7, which are often seen as later additions. In my view, this is a misjudgment given that both verses make a fundamental contribution to the rhetoric of the passage as a whole.

Rudolph once ironically but aptly commented that v. 3 has seen 'a long history of suffering'.[31] The main reasons for its dismissal were that it features only one rhetorical question compared to the doublets found in the following verses, that it conveys no threat and that its content is too trivial.[32] However, given that vv. 3-6 consist of seven rhetorical questions, a characteristically Amosian feature, as we have seen above, one verse must by necessity stand out as, regrettably one is almost tempted to say, seven happens to be an odd number. Furthermore, as far as the peaceful character and the triviality of its content are concerned, these have been rightly judged intentional by Paul, noting that v. 3 is meant 'to lure the audience into the prophet's train of thought'.[33]

The real sticking point, however, is v. 7, which has often been regarded as a gloss because it is said to interrupt the series of questions, to contain

31. Rudolph, *Joel, Amos, Obadja, Jona*, p. 155.
32. Cf. Gese, 'Kleine Beiträge', p. 425; and S. Mittmann, 'Gestalt und Gehalt einer prophetischen Selbstrechtfertigung (Amos 3,3-8)', *TQ* 151 (1971), pp. 134-45 (135).
33. Paul, *Amos*, p. 109.

'deuteronomistic' vocabulary, to be composed in prose (the remainder of Amos 3.3-8 is poetry) and to deviate from the cause and effect pattern.[34] Yet, a closer look at the development of the argument in Amos 3.3-8 indicates that v. 7 is by no means an intrusive gloss but an important part of Amos's case. Indeed, Hayes has made a strong case for its authenticity, noting:

> (1) Syntactically, one would expect a statement about authority to take the form of an assertion rather than a question. (2) Prose is more assertive than poetry; the break from poetry to prose highlights the assertion as assertion. (3) The parallel between this text and deuteronomistic passages does not prove anything more than a shared perspective and vocabulary.[35]

Pointing to the rhetorical function of v. 7, Andersen and Freedman have stressed that 'the fact that the prophet shifts here from metaphoric language to the substance of his argument…is sufficient to explain the break in the previously established pattern'.[36] And Finley rightly asks, 'does an interruption in form have to mean a secondary intrusion? As a literary device, might it not also indicate climax?' Providing the answer himself, he concludes that 'v. 7 does form the climax to vv. 3-6 and sets them off from v. 8'.[37]

---

34. Cf. W. Baumgartner, 'Amos 3 ₃₋₈', *ZAW* 33 (1913), pp. 78-80 (78); Lehming, 'Erwägungen', p. 152; Wolff, *Joel and Amos*, p. 181; Rudolph, *Joel, Amos, Obadja, Jona*, p. 157; McKeating, *Books of Amos, Hosea and Micah*, p. 27; Martin-Achard, 'End', p. 29; Gese, 'Kleine Beiträge', pp. 424-25; Wolff, *Amos' geistige Heimat*, p. 5; G. Pfeifer, 'Unausweichliche Konsequenzen. Denkformenanalyse von Amos iii 3-8', *VT* 33 (1983), pp. 341-47 (342); Willi-Plein, *Vorformen*, pp. 21-23; W. Eichrodt, 'Die Vollmacht des Amos. Zu einer schwierigen Stelle im Amosbuch', in H. Donner, R. Hanhart and R. Smend (eds.), *Beiträge zur alttestamentlichen Theologie: Festschrift für Walther Zimmerli zum 70. Geburtstag* (Göttingen: Vandenhoeck & Ruprecht, 1977), pp. 124-31 (125); A. Schenker, 'Steht der Prophet unter dem Zwang zu weissagen, oder steht Israel vor der Evidenz der Weisung Gottes in der Weissagung des Propheten? Zur Interpretation von Amos 3,3-8', *BZ* NS 30 (1986), pp. 250-56 (251); H. Mowvley, *The Books of Amos and Hosea* (Epworth Commentaries; London: Epworth Press, 1991), p. 39; and J. Pschibille, *Hat der Löwe erneut gebrüllt? Sprachliche, formale und inhaltliche Gemeinsamkeiten in der Verkündigung Jeremias und Amos'* (Biblisch-theologische Studien, 41; Neukirchen–Vluyn: Neukirchener Verlag, 2001), p. 130.

35. Hayes, *Amos*, pp. 126-27; see also Gitay, 'Study', p. 305; and Stuart, *Hosea–Jonah*, p. 325.

36. Andersen and Freedman, *Amos*, p. 392.

37. Finley, *Joel, Amos, Obadiah*, p. 186. Others who have understood v. 7 to be an integral part of Amos 3.3-8 include Harper, *Commentary*, pp. 71-73; Gressmann,

Turning then to the structure of Amos 3.3-8, it is worth noting that the entire piece consists of a series of *bistichoi*, albeit of varying design and length (cf. Figure 19 below).

3 הילכו שנים יחדו	בלתי אם־נועדו
4 הישאג אריה ביער	וטרף אין לו
היתן כפיר קולו ממענתו	בלתי אם־לכד
5 התפל צפור על־פח הארץ	ומוקש אין לה
היעלה־פח מן־האדמה	ולכוד לא ילכוד
6 אם־יתקע שופר בעיר	ועם לא יחרדו
אם־תהיה רעה בעיר	ויהוה לא עשה
7 כי לא יעשה אדני יהוה דבר	כי אם־גלה סודו אל־עבדיו הנביאים
8 אריה שאג	מי לא יירא
אדני יהוה דבר	מי לא ינבא

Figure 19. *An Outline of the Bistichoi in Amos 3.3-8*

As Limburg has pointed out, here we have another 7+1 series (i.e., seven rhetorical questions followed by the passage's focal point).[38] The first five

---

Geschichtsschreibung, pp. 338-39; E.A. Edghill, *The Book of Amos* (ed. G.A. Cooke; Westminster Commentaries; London: Methuen, 2nd edn, 1926); pp. 30-31; Theis, 'Der Prophet Amos', pp. 119-20; Robinson, 'Hosea bis Micha', pp. 80-83; Maag, *Text*, p. 14; and M. Bič, *Das Buch Amos* (Berlin: Evangelische Verlagsanstalt, 1969), pp. 68-69.

Rather peculiar is the treatment of the whole issue by Schenker who, without actually discussing the authenticity of v. 7, assumes that it is secondary. He does, however, discuss the proposals of Vermeylen, *Du prophète Isaïe*, pp. 525-28; and B. Renaud, 'Genèse et théologie d'Amos 3,3-8', in A. Caquot and M. Delcor (eds.), *Mélanges bibliques et orienteaux en l'honneur de M. Henri Cazelles* (AOAT, 212; Neukirchen–Vluyn: Neukirchener Verlag, 1981), pp. 353-72 (356-61), who based on stylistic considerations regard vv. 3, 7 and 8 as editorial additions. Rejecting their conclusions, Schenker, 'Prophet', p. 251, quite perceptively comments: 'Die Gefahr ist, daß man als Kriterien der Einheitlichkeit oder Uneinheitlichkeit einen Maßstab des prophetischen Denk- und Sprachstils setzt, der uns nirgends objektiv gegeben ist, sondern den wir uns selber subjektiv zurechtlegen…[Doch] stellt sich die Frage, ob die unverkennbaren Unterschiede innerhalb eines Bereiches kompositorischer Freiheit… liegen können oder nicht…[So] liegt es näher, diese Verse vorerst als Einheit zu betrachten, bes. wenn sie als solche Einheit einen guten Sinn ergeben.' These, as already said, are perceptive remarks, yet one is left wondering whether they could not apply equally well to Schenker's own handling of v. 7.

38. Limburg, 'Sevenfold Structures', p. 220, who regards v. 7 as a 'parenthetical comment' followed by the climax in v. 8 (cf. also Dorsey, 'Literary Architecture', p. 311; and Paul, *Amos*, pp. 105-106).

questions in vv. 3-5 are introduced by הֲ followed by a negation in the
second part of the sentence (בלתי אם, וְ...אִין or וְ...לֹא). The last two
questions, on the other hand, start with אם followed by the construction
וְ–subject–לֹא–verb. This structural deviation points to the passage's thematic development (cf. Figure 20).

General description	Structure of first part	Structure of second part	Function
a) five rhetorical questions (vv. 3-5)	Introduced by הֲ	negation: בלתי אם, וְ...לֹא or אִין	*introductory and preparatory* questions
b) two rhetorical questions (v. 6)	Introduced by אם	וְ + subject + לֹא + verb	*thematic development*, marked by structural alterations[39]
c) prose statement (v. 7)	Introduced by כי לֹא	introduced by אם כי	*explanation* of God's purposes requiring an assertion[40]
d) statements and rhetorical questions (v. 8)	subject + verb	מי לֹא + verb	the passage's *focal point*, again marked by structural variation[41]

Figure 20. *The Structure of Amos 3.3-8*

The overall structure of Amos 3.3-8 falls into four parts, which correspond
to the gradual development of the argument. The first part, vv. 3-5, has an
introductory function designed to prepare the audience for the eventual

39. Cf. Finley, *Joel, Amos, Obadiah*, p. 183: 'The change in structure from *he*-
interrogative to coordinating *'im* marks the change in focus from lions and fowling to
distress in a city.' Hubbard, *Joel and Amos*, p. 149, similarly points out that the form of
the questions intensifies in v. 6 (see also Gitay, 'Study', p. 304). E.L. Greenstein, 'How
Does Parallelism Mean?', in *A Sense of Text: The Art of Language in the Study of
Biblical Literature. Papers from a Symposium at The Dropsie College for Hebrew and
Cognate Learning, May 11, 1982* (JQRSup; Winona Lake, IN: Eisenbrauns, 1983), pp.
41-70 (62-63), has stressed that the two lines in v. 6 are exactly parallel in structure
(which is not true for vv. 4-5). Their structural arrangement is as follows.

אִם־ יִתָּקַע שׁוֹפָר בְּ עִיר וְ עָם לֹא יֶחֱרָדוּ
אִם־ תִּהְיֶה רָעָה בְּ עִיר וְ יהוה לֹא עָשָׂה

Calling this the 'sharpening of a focus and the tightening of a vise', Greenstein concludes that 'the line of thought that the prophet develops beginning in v. 3 culminates
in the logic of v. 6'.
40. See Hayes, *Amos*, pp. 126-27, who agrees that 'one would expect a statement
about authority to take the form of an assertion rather than a question'.
41. Eichrodt, 'Vollmacht', p. 128, commenting on the meter of v. 8, underlines that
'durch die Änderung der bisher angewandten fünfhebigen Zeile in die vierhebige läßt
der Sprechende das ihm selbst wiederfahrende [*sic*] Geschehen dem Hörer entgegen-
treten'. Harper, *Commentary*, p. 73, similarly, regards v. 8 as 'the last [utterance] of the
rapidly rising climax' (cf. also Hayes, *Amos*, p. 127).

punchline. The series of rhetorical questions drawn from common experience is surely not intended as an allegory.[42] Each question refers to events that are closely related, a literary expression employed 'in order to draw [the] unexpecting audience logically and skillfully into the flow of a persuasive and penetrating presentation of the inextricable relationship of all events and happenings'.[43]

The series' internal development is climactic[44] with a peaceful beginning (v. 3)[45] being followed first by animal struggle (v. 4) before eventually giving way to conflict between animals and humans (v. 5).[46] Mittmann has rightly stressed the preparatory function of the images of hunting found in the first strophe, noting that their threatening atmosphere,[47] inexorable cause-and-effect pattern and inescapable logic prime the audience for what is to follow.[48]

The second part, consisting of the next pair of rhetorical questions in v. 6, clearly is a transitional element, as has been recognized by Finley, noting that 'the second half [of the verse] brings this part of the passage to a climax, at the same time making a transition into the underlying thought behind the entire section'.[49] Wolff has captured its rhetorical effect well, describing it as the 'zero[ing] in on the world of experience of [Amos's] hearers' because now 'humanity becomes the endangered species'.[50] However, while v. 6a focuses on the interpersonal realm, v. 6b ascends to the divine–human sphere of contact,[51] exploiting the audience's belief that, ultimately, it must be Yahweh who is responsible for any disaster that

42. Thus against D.S. Shapiro, 'The Seven Questions of Amos', *Tradition* 20 (1982), pp. 327-31; and Finley, *Joel, Amos, Obadiah*, p. 180; but with Pfeifer, 'Unausweichliche Konsequenzen', p. 342; and Rudolph, *Joel, Amos, Obadja, Jona*, p. 154.

43. Thus Paul, *Amos*, p. 104.

44. Cf. Gese, 'Kleine Beiträge', p. 426; and Polley, *Amos*, p. 13. Mittmann, 'Gestalt', p. 138, however, found himself unable to detect any climactic development.

45. Hayes, *Amos*, p. 124, describes v. 3 as 'an interrogative statement which may be seen as a neutral or rather banal way of getting the series going' (see also Paul, *Amos*, p. 106; and Andersen and Freedman, *Amos*, p. 388).

46. Cf. Wolff, *Joel and Amos*, p. 183; and Paul, *Amos*, p. 106.

47. According to Andersen and Freedman, *Amos*, p. 389, 'the entire series is pervaded by an atmosphere of terror'.

48. Mittmann, 'Gestalt', p. 143; cf. also Martin-Achard, 'End', p. 29.

49. Finley, *Joel, Amos, Obadiah*, p. 184; see also Andersen and Freedman, *Amos*, pp. 389-90.

50. Wolff, *Joel and Amos*, p. 186.

51. Cf. Paul, *Amos*, p. 106.

might befall a city.[52] According to Smith, it is precisely this move, which 'springs the trap and foreshadows the final climax in 3.8'.[53]

Yet, before coming to his main point, Amos deems it necessary to stress that Yahweh would never punish his people without warning them first.[54] No, he reveals his plans to the prophets who, in turn, are responsible for warning the people. Thus, v. 7 prolongs the transitional element,[55] being closely connected to the preceding statement in v. 6b. As the following figure indicates, v. 7a in fact re-employs the vocabulary of v. 6b,[56] which suggests that v. 7 is intended to clarify and comment on that earlier statement.[57]

(v. 6bβ)   ויהוה   לא עשׂה
(v. 7a)   כי   לא יעשׂה אדני יהוה דבר

Figure 21. *The Interrelation of Amos 3.6bβ and 7a*

Up to this point Amos has already made two important points. First, if there is a disaster in the city, then it is no one else but Yahweh who is

52. W. Dietrich and C. Link, *Die dunklen Seiten Gottes*. I. *Willkür und Gewalt* (Neukirchen–Vluyn: Neukirchener Verlag, 3rd edn, 2000), p. 151, have traced this belief to the wholesale rejection of dualism, which leads to the conviction that Yahweh is responsible for both, light (אור) and darkness (חשׁך), weal (שׁלום) and woe (רע; cf. Isa. 45.7). See also Mittmann, 'Gestalt', p. 137; Rudolph, *Joel, Amos, Obadja, Jona*, p. 154; Eichrodt, 'Vollmacht', p. 126, according to whom Amos 3.6b reflects a 'typisch gemeinisraelitische Glaubenslehre'; and Pfeifer, 'Unausweichliche Konsequenzen', p. 345, who notes that Amos expects his hearers to agree with him on this point. For a different view, see Stuart, *Hosea–Jonah*, p. 325; and Gitay, 'Study', p. 296.

53. Smith, *Amos*, p. 110.

54. See Shapiro, 'Seven Questions', p. 330. סוד denotes the heavenly council where prophets receive the divine word. Cf. P.D. Miller, Jr, 'The World and Message of the Prophets: Biblical Prophecy in Its Context', in Mays, Petersen and Richards (eds.), *Old Testament Interpretation*, pp. 97-112 (103); J.D.W. Watts, 'Images of Yahweh: God in the Prophets', in R.L. Hubbard, Jr and R.K. Johnston (eds.), *Studies in Old Testament Theology* (Dallas: Word Books, 1992), pp. 135-47 (136-37); Lindblom, *Prophecy*, pp. 112-13; and W. McKane, *Prophets and Wise Men* (SBT, 44; London: SCM Press, 1965), p. 124.

55. According to Hubbard, *Joel and Amos*, p. 149, the literary purpose of v. 7 'may be to postpone the climax and thus to enhance the suspense of the sequence of questions'.

56. See Paul, *Amos*, p. 108; and Andersen and Freedman, *Amos*, p. 393.

57. See Hubbard, *Joel and Amos*, p. 149, who notes that v. 7 'serves as a link between the question on divine activity (v. 6) and the climactic one on the inescapable duties of the prophet'. See also Hayes, *Amos*, p. 126; and Gitay, 'Study', p. 305.

responsible for it. Secondly, Israel's God is 'not going to do anything' (לֹא עָשָׂה דָבָר) without warning his people through his servants, the prophets. However, if this is so, then how can a prophet remain silent once Yahweh has spoken? This is the point made by the rhetorical questions in v. 8, the climax of the whole section.[58] The answers are obvious—if a lion roars, people will be afraid; if Yahweh speaks, one has to prophesy[59]—but the questions force the audience to admit that Amos had no other choice but to proclaim his dire message. This, the focal point of the entire unit,[60] is again structurally marked, as has been observed by Wolff, drawing attention to the terseness of the two bicola and noting that only here is the crucial issue stated in form of a thesis, namely that 'Yahweh has spoken' (אֲדֹנָי יְהוָה דִּבֶּר).[61] Mittmann also points to the shift to another meter as well as to the re-employment of the lion metaphor, concluding:

58. Vv. 7-8 are closely linked by means of the phrase אֲדֹנָי יְהוָה דָּבָר in 7aβ and אֲדֹנָי יְהוָה דִּבֶּר in 8bα as well as the terms הַנְּבִיאִים in v. 7 and יִנָּבֵא in v. 8 (see Paul, *Amos*, p. 108). Andersen and Freedman, *Amos*, p. 393, have pointed out that this catch word method is used throughout the poem: see לְכַד (v. 4) ‖ ולכוד...ילכוד (v. 5); פָּח (v. 5a) ‖ פָּח (v. 5b); בְּעִיר (v. 6a) ‖ בְּעִיר (v. 6b); אַרְיֵה (v. 4) ‖ אַרְיֵה (v. 8).

59. Schenker, 'Prophet', p. 250, speaks of coercion ('Nötigung'); and Jeremias, 'Interrelationship', p. 182, notes that the word of disaster is 'forced upon Amos'; cf. also Wolff, 'Das unwiderstehliche Wort', pp. 10-11; and H. Gunkel, 'Die geheimen Erfahrungen der Propheten', in Neumann (ed.), *Das Prophetenverständnis*, pp. 109-43 (138-39).

60. Cf. Baumgartner, 'Amos 3 3-8', p. 78; and Pfeifer, 'Unausweichliche Konsequenzen', p. 342, who argues against dividing this unit into two parts (vv. 3-6, and [7-]8), as has been suggested by some interpreters. S. Daiches, 'Amos iii. 3-8', *ExpTim* 26 (1914–15), p. 237, on the other hand, believes that vv. 7-8 are 'additional observations', which are 'not vital to the subject'.

61. Wolff, *Joel and Amos*, p. 183; cf. also Gese, 'Kleine Beiträge', p. 427. Wolff regards v. 7 as a later addition yet affirms the transitional character of v. 6 as well as the climactic character of v. 8 (Wolff, *Joel and Amos*, pp. 182-83). According to him: 'the initial mention of Yahweh in v 6b functions as the vitally important premise to the conclusion properly drawn in v 8b. Indeed, it might well be precisely the alteration in style which indicates that the point of this series of questions is revealed only in v. 8…The change to a new syntactical structure at the end of our oracle is meant to emphasize the new thesis there advanced.' A few pages down (p. 186) he elaborates on this, noting: 'two novel stylistic features show that [the] goal [of the series] is attained with v 8. First of all, the sentences no longer begin with an interrogative participle (which in every case had been followed by a verb in the imperfect); now the initial clauses are statements of fact, formulated in the perfect. Secondly, the questions concerning consequential relationship are raised in the second cola, and are formulated in a pointedly direct, personal way…'

these means serve to bring about an effective rhetorical intensification. After the monotony of the preceding six questions of a similar style, the hearer is surprised and startled by the sudden change…it almost testifies to rhetorical ingenuity how in v. 8a due to the surprising and at the same time retarding relapse into metaphorical speech the suspense undergoes some final intensification before the concluding key statement in v. 8b.[62]

b. *Rhetorical Function*

How then does Amos 3.3-8 fit into its context, and what is its function for the discourse in 3.1-15 as a whole? Making one's way through the book, one is struck by the rather abrupt shift from the announcement of judgment in v. 2 to a series of rhetorical questions in vv. 3-6, which appear to come completely out of the blue. Why, one wonders, does the prophet suddenly start to ask what seem to be irrelevant and indeed almost stupid questions? Of course, this eventually does become clear in vv. 6-8, and it is these verses that allow us to come to a conclusion concerning the rhetorical function of Amos 3.3-8, noting that Amos apparently had to defend his proclamation of the divine punishment.

Amos's announcement of Yahweh's punitive visit in v. 2 (as well as the judgment speech in 2.6-16) obviously led the audience to question his authority. To be sure, the text does not explicitly confirm this, yet this has not prevented scholars from coming to the stated conclusion. Hubbard, for instance, surmises that 'there must have been some formal protest lodged contesting both the negative promise and Amos' right to deliver it'.[63] Paul, similarly, concludes:

> in defense of his previous oracle announcing impending punishment of the elected people (3.1-2), [Amos] forcefully and cogently argues that prophecy is not a self-generating act; rather, the prophet is irresistibly compelled to deliver God's words.[64]

And, to give just one further example, Gitay too claims that:

> the introduction, presenting the stunning issue of the people's punishment, needs confirmation… The chain of rhetorical questions which follow the introduction stresses Amos' position and is intended to refute the basic opinion of the audience that God will not punish them.[65]

---

62. Mittmann, 'Gestalt', p. 141.
63. Hubbard, *Joel and Amos*, p. 148.
64. Paul, *Amos*, 105.
65. Gitay, 'Study', p. 300. For similar judgments, cf. Rudolph, *Joel, Amos, Obadja, Jona*, pp. 151-52; Wolff, *Joel and Amos*, pp. 181, 184; Smith, *Amos*, pp. 97, 106-107;

While these conclusions are not without historical warrant—the prophetic books after all abound with conflict stories, disputation speeches and similar indications of lively disputes—it should be noted that they are also an apt interpretation of the text's arrangement, which implicitly portrays the prophet's audience as evoking Amos's reaction recorded in vv. 3-8. How could he dare to declare such horrible things? How could he have known that Yahweh was going to punish his chosen people? Why could he not just shut up and remain silent? These are the questions that Amos had to answer. And he does this quite adroitly by asking questions himself, thus forcing the audience itself 'to take an active role in the persuasion process'.[66] As Labuschagne has stressed:

> the rhetorical question is one of the most forceful and effectual ways employed in speech for driving home some idea or conviction. Because of its impressive and persuasive effect the hearer is not merely listener: he is forced to frame the expected answer in his mind, and by doing so he actually becomes a co-expressor of the speaker's conviction.[67]

In Amos 3.3-8 in particular, the rhetorical effect of the rhetorical questions is heightened by the use of a whole series of them.[68] Moreover, the steady movement from apparently inconspicuous examples (vv. 3-5) to cases that involve the prophet's audience more directly (v. 6-8) results in another rhetorical trap, comparable to the one represented by the OAN in Amos 1–2. Having been pushed to agree that no, a snare does not spring into action unless something has gone into it, that yes, if a trumpet is blown in a city, its citizens will be afraid of the impending war, and that a lion's roar will indeed lead to universal fear, the audience cannot but concede that if Yahweh has spoken, one must prophesy. And this is true, of course, no matter how uncomfortable the message. If Yahweh is intent on punishing his people, then Amos, his prophet, has no choice but to convey what has been revealed to him.

Martin-Achard, 'End', p. 28; Melugin, 'Formation', p. 381; and Jeremias, 'Interrelationship', p. 182, who speaks of the 'legitimizing function' of the questions.

66. Thus Gitay, 'Deutero-Isaiah', p. 197.

67. C.J. Labuschagne, *The Incomparability of Yahweh in the Old Testament* (Pretoria Oriental Series, 5; Leiden: E.J. Brill, 1966), p. 23.

68. See K.M. Craig, Jr, 'Interrogatives in Haggai–Zechariah: A Literary Thread?', in Watts and House (eds.), *Forming Prophetic Literature*, pp. 224-44 (230), who emphasizes the heightening effect of sequential questions.

3. *Amos 3.9-11*

a. *Exegetical Observations and Structure*

According to Dorsey, this unit is to be sub-divided into three parts, which are themselves arranged chiastically (with A = v. 9, B = v. 10 and A' = v. 11),[69] thus forming a small chiasm within the larger one Dorsey claims to have instead discovered in Amos 3 as a whole. However, upon closer inspection, it quickly becomes apparent that the similarities of the outer parts of this smaller chiasm are in fact limited to the recurrence of the term ארמנות. Thematically, the foci are quite different. In v. 9, the inhabitants of the fortresses (ארמנות) of Ashdod and Egypt are called upon to assemble on Mount Samaria in order to assess the oppression found in Israel's capital. Verse 11, on the other hand, speaks about the impending destruction of Israel's fortresses (ארמנות).

Dorsey's analysis is further weakened by the fact that the term ארמנות appears also in v. 10, where it is said that the Israelites store up violence and robbery in their own fortresses. To add to this, Dorsey also errs in claiming that each of the proposed seven parts of Amos 3 contains a divine speech formula,[70] as there is none to be found in v. 9. Overall, it therefore seems best to accept the standard form-critical analysis, which regards vv. 9-11 as one unit, which, while not being arranged chiastically, is governed by the *Leitmotiv* ארמנות. Its arrangement is best described as linear, displaying a progressive development, as can be seen in the following outline of the passage's argument.

Someone is to proclaim in the strongholds of Ashdod and Egypt (v. 9a)
→   that they are to gather on Mount Samaria (v. 9bα)
→   in order to assess the oppression found in Israel's capital (v. 9bβ).
→   Then Yahweh explains the reasons for the oppression (v. 10),
→   as a result of which an enemy shall surround the land, (v. 11a)
→   destroy the Israelite defences, (v. 11bα)
→   and plunder her fortresses (v. 11bβ).

Figure 22. *Linear, Progressive Development in Amos 3.9-11*

Amos 3.9-11 is a good example of a poetic text establishing what Alter has called 'a miniature narrative continuum'.[71] Particularly interesting in

---

69. Dorsey, 'Literary Architecture', p. 310.
70. Dorsey, 'Literary Architecture', p. 310.
71. Alter, 'Characteristics', p. 618.

this respect is v. 11, which depicts Samaria's conquest in three acts.[72] Gitay has described its poetic nature well, pointing out that 'the description of punishment is constructed by a verse of three lines, depicting a military campaign: siege, defeat and plunder. The lines are short, with no detailed description; hence construction dramatizes the quickness of the fall'.[73]

It is also striking how quickly the oracle as a whole progresses from the calling of witnesses (v. 9a) to the announcement of punishment (v. 11). As Pfeifer has noted, stressing what he calls the passage's inexorable determination ('unerbittliche Konsequenz'):

> there is no pause, no awaiting what kind of assessment the witnesses, were they to come, would make, what judgment they would reach. Instead, the brief and yet exhaustive description of the state of affairs, limited as it is to the essentials, is followed immediately by Yahweh's sentence: an enemy will come and conquer the land, raze the fortresses, plunder the palaces.[74]

The passage's rhetorical structure is thus best charted as follows.

9 השמיעו על־ארמנות באשדוד
ועל־ארמנות בארץ מצרים ואמרו

האספו על־הרי שמרון

וראו מהומת רבות בתוכה
ועשוקים בקרבה

10 ולא־ידעו עשות־נכחה
נאם־יהוה
האוצרים חמס ושד בארמנותיהם

11 לכן כה אמר אדני יהוה
צר וסביב הארץ

והורד ממך עזך

ונבזו ארמנותיך

Figure 23. *The Rhetorical Structure of Amos 3.9-11*

Although the term ריב does not appear in these verses, the form-critical classification of the passage as a courtroom scene is helpful and illuminat-

72. Cf. G. Pfeifer, 'Die Denkform des Propheten Amos (iii 9-11)', *VT* 34 (1984), pp. 476-81 (478).
73. Gitay, 'Study', p. 307.
74. Pfeifer, 'Denkform', p. 480.

ing. It has been advocated, for instance, by Sinclair, who has suggested the following outline.

    I. Description of the judgment scene (v. 9a)
    II. Speech of the judge (v. 9b)
        A. Address to the defendant
        B. Pronouncement of guilt (indictment) (v. 10)
        C. Sentence (v. 11)

Figure 24. *The Courtroom Scene in Amos 3.9-11*[75]

However, this analysis, helpful and illuminating though it is, does not really bring out the text's provocative dimension. After all, Amos is here portrayed as commanding some unspecified emissaries to invite the leaders of Egypt and Ashdod, people who neither know Yahweh nor keep his laws, to witness against Yahweh's own chosen people.[76] This must have shocked Amos's Israelite audience, who no doubt would have considered themselves morally superior to these pagan witnesses,[77] who, as Rudolph ironically remarks, were 'experts in terms of oppression'.[78] However, as such, they had to admit that the Israelites' performances were up to their own.[79] Dearman similarly surmises that Ashdod and Egypt have been chosen as two former oppressors of Israel, who 'are called as witnesses…to see the capital city of Samaria now playing a similar role of oppression'.[80]

As far as the rhetorical force of the commands of v. 9 is concerned, Finley aptly notes that 'the effect lends much more vividness to the scene than a simple statement that even the Gentile nations would know Israel was guilty of inhuman actions.'[81] It might also be significant that two wit-

75. L.A. Sinclair, 'The Courtroom Motif in the Book of Amos', *JBL* 85 (1966), pp. 351-53 (352). McKeating, *Books of Amos, Hosea and Micah*, p. 29, similarly speaks of a trial.

76. See Stuart, *Hosea–Jonah*, p. 329; and Finley, *Joel, Amos, Obadiah*, p. 187. Andersen and Freedman, *Amos*, p. 374, relate the request to summon witnesses to the heavenly proceedings in v. 7, noting that 'it is likely that they are instructions given by God directly to some of those attending the heavenly council'.

77. Hubbard, *Joel and Amos*, p. 151; see also Harper, *Commentary*, pp. 74, 76; and Paul, *Amos*, p. 115.

78. Rudolph, *Joel, Amos, Obadja, Jona*, p. 163.

79. Thus again Rudolph, *Joel, Amos, Obadja, Jona*, p. 163.

80. Dearman, *Property Rights*, p. 26.

81. Finley, *Joel, Amos, Obadiah*, p. 188; cf. also Rudolph, *Joel, Amos, Obadja,*

nesses are invited, as this was the number required in a capital case (Num. 35.30; Deut. 17.6; 19.5; 1 Kgs 21.10-13). In this particular instance, the witnesses are summoned to have a look at the great terror (מהומת רבות) that is going on in Samaria. Indeed, the immense wickedness of Samaria's leaders, who, with what has been called 'acid criticism',[82] are here portrayed as storing up violence and robbery (אצר חמס ושד), compels Yahweh to conclude that they quite simply do not know how to do what is right (נכחה).[83]

Because of (לכן) their offences, Yahweh declares that they will be severely punished. Attention needs to be drawn to the divine speech formula כה אמר אדני יהוה, which stresses the divine origin of the following announcement of judgment, as well as to the fact that v. 11 addresses the audience directly. As Gitay has noted, 'the function of the sudden transition from the third person to the second, called *aversio*, is to emphasize and to raise emotion',[84] thus providing another example of what Aristotle had described as the rhetorician's use of *pathos* (cf. also Amos 2.10-11). The judgment itself is in the form of *lex talionis*[85] but there is also a sense of irony here in that 'the houses of the robbers will themselves be robbed'.[86] All the riches will thus turn out to have been collected in vain, just as the violence and robbery (חמס ושד; v. 10) will not have achieved anything in the end.

b. *Rhetorical Function*
Like the preceding parts, vv. 9-11 too play an important role for the argument of Amos 3.1-15 as a whole. As noted earlier, the discourse opened with Amos's paradoxical announcement that Yahweh will punish

Jona, p. 163; and Smith, *Amos*, p. 119.

82. Thus Wolff, *Joel and Amos*, p. 193; see also Smith, *Amos*, p. 120; and Andersen and Freedman, *Amos*, p. 375.

83. Harper, *Commentary*, p. 77, rightly stresses that the emphasis is on not knowing. The phrase נאם־יהוה in this context underlines that this is Yahweh's own assessment of the situation. Thus also Rofé, *Introduction*, p. 57, who notes that 'if the words "declares the Lord" in v. 10, are indeed original, they show that the Lord drew his conclusions from the facts denounced by the prophet'. Paul, *Amos*, p. 177, on the other hand, regards its insertion as a 'delaying tactic', which however seems less probable.

84. Gitay, 'Study', p. 306.

85. See Paul, *Amos*, p. 118; Smith, *Amos*, p. 121; and Andersen and Freedman, *Amos*, p. 375.

86. Wolff, *Joel and Amos*, p. 194.

Israel precisely because (עַל־כֵּן) they are his chosen people. As this declaration apparently caused some controversy, the prophet feels compelled to assure his audience that this is indeed the divine message and that he has no choice but to proclaim it (vv. 3-8). Yet, the actual focus in Amos 3 is on the divine punishment as such, which is brought up at the beginning and the end of the discourse (cf. vv. 1-2, 12-15). In fact, this issue is to the fore also in the courtroom scene in vv. 9-11, which, as Wolff has noted:

> following upon the inserted legitimation dispute (3.3-6+8), provides the first commentary on the statement of principle found at the beginning of the collection of 'the words of Amos from Tekoa' (3.1-2). It spells out concretely which crimes Yahweh will punish and how he will do it.[87]

By pointing out that vv. 9-11 develop the punishment theme introduced in v. 2, specify some of the reasons for the divine intervention and indicate its nature, Wolff has already drawn attention to some of the passage's key functions. Yet, in addition to all this, the courtroom scene also adds a powerful rhetorical flourish. As has already been noted above, Amos's call for the people of Ashdod and Egypt to witness against Israel is designed to impress the severity of Yahweh's charges on his audience. If even those foreign 'experts in terms of oppression' would testify against Israel, then the situation must certainly be very grave, as indeed the judge's verdict in v. 11 implies.

4. *Amos 3.12*

a. *Exegetical Observations and Structure*

Amos 3.12, short though it is, constitutes one of the five sub-units of the discourse in Amos 3, belonging neither to the preceding courtroom scene in vv. 9-11 nor to the following announcement of judgment in vv. 13-15.[88] The beginning of this sub-unit is marked by the divine speech formula כה אמר יהוה while the introductory שִׁמְעוּ in v. 13 indicates the commencement of the following oracle. Thematically, v. 12 also stands out in that Amos's sarcastic comment on the issue of rescue, using an illustration drawn from the pastoral sphere of shepherding, clearly does not constitute

---

87. Wolff, *Joel and Amos*, p. 192 (translation modified); against Noble, 'Literary Structure', p. 217 n. 29, who regards vv. 9-11 as an anticlimax.

88. Cf. G. Pfeifer, '"Rettung" als Beweis der Vernichtung (Amos 3,12)', *ZAW* 100 (1988), pp. 269-77 (274); and Gese, 'Kleine Beiträge', p. 427; but against Smith, *Amos*, p. 121.

a continuation of the preceding courtroom motif.

The illustration in v. 12 is given in a comparative clause with כאשר in the protasis and כן in the apodosis (see Figure 25).[89] Following these particles in both parts of the sentence, the verb נצל indicates the theme of the illustration, which is the issue of rescue or deliverance.[90] However, it quickly becomes clear that Amos's statement is highly ironic.[91] Because just as the small remains of an animal[92] that a shepherd has been able to rescue from a lion's mouth only serve to confirm its loss (Exod. 22.13; 1 Sam. 17.34-35; also CH §266[93] and Gen. 31.39), so the worthless parts of once luxurious furniture will only attest to the former existence of some wealthy people. 'Only the memory of a comfortable life is "rescued"', as Wolff once put it.[94]

כה אמר יהוה

| (aβ) שתי כרעים או בדל־אזן | (aα) כאשר יציל הרעה מפי הארי |
| (bβ) בפאת מטה ובדמשק ערש | (bα) כן ינצלו בני ישראל הישבים בשמרון |

Figure 25. *The Structure of Amos 3.12*

The precise implications of Amos's illustration are, to some extent at least, difficult to determine. While it seems clear that Amos is denying that there will be any real rescue or deliverance from the impending divine judgment, the final phrase of v. 12, בפאת מטה ובדמשק ערש, presents a number of difficulties. Hayes even regards it as 'a major *crux interpretum* in Old Testament studies'[95]—for three reasons. First, exegetes are not sure to which part of the sentence v. 12bβ is attributive. Secondly, there is a dispute over the interpretation of the two prepositional prefixes in בפאת and בדמשק. And thirdly, the meaning of the *hapax legomenon* דמשק itself

89. See JM §174a+b.

90. On נצל see F.L. Hossfeld and B. Kalthoff, 'הִצִּילָה, נצל', in *TDOT*, IX, pp. 533-40.

91. Stuart, *Hosea–Jonah*, p. 331, speaks of a 'mocking, scornful tone'. See also Cripps, *Commentary*, p. 161; Smith, *Amos*, p. 122; Andersen and Freedman, *Amos*, p. 373; and Pfeifer, 'Rettung', p. 276.

92. Paul, *Amos*, p. 119, interprets the references to the legs and the piece of an ear as a merism: 'from top (ear) to bottom (leg), almost nothing whatsoever will be saved'.

93. R. Haase, *Die keilschriftlichen Rechtssammlungen in deutscher Fassung* (Wiesbaden: Otto Harrassowitz, 2nd edn, 1979), p. 56.

94. Wolff, *Joel and Amos*, p. 198; cf. also Pfeifer, 'Rettung', p. 271; and Paul, *Amos*, p. 120.

95. Hayes, *Amos*, p. 133.

is far from clear. There is no lack of proposals but in my opinion, the most convincing solution is the one offered by Rabinowitz and Moeller.[96] Commenting on the first of these problems, Moeller has argued that v. 12:

> is composed of two parallel main clauses [a + b] which express a comparison... [The] literary structure demands that the final phrases of clause two [bβ]...stand in parallel to the final phrase of clause one [aβ]. It also demands that, just as the final phrase of the first clause [aβ] is attributive to the main verb, the final compound phrase of the second clause [bβ] be understood as being attributive to the main verb in its clause.[97]

Moeller's proposal has been challenged by Andersen and Freedman, who deny that v. 12a and 12b are parallel because 'v 12b does not have anything to match the lion or the shepherd [and because] it changes the active *yaṣṣîl* to the passive or reflexive *yinnāṣĕlû*'.[98] Correct though these observations are, Andersen and Freedman's criticism is marred by their inadequate definition of parallelism. As Greenstein has pointed out, 'in order to reveal a repetition of syntactic patterning one must of necessity examine not only the surface structure of the line but also its more abstract underlying relations'.[99] Parallelism, that is to say, 'may not be evident superficially, but it may be present deep down'.[100] The following example, taken from Psalm 105.17, illustrates this principle well:

He (God) sent a man ahead of them	שלח לפניהם איש
Joseph was sold as a slave	לעבד נמכר יוסף

As Greenstein notes, 'on the surface the two lines differ in syntactic structure. However, if one removes the passivization involved in the second line, a case of parallelism materializes.'[101] This Greenstein outlines as follows:

| (he) | sent | before | them | a man | איש | הם | לפני | שלח |
| (he) | sold | as | | a slave | Joseph | יוסף | עבד | ל | נמכר |

Applied to Amos 3.12, the removal of the passivization in v. 12b similarly exposes the parallel structure of the two halves of that verse.

Turning to the remaining two problems of interpretation, it should be

96. I. Rabinowitz, 'The Crux at Amos iii 12', *VT* 11 (1961), pp. 228-31; and H.R. Moeller, 'Ambiguity at Amos 3.12', *BT* 15 (1964), pp. 31-34. For further suggestions, see the commentaries *ad loc*.
97. Moeller, 'Ambiguity', p. 32.
98. Andersen and Freedman, *Amos*, p. 409.
99. Greenstein, 'Parallelism', p. 46.
100. Greenstein, 'Parallelism', p. 47.
101. Greenstein, 'Parallelism', p. 48.

noted that Rabinowitz proposed to amend the problematic term וּבִדְמֶשֶׁק to
וּבַד מֹשֶׁק, meaning 'and a piece from a leg'. According to this interpretation, the beth is simply the first letter of the noun בַּד, whereas the beth in
בְּפְאַת is a *beth essentiae* whose force extends to both members of v.
12bβ.[102] The whole expression would then mean that the Israelites, those
who live in Samaria, would be rescued 'like a piece of a couch and a part
from the leg of a bed'. Summarizing the advantages of this rendering,
Moeller points out:

> (1) it interprets the problem phrase in terms of words known to be in the
> classical Hebrew vocabulary, without alteration of the consonants of the
> text; (2) it interprets the passage in keeping with the regular norms of
> Hebrew syntax…; (3) the obviously-intended comparative parallelism
> between the final phrases of the two clauses is restored; and (4) the
> resulting sense fits the demands of both the immediate linguistic and the
> larger sense contexts much better than other suggestions which have been
> offered.[103]

Paul rejects the proposal of Rabinowitz and Moeller, noting that שׁוֹק never
refers to the 'foot' of a bed.[104] Yet, this reservation notwithstanding, he
still arrives at a very similar solution, pointing out:

> even though the etymology and meaning of the word are still unknown,
> most likely it refers to another part of the bed. In the light of the first half of
> the verse, in which the prophet uses the imagery from bottom (legs) to top
> (ear) to create an anatomical merism, it stands to reason that here, too, he
> names chiastically the two opposite sides of the bed, from top to bottom:
> פְּאַת ('front/head') and דְּמֶשֶׁק, which in the present context would then
> represent the 'rear/foot' of the bed.[105]

Pfeifer largely agrees with Rabinowitz and Moeller but understands
דְּמֶשֶׁק as referring to Damascus (usually spelled דַּמֶּשֶׂק),[106] noting that it
might reflect a dialectical difference or be 'a fashionable foreign word for
a fashionable foreign bed'. Yet, this is unlikely, as Moeller and Finley
have shown, listing a number of reasons for the improbability of reading
'Damascus'.[107]

102. See Moeller, 'Ambiguity', pp. 33-34.
103. Moeller, 'Ambiguity', p. 34. This solution has also been adopted by Smith,
Amos, pp. 116, 123.
104. Paul, *Amos*, p. 121.
105. Paul, *Amos*, p. 122.
106. Pfeifer, 'Rettung', pp. 273-74.
107. See Moeller, 'Ambiguity', pp. 32-33; Finley, *Joel, Amos, Obadiah*, pp. 191-92;

Wolff and Hayes, on the other hand, have criticized the solution suggested by Rabinowitz and Moeller. Like Paul, Wolff has pointed out that שׁק is never used for the leg of a bed, adding that 'after the simile in v 12a such a new pictorial expression is neither to be expected nor is it clearly understandable'.[108] However, while Wolff is right that שׁק is not otherwise used for the leg of a bed, it does not follow that the term could not be used in such a way.[109] And as far as the suggested metaphorical use of שׁק is concerned, even the most careful perusal of Wolff's comments does not reveal why this should be so unexpected and unintelligible. Wolff himself in the end adopted Gese's suggestion to amend the phrase to בַּאֲמֶשֶׁת ('at the headboard'),[110] thus avoiding the 'problem' of the unusual use of שׁק. Yet, for this he has to assume a major scribal error, whereas Rabinowitz and Moeller's solution preserves the consonantal text as it has come down to us.

Hayes, for his part, is adamant that 'the statements in the verse are not constructed so that the last four words are parallel to "two legbones or a piece of an ear"'.[111] Thus, while in 12aβ we have the particle או, the two phrases in 12bβ are joined by a waw. Hayes maintains that דְּמֶשֶׁק means 'Damascus' and that v. 12bβ is best translated as 'and in Damascus (is) a bed'. This he takes to mean that 'Samaria will be salvaged along with some fragments of bedding but their place of sleeping will be in Damascus; that is, they will be exiled from the land'.[112] Yet, apart from the fact that this still leaves us with an unusual spelling for Damascus, Hayes fails to recognize the parallel construction of the two phrases in v. 12bβ itself. In both cases, the initial preposition beth is followed by a noun, which in turn is succeeded by another noun designating a bed (מטה or ערשׂ). This would seem to suggest that Rabinowitz and Moeller's rendering of ובדמשׁק ערשׂ (or indeed ובד משׁק ערשׂ) as 'and a piece from a leg of a bed' is still the most convincing solution to this *crux interpretum*.[113]

---

and also Smith, *Amos*, pp. 122-23. Already Wellhausen, *Die kleinen Propheten*, p. 77, had suggested that דמשׁק might be a corruption of some word corresponding to פאה.

108. Wolff, *Joel and Amos*, p. 196.

109. Cf. Andersen and Freedman, *Amos*, p. 409, who have argued that שׁק could be metaphorical, which would be quite appropriate in the context.

110. Gese, 'Kleine Beiträge', pp. 427-32, who understood בדמשׁק as 'eine Analogiebildung zu dem vorhergehenden בשׁמרון' (p. 428).

111. Hayes, *Amos*, p. 135.

112. Hayes, *Amos*, p. 135.

113. For further discussions see Harper, *Commentary*, pp. 80-83; Cripps, *Commentary*, pp. 291-92; Rudolph, *Joel, Amos, Obadja, Jona*, pp. 159-60; Finley, *Joel,*

Rhetorical Function

The sudden shift from the announcement of the divine punishment in v. 11 to this talk of (no) rescue in v. 12 may at first appear somewhat surprising. After all, vv. 13-15 would be a natural conclusion to vv. 9-11, stressing as they do the consequences of the enemy invasion. Yet, given that the discourse in Amos 3 consists of a variety of speech forms representing some eloquent rhetorical moves on the part of the prophet, it would be rash to conclude that the illustration in v. 12 is out of place in its present context. Like the provocative summoning of foreign witnesses in vv. 9-11, the talk of remains of furniture being rescued from the rubble left by the invading enemy also contributes to Amos's main point: that the Israelites will have to face the divine judgment in all its severity. While the preceding verses made it clear that Yahweh's punishment is justified—even by the Philistines' and the Egyptians' standards would one come to that conclusion— the sarcastic illustration in v. 12 stresses that there will be no rescue.

As some have noted, this appears to be another case of the prophet responding to his audience's objections, who were confident that Yahweh would deliver them from the enemy attack threatened in the preceding announcement of judgment. For instance, Pfeifer has argued that

> Amos picks up the words of his hearers; he takes up the talk of rescue and confirms it. Yes, there will be a rescue from the impending judgment of God over Israel but what will be rescued is some debris of their furnishings, which witnesses to the life to which they once belonged... This 'rescue' is only proof of the destruction.[114]

The short statement in v. 12 thus contributes to the presentation of 'the cut-and-thrust of a prophet in debate with his audience', to phrase it in Davies's words.[115]

Amos, Obadiah, pp. 191-92; Hubbard, *Joel and Amos*, p. 152; and S. Mittmann, 'Amos 3,12-15 und das Bett der Samarier', *ZDPV* 92 (1976), pp. 149-67. Gese, 'Kleine Beiträge', p. 429, lists yet more proposals and discusses the interpretations of LXX, Vg, and Tg in some detail. O. Loretz, 'Vergleich und Kommentar in Amos 3,12', *BZ* NS 20 (1976), pp. 122-25, regards the disputed phrase, together with large parts of the verse, as a prosaic gloss, but see Mittmann, 'Amos 3,12-15', p. 150, for a critique of Loretz's treatment of v. 12.

114. Pfeifer, 'Rettung', p. 276; cf. also Rudolph, *Joel, Amos, Obadja, Jona*, p. 164; and Wolff, *Joel and Amos*, p. 197.

115. Davies used this expression in his (critical) discussion of Wolff's suggestion that Hos. 4–11 consists of a number of 'Auftrittsskizzen' (see Davies, *Hosea*, p. 103).

Andersen and Freedman regard v. 12 as the centrepiece of the entire discourse, noting that 'it represents the last scene in the process of destruction threatened and described in vv. 11 and 14-15'.[116] However, it also serves well as an introduction to the concluding verses with their focus on the divine punishment. And, as Melugin has pointed out, v. 12 fits well into the context of Amos 3 as a whole, which it apparently presupposes. After all, 'its use of the messenger formula, as well as the language about household furnishings and the verb *yšb*, relates to both vv. 9-11 and vv. 13-15. The mention of the "lion" in v. 12 is reminiscent of vv. 3-8 (4, 8)'.[117]

5. *The Rhetorical Structure of Amos 3*

The discourse in Amos 3 is bracketed by two announcements of punishment, each of which is introduced by שִׁמְעוּ and uses the key word פְּקֹד to allude to the impending judgment. The inclusio highlights the passage's central message while at the same time lending unity to a discourse, whose individual parts are increasingly seen to be integral components of this judgment speech.[118] The three sections sandwiched in between the outer parts serve to underline that the prophet's message is indeed the divine word, which Amos has to proclaim as a warning to the people of Israel (vv. 3-8), that the divine judgment is justified, even by the standards of Israel's neighbours (vv. 9-11), and that the Israelites' hope for a rescue from the catastrophe will not be realized (v. 12). Moving from the introductory part in vv. 1-2 to the subsequent series of rhetorical questions in vv. 3-8, it might at first appear as though Amos has abandoned his initial theme. Yet, in the following sections, he gradually returns to his main issue, which he revisits from different angles, before finally reaffirming his initial declaration that Yahweh is going to punish the people of Israel. The whole discourse thus unfolds as follows.

---

116. Andersen and Freedman, *Amos*, p. 405.

117. Melugin, 'Formation', p. 382. His conclusion that it 'was created by a redactor who already had the material in ch. 3 before him' is less evident, however. While describing a possible scenario, one should not rule out the possibility of v. 12 being a genuine part of the Amos tradition, which has been placed in its current setting by the book's editors in their desire to capture and present the prophet's debate with his eighth-century audience.

118. Thus, for instance, Lubsczyk, *Auszug Israels*, p. 46.

A   Initial declaration: Yahweh is going to punish his chosen people
    (vv. 1-2)
    introduced by: שמעו; key word: פקד
        B   Argumentation: Yahweh's words have to be announced as a
            warning (vv. 3-8)
            C   Provocative confirmation: even foreign witnesses will confirm
                the need for punishment (vv. 9-11)
                key word: ארמנות
            D   Sarcastic refutation: there will be no rescue (v. 12)
E   Reaffirmation of the initial declaration: Yahweh will indeed punish Israel
    (vv. 13-15)
    introduced by: שמעו; key word: פקד

Figure 26. *The Rhetorical Structure of Amos 3*

The advantage of this outline over against the chiastic arrangement proposed by Dorsey is that it draws attention to the development of the
argument rather than simply highlighting features of repetition. It also
avoids linking parts B (vv. 3-8) and D (v. 12), which as I have already
pointed out do not feature many parallels apart from two rather different
references to lions and their prey.[119] Another chiastic arrangement has
been suggested by Wendland, dividing the chapter into two parts, each of
which he believes to feature an A–B–A' structure.[120] Both parts are
marked by the use of inclusios—דבר יהוה and אדני יהוה דבר in vv. 1a,
8b,[121] on the one hand; and ארמנות in vv. 9-11 complemented by the corresponding בתים in vv. 13-15, on the other. Thus, according to Wendland,
the structure of Amos 3 can be outlined as follows:

Cycle one: the threat of imminent punishment (1-8)
    A   Introduction 'Listen…Yahweh has spoken' (1-2)
        B   Illustration: seven rhetorical questions with a progressive intensi-
            fication (3-6)
    A' Conclusion: climax—the lion (Yahweh) roars through his prophets
        (7-8)

Cycle two: the punishment is specified (9-15)
    A   Introduction: call to witness, indictment, verdict (9-11)
        B   Illustration: vivid simile (12)
    A' Conclusion: the indictment and verdict of unit A is continued (13-15)

Figure 27. *Amos 3 as Two Chiastic Cycles (Wendland)*

119. See section 2.a above.
120. Wendland, 'Word', pp. 11-12.
121. For this inclusio, see also Melugin, 'Formation', p. 381.

However, Wendland's analysis is flawed in that it overlooks the inclusio
provided by vv. 1-2 and vv. 13-15, which in addition to the repetition of
both שמעו and פקד also features clear thematic correspondences. This is
not the case with regard to Wendland's first cycle. Thus, while the phrases
דבר יהוה and אדני יהוה דבר in vv. 1, 8 do provide a formal inclusio, there
is at best only some superficial correspondence between the introductory
announcement of punishment in vv. 1-2 and Amos's conclusion in vv. 7-8
that if Yahweh has spoken he cannot but prophesy. It also seems preferable to stick with the traditional form-critical analysis, according to which
vv. 1-2, on the one hand, and vv. 3-8, on the other, constitute two distinct
units.

Wendland's case is much stronger with regard to the second cycle since
vv. 13-15 clearly develop the punishment theme of vv. 9-11. Yet, a closer
look reveals that the concluding section does not elaborate on the indictment, as Wendland's outline suggests. The focus is rather exclusively on
the verdict or, to be more precise, on its consequences, as vv. 13-15 stress
that the stripping of Israel's defences (cf. v. 11) will be followed by the
destruction of the people's luxurious residences. However, while it might
thus just be possible to regard vv. 9-15 as a chiastic arrangement, it has to
be said that Wendland's analysis obscures not only the more important
correspondences between vv. 1-2 and vv. 13-15 but also the argumentative
structure of the discourse as a whole. And as far as the function of vv. 13-
15 in particular is concerned, I am more inclined to follow Gitay, who
appropriately calls the section 'the epilogue to the discourse.'[122]

It should also be noted in this context that the above analysis has confirmed form-critical findings that regard Amos 3 as a string of five distinct
oracles or forms of speech. In fact, the five sections that make up this
chapter are quite diverse both in form and content. Yet this notwithstanding, I remain sceptical about earlier claims, made by Gunkel and others,
that these short sayings were originally delivered independently. Having
said that, however, I should add that it does not follow that the prophetic
discourse in Amos 3 represents one of Amos's original speeches. As I
have already pointed out above, it seems more likely that what we are
dealing with in the book of Amos is a mixture of edited collections of
oracles (taken perhaps from different speeches) as well as abstracts or
summaries of prophetic discourses.[123] To phrase it differently, what we
have are not the *ipsissima verba* of the prophet Amos but his *ipsissima*

---

122. Gitay, 'Study', p. 301.
123. See the discussion in Chapter 2, section 1.a above.

vox, that is, a collection of material that captures Amos's original message while presenting it in a new way.

However, even or maybe especially in their new setting, the variety of speech forms (or rhetorical devices) testify to the prophet's skill in relating his difficult message to an unresponsive audience. Equally importantly, the condensation and arrangement of these 'Amosian sound bites' also reveals the editorial skill, which has put us as readers in a position to relive the debate between the prophet and his eighth-century hearers. As we have seen, in Amos 3 the stringing together of five rather diverse speech forms with different *Sitze im Leben* has helped to reproduce the intensity of the dialogue between the prophet and his addressees, in which both parties are seen to respond to and argue with one another.

Finally, I would like to draw attention to the fact that the above analysis of Amos 3 confirms what was said in Chapter 1, namely, that anyone undertaking structural investigations would do well to look for more than just one particular structural device, such as an inclusio. And apart from the need to look for a convergence of a variety of structural indicators (in our particular case the introductory formulas in 3.1 and 4.1 as well as the inclusio provided by the verb פקד in 3.2, 14), one should bear in mind that a text's structure is meant to be subservient to its message. For this reason, structural investigations should never become an end in themselves.

6. *The Rhetorical Function of Amos 3*

Having looked at the rhetorical structure and function of each of the five parts that make up Amos 3 as well as the rhetorical structure of the chapter as a whole, what yet remains to be done is to consider the chapter's role in the presentation of the debate found in the book of Amos. As, for instance, Dorsey has pointed out, 'the unit appears to be positioned here to develop one of the themes introduced in the final stanza of the previous message, viz., the judgment of Israel'.[124]

Indeed, Amos 3, while clearly being a distinct discourse on its own, displays close links with the OAN in Amos 1.3–2.16. The most important of these is the term ארמון,[125] which occurs exclusively in Amos 1–3 with only one exception in 6.8.[126] In the first two chapters, the prophet formu-

124. Dorsey, 'Literary Architecture', p. 310; cf. also Andersen and Freedman, *Amos*, p. 369.
125. Cf. Hubbard, *Joel and Amos*, p. 147; and Melugin, 'Formation', p. 383.
126. The term appears in Amos 1.4, 7, 10, 12, 14; 2.2, 5; 3.9 (twice), 10, 11; 6.8. Of

A Prophet in Debate

laically announces that Yahweh is going to send a fire to devour the strongholds of the foreign nations in question. However, this notion is missing from the Israel strophe, as Amos 2.13-16 focuses mainly on the ineluctability of the divine punishment rather than on its nature.[127] The following section then opens with another announcement of punishment (Amos 3.1-2), which, for reasons that have been discussed earlier, is not developed until v. 11. Inviting representatives from the ארמנות of Egypt and Ashdod, who are called to witness the crimes committed within the ארמנות of Samaria, Amos finally announces that Israel's own ארמנות shall be plundered by an enemy.

The courtroom scene in vv. 9-11 thus provides a strong link with the previous discourse, thereby indicating that Amos 3 develops the theme of Israel's judgment introduced in 2.6-16. Hayes has come to similar conclusions with regard to 3.9-11, arguing that 'the oppression and outrage referred to in this text are no doubt to be seen as synonymous with the list of wrongdoings denounced in 2.6-8'.[128] However, the terminological and thematic links and correspondences are not confined to vv. 9-11. Another important connection is provided by the term פשע, which designates the wrongdoings of each of the accused nations in Amos 1–2, including Israel (cf. 2.6). The same term recurs in 3.14, where it once again sums up the people's evil actions, thus tying the extended accusation against Israel (2.6–3.15) together.[129] Rudolph is therefore right to relate vv. 14-15 to the Israel oracle in Amos 2, claiming that this small section connects with the notions expressed in 2.6-16 and serves to develop the threat of judgment in vv. 13-16.[130]

Another theme that connects the Israel strophe in Amos 2 with the discourse in Amos 3 is the issue of the prophets and Israel's dealings with them. Whereas in 2.11-12 the silencing of the prophets by the Israelites is given as one of the reasons for the judgment to come, in 3.3-8 Amos feels

---

the 32 occurrences of this expression in the Old Testament, no less than 12 are found in the book of Amos.

127. Amos 2.13 might be an allusion to an earthquake, however.

128. Hayes, *Amos*, p. 128.

129. See Rudolph, *Joel, Amos, Obadja, Jona*, p. 162; Hubbard, *Joel and Amos*, p. 147; and Melugin, 'Formation', pp. 383-84, who has pointed out that the term פשע is used predominantly in Amos 1–3 (1.3, 6, 9, 11, 13; 2.1, 4, 6; 3.14). The only two occurrences in the rest of the book are in 4.4 and 5.12. See also Smith, *Amos*, p. 125; and Andersen and Freedman, *Amos*, pp. 377, 411.

130. Rudolph, *Joel, Amos, Obadja, Jona*, p. 165.

4. *Amos 3*   249

compelled to defend his own prophetic ministry, claiming that he has no choice but to proclaim the divine message.[131] In addition, both passages mention the exodus theme, using the phrase הֶעֱלֵיתִי מֵאֶרֶץ מִצְרַיִם to refer to the delivery of Yahweh's chosen people out of Egypt (cf. 2.10; 3.1).[132] Based on this correspondence and the continuation of the judgment theme, Paul has argued for vv. 1-2 to be 'a sort of minirecapitulation of some of the main motifs and expressions of the first two chapters'.[133] Finally, it should also be noted that the comparison of Yahweh's voice to a lion's roar in 3.4, 8 connects Amos 3 back to the book's motto in 1.2.

Having discussed the correspondences between the OAN in Amos 1–2 and the following discourse in Amos 3, the transition in 3.1-2 in particular deserves a closer look. Throughout this chapter, I have drawn attention to how the stringing together of a variety of prophetic oracles in Amos 3 captures the dialogical character of the prophetic ministry, as each subsection appears to presuppose and react to some kind of comment or objection by Amos's hearers. The same appears to be the case in 3.1-2. With Amos comparing Israel's social evils to the crimes of her neighbours and even threatening a divine punishment, it would seem only natural for his addressees to rely on their special status as God's chosen people.[134]

It is to this that the words in 3.1-2 respond. Hoffman has argued that in his reference to the exodus, Amos actually employs 'a popular expression, which he quotes ironically, or at least polemically'.[135] This he does in

131. Cf. Dorsey, 'Literary Architecture', p. 310; Hubbard, *Joel and Amos*, p. 147; and Andersen and Freedman, *Amos*, p. 378.

132. Andersen and Freedman, *Amos*, p. 378; Paul, *Amos*, p. 101; Finley, *Joel, Amos, Obadiah*, p. 180; Hubbard, *Joel and Amos*, p. 147; and Pfeifer, 'Amos und Deuterojesaja', p. 441. Smith, *Amos*, p. 104, has pointed out that the 'connection with 2.10 is lost if 3.1b is omitted as a secondary gloss', adding that 'if all of 3.1 is part of God's message (instead of a prophetic introduction) one of the major reasons for omitting 3.1b is removed'.

133. Paul, *Amos*, pp. 100-101. According to Melugin, 'Formation', p. 383, all these correspondences should be attributed to 'the composer of 1.3-2.16 [who] has created this passage as an introduction to 3.1ff. by using language which is employed elsewhere in his collected material'.

134. See Rudolph, *Joel, Amos, Obadja, Jona*, p. 153, who notes that Amos 'erlebte …gewiß immer wieder, daß ihm die Erwählungstatsache entgegengehalten wurde'. See also Harper, *Commentary*, p. 64; Cripps, *Commentary*, pp. 149-50; Paul, *Amos*, p. 101; Smith, *Amos*, p. 97; Martin-Achard, 'End', p. 28; and Melugin, 'Formation', p. 381.

135. Hoffman, 'North Israelite Typological Myth', p. 180. Hoffman points out that we find a similar reference to the exodus in Jer. 16.14; 23.7, where it features as an oath formula (see also C.F. Keil, *Jeremiah, Lamentations* [COT, 8; repr., Peabody,

order to underline that even the people's special privileges will turn against them because of their unacceptable behaviour. Vollmer too has seen the dialogical dimension of Amos 3.2, a verse he regards as an 'expression of the discussion' between the prophet and his audience. He even believes that the statement in 3.2a:

> when seen in connection with Amos's proclamation, can only be understood as a concession to his hearers, which Amos makes without identifying with it. The half-verse is only comprehensible as an objection, which is levelled against Amos because of his proclamation of judgement.[136]

This illustrates that the dialogical component is not just intrinsic to Amos 3 but extends to the macrostructural level connecting, as in the example under discussion, the book's major discourses, which thus become the individual discussion rounds of the debate that runs through the book of Amos as a whole.

MA: Hendrickson, 1996], p. 168). This strengthens the idea that we are dealing with a phrase that belongs to the repertoire of popular tradition.

136. Vollmer, *Geschichtliche Rückblicke und Motive*, p. 31.

Chapter 5

Amos 4

A review of exegetical discussions of Amos 4 quickly indicates that there
is no consensus about the passage's structure. Often, either vv. 6-13[1] or
vv. 4-13[2] are seen as distinct entities but in recent years some have, I
believe, succeeded in making a case for the whole chapter to be regarded
as a unity.[3] However, as in the above discussion of Amos 3, I am not
going to argue for the chapter to be seen as one of the prophet's original
speeches. Instead, I am interested in its present form, that is, in how its
structure, message and rhetoric work together to achieve the passage's
specific mode of persuasion.

1. *Amos 4.1-3*

a. *Exegetical Observations and Structure*
The interpretation of the first three verses is aggravated by some major textual problems, which have given rise to three main questions. First, what
are we to make of the phrase פרות הבשן in v. 1 and why is it followed by

1.   Mays, *Amos*, pp. 76-83; Weiser, *Buch der zwölf kleinen Propheten*, pp. 153-57;
Wolff, *Joel and Amos*, pp. 211-15; and Pfeifer, *Theologie*, p. 53.
2.   Harper, *Commentary*, pp. 90-105; Rudolph, *Joel, Amos, Obadja, Jona*, pp. 169-
83; Stuart, *Hosea–Jonah*, pp. 333-40; Smith, *Amos*, pp. 133-50; Paul, *Amos*, pp. 137-
56; Carroll R., *Contexts*, pp. 206-21; and Jeremias, *Book of Amos*, pp. 67-76.
3.   The initial 3 verses present the main problem because of their thematic links
with the previous oracles. However, as I have argued in Chapter 1, the introductory
phrase שמעו הדבר הזה in 4.1 indicates a major break at this point. Amos 4 is also
regarded as a unity by J.L. Crenshaw, '*Wedōrēk 'al-bāmŏtê 'āreṣ*', *CBQ* 34 (1972),
pp. 39-53 (42); Melugin, 'Formation', pp. 377-78; Barstad, *Religious Polemics*, pp. 37-
75; Limburg, 'Sevenfold Structures', p. 218; Wendland, 'Word', pp. 12-14; Hubbard,
Joel and Amos, pp. 154-63; Finley, *Joel, Amos, Obadiah*, pp. 197-219; Dempster,
'Lord', p. 175; Dorsey, 'Literary Architecture', pp. 311-12; and Niehaus, 'Amos',
p. 328.

an alternation of masculine and feminine forms in vv. 1-3? Secondly, what kind of judgment is depicted by the phrases צנות and סירות דוגה in v. 2? And thirdly, what is the meaning of ההרמונה in v. 3? While the latter two problems are of minor importance for our purposes—it is in any case clear that vv. 2-3 envisage a divine judgment—the first question significantly affects the interpretation of Amos 4.1-3 and thus merits closer attention. Two major solutions have been proposed:

1. The majority of commentators have taken the oracle as an attack against the upper-class women of Samaria, who are rebuked because of their extravagant and oppressive lifestyle.[4] Bashan was known for its rich pastures and fat animals (cf. Deut. 32.14; Ezek. 39.18; Mic. 7.14; Ps. 22.13), and Smith has drawn attention to the fact that in Isa. 2.13 the oaks of Bashan symbolize the proud and haughty while the bulls of Bashan in Ps. 22.12 epitomize violence and strength.[5] Advocates of this view also point to the social crimes listed in v. 1. According to this interpretation, אדנים in v. 1b refers to the women's husbands, who are expected to keep their wives' drinks coming. However, the more common terms to refer to a husband are איש or בעל,[6] and the use of אדון may well be sarcastic, indicating that while their husbands are called lords,

---

4. Thus Harper, *Commentary*, p. 86; Cripps, *Commentary*, p. 165; Wolff, *Joel and Amos*, p. 205; Paul, *Amos*, p. 128; Hayes, *Amos*, p. 139; Weiser, *Buch der zwölf kleinen Propheten*, p. 150; King, *Amos, Hosea, Micah*, p. 126; Smith, *Amos*, pp. 127-28; Finley, *Joel, Amos, Obadiah*, p. 198; Hubbard, *Joel and Amos*, p. 155; Soggin, *Prophet Amos*, pp. 69-70; Stuart, *Hosea–Jonah*, p. 332; Niehaus, 'Amos', p. 392; Reimer, *Recht*, p. 88; Sawyer, *Prophecy*, p. 42; Jemielity, *Satire*, p. 89; McComiskey, 'Amos', p. 302; Feinberg, *Minor Prophets*, p. 98; McKeating, *Books of Amos, Hosea and Micah*, p. 32; and Jeremias, *Book of Amos*, p. 63.

Some have argued that the phrase פרות הבשן is not meant to be taken in a derogatory sense but that it indicates quality (for this view, see Rudolph, *Joel, Amos, Obadja, Jona*, p. 167; Hammershaimb, *Book of Amos*, p. 65; Pfeifer, *Theologie*, p. 50; Martin-Achard, 'End', p. 33; M. Holland, *Joel, Amos und Obadja* [Wuppertal: Brockhaus, 1991], p. 134; and Mays, *Amos*, p. 72). However, J. Limburg, *Hosea–Micah* (Interpretation; Atlanta: John Knox Press, 1988), p. 99, has rightly stressed that Amos's words 'were spoken in public, in the context of confrontation' and that 'it is difficult to imagine that those who heard them would take them as a compliment'.

5. Smith, *Amos*, p. 128.

6. According to Reimer, *Recht*, pp. 89-90, אדנים is a *pluralis reverentiae* and the quote in v. 1 is a request by the women at the court, demanding the king to supply them with enough to drink. Niehaus, 'Amos', p. 392, on the other hand, thinks of 'husbands of high rank or social standing'.

the women's orders clearly indicate otherwise.[7]

Yet, scholars advocating this interpretation have found it difficult to explain the curious combination of feminine and masculine forms in vv. 1-3. Wellhausen and Elliger, to name but two representatives, have suggested that the masculine forms be turned into feminine ones[8] while Reimer has argued that the alternating forms are traces of subsequent editorial work, the aim of which may have been to connect the passage to the following section with its religious focus.[9] Yet, if this was the editors' aim, one wonders why they kept some of the feminine forms rather than tidying the text up properly. There may be no definite solution to this issue but it should be noted that, for instance, the masculine suffix of שמעו (v. 1) may simply be due to the term being used as a set phrase in the book of Amos.[10] As regards אדניהם in v. 1 and עליכם and אתכם in v. 2, it is important to note that biblical Hebrew frequently employs masculine pronouns to refer to feminine subjects or objects.[11]

2. This then takes us to the second interpretation of vv. 1-3, according to which it is the ruling classes in general that are indicted in these verses. In this reading, the feminine forms are understood as a figure of speech and the characterization of Israel's ruling elite as female cattle, an insulting and provocative epithet, is taken to be the very point Amos intended to make.[12] As Andersen and Freedman have pointed out:

---

7. See Rudolph, *Joel, Amos, Obadja, Jona*, p. 167; Weiser, *Buch der zwölf kleinen Propheten*, p. 150; Deissler, *Zwölf Propheten*, p. 107; Carroll R., *Contexts*, pp. 201-202; and Smith, *Amos*, pp. 128-29, who calls this 'a derogatory remark about the husband's authority'.

8. See Wellhausen, *Die kleinen Propheten*, p. 78; and *BHS ad loc*. This seems a bit rash, however, because as A. Wolters, 'Cross-Gender Imagery in the Bible', *BBR* 8 (1998), pp. 217-28, has shown, what he calls 'cross-gender imagery' is a widespread phenomenon not only in biblical and other ancient texts (Mesopotamian as well as Greek) but also in contemporary speech and literature.

9. Reimer, *Recht*, p. 95.

10. See Amos 3.1; 5.1; 8.4 and also GK §§110k, 144a for the use of the 2nd masc. sg. ipv. with a feminine subject.

11. See GK §135o. Commenting on אדניהם and referring to W.G.E. Watson, *Classical Hebrew Poetry: A Guide to Its Techniques* (JSOTSup, 26; Sheffield: JSOT Press, 1984), pp. 231-32, Carroll R., *Contexts*, p. 202 n. 1, has suggested that the switch to the use of the masculine suffix 'might be an instance of rhyming to maintain the *wt-ym* pattern of the previous line'.

12. This had already been the view of Calvin, *Minor Prophets*, pp. 224, who believed that Amos did not think Israel's leaders 'worthy of the name of men'; cf. also L. Bauer, 'Einige Stellen des Alten Testaments bei Kautzsch 4. Aufl. im Licht des

the use of animal names—buffalo, ram, stag, stallion, bull (*šôr*)—for strong brave men, especially warriors, was popular among North Semitic peoples… To call men who fancied themselves such heroes 'cows' would then be a parody and an insult. Such a taunt or curse is found in other texts, where soldiers behave like women. The military background of v 2 supports this result.[13]

Scholars taking this line of approach tend to favour a cultic interpretation that invests both the phrase פרות הבשן and the words הביאה ונשתה with cultic significance. For instance, Barstad has argued that:

> *pārôṯ habbāšān* is an address to the whole people. Behind this designation there is hidden a polemic against the Baal cult because *pārâ* needs to be understood as a prophetic 'invective' against the adherents of the fertility cult, possibly even as a technical term for the participants in the hieros gamos of the fertility cult…[14]

Several points have been made in support of this interpretation. First, the larger context in Amos 3.1-15; 4.4-13 clearly suggests that Amos is addressing the people as a whole.[15] Secondly, the repetition of the introductory שמעו formula, which in Amos 3.1; 5.1; 8.4 addresses all of Israel, suggests that פרות הבשן too might refer to the Israelites in general.[16] Thirdly, the alternating use of masculine and feminine forms is taken to indicate that members of both genders are targeted in these verses.[17]

heiligen Landes', *TSK* 100 (1927–28), pp. 426-38 (437).

13. Andersen and Freedman, *Amos*, p. 421; cf. also J.D.W. Watts, 'A Critical Analysis of Amos 4.1ff.', in McGaughy (ed.), *SBLASP* 108.2, pp. 489-500 (496).

14. H.M. Barstad, 'Die Basankühe in Amos iv 1', *VT* 25 (1975), pp. 286-97 (296); cf. *idem, Religious Polemics*, p. 40; and Koch, *Prophets*, p. 46, who also favours a cultic interpretation but believes that the addressees are exclusively female. He argues that Amos 'may be mockingly picking up a cultic name the women gave themselves, since they imagined themselves to be the worshippers of the mighty bull of Samaria (Hos. 8.5f.)'. Koch's view is supported by P.F. Jacobs, ' "Cows of Bashan"—A Note on the Interpretation of Amos 4.1', *JBL* 104 (1985), pp. 109-10.

15. Cf. Barstad, 'Basankühe', p. 290; and *idem, Religious Polemics*, p. 40.

16. Barstad draws our attention to בתולת ישראל in Amos 5.2 as a similar metaphorical term for all of Israel (cf. 'Basankühe', p. 291; and *Religious Polemics*, pp. 40-41). He also points to the similarity of the phrases הישבים בשמרון in 3.12 and בהר שמרון in 4.1 ('Basankühe', p. 290), arguing that since the former refers to the whole people, the latter should be understood in the same way.

17. Thus Andersen and Freedman, *Amos*, p. 420; and Smith, 'Amos, Obadiah', p. 84. A.J. Williams, 'A Further Suggestion about Amos iv 1-3', *VT* 29 (1979), pp. 206-11 (206 n. 1), believes that the text's ambiguity might be intentional, making it possible for both the Israelites in general and the upper-class females in particular to be

Fourthly, the words פרה and בשׁן are both found in contexts that deal with cultic activities.[18] Fifthly, it is argued that אדון in v. 1 can just as easily refer to a foreign deity as to the husbands of some upper-class women,[19] especially as the masculine suffix of אדניהם suggests male addressees.[20]

Amos 2.8, which has Amos condemn the people's practice of drinking wine in the house of their God, is taken as further evidence in favour of a cultic interpretation. It has been pointed out that Amos 2.8 and 4.1 both contain references to 'drinking' (ישׁתו in 2.8 and ונשׁתה in 4.1) as well as to 'their God' or 'their Lord' (אלהיהם in 2.8 and אדניהם in 4.1). This, together with the arguments rehearsed above, has led some to conclude that Amos 2.6-8 and 4.1-3 (4-5) both speak of social *and* cultic offences. In support of a cultic understanding of Amos 4.1-3, Watts has also claimed that the words הביאה ונשׁתה, which he prefers to translate as 'Come. Let us drink!', refer to Baalistic rites.[21]

the prophet's targets. F. Praetorius, 'Zum Texte des Amos', *ZAW* 34 (1914), pp. 42-44 (43); and Holland, *Joel, Amos und Obadja*, p. 135, have suggested that the alternation between masculine and feminine forms might be significant, at least with regard to v. 2, which Praetorius paraphrases as follows: 'und man wird euch (Männer) an den Schilden wegnehmen, und euch (Weiber) bis auf die letzte an den Kochtöpfen.' However, this still leaves the remaining cases unexplained.

18. Thus Barstad, 'Basankühe', p. 293, referring to the use of בשׁן in Ps. 68.15-17; and Williams, 'Further Suggestion', pp. 210-211, who notes that 'in Ps. lxviii 15 a certain rivalry between Mount Zion and the hills of Bashan is implied which no doubt has cultic overtones'. He adds that 'the reference to "bulls" in Ps. xxii 13 should also be noted' and that 'there may be a reference to a foreign cultic tradition originating in the region of Bashan' (however, see Melugin, 'Formation', pp. 382-83, who regards the 'bulls of Bashan', together with the dogs and lions in Ps. 22.13, as 'images of the supplicant's enemies rather than cultic figures'). On the cultic overtones of בשׁן see also G. del Olmo Lete, 'Bashan', in van der Toorn, Becking and van der Horst (eds.), *Dictionary of Deities and Demons in the Bible*, pp. 161-63.

With regard to פרה, Barstad, 'Basankühe', pp. 293-94, refers to Hos. 4.16 where he believes the term to have cultic implications. Thus, while פרה סררה is usually translated as 'stubborn heifer', Barstad prefers to render סרר as 'licentious' or 'randy'. He also points to Jer. 2.24, but there the term in question is פֶּרֶה rather than פָּרָה. Overall, the evidence does not appear to be conclusive, leaving me inclined to follow Melugin, 'Formation', pp. 382-83, who has underlined that neither the reference to the mountain of Samaria nor the mention of the 'cows of Bashan' are unequivocally cultic.

19. Barstad, 'Basankühe', p. 292, has pointed out that the term sometimes refers to Baal (see also *idem, Religious Polemics*, p. 41).

20. See Andersen and Freedman, *Amos*, p. 422; and Watts, 'Critical Analysis', p. 496.

21. Watts, 'Critical Analysis', p. 496. Unfortunately, however, he does not present

At present, it seems that neither the addressees nor the nature of the offences can be identified with absolute certainty. Yet, it should be noted that even if there were cultic overtones in Amos 4.1-3, the focus nevertheless appears to be on the ruling classes' exploitative lifestyle. As Koch so aptly notes, 'like replete cattle [Amos's addressees] wilfully trample down their pastures, the lower classes of the people, on whom their existence in fact depends.'[22]

Amos here portrays Israel's leaders as nurturing their own self-indulgence at the expense of the poor and needy, who are incessantly oppressed and exploited.[23] Whereas עשק refers to direct and indirect forms of exploitation of human working power,[24] רצץ implies the use of excessive violence. This can be seen, for instance, from Judg. 9.53 and Ps. 74.14, where רצץ denotes the crushing of the heads of Abimelech and Leviathan.[25] Niehaus has argued for the two terms to function as 'a hendiadys meaning "cruel oppression"',[26] and Jeremias has pointed out 'that Amos is concerned not with individual instances of injustice, but rather with the devastation of the existence of entire families'.[27] Based on the occurrence of עשק and מְרוּצָה in Jer. 22.17, Reimer has argued that what Amos had in mind was compulsory labour.[28]

As regards the victims of the offences condemned in Amos 4.1, they are identified as the דלים and אביונים, the poor and the marginalized, those who lack social standing and have no influence in society.[29] According to

any evidence to support his claim. Barstad, *Religious Polemics*, p. 42, on the other hand, has argued that the phrase refers to the *marzeaḥ*.

22. Koch, *Prophets*, p. 46; cf. also Mays, *Amos*, p. 72.

23. The notion of continuity is conveyed by the use of participles (cf. GK §116a). According to Niehaus, 'Amos', p. 392, the series of three participles parallels 'the pattern of an ancient Near Eastern divine or royal titulary'.

24. See Reimer, *Recht*, p. 89.

25. See also Ezek. 29.7 (where רצץ parallels שבר); Judg. 10.8 (where it is used alongside of רעץ); and Eccl. 12.6; Isa. 58.6 (where it appears in combination with נתק). Wolff, *Joel and Amos*, p. 206, described עשק as abuse 'through oppression and extortion' and רצץ as abuse 'through striking and beating' and Harper, *Commentary*, p. 88, notes that 'רצץ refers...to open attack and assault'.

26. Niehaus, 'Amos', p. 392.

27. Jeremias, *Book of Amos*, p. 45.

28. Reimer, *Recht*, p. 89. עשק and רצץ are also paired up in Deut. 28.33; 1 Sam. 12.3-4; Jer. 22.17 and Hos. 5.11.

29. See Fabry, 'דל', pp. 208-30; and Botterweck, 'אֶבְיוֹן', pp. 27-41, for further discussion of the two terms.

the law, they should have been treated with justice and compassion (Deut. 15.4-11; 24.14) but the exact opposite is the case. Returning once more to the culprits, Brenner has complained that 'apparently, when women allegedly have political and social influence, injustice reigns'.[30] However, apart from the fact that it is by no means clear that the פרות הבשן are actually (and exclusively) female, Brenner's comments are clearly a red herring in that it would be wrong to suggest that Amos is singling out Israel's women as the main culprits. If anything, Amos 4.1-3 merely indicates that the female members of Israel's upper classes were not exempt from the prophet's criticisms.

Wolff, in his important article 'Das Zitat im Prophetenspruch', has drawn attention to the intensifying rhetoric of the indictment of 4.1, highlighting in particular the function of the quote in v. 1d. Arguing that one function of prophetic quotes is to indicate a climax, he has pointed out that the motivation for the subsequent announcement of judgment in vv. 2-3 is given in three climactic steps. Thus, the insolent address 'cows of Bashan' is followed by two participles, which describe the despicable behaviour of the addressees, before being eclipsed by the actual climax provided by the quote in v. 1d, in which the prophet's targets all but condemn themselves by their own words.[31]

The judgment section in vv. 2-3 is also rhetorically marked, being introduced by a divine oath, which אדני יהוה is said to swear by his own holiness. Wolff has pointed out that 'when the oath formula replaces the messenger formula, the irrevocable nature of that which is proclaimed is set forth in the strongest terms'.[32] The longer form of the divine name אדני יהוה in this particular case carries an ironic touch (whether intentional or not) in as much as it stands in contrast to the reference to אדניהם in v. 1. Thus, whereas the Israelite women demand 'their lords' to get them something to drink, what they will get will come from an altogether different source; it will come from their real lord, אדני יהוה—and it won't be what they had been asking for.[33]

---

30. A. Brenner, 'Introduction', in *idem* (ed.), *A Feminist Companion to The Latter Prophets*, pp. 21-37 (23).

31. Wolff, 'Zitat', p. 79.

32. Wolff, *Joel and Amos*, p. 206; cf. also *idem*, 'Einführung', p. 15, for his observation that when an oracle is not identified as a divine utterance in its introduction, at least the proclamation concerning the future is said to be of divine origin (cf. v. 2aα).

33. See Paul, *Amos*, p. 130; and Carroll R., *Contexts*, p. 202 (n. 2). Wolff, *Joel and Amos*, pp. 190, 203, who proposed to delete אדני, completely missed its ironic

The Old Testament prophetic corpus features no more than six comparable oath formulas. Half of these appear in the book of Amos (4.2; 6.8 and 8.7) and the remaining three are to be found in Isa. 14.24; 62.8 and Jer. 51.14. In each of the Amosian cases, Yahweh swears by something different: by his holiness in 4.2,[34] by his life in 6.8 and by the pride of Jacob in 8.7. And in each case, the oath is followed by a judgment speech. This is noteworthy, representing as it does an Amosian particularity. In the other prophetic instances in Isaiah and Jeremiah, the oath formulas introduce oracles that reserve the divine punishment for Israel's enemies, promising salvation for the people of God.

Another interesting feature in v. 2 is the expression ימים באים, which indicates the dawn of a 'new era',[35] an era of divine judgment, an era that will upset the expectations of those, who regard themselves as God's favourites. Having already noted the ironic connotations attached to the recurrence of אדני in v. 2, attention should also be drawn to another conspicuous repetition, namely, the reappearance of the verb בוא. Whereas in v. 1 the Israelite women commanded their husbands to bring something to drink (הביאה), what they will in fact get is days of punishment, which will come to them (באים).[36]

I have already indicated that the interpretative problems posed by the judgment section in vv. 2-3, which in Hayes's view are an interpreter's nightmare,[37] need not be discussed in detail. The first difficulty concerns the nature of the divine judgment in general and the terms צנות and סירות דוגה in particular. While there is uncertainty about their precise meaning, the majority of interpreters believe that Amos is talking about a

---

overtones in v. 2. See also Dempster, 'Lord', p. 178, for a list of the different forms of the divine name that are used in Amos 4.1-13.

34. Outside the prophetic corpus, Yahweh also swears by his holiness in Ps. 89.36.

35. Cf. Paul, *Amos*, p. 130; Wolff, *Joel and Amos*, p. 206; Hubbard, *Joel and Amos*, p. 156; and Stuart, *Hosea–Jonah*, p. 332. According to Mays, *Amos*, p. 72, the phrase is 'used to designate the imminent inbreaking time when Yahweh would effect his great setting-right, whether for woe (8.11) or weal (9.13)'. According to Watts, 'Critical Analysis', p. 493, the phrase ימים באים is related to the concept of the יום יהוה.

36. Cf. Paul, *Amos*, p. 130 n. 19; and Wolff, 'Zitat', p. 79, who aptly, if somewhat awkwardly, translates the respective phrases as follows: 'Laßt uns zu trinken *kommen*! Ja, Tage *kommen* über euch, da schleppt man euch fort...' According to Wolff, the concatenation confirms his thesis that the women's quote receives a certain emphasis within the indictment.

37. Hayes, *Amos*, p. 139.

deportation.[38] It is also evident that the prophet's vivid description is meant to emphasise the brutality and totality of the judgment. The latter aspect is underlined by the fact that even those 'who are unwilling, the obstinate remnant of them'[39] will be led away. In a scenario that has been described as the next stage of the enemy invasion, following the city's siege and conquest in 3.11,[40] no one will be able to escape the deportation. They will all leave the city unhindered, as each one of them will be made to walk in a straight line through one of the countless breaches in the walls (cf. Josh. 6.20).[41]

This then takes us to the last of the interpretative problems mentioned

---

38. Concerning the nature of the punishment, several solutions have been proposed: (1) G.R. Driver, 'Babylonian and Hebrew Notes', *WO* 2 (1954), pp. 20-21; and McComiskey, 'Amos', p. 303, believe that Amos envisages the removal of corpses on large shields. (2) A sizeable number of scholars follow what appears to be the traditional interpretation, namely, that some kinds of hooks are used. Advocates of this view include Williams, 'Further Suggestion', p. 208; Harper, *Commentary*, p. 87; Cripps, *Commentary*, p. 167; Rudolph, *Joel, Amos, Obadja, Jona*, p. 161; Hammershaimb, *Book of Amos*, p. 66; Smith, *Amos*, p. 130; Finley, *Joel, Amos, Obadiah*, pp. 200-201; and Feinberg, *Minor Prophets*, p. 99. (3) Another possibility is the use of ropes, which has been suggested by S.J. Schwantes, 'Note on Amos 4 $_{2b}$', *ZAW* 79 (1967), pp. 82-83; and Wolff, *Joel and Amos*, pp. 206-207. (4) Finally, S.M. Paul, 'Fishing Imagery in Amos 4.2', *JBL* 97 (1978), pp. 183-90 (185-88), has argued that the text describes a carrying away in baskets or pots.

According to Brenner, 'Introduction', p. 23, who partly follows the LXX, which renders the words ופרצים תצאנה אשה in v. 3 as καὶ ἐξενεχθήσεσθε γυμναί, the women are 'brought out naked, and thrown into the harem', which seems rather fanciful, however. Some of the studies mentioned above offer detailed investigations of the *hapax legomena* in v. 2 and Paul, *Amos*, pp. 130-35, also has an extensive discussion of the various interpretative options.

39. Thus Hasel, *Remnant*, p. 183. While the usual term for 'remnant' is שארית (cf. Amos 1.8; 5.15; 9.12), אחרית can also take on this connotation (e.g., Amos 9.1; and see Harper, *Commentary*, p. 87; Cripps, *Commentary*, p. 167; Wolff, *Stunde des Amos*, pp. 118-20; Carroll R., *Contexts*, p. 202 n. 4; and Rudolph, *Joel, Amos, Obadja, Jona*, pp. 161, 168, who notes that Amos uses this 'rhetorische Figur, um die Totalität der Katastrophe zu veranschaulichen'). Some commentators have argued that the term refers to the backside or rear end of an animal, but as this meaning is not otherwise attested, an 'emendation' to אחֹרֵי has been suggested (cf. Exod. 26.12; 33.23; 1 Kgs 7.25; Ezek. 8.16). However, Hasel, *Remnant*, p. 182, has rightly pointed out that this interpretation contradicts the term's other uses in the book of Amos.

40. Cf. Reimer, *Recht*, p. 92.

41. פרצים is an *accusativus loci* (cf. GK §118 d+h). Its prominent position at the beginning of the sentence draws attention to the destroyed wall with its many breaches.

above as well as to the structure of Amos 4.1-3 as a whole. With regard to the former, it should suffice to note that הַהַרְמֹנָה, the *hapax legomenon* that concludes the present judgment oracle, in all likelihood denotes a location,[42] thus paralleling Amos 5.27, where a deportation 'beyond Damascus' is in view. And as far as the latter is concerned, the structure of this introductory oracle can be outlined as follows.

Introductory address	שִׁמְעוּ(m. pl.)הַדָּבָר הַזֶּה (f. pl.)פָּרוֹת הַבָּשָׁן אֲשֶׁר בְּהַר שֹׁמְרוֹן
Detailed accusation	הָעֹשְׁקוֹת דַּלִּים(f. pl.)
(elaboration on addressee)	הָרֹצְצוֹת אֶבְיוֹנִים(f. pl.)
	הָאֹמְרֹת(f. pl.)(suff. m. pl.)לַאֲדֹנֵיהֶם הָבִיאָה וְנִשְׁתֶּה
Announcement of punishment	
Introduction: divine oath formula	נִשְׁבַּע אֲדֹנָי יְהוִה בְּקָדְשׁוֹ
Announcement of a new era	כִּי הִנֵּה יָמִים בָּאִים(m. pl.)עֲלֵיכֶם
Detailed description of punishment	וְנִשָּׂא(m. pl.)אֶתְכֶם בְּצִנּוֹת
	(suff. f. pl.)וְאַחֲרִיתְכֶן בְּסִירוֹת דּוּגָה
	וּפְרָצִים(f. pl.)תֵּצֶאנָה(f. sg.)אִשָּׁה נֶגְדָּהּ
	(f. pl.)וְהִשְׁלַכְתֶּנָה הַהַרְמוֹנָה
Concluding oracle formula	נְאֻם־יְהוָה

Figure 28. *The Structure of Amos 4.1-3*[43]

42. Thus, for instance, Harper, *Commentary*, pp. 88-89; Paul, *Amos*, p. 136; Williams, 'Further Suggestion', p. 210; and McKeating, *Books of Amos, Hosea and Micah*, p. 32. D.N. Freedman and F.I. Andersen, 'Harmon in Amos 4.3', *BASOR* 198 (1970), p. 41, identify Harmon with modern Hermel near Kadesh on the Orontes. According to Pfeifer, *Theologie*, p. 51 n. 67, הַרְמוֹן might be a dialectal form of חֶרְמוֹן. However, Hayes, *Amos*, p. 142, prefers to read הַמַּדְמֵנָה 'the dung-pit, garbage heap' instead of הַהַרְמוֹנָה (cf. also NEB; NJPSV); and van der Wal, 'Structure of Amos', pp. 109-10; and Reimer, *Recht*, p. 93, have suggested emending the text to הָאַרְמוֹנָה. As Reimer notes, 'mit der Annahme, daß es sich bei dem letzten Wort in der Strafansage Am 4,3b um *'armenôt* / "Palastbauten" handelt, gewinnen wir einen durch das Stilmittel der "inclusio" in sich abgerundeten Textkomplex'.

As far as הִשְׁלַכְתֶּנָה is concerned, it seems best to follow the LXX, whose rendering ἀπορριφήσεσθε presupposes the passive הָשְׁלַכְתֶּנָה, 'and you will be thrown out' (cf. Reimer, *Recht*, p. 93; Rudolph, *Joel, Amos, Obadja, Jona*, p. 162; Paul, *Amos*, p. 136; Finley, *Joel, Amos, Obadiah*, p. 202; Hammershaimb, *Book of Amos*, p. 67; Soggin, *Prophet Amos*, p. 68; Stuart, *Hosea–Jonah*, p. 328; Holland, *Joel, Amos und Obadja*, pp. 133-34; and Carroll R., *Contexts*, p. 203 n. 1). The final ה might be a case of dittography, occasioned by the following word (cf. GK §44k). However, Niehaus, 'Amos', p. 394, prefers to retain the hiphil because it is the *lectio difficilior*.

43. Cf. also the outlines suggested by Westermann, *Basic Forms*, p. 174; and G.M. Tucker, 'Prophetic Speech', *Int* 32 (1978), pp. 31-45 (40).

b. *Rhetorical Function*

Like Amos 3.1-2, the oracle in Amos 4.1-3 also functions as an introduction to the following prophetic discourse. Both passages begin with a שמעו
phrase (3.1; 4.1) followed by a description of the addressees. They both
end with an announcement of punishment, which provides a provocative
entry into the subsequent discourse. Yet, there are differences too. In 4.1-
3, there is a comparatively detailed accusation (v. 1) whereas Amos 3.1-2
only vaguely refers to the people's iniquities. More importantly, the
addressees appear to be different, with Amos 3.1 calling them בני ישראל
and 4.1 speaking of the פרות הבשן.

To revisit the above discussion of the latter phrase's referents, Jeremias
has stressed that the context disallows the narrow definition, according to
which the phrase פרות הבשן refers to Israel's upper-class women. As he
points out, 'the individual sayings all stand under the auspices of 3.1-8 (and
4.6-13), which are directed at the people of God as a whole'.[44] In addition,
the use of the masculine pronoun in the phrase כי הנה ימים באים עליצם
also indicates that what the prophet had in mind was a mixed-gender audience.[45] However, it is also interesting to note that 4.1d refers to the
addressees in the third person (cf. אדניהם), which has led Hardmeier to
point out that Amos is talking about people who were in fact absent at the
time of him delivering his speech.[46]

This is an important point and it leads me to conclude that v. 1 may
indeed be speaking of some well-to-do women after all. However, and this
should not be overlooked, the textual context as a whole (possibly
including Amos 4.2-3) is clearly addressing a wider audience. The consequences of these observations are twofold. First, it seems as though the
malicious behaviour of the פרות הבשן is mentioned as another example of
the people's sin, just as, for instance, the charges brought against Israel in
Amos 2.6-8 in fact only concerned a specific stratum of Israel's society.
Secondly, for Amos to address a group of people, who were either absent
or who comprised only a relatively small portion of his audience (this
being another possible explanation for the use of the third person), might
have been a clever rhetorical move. It would have led the majority of his
hearers to breathe a sigh of relief, as they did not see themselves implicated by the prophet's words, only for them to find out seconds later that
the divine noose was tightening around them after all.

44. Jeremias, *Book of Amos*, p. 57.
45. Jeremias, *Book of Amos*, p. 64.
46. Hardmeier, *Texttheorie*, p. 379.

Amos's radical and indeed partly insulting language adds to the rhetorical impact of the passage.[47] It should therefore not be seen as a mere emotional outburst but as an attempt to provoke his addressees into rethinking their lifestyle and behaviour. Jemielity has drawn attention to the similarities between this prophetic use of language and satire, noting:

> whatever intensity the prophetic text conveys, unmistakable traces of artfulness also appear, signs of that careful attention to the ordering of language which suggest that the prophetic text, like the satiric, is not so much emotion as emotion recollected in tranquility.[48]

Another way of looking at the פרות הבשׁן reference is to regard it as a caricature, which is the stance taken by Weippert.[49] Defined as a distorted image that, by overplaying certain character traits, exposes political, social or moral deficiencies, caricature's very distortion of reality is intended to generate discussion and reassessment.[50] Applied to the function of our specific example and coming back to the initial oracle in 4.1-3 in general, it thus appears that, like the opening of the previous discourse in Amos 3, it too would have sparked, and in all likelihood was intended to spark, another round in the prophet's debate with his audience.

2. *Amos 4.4-5*

a. *Exegetical Observations and Structure*
Without any transition or introduction, Amos then goes on to invite the people to come to Bethel and Gilgal. Both—the former being Israel's national sanctuary or the king's sanctuary, as the priest Amaziah preferred

---

47. Cf. Wolff, 'Begründungen', pp. 12-13, who notes that 'die Hörer bekommen ihre Schuld an den Kopf geworfen'.

48. Jemielity, *Satire*, p. 89.

49. Weippert, 'Amos', p. 10 n. 20.

50. On caricature, cf. G. von Wilpert, *Sachwörterbuch der Literatur* (Stuttgart: Kröner, 5th edn, 1969), p. 278, who has the following definition: 'Karikatur (ital. *caricare* = überladen, -treiben), Zerrbild, das durch Überbetonung einzelner, dennoch erkennbarer Charakterzüge komisch oder satirisch wirkt, dient durch die einseitige Verzerrung neben dem Spott oft auch der Kritik, mit der Absicht, durch Aufdeckung verurteilenswerter Schwächen und Mißstände auf politischem, sozialem oder sittlichem Gebiet zu deren Abstellung anzuregen.'

The quote is from K. Seybold, 'Die Verwendung der Bildmotive in der Prophetie Zefanjas', in Weippert, Seybold and Weippert, *Beiträge zur prophetischen Bildsprache*, pp. 30-54 (32-34).

to call it (Amos 7.13)—were important cult centres.[51] Imitating a 'priestly
invitation to worship',[52] Amos sarcastically calls the Israelites not to come
to these places and worship, but to come and sin.[53] Thus, whereas the
purpose of such a pilgrimage should have been, and in the eyes of the
prophet's audience would have been, thanksgiving and the fulfilment of
vows, Amos equates the Israelites' cultic performances with the war
crimes condemned in Amos 1–2, both of which are described as פֶּשַׁע.

The sinfulness of the worship is underlined by the ironic command to
multiply their sins (הַרְבּוּ לִפְשֹׁעַ)[54] as well as by the use of another heptad,
in this instance consisting of seven imperatives,[55] which, again ironically,
calls on the people to outperform the law's cultic requirements. Mocking
their attitude, especially their reliance on outward gestures, Amos asks the
Israelites to offer sacrifices every morning instead of once a year and give

---

51. Bethel is mentioned in Amos 3.14; 4.4; 5.5, 6; 7.10, 13 and Gilgal appears in
Amos 4.4; 5.5. On the two places, see also King, *Amos, Hosea, Micah*, pp. 40-41; and
Barstad, *Religious Polemics*, p. 49-54.

52. Cf. J. Begrich, 'Die priesterliche Tora', in P. Volz, F. Stummer and J. Hempel
(eds.), *Werden und Wesen des Alten Testaments. Vorträge gehalten auf der Internationalen Tagung alttestamentlicher Forscher zu Göttingen vom 4.-10. September
1935* (BZAW, 66; Berlin: Alfred Töpelmann, 1936), pp. 63-88 (77); followed by
Pfeifer, *Theologie*, p. 52; Jemielity, *Satire*, pp. 54-55, 91; Wolff, *Joel and Amos*,
p. 218; *idem*, 'Prophet und Institution im Alten Testament', in *idem*, *Studien zur
Prophetie*, pp. 50-64 (59); Rudolph, *Joel, Amos, Obadja, Jona*, p. 175; Mays, *Amos*,
p. 74; Paul, *Amos*, p. 138; Hayes, *Amos*, p. 142; Hubbard, *Joel and Amos*, p. 157;
Soggin, *Prophet Amos*, p. 71; Stuart, *Hosea–Jonah*, p. 337; Weiser, *Buch der zwölf
kleinen Propheten*, p. 151; and Deissler, *Zwölf Propheten*, p. 108. Proper summonses
to worship can be found in Lev. 7.22-25; 19.58; Deut. 14.4-8, 21; Isa. 2.3 and Ps.
122.1.

53. Cf. Alonso Schökel, *Manual of Hebrew Poetics*, p. 160, who lists this passage
as an illustration of sarcasm. Jeremias, *Book of Amos*, p. 68, too, regarding פֶּשַׁע as 'the
harshest word in the Old Testament…for offences against human beings', considers
Amos's use of it in this context 'a bitter sarcasm'. Limburg, *Hosea–Micah*, p. 102, on
the other hand, speaks of 'language unmatched for irony in the Bible'.

54. For the construction, see GK §114n; see also Carroll R., *Contexts*, p. 206; and
Wolff, *Joel and Amos*, p. 218.

55. See Limburg, 'Sevenfold Structures', p. 220; and Paul, *Amos*, p. 140. The fifth
verb, the piel infinitive absolute קַטֵּר, also functions as an imperative; for which cf. GK
§113z, bb; JM §123x; and Freedman, 'Deliberate Deviation', pp. 47-48, who regards it
as a deliberate deviation from an established pattern. Noting that in Exod. 20.8 and
Deut. 5.12 זָכוֹר and שָׁמוֹר replace the fuller זָכוֹר תִּזְכְּרוּ and שָׁמוֹר תִּשְׁמְרוּ, Freedman
concludes that the infinitive absolute in a series of imperatives effectively serves as a
substitute for the normal form of the imperative.

their tithes every three days rather than once in three years.[56] By the same token, he calls on his audience to offer thank offerings along with freewill offerings[57] but what is missing, rather conspicuously, is any mention of sin offerings or indeed anything related to the issues of sin and repentance.[58] What Amos does stress, referring to '*your* offerings', '*your* tithes', and so on, is the people's egotism, which is at the heart of their remarkable display of religious zeal.

Exegetes are divided as to whether Amos denounces the people for burning leavened thank offerings. Yet, since the prophet does not appear to be attacking improper offering practices but the people's reliance on excessive cultic performances, this does not seem likely.[59] What Amos

56. This interpretation, which has also been advocated by Cripps, *Commentary*, p. 170; Paul, *Amos*, p. 140; Soggin, *Prophet Amos*, p. 71; Stuart, *Hosea–Jonah*, p. 338; Niehaus, 'Amos', p. 396; J.A. Motyer, *The Message of Amos* (Leicester: IVP, 1974), p. 95 n. 4; and Smith, *Amos*, p. 143, takes the phrases לבקר and לשלשת ימים to be distributive, meaning 'every morning' and 'every three days' (cf. R.J. Williams, *Hebrew Syntax: An Outline* [Toronto: University of Toronto Press, 2nd edn, 1976], p. 103).

Others, such as Wolff, *Joel and Amos*, p. 219; Rudolph, *Joel, Amos, Obadja, Jona*, p. 176; Hammershaimb, *Book of Amos*, p. 69; and Carroll R., *Contexts*, p. 208, have argued that they refer to the day of arrival at a pilgrimage festival (לבקר) or the festival's third day (לשלשת ימים—cf. Exod. 19.10-16; Hos. 6.1-2, for references to such a pilgrimage festival). If this were correct, Amos would be mocking the people's punctiliousness. However, Cripps, *Commentary*, p. 170; Paul, *Amos*, p. 140; and McKeating, *Books of Amos, Hosea and Micah*, p. 34, have pointed out that the custom of presenting tithes two days after the pilgrim's arrival at the sanctuary is not attested anywhere else.

57. On these offerings, which are two different types of peace offering, see G.J. Wenham, *The Book of Leviticus* (NICOT; Grand Rapids: Eerdmans, 1979), pp. 76-81, 123-25.

58. Cf. Carroll R., *Contexts*, p. 209.

59. Thus also Andersen and Freedman, *Amos*, p. 433 (referring to Lev. 7.11-13); Paul, *Amos*, p. 141; Hammershaimb, *Book of Amos*, p. 70; Hayes, *Amos*, p. 144 (who prefers to understand קטר in a generic sense, 'to offer a sacrifice', in which case there would be no reference to the *burning* of leaven); Rudolph, *Joel, Amos, Obadja, Jona*, p. 176 n. 11; K. Elliger, *Leviticus* (HAT, 1.4; Tübingen: J.C.B. Mohr [Paul Siebeck], 1966), p. 46 n. 16; and Finley, *Joel, Amos, Obadiah*, pp. 207-208, who has argued: 'the prohibition against using leaven in a burnt offering applies to the cereal offering (Lev. 2), not to the peace offering (Lev. 7.11-36). Leavened bread was required as part of a thanksgiving offering, a subdivision of the peace offering (Lev. 7.11-15). Leavened bread thus seems to be a distinguishing feature of this offering. The Mosaic commandment does not mention burning of the leavened bread, but a portion of each

does criticize, however, is the publicizing of freewill offerings, which Hayes regards as invitations to others to join in what he has called a 'gala barbecue'.[60] By repeatedly commanding the people to advertise these offerings (קראו...הׁשמיעו), Amos highlights the Israelites' eagerness for the praise of their compatriots.[61] And, corresponding to the previous references to '*your* sacrifices' and '*your* tithes' in v. 4, Amos's conclusion כי כן אהבתם indicates what is uppermost in his audience's minds, namely to do what pleases *them*.[62] Indeed, this concluding statement is highly ironic, as Mays has pointed out, noting:

> at the conclusion some declaratory formula spoken as the basis for the summons to worship would be expected: 'for I am Yahweh your God' or a reference to Yahweh's will or pleasure in the cult. But instead Israel's own pleasure in the cult is thrust into the place of the divine... The shift is in effect a charge that the sacrificial cult has nothing to do with Yahweh... However pious and proper all their religious acts, the sacrifices and offerings are no submission of life to the Lord, but merely an expression of their own love of religiosity.[63]

The oracle closes with an extended form of the oracle formula (נאם אדני יהוה), thus drawing attention to the source of this devastating criticism of the Israelites' overreaching cultic performances.[64] Its structure can be outlined as follows.

---

segment of the offering goes toward a "contribution to Yahweh." The thank offering may be exceptional, then, in that leavened bread could be part of a burnt offering.' Those who believe that מחמץ does denote an offence include Carroll R., *Contexts*, pp. 208-209 (see p. 209, n. 1); Stuart, *Hosea–Jonah*, p. 338; Niehaus, 'Amos', pp. 396-97; and Motyer, *Message*, p. 95 n. 5, who claims that 'Amos makes his case here by joining together the words "offer (lit. 'burn') that which is leavened", the very thing the law forbade'. According to Keil, *Minor Prophets*, pp. 182-83; and Harper, *Commentary*, pp. 92-93, Amos refers to overzealousness, 'a new custom, just now being developed', but for a critique of this view, see Finley, *Joel, Amos, Obadiah*, p. 208.

    60. Hayes, *Amos*, p. 144.
    61. See Smith, 'Amos, Obadiah', p. 88, who notes that 'together the terms [קראו and הׁשמיעו] suggest a prideful and boastful attitude towards their generous sacrifices and offerings'.
    62. Carroll R., *Contexts*, p. 210, has rightly pointed out that this being the eighth verb after 7 commands, it functions as the climax of yet another 7+1 series (see also Limburg, 'Sevenfold Structures', p. 220).
    63. Mays, *Amos*, pp. 74-76; cf. also H.W. Wolff, 'Hauptprobleme alttestamentlicher Prophetie', in *idem, Gesammelte Studien*, pp. 206-31 (222); and Schmidt, 'Prophetische "Grundgewissheit"', p. 552 n. 27.
    64. Cf. Carroll R., *Contexts*, p. 210; and Dempster, 'Lord', pp. 178-79.

General invitation to come and sin	4 (1)בָּאוּ בֵית־אֵל (2)וּפִשְׁעוּ
	הַגִּלְגָּל (3) הַרְבּוּ לִפְשֹׁעַ
Specific summonses	(4)וְהָבִיאוּ לַבֹּקֶר זִבְחֵיכֶם
to fulfil cultic demands	לִשְׁלֹשֶׁת יָמִים מַעְשְׂרֹתֵיכֶם
	5 (5)וְקַטֵּר מֵחָמֵץ תּוֹדָה
	(6)וְקִרְאוּ נְדָבוֹת
	(7)הַשְׁמִיעוּ
The reason for the people's eagerness	כִּי כֵן אֲהַבְתֶּם בְּנֵי יִשְׂרָאֵל
Concluding oracle formula	נְאֻם אֲדֹנָי יְהוִה

Figure 29. *The Structure of Amos 4.4-5*[65]

b. *Rhetorical Function*

The transition from the initial oracle in 4.1-3 to the present one may seem somewhat abrupt, given the lack of connectives, such as כִּי or לָכֵן, as well as the change of topic. Yet, the combination of social issues (vv. 1-3) with religious or cultic ones (vv. 4-5) is a recurrent feature in the book of Amos, as has been stressed, for instance, by Hubbard speaking of the 'twin themes of oppressive wealth and abuse of worship'.[66] From a rhetorical point of view, it should also be noted that the present arrangement results in an interesting ironic effect, as the people are said to display an impressive religious drive that goes far beyond the requirements of the law while at the same time disobeying the heart of the law by exploiting and abusing the poor.[67]

As far as the passage's rhetorical strategy is concerned, there are some noticeable similarities with Amos 3. Here, as in the previous discourse, an initial announcement of judgment is followed by a section that appears to interrupt the flow of thought. This is true of the series of rhetorical questions in 3.3-8 as well as the imitation of a priestly call to worship in 4.4-5. However, their respective rhetorical function and significance become clearer in the light of the shocking and controversial nature of the introductory announcements of judgment (in 3.1-2, the provocative effect results from Amos's reinterpretation of the exodus tradition whereas in 4.1-3, the insulting epithet פָּרוֹת הַבָּשָׁן will have raised some eyebrows). That is to say, both proclamations of judgment were likely to have raised objections on the part of Amos's audience and the internal textual arrangement of the two discourses in Amos 3–4 suggests that 3.3-8 and

---

65. The numbers indicate the 7 verbs with imperatival force.
66. Hubbard, *Joel and Amos*, p. 154. See especially Amos 2.6-8; 5.21-24.
67. See Niehaus, 'Amos', p. 396.

4.4-5 are to be seen as the prophet's responses to these objections.

Commenting on the transition from Amos 4.1-3 to vv. 4-5, Smith has pointed out that even the lack of a response to the prophet's words of judgment in vv. 1-3 would have been some kind of response. As Smith notes, 'if the response was anything other than a move to repent, Amos would need to persuade his audience that their actions were inadequate'.[68] Yet, the portrayal of Amos imitating and indeed abusing the priestly call to worship can also be taken as the prophet's answer to the Israelites' actual refutation of his words of judgment. Punctilious as they were in their observance of the cultic requirements they believed that they would not have to face Yahweh's punitive intervention. Amos responds to this with heavy irony, inviting the people to come and revel in a 'gala barbecue' consisting of a multitude of offerings and sacrifices, only to condemn their religious zeal, quite brutally, as פשע, as something akin to the horrible war crimes committed by Israel's enemies.

Yet, in addition to the implied reaction of the prophet's audience, there is another connection between vv. 1-3 and vv. 4-5. As Paul has noted, both sections feature the verbal root בוא, which appears in vv. 1, 2 and 4 (where it occurs twice).[69] We have already seen that the use of this verb leads to an interesting irony in vv. 1-3, as the women's demand receives an unexpected response from an unexpected source in that Yahweh threatens to send them days of punishment. The ironic disparity between the people's behaviour and attitude and that of Yahweh continues in the present passage, as Amos invites the Israelites to 'come' (באו) only to sin (פשעו) and 'bring' (הביאו) what pleases them (כי כן אהבתם), even though offerings and sacrifices were meant to be pleasing to Yahweh. The whole sequence thus runs like this:

- The women demand that their husbands *bring* something to drink (הביאה ונשתה).
- What they get, however, is days of judgment *coming* upon them (ימים באים עליכם).
- To *come* (באו) to Bethel and Gilgal is not going to avert the judgment because it is tantamount to sinning (פשעו).
- And to *bring* (הביאו) offerings and sacrifices does not help either, as the people's motivation is entirely selfish (cf. כי כן אהבתם).

Hayes has pointed to yet another connection between the first two sections of Amos 4, noting:

---

68. Smith, *Amos*, p. 133.
69. Paul, *Amos*, p. 138.

the sacrifices implicated in this text [vv. 4-5] are those primarily consumed by the worshippers. The worship was thus treated by the prophet as constituting another example of extravagant self-indulgence. Thus, this pericope is a natural continuation of the material in 3.13–4.3 especially 3.15 and 4.1... The context indicates that the sacrifices were condemned as another example of the self-indulgence of the ruling establishment (see 3.15; 4.1)... The lower classes of Israelite society were probably incapable of such sacrificial extravagance because of the expense involved...[70]

However, while this focus on the misconduct of the upper classes might be the main thrust of the prophet's criticism, Amos's message resists attempts to reduce it to a neat liberation paradigm. As Carroll R. has emphasized, the 'masses of people' are sometimes included in the prophetic critique in that the frequent interweaving of social and cult-related criticism points to a joined participation of the rich and the poor in the nation's guilt.[71] This 'complicity in the nationalistic cult and social sin', according to Carroll R., makes 'simplistic categorizations of the larger populace as simply victims of an unjust system' impossible.[72] He goes on to say:

> irony reigns, as cultic celebrations mask the harsh facts of national failures. This superficial faith in a benevolent deity is not limited to an elite or to the monarchy and its propagandists. The prophetic text portrays this as a generalized belief and an integral part of the complex understanding of social life and of the divine. The world in Amos is fervently and actively religious, yet this Yahwism is a mixture of joyous nationalism and communal self-satisfaction (with perhaps also a hint of underlying or accompanying non-Yahwistic beliefs and practices; 2.8; 4.13; 5.6; 26; 8.14). The rulers and the governed share the Yahwistic faith at different levels and in various ways, as all move about in a world that claims YHWH but does not truly meet him at the sanctuaries.[73]

3. Amos 4.6-11

a. *Exegetical Observations and Structure*
Once again, Amos is portrayed as employing a series of similarly constructed components (vv. 6-11; cf. 1.3–2.16 and 3.3-8), in this instance

70. Hayes, *Amos*, pp. 142, 145.
71. For this interweaving of social and cultic offences cf. 4.1-3 ⇔ vv. 4-5; 5.4-5 ⇔ vv. 6-7 and 5.21-23 ⇔ v. 24.
72. Carroll R., 'Prophetic Text', p. 86. On the significance of Amos's cultic criticism, see also K. Barth, *Die Kirchliche Dogmatik. IV/2. Die Lehre von der Versöhnung* (Zürich: EVZ-Verlag, 1955), pp. 507-508.
73. Carroll R., 'Prophetic Text', p. 92; cf. *idem*, 'War and Utopia', pp. 114-15.

consisting of five strophes. These five parts can be grouped together under three headings with the first four sections representing two pairs.[74] On the other hand, the strophes speak of seven plagues[75]—famine (v. 6), drought (vv. 7-8), blight and locusts (v. 9), pestilence and sword (v. 10) and over-throw (v. 11)—which are presented as divine interventions against Israel.[76] The plagues are furthermore portrayed as a climactic sequence heading towards a final, decisive blow.[77] Taken as a whole, the series speaks of

74. See A. Weiser, 'Zu Amos 4 6-13', *ZAW* 46 (1928), pp. 49-59 (53-57); followed by Jeremias, *Book of Amos*, p. 70.

75. Some have underlined the parallels between Amos 4.6-11 and Lev. 26.14-45; Deut. 28.15-68 and 1 Kgs 8.33-37. See, e.g., Wolff, *Joel and Amos*, p. 213, for a detailed list of similarities and Mays, *Amos*, pp. 79, 80, who has pointed out that the 'cogency of reciting this narrative as a record of Israel's failure to respond to Yahweh presupposes that Amos had a basis for recognizing the blows as the personal overtures of Yahweh, and that the people should have recognized them as such and responded. The context in which these disasters could possess such significance is the covenant tradition... Of course there is no literary dependence of Amos on the later composi-tions preserved in Deut. 28 and Lev. 26... Amos' narrative of disasters is a rather free construction using some traditional curses and depending on the general tradition that Yahweh acts in typical ways to punish those who are disloyal to the covenant. In using the curse tradition to tell a narrative Amos makes a distinctive and new use of the curse materials.'

Hubbard, *Joel and Amos*, p. 161, similarly comments that 'Amos has given the covenant curse a special twist by interpreting it...as a lens through which to look at past judgment...'. However, Vollmer, *Geschichtliche Rückblicke und Motive*, p. 18; and O'Rourke Boyle, 'Covenant Lawsuit', p. 354, have urged more caution in appeal-ing to the analogy provided by the covenant curses. As O'Rourke Boyle notes: 'to concentrate on the similarity of language to the covenant curses is to miss the intention of the author altogether. The emphasis is upon Yahweh's authorship of the events and upon the Israelites' failure to recognize him through them and return repentant.'

76. Amos is, of course, speaking of past events, as Weiser, 'Zu Amos 4 6-13', p. 52, has underlined because 'würde das Stück von zukünftigen Plagen, und mit ihm natürlich auch der Kehrvers von ihrer Erfolglosigkeit reden, so würde damit Jahwe seine eigene Ohnmacht zugeben, und jegliche weitere Gerichtsdrohung zur selben Wirkungslosigkeit verdammt sein'.

77. The passage's climactic arrangement has been noted by Andersen and Freed-man, *Amos*, p. 417; Gese, 'Komposition', pp. 85-86; J.L. Crenshaw, ' "A Liturgy of Wasted Opportunity" (Am. 4.6-12; Isa. 9.7–10.4; 5.25-29)', *Semitics* 1 (1970), pp. 27-37 (31); Jeremias, *Book of Amos*, p. 72; Carroll R., *Contexts*, p. 211; Vollmer, *Geschichtliche Rückblicke und Motive*, p. 17; Hubbard, *Joel and Amos*, p. 158; Stuart, *Hosea–Jonah*, p. 339; and W. Brueggemann, 'Amos iv 4-13 and Israel's Covenant Worship', *VT* 15 (1965), pp. 1-15 (7).

Yahweh's desperate and unsuccessful struggle to induce his people to turn back to him.

Hunger and Thirst (vv. 6-8). The first two strophes have a strikingly similar opening, i.e. וגם אני/אנכי נתתי/מנעתי ל/מכם (vv. 6, 7), which serves to highlight the contrast between the people's inappropriate cultic activities in vv. 4-5 and the divine interventions outlined in vv. 6-11.[78] The people's self-gratifying behaviour (cf. כי כן אהבתם בני ישראל in v. 5) is thus countered by Yahweh's interventional activities (וגם אני נתתי לכם, v. 6). Yet, the two strophes in v. 6 and vv. 7-8 are also linked by the complementary concepts of hunger and thirst. Thus, while the first sarcastically speaks of the people's 'cleanness of teeth', according to Rudolph an 'expression of bitter gallows humour'[79], the second features a vivid portrayal of a God-sent drought, emphasizing the people's desperate struggle to quench their thirst.

Strophe 1: famine (v. 6). Apart from the ironical reference to the people's clean teeth, what is noteworthy is the extent of the plague, as this receives particular emphasis, with Amos stressing that כל-עריכם as well as כל מקומתיכם have been affected by it.

Strophe 2: drought (vv. 7-8). This, the most complex strophe in the entire series,[80] has Amos pointing to a lack of rain at the crucial time

---

For a different view, see W. Rudolph, 'Amos 4,6-13', in H.J. Stoebe, J.J. Stamm and E. Jenni (eds.), *Wort—Gebot—Glaube: Beiträge zur Theologie des Alten Testaments, Walter Eichrodt zum 80. Geburtstag* (ATANT, 59; Zürich: Zwingli, 1970), pp. 27-38 (32); Mays, *Amos*, p. 78; and Reventlow, *Amt*, p. 84, who thinks that 'in dem Abschnitt V. 6-11 herrscht…das vollkommene Gleichmaß, fast die Monotonie'.

78. Cf. Harper, *Commentary*, p. 96; Cripps, *Commentary*, p. 171; Smith, *Amos*, p. 144; Soggin, *Prophet Amos*, p. 74; Jeremias, *Book of Amos*, p. 69; Melugin, 'Formation', p. 380; Carroll R., *Contexts*, p. 210; and Vollmer, *Geschichtliche Rückblicke und Motive*, p. 10, who has, however, suggested deleting the words וגם אנכי in 4.7.

79. Rudolph, 'Amos 4,6-13', p. 32 ('ein Ausdruck bitteren Galgenhumors').

80. Sometimes, this complexity is seen as an indication of a glossator's activity. For instance, Rudolph, 'Amos 4,6-13', p. 29 n. 5, has argued that 'v. 7b ist der Zusatz eines Pedanten, der feststellen wollte, daß sich das Regnen oder Nichtregnen auch auf das umliegende Land auswirkt.' (see also Weiser, 'Zu Amos 4 6-13', pp. 53-54; and Harper, *Commentary*, p. 96). However, Pfeifer, *Theologie*, p. 54 n. 72, has pointed out that 'W. Rudolph, …der V. 7b als pedantische Glosse ausscheiden möchte, übersieht, daß es sich um einen dritten Fall handelt'.

Vollmer, *Geschichtliche Rückblicke und Motive*, p. 10, has come up with an interesting interpretation of v. 8, noting that 'zwei, drei Städte wankten nicht deswegen

during the last three months before the harvest, which has had catastrophic consequences for the people. Rudolph describes its rhetorical impact well, noting that 'the prophet again vividly confronts his hearers with those dreary images of the ones who had got less than their fair share setting out, with the unsteady gait of the exhausted, to visit their luckier neighbours'.[81] In similar vein, Paul has pointed out that while 'the correct nuance of the verb [נוע] is 'to reel, to stagger,' describing the tipsy tottering of a drunkard', here the people 'are portrayed as taking a zigzag course not because of drunkenness but due to dehydration'.[82]

The detailed portrayal of the calamity and its consequences serves to underline the graveness of the experience.[83] However, attention should also be drawn to the strophe's alternation between field and city, which has been noted by Carroll R., stressing that it communicates the extent of the disaster, which impacts the entire country. Carroll R. has outlined the progression of thought in vv. 7-8 as follows:

4.7a	field:	rain withheld before the harvest (disaster)
b	city:	uneven rainfall among the cities (disaster)
a'	field:	uneven rainfall, crops withered (disaster + result)
4.8b'	city:	people wandered, were not satisfied (result)[84]

Finally, commenting on Amos's claim that time and again some parts of the country lacked rain while others were rained upon,[85] Hayes has argued that this accurately reflects the climactic conditions of the region, which 'has an enormous diversity in climate'.[86]

---

zu einer Stadt, weil über der einen Stadt Regen fiel, über der anderen nicht…, sondern weil die eine Stadt über bessere Zisternen und damit einen größeren Wasservorrat verfügte als die anderen'. Interesting though this is, Vollmer fails to provide any supporting evidence for his claim.

81. Rudolph, 'Amos 4,6-13', p. 32.

82. Paul, *Amos*, p. 145.

83. See Feinberg, *Minor Prophets*, p. 101; and McComiskey, 'Amos', p. 306. According to Paul, *Amos*, p. 144, the detailed description also serves to stress 'the divine origin of the disaster'.

84. Carroll R., *Contexts*, p. 212.

85. This interpretation regards the imperfect forms as iterative. See Rudolph, 'Amos 4,6-13', p. 32; Paul, *Amos*, p. 144 n. 48; Smith, *Amos*, p. 137; and Jeremias, *Book of Amos*, p. 46 n. 4, who notes that 'the perfect in v. 7aα lists factual circumstances in a summary fashion, while the iteratives in v. 7aβb and 8a provide the more exact details or the results'.

86. Hayes, *Amos*, p. 146.

Destructive Forces (vv. 9-10). The second pair of strophes differs from the first in that each strophe portrays two calamities. Furthermore, whereas the calamities mentioned in vv. 6-8 are caused by Yahweh taking something away from the people (bread[87] and rain), now he is said to have given them something in their place, namely, grain diseases, locusts, pestilence and the sword. As Weiser has noted,[88] there appears to be a climactic movement in these verses, with the insatiable locusts, who devour everything from gardens and vineyards to fig trees and olive trees, being followed by a pestilence after the manner of Egypt, the killing of Israel's choicest young men and the penetrating stench caused by the corpses on the battlefield.

Strophe 3: blight and locusts (v. 9). The phrases שִׁדָּפוֹן and יֵרָקוֹן always occur together, denoting grain diseases such as blight or mildew (Deut. 28.22; 1 Kgs 8.37; 2 Chron. 6.28; Hag. 2.17), which destroy the crops and with them the hope of securing food for the coming year. For the term הַרְבּוֹת, which is often thought to be problematic, a number of emendations have been proposed. The most prominent one, which originates with Wellhausen and has been adopted, for instance, by the NRSV, suggests to read הֶחֱרַבְתִּי instead.[89] The NRSV thus renders v. 9 as:

> I struck you with blight and mildew;
> I laid waste your gardens and your vineyards;
> the locust devoured your fig trees and your olive trees...

However, in order to arrive at Wellhausen's conclusion, several changes to the consonantal text are required.[90] In addition, some commentators have pointed out that the ancient versions clearly support the masoretic text even though they apparently had great difficulties making sense of it.[91]

---

87. Ironically, however, the withholding of bread is referred to as the giving of clean teeth.

88. Weiser, 'Zu Amos 4 6-13', p. 55.

89. See Wellhausen, *Die kleinen Propheten*, p. 80; whose proposal has been accepted, among others, by Maag, *Text*, pp. 21-22; Weiser, 'Zu Amos 4 6-13', p. 55; Pfeifer, *Theologie*, p. 54 n. 73; Vollmer, *Geschichtliche Rückblicke und Motive*, p. 11; Harper, *Commentary*, p. 99; Cripps, *Commentary*, p. 173; Wolff, *Joel and Amos*, p. 210; Mays, *Amos*, p. 76; Hubbard, *Joel and Amos*, p. 159; and Jeremias, *Book of Amos*, p. 66 n. 6.

90. In addition to the changes to the disputed term, *BHS* suggests deleting the waw of ותאניכם.

91. See Paul, *Amos*, p. 147; and Finley, *Joel, Amos, Obadiah*, p. 214. Stuart, *Hosea–Jonah*, p. 336; and Niehaus, 'Amos', p. 401, have also objected to the

And it should also be noted that it is possible to retain הָרְבּוֹת, which can be understood as an adjective referring to a mass of gardens, vineyards, etc.,[92] thus suggesting a translation such as:

> I struck you with blight and mildew;
> your many gardens, vineyards, fig trees and olive trees the locust devoured.

The imperfect יאֹכַל, another iterative, underlines the repeated devastation of the country's agricultural products through locust invasions. The description also emphasizes the completeness of the destruction. As their entire agriculture was affected, the people's food supply was under serious threat. Again, there appears to be a climactic movement in this strophe, as has been pointed out by Jeremias, noting that it 'moves from more frequently experienced harvest damage...to the dreaded plague of locusts (cf. esp. Joel 1.4), and from grain as daily food, to vegetables and fruits from the gardens, to the luxury of figs, oil and wine'.[93]

Strophe 4: pestilence and sword (v. 10). In strophe four, two paratactic clauses (שׁלּחתי...הרגתי...) are followed by a waw-consecutive (וָאַעֲלֶה). The construction serves to paint a realistic picture of a defeated army in its camp, where men have been killed by the sword and a pestilence has arisen,[94] which has resulted in a terrible stench wafting through the camp.[95]

---

suggested emendation of הָרְבּוֹת.

92. See Paul, *Amos*, p. 147; and Finley, *Joel, Amos, Obadiah*, pp. 210, 214. הָרְבּוֹת is also used as an adjective in Prov. 25.27 (see O. Plöger, *Sprüche Salomos [Proverbia]* [BKAT, 17; Neukirchen–Vluyn: Neukirchener Verlag, 1984], p. 295). It can also be employed in a finite sense, as in Deut. 17.16; 28.63; Prov. 22.16 and 1 Chron. 27.23, but for this it needs to be preceded by a finite verb followed by either לְ or לְמַעַן. Other options include regarding it as an equivalent to the infinitive absolute, in which case it should be translated adverbially (i.e. 'repeatedly'; cf. Paul, *Amos*, p. 137), or as a substantive referring to 'the multitude of your gardens etc.' (Niehaus, 'Amos', p. 401). According to Carroll R., *Contexts*, p. 213, the use of הָרְבּוֹת leads to an irony in that the people are said to 'multiply sin (*hrbw*, 4.4a), even as their multiple gardens were devoured'.

93. Jeremias, *Book of Amos*, p. 73.

94. Plague and sword often go together (cf. Exod. 5.3; Lev. 26.25 and Deut. 28.49-59).

95. Cf. Andersen and Freedman, *Amos*, p. 437. Weiser, 'Zu Amos 4 6-13', p. 55, prefers to eliminate the notion of the stench because 'lange bei einem Bild zu verweilen, ist nicht die stilistische Eigenart dieses Stückes'. Yet, this overlooks that one of the characteristics of these strophes is precisely that they are not build according to a firm pattern. And as Kraft, 'Further Observations', p. 73, has pointed out, 'variety in strophic organization normally indicates, not chaos, but artistic design'.

The description of the stench rising into the Israelites' nostrils[96] adds rhetorical flourish and illustrates once again Amos's fondness for vivid language.

Yet, this is not the only rhetorical feature that deserves attention. Amos also stresses the gravity of the pestilence by characterizing it as a pestilence בְּדֶרֶךְ מִצְרַיִם, 'after the manner of Egypt' (cf. Exod. 15.26; Deut. 7.15; 28.60; Isa. 10.24-26; Ezek. 20.30).[97] And he emphasizes the tragic outcome of the enemy attack, which is said to lead to the בַּחוּרִים ('young men' or 'elite troops') being killed and the battle-horses being carried away, thus resulting in the loss of the best of their warriors as well as their all-important cavalry.[98] Finally, by making Yahweh the subject of all the

Commenting on בָּאֵשׁ, Rudolph, *Joel, Amos, Obadja, Jona*, p. 171, has argued that 'das seltene Wort von M hat vor dem geläufigen בְּאֵשׁ von G ("ich ließ in Feuer aufgehen") weitaus den Vorzug...' (see also Soggin, *Prophet Amos*, p. 75).

96. Some exegetes, following the LXX, prefer to delete the waw in וּבָאפְּכֶם (cf., e.g., Vollmer, *Geschichtliche Rückblicke und Motive*, p. 12; and Soggin, *Prophet Amos*, p. 75). Others, on the other hand, have argued that the deletion is unnecessary and that the waw should be understood as an emphatic or explanatory waw (cf. GK §154a n. 1b; Mays, *Amos*, p. 76; Wolff, *Joel and Amos*, p. 210; Finley, *Joel, Amos, Obadiah*, p. 213; Stuart, *Hosea–Jonah*, p. 336; and Carroll R., *Contexts*, p. 214). Rudolph, *Joel, Amos, Obadja, Jona*, p. 171, has rejected this interpretation, claiming, 'daß ו hier das hervorhebende oder erläuternde ו sein soll ("und zwar in eure Nase"), wirkt lächerlich, da das Riechen mit der Nase keiner Erläuterung bedarf'. Rudolph is, of course, correct to point out that there is no need to explain that it is the nose into which the stench rises. He overlooks, however, that the stress may be not on the noun but on the suffix, i.e., on the fact that the stench rises into *your* noses, in which case the waw would be entirely appropriate.

97. Rudolph, 'Amos 4,6-13', p. 33, notes that 'bei dem Hinweis auf Ägypten ist nicht an die fünfte Plage von Ex 9,3-7 gedacht, die nur das Vieh betraf, sondern an die Tötung der Erstgeburt...so daß man fragen kann, ob Amos nicht ein Wortspiel zwischen בחור und בְּכוֹר beabsichtigt hat' (see also Carroll R., *Contexts*, p. 213; and Smith, *Amos*, p. 145). Andersen and Freedman, *Amos*, pp. 442-43, note that there might be an allusion to Deut. 28.60, where covenant rebels are threatened with the diseases of Egypt. According to Hayes, *Amos*, p. 147, however, the reference 'is simply a general statement about a plague like those for which Egypt was famous' (thus also Cripps, *Commentary*, p. 174).

98. The reference to the carrying away of the people's horses is sometimes regarded as an anti-climactic gloss following, as it does, the killing of the elite troops (for this view, see Harper, *Commentary*, p. 100; Cripps, *Commentary*, p. 174 [n. 2]; Rudolph, *Joel, Amos, Obadja, Jona*, p. 171; and Vollmer, *Geschichtliche Rückblicke und Motive*, p. 11). However, already Wellhausen, *Die kleinen Propheten*, p. 80, has pointed out that in

actions (see שׁלחתי...הרגתי...ואעלה), the prophet accentuates the divine origin of the calamities.

Climactic Overthrow (v. 11). The final strophe is clearly the climax of the whole piece in that the destruction of Sodom and Gomorrah is the example par excellence of God's wrath, 'the archetype of total calamity'.[99] As Jemielity notes, commenting on vv. 10-11:

> drawing on the hated role of Egypt and the despised place of Sodom and Gomorrah in their history, Amos, ironically, has Israel play the role of these three despised nations in experiencing like them the ineffectual chastisement of the LORD and soon to experience like them the doom of the LORD... *Israel is the new Egypt, the new Sodom and Gomorrah.*[100]

Strophe 5: overthrow (v. 11). Finally, Amos reminds his audience that Yahweh had even overthrown[101] some of them[102] as he had once over-

those days horses were rare and highly prized. According to S. Dalley, 'Foreign Chariotry and Cavalry in the Armies of Tiglat-Pileser III and Sargon II', *Iran* 47 (1985), pp. 31-48, Israel was famous for its chariots. And P.C. Craigie, *Psalms 1–50* (WBC, 19; Waco, TX: Word Books, 1983), p. 187, has stressed that chariots and horses 'represented the most powerful military resources available in the ancient Near Eastern practice of warfare'. See also D.R. Ap-Thomas, 'All the King's Horses?', in J.I. Durham and J.R. Porter (eds.), *Proclamation and Presence: Old Testament Essays in Honour of Gwynne Henton Davies* (Macon, GA: Mercer University Press, new corr. edn, 1983), pp. 135-51; and Feinberg, *Minor Prophets*, p. 101, who speaks of 'their boasted cavalry'.

Sometimes, שׁבי is emended to צבי ('beauty, pomp') because the root שׁבה usually refers to human beings (see, e.g., Maag, *Text*, pp. 21-22). However, Paul, *Amos*, p. 148, has rejected this, noting that the root is also used with reference to animals in Exod. 22.9.

99. Thus Hayes, *Amos*, p. 147.

100. Jemielity, *Satire*, p. 91 (my italics).

101. The objects of such an overthrow are often cities or nations, such as Jerusalem in 2 Kgs 21.13, Nineveh in Jon. 3.4, Babylon in Isa. 13.19; Jer. 50.40, Edom in Jer. 49.18 and Israel in Deut. 29.22. Rudolph, 'Amos 4,6-13', p. 34, notes: 'die Folge der מהפכה ist, daß an der betroffenen Stätte niemand mehr siedeln kann (Jes 13,19; Jer 49,18; 50,40), weil nichts mehr wächst (Dt 29,22) und so eine Wüstenei entsteht (Jes 1,7)'. In Amos, the root הפך also appears in 5.7, 8; 6.12 and 8.10.

102. The beth of בכם is used in a partitive sense indicating that, as with the second plague, the disaster was partial (see Harper, *Commentary*, p. 102; Cripps, *Commentary*, p. 175; Andersen and Freedman, *Amos*, p. 444; and Finley, *Joel, Amos, Obadiah*, p. 213). There is no need to change בכם to בתכם ('your houses'), as suggested by Elliger in *BHS*.

thrown Sodom and Gomorrah. According to Paul, the 'point of comparison between the tale in Genesis and the verse in Amos is the suddenness and thoroughness of the destruction'.[103] And once again, speaking of a מהפכת אלהים, Amos highlights Yahweh's initiative in the punishment.[104] However, the words ותהיו כאוד מצל משׂרפה, a proverbial expression signifying a narrow escape (Zech. 3.2; Isa. 7.4), also make it clear that Yahweh did not desire to annihilate his people. Rather, the point of this and all previous judgments was meant to be for Israel to learn their lesson and return to their God. In fact, Yahweh's desire to uphold his people would be even clearer, if Andersen and Freedman are correct in maintaining that מצל speaks of a rescue, not just a survival.[105] Yet, as the refrain ולא־שׁבתם עדי נאם־יהוה emphasizes time and again, the divine interventions had all been in vain, as the people would not be induced to return to their God.

A comparison of Amos 4.6-11 with the oracles in Amos 1–2 indicates that the five strophes dealing with Yahweh's punitive interventions against Israel exhibit much less uniformity than the OAN. There are, however, two recurring features in 4.6-11, which lend unity to the whole series. Thus, all strophes open with a first person masculine singular perfect verb (i.e., נתתי in v. 6, מנעתי in v. 7, הכיתי in v. 9, שׁלחתי in v. 10 and הפכתי in v. 11) stressing the divine initiative in punishing Israel, and they all close with the refrain ולא־שׁבתם עדי followed by the oracle formula נאם־יהוה.

The refrain receives particular emphasis, as its verbatim repetition alerts readers to the people's unwillingness to return to their God. As Mays has so perceptively put it, 'the refrain interprets the disasters as Yahweh's quest for Israel's return to him and rings like a lament in its reiteration of the failure of the quest'.[106] Employing עדי rather than אלי, the prophet stresses that what was desired was not only a change of direction, a turning *towards* Yahweh, but a full return *to* their God.[107] And drawing

103. Paul, *Amos*, p. 149; according to Niehaus, 'Amos', p. 403, it is the result of the judgment.

104. However, Paul, *Amos*, p. 149, is right to stress that the term 'expresses not only the source of the catastrophe but also its incomparable enormity and immensity'.

105. Andersen and Freedman, *Amos*, p. 444.

106. Mays, *Amos*, p. 78; see also Smith, *Amos*, p. 135. A.S. Kapelrud, 'God as Destroyer in the Preaching of Amos and in the Ancient Near East', *JBL* 71 (1952), pp. 33-38 (36), stresses Yahweh's willingness to show mercy, noting that 'he had given them warning several times, through different means, in order to make them stop and think, but in vain'.

107. See Crenshaw, 'Liturgy', p. 33; Vollmer, *Geschichtliche Rückblicke und*

attention to the connection of vv. 6-11 with the subsequent warning in vv.
12-13, Crenshaw has underlined that the refrain 'points forward to the
final judgment, the real focus of the passage'.[108] Finally, the repetition of
the oracle formula נאם־יהוה at the end of each strophe indicates that this
assessment of Israel's history is not the prophet's but that of Yahweh
himself.

Hunger and Thirst (vv. 6-8)

Calamity 1	וגם־אני נתתי לכם נקיון שנים בכל־עריכם	6
	וחסר לחם בכל מקומתיכם	
Refrain	ולא־שבתם עדי	
Concluding oracle formula	נאם־יהוה	

Calamity 2	וגם אנכי מנעתי מכם את־הגשם בעוד שלשה חדשים לקציר	7
(detailed description)	והמטרתי על־עיר אחת ועל־עיר אחת לא אמטיר	
	חלקה אחת תמטר וחלקה אשר־לא־תמטיר עליה תיבש	
Consequence	ונעו שתים שלש ערים אל־עיר אחת לשתות מים ולא ישבעו	8
Refrain	ולא־שבתם עדי	
Concluding oracle formula	נאם־יהוה	

Destructive Forces (vv. 9-10)

Calamity 3	הכיתי אתכם בשדפון ובירקון	9

Calamity 4	הרבות גנותיכם וכרמיכם ותאניכם וזיתיכם יאכל הגזם	
Refrain	ולא־שבתם עדי	
Concluding oracle formula	נאם־יהוה	

Calamity 5	שלחתי בכם דבר בדרך מצרים	10

Calamity 6	הרגתי בחרב בחוריכם עם שבי סוסיכם	
Consequence	ואעלה באש מחניכם ובאפכם	
Refrain	ולא־שבתם עדי	
Concluding oracle formula	נאם־יהוה	

Climactic Overthrow (v. 11)

Calamity 7	הפכתי בכם כמהפכת אלהים את־סדם ואת־עמרה	11

Motive, p. 14; H.W. Wolff, 'Das Thema "Umkehr" in der alttestamentlichen Prophetie', in Wolff, *Gesammelte Studien*, pp. 130-50 (145); *idem*, *Stunde des Amos*,
p. 138; Weiser, 'Zu Amos 4 6-13', p. 59 n. 1; Harper, *Commentary*, p. 98; Budde, 'Text
und Auslegung', p. 97; Hammershaimb, *Book of Amos*, p. 71; and Paul, *Amos*, p. 144,
who notes that the use of עד with שוב is limited to references to a return to God (see
Deut. 4.30; 30.2; Isa. 9.12; 19.22; Hos. 14.2; Joel 2.12; Job 22.23 and Lam. 3.40).

108. Crenshaw, 'Liturgy', p. 35.

Consequence	ותהיו כאוד מצל משׂרפה
Refrain	ולא־שׁבתם עדי
Concluding oracle formula	נאם־יהוה

Figure 30. *The Strophic Arrangement and the Structure of Amos 4.6-11*

b. *Rhetorical Function*

As already indicated above, vv. 6-11 are connected to the preceding sar-castic imitation of a priest's call to worship by means of the introductory words וגם־אני.[109] This juxtaposition of Amos's criticism of the people's cultic activities and Yahweh's complaint that they never actually sought him emphasizes that religiosity is not the same as repentance and that the bringing of many sacrifices and an abundance of tithes does not constitute a return to Yahweh. Or, looking at it from a slightly different angle, Vollmer has noted:

> Israel's ill-judged behaviour towards Yahweh in the cult (vv. 4-5) is contrasted in vv. 6-11 with Yahweh's behaviour towards Israel in the past. Whereas vv. 4-5 are entirely dominated by the 'you' of Israel, vv. 6-11 by contrast speak of the 'I' of Yahweh.[110]

Indeed, highlighting the passage's dialogical character, Vollmer adds that 'it is questionable whether vv. 4-5...are likely to be an independent unit... The Yahwistic cult was considered holy by the Israelites. When Amos calls it a sin, he needs to substantiate this claim. This substantiation is found in 4.6-11.'[111] Rudolph has similarly concluded that 'the section [i.e. vv. 6-13] has grown out of a discussion',[112] noting that its

109. This has been noted, for instance, by Andersen and Freedman, *Amos*, p. 445; and Crenshaw, 'Liturgy', p. 31. Some have stressed the secondary nature of this con-nection (thus Weiser, 'Zu Amos 4 6-13', p. 50; and Jeremias, 'Amos 3–6: Beobach-tungen', p. 129), which only confirms the point made in Chapter 2 (section 1.a) that the book of Amos is best understood as an edited collection of prophetic speeches, oracles and visions.

110. Vollmer, *Geschichtliche Rückblicke und Motive*, pp. 13-14.

111. Vollmer, *Geschichtliche Rückblicke und Motive*, pp. 14-15. For a different view, cf. Jeremias, *Book of Amos*, p. 67, who claims that 'Amos 4.4f. was conceivably and probably an originally independent rhetorical unit, while 4.6ff. was not'. Soggin, *Prophet Amos*, p. 76, on the other hand, ventures that vv. 6-11 are 'substantially a self-contained unity'. What these conflicting opinions indicate is just how difficult it is to come to any well-founded conclusions about the oracles' original forms and settings.

112. Rudolph, 'Amos 4,6-13', p. 28.

background is the objection by the prophet's hearers that his harsh warnings and threats were out of place because the period of bloom, in which one lived, proved that Yahweh was satisfied with his people. Amos retorts that only someone who knowingly shuts the eyes to reality could talk like that. In five strophes (vv. 6-11), he lists the troubles and plagues from the last decades, which should have been a reminder for them to examine their optimistic delusion and ask themselves whether they truly did not have any reason to give up their overbearing self-complacency.[113]

Thus, the debate between the prophet and his audience continues in vv. 6-11, as Amos makes another attempt to make the people understand that their behaviour is unacceptable to Yahweh, something they should have realized long ago, given the deity's frequent punitive interventions in the past. Ironically, as Carroll R. has pointed out, the sacrifices mentioned in 4.4-5 are those that 'express gratitude for divine blessing and protection, yet 4.6-11 put the lie to that misconception of Yahweh's involvement in the national history',[114] as Amos presents what amounts to 'a parody of the saving history', to put it in von Rad's words.[115]

The elaborate list of God-sent calamities in vv. 6-11 gives the impression that there were plenty of them, which again connects well to the previous section, where the Israelites are said to have inundated Yahweh with plenty of offerings, sacrifices and tithes. Again ironically, neither barrage achieved the desired outcome. While all the people's gifts could not establish a real relationship with their God, the divine interventions did not result in the restoration of this relationship either. Finally, it should also be noted that Melugin has pointed to a verbal link between vv. 6-11 and the initial oracle in vv. 1-3, arguing:

> the most striking similarity in language is the parallel between 'bring that we may drink' (v 1) and 'two or three cities wandered to one city to drink water and were not satisfied' (v 8). [...] the redactor who joined vv 1-3 with vv 4-5 and vv 6-12 seems to have intended a contrast between the wealthy women who, before the destruction announced in vv 2-3, were able to say,

113. Rudolph, 'Amos 4,6-13', p. 31; see also Weiser, *Buch der zwölf kleinen Propheten*, p. 155; and Deissler, *Zwölf Propheten*, p. 109, who similary comments: 'wenn der Text auf Amos zurückgeht, ist als Anlaß für diesen geschichtstheologischen Rückblick eine Einrede der Zuhörer anzunehmen, in der sie auf die "Segenszeit" (unter Jerobeam II.) als Kontrast zu Amos' pessimistischen Schelt- und Drohreden hinweisen'.

114. Carroll R., *Contexts*, p. 218.

115. Von Rad, *Old Testament Theology*, II, p. 181.

'Bring that we may drink!' and the situation in which cities could not find water to drink.[116]

4. *Amos 4.12-13*

a. *Exegetical Observations and Structure*

The conclusion to the prophetic discourse in Amos 4 opens with the words לכן כה, which link it to the preceding recital of Yahweh's punitive interventions in vv. 6-11.[117] The one speaking is still the deity but the imperfect אעשה indicates that the focus has now shifted from the recounting of past events (vv. 6-11) to what is going to happen in the future. Yet, while it is clear that some kind of judgment must be in view, the phrases כה אעשה־לך and זאת אעשה־לך have given rise to a variety of interpretations. The main question concerns the referent of the particles כה and זאת, which some have taken to be a judgment announced earlier in the book.[118] According to others, the particles refer to the calamities mentioned in vv. 6-11[119] or, more narrowly, to the final one in v. 11.[120] Yet others believe that they point forward to the ominous meeting with Israel's God in 4.12bβ,[121] that they were accompanied by a pointing or threatening gesture,[122] that the prophetic threat was deliberately vague or that some part of it has been lost.[123]

116. Melugin, 'Formation', p. 383.

117. Cf. Rudolph, *Joel, Amos, Obadja, Jona*, p. 180; Mays, *Amos*, p. 81; Andersen and Freedman, *Amos*, p. 413; Deissler, *Zwölf Propheten*, p. 110; and Vollmer, *Geschichtliche Rückblicke und Motive*, p. 16. In the book of Amos, לכן always introduces a threat of punishment (cf. 3.11; 5.16; 7.17 [לכן כה־אמר יהוה] as well as 4.12; 5.11, 13; 6.7 [לכן]).

118. Thus Smith, *Amos*, p. 147, who finds this previous announcement in Amos 3.2 and O'Rourke Boyle, 'Covenant Lawsuit', pp. 349, 358, who refers to 3.11-12, 12bc-14.

119. Andersen and Freedman, *Amos*, pp. 450-52.

120. Jeremias, *Book of Amos*, p. 74.

121. Rudolph, *Joel, Amos, Obadja, Jona*, p. 181.

122. Wolff, *Joel and Amos*, pp. 217-18; *idem*, 'Das Ende des Heiligtums in Bethel', in *idem*, *Gesammelte Studien*, pp. 442-53 (esp. 450-53); Hammershaimb, *Book of Amos*, p. 74; Hubbard, *Joel and Amos*, pp. 161-62; and Paul, *Amos*, p. 150, who rejects Wolff's claim that the prophet was referring to the ruined temple at Bethel, which had been destroyed during the Josianic reform.

123. Thus Harper, *Commentary*, p. 103; Cripps, *Commentary*, p. 175; Weiser, *Buch der zwölf kleinen Propheten*, p. 156; *idem*, 'Zu Amos 4 6-13', p. 57; J.L. Crenshaw, '*YHWH Ṣeba'ôt šemô*: A Form-Critical Analysis', *ZAW* 81 (1969), pp. 156-75 (161);

Some exegetes have been troubled by the repetitiveness of the two phrases but I concur with Carroll R. that a stylistic or rhetorical explanation is preferable to the assumption of a textual conflation.[124] In fact, Carroll R. has also offered a suggestive explanation for the use of כה and זאת by noting that 'the colon develops suspense by postponing definition. What is "this"? Will there be more of the same suffered in 4.6-11? The reader must push on.'[125] Thus, employing a rhetorical perspective that pays attention to the text's effect on its hearers or readers, Carroll R.'s solution combines two of the interpretations listed above, i.e. the ones that regard the phrases as deliberately vague or as pointing forward. And it is precisely these two factors, the vagueness and the prolepsis, that serve to create the desired suspense.

Following the ominous notion that Yahweh is going to do something to the people, they are instructed to prepare themselves for a meeting with their God. Given the Israelites' previous refusal to turn to Yahweh (vv. 6-11), this instruction does not lack in irony.[126] However, apart from this ironic twist, the final line of v. 12, and in particular the phrase הכון לקראת, also adds to the overall sense of uncertainty. What is this meeting with God going to be like? Brueggemann has pointed to the terms' military connotations as well as to their connection with the holy war tradition,[127] noting that כון can describe the preparations for war while לקראת 'refers to going out into "the field" to engage the enemy'.[128] However, stressing that the phrases also occur in what he calls 'positive' contexts—הכון appears in

Feinberg, *Minor Prophets*, p. 102; Holland, *Joel, Amos und Obadja*, p. 142; Vollmer, *Geschichtliche Rückblicke und Motive*, p. 12; and Mays, *Amos*, p. 81.

124. McComiskey, 'Hymnic Elements', p. 142, also discusses these two options, noting that 'either this statement is a literary device calculated by the author to create an aura of uncertainty by purposefully omitting a reference to the judgment, or it is textually corrupt'. However, pointing to similar examples of Amos creating a deliberate uncertainty, McComiskey thinks that there are strong reasons for assuming the phrases in Amos 4.12 to have been meant to be vague ('Hymnic Elements', pp. 142-43).

125. Carroll R., *Contexts*, p. 215 (n. 2).

126. Cf. Weiser, 'Zu Amos 4 6-13', p. 57. According to H.W. Wolff, 'Zur Gotteserfahrung der Propheten', in *idem, Studien zur Prophetie*, pp. 25-38 (36), 'die Zukunft… wird unentrinnbar die Begegnung mit Jahwe bringen. Das Ende bringt seine unerwünschte, seine unerwartete, aber unausweichliche Ankunft' (see also Wolff, 'Endzeitvorstellungen', p. 68).

127. Brueggemann, 'Amos iv 4-13', pp. 1-15.

128. Brueggemann, 'Amos iv 4-13', p. 4.

covenant texts (e.g. Exod. 19.11, 15; 34.2) while לקראת features in an encounter between a suzerain and his vassal aimed at renewing the covenant[129]—Brueggemann actually favours a 'positive' reading for Amos 4.12, interpreting the prophet's command as an appeal to renew the covenant.[130]

However, Carny has rightly criticized Brueggemann for favouring 'the meaning of הכון and לקראת which is conveyed by a minority of instances, neglecting as "secondary" the meaning in which these words occur most often in the Bible'.[131] This observation, together with the thrust of the argument in Amos 4, and indeed the whole book up to this point, seems to suggest that הכון לקראת in 4.12 hints at a punishment that is going to eclipse the calamities described in vv. 6-11.[132] Yet, it must be stressed that a certain (perhaps intentional) ambiguity remains.[133] Other noteworthy

129. Brueggemann, 'Amos iv 4-13', p. 5.

130. Brueggemann, 'Amos iv 4-13', pp. 5-6.

131. P. Carny, 'Doxologies—A Scientific Myth', *Hebrew Studies* 18 (1977), pp. 149-59 (153). See Josh. 8.4; Isa. 14.21; Jer. 51.12; Ezek. 7.14; 38.7; Ps. 7.13 and Prov. 21.31 for הכון; as well as Num. 21.23; Josh. 8.14; 11.20; Judg. 7.24; 20.31; 1 Sam. 4.1-2; 17.21, 48, 55; 23.28; 2 Sam. 10.9-10; 18.6; Ps. 35.3 and Job 39.21 for לקראת.

132. Thus also Rudolph, 'Amos 4,6-13', p. 35, who stresses that 'während in der Sinai-Situation trotz der die Theophanie begleitenden tremenda der heilwirkende Gott in Erscheinung tritt, wird hier auf den richtenden und strafenden vorbereitet. Es geht hier also keineswegs um Bundeserneuerung...sondern allein um Strafankündigung' (see also Hunter, *Lord*, p. 121; Mays, *Amos*, p. 82; Hayes, *Amos*, pp. 148-49; and Smith, *Amos*, p. 147, who speaks of a 'theophany of judgment').

G.W. Ramsey, 'Amos 4.12—A New Perspective', *JBL* 89 (1970), pp. 187-91, on the other hand, has argued for Amos 4.12 to be interpreted in the context of a *rîb*, claiming that Israel is tauntingly commanded to 'prepare to call "your" gods, O Israel!' (p. 190). In this reading, לקראת is rendered as 'to call' and אלהיך is understood as a reference to foreign gods. However, R. Youngblood, 'לקראת in Amos 4.12', *JBL* 90 (1971), p. 98, while backing Ramsey's interpretation of the passage, has demonstrated that לקראת, which occurs 121 times in the Old Testament, never means 'to call'. In order nevertheless to arrive at Ramsey's interpretation, Youngblood conjectures that there is a textual corruption, which is due to a haplography, and that the text should read לקרא את. Yet, Soggin, *Prophet Amos*, p. 75, has rightly refuted these claims, stressing that the text makes perfect sense as it stands and that there is nothing in the context to suggest that Amos is rebuking the people for following foreign deities. The exact opposite is the case: the Israelites are criticized for their overenthusiastic yet misguided participation in ritual practices pertaining to the Yahwistic cult (cf. 4.4-5).

133. According to Carny, 'Doxologies', p. 153, the discourse is intended to bring about repentance even though 'it is not in the habit of Amos to conclude his descriptions of destruction with an appeal for repentance. This he leaves for his audience to figure out. It is his personal style to conclude his orations with a description of terrible

features in v. 12 are the shift from the plural (שבתם) to the singular (הכון) as well as the use of the personal pronoun in combination with God, '*your God*' (אלהיך), both of which point to the people's personal accountability to their covenant God.

The final verse, which is one of the book's hymn fragments (the others being 5.8-9 and 9.5-6), is widely considered a doxology in praise of the Creator God.[134] In this view, the previous *catalogus calamitatum*[135] is concluded by v. 12, which contains an unspecified threat of punishment. The hymn fragment in v. 13, by contrast, is seen as not or only loosely

doom, apparently inevitable, and he is never tempted to commit the rhetorically serious mistake of mitigating the strong effect in any way.' For a similar view, see Barstad, *Religious Polemics*, p. 60; Vollmer, *Geschichtliche Rückblicke und Motive*, pp. 16-17; and A.J. Heschel, *The Prophets* (New York: Harper & Row, 1962), p. 12, who claims that 'every prediction of disaster is in itself an exhortation to repentance'. See also the disussion in Chapter 2, section 2.c., as well as Möller, 'Words of (In-)evitable Certitude'; and Polley, *Amos*, ch. 7.

134.   On the hymn fragments, see Horst, 'Doxologien', pp. 45-54; T.H. Gaster, 'An Ancient Hymn in the Prophecies of Amos', *Journal of the Manchester Egyptian and Oriental Society* 19 (1935), pp. 23-26; Watts, 'Old Hymn', pp. 33-39; *idem, Vision and Prophecy*, pp. 9-27; S.B. Frost, 'Asseverations by Thanksgiving', *VT* 8 (1958), pp. 380-90; F. Crüsemann, *Studien zur Formgeschichte von Hymnus und Danklied in Israel* (WMANT, 32; Neukirchen–Vluyn: Neukirchener Verlag, 1969), pp. 97-106; Berg, *Hymnenfragmente*; Koch, 'Rolle', pp. 504-37; Crenshaw, *Hymnic Affirmation*; Bergler, *Die hymnischen Passagen*; C.I.K. Story, 'Amos—Prophet of Praise', *VT* 30 (1980), pp. 67-80; McComiskey, 'Hymnic Elements', pp. 139-57; G. Pfeifer, 'Jahwe als Schöpfer der Welt und Herr ihrer Mächte in der Verkündigung des Propheten Amos', *VT* 41 (1991), pp. 475-81; S.E. Gillingham, ' "Der die Morgenröte zur Finsternis macht": Gott und Schöpfung im Amosbuch', *EvT* 53 (1993), pp. 109-23 (114-16); Mathys, *Dichter und Beter*; as well as the detailed comments in Botterweck, 'Authentizität', pp. 182-86; Hasel, *Understanding*, pp. 83-89; Wolff, *Joel and Amos*, pp. 215-17; Mays, *Amos*, pp. 83-84; Paul, *Amos*, pp. 152-53; Finley, *Joel, Amos, Obadiah*, pp. 329-33; and Jeremias, *Book of Amos*, pp. 76-79.

Frequently, questions of authenticity have been at the top of scholars' agendas, with many an exegete consigning the hymn fragments to an exilic or postexilic date due to their elevated theology and distinctive vocabulary. According to Paul, *Amos*, p. 152, the first to question their authenticity was B. Duhm, *Die Theologie der Propheten als Grundlage für die innere Entwicklungsgeschichte der israelitischen Religion* (Bonn: Marcus, 1875), p. 119 (see also Wellhausen, *Die kleinen Propheten*, p. 80; and Mays, *Amos*, pp. 82-84). Hayes, *Amos*, p. 149, has pointed out that 'practically all interpreters agree that all three hymnic texts have features in common and share some type of relationship', an estimate shared by Hasel, *Understanding*, p. 84.

135.   Thus Rudolph, 'Amos 4,6-13', p. 34.

connected to the preceding material.[136] Adopting Horst's notion of an *exhomologesis*, which is both a confession and a doxology and which has come to be known as 'doxology of judgment',[137] v. 13 is often seen as an editorial addition intended to praise God for the punishment that is threatened in v. 12 and which a subsequent generation of readers had come to regard as just and deserved.[138]

However, this view has not found universal acclaim. For instance, Carny has argued that v. 12, in and by itself, cannot stand as a conclusion to the preceding series of calamities and that the phrase כי הנה in v. 13 indicates the adjunction of an explanation as to why the people have to be prepared for their meeting with God. Rudolph has come to similar conclusions, arguing that the doxology in v. 13, which is connected to the previous verse by means of the substantiating כי, provides an apt and effective closure to vv. 6-12.[139] And Paul has pointed out that 'the present

---

136. Thus, e.g., Horst, 'Doxologien', p. 45; Weiser, *Buch der zwölf kleinen Propheten*, p. 156; Barstad, 'Basankühe', p. 290; and Mathys, *Dichter und Beter*, pp. 106-107. According to Gaster, 'Ancient Hymn', p. 23, all three hymnic pieces 'obtrude upon the contexts in which they are to be found'.

137. Horst, 'Doxologien', pp. 50-54, who has been followed by many. See, e.g., von Rad, 'Gerichtsdoxologie', pp. 28-37; Jeremias, *Book of Amos*, p. 76; Crenshaw, '*Wedōrēk 'al-bāmŏtê 'āreṣ*', p. 44; and *idem, Hymnic Affirmation*, pp. 141-43, who claims that 'the doxologies were added to the prophetic text for use on special days of penitence and confession, and their function was later taken over by cultic prayers instead of prophetic word of judgment plus doxology' (p. 143). For a criticism of this view, see Koch, 'Rolle', p. 506. A similar opinion had already been advanced by C. Steuernagel, *Lehrbuch der Einleitung in das Alte Testament* (Tübingen: J.C.B. Mohr, 1912), p. 616, who regarded the hymn fragment as a 'liturgischer Zusatz, der wohl das Ende eines Leseabschnittes im Synagogengottesdienst markiert' (as quoted in Botterweck, 'Authentizität', p. 182 n. 42).

Recently, Noble, 'Literary Structure', p. 216, has advocated a deletion of v. 13 because it 'would cut across the palistrophic structure' and 'would not be balanced by a corresponding connection'. 'Presumably', Noble concludes, 'it was added by a later redactor…who did not realize that it disrupted the overall pattern.' Without entering into another discussion of palistrophic structures at this point, it seems pertinent to suggest that it might be Noble's structural analysis rather than the text, which requires adjustment.

138. Thus, e.g., Weiser, 'Zu Amos 4 6-13', p. 58; and Vollmer, *Geschichtliche Rückblicke und Motive*, p. 13. See also the discussion in Chapter 2, section 1.b., as well as Möller, 'Hear this Word', pp. 512-15.

139. Rudolph, *Joel, Amos, Obadja, Jona*, p. 181; see also Cramer, *Amos*, p. 90; and Cripps, *Commentary*, p. 176.

doxology, Amos 4.13, styled in participial fashion, follows naturally upon the previous verses by emphasizing the power and might of the omnipotent God of creation whom Israel is about to confront in final judgment'.[140] As such, it gives 'dramatic and climactic force to the [preceding] oracle'.[141]

In exceptional rhetorical style, the reason as to why the people are to prepare themselves for their encounter with the deity is given in the description of Yahweh's awesome power and might. He is the creator of the world, as the two initial participles emphasize.[142] He is the one who formed the mountains (יצר is also used to describe a potter's activity) and created (ברא) the wind (רוח).[143] Rudolph has summarized the implications of this statement well, noting:

> if Yahweh is the creator of the mountains and the wind, then thus are juxtaposed the most solid and the most mobile and also that, which cannot be overlooked, and that, which can never be seen. The conjoining of contrasts always indicates totality...so the first two participial sentences denote Yahweh as the creator of the universe.[144]

140. Paul, *Amos*, p. 153. In the book of Amos, references to God as creator always reinforce threats of divine punishment (cf. 5.8-9 and 9.5-6).

141. Thus J. Muilenburg, 'The Linguistic and Rhetorical Usages of the Particle כי in the Old Testament', *HUCA* 32 (1961), pp. 135-60 (137).

142. Cf. Carny, 'Doxologies', p. 155, who has pointed out that the participles have no active aspect but are adjectives that describe divine attributes. According to Niehaus, 'Amos', p. 407, the present list of participles, which function as divine epithets or titles, resembles ancient Near Eastern divine titularies.

143. There is an obvious link here with Gen. 1–3, where we also find the terms יצר, ברא and רוח. On ברא see J. Bergman *et al.*, 'בָּרָא', in *TDOT*, II, pp. 242-49. As far as the use of רוח is concerned, I believe Paul, *Amos*, p. 154 n. 144, is right to suggest that in the present context, where cosmic activities are in view, the reference is to the creation of the wind rather than to the spirit (cf. also Hammershaimb, *Book of Amos*, pp. 74-75). However, Wolff, *Joel and Amos*, p. 223, does have a point in stressing: 'it is probably advisable to keep in mind the polarity of meaning in the Hebrew word רוח ("wind—spirit"), particularly here at the point of transition between the first and the third participial cola of our hymn. [...] The next statement leads us unequivocally to mankind. God is praised because he establishes contact with humankind in his word.'

See also Carroll R., *Contexts*, p. 217 n. 2; and D. Lys, *'Rûach', le souffle dans l'Ancien Testament: Enquête anthropologique à travers l'histoire théologique d'Israël* (Études d'histoire et de philosophie religieuses, 56; Paris: Presses Universitaires de France, 1962), p. 66, who notes that 'celui qui a formé les montagnes a créé le souffle (= vent); et celui qui a créé le souffle (= respiration) fait connaître à l'homme ses pensées' (as quoted in Berg, *Hymnenfragmente*, p. 274 n. 17).

144. Rudolph, 'Amos 4,6-13', p. 36. On the mountains' impact on the Hebrew

Leaving behind the sphere of creation, the third participle portrays the deity as a God who reveals his plans to humankind, a concept that also underlies the raising up of prophets in Amos 2.11 and is boldly expressed in Amos's claim that Yahweh does nothing without disclosing his intentions to the prophets (cf. 3.7).[145] The pronoun of שֵׂחוֹ most likely refers to God himself, who reveals his own thoughts to humankind.[146] This interpretation is confirmed by the use of the participle מַגִּיד, which suggests a revelation.[147]

Following the syndetical connection of the preceding participles (i.e., יוֹצֵר...וּבֹרֵא...וּמַגִּיד), the break occasioned by the asyndetically conjoined phrase in v. 13 bα (...עֹשֵׂה שַׁחַר עֵיפָה) appears to be significant. Carny has taken it to mark the beginning of a new topic, suggesting that the foregoing phrase וּמַגִּיד לְאָדָם מַה־שֵׂחוֹ

> serves to separate God's manifestation in the past through the act of creation and his control of the universe, which is a positive manifestation, from the acts that he is about to perform: the reversal of the laws of nature ending up in total destruction.[148]

writers see L. Alonso Schökel, *Das Alte Testament als literarisches Kunstwerk* (Cologne: Bachem, 1971), p. 348; and Berg, *Hymnenfragmente*, pp. 272-73.

145. Thus the *hapax legomenon* שֵׂחַ, a derivate from שִׂיחַ (cf. Cripps, *Commentary*, p. 177; Wolff, *Joel and Amos*, p. 211; Rudolph, *Joel, Amos, Obadja, Jona*, p. 171; and Jeremias, *Book of Amos*, p. 66 n. 9), parallels סוֹד in 3.7, which also speaks of Yahweh's plans. On שֵׂחַ, see S. Mowinckel, 'The Verb *śiaḥ* and the Nouns *śiaḥ, śiḥā*', *ST* 15 (1961), pp. 1-10; and H.-P. Müller, 'Die hebräische Wurzel שׂיחַ', *VT* 19 (1969), pp. 361-71.

146. Against Rudolph, *Joel, Amos, Obadja, Jona*, pp. 181-82; Hammershaimb, *Book of Amos*, p. 75; Story, 'Amos', pp. 69 (n. 6), 80; McComiskey, 'Amos', p. 308; and Niehaus, 'Amos', p. 407.

147. Cf. Wolff, *Joel and Amos*, p. 224; Hammershaimb, *Book of Amos*, p. 75; Finley, *Joel, Amos, Obadiah*, pp. 217-18; Jeremias, *Book of Amos*, p. 79; and Pfeifer, 'Jahwe', p. 479. However, Berg, *Hymnenfragmente*, pp. 286-87, arguing that the pronoun refers to human thoughts, has offered the following paraphrase of וּמַגִּיד לְאָדָם מַה־שֵׂחוֹ: 'der dem Menschen kundtut (kundgetan hat), was (= Jahwes Taten in Schöpfung und Geschichte) "Gegenstand" seines (= des Menschen) Sinnens ist.' Yet, this interpretation has been criticized by Mathys, *Dichter und Beter*, p. 111 n. 51; and Pfeifer, *Theologie*, p. 56 n. 79, who has objected: 'das Wort auf den Sinn des Menschen zu beziehen, …ist in diesem Zusammenhang weniger ratsam, da es ja um eine Ankündigung künftigen Handeln Gottes geht'.

148. Carny, 'Doxologies', p. 155-56. However, some have proposed to emend the line in order to relate it too to the realm of nature. See Gaster, 'Ancient Hymn', pp. 24-25; Harper, *Commentary*, p. 104; Müller, 'Die hebräische Wurzel שׂיחַ', p. 369; and

This shift from 'creation-talk' to 'destruction-talk' also coincides with a change in the audience's putative response to Amos's words. While his hearers would have agreed that Yahweh is the former of the mountains, the creator of the wind and the self-revealing deity the prophet makes him out to be, they probably would not have known him as the 'turner of dawn into darkness'. And though they might have thought of their God as the one who treads in triumph on the heights of the earth, they would not have understood this as having negative implications for them.

Thirdly, the asyndetic arrangement highlights a change in perspective, as Yahweh's past acts of creation are eclipsed by something that he is about to do in the near future. This has been pointed out by Koch, noting that the deity's 'striding over the (cultic) heights or his treading on them… indicates…not a single primordial act but either a future action or some frequently repeated proceedings'.[149]

Based on the observations detailed in the above analysis, v. 13 is best translated along the following lines:

> For behold,
>> the former of the mountains
>> and the creator of the wind
>> and the revealer of his thoughts to humankind
>>> is the one, who is going to turn [i.e. the turner of] dawn into darkness
>>> and tread [i.e. the treader] on the heights of the earth
>>>> —Yahweh, the God of hosts, is his name!

Amos thus declares that Israel's God is going to bring about a deadly darkness,[150] which is a recurring threat in his prophecy (e.g. Amos 5.18, 20;

Horst, 'Doxologien', p. 49, who has argued that it speaks about the creation of the vegetation. Emending MT to וַ(מְ)מַגִּד לְאָדָם מַה־חֶשְׁחוֹ, Horst translates it as 'der den Menschen reichlich spendet, was sie begehren bzw. bedürfen'. However, Crenshaw, '*Wedōrēk 'al-bāmŏtê 'āreṣ*', p. 42, has rightly stressed that there is no need for an emendation, noting that the text makes perfect sense as it stands.

149. Koch, 'Rolle', p. 509.

150. עיפה is a *hapax legomenon*, but cf. עיפתה (Job 10.21), מעוף (Isa. 8.22) and תעפה (Job 11.17). Berg, *Hymnenfragmente*, p. 288, comparing עיפה with עיפתה, has suggested that 'dabei mag des [*sic*] Grauenvolle, das in *'êpātāh* enthalten und überhaupt mit der Vorstellung der nächtlichen Dunkelheit ohne irgendein Licht verbunden ist, bei *'êpāh* mitschwingen'. Koch, 'Rolle', p. 513, has similarly characterized עיפה as designating a 'todbringendes Übel'.

Some have asked whether God is portrayed as turning morning into darkness or as making morning out of darkness. For instance, Paul, *Amos*, p. 155, arguing that שחר means 'darkness' while עיפה indicates the 'glimmering dawn', prefers to translate the

8.9). In response to the Israelites' behaviour, the creator of the world will even reverse the laws of nature in order to punish his people. A judgmental reading of v. 13 is also suggested by the phrase וְדֹרֵךְ עַל־בָּמֳתֵי אָרֶץ, which, as Paul has noted, employs the 'imagery of a mighty conqueror'.[151] However, if this is the case, then Hayes is correct to conclude that v. 13 'clearly fits its context and brings the thought of verse 12 to a logical conclusion'.[152] This has also been stressed by McComiskey, who notes:

> the theophanic depiction in the doxology of Amos 4.13…immediately follows the announcement that an encounter between Yahweh and the people is imminent. The theme of the hymn is exactly consonant with the theme of the immediately preceding context and is thus in conceptual agreement with it.[153]

To be sure, the hymn fragments, Amos 4.13 included, do stand out because of their distinctive vocabulary, which is probably due to Amos employing some older poetic material.[154] Yet, McComiskey's reference to the thematic and conceptual similarities between v. 13 and its context aptly points to

phrase as 'he who turns blackness into daybreak'. And according to Rudolph, *Joel, Amos, Obadja, Jona*, p. 182, 'geht es in den beiden letzten Partizipialsätzen um das sich täglich wiederholende Wunder des Sonnenaufgangs'.

However, both the syntax as well as the context of the phrase favour the former view, that the text refers to a divine reversal of light into darkness. Cf. GK §117ii; Koch, 'Rolle', p. 508 n. 16; and Berg, *Hymnenfragmente*, p. 289, who has pointed out that 'bei der Deutung und Übersetzung von W. Rudolph dürfte man, analog zu Am 5,8ba, vor *šḥr* den Dativpartikel "*lᵉ*" erwarten.' On שַׁחַר, see L. Köhler, 'Die Morgenröte im Alten Testament', *ZAW* 44 (1926), pp. 56-59.

151. Paul, *Amos*, p. 156. D.J.A. Clines, *Job 1–20* (WBC, 17; Dallas: Word Books, 1989), p. 231, has noted that 'the same idiom for trampling on the backs of defeated foes occurs in Deut 33.29; Amos 4.13; Mic 1.3'. In Deut. 33.29, the triumphal connotation is most obvious. Job 9.8 portrays God as treading on the back of his archenemy, the sea monster, and Mic. 1.3-4 speaks of God's treading on the high places of the earth causing an earthquake. See also Crenshaw, '*Wedōrēk 'al-bāmŏtê 'āreṣ*', p. 43; Berg, *Hymnenfragmente*, pp. 291-93; Koch, 'Rolle', pp. 509-13; K. Koch *et al.*, 'דֶּרֶךְ, אֹרַח, שְׁבִיל, נְתִיבָה, נְתִיב, מַעְגָּל, הֵלַךְ, הֲלִיכָה, הֲלִיךְ, מְסִלָּה, חוּץ, שׁוּק, דָּרַךְ', in *TDOT*, III, pp. 270-93; as well as K.-D. Schunck, 'בָּמָה', in *TDOT*, II, pp. 139-45. One of the questions concerning the phrase בָּמֳתֵי אָרֶץ is whether it entails a cultic dimension. See in this context בָּמוֹת יִשְׂחָק in Amos 7.9 as well as Pfeifer, 'Jahwe', p. 479.

152. Hayes, *Amos*, p. 150.

153. McComiskey, 'Hymnic Elements', p. 141 (see also p. 154).

154. However, McComiskey, 'Hymnic Elements', p. 154, believes that 'the doxologies are poetic representations of theological truth written by Amos himself to give awesome validation to the content of the oracle that precedes each doxology'.

the prophet's rhetorical skill in using this hymnic material as a climactic reference to the impending divine judgment already hinted at in v. 12.[155] This interpretation receives further confirmation once the book of Amos is read as a literary whole rather than a random collection of oracles. Moving on from 4.13 to the words שמעו את־הדבר הזה אשר אנכי נשא עליכם קינה בית ישראל in 5.1, it appears that the threatened encounter between Yahweh and his people has not only taken place, but has had some grave consequences, which lead Amos to bewail the death of בתולת ישראל.

Finally, coming back again to 4.13, attention should also be drawn to the concluding declaration יהוה אלהי־צבאות שמו. As Brueggemann has noted, 'the use of the name at this climactic point is a reminder of the terror of the God of Sinai who came again and again into the history of Israel'.[156] Or, to put it in Smith's words, the hymn closes 'in almost oath-like fashion...with the certainty that Yahweh's authority and character stand behind it'.[157] This then brings us to the rhetorical structure of Amos 4 as a whole, which can be outlined as follows.

Unspecified reason for exhortation	12 לכן כה אעשה־לך ישראל
	עקב כי־ זאת אעשה־לך
Exhortation	הכון לקראת־אלהיך ישראל
Reason for the exhortation	13 כי הנה
God's (traditional) attributes	יוצר הרים ובראׄ רוח ומגיד לאדם מה־שחו
God's future actions	עשה שחר עיפה ודרך על־במתי ארץ
Climactic conclusion	יהוה אלהי־צבאות שמו

Figure 31. *The Rhetorical Structure of Amos 4.12-13*

b. *Rhetorical Function*

Introduced by the phrase לכן כה, vv. 12-13 provide a climactic closure for the prophetic discourse in Amos 4, or to look at it from another angle, one might say, with Mays, that vv. 6-11 are an indictment, which 'serves as a basis for the announcement of judgment in v. 12'.[158] However, if this is indeed the case, we are presented here with another seven-plus-one

---

155. Thus also Cripps, *Commentary*, pp. 296-97; and Koch, 'Rolle', p. 512, who speaks of a 'Vernichtungstheofanie' (cf. also p. 515).

156. Brueggemann, 'Amos iv 4-13', p. 13.

157. Smith, *Amos*, p. 148; see also Hammershaimb, *Book of Amos*, p. 75; Finley, *Joel, Amos, Obadiah*, p. 216; Carroll R., *Contexts*, p. 217; and Dempster, 'Lord', pp. 179-80.

158. Mays, *Amos*, p. 78; see also Martin-Achard, 'End', p. 36.

series,[159] in this instance consisting of seven bygone disasters followed by a climactic future encounter between Yahweh and his people.

Dempster has pointed to yet another connection between vv. 12-13 and the end of the preceding section (v. 11), stressing that both refer to God as אלהים. Thus, while in the first three quarters of the discourse either יהוה or אדני יהוה are used as divine epithets, in vv. 11-13 the deity is referred to by the generic term אלהים. Dempster notes:

> in the context, the name functions to mark an abrupt transition—the onset of climax. Yahweh (4, 6, 8, 9, 10) is the God (אלהים 11) who destroyed the cities of the plain. This Yahweh (11) is Israel's God (אלהיך 12)! And He is none other than the Lord God of Hosts (יהוה אלהי־צבאות 13).[160]

However, in addition to the connections between vv. 6-11 and the climactic conclusion to this list of calamities in vv. 12-13 attention needs to be drawn also to the ironic contrast between the closing verses and the mock call to worship in vv. 4-5. Whereas Amos's imitation of a priestly invitation to worship stresses the futility of approaching Yahweh with a plethora of sacrifices, offerings and tithes, in vv. 12-13 the prophet indicates that there will nevertheless be a true encounter with the deity. As Stuart notes, 'what the Israelites improperly sought by worshipping at Gilgal and Bethel (v 4) they will genuinely get, although in a way they would never have chosen, when Yahweh reveals himself to them (v 13)'.[161]

5. The Rhetorical Structure and Function of Amos 4

Turning to the rhetorical structure and function of Amos 4 as a whole, it should first be noted that there are some interesting correspondences between the two outer parts of this prophetic discourse. This has been pointed out by Hubbard, who stresses:

> the judgment speech of 4.1-13 begins and ends with descriptive participles. In verse 1 the women are indicted as oppressing, crushing and begging; in verse 13 God is lauded as creating, declaring, making and treading. We cannot be sure that Amos intended such a contrast, but the idea of it is certainly in line with everything he has said about the ultimate and tragic difference between God's ways and those of his people.[162]

159. See Limburg, 'Sevenfold Structures', p. 220; and Paul, *Amos*, p. 151.
160. Dempster, 'Lord', pp. 179-80.
161. Stuart, *Hosea–Jonah*, p. 336.
162. Hubbard, *Joel and Amos*, p. 163.

One might say that the use of descriptive participles in vv. 1 and 13 provides an inclusio for the discourse in Amos 4. Indeed, this judgment
receives further confirmation by the fact that both verses allude to
mountains. Thus, while the accused women of v. 1 are associated with
הר שמרון, Yahweh is introduced in v. 13 as the יוצר הרים.[163] However, in
line with my cautionary comments on the detection of inclusios in Chapter
1,[164] it should be noted that the present inclusio in Amos 4.1, 13 can only
be recognized once the passage's outer boundaries have already been
drawn. As both participles as well as references to mountains (e.g. 3.9;
4.1, 13; 6.1; 9.13) occur frequently throughout the book of Amos, neither
could, by themselves, be taken as reliable structural indicators.

The structural unity of Amos 4 is reinforced by yet another seven-plus-
one series. While vv. 6-13 speak of seven past calamities to be followed
by a climactic meeting with Yahweh, vv. 1-11 feature seven oracle
formulas (נאם יהוה) followed by the phrase יהוה אל הי־צבאות שמו in v.
13.[165] Brueggemann has stressed that this phrase 'serves a function not
unlike *ne'um YHWH* in vv. 6-11',[166] and Muilenburg has emphasized that
the final component of a series often 'breaks the repetitive sequence' and
'gives point and force to the whole series'.[167] The repeated references to
Yahweh's speaking underline that it is the deity himself who condemns
the misdemeanours of Israel's upper-class women, the people's meaning-
less religious frenzy and their refusal to return to him. Indeed, it is because
of these that Israel is now called upon to prepare for what threatens to be a
disastrous encounter with their God. As Hubbard has noted:

> all of the awful terror which God displayed to Israel in covenant grace at
> Sinai will now be unleashed in judgment against him because of the triple
> indictment—the ruthless opulence of Samaria's women (4.1-3), the empty,
> self-centred rituals of Bethel and Gilgal (4.4-5), and the refusal to read the
> invitation to repentance in the messages of judgment (4.6-11).[168]

---

163. See Paul, *Amos*, p. 154 n. 146 and p. 156. Koch, 'Rolle', p. 512-14, has also
drawn attention to the 'Stichwortanschluß' of v. 13 with v. 1 (i.e., הר || הרים). Noting
the additional reference to the במתי ארץ in v. 13 as well as the cultic thrust of vv. 4-5,
Koch has concluded that Amos is threatening the destruction of the cultic heights at
Bethel, Gilgal and Samaria.

164. See section 2.c.

165. See Dorsey, 'Literary Architecture', p. 311; and Wendland, 'Word', p. 13.

166. Brueggemann, 'Amos iv 4-13', p. 13.

167. J. Muilenburg, 'A Study in Hebrew Rhetoric: Repetition and Style', in *Congress
Volume, Copenhagen 1953* (VTSup, 1; Leiden: E.J. Brill, 1953), pp. 97-111 (107).

168. Hubbard, *Joel and Amos*, p. 161; cf. also Dorsey, 'Literary Architecture', p. 312.

The discourse as a whole thus points to the crisis that exists in the relationship between Yahweh and his people. It is, as Carny has argued, 'a unified oration, relating the deeds and attitudes of the people, belonging to the dominant classes, who had failed to interpret correctly God's warnings as manifested in the terrible events of the past'.[169]

With respect to both the rhetorical structure and the rhetorical strategy of Amos 4, attention should be drawn to the similarities between this discourse and the preceding one in Amos 3. Both open with an announcement of judgment, which triggers the ensuing discussion. We have already seen that Amos 3.1-2 functions as a provocative summary reference to the divine punishment but something similar can be said also of 4.1-3. Here, as in 3.1-2, the stress is on the punishment, as its framing by the solemn introduction נשבע אדני יהוה בקדשו כי הנה ימים באים עליכם and the concluding oracle formula נאם־יהוה indicate. And whereas the previous discourse opened with the surprising suggestion that Israel would be punished *because of* their special status as Yahweh's chosen people, here the sarcastic reference to the פרות הבשן as well as the threat of an exceedingly brutal punishment will have given rise to objections on the part of Amos's audience.

In both discourses, Amos then goes on to argue his case, adopting, however, different strategies. Thus, while in 3.3-8 he makes the point that, as Yahweh's prophet, he cannot but proclaim what he had been told, in 4.4-5 Amos justifies his message of punishment by censuring the people's empty, self-serving cultic observances. The following parts in 3.9-11 and 4.6-11 then serve to confirm the need for a divine intervention. In 3.9-11, foreign witnesses are invited to assess the social crimes committed by the Israelites, while in 4.6-11 God's people are themselves challenged to think about their own history. It teaches that Yahweh's numerous punishments have not made any difference, which is why now a decisive encounter with the deity must take place (vv. 12-13).

The dramatic illustration of the extent of the divine punishment in 3.12 has no parallel in Amos 4, yet that does not take anything away from the fact that the two discourses share many structural and rhetorical similarities. Indeed, this is confirmed by the endings in 3.13-15 and 4.12-13, which, while different in terms of their surface structure, function in similar ways in providing a concluding threat of judgment. On the basis of

---

169. Carny, 'Doxologies', p. 157. Barstad, *Religious Polemics*, p. 59, similarly regards Amos 4 as a 'coherent speech unit', which, he believes, delivers a polemic against 'non-Yahwistic or Yahwistic/syncretistic cults'.

these observations, the rhetorical structure of Amos 4 can thus be outlined as follows.

A Opening declaration: those who exploit the poor will be punished (vv. 1-3)
   closed by נאם־יהוה
   B Ironic invitation: come and sin (vv. 4-5)
      closed by נאם אדני יהוה
         C Historical confirmation: Yahweh's past punishments did not
            make the people return to him (vv. 6-11)
            each strophe is closed by נאם־יהוה
D Concluding 'invitation': be prepared to meet the LORD (vv. 12-13)
   closed by יהוה אלהי־צבאות שמו

Figure 32. *The Rhetorical Structure of Amos 4*

This concludes my investigation of Amos 1–4, the aim of which was to illustrate the exegetical implications of the rhetorical-critical approach advocated in the present study. The summary of the debate between Amos and his audience presented in Chapter 2 has shown that the communication-theoretical approach advanced in the study in hand can also be fruitfully applied to the rest of the book, including the vision cycle in 7.1–8.3 and the subsequent discourses in 8.4-14 and 9.1-15.[170]

170. See also in this context Möller, 'Hear this Word', pp. 499-518; and *idem*, 'Rehabilitation', pp. 41-55.

CONCLUSIONS

In the present study, I have looked at Amos's literary structure and rhetoric of persuasion, arguing that the book has not been compiled only in order to preserve the prophet's words. I have also challenged the common redaction-critical view, which regards the book as the result of a lengthy redactional process, involving several generations of redactors, who continually adapted their text to guarantee its relevance for changing times and circumstances. Against this view, I have argued that the book might well have been compiled relatively shortly after Amos's time, and that it was intended to capture or present the debate between Amos and his original eighth-century Israelite audience.

Interpreting the book within a communication-theoretical framework and employing the methodological tools provided by rhetorical criticism, I have suggested that it has been compiled for a specific persuasive purpose. That is to say, those responsible for the book of Amos in its present form sought to present the debate between Amos and the Israelites in order for it to function as a warning for a pre-exilic Judaean audience. To be more specific, when read in the light of the catastrophic events of 722 BCE, the presentation of Amos struggling—and failing—to convince his contemporaries of the imminent divine judgment becomes a powerful warning, admonishing Judaean readers or hearers not to repeat the stubborn attitude of their northern brothers and sisters, lest they too face punishment.

In the introductory chapter, I have outlined my definition of rhetorical criticism, its interpretative potential and the interpretative tasks it engenders. This was done partly by contrasting the approach with the tenets, aims and interests that characterize redaction criticism. I have also looked at the reader's role in the interpretative process as well as outlined the methodological steps engendered by the rhetorical-critical enquiry. Chapter 2, in turn, discussed the book's macrostructure, beginning with a review of some recent proposals. An approach was then advocated that takes into account the 'oral world' of the book's original hearers, seeking to establish what kind of structural markers would have been recognizable in such an oral setting. In Chapter 3, the rhetorical situation and the rhetorical problem that caused the production of the book of Amos were considered. This was followed by a discussion of its overall rhetorical strategy, which, as I have pointed out, is best described in terms of a presentation of the debating prophet intended to function as a warning to pre-exilic Judaean readers. Chapters 4–6 then looked at Amos 1–4, applying the rhetorical-critical notions outlined above.

Towards the end of the introductory chapter, I outlined five methodological steps of rhetorical-critical enquiry, the last of which I have not yet addressed. I noted that, having analysed *how* the rhetoric of the work under consideration 'operates', the critic also needs to evaluate its 'rhetorical effectiveness'. It needs to be asked, that is to say, whether, or to what degree, the utterance is a fitting response to the exigency that occasioned it. This can be gauged by establishing whether the rhetorical utterance successfully modified the exigency or at least had the potential of doing so. This proviso is necessary, as the rhetorical effectiveness of an utterance evidently does not depend on internal factors (such as its genre, structure, etc.) alone. To mention but one external factor, it is influenced also by the audience's disposition towards the originator(s) of the utterance and the message that utterance conveys.

Applying the scenario I suggested earlier, that the book was meant to admonish a pre-exilic Judaean audience not to repeat the mistakes of the Israelites who would not listen to the prophet Amos, the following conclusions can be drawn. Based on what we know about the history of eighth- and seventh-century Judah, it is evident that the book of Amos did not successfully modify the exigency that had caused its compilation. That is to say, the Judaeans ultimately did experience a fate similar to that of their northern brothers and sisters, which would suggest that they would not be warned by what had happened to Israel. Of course, our limited historical knowledge does not allow us to rule out that the book may have made an impact on *some* of its hearers. Yet, while this may have been the case, this is a highly conjectural scenario, which does not yield much of an answer to the question of the book's rhetorical effectiveness.

However, as has already been pointed out, for a rhetorical utterance to be an appropriate response to an exigency, it is not actually necessary for the latter to be modified. All that is in fact required is that the utterance has the potential of modifying that exigency. And this clearly seems to be the case, as far as the book of Amos is concerned. That is to say, at a time when, for instance, the prophet Isaiah, criticizing the Judaean elite for their

296 A Prophet in Debate

social crimes and luxurious lifestyle, announced the divine judgment as a consequence of the people's wrongdoings, the book of Amos would have been a powerful means for backing up that message. By drawing attention to the Israelites' intolerable behaviour as well as to Yahweh's eventual punishment of his stubborn people, it would have pointed to an alarming precedent, suggesting that something similar might be in store for the Judaeans, if they too refused to be warned by their prophets. Let me add, finally, that, if asked how exactly the book would have been used in that situation, I would envisage a public reading, quite possibly in the Jerusalem temple.

BIBLIOGRAPHY

1. *Primary Sources, Texts and Versions*

Aristotle, *The Art of Rhetoric* (trans. J.H. Freese; LCL, 193; Cambridge, MA: Harvard University Press, 1926).

Augustine, *Confessions* (trans. W. Watts; LCL, 26-27; 2 vols.; Cambridge, MA: Harvard University Press, 1912).

Cathcart, K.J., and R.P. Gordon (eds.), *The Targum of the Minor Prophets: Translated, with a Critical Introduction, Apparatus, and Notes* (The Aramaic Bible, 14; Edinburgh: T. & T. Clark, 1989).

Cicero, *Brutus. Orator* (trans. G.L. Hendrickson and H.M. Hubbell; LCL, 342; Cambridge, MA: Harvard University Press, 1939).

—*De Oratore: Books I–II* (trans. E.W. Sutton and H. Rackham; LCL, 348; Cambridge, MA: Harvard University Press, 1942).

—*De Oratore: Book III. De Fato. Paradoxa Stoicorum. De Partitione Oratoria* (trans. H. Rackham; LCL, 349; Cambridge, MA: Harvard University Press, 1942).

Haase, R., *Die keilschriftlichen Rechtssammlungen in deutscher Fassung* (Wiesbaden: Otto Harrassowitz, 2nd edn, 1979).

Hoftijzer, J. (ed.), *Aramaic Texts from Deir ʿAlla* (Documenta et monumenta orients antiqui, 19; Leiden: E.J. Brill, 1976).

Josephus, *Jewish Antiquities* (trans. H.St.J. Thackeray, R. Marcus and L.H. Feldman; LCL, 242, 281, 326, 365, 410, 433, 456; 7 vols.; Cambridge, MA: Harvard University Press, 1930–65).

—*The Life. Against Apion* (trans. H.St.J. Thackeray; LCL, 186; Cambridge, MA: Harvard University Press, 1926).

Kittel, R. (ed.), *Biblia Hebraica* (Stuttgart: Württembergische Bibelanstalt, 1937).

Lambert, W.G., *Babylonian Wisdom Literature* (Oxford: Clarendon Press, 1960).

Lichtheim, M. (ed.), *Ancient Egyptian Literature: A Book of Readings* (3 vols.; Berkeley: University of California Press, 1973–80).

Martial, *Epigrams* (ed. and trans. D.R. Shackleton Bailey; LCL, 94–95, 480; 3 vols.; Cambridge, MA: Harvard University Press, 1993).

Philo, *Works* (trans. F.H. Colson and G.H. Whitaker; LCL, 226, 227, 247, 261, 275, 289, 320, 341, 363, 379; 10 vols.; Cambridge, MA: Harvard University Press, 1929–62).

Plato, *Euthyphro. Apology. Crito. Phaedo. Phaedrus* (trans. H.N. Fowler; LCL, 36; Cambridge, MA: Harvard University Press, 1990).

—*Theaetetus. Sophist* (trans. H.N. Fowler; LCL, 123; Cambridge, MA: Harvard University Press, 1987).

Pliny, *Letters and Panegyricus* (trans. B. Radice; LCL, 55, 59; 2 vols.; Cambridge, MA: Harvard University Press, 1969).

Rahlfs, A. (ed.), *Septuaginta* (Stuttgart: Deutsche Bibelgesellschaft, 1979).

Sperber, A., *The Bible in Aramaic Based on Old Manuscripts and Printed Texts*. III. *The Latter Prophets According to Targum Jonathan* (Leiden: E.J. Brill, 1962).

Ziegler, J. (ed.), *Duodecim prophetae* (Septuaginta: Vetus Testamentum Graecum Auctoritate Academiae Scientiarum Gottingensis editum, 13; Göttingen: Vandenhoeck & Ruprecht, 3rd edn, 1984).

2. Reference Works

Abrams, M.H., *A Glossary of Literary Terms* (Fort Worth, TX: Harcourt Brace College, 6th edn, 1993).

Bauer, W., *Griechisch–deutsches Wörterbuch zu den Schriften des Neuen Testaments und der frühchristlichen Literatur* (ed. K. Aland and B. Aland; Berlin: W. de Gruyter, 6th rev. edn, 1988).

Bühlmann, W., and K. Scherer, *Stilfiguren der Bibel: Ein kleines Nachschlagewerk* (Fribourg: Schweizerisches Katholisches Bibelwerk, 1973).

Bullinger, E.W., *Figures of Speech Used in the Bible Explained and Illustrated* (London: Eyre & Spottiswoode, 1898; repr., Grand Rapids: Baker Book House, 1968).

Even-Shoshan, A. (ed.), *A New Concordance of the Bible: Thesaurus of the Language of the Bible, Hebrew and Aramaic Roots, Words, Proper Names, Phrases and Synonyms* (Jerusalem: Kiryat Sefer, 1990).

Jastrow, M., *A Dictionary of the Targumim, the Talmud Babli and Yerushalmi, and the Midrashic Literature* (2 vols.; Brooklyn: Shalom, 1967).

Kunzmann, P., F.P. Burkard and F. Wiedmann, *dtv-Atlas zur Philosophie: Tafeln und Texte* (Munich: Deutscher Taschenbuch Verlag, 3rd edn, 1993).

Lisowsky, G., and L. Rost, *Konkordanz zum hebräischen Alten Testament* (Stuttgart: Württembergische Bibelanstalt, corr. edn, 1958).

Pfeifer, G., *Hebräische Wortkonkordanz zum Amosbuch* (Frankfurt: Peter Lang, 1998).

Sanderson, J.E., 'War, Peace, and Justice in the Hebrew Bible: A Representative Bibliography', in G. von Rad, *Holy War in Ancient Israel* (ed. and trans. M.J. Dawn; Grand Rapids: Eerdmans, 1991), pp. 135-66.

Thompson, H.O., *The Book of Amos: An Annotated Bibliography* (ATLA Bibliographies, 42; Lanham, MD: Scarecrow Press, 1997).

Wal, A. van der, *Amos: A Classified Bibliography* (Applicatio, 3; Amsterdam: Free University Press, 3rd edn, 1986).

Wal, A. van der, and E. Talstra, *Amos: Concordance and Lexical Surveys* (Applicatio, 2; Amsterdam: Free University Press, 1984).

Watson, D.F., and A.J. Hauser, *Rhetorical Criticism of the Bible: A Comprehensive Bibliography with Notes on History and Method* (BIS, 4; Leiden: E.J. Brill, 1994).

Watson, W.G.E., *Classical Hebrew Poetry: A Guide to Its Techniques* (JSOTSup, 26; Sheffield: JSOT Press, 1984).

Williams, R.J., *Hebrew Syntax: An Outline* (Toronto: University of Toronto Press, 2nd edn, 1976).

Wilpert, G. von, *Sachwörterbuch der Literatur* (Stuttgart: Kröner, 5th edn, 1969).

3. *Commentaries on Amos*

Achtemeier, E., *Minor Prophets I* (NIBC, 17; Peabody, MA: Hendrickson, 1996).

Alonso Schökel, L., and J.L. Sicre Diaz, *Profetas: Introducciones y comentario*. II. *Ezequiel, Doce Profetas Menores, Daniel, Baruc, Carta de Jeremías* (Nueva Biblia Española; Madrid: Ediciones Cristiandad, 2nd edn, 1980).

Amsler, S., 'Amos', in E. Jacob, C.-A. Keller and S. Amsler, *Osée, Joël, Amos, Abdias, Jonas* (CAT, 11a; Neuchâtel: Delachaux & Niestlé, 1965), pp. 157-247.

Andersen, F.I., and D.N. Freedman, *Amos: A New Translation with Introduction and Commentary* (AB, 24a; New York: Doubleday, 1989).

Barré, M.L., 'Amos', in R.E. Brown, J.A. Fitzmyer and R.E. Murphy (eds.), *The New Jerome Bible Commentary* (London: Geoffrey Chapman, 1989), pp. 209-16.

Bič, M., *Das Buch Amos* (Berlin: Evangelische Verlagsanstalt, 1969).

Birch, B.C., *Hosea, Joel, and Amos* (Westminster Bible Companion; Louisville, KY: Westminster/John Knox Press, 1997).

Bovati, P., and R. Meynet, *Le livre du prophète Amos* (RhétBib, 2; Paris: Cerf, 1994).

Budde, K., 'Zu Text und Auslegung des Buches Amos', *JBL* 43 (1924), pp. 46-131; and *JBL* 44 (1925), pp. 63-122.

Calvin, J., *A Commentary on the Twelve Minor Prophets*. II. *Joel, Amos and Obadiah* (trans. J. Owen; repr., Edinburgh: Banner of Truth Trust, 1986 [1846]).

Chisholm, R.B., Jr, *Interpreting the Minor Prophets* (Grand Rapids: Zondervan, 1990).

Coggins, R.J., *Joel and Amos* (NCB; Sheffield: Sheffield Academic Press, 2000).

Craigie, P.C., *The Twelve Prophets*. I. *Hosea, Joel, Amos, Obadiah, and Jonah* (Edinburgh: Saint Andrew Press, 1984).

Cripps, R.S., *A Critical and Exegetical Commentary on the Book of Amos* (London: SPCK, 1929).

Deissler, A., *Zwölf Propheten*. I. *Hosea, Joël, Amos* (Neue Echter Bibel, 4; Würzburg: Echter Verlag, 3rd edn, 1992).

Driver, S.R., *The Books of Joel and Amos with Introduction and Notes* (Cambridge: Cambridge University Press, 1897).

Duhm, B., 'Anmerkungen zu den zwölf Propheten', *ZAW* 31 (1911), pp. 1-43, 81-110, 161-204.

Edghill, E.A., *The Book of Amos* (ed. G.A. Cooke; Westminster Commentaries; London: Methuen, 2nd edn, 1926).

Feinberg, C.L., *The Minor Prophets* (repr. of *The Major Messages of the Minor Prophets* [5 vols., 1948–52]; Chicago: Moody Press, 1990).

Finley, T.J., *Joel, Amos, Obadiah* (Wycliffe Exegetical Commentary; Chicago: Moody Press, 1990).

Fosbroke, H.E.W., 'The Book of Amos: Introduction and Exegesis', in G.A. Buttrick *et al.* (eds.), *IB*, VI (New York: Abingdon Press, 1956), pp. 761-853.

Gowan, D.E., 'The Book of Amos: Introduction, Commentary, and Reflections', in L.E. Keck *et al.* (eds.), *NIB*, VII (Nashville: Abingdon Press, 1996), pp. 337-431.

Gressmann, H., *Die älteste Geschichtsschreibung und Prophetie Israels (von Samuel bis Amos und Hosea)* (SAT, 2.1; Göttingen: Vandenhoeck & Ruprecht, 2nd edn, 1921).

Guthe, H., 'Der Prophet Amos', in E. Kautzsch and A. Bertholet (eds.), *Die Heilige Schrift des Alten Testaments*, II (Tübingen, 4th edn, 1923; repr., Hildesheim: Georg Olms, 1971), pp. 30-47.

Hammershaimb, E., *The Book of Amos: A Commentary* (Oxford: Basil Blackwell, 1970).

Harper, W.R., *A Critical and Exegetical Commentary on Amos and Hosea* (ICC; Edinburgh: T. & T. Clark, 1905).

Hayes, J.H., *Amos—The Eighth-Century Prophet: His Times and His Preaching* (Nashville: Abingdon Press, 1988).

Holland, M., *Joel, Amos und Obadja* (Wuppertal: Brockhaus, 1991).

Hubbard, D.A., *Joel and Amos: An Introduction and Commentary* (TOTC; Leicester: IVP, 1989).

Hyatt, J.P., 'Amos', in M. Black and H.H. Rowley (eds.), *Peake's Commentary on the Bible* (London: Nelson, 1962), pp. 617-25.

Jeremias, J., *The Book of Amos: A Commentary* (trans. D.W. Stott; OTL; Louisville, KY: Westminster/John Knox Press, 1998).

—*Der Prophet Amos* (ATD, 24.2; Göttingen: Vandenhoeck & Ruprecht, 1995).

Keil, C.F., *The Minor Prophets* (COT, 10; Edinburgh: T. & T. Clark, 1866–91; repr., Peabody, MA: Hendrickson, 1996).

Koch, K., et al., *Amos untersucht mit den Methoden einer strukturalen Formgeschichte* (AOAT, 30; 3 vols.; Kevelaer: Butzon & Bercker, 1976).

Leeuwen, C. van, *Amos* (De Prediking van het Oude Testament; Nijkerk: Callenbach, 1985).

Limburg, J., *Hosea–Micah* (Interpretation; Atlanta: John Knox Press, 1988).

Marti, K., *Das Dodekapropheton erklärt* (KHAT, 13; Tübingen: J.C.B. Mohr, 1904).

Martin-Achard, R., 'The End of the People of God: A Commentary on the Book of Amos', in idem and S.P. Re'emi, *God's People in Crisis: A Commentary on the Book of Amos and a Commentary on the Book of Lamentations* (ITC; Edinburgh: Handsel Press, 1984), pp. 1-71.

Mays, J.L., *Amos: A Commentary* (OTL; Philadelphia: Westminster Press, 1969).

McComiskey, T.E., 'Amos', in F.E. Gaebelein et al. (eds.), *The Expositor's Bible Commentary*. VII. *Daniel–Minor Prophets* (Grand Rapids: Zondervan, 1985), pp. 267-331.

McKeating, H., *The Books of Amos, Hosea and Micah* (Cambridge Bible Commentary; Cambridge: Cambridge University Press, 1971).

Motyer, J.A., *The Message of Amos* (Leicester: IVP, 1974).

Mowvley, H., *The Books of Amos and Hosea* (Epworth Commentaries; London: Epworth Press, 1991).

Niehaus, J.J., 'Amos', in T.E. McComiskey (ed.), *The Minor Prophets: An Exegetical and Expository Commentary*. I. *Hosea, Joel, and Amos* (Grand Rapids: Baker Book House, 1992), pp. 315-494.

Nowack, W., *Die kleinen Propheten übersetzt und erklärt* (HKAT, 3.4; Göttingen: Vandenhoeck & Ruprecht, 2nd edn, 1903).

Orelli, C. von, *Die zwölf kleinen Propheten* (Kurzgefasster Kommentar zu den heiligen Schriften Alten und Neuen Testamentes sowie zu den Apokryphen, A.5.2; Munich: Beck, 2nd edn, 1896).

Paul, S.M., *Amos: A Commentary on the Book of Amos* (Hermeneia; Minneapolis: Fortress Press, 1991).

Pusey, E.B., *The Minor Prophets with a Commentary Explanatory and Practical, and Introductions to the Several Books*. II. *Amos* (London: James Nisbet, 1906).

Robinson, T.H., 'Hosea bis Micha', in idem and F. Horst, *Die Zwölf Kleinen Propheten* (HAT, 1.14; Tübingen: J.C.B. Mohr [Paul Siebeck], 2nd edn, 1954), pp. 1-152.

Rudolph, W., *Joel, Amos, Obadja, Jona* (KAT, 13.2; Gütersloh: Gütersloher Verlagshaus Gerd Mohn, 1971).

Sellin, E., *Das Zwölfprophetenbuch*. I. *Hosea-Micha* (KAT, 12.1; Leipzig: Deichert, 3rd edn, 1929).

Smith, B.K., 'Amos, Obadiah', in *idem* and F.S. Page, *Amos, Obadiah, Jonah* (New American Commentary, 19b; Broadman & Holman, 1995), pp. 23-201.

Smith, G.A., *The Book of the Twelve Prophets Commonly Called the Minor*. I. *Amos, Hosea and Micah. With an Introduction and a Sketch of Prophecy in Early Israel* (Expositor's Bible; London: Hodder & Stoughton, 1908).

Smith, G.V., *Amos: A Commentary* (LBI; Grand Rapids: Zondervan, 1989).

Soggin, J.A., *The Prophet Amos: A Translation and Commentary* (trans. J. Bowden; London: SCM Press, 1987).

Stuart, D., *Hosea–Jonah* (WBC, 31; Waco, TX: Word Books, 1987).

Sweeney, M.A., *The Twelve Prophets*. I. *Hosea, Joel, Amos, Obadiah, Jonah* (Berit Olam; Collegeville, MN: Michael Glazier, 2000).

Theis, J., 'Der Prophet Amos', in J. Lippl and J. Theis, *Die zwölf kleinen Propheten*. 1. *Osee, Joel, Amos, Abdias, Jonas, Michäas* (HSAT, 8.3.1; Bonn: Peter Hanstein, 1937), pp. 107-37.

Waard, J. de, and W.A. Smalley, *A Handbook on the Book of Amos* (UBSHS; New York: United Bible Societies, 1979).

Weiser, A., *Das Buch der zwölf kleinen Propheten*. 1. *Die Propheten Hosea, Joel, Amos, Obadja, Jona, Micha* (ATD, 24; Göttingen: Vandenhoeck & Ruprecht, 8th edn, 1985).

Wellhausen, J., *Die kleinen Propheten übersetzt und erklärt* (Berlin: W. de Gruyter, 4th edn, 1963).

Wolff, H.W., *Dodekapropheton*. II. *Joel und Amos* (BKAT, 14.2; Neukirchen–Vluyn: Neukirchener Verlag, 3rd edn, 1985).

—*Joel and Amos: A Commentary on the Books of the Prophets Joel and Amos* (ed. S.D. McBride, Jr; trans. W. Janzen, S.D. McBride, Jr and C.A. Muenchow; Hermeneia; Philadelphia: Fortress Press, 1977).

4. *Other Works Cited*

Abrams, M.H., 'Orientation of Critical Theories', in D. Lodge (ed.), *20th Century Criticism: A Reader* (London: Longman, 1972), pp. 1-26.

Achtemeier, P.J. (ed.), *SBLASP* 114.1 (Missoula: Scholars Press, 1978).

Ackroyd, P.R., 'Isaiah I–XII: Presentation of a Prophet', in *Congress Volume, Göttingen 1977* (VTSup, 29; Leiden: E.J. Brill, 1978), pp. 16-48.

—'A Judgment Narrative Between Kings and Chronicles? An Approach to Amos 7.9-17', in Coats and Long (eds.), *Canon and Authority*, pp. 71-87.

Alonso Schökel, L., *Das Alte Testament als literarisches Kunstwerk* (Cologne: Bachem, 1971).

—*The Inspired Word: Scripture in the Light of Language and Literature* (New York: Herder & Herder, 1965).

—*A Manual of Hebrew Poetics* (SubBib, 11; Rome: Editrice Pontificio Istituto Biblico, 1988).

Alonso Schökel, L., with J.M. Bravo, *A Manual of Hermeneutics* (ed. B.W.R. Pearson; trans. L.M. Rosa; BibSem, 54; Sheffield: Sheffield Academic Press, 1998).

Alter, R., *The Art of Biblical Narrative* (New York: Basic Books, 1981).

—*The Art of Biblical Poetry* (New York: Basic Books, 1985).

—'The Characteristics of Ancient Hebrew Poetry', in *idem* and Kermode (eds.), *The Literary Guide to the Bible*, pp. 611-24.

—'Introduction to the Old Testament', in *idem* and Kermode (eds.), *The Literary Guide to the Bible*, pp. 11-35.

—*The World of Biblical Literature* (London: SPCK, 1992).

Alter, R., and F. Kermode (eds.), *The Literary Guide to the Bible* (London: Fontana, 1987).

Althusser, L., 'From *Capital* to Marx's Philosophy', in *idem* and E. Balibar, *Reading Capital* (trans. B. Brewster; New York: Verso, 1970), pp. 11-39.

Amador, J.D.H., 'Where Could Rhetorical Criticism (Still) Take Us?', *CRBS* 7 (1999), pp. 195-222.

Amsler, S., 'Amos et les droits de l'homme', in Doré, Grelot and Carrez (eds.), *De la Tôrah au Messie*, pp. 181-87.

Andersen, F.I., *The Sentence in Biblical Hebrew* (Janua Linguarum, Series Practica, 231; The Hague: Mouton, 1974).

Andersen, Ø., *Im Garten der Rhetorik: Die Kunst der Rede in der Antike* (trans. B. Mannsperger and I. Tveide; Darmstadt: Wissenschaftliche Buchgesellschaft, 2001).

Anderson, B.W., 'The New Frontier of Rhetorical Criticism. A Tribute to James Muilenburg', in Jackson and Kessler (eds.), *Rhetorical Criticism*, pp. ix-xviii.

Anderson, J.C., and J.L. Staley (eds.), *Taking it Personally: Autobiographical Biblical Criticism* (Semeia, 72; Atlanta: Scholars Press, 1995).

Applegate, J., 'Narrative Patterns for the Communication of Commissioned Speech in the Prophets: A Three-Scene Model', in G.J. Brooke and J.-D. Kaestli (eds.), *Narrativity in Biblical and Related Texts. La narrativité dans la Bible et les textes apparentés* (BETL, 149; Leuven: Leuven University Press, 2000), pp. 69-88.

Ap-Thomas, D.R., 'All the King's Horses?', in J.I. Durham and J.R. Porter (eds.), *Proclamation and Presence: Old Testament Essays in Honour of Gwynne Henton Davies* (Macon, GA: Mercer University Press, new corr. edn, 1983), pp. 135-51.

Arieti, J.A., 'The Vocabulary of Septuagint Amos', *JBL* 93 (1974), pp. 338-47.

Asen, B.A., 'No, Yes and Perhaps in Amos and the Yahwist', *VT* 43 (1993), pp. 433-41.

Auld, A.G., *Amos* (OTG; Sheffield: JSOT Press, 1986).

—'Amos and Apocalyptic: Vision, Prophecy, Revelation', in Garrone and Israel (eds.), *Storia e Tradizioni di Israele*, pp. 1-13.

—'Prophecy in Books: A Rejoinder', *JSOT* 48 (1990), pp. 31-32.

—'Prophets through the Looking Glass: A Response to Robert Carroll and Hugh Williamson', *JSOT* 27 (1983), pp. 41-44.

—'Prophets through the Looking Glass: Between Writings and Moses', *JSOT* 27 (1983), pp. 3-23.

Aurelio, T., *Disclosures in den Gleichnissen Jesu: Eine Anwendung der Disclosure-Theorie von I. T. Ramsey, der modernen Metaphorik und der Sprechakte auf die Gleichnisse Jesu* (Regensburger Studien zur Theologie, 8; Frankfurt: Peter Lang, 1977).

Austin, J.L., *How to Do Things With Words* (Oxford: Clarendon Press, 2nd edn, 1975).

Bach, R., '…Der, der Bogen zerbricht, Spiesse zerschlägt und Wagen mit Feuer verbrennt', in Wolff (ed.), *Probleme biblischer Theologie*, pp. 13-26.

—'Gottesrecht und weltliches Recht in der Verkündigung des Propheten Amos', in W. Schneemelcher (ed.), *Festschrift für Günther Dehn* (Neukirchen–Vluyn: Erziehungs-verein, 1957), pp. 23-34.

Baker, W.R., *Personal Speech-Ethics in the Epistle of James* (WUNT, 2.68; Tübingen: J.C.B. Mohr, 1995).

Bakhtin, M., *The Dialogic Imagination: Four Essays* (ed. M. Holquist; trans. C. Holquist and M. Holquist; University of Texas Press Slavic Series, 1; Austin: University of Texas Press, 1981).

Balla, E., *Die Droh- und Scheltworte des Amos* (Leipzig: Edelmann, 1926).

Barr, J., *The Semantics of Biblical Language* (Oxford: Oxford University Press, 1961).

—'The Synchronic, the Diachronic and the Historical: A Triangular Relationship?', in de Moor (ed.), *Synchronic or Diachronic?*, pp. 1-14.

Barré, M.L., 'Amos 1.11 Reconsidered', *CBQ* 47 (1985), pp. 420-27.

—'The Meaning of *l' 'šybnw* in Amos 1.3–2.6', *JBL* 105 (1986), pp. 611-31.

Barstad, H.M., 'Die Basankühe in Amos iv 1', *VT* 25 (1975), pp. 286-97.

—'No Prophets? Recent Developments in Biblical Prophetic Research and Ancient Near Eastern Prophecy', *JSOT* 57 (1993), pp. 39-60.

—*The Religious Polemics of Amos: Studies in the Preaching of Am 2,7B-8; 4,1-13; 5,1-27; 6,4-7; 8,14* (VTSup, 34; Leiden: E.J. Brill, 1984).

Bartelmus, R., T. Krüger and H. Utzschneider (eds.), *Konsequente Traditionsgeschichte. Festschrift für Klaus Baltzer zum 65. Geburtstag* (OBO, 126; Freiburg: Universitätsverlag, 1993).

Barth, K., *Die Kirchliche Dogmatik. IV/2. Die Lehre von der Versöhnung* (Zürich: EVZ-Verlag, 1955).

Barthes, R., *Le plaisir du texte* (Paris: Seuil, 1973).

Bartholomew, C.G., *Reading Ecclesiastes: Old Testament Exegesis and Hermeneutical Theory* (AnBib, 139; Rome: Editrice Pontificio Istituto Biblico, 1998).

Bartholomew, C.G., C. Greene and K. Möller (eds.), *After Pentecost: Language and Biblical Interpretation* (SHS, 2; Carlisle: Paternoster Press; Grand Rapids: Zondervan, 2001).

—*Renewing Biblical Interpretation* (SHS, 1; Carlisle: Paternoster Press; Grand Rapids: Zondervan, 2000).

Bartlett, J.R., 'The Brotherhood of Edom', *JSOT* 4 (1977), pp. 2-27.

Barton, J., *Amos's Oracles against the Nations: A Study of Amos 1.3–2.5* (SOTSMS, 6; Cambridge: Cambridge University Press, 1980).

—'Classifying Biblical Criticism', *JSOT* 29 (1984), pp. 19-35.

—'History and Rhetoric in the Prophets', in Warner (ed.), *Bible as Rhetoric*, pp. 51-64.

—*Isaiah 1–39* (OTG; Sheffield: Sheffield Academic Press, 1995).

—*Reading the Old Testament: Method in Biblical Study* (London: Darton, Longman & Todd, 2nd edn, 1996).

Bauer, L., 'Einige Stellen des Alten Testaments bei Kautzsch 4. Aufl. im Licht des heiligen Landes', *TSK* 100 (1927–28), pp. 426-38.

Baumann, A., 'אָבֵל ,אָבַל ,אֲבֵל', in *TDOT*, I, pp. 44-48.

Baumann, E., *Der Aufbau der Amosreden* (BZAW, 7; Giessen: Rickert, 1903).

Baumgärtel, F., 'Die Formel *ne'um jahwe*', *ZAW* 73 (1961), pp. 277-90.

Baumgartner, W., 'Amos 3 $_{3-8}$', *ZAW* 33 (1913), pp. 78-80.

Beardsley, M.C., *Aesthetics: Problems in the Philosophy of Criticism* (New York: Harcourt, Brace & World, 1958).

—*The Possibility of Criticism* (Detroit: Wayne State University Press, 1970).

Beaucamp, E., 'Amos 1–2: Le pèsha' d'Israel et celui des Nations', *ScEs* 21 (1969), pp. 435-41.

Beek, M.A., 'The Religious Background of Amos 2.6-8', in *OTS*, 5 (Leiden: E.J. Brill, 1948), pp. 132-41.

Beentjes, P.C., 'Oracles Against the Nations: A Central Issue in the "Latter Prophets"', *Bijdragen, tijdschrift voor filosofie en theologie* 50 (1989), pp. 203-209.

Begrich, J., 'Die priesterliche Tora', in P. Volz, F. Stummer and J. Hempel (eds.), *Werden und Wesen des Alten Testaments. Vorträge gehalten auf der Internationalen Tagung alttestamentlicher Forscher zu Göttingen vom 4.-10. September 1935* (BZAW, 66; Berlin: Alfred Töpelmann, 1936), pp. 63-88.

—*Studien zu Deuterojesaja* (BWANT, 4.25; Stuttgart: W. Kohlhammer, 1938).

Benson, A., ' "From the Mouth of the Lion": The Messianism of Amos', *CBQ* 19 (1957), pp. 199-212.

Bentzen, A., 'The Ritual Background of Amos 1,2–2,16', in P.A.H. de Boer (ed.), *OTS*, 8 (Leiden: E.J. Brill, 1950), pp. 85-99.

Ben Zvi, E., 'The Dialogue between Abraham and Yhwh in Gen. 18.23-32: A Historical-Critical Analysis', *JSOT* 53 (1992), pp. 27-46.

—*A Historical-Critical Study of the Book of Obadiah* (BZAW, 242; Berlin: W. de Gruyter, 1996).

—*A Historical-Critical Study of the Book of Zephaniah* (BZAW, 198; Berlin: W. de Gruyter, 1991).

Berg, W., *Die sogenannten Hymnenfragmente im Amosbuch* (Europäische Hochschulschriften, 23.45; Bern: Herbert Lang, 1974).

Bergen, R.D. (ed.), *Biblical Hebrew and Discourse Linguistics* (Dallas: SIL, 1994).

Bergler, S., *Die hymnischen Passagen und die Mitte des Amosbuches: Ein Forschungsbericht* (Magisterschrift, Tübingen, 1978).

Bergman, J. *et al.*, 'בָּרָא', in *TDOT*, II, pp. 242-49.

Berlin, A., *The Dynamics of Biblical Parallelism* (Bloomington: Indiana University Press, 1985).

—*Poetics and Interpretation of Biblical Narrative* (Winona Lake, IN: Eisenbrauns, 1994).

Bernhardt, K.-H. (ed.), *Schalom: Studien zu Glaube und Geschichte Israels. Festschrift für Alfred J. Jepsen zum 70. Geburtstag dargebracht* (Stuttgart: Calwer, 1971).

Berquist, J.L., 'Dangerous Waters of Justice and Righteousness: Amos 5.18-27', *BTB* 23 (1993), pp. 54-63.

Berridge, J.M., 'Zur Intention der Botschaft des Amos: Exegetische Überlegungen zu Am. 5', *TZ* 32 (1976), pp. 321-40.

Berry, D.K., *The Psalms and their Readers: Interpretive Strategies for Psalm 18* (JSOTSup, 153; Sheffield: JSOT Press, 1993).

Bertholet, A., 'Zu Amos 1.2', in *Theologische Festschrift. G. Nathanael Bonwetsch zu seinem 70. Geburtstag* (Leipzig: Deichert, 1918), pp. 1-12.

Beuken, W.A.M., *Haggai–Sacharja 1–8: Studien zur Überlieferungsgeschichte der frühnachexilischen Prophetie* (StSN, 10; Assen: Van Gorcum, 1967).

Bible and Culture Collective (G. Aichele *et al.*), *The Postmodern Bible* (New Haven: Yale University Press, 1995).

Bič, M., 'Der Prophet Amos—ein Haepatoskopos?', *VT* 1 (1951), pp. 293-96.

Bitzer, L.F., 'The Rhetorical Situation', in W.R. Fisher (ed.), *Rhetoric: A Tradition in Transition. In Honor of Donald C. Bryant* (East Lansing, MI: Michigan State University Press, 1974), pp. 247-60.

Bjørndalen, A.J., 'Erwägungen zur Zukunft des Amazja und Israels nach der Überlieferung Amos 7,10-17', in R. Albertz *et al.* (eds.), *Werden und Wirken des Alten Testaments. Festschrift für Claus Westermann zum 70. Geburtstag* (Göttingen: Vandenhoeck & Ruprecht, 1980), pp. 236-51.

—'Jahwe in den Zukunftsaussagen des Amos', in J. Jeremias and L. Perlitt (eds.), *Die Botschaft und die Boten. Festschrift für Hans Walter Wolff zum 70. Geburtstag* (Neukirchen–Vluyn: Neukirchener Verlag, 1981), pp. 181-202.

—'Zu den Zeitstufen der Zitatformel...אמר הכ im Botenverkehr', *ZAW* 86 (1974), pp. 393-403.

Black, C.C., 'Rhetorical Criticism', in Green (ed.), *Hearing the New Testament*, pp. 256-77.

—'Rhetorical Criticism and Biblical Interpretation', *ExpTim* 100 (1988–89), pp. 252-58.

Blenkinsopp, J., *A History of Prophecy in Israel* (Philadelphia: Westminster Press, 1983).

Böckler, A., *Gott als Vater im Alten Testament: Traditionsgeschichtliche Untersuchungen zur Entstehung und Entwicklung eines Gottesbildes* (Gütersloh: Gütersloher Verlagshaus, 2000).

Boda, M.J., 'Chiasmus in Ubiquity: Symmetrical Mirages in Nehemiah 9', *JSOT* 71 (1996), pp. 55-70.

Bodine, W.R. (ed.), *Linguistics and Biblical Hebrew* (Winona Lake, IN: Eisenbrauns, 1992).

Boehmer, J., 'Amos nach Gedankengang und Grundgedanken', *Nieuwe Theologische Studien* 10 (1927), pp. 1-7.

Bons, E., *Das Buch Hosea* (Neuer Stuttgarter Kommentar: Altes Testament, 23.1; Stuttgart: Katholisches Bibelwerk, 1996).

—'Das Denotat von כזביהם "ihre Lügen" im Judaspruch Am 2,4-5', *ZAW* 108 (1996), pp. 201-13.

Booth, W.C., 'Rhetorical Critics Old and New', in L. Lerner (ed.), *Deconstructing Literature* (Oxford: Basil Blackwell, 1983), pp. 123-41.

—*The Rhetoric of Fiction* (Harmondsworth: Penguin Books, 2nd edn, 1983).

—'The Rhetoric of Fiction and the Poetics of Fiction', *Novel: A Forum on Fiction* 1 (1968), pp. 105-17.

—*A Rhetoric of Irony* (Chicago: University of Chicago Press, 1974).

Bosman, H.L., 'מָרְזֵחַ', in *NIDOTTE*, II, pp. 1102-1103.

Botha, J.E., *Jesus and the Samaritan Woman: A Speech-Act Reading of John 4.1-42* (NovTSup, 65; Leiden: E.J. Brill, 1991).

Botterweck, G.J., 'אֶבְיוֹן', in *TDOT*, I, pp. 27-41.

—'Zur Authentizität des Buches Amos', *BZ* NS 2 (1958), pp. 176-89.

Braulik, G., 'Zur Funktion von Siebenergruppierungen im Endtext des Deuteronomiums', in F.V. Reiterer (ed.), *Ein Gott, eine Offenbarung: Beiträge zur biblischen Exegese, Theologie und Spiritualität. Festschrift für Notker Füglister OSB zum 60. Geburtstag* (Würzburg: Echter Verlag, 1991), pp. 37-50.

—'Die Theorien über das Deuteronomistische Geschichtswerk ("DtrG")', in Zenger *et al.* (eds.), *Einleitung in das Alte Testament*, pp. 127-31.

Brekelmans, C., 'Deuteronomistic Influence in Isaiah 1–12', in J. Vermeylen (ed.), *Le livre d'Isaïe: Les oracles et leurs relectures, unité et complexité de l'ouvrage* (BETL, 81; Leuven: Leuven University Press, 1989), pp. 167-76.

Brenner, A., 'Introduction', in *idem* (ed.), *A Feminist Companion to The Latter Prophets*, pp. 21-37.

—'Preface', in *idem* (ed.), *A Feminist Companion to The Latter Prophets*, pp. 13-19.

Brenner, A. (ed.), *A Feminist Companion to The Latter Prophets* (FCB, 8; Sheffield: Sheffield Academic Press, 1995).

Bright, J., 'A New View of Amos', *Int* 25 (1971), pp. 355-58.

Brinton, A., 'Situation in the Theory of Rhetoric', *Philosophy & Rhetoric* 14 (1981), pp. 234-48.

Brown, G., and G. Yule, *Discourse Analysis* (Cambridge Textbooks in Linguistics; Cambridge: Cambridge University Press, 1983).

Bruce, F.F., *The Acts of the Apostles* (Leicester: Apollos, 3rd edn, 1990).

Brueggemann, W., 'Amos' Intercessory Formula', *VT* 19 (1969), pp. 385-99.

—'Amos iv 4-13 and Israel's Covenant Worship', *VT* 15 (1965), pp. 1-15.

—*Hopeful Imagination: Prophetic Voices in Exile* (Philadelphia: Fortress Press, 1986).

—'The Prophet as a Destabilizing Presence', in *idem*, *A Social Reading of the Old Testament: Prophetic Approaches to Israel's Communal Life* (ed. P.D. Miller; Minneapolis: Fortress Press, 1994), pp. 221-44.

—*The Prophetic Imagination* (Philadelphia: Fortress Press, 1978).

—'Response to James L. Mays, "The Question of Context"', in McCann (ed.), *The Shape and Shaping of the Psalter*, pp. 29-41.

—*Texts under Negotiation: The Bible and Postmodern Imagination* (Minneapolis: Fortress Press, 1993).

—*Theology of the Old Testament: Testimony, Dispute, Advocacy* (Minneapolis: Fortress Press, 1997).

Brunt, J.C., 'More on the Topos as a New Testament Form', *JBL* 104 (1985), pp. 495-500.

Bryan, D.B., 'Texts Relating to the Marzeaḥ: A Study of an Ancient Semitic Institution' (Unpubl. diss., The Johns Hopkins University, Baltimore, 1973).

Buber, M., *The Prophetic Faith* (trans. C. Witton-Davies; New York: Macmillan, 1949).

Budde, K., 'Amos 1 ₂', *ZAW* 30 (1910), pp. 37-41.

—'Die Überschrift des Buches Amos und des Propheten Heimat', in G.A. Kohut (ed.), *Semitic Studies in Memory of Rev. Dr. Alexander Kohut* (Berlin: Calvary, 1897), pp. 106-10.

Bultmann, R., 'ἀναγινώσκω, ἀνάγνωσις', in *TWNT*, I, p. 347.

—'πένθος, πενθέω', in *TWNT*, VI, pp. 40-43.

Burger, J.A., 'Amos: A Historical-geographical View', *Journal for Semitics* 4 (1992), pp. 130-50.

Buss, M.J., 'Potential and Actual Interactions Between Speech Act Theory and Biblical Studies', in White (ed.), *Speech Act Theory*, pp. 125-34.

Byargeon, R.W., 'Amos: The Man and His Times', *Southwestern Journal of Theology* 38.1 (1995), pp. 4-10.

Callow, J., 'Units and Flow in the Song of Songs 1.2–2.6', in Bergen (ed.), *Biblical Hebrew*, pp. 462-88.

Campbell, E.F., 'Archaeological Reflections on Amos's Targets', in Coogan (ed.), *Scripture and Other Artifacts*, pp. 32-52.

Carny, P., 'Doxologies—A Scientific Myth', *Hebrew Studies* 18 (1977), pp. 149-59.

Carpenter, E., and M.A. Grisani, 'כוב', in *NIDOTTE*, II, pp. 619-21.

—'פשׁע', in *NIDOTTE*, III, pp. 706-10.

Carroll, R.P., 'Arguing About Jeremiah: Recent Studies and the Nature of a Prophetic Book', in J.A. Emerton (ed.), *Congress Volume, Leuven 1989* (VTSup, 43; Leiden: E.J. Brill, 1991), pp. 222-35.

—'Night Without Vision: Micah and the Prophets', in F. García Martínez, A. Hilhorst and C.J. Labuschagne (eds.), *The Scriptures and the Scrolls: Studies in Honour of A.S. van der Woude on the Occasion of his 65th Birthday* (VTSup, 49; Leiden: E.J. Brill, 1992), pp. 74-84.

—'Poets not Prophets: A Response to "Prophets through the Looking Glass"', *JSOT* 27 (1983), pp. 25-31.

—'Whose Prophet? Whose History? Whose Social Reality? Troubling the Interpretative

Community Again: Notes towards a Response to T.W. Overholt's Critique', *JSOT* 48 (1990), pp. 33-49.

Carroll R., M.D., *Contexts for Amos: Prophetic Poetics in Latin American Perspective* (JSOTSup, 132; Sheffield: JSOT Press, 1992).

—'דלל', in *NIDOTTE*, I, pp. 951-54.

—'God and His People in the Nations' History: A Contextualised Reading of Amos 1–2', *TynBul* 47 (1996), pp. 39-70.

—'The Prophetic Text and the Literature of Dissent in Latin America: Amos, García Márquez, and Cabrera Infante Dismantle Militarism', *BibInt* 4 (1996), pp. 76-100.

—'Reflecting on War and Utopia in the Book of Amos: The Relevance of a Literary Reading of the Prophetic Text for Central America', in *idem*, D.J.A. Clines and P.R. Davies (eds.), *The Bible in Human Society: Essays in Honour of John Rogerson* (JSOTSup, 200; Sheffield: Sheffield Academic Press, 1995), pp. 105-21.

Cassirer, E., *Philosophie der symbolischen Formen* (4 vols.; Darmstadt: Wissenschaftliche Buchgesellschaft, new edn, 1994).

Cazelles, H., 'L'arrière-plan historique d'Amos 1,9-10', in Shinan (ed.), *Proceedings of the Sixth World Congress of Jewish Studies*, I, pp. 71-76.

Ceresko, A.R., 'The A:B::B:A Word Pattern in Hebrew and Northwest Semitic, with Special Reference to the Book of Job', *UF* 7 (1975), pp. 73-88.

—'The Chiastic Word Pattern in Hebrew', *CBQ* 38 (1976), pp. 303-11.

—'The Function of Chiasmus in Hebrew Poetry', *CBQ* 40 (1978), pp. 1-10.

—'Janus Parallelism in Amos's "Oracles Against the Nations" (Amos 1.3–2.16)', *JBL* 113 (1994), pp. 485-90.

Chambers, T.W., 'The Literary Character of Amos', *The Old Testament Student* 3.1 (1883), pp. 2-6.

Childs, B.S., 'The Canonical Shape of the Prophetic Literature', *Int* 32 (1978), pp. 46-55.

—'Deuteronomic Formulae of the Exodus Tradition', *VT* 17 (1967), pp. 30-39.

—*Introduction to the Old Testament as Scripture* (Philadelphia: Fortress Press, 1979).

Chisholm, R.B., Jr, '"For Three Sins… Even For Four": The Numerical Sayings of Amos', *BSac* 147 (1990), pp. 188-97.

Christensen, D.L., 'The Prosodic Structure of Amos 1–2', *HTR* 67 (1974), pp. 427-36.

—*Transformations of the War Oracle in Old Testament Prophecy: Studies in the Oracles against the Nations* (HDR, 3; Missoula: Scholars Press, 1975).

Clark, D.J., 'Vision and Oracle in Zechariah 1–6', in Bergen (ed.), *Biblical Hebrew*, pp. 529-60.

Classen, C.J., 'St Paul's Epistles and Ancient Greek and Roman Rhetoric', in S.E. Porter and T.H. Olbricht (eds.), *Rhetoric and the New Testament: Essays from the 1992 Heidelberg Conference* (JSNTSup, 90; Sheffield: JSOT Press, 1993), pp. 265-91.

Clauss, M., *Gesellschaft und Staat in Juda und Israel* (Eichstätter Hochschulreden, 48; Munich: Minerva, 1985).

Clements, R.E., 'Amos and the Politics of Israel', in Garrone and Israel (eds.), *Storia e Tradizioni di Israele*, pp. 49-64.

—*Prophecy and Covenant* (SBT, 43; London: SCM Press, 1965).

—'Prophecy as Literature: A Re-appraisal', in D.G. Miller (ed.), *The Hermeneutical Quest. Essays in Honor of J.L. Mays for his 65th Birthday* (PTMS, 4; Allison Park: Pickwick Press, 1986), pp. 56-76.

—'The Prophet and his Editors', in D.J.A. Clines, S.E. Fowl and S.E. Porter (eds.), *The Bible in Three Dimensions: Essays in Celebration of Forty Years of Biblical Studies in the University of Sheffield* (JSOTSup, 87; Sheffield: JSOT Press, 1990), pp. 203-20.

Clifford, R.J., *Fair Spoken and Persuading: An Interpretation of Second Isaiah* (New York: Paulist Press, 1984).

—'Rhetorical Criticism in the Exegesis of Hebrew Poetry', in P.J. Achtemeier (ed.), *SBLSP*, 19 (Missoula: Scholars Press, 1980), pp. 17-28.

Clines, D.J.A., *Ezra, Nehemiah, and Esther* (NCB; Grand Rapids: Eerdmans, 1984).

—'Introduction', in idem, *What Does Eve Do to Help? and Other Readerly Questions to the Old Testament* (JSOTSup, 94; Sheffield: Sheffield Academic Press, 1990), pp. 9-24.

—*Job 1–20* (WBC, 17; Dallas: Word Books, 1989).

—'Was There an *'bl* II "Be Dry" in Classical Hebrew?', *VT* 42 (1992), pp. 1-10.

Clines, D.J.A., D.M. Gunn and A.J. Hauser (eds.), *Art and Meaning: Rhetoric in Biblical Literature* (JSOTSup, 19; Sheffield: JSOT Press, 1982).

Coats, G.W., and B.O. Lang (eds.), *Canon and Authority: Essays in Old Testament Religion and Theology* (Philadelphia: Fortress Press, 1977).

Cohen, S., 'The Political Background of the Words of Amos', *HUCA* 36 (1965), pp. 153-60.

Collins, T., *The Mantle of Elijah: The Redaction Criticism of the Prophetical Books* (BibSem, 20; Sheffield: JSOT Press, 1993).

Condamin, A., *Poèmes de la Bible: Avec une introduction sur la strophique hébraïque* (Paris: Beauchesne, 1933).

Conrad, E.W., 'The End of Prophecy and the Appearance of Angels/Messengers in the Book of the Twelve', *JSOT* 73 (1997), pp. 65-79.

—'Prophet, Redactor and Audience: Reforming the Notion of Isaiah's Formation', in R.F. Melugin and M.A. Sweeney (eds.), *New Visions of Isaiah* (JSOTSup, 214; Sheffield: Sheffield Academic Press, 1996), pp. 306-26.

Coogan, M.D. (ed.), *Scripture and other Artifacts: Essays in Honor of Philip J. King* (Louisville, KY: Westminster/John Knox Press, 1994).

Coote, R.B., 'Amos 1.11: *rhmyw*', *JBL* 90 (1971), pp. 206-208.

—*Amos among the Prophets: Composition and Theology* (Philadelphia: Fortress Press, 1981).

Corbett, E.P.J., *Classical Rhetoric for the Modern Student* (New York: Oxford University Press, 3rd edn, 1990).

—*Rhetorical Analyses of Literary Works* (New York: Oxford University Press, 1969).

Cornelius, I., 'נֶקֶד', in *NIDOTTE*, III, p. 151.

Cotterell, P., 'Linguistics, Meaning, Semantics, and Discourse Analysis', in *NIDOTTE*, I, pp. 134-60.

Craig, K.M., Jr, 'Interrogatives in Haggai–Zechariah: A Literary Thread?', in Watts and House (eds.), *Forming Prophetic Literature*, pp. 224-44.

Craigie, P.C., 'Amos the *nōqēd* in the Light of Ugaritic', *SR* 11 (1982), pp. 29-33.

—*Psalms 1–50* (WBC, 19; Waco, TX: Word Books, 1983).

Cramer, K., *Amos: Versuch einer theologischen Interpretation* (BWANT, 51; Stuttgart: W. Kohlhammer, 1930).

Crenshaw, J.L., 'Amos and the Theophanic Tradition', *ZAW* (1968), pp. 203-15.

—*Hymnic Affirmation of Divine Justice: The Doxologies of Amos and Related Texts in the Old Testament* (SBLDS, 24; Missoula: Scholars Press, 1975).

—'The Influence of the Wise upon Amos: The "Doxologies of Amos" and Job 5 9-16; 9 5-10', *ZAW* 79 (1967), pp. 42-52.

—'"A Liturgy of Wasted Opportunity" (Am. 4.6-12; Isa. 9.7–10.4; 5.25-29)', *Semitics* 1 (1970), pp. 27-37.

—'*Wedōrēk 'al-bāmŏtê 'āreṣ*', *CBQ* 34 (1972), pp. 39-53.

—'*YHWH Ṣeba'ôt šemô*: A Form-Critical Analysis', *ZAW* 81 (1969), pp. 156-75.

Crocker, P.T., 'History and Archaeology in the Oracles of Amos', *Buried History: A Quarterly Newsletter of the Australian Institute of Archaeology* 23 (1987), pp. 7-15.

Cross, F.M., *Canaanite Myth and Hebrew Epic: Essays in the History of the Religion of Israel* (Cambridge, MA: Harvard University Press, 1973).

Crüsemann, F., *Studien zur Formgeschichte von Hymnus und Danklied in Israel* (WMANT, 32; Neukirchen–Vluyn: Neukirchener Verlag, 1969).

—'Vorwort', in Schwantes, *Das Land kann seine Worte nicht ertragen*, pp. 8-11.

Daiches, S., 'Amos iii. 3-8', *ExpTim* 26 (1914–15), p. 237.

Dalley, S., 'Foreign Chariotry and Cavalry in the Armies of Tiglat-Pileser III and Sargon II', *Iran* 47 (1985), pp. 31-48.

Darr, K.P., 'Literary Perspectives on Prophetic Literature', in Mays, Petersen and Richards (eds.), *Old Testament Interpretation*, pp. 127-43.

Davies, G.H., 'Amos—The Prophet of Re-Union', *ExpTim* 92 (1980–81), pp. 196-200.

Davies, G.I., *Hosea* (OTG; Sheffield: JSOT Press, 1993).

Dawson, D.A., *Text-Linguistics and Biblical Hebrew* (JSOTSup, 177; Sheffield: Sheffield Academic Press, 1994).

Day, J., 'Pre-Deuteronomic Allusions to the Covenant in Hosea and Psalm lxxviii', *VT* 36 (1986), pp. 1-12.

Dearman, J.A., *Property Rights in the Eighth-Century Prophets: The Conflict and Its Background* (SBLDS, 106; Atlanta: Scholars Press, 1988).

Deissler, A., *Dann wirst du Gott erkennen: Die Grundbotschaft der Propheten* (Freiburg: Herder, 1987).

Dell, K.J., 'The Misuse of Forms in Amos', *VT* 45 (1995), pp. 45-61.

Dempster, S., 'Amos 3: Apologia of a Prophet', *BRT* 5 (1995), pp. 35-51.

—'The Lord is His Name: A Study of the Distribution of the Names and Titles of God in the Book of Amos', *RB* 98 (1991), pp. 170-89.

Dietrich, M., and O. Loretz, 'Die ugaritische Berufsgruppe der *NQDM* und das Amt des *RB NQDM*', *UF* 9 (1977), pp. 336-37.

Dietrich, W., 'JHWH, Israel und die Völker beim Propheten Amos', *TZ* 48 (1992), pp. 315-28.

Dietrich, W., and C. Link, *Die dunklen Seiten Gottes. I. Willkür und Gewalt* (Neukirchen–Vluyn: Neukirchener Verlag, 3rd edn, 2000).

Dijkema, F., 'Le fond des prophéties d'Amos', in *OTS*, 2 (Leiden: E.J. Brill, 1943), pp. 18-34.

Dines, J., 'Reading the Book of Amos', *ScrB* 16 (1986), pp. 26-32.

Dobbs-Allsopp, F.W., 'Rethinking Historical Criticism', *BibInt* 7 (1999), pp. 235-71.

Domeris, W.R., 'אֶבְיוֹן', in *NIDOTTE*, I, pp. 228-32.

Donner, H., 'Die soziale Botschaft der Propheten im Lichte der Gesellschaftsordnung in Israel', in Neumann (ed.), *Das Prophetenverständnis*, pp. 493-514.

Doré, J., P. Grelot and M. Carrez (eds.), *De la Tôrah au Messie: Études d'exégèse et d'herméneutique bibliques offertes à Henri Cazelles* (Paris: Desclée, 1981).

Dorsey, D.A., 'Literary Architecture and Aural Structuring Techniques in Amos', *Bib* 73 (1992), pp. 305-30.

Dozeman, T.B., 'Old Testament Rhetorical Criticism', in *ABD*, V, pp. 712-15.

Driver, G.R., 'Babylonian and Hebrew Notes', *WO* 2 (1954), pp. 20-21.

—'Confused Hebrew Roots', in B. Schindler and A. Marmorstein (eds.), *Occident and Orient, Being Studies in Semitic Philology and Literature, Jewish History and Philosophy and Folklore in the Widest Sense, in Honour of Haham Dr. M. Gaster's 80th Birthday* (London: Taylor's Foreign Press, 1936), pp. 73-82.

Duhm, B., *Die Theologie der Propheten als Grundlage für die innere Entwicklungsgeschichte der israelitischen Religion* (Bonn: Marcus, 1875).

Duke, R.K., *The Persuasive Appeal of the Chronicler: A Rhetorical Analysis* (JSOTSup, 88; BLS, 25; Sheffield: Almond Press, 1990).

Dumbrell, W.J., 'עָנָה', in *NIDOTTE*, III, pp. 454-64.

Du Plessis, J.G., 'Clarity and Obscurity: A Study in Textual Communication of the Relation between Sender, Parable, and Receiver in the Synoptic Gospels' (D. Theol. dissertation, University of Stellenbosch, 1985).

—'Speech Act Theory and New Testament Interpretation with Special Reference to G.N. Leech's Pragmatic Principles', in P.J. Hartin and J.H. Petzer (eds.), *Text and Interpretation: New Approaches in the Criticism of the New Testament* (Leiden: E.J. Brill, 1991), pp. 129-42.

Dürr, L., *Die Wertung des göttlichen Wortes im Alten Testament und im antiken Orient. Zugleich ein Beitrag zur Vorgeschichte des neutestamentlichen Logosbegriffes* (MVAG, 42.1; Leipzig: J.C. Hinrichs, 1938).

Eagleton, T., 'J.L. Austin and the Book of Jonah', in R.M. Schwartz (ed.), *The Book and the Text: The Bible and Literary Theory* (Oxford: Basil Blackwell, 1990), pp. 231-36.

—*Literary Theory: An Introduction* (Oxford: Basil Blackwell, 2nd edn, 1996).

Eco, U., 'Between Author and Text', in *idem et al.*, *Interpretation and Overinterpretation*, pp. 67-88.

—*Die Grenzen der Interpretation* (trans. G. Memmert; Munich: Deutscher Taschenbuch Verlag, 1995).

—'Interpretation and History', in *idem et al.*, *Interpretation and Overinterpretation*, pp. 23-43.

—*Lector in fabula: Die Mitarbeit der Interpretation in erzählenden Texten* (Munich: Deutscher Taschenbuch Verlag, 1990).

—*Nachschrift zum 'Namen der Rose'* (trans. B. Kroeber; Munich: Deutscher Taschenbuch Verlag, 8th edn, 1987).

—*The Open Work* (trans. A. Cancogni; London: Hutchinson Radius, 1989).

—*The Search for the Perfect Language* (trans. J. Fentress; London: Fontana, 1997).

Eco, U., *et al.*, *Interpretation and Overinterpretation* (ed. S. Collini; Cambridge: Cambridge University Press, 1992).

Ehninger, D., 'A Synoptic View of Systems of Western Rhetoric', *QJS* 61 (1975), pp. 448-53.

Eichrodt, W., *Theologie des Alten Testaments* (2 vols.; Stuttgart: Klotz, 1962–64).

—'Die Vollmacht des Amos. Zu einer schwierigen Stelle im Amosbuch', in H. Donner, R. Hanhart and R. Smend (eds.), *Beiträge zur alttestamentlichen Theologie: Festschrift für Walther Zimmerli zum 70. Geburtstag* (Göttingen: Vandenhoeck & Ruprecht, 1977), pp. 124-31.

Eising, H., 'נָאַם', in *ThWAT*, V, pp. 119-23.

Eissfeldt, O., 'Etymologische und archäologische Erklärung alttestamentlicher Wörter', *OrAnt* 5 (1966), pp. 166-71.

—*The Old Testament: An Introduction* (trans. P.R. Ackroyd; New York: Harper & Row, 1965).

Elliger, K., *Leviticus* (HAT, 1.4; Tübingen: J.C.B. Mohr [Paul Siebeck], 1966).

Emerton, J.A., 'An Examination of Some Attempts to Defend the Unity of the Flood Narrative in Genesis', *VT* 37 (1987), pp. 401-420; and *VT* 38 (1988), pp. 1-21.

Eslinger, L., 'The Education of Amos', *HAR* 11 (1987), pp. 35-57.

—*House of God or House of David: The Rhetoric of 2 Samuel 7* (JSOTSup, 164; Sheffield: JSOT Press, 1994).

Eubanks, S.W., 'Amos: Artist in Literary Composition' (unpubl. dissertation, Louisville, KY: Southern Baptist Theological Seminary, 1942).

Fabry, H.-J., 'דַּל, דָּלַל, דַּלָּה, דַּלָּה, זְלַל', in *TDOT*, III, pp. 208-30.

—'מֶרְזַח', in *TWAT*, V, pp. 11-16.

Fendler, M., 'Zur Sozialkritik des Amos: Versuch einer wirtschafts- und sozialgeschichtlichen Interpretation alttestamentlicher Texte', *EvT* 33 (1973), pp. 32-53.

Fensham, F.C., 'Common Trends in Curses of the Near Eastern Treaties and *Kudurru*-Inscriptions Compared with Maledictions of Amos and Isaiah', *ZAW* 75 (1963), pp. 155-75.

Fey, R., *Amos und Jesaja: Abhängigkeit und Eigenständigkeit des Jesaja* (WMANT, 12; Neukirchen–Vluyn: Neukirchener Verlag, 1963).

Fichtner, J., 'Jesaja unter den Weisen', *TLZ* 74 (1949), pp. 75-80.

Finley, T.J., and G. Payton, 'A Discourse Analysis of Isaiah 7–12', *JOTT* 6 (1993), pp. 317-35.

Fish, S., *Is There a Text in This Class? The Authority of Interpretive Communities* (Cambridge, MA: Harvard University Press, 1980).

Fishbane, M., 'Additional Remarks on *rhmyw* (Amos 1.11)', *JBL* 91 (1972), pp. 391-93.

—*Biblical Interpretation in Ancient Israel* (Oxford: Clarendon Press, 1985).

—'The Treaty-Background of Amos 1.11 and Related Matters', *JBL* 89 (1970), pp. 313-18.

Fleischer, G., *Von Menschenverkäufern, Baschankühen und Rechtsverkehrern: Die Sozialkritik des Amosbuches in historisch-kritischer, sozialgeschichtlicher und archäologischer Perspektive* (BBB, 74; Frankfurt: Athenäum, 1989).

Fohrer, G., 'Bemerkungen zum neueren Verständnis der Propheten', in Neumann (ed.), *Das Prophetenverständnis*, pp. 475-92.

—'Prophetie und Magie', *ZAW* 78 (1966), pp. 25-47.

—'Überlieferungskritik, Kompositions- und Redaktionskritik, Zeit- und Verfasserfrage', in *idem et al.*, *Exegese des Alten Testaments*, pp. 119-50.

—'Zion–Jerusalem im Alten Testament', in *TWNT*, VII, pp. 292-318.

Fohrer, G., *et al.*, *Exegese des Alten Testaments: Einführung in die Methodik* (UTB, 267; Heidelberg: Quelle & Meyer, 5th rev. edn, 1989).

Foley, J.M., *Immanent Art: From Structure to Meaning in Traditional Oral Epic* (Bloomington: Indiana University Press, 1991).

Fowler, R.M., 'Who Is "The Reader" in Reader Response Criticism?', in House (ed.), *Beyond Form Criticism*, pp. 376-94.

Fox, M.V., 'The Rhetoric of Ezekiel's Vision of the Valley of the Bones', in Gordon (ed.), *'The Place Is Too Small for Us'*, pp. 176-90.

Freedman, D.N., 'The Burning Bush', *Bib* 50 (1969), p. 246.

—'Confrontations in the Book of Amos', *PSB* 11 (1990), pp. 240-52.

—'Deliberate Deviation from an Established Pattern of Repetition in Hebrew Poetry as a Rhetorical Device', in *Proceedings of the Ninth World Congress of Jewish Studies. Division A: The Period of the Bible* (Jerusalem: World Union of Jewish Studies, 1986), pp. 45-52.

Freedman, D.N., and F.I. Andersen, 'Harmon in Amos 4.3', *BASOR* 198 (1970), p. 41.

Freedman, D.N., and A. Welch, 'Amos's Earthquake and Israelite Prophecy', in Coogan (ed.), *Scripture and Other Artifacts*, pp. 188-98.

Fritz, V., 'Amosbuch, Amos-Schule und historischer Amos', in *idem*, Pohlmann and Schmitt (eds.), *Prophet und Prophetenbuch*, pp. 29-43.

—'Die Fremdvölkersprüche des Amos', *VT* 37 (1987), pp. 26-38.

Fritz, V., K.-F. Pohlmann and H.-C. Schmitt (eds.), *Prophet und Prophetenbuch. Festschrift für Otto Kaiser zum 65. Geburtstag* (BZAW, 185; Berlin: W. de Gruyter, 1989).

Frost, S.B., 'Asseverations by Thanksgiving', *VT* 8 (1958), pp. 380-90.

Frye, N., *The Great Code: The Bible and Literature* (San Diego: Harcourt Brace Jovanovich, 1983).

—'Rhetorical Criticism: Theory of Genres', in *idem, Anatomy of Criticism: Four Essays* (Harmondsworth: Penguin Books, 1990), pp. 241-337.

Fuhrmann, M., *Die antike Rhetorik: Eine Einführung* (Zürich: Artemis & Winkler, 4th edn, 1995).

Fuhs, H.F., 'Amos 1,1: Erwägungen zur Tradition und Redaktion des Amosbuches', in H.-J. Fabry (ed.), *Bausteine biblischer Theologie: Festgabe für G. Johannes Botterweck zum 60. Geburtstag dargebracht von seinen Schülern* (BBB, 50; Cologne: Peter Hanstein: 1977), pp. 271-89.

García-Treto, F.O., 'A Reader-Response Approach to Prophetic Conflict: The Case of Amos 7.10-17', in J.C. Exum and D.J.A. Clines (eds.), *The New Literary Criticism and the Hebrew Bible* (JSOTSup, 143; Sheffield: JSOT Press, 1993), pp. 114-24.

Garrone, D., and F. Israel (eds.), *Storia e Tradizioni di Israele: Scritti in Onore di J. Alberto Soggin* (Brescia: Paideia, 1991).

Gaster, T.H., 'An Ancient Hymn in the Prophecies of Amos', *Journal of the Manchester Egyptian and Oriental Society* 19 (1935), pp. 23-26.

Genette, G., 'Rhetoric Restrained', in *idem, Figures of Literary Discourse* (trans. A. Sheridan; New York: Columbia University Press, 1982), pp. 103-26.

Gerstenberger, E.S., 'עָנָה II, עֲנָה, עֱנוּת, עֹנָה, תַּעֲנִית, עֳנִי, עָנָו', in *ThWAT*, VI, pp. 247-70.

Gese, H., 'Kleine Beiträge zum Verständnis des Amosbuches', *VT* 12 (1962), pp. 417-38.

—'Komposition bei Amos', in J.A. Emerton (ed.), *Congress Volume, Vienna 1980* (VTSup, 32; Leiden: E.J. Brill, 1981), pp. 74-95.

Geyer, J.B., 'Mythology and Culture in the Oracles Against the Nations', *VT* 36 (1986), pp. 129-45.

Gibbons, S., *Cold Comfort Farm* (Harmondsworth: Penguin Books, 1938).

Gibson, J.C.L., *Language and Imagery in the Old Testament* (London: SPCK, 1998).

Giles, T., '*Dal* and *'ebyon*: The Poor and the Needy in the Book of Amos', *BRT* 1 (1991), pp. 12-20.

Gillingham, S.E., ' "Der die Morgenröte zur Finsternis macht": Gott und Schöpfung im Amosbuch', *EvT* 53 (1993), pp. 109-23.

Ginsberg, H.L., *The Israelian Heritage of Judaism* (New York: Jewish Theological Seminary, 1982).

—' "Roots Below and Fruit Above" and Related Matters', in D.W. Thomas and W.D. McHardy (eds.), *Hebrew and Semitic Studies: Presented to Godfrey Rolles Driver in Celebration of his Seventieth Birthday, 20 August 1962* (Oxford: Clarendon Press, 1963), pp. 72-76.

Gitay, Y., 'Deutero-Isaiah: Oral or Written?', *JBL* 99 (1980), pp. 185-97.

—*Isaiah and His Audience: The Structure and Meaning of Isaiah 1–12* (StSN, 30; Assen: Van Gorcum, 1991).

—*Prophecy and Persuasion: A Study of Isaiah 40–48* (Forum theologiae linguisticae, 14; Bonn: Linguistica Biblica, 1981).

—'Reflections on the Study of the Prophetic Discourse: The Question of Isaiah 1.2-20', *VT* 33 (1983), pp. 207-21.

—'Rhetorical Criticism', in S.L. McKenzie and S.R. Haynes (eds.), *To Each Its Own Meaning: An Introduction to Biblical Criticisms and Their Application* (London: Geoffrey Chapman, 1993), pp. 135-49.

—'A Study of Amos's Art of Speech: A Rhetorical Analysis of Amos 3.1-15', *CBQ* 42 (1980), pp. 293-309.

Goldingay, J.E., 'Isaiah 42.18-25', *JSOT* 67 (1995), pp. 43-65.

—'The Logic of Intercession', *Theology* 101 (1998), pp. 262-70.

Good, E.M., *Irony in the Old Testament* (BLS; Sheffield: Almond Press, 2nd edn, 1981).

Gordis, R., 'The Composition and Structure of Amos', in *idem, Poets, Prophets and Sages: Essays in Biblical Interpretation* (Bloomington: Indiana University Press, 1971), pp. 217-29.

—'Edom, Israel and Amos—An Unrecognized Source for Edomite History', in A.I. Katsh and L. Lemoy (eds.), *Essays on the Occasion of the Seventieth Anniversary of the Dropsie University* (Philadelphia: Dropsie University, 1979), pp. 109-32.

—'The Heptads as an Element of Biblical and Rabbinic Style', *JBL* 62 (1943), pp. 17-26.

—'Some Hitherto Unrecognized Meanings of the Verb *Shub*', *JBL* 52 (1933), pp. 153-62.

—'Studies in the Book of Amos', *PAAJR* 46–47 (1979–80), pp. 201-46.

Gordon, R.P. (ed.), *'The Place Is Too Small for Us': The Israelite Prophets in Recent Scholarship* (SBTS, 5; Winona Lake, IN: Eisenbrauns, 1995).

Gosse, B., 'Le recueil d'oracles contre les nations du livre d'Amos et l'"histoire deutéronomique"', *VT* 38 (1988), pp. 22-40.

Gottlieb, H., 'Amos und Jerusalem', *VT* 17 (1967), pp. 430-63.

Gottwald, N.K., *All the Kingdoms of the Earth: Israelite Prophecy and International Relations in the Ancient Near East* (New York: Harper & Row, 1964).

Graffy, A., *A Prophet Confronts His People: The Disputation Speech in the Prophets* (AnBib, 104; Rome: Biblical Institute Press, 1984).

Gray, J., 'The Day of Yahweh in Cultic Experience and Eschatological Prospect', *SEÅ* 39 (1974), pp. 5-37.

Green, J.B., 'Discourse Analysis and New Testament Interpretation', in Green (ed.), *Hearing the New Testament*, pp. 175-96.

Green, J.B. (ed.), *Hearing the New Testament: Strategies for Interpretation* (Grand Rapids: Eerdmans, 1995).

Greenfield, J.C., 'The *Marzeaḥ* as a Social Institution', *Acta antiqua academiae scientarum hungaricae* 22 (1974), pp. 451-55.

Greenstein, E.L., 'How Does Parallelism Mean?', in *A Sense of Text: The Art of Language in the Study of Biblical Literature. Papers from a Symposium at The Dropsie College for Hebrew and Cognate Learning, May 11, 1982* (JQRSup; Winona Lake, IN: Eisenbrauns, 1983), pp. 41-70.

Greenwood, D., 'Rhetorical Criticism and Formgeschichte: Some Methodological Considerations', *JBL* 89 (1970), pp. 418-26.

Gressmann, H., *Der Ursprung der israelitisch-jüdischen Eschatologie* (FRLANT, 6; Göttingen: Vandenhoeck & Ruprecht, 1905).

Grether, O., *Name und Wort Gottes im Alten Testament* (BZAW, 64; Giessen: Alfred Töpelmann, 1934).

Grice, H.P., 'Logic and Conversation', in P. Cole and J.L. Morgan (eds.), *Syntax and Semantics. III. Speech-Acts* (New York: Academic Press, 1975), pp. 41-58.

—'Utterance-Meaning, Sentence-Meaning, and Word-Meaning', in J.R. Searle (ed.), *The Philosophy of Language* (London: Oxford University Press, 1971), pp. 54-70.

Gross, W., 'Die Herausführungsformel: Zum Verhältnis von Formel und Syntax', *ZAW* 86 (1974), pp. 425-53.

Gross, W. (ed.), *Jeremia und die 'deuteronomistische Bewegung'* (BBB, 98; Weinheim: Beltz Athenäum, 1995).

Gunkel, H., 'Die geheimen Erfahrungen der Propheten', in Neumann (ed.), *Das Prophetenverständnis*, pp. 109-43.

—'The Prophets as Writers and Poets' (trans. J.L. Schaaf), in D.L. Petersen (ed.), *Prophecy in Israel: Search for an Identity* (Issues in Religion and Theology, 10; Philadelphia: Fortress Press, 1987), pp. 22-73.

Gunn, D.M., and D.N. Fewell, *Narrative in the Hebrew Bible* (OBS; Oxford: Oxford University Press, 1993).

Habel, N., 'The Form and Significance of the Call Narratives', *ZAW* 77 (1965), pp. 297-323.

Hancher, M., 'Performative Utterances, the Word of God, and the Death of the Author', in White (ed.), *Speech Act Theory*, pp. 27-40.

Haran, M., 'The Graded Numerical Sequence and Phenomenon of "Automatism" in Biblical Poetry', in *Congress Volume, Uppsala 1971* (VTSup, 22; Leiden: E.J. Brill, 1972), pp. 238-67.

—'Observations on the Historical Background of Amos 1.2–2.6', *IEJ* 18 (1968), pp. 201-12.

—'The Rise and Decline of the Empire of Jeroboam ben Joash', *VT* 17 (1967), pp. 266-97.

Hardmeier, C., 'Die judäische Unheilsprophetie: Antwort auf einen Gesellschafts- und Normenwandel im Israel des 8. Jahrhunderts vor Christus', *Der altsprachliche Unterricht* 26 (1983), pp. 20-44.

—*Texttheorie und biblische Exegese: Zur rhetorischen Funktion der Trauermetaphorik in der Prophetie* (BEvT, 79; Munich: Chr. Kaiser Verlag, 1978).

Harré, R., and R. Lamb (eds.), *The Encyclopedic Dictionary of Psychology* (Oxford: Basil Blackwell, 1983).

Harrison, R.K., *Jeremiah and Lamentations: An Introduction and Commentary* (TOTC; Leicester: IVP, 1973).

Hasel, G.F., 'The Alleged "No" of Amos and Amos' Eschatology', *AUSS* 29 (1991), pp. 3-18.

—*The Remnant: The History and Theology of the Remnant Idea from Genesis to Isaiah* (AUMSR, 5; Berrien Springs: Andrews University Press, 3rd edn, 1980).

—*Understanding the Book of Amos: Basic Issues in Current Interpretations* (Grand Rapids: Baker Book House, 1991).

Hayden, R.E., 'אבל', in *NIDOTTE*, I, p. 248.

—'בשׁ', in *NIDOTTE*, II, pp. 393-94.

Hayes, J.H., 'Amos's Oracles Against the Nations (1.2–2.16)', *RevExp* 92 (1995), pp. 153-67.

—'The Oracles against the Nations in the Old Testament: Their Usage and Theological Importance' (Th.D. dissertation, Princeton Theological Seminary, 1964).

—'The Usage of Oracles against Foreign Nations in Ancient Israel', *JBL* 87 (1968), pp. 81-92.

Hehn, J., 'Zur Bedeutung der Siebenzahl', in K. Budde (ed.), *Vom Alten Testament. Karl Marti zum siebzigsten Geburtstage* (BZAW, 41; Giessen: Alfred Töpelmann, 1925), pp. 128-36.

—*Siebenzahl und Sabbat bei den Babyloniern und im Alten Testament: Eine religions-geschichtliche Studie* (Leipziger semitistische Studien, 2.5; Leipzig: J.C. Hinrichs, 1907).

Henry, M.L., 'Pferd', in *BHH*, III, pp. 1438-39.

Herder, J.G., *Vom Geist der ebräischen Poesie: Eine Einleitung für die Liebhaber derselben, und der ältesten Geschichte des menschlichen Geistes* (2 vols.; Dessau, 1782–83).

Hermisson, H.-J., *Studien zur israelitischen Spruchweisheit* (WMANT, 28; Neukirchen–Vluyn: Neukirchener Verlag, 1968).

Herrmann, J., 'Das Gebet im AT', in *TWNT*, II, pp. 782-99.

Heschel, A.J., *The Prophets* (New York: Harper & Row, 1962).

Hillers, D.R., 'Palmyrene Aramaic Inscriptions and the Old Testament, especially Amos 2.8', *ZAH* 8 (1995), pp. 55-62.

Hirsch, E.D., Jr, *Validity in Interpretation* (New Haven: Yale University Press, 1967).

Hobbs, T.R., 'Amos 3 $_{1b}$ and 2 $_{10}$', *ZAW* 81 (1969), pp. 384-87.

Höffken, P., 'Eine Bemerkung zum "Haus Hasaels" in Amos 1 $_4$', *ZAW* 94 (1982), pp. 413-15.

—*Untersuchungen zu den Begründungselementen der Völkerorakel des Alten Testaments* (Bonn, 1977).

Hoffman, Y., 'A North Israelite Typological Myth and a Judaean Historical Tradition: The Exodus in Hosea and Amos', *VT* 39 (1989), pp. 169-82.

Hogg, H.W., 'The Starting Point of the Religious Message of Amos', in P.S. Allen and J. de M. Johnson (eds.), *Transactions of the Third International Congress for the History of Religions*, I (Oxford: Clarendon Press, 1908), pp. 325-27.

Horst, F., 'Die Doxologien im Amosbuch', *ZAW* 47 (1929), pp. 45-54.

Hossfeld, F.L., and B. Kalthoff, 'הִצִּיל, נצל', in *TDOT*, IX, pp. 533-40.

House, P.R., 'Amos and Literary Criticism', *RevExp* 92 (1995), pp. 175-87.

—*The Unity of the Twelve* (JSOTSup, 97; BLS, 27; Sheffield: Almond Press, 1990).

—*Zephaniah: A Prophetic Drama* (BLS, 16; Sheffield: Almond Press, 1988).

House, P.R. (ed.), *Beyond Form Criticism: Essays in Old Testament Literary Criticism* (SBTS, 2; Winona Lake, IN: Eisenbrauns, 1992).

Houston, W., 'What Did the Prophets Think They Were Doing? Speech Acts and Prophetic Discourse in the Old Testament', in Gordon (ed.), *'The Place Is Too Small for Us'*, pp. 133-53.

Howard, D.M., Jr, 'Rhetorical Criticism in Old Testament Studies', *BBR* 4 (1994), pp. 87-104.

Huffmon, H.B., 'The Social Role of Amos' Message', in *idem*, F.A. Spina and A.R.W. Green (eds.), *The Quest for the Kingdom of God: Studies in Honor of George E. Mendenhall* (Winona Lake, IN: Eisenbrauns, 1983), pp. 109-16.

Humbert, P., 'Dieu fait sortir', *TZ* 18 (1962), pp. 357-61.

Hunter, A.V., *Seek the Lord! A Study of the Meaning and Function of the Exhortations in Amos, Hosea, Isaiah, Micah, and Zephaniah* (Baltimore: St Mary's Seminary & University, 1982).

Hutchinson, T. (ed.), *The Poems of William Wordsworth with Introductions and Notes* (London: Oxford University Press, 1923).

Isbell, C.D., 'A Note on Amos 1.1', *JNES* 36 (1977), pp. 213-14.

Iser, W., *Der Akt des Lesens: Theorie ästhetischer Wirkung* (UTB, 636; Munich: Fink, 3rd edn, 1990).

Jackson, J.J., and M. Kessler (eds.), *Rhetorical Criticism: Essays in Honor of James Muilenburg* (PTMS, 1; Pittsburgh: Pickwick Press, 1974).

Jacob, E., *Theology of the Old Testament* (trans. A.W. Heathcote and P.J. Allcock; London: Hodder & Stoughton, 1958).

Jacobs, P.F., ' "Cows of Bashan"—A Note on the Interpretation of Amos 4.1', *JBL* 104 (1985), pp. 109-10.

Jahnow, H., *Das hebräische Leichenlied im Rahmen der Völkerdichtung* (BZAW, 36; Giessen: Alfred Töpelmann, 1923).

Jarick, J., 'Prophets and Losses: Some Themes in Recent Study of the Prophets', *ExpTim* 107 (1995–96), pp. 75-77.

Jaruzelska, I., *Amos and the Officialdom in the Kingdom of Israel: The Socio-economic Position of the Officials in the Light of the Biblical, the Epigraphic and Archaeological Evidence* (Uniwersytet im. Adama Mickiewicza w Poznaniu, Seria Socjologie, 25; Poznań: Adam Mickiewicz University Press, 1998).

—'Social Structure in the Kingdom of Israel in the Eighth Century B.C. as Reflected in the Book of Amos', *Folia orientalia* 29 (1992–93), pp. 91-117.

Jeffrey, D.L., *People of the Book: Christian Identity and Literary Culture* (Grand Rapids: Eerdmans, 1996).

Jemielity, T., *Satire and the Hebrew Prophets* (Literary Currents in Biblical Interpretation; Louisville, KY: Westminster/John Knox Press, 1992).

Jenson, P.P., ' אַרְבַּע', in *NIDOTTE*, I, pp. 495-97.

Jepsen, A., 'מֶחֱזֶה, מַחֲזֶה, חִזָּיוֹן, חָזוּת, חֲזוֹת, חָזוֹן, חֹזֶה, חָזָה', in *TDOT*, IV, pp. 280-90.

Jeremias, J., 'Amos 3–6: Beobachtungen zur Entstehungsgeschichte eines Prophetenbuches', *ZAW* 100, Suppl. (1988), pp. 123-38.

—'Amos 3–6: From the Oral Word to the Text', in G.M. Tucker, D.L. Peterson and R.R. Wilson (eds.), *Canon, Theology, and Old Testament Interpretation: Essays in Honor of Brevard S. Childs* (Philadelphia: Fortress Press, 1988), pp. 217-29.

—'Zur Entstehung der Völkersprüche im Amosbuch', in *idem, Hosea und Amos*, pp. 172-82.

—'Grundtendenzen gegenwärtiger Prophetenforschung', in *idem, Hosea und Amos*, pp. 1-19.

—*Hosea und Amos: Studien zu den Anfängen des Dodekapropheton* (FAT, 13; Tübingen: J.C.B. Mohr [Paul Siebeck], 1996).

—'The Interrelationship Between Amos and Hosea', in Watts and House (eds.), *Forming Prophetic Literature*, pp. 171-86.

—*Kultprophetie und Gerichtsverkündigung in der späten Königszeit Israels* (WMANT, 35; Neukirchen–Vluyn: Neukirchener Verlag, 1970).

—'Die Mitte des Amosbuches (Am 4,4-13; 5,1-17), in *idem, Hosea und Amos*, pp. 198-213.

—'Das Proprium der alttestamentlichen Prophetie', in *idem, Hosea und Amos*, pp. 20-33.

—*Theophanie: Die Geschichte einer alttestamentlichen Gattung* (WMANT, 10; Neukirchen–Vluyn: Neukirchener Verlag, 2nd edn, 1977).

—'Tod und Leben in Amos 5,1-17', in *idem, Hosea und Amos*, pp. 214-30.

—'Das unzugängliche Heiligtum: Zur letzten Vision des Amos (Am 9,1-4)', in Bartelmus, Krüger and Utzschneider (eds.), *Konsequente Traditionsgeschichte*, pp. 155-67.

—'Völkersprüche und Visionsberichte im Amosbuch', in Fritz, Pohlmann and Schmitt (eds.), *Prophet und Prophetenbuch*, pp. 82-97.

—'"Zwei Jahre vor dem Erdbeben" (Am 1,1)', in *idem, Hosea und Amos*, pp. 183-97.

Johnson, B., 'צַדִּיק, צְדָקָה, צֶדֶק, צָדֵק', in *ThWAT*, VI, pp. 898-924.

Jones, G.H., 'An Examination of Some Leading Motifs in the Prophetic Oracles Against Foreign Nations' (dissertation, University of Wales at Bangor, 1970).

Jozaki, S., 'The Secondary Passages of the Book of Amos', *Kwansei Gakuin University Annual Studies* 4 (1956), pp. 25-100.

Kallner-Amiran, D.H., 'A Revised Earthquake Catalogue of Palestine', *IEJ* 1 (1950–51), pp. 223-246; and *IEJ* 2 (1952), pp. 48-65.

Kapelrud, A.S., *Central Ideas in Amos* (Oslo: Aschehoug, 1956).

—'God as Destroyer in the Preaching of Amos and in the Ancient Near East', *JBL* 71 (1952), pp. 33-38.

—'The Number Seven in Ugaritic Texts', *VT* 18 (1968), pp. 494-99.

Kedar-Kopfstein, B., 'קוֹל', in *ThWAT*, VI, pp. 1237-52.

Keel, O., 'Rechttun oder Annahme des drohenden Gerichts? Erwägungen zu Amos, dem frühen Jesaja und Micha', *BZ* NS 21 (1977), pp. 200-18.

Keil, C.F., *Jeremiah, Lamentations* (COT, 8; repr., Peabody, MA: Hendrickson, 1996).

Kellermann, U., 'Der Amosschluss als Stimme deuteronomistischer Heilshoffnung', *EvT* 29 (1969), pp. 169-83.

Kennedy, G.A., *The Art of Persuasion in Greece* (Princeton: Princeton University Press, 1963).

—*The Art of Rhetoric in the Roman World 300 B.C.–A.D. 300* (Princeton: Princeton University Press, 1972).

—*Classical Rhetoric and Its Christian and Secular Tradition from Ancient to Modern Times* (Chapel Hill: University of North Carolina Press, 1980).

—*Greek Rhetoric under Christian Emperors* (Princeton: Princeton University Press, 1983).

—*A New History of Classical Rhetoric: An Extensive Revision and Abridgment of* The Art of Persuasion in Greece, The Art of Rhetoric in the Roman World *and* Greek Rhetoric under Christian Emperors *with Additional Discussion of Late Latin Rhetoric* (Princeton: Princeton University Press, 1994).

—*New Testament Interpretation through Rhetorical Criticism* (Chapel Hill: University of North Carolina Press, 1984).

Kernan, A.B., *The Plot of Satire* (New Haven: Yale University Press, 1965).

Kessler, M., 'An Introduction to Rhetorical Criticism of the Bible: Prolegomena', *Semitics* 7 (1980), pp. 1-27.

—'A Methodological Setting for Rhetorical Criticism', in Clines, Gunn and Hauser (eds.), *Art and Meaning*, pp. 1-19.

Kida, K., 'The Sovereignty of God and the Destiny of the Nations in the Prophecies of Amos, Isaiah and Jeremiah', in Bartelmus, Krüger and Utzschneider (eds.), *Konsequente Traditionsgeschichte*, pp. 169-81.

Kikawada, I.M., 'Some Proposals for the Definition of Rhetorical Criticism', *Semitics* 5 (1977), pp. 67-91.

King, P.J., *Amos, Hosea, Micah: An Archaeological Commentary* (Philadelphia: Westminster Press, 1988).

—'The *Marzeah* Amos Denounces', *BARev* 15.4 (1988), pp. 34-44.

Klein, R.W., *1 Samuel* (WBC, 10; Waco, TX: Word Books, 1983).

Kleven, T., 'The Cows of Bashan: A Single Metaphor at Amos 4.1-3', *CBQ* 58 (1996), pp. 215-27.

Knierim, R.P., *Die Hauptbegriffe für Sünde im Alten Testament* (Gütersloh: Gütersloher Verlagshaus Gerd Mohn, 1965).

—' "I Will Not Cause It to Return" in Amos 1 and 2', in Coats and Long (eds.), *Canon and Authority*, pp. 163-75.

—'Old Testament Form Criticism Reconsidered', *Int* 27 (1973), pp. 435-68.

Koch, K., 'Die Entstehung der sozialen Kritik bei den Propheten', in Wolff (ed.), *Probleme biblischer Theologie*, pp. 236-57.

—*The Prophets*. I. *The Assyrian Period* (trans. M. Kohl; London: SCM Press, 1982).

—'Die Rolle der hymnischen Abschnitte in der Komposition des Amos-Buches', *ZAW* 86 (1974), pp. 504-37.

—*Was ist Formgeschichte? Methoden der Bibelexegese* (Neukirchen–Vluyn: Neukirchener Verlag, 3rd edn, 1974).

Koch, K., *et al.*, 'אֹרַח, שְׁבִיל, נְתִיבָה, נָתִיב, מַעְגָּל, הַלִיכָה, הָלַךְ, מְסִלָּה, חוּץ, שׁוּק, דֶּרֶךְ, דָּרַךְ', in *TDOT*, III, pp. 270-93.

Köckert, M., 'Das Gesetz und die Propheten in Amos 1–2', in J. Hausmann and H.-J. Zobel (eds.), *Alttestamentlicher Glaube und Biblische Theologie. Festschrift für Horst Dietrich Preuss zum 65. Geburtstag* (Stuttgart: W. Kohlhammer, 1992), pp. 145-54.

Koenen, K., *Heil den Gerechten—Unheil den Sündern! Ein Beitrag zur Theologie der Prophetenbücher* (BZAW, 229; Berlin: W. de Gruyter, 1994).

Köhler, L., *Deuterojesaja (Jes 40–55) stilkritisch untersucht* (BZAW, 37; Giessen: Alfred Töpelmann, 1923).

—'Die Morgenröte im Alten Testament', *ZAW* 44 (1926), pp. 56-59.

Kornfeld, W., 'Die Gesellschafts- und Kultkritik alttestamentlicher Propheten', in R. Schulte (ed.), *Leiturgia—Koinonia—Diakonia. FS Kardinal F. König* (Vienna: Herder, 1980), pp. 181-200.

Kraft, C.F., 'Some Further Observations Concerning the Strophic Structure of Hebrew Poetry', in E.C. Hobbs (ed.), *A Stubborn Faith: Papers on Old Testament and Related Subjects. Presented to Honor William Andrew Irwin* (Dallas: Southern Methodist University Press, 1956), pp. 62-89.

Kraus, H.-J., *Geschichte der historisch-kritischen Erforschung des Alten Testaments* (Neukirchen–Vluyn: Neukirchener Verlag, 4th edn, 1988).

—'Die prophetische Botschaft gegen das soziale Unrecht Israels', *EvT* 15 (1955), pp. 295-307.

Krause, H.-H., 'Der Gerichtsprophet Amos, ein Vorläufer des Deuteronomisten', *ZAW* 50 (1932), pp. 221-39.

Krause, M., *Das Verhältnis von sozialer Kritik und kommender Katastrophe in den Unheilsprophezeiungen des Amos* (Hamburg, 1972).

Kuenen, A., *De Profeten en de Profetie onder Israël: Historisch-dogmatische studie* (2 vols.; Leiden: Engels, 1875).

Kugel, J., *The Idea of Biblical Poetry: Parallelism and Its History* (New Haven: Yale University Press, 1981).

Kuhl, C., ' "Die Wiederaufnahme"—ein literarkritisches Prinzip?', *ZAW* 64 (1952), pp. 1-11.

Kuhn, T., *The Structure of Scientific Revolutions* (Chicago: University of Chicago Press, 2nd edn, 1970).

Kutsch, E., ' "Trauerbräuche" und "Selbstminderungsriten" im Alten Testament', *Theologische Studien* 78 (1965), pp. 23-42.

Labuschagne, C.J., *The Incomparability of Yahweh in the Old Testament* (Pretoria Oriental Series, 5; Leiden: E.J. Brill, 1966).

—'The Pattern of the Divine Speech Formulas in the Pentateuch: The Key to Its Literary Structure', *VT* 32 (1982), pp. 268-96.

Landy, F., 'Vision and Poetic Speech in Amos', *HAR* 11 (1987), pp. 223-46.

Lang, B., *Monotheism and the Prophetic Minority: An Essay in Biblical History and Sociology* (SWBA, 1; Sheffield: Almond Press, 1983).

—'Sklaven und Unfreie im Buch Amos (ii 6, viii 6)', *VT* 31 (1981), pp. 482-88.

Lausberg, H., *Elemente der literarischen Rhetorik* (Munich: Hueber, 8th edn, 1984).

—*Handbuch der literarischen Rhetorik: Eine Grundlegung der Literaturwissenschaft* (2 vols.; Munich: Hueber, 1960).

Leeuwen, C. van, 'Amos 1.2, Épigraphe du livre entier ou introduction aux oracles des chapitres 1–2?', in M. Boertien (ed.), *Verkenningen in een Stromgebied. Proeven von oudtestamentisch Onderzoek. Festschrift M.A. Beek* (Amsterdam: Theologisch Instituut, 1974), pp. 93-101.

—'The Prophecy of the *Yōm YHWH* in Amos V 18-20', in A.S. van der Woude (ed.), *Language and Meaning: Studies in Hebrew Language and Biblical Exegesis* (OTS, 19; Leiden: E.J. Brill, 1974), pp. 113-34.

Leeuwen, R.C. van, 'The Sage in the Prophetic Literature', in J.G. Gammie and L.G. Perdue (eds.), *The Sage in Israel and the Ancient Near East* (Winona Lake, IN: Eisenbrauns, 1990), pp. 295-306.

Lehming, S., 'Erwägungen zu Amos', *ZTK* 55 (1958), pp. 145-69.

Lenchak, T.A., *'Choose Life!' A Rhetorical-Critical Investigation of Deuteronomy 28,69–30,20* (AnBib, 129; Rome: Editrice Pontificio Istituto Biblico, 1993).

Lentricchia, F., *Criticism and Social Change* (Chicago: University of Chicago Press, 1983).

Levin, C., 'Amos und Jerobeam I.', *VT* 45 (1995), pp. 307-17.

Levine, M.P., 'Review of Nicholas Wolterstorff's *Divine Discourse*', *Mind* 106 (1997), pp. 359-63.

Lewis, C.S., *'De descriptione temporum'*, in idem, *Selected Literary Essays* (ed. W. Hooper; Cambridge: Cambridge University Press, 1969), pp. 1-14.

Lewis, R.L., 'The Persuasive Style and Appeals of the Minor Prophets Amos, Hosea, and Micah' (dissertation, University of Michigan, 1959).

Limburg, J., 'Sevenfold Structures in the Book of Amos', *JBL* 106 (1987), pp. 217-22.

Lindblom, J., *Die literarische Gattung der prophetischen Literatur* (Uppsala Universitetsårskrift Theologi, 1; Uppsala: Lundquist, 1924).

—*Prophecy in Ancient Israel* (Oxford: Basil Blackwell, 1962).

—'Wisdom in the Old Testament Prophets', in M. Noth and D.W. Thomas (eds.), *Wisdom in Israel and in the Ancient Near East: Presented to Prof. H.H. Rowley by the Society for Old Testament Study* (VTSup, 3; Leiden: E.J. Brill, 1955), pp. 192-204.

Lodge, D., *The Art of Fiction* (Harmondsworth: Penguin Books, 1992).

—'Beginning', in idem, *The Art of Fiction*, pp. 3-8.

—'Suspense', in idem, *The Art of Fiction*, pp. 13-16.

Lohfink, N., 'Bund als Vertrag im Deuteronomium', *ZAW* 107 (1995), pp. 215-39.

—'Gab es eine deuteronomistische Bewegung?', in Gross (ed.), *Jeremia und die 'deuteronomistische Bewegung'*, pp. 313-82.

Löhr, M., *Untersuchungen zum Buche Amos* (BZAW, 4; Giessen: Rickert, 1901).

Loretz, O., 'Ugaritisch-biblisch *mrzḥ*: "Kultmahl, Kultverein" in Jer 16,5 und Am 6,7', in L. Ruppert, P. Weimar and E. Zenger (eds.), *Künder des Wortes: Beiträge zur Theologie der Propheten. Josef Schreiner zum 60. Geburtstag* (Würzburg: Echter Verlag, 1982), pp. 87-93.

—'Vergleich und Kommentar in Amos 3,12', *BZ* NS 20 (1976), pp. 122-25.

Lowth, R., *Lectures on the Sacred Poetry of the Hebrews* (London: Tegg, 1835).

Lubsczyk, H., *Der Auszug Israels aus Ägypten: Seine theologische Bedeutung in prophetischer und priesterlicher Überlieferung* (Erfurter Theologische Studien, 11; Leipzig: St. Benno, 1963).

Lundblom, J.R., *Jeremiah: A Study in Ancient Hebrew Rhetoric* (SBLDS, 18; Missoula: Scholars Press, 1975).

Lust, J., 'Remarks on the Redaction of Amos V 4-6, 14-15', in B. Albrektson *et al.* (eds.), *Remembering All the Way ...: A Collection of Old Testament Studies Published on the Occasion of the Fortieth Anniversary of the Oudtestamentisch Werkgezelschap in Nederland* (OTS, 21; Leiden: E.J. Brill, 1981), pp. 129-54.

Lyons, J., *Introduction to Theoretical Linguistics* (Cambridge: Cambridge University Press, 1968).

Lys, D., *'Rûach', le souffle dans l'Ancien Testament: Enquête anthropologique à travers l'histoire théologique d'Israël* (Études d'histoire et de philosophie religieuses, 56; Paris: Presses Universitaires de France, 1962).

Maag, V., 'Amos', in *RGG*, I, pp. 328-31.

—*Text, Wortschatz und Begriffswelt des Buches Amos* (Leiden: E.J. Brill, 1951).

Mack, B.L., *Rhetoric and the New Testament* (GBS; Minneapolis: Fortress Press, 1990).

Majercik, R., 'Rhetoric and Oratory in the Greco-Roman World', in *ABD*, V, pp. 710-12.

Malamat, A., 'Amos 1.5 in the Light of the Til Barsip Inscriptions', *BASOR* 129 (1953), pp. 25-26.

Manguel, A., *A History of Reading* (London: Flamingo, 1996).

Marco, A. di, 'Der Chiasmus in der Bibel: Ein Beitrag zur strukturellen Stilistik', *LB* 36 (1975), pp. 21-97; and *LB* 37 (1976), pp. 49-68.

Margulis, B.B., 'Studies in the Oracles Against the Nations' (dissertation, Brandeis University, Waltham, MA, 1966).

Markert, L., *Struktur und Bezeichnung des Scheltworts: Eine gattungskritische Studie anhand des Amosbuches* (BZAW, 140; Berlin: W. de Gruyter, 1977).

Markert, L., and G. Wanke, 'Die Prophetinterpretation: Anfragen und Überlegungen', *KD* 22 (1976), pp. 191-220.

Marks, H., 'The Twelve Prophets', in Alter and Kermode (eds.), *The Literary Guide to the Bible*, pp. 207-33.

Marti, K., 'Zur Komposition von Amos 1 $_3$–2 $_3$', in W. Frankenberg and F. Küchler (eds.), *Abhandlungen zur semitischen Religionskunde und Sprachwissenschaft: Wolf Wilhelm Graf von Baudissin zum 26. September 1917 überreicht von Freunden und Schülern* (BZAW, 33; Giessen: Alfred Töpelmann, 1918), pp. 323-30.

Martin-Achard, R., *Amos: L'homme, le message, l'influence* (Publications de la Faculté de Théologie de l'Université de Genève, 7; Geneva: Labor et Fides, 1984).

Mason, R., *Propaganda and Subversion in the Old Testament* (London: SPCK, 1997).

Mathys, H.-P., *Dichter und Beter: Theologen aus spätalttestamentlicher Zeit* (OBO, 132; Freiburg: Universitätsverlag, 1994).

Mauchline, J., 'Implicit Signs of a Persistent Belief in the Davidic Empire', *VT* 20 (1970), pp. 287-303.

Mays, J.L., D.L. Peterson and K.H. Richards (eds.), *Old Testament Interpretation: Past, Present, and Future. Essays in Honour of Gene M. Tucker* (Edinburgh: T. & T. Clark, 1995).

McAlpine, T.H., 'The Word Against the Nations', *Studia biblica et theologica* 5.1 (1975), pp. 3-14.

McCann, J.C. (ed.), *The Shape and Shaping of the Psalter* (JSOTSup, 159; Sheffield: JSOT Press, 1993).

McComiskey, T.E., 'The Hymnic Elements of the Prophecy of Amos: A Study of Form-Critical Methodology', *JETS* 30 (1987), pp. 139-57.

McGaughy, L.C. (ed.), *SBLASP* 108.2 (Missoula: SBL, 1972).

McKane, W., *A Critical and Exegetical Commentary on Jeremiah. I. Introduction and Commentary on Jeremiah I–XXV* (ICC; Edinburgh: T. & T. Clark, 1986).

—*Prophets and Wise Men* (SBT, 44; London: SCM Press, 1965).

McKnight, E.V., *Postmodern Use of the Bible: The Emergence of Reader-Oriented Criticism* (Nashville: Abingdon Press, 1988).

McLaughlin, J.L., review of *Le livre du prophète Amos* (RhétBib, 2; Paris: Cerf, 1994), by P. Bovati and R. Meynet, in *Bib* 77 (1996), pp. 114-17.

Meek, T.J., 'The Accusative of Time in Amos 1.1', *JAOS* 61 (1941), pp. 63-64, 190-91.

Meier, S.A., *Speaking of Speaking: Marking Direct Discourse in the Hebrew Bible* (VTSup, 46; Leiden: E.J. Brill, 1992).

Melugin, R.F., 'The Formation of Amos: An Analysis of Exegetical Method', in Achtemeier (ed.), *SBLASP* 114.1, pp. 369-91.

—'Muilenburg, Form Criticism, and Theological Exegesis', in M.J. Buss (ed.), *Encounter with the Text: Form and History in the Hebrew Bible* (Semeia Supplements, 8; Philadelphia: Fortress Press; Missoula: Scholars Press, 1979), pp. 91-100.

—'The Typical Versus the Unique Among the Hebrew Prophets', in McGaughy (ed.), *SBLASP* 108.2, pp. 331-41.

Meynet, R., *Rhetorical Analysis: An Introduction to Biblical Rhetoric* (JSOTSup, 256; Sheffield: Sheffield Academic Press, 1998).

Milgrom, J., 'Did Isaiah Prophesy during the Reign of Uzziah?', *VT* 14 (1964), pp. 178-82.

Miller, J.H., *Thomas Hardy: Distance and Desire* (Cambridge, MA: Belknap/Harvard University Press, 1970).

Miller, P.D., Jr, 'The World and Message of the Prophets: Biblical Prophecy in Its Context', in Mays, Petersen and Richards (eds.), *Old Testament Interpretation*, pp. 97-112.

Mittmann, S., 'Amos 3,12-15 und das Bett der Samarier', *ZDPV* 92 (1976), pp. 149-67.

—'Gestalt und Gehalt einer prophetischen Selbstrechtfertigung (Amos 3,3-8)', *TQ* 151 (1971), pp. 134-45.

Moeller, H.R., 'Ambiguity at Amos 3.12', *BT* 15 (1964), pp. 31-34.

Möller, K., ' "Hear this Word against You": A Fresh Look at the Arrangement and the Rhetorical Strategy of the Book of Amos', *VT* 50 (2000), pp. 499-518.

—'Reconstructing and Interpreting Amos's Literary Prehistory: A Dialogue with Redaction Criticism', in C. Bartholomew *et al.* (eds.), *'Beyond' the Text: History and Biblical Interpretation* (SHS, 4; Carlisle: Paternoster Press; Grand Rapids: Zondervan, forthcoming, 2003).

—'Rehabilitation eines Propheten: Die Botschaft des Amos aus rhetorischer Perspektive unter besonderer Berücksichtigung von Am. 9,7-15', *EuroJT* 6 (1997), pp. 41-55.

—'Renewing Historical Criticism', in Bartholomew, Greene and Möller (eds.), *Renewing Biblical Interpretation*, pp. 145-71.

—review of *Reading the Old Testament: Method in Biblical Study* (London: Darton, Longman & Todd, 2nd edn, 1996), by J. Barton, in *EuroJT* 6 (1997), pp. 172-74.

—'Words of (In-)evitable Certitude? Reflections on the Interpretation of Prophetic Oracles of Judgement', in Bartholomew, Greene and Möller (eds.), *After Pentecost*, pp. 352-86.

Moor, J.C. de (ed.), *Synchronic or Diachronic? A Debate on Method in Old Testament Exegesis. Papers Read at the Ninth Joint Meeting of Het Oudtestamentisch Werkgezelschap in Nederland en Belgie and the Society for Old Testament Study Held at Kampen, 1994* (OTS, 34; Leiden: E.J. Brill, 1995).

Morgenstern, J., 'Amos Studies I', *HUCA* 11 (1936), pp. 19-140.

—'Amos Studies II: The Sin of Uzziah, the Festival of Jeroboam and the Date of Amos', *HUCA* 12/13 (1937–38), pp. 1-53.

—'Amos Studies IV: The Addresses of Amos—Text and Commentary', *HUCA* 32 (1961), pp. 295-350.

—*Amos Studies. I. Parts I, II, and III* (Cincinnati: Hebrew Union College, 1942).

Mosis, R., 'כּוֹזְבָא, כָּזִיב, אַכְזִיב, כָּזִב, כֹּזְבִי, כִּדְבָה, אַכְזָב, כָּזָב, כָּזַב, כֹּזֵב', in *TDOT*, VII, pp. 104-21.

Mowinckel, S., 'Drive and/or Ride in O.T.', *VT* 12 (1962), pp. 278-99.

—'The Verb *śiaḥ* and the Nouns *śiaḥ*, *śiḥā*', *ST* 15 (1961), pp. 1-10.

Mühlhäusler, P., 'Language: Variation Theories', in Harré and Lamb (eds.), *Encyclopedic Dictionary of Psychology*, p. 332.

—'Linguistics: Synchronic', in Harré and Lamb (eds.), *Encyclopedic Dictionary of Psychology*, p. 355.

Muilenburg, J., 'Form Criticism and Beyond', *JBL* 88 (1969), pp. 1-18.

—'The Linguistic and Rhetorical Usages of the Particle כִּי in the Old Testament', *HUCA* 32 (1961), pp. 135-60.

—'A Study in Hebrew Rhetoric: Repetition and Style', in *Congress Volume, Copenhagen 1953* (VTSup, 1; Leiden: E.J. Brill, 1953), pp. 97-111.

Mulder, M.J., 'Carmel', in van der Toorn, Becking and van der Horst (eds.), *Dictionary of Deities and Demons in the Bible*, pp. 182-85.

—'כַּרְמֶל', in *TDOT*, VII, pp. 325-36.

—'Kuenen und der "ethische Monotheismus" der Propheten des 8. Jahrhunderts v. Chr.', in P.B. Dirksen and A. van der Kooij (eds.), *Abraham Kuenen (1828–1891): His Major Contributions to the Study of the Old Testament. A Collection of Old Testament Studies Published on the Occasion of the Centenary of Abraham Kuenen's Death (10 December 1991)* (OTS, 29; Leiden: E.J. Brill, 1993), pp. 65-90.

Müller, H.-P., 'Die hebräische Wurzel שׂיח', *VT* 19 (1969), pp. 361-71.

—'Ein Paradigma zur Theorie der alttestamentlichen Wissenschaft: Amos, seine Epigonen und Interpreten', *NZSTR* 33 (1991), pp. 112-38.

—'Phönizien und Juda in exilisch-nachexilischer Zeit', *WO* 6.2 (1971), pp. 189-204.

—*Ursprünge und Strukturen alttestamentlicher Eschatologie* (BZAW, 109; Berlin: Alfred Töpelmann, 1969).

—'Die Wurzeln *'yq, y'q* und *'wq*', *VT* 21 (1971), pp. 556-64.

Müller, P., *'Verstehst du auch, was du liest?' Lesen und Verstehen im Neuen Testament* (Darmstadt: Wissenschaftliche Buchgesellschaft, 1994).

Muntingh, L.M., 'Political and International Relations of Israel's Neighbouring Peoples According to the Oracles of Amos', in *Studies on the Books of Hosea and Amos* (OTWSA, 7/8; Potchefstroom: Pro Rege-Pers Beperk, 1966), pp. 134-42.

Murphy, R.E., 'Reflections on Contextual Interpretation of the Psalms', in McCann (ed.), *The Shape and Shaping of the Psalter*, pp. 21-28.

Murtonen, A., 'The Prophet Amos—A Hepatoscoper?', *VT* 2 (1952), pp. 170-71.

Nägele, S., *Laubhütte Davids und Wolkensohn: Eine auslegungsgeschichtliche Studie zu Amos 9,11 in der jüdischen und christlichen Exegese* (AGJU, 24; Leiden: E.J. Brill, 1995).

Negoitặ, A., and H. Ringgren, 'הִגָּיוֹן, הָגוּת, הֶגֶה, הָגָה', in *TDOT*, III, pp. 321-24.

Neher, A., *Amos: Contribution à l'étude du prophètisme* (Paris: Vrin, 1950).

Neufeld, D., *Reconceiving Texts as Speech Acts: An Analysis of 1 John* (BIS, 7; Leiden: E.J. Brill, 1994).

Neumann, P.H.A. (ed.), *Das Prophetenverständnis in der deutschsprachigen Forschung seit Heinrich Ewald* (WdF, 307; Darmstadt: Wissenschaftliche Buchgesellschaft, 1979).

Neumann, P.K.D., *Hört das Wort Jahwäs. Ein Beitrag zur Komposition alttestamentlicher Schriften* (Hamburg: Stiftung Europa-Kolleg, 1975).

Niditch, S., *Oral World and Written Word: Ancient Israelite Literature* (Library of Ancient Israel; Louisville, KY: Westminster/John Knox Press, 1996).

Niehaus, J.J., *God at Sinai: Covenant and Theophany in the Bible and Ancient Near East* (SOTBT; Carlisle: Paternoster Press, 1995).

Niehr, H., 'Die Reform des Joschija. Methodische, historische und religionsgeschichtliche Aspekte', in Gross (ed.), *Jeremia und die 'deuteronomistische Bewegung'*, pp. 33-55.

Niemann, H.M., 'Theologie in geographischem Gewand: Zum Wachstumsprozess der Völkerspruchsammlung Amos 1–2', in *idem*, M. Augustin and W.H. Schmidt (eds.), *Nachdenken über Israel, Bibel und Theologie: Festschrift für Klaus-Dietrich Schunck zu seinem 65. Geburtstag* (BEATAJ, 37; Frankfurt: Peter Lang, 1994), pp. 177-96.

Noble, P.R., 'Amos' Absolute "No"', *VT* 47 (1997), pp. 329-40.

—'The Function of *n'm Yhwh* in Amos', *ZAW* 108 (1996), pp. 623-26.

—'Israel among the Nations', *HBT* 15 (1993), pp. 56-82.

—' "I Will Not Bring 'It' Back" (Amos 1.3): A Deliberately Ambiguous Oracle?', *ExpTim* 106 (1994–95), pp. 105-109.

—'The Literary Structure of Amos: A Thematic Analysis', *JBL* 114 (1995), pp. 209-26.

Nogalski, J.D., 'A Teaching Outline for Amos', *RevExp* 92 (1995), pp. 147-51.

North, F.S., 'The Expression "the Oracle of Yahweh" as an Aid to Critical Analysis', *JBL* 71 (1952).

Noth, M., 'Das Krongut der israelitischen Könige und seine Verwaltung', *ZDPV* 50 (1927), pp. 211-44.

Nötscher, F., *Das Buch Jeremias übersetzt und erklärt* (HSAT, 7.2; Bonn: Peter Hanstein, 1934).

O'Connell, R.H., *Concentricity and Continuity: The Literary Structure of Isaiah* (JSOTSup, 188; Sheffield: Sheffield Academic Press, 1994).

—'Telescoping N+1 Patterns in the Book of Amos', *VT* 46 (1996), pp. 56-73.

Odell, M.S., 'The Prophets and the End of Hosea', in Watts and House (eds.), *Forming Prophetic Literature*, pp. 158-70.

Oettli, S., *Amos und Hosea: Zwei Zeugen gegen die Anwendung der Evolutionstheorie auf die Religion Israels* (BFCT, 5.4; Gütersloh: Bertelsmann, 1901).

Ogden, D.K., 'The Earthquake Motif in the Book of Amos', in K.-D. Schunck and M. Augustin (eds.), *Goldene Äpfel in silbernen Schalen. Collected Communications to the XIIIth Congress of the International Organization for the Study of the Old Testament, Leuven 1989* (BEATAJ, 20; Frankfurt: Peter Lang, 1992), pp. 69-80.

Oliver, A., 'אבל', in *NIDOTTE*, I, pp. 243-48.

Olmo Lete, G. del, 'Bashan', in van der Toorn, Becking and van der Horst (eds.), *Dictionary of Deities and Demons in the Bible*, pp. 161-63.

O'Rourke Boyle, M., 'The Covenant Lawsuit of the Prophet Amos: iii 1–iv 13', *VT* 21 (1971), pp. 338-62.

Oswalt, J.N., *The Book of Isaiah: Chapters 1–39* (NICOT; Grand Rapids: Eerdmans, 1986).

Overholt, T.W., ' "It is Difficult to Read"', *JSOT* 48 (1990), pp. 51-54.

—'Prophecy in History: The Social Reality of Intermediation', *JSOT* 48 (1990), pp. 3-29.

Owens, J.J., 'Exegetical Studies in the Book of Amos', *RevExp* 63 (1966), pp. 429-40.

Park, A.W., *The Book of Amos as Composed and Read in Antiquity* (Studies in Biblical Literature, 37; New York: Peter Lang, 2001).

Parunak, H. van Dyke, 'Oral Typesetting: Some Uses of Biblical Structure', *Bib* 62 (1981), pp. 153-68.

—'Some Axioms for Literary Architecture', *Semitics* 8 (1983), pp. 1-16.

—'Some Discourse Functions of Prophetic Quotation Formulas in Jeremiah', in Bergen (ed.), *Biblical Hebrew*, pp. 489-519.

Patrick, D., *The Rhetoric of Revelation in the Hebrew Bible* (Overtures to Biblical Theology; Minneapolis: Fortress Press, 1999).

Patrick, D., and A. Scult, *Rhetoric and Biblical Interpretation* (JSOTSup, 82; BLS, 26; Sheffield: Sheffield Academic Press, 1990).

Patte, D., 'Speech Act Theory and Biblical Exegesis', in White (ed.), *Speech Act Theory*, pp. 85-102.

Paul, S.M., 'Amos 1.3–2.3: A Concatenous Literary Pattern', *JBL* 90 (1971), pp. 397-403.

—'Amos 3.3-8: The Irresistible Sequence of Cause and Effect', *HAR* 7 (1983), pp. 203-20.

—'Amos iii 15—Winter and Summer Mansions', *VT* 28 (1978), pp. 358-60.

—'Fishing Imagery in Amos 4.2', *JBL* 97 (1978), pp. 183-90.

—'A Literary Reinvestigation of the Authenticity of the Oracles Against the Nations of Amos', in Doré, Grelot and Carrez (eds.), *De la Tôrah au Messie*, pp. 189-204.

Perelman, C., *The Realm of Rhetoric* (trans. W. Kluback; Notre Dame: University of Notre Dame Press, 1982).

Perelman, C., and L. Olbrechts-Tyteca, *The New Rhetoric: A Treatise on Argumentation* (trans. J. Wilkinson and P. Weaver; Notre Dame: University of Notre Dame Press, 1969).

Perrin, N., *What is Redaction Criticism?* (GBS; Philadelphia: Fortress Press, 1970).

Peters, J.P., *The Psalms as Liturgies* (New York: Macmillan, 1922).

Petersen, D.L., *The Roles of Israel's Prophets* (JSOTSup, 17; Sheffield: JSOT Press, 1981).

Pfeifer, G., 'Amos und Deuterojesaja denkformenanalytisch verglichen', *ZAW* 93 (1981), pp. 439-43.

—'Die Ausweisung eines lästigen Ausländers: Amos 7 $_{10\text{-}17}$', *ZAW* 96 (1984), pp. 112-18.

—'Denkformenanalyse als exegetische Methode, erläutert an Amos 1 $_2$–2 $_{16}$', *ZAW* 88 (1976), pp. 56-71.

—'Die Denkform des Propheten Amos (iii 9-11)', *VT* 34 (1984), pp. 476-81.

—'Die Fremdvölkersprüche des Amos—Spätere *vaticinia ex eventu*?', *VT* 38 (1988), pp. 230-33.

—' "Ich bin in tiefe Wasser geraten, und die Flut will mich ersäufen" (Psalm lxix 3)—Anregungen und Vorschläge zur Aufarbeitung wissenschaftlicher Sekundärliteratur', *VT* 37 (1987), pp. 327-39.

—'Das Ja des Amos', *VT* 39 (1989), pp. 497-503.

—'Jahwe als Schöpfer der Welt und Herr ihrer Mächte in der Verkündigung des Propheten Amos', *VT* 41 (1991), pp. 475-81.

—' "Rettung" als Beweis der Vernichtung (Amos 3,12)', *ZAW* 100 (1988), pp. 269-77.

—*Die Theologie des Propheten Amos* (Frankfurt: Peter Lang, 1995).

—'Über den Unterschied zwischen Schriftstellern des zwanzigsten Jahrhunderts nach und des ersten Jahrtausends vor Christus. Zur Entstehung des Amosbuches', *VT* 41 (1991), pp. 123-27.

—'Unausweichliche Konsequenzen. Denkformenanalyse von Amos iii 3-8', *VT* 33 (1983), pp. 341-47.

Plöger, O., *Sprüche Salomos (Proverbia)* (BKAT, 17; Neukirchen–Vluyn: Neukirchener Verlag, 1984).

Pöhlmann, H.G., *Abriss der Dogmatik: Ein Kompendium* (Gütersloh: Gütersloher Verlagshaus Gerd Mohn, 5th edn, 1990).

Polley, M.E., *Amos and the Davidic Empire: A Socio-Historical Approach* (New York: Oxford University Press, 1989).

Pope, M.H., 'A Divine Banquet at Ugarit', in J.M. Efird (ed.), *The Use of the Old Testament in the New and Other Essays: Studies in Honor of William Franklin Stinespring* (Durham, NC: Duke University Press, 1972), pp. 170-203.

—'Seven, Seventh, Seventy', in *IDB*, IV, pp. 294-95.

Praetorius, F., 'Zum Texte des Amos', *ZAW* 34 (1914), pp. 42-44.

Preuss, H.D., 'שֵׁבָ, יָבְשָׁה, יַבֶּשֶׁת', in *TDOT*, V, pp. 373-79.

—*Jahweglaube und Zukunftserwartung* (BWANT, 87; Stuttgart: W. Kohlhammer, 1968).

—*Theologie des Alten Testaments* (2 vols.; Stuttgart: W. Kohlhammer, 1991–92).

Priest, J., 'The Covenant of Brothers', *JBL* 84 (1965), pp. 400-406.

Procksch, O., ' "Wort Gottes" im AT', in *TWNT*, IV, pp. 89-100.

Pschibille, J., *Hat der Löwe erneut gebrüllt? Sprachliche, formale und inhaltliche Gemeinsamkeiten in der Verkündigung Jeremias und Amos'* (Biblisch-theologische Studien, 41; Neukirchen–Vluyn: Neukirchener Verlag, 2001).

Rabinowitz, I., 'The Crux at Amos iii 12', *VT* 11 (1961), pp. 228-31.

Rad, G. von, 'Gerichtsdoxologie', in Bernhardt (ed.), *Schalom*, pp. 28-37.

—*Old Testament Theology* (trans. D.M.G. Stalker; 2 vols.; Edinburgh: Oliver & Boyd, 1962–65).

—'The Origin of the Concept of the Day of Yahweh', *JSS* 4 (1959), pp. 97-108.

—*Theologie des Alten Testaments* (2 vols.; Munich: Chr. Kaiser Verlag, 10th edn, 1992–93).

—*Weisheit in Israel* (Gütersloh: Gütersloher Verlagshaus Gerd Mohn, new edn, 1992).

Radday, Y.T., 'Chiasmus in Hebrew Biblical Narrative', in Welch (ed.), *Chiasmus in Antiquity*, pp. 50-117.

Ramsey, G.W., 'Amos 4.12—A New Perspective', *JBL* 89 (1970), pp. 187-91.

Reid, S.B., 'Psalm 50: Prophetic Speech and God's Performative Utterances', in *idem* (ed.), *Prophets and Paradigms: Essays in Honor of Gene M. Tucker* (JSOTSup, 229; Sheffield: Sheffield Academic Press, 1996), pp. 217-30.

Reimer, D.J., 'צדק', in *NIDOTTE*, III, pp. 744-69.

Reimer, H., *Richtet auf das Recht! Studien zur Botschaft des Amos* (SBS, 149; Stuttgart: Katholisches Bibelwerk, 1992).

Renaud, B., 'Genèse et théologie d'Amos 3,3-8', in A. Caquot and M. Delcor (eds.), *Mélanges bibliques et orienteaux en l'honneur de M. Henri Cazelles* (AOAT, 212; Neukirchen–Vluyn: Neukirchener Verlag, 1981), pp. 353-72.

Rendtorff, R., 'Zu Amos 2 $_{14-16}$', *ZAW* 85 (1973), pp. 226-27.

—'Between Historical Criticism and Holistic Interpretation: New Trends in Old Testament Exegesis', in *idem*, *Canon and Theology*, pp. 25-30.

—'Botenformel und Botenspruch', *ZAW* 74 (1962), pp. 165-77.

—*Canon and Theology* (ed. M. Kohl; Edinburgh: T. & T. Clark, 1994).

—'Forty Years On: Four Decades of Old Testament Scholarship as I Have Experienced Them in Heidelberg and Elsewhere', in *idem*, *Canon and Theology*, pp. 207-19.

—'Zum Gebrauch der Formel *ne'um jahwe* im Jeremiabuch', *ZAW* 66 (1954), pp. 27-37.

—'The Importance of the Canon for a Theology of the Old Testament', in *idem*, *Canon and Theology*, pp. 46-56.

—'Isaiah 6 in the Framework of the Composition of the Book', in *idem*, *Canon and Theology*, pp. 170-80.

—'Old Testament Theology: Some Ideas for a New Approach', in *idem*, *Canon and Theology*, pp. 1-16.

Renz, T., *The Rhetorical Function of the Book of Ezekiel* (VTSup, 76; Leiden: E.J. Brill, 1999).

Reventlow, H. Graf, *Das Amt des Propheten bei Amos* (FRLANT, 80; Göttingen: Vandenhoeck & Ruprecht, 1962).

—*Hauptprobleme der alttestamentlichen Theologie im 20. Jahrhundert* (EdF, 173; Darmstadt: Wissenschaftliche Buchgesellschaft, 1982).

Richardson, H.N., 'Amos 2.13-16: Its Structure and Function in the Book', in Achtemeier (ed.), *SBLASP* 114.1, pp. 361-67.

—'*skt* (Amos 9.11): "Booth" or "Succoth"?', *JBL* 92 (1973), pp. 375-81.

Richter, W., *Die sogenannten vorprophetischen Berufungsberichte* (FRLANT, 101; Göttingen: Vandenhoeck & Ruprecht, 1970).

Ricœur, P., *Interpretation Theory: Discourse and the Surplus of Meaning* (Fort Worth: Texas Christian University Press, 1976).
—*The Symbolism of Evil* (Boston: Beacon Press, 1967).
—'Toward a Hermeneutic of the Idea of Revelation', *HTR* 70 (1977), pp. 1-37.
Rieger, J., *Die Bedeutung der Geschichte für die Verkündigung des Amos und Hosea* (Giessen: Alfred Töpelmann, 1929).
Riesner, R., *Jesus als Lehrer: Eine Untersuchung zum Ursprung der Evangelien-Überlieferung* (WUNT, 2.7; Tübingen: J.C.B. Mohr [Paul Siebeck], 3rd edn, 1988).
Ringgren, H., 'Israelite Prophecy: Fact or Fiction?', in J.A. Emerton (ed.), *Congress Volume, Jerusalem 1986* (VTSup, 40; Leiden: E.J. Brill, 1988), pp. 204-10.
Ringgren, H., and H. Seebass, 'פֶּשַׁע, פֶּשַׁע', in *ThWAT*, VI, pp. 791-810.
Robbins, V.K., *Jesus the Teacher: A Socio-Rhetorical Interpretation of Mark* (repr., Minneapolis: Fortress Press, 1992).
—*New Boundaries in Old Territory: Forms and Social Rhetoric in Mark* (New York: Lang, 1994).
—*The Tapestry of Early Christian Discourse: Rhetoric, Society and Ideology* (London: Routledge, 1996).
Rofé, A., *Introduction to the Prophetic Literature* (trans. J.H. Seeligmann; BibSem, 21; Sheffield: Sheffield Academic Press, 1997).
Rohland, E., 'Die Bedeutung der Erwählungstraditionen Israels für die Eschatologie der alttestamentlichen Propheten' (dissertation, University of Heidelberg, 1956).
Rosenbaum, S.N., *Amos of Israel: A New Interpretation* (Macon, GA: Mercer University Press, 1990).
—'Northern Amos Revisited: Two Philological Suggestions', *Hebrew Studies* 18 (1977), pp. 132-48.
Rost, L., 'Zu Amos 7,10-17', in *Festgabe für Theodor Zahn* (Leipzig: Deichert, 1928), pp. 229-36.
Roth, W.M.W., *Numerical Sayings in the Old Testament: A Form-Critical Study* (VTSup, 13; Leiden: E.J. Brill, 1965).
—'The Numerical Sequence x/x+1 in the Old Testament', *VT* 12 (1962), pp. 300-11.
Rottzoll, D.U., *Studien zur Redaktion und Komposition des Amosbuchs* (BZAW, 243; Berlin: W. de Gruyter, 1996).
Rudolph, W., 'Amos 4,6-13', in H.J. Stoebe, J.J. Stamm and E. Jenni (eds.), *Wort—Gebot—Glaube: Beiträge zur Theologie des Alten Testaments, Walter Eichrodt zum 80. Geburtstag* (ATANT, 59; Zürich: Zwingli, 1970), pp. 27-38.
—'Die angefochtenen Völkersprüche in Amos 1 und 2', in Bernhardt (ed.), *Schalom*, pp. 45-49.
Rüterswörden, U., *Die Beamten der israelitischen Königszeit: Eine Studie zu śr und vergleichbaren Begriffen* (BWANT, 117; Stuttgart: W. Kohlhammer, 1985).
Rüthi, A.E., 'Reiter/Reiterei', in *BHH*, III, pp. 1584-85.
Ryken, L., 'Amos', in *idem* and T. Longman III (eds.), *A Complete Literary Guide to the Bible* (Grand Rapids: Zondervan, 1993), pp. 337-47.
Safrai, S., 'Education and the Study of the Torah', in *idem* and M. Stern (eds.), *The Jewish People in the First Century: Historical Geography, Political History, Social, Cultural and Religious Life and Institutions* (Compendia rerum Iudaicarum ad Novum Testamentum, Section 1; 2 vols.; Assen: Van Gorcum, 1974–76), II, pp. 945-70.
Sarna, N.M., *On the Book of Psalms: Exploring the Prayers of Ancient Israel* (New York: Schocken Books, 1995).
Sasson, J.M., 'A Genealogical "Convention" in Biblical Chronography?', *ZAW* 90 (1978), pp. 171-85.

Sauer, G., 'Amos 7,10-17 und mesopotamischer Briefstil', in J.J. Adler (ed.), *Haim M.I. Gevaryahu Memorial Volume* (Jerusalem: World Jewish Bible Center, 1990), pp. 119-28.

Saussure, F. de, *Cours de linguistique générale* (Wiesbaden: Otto Harrassowitz, 1967).

Sawyer, J.F.A., *Prophecy and the Prophets of the Old Testament* (OBS; Oxford: Oxford University Press, 1987).

Schäfer-Lichtenberger, C., *Stadt und Eidgenossenschaft im Alten Testament: Eine Auseinandersetzung mit Max Webers Studie 'Das antike Judentum'* (BZAW, 156; Berlin: W. de Gruyter, 1983).

Scharbert, J., *Der Schmerz im Alten Testament* (BBB, 8; Bonn: Peter Hanstein, 1955).

Schart, A., *Die Entstehung des Zwölfprophetenbuchs: Neubearbeitungen von Amos im Rahmen schriftenübergreifender Redaktionsprozesse* (BZAW, 260; Berlin: W. de Gruyter, 1998).

Schenker, A., 'Gerichtsverkündigung und Verblendung bei den vorexilischen Propheten', *RB* 93 (1986), pp. 563-80.

—'Steht der Prophet unter dem Zwang zu weissagen, oder steht Israel vor der Evidenz der Weisung Gottes in der Weissagung des Propheten? Zur Interpretation von Amos 3,3-8', *BZ* NS 30 (1986), pp. 250-56.

Schilling, O., 'Das Wort Gottes im AT', *Erfurter Theologische Studien* 12 (1962), pp. 7-26.

Schleiermacher, F.D.E., *Hermeneutics: The Handwritten Manuscripts* (ed. H. Kimmerle; Missoula: Scholars Press, 1977).

Schmid, H.H., 'Amos: Zur Frage nach der "geistigen Heimat" des Propheten', *WuD* 10 (1969), pp. 85-103.

Schmidt, H., 'Die Herkunft des Propheten Amos', in K. Marti (ed.), *Beiträge zur alttestamentlichen Wissenschaft: Karl Budde zum siebzigsten Geburtstag* (BZAW, 34; Giessen: Alfred Töpelmann, 1920), pp. 158-71.

Schmidt, J.M., 'Ausgangspunkt und Ziel prophetischer Verkündigung im 8. Jahrhundert', *Verkündigung und Forschung* (Beihefte zu *EvT*, 22; Gütersloh: Chr. Kaiser Verlag, 1977), pp. 65-82.

Schmidt, W.H., *Alttestamentlicher Glaube in seiner Geschichte* (Neukirchener Studienbücher, 6; Neukirchen–Vluyn: Neukirchener Verlag, 6th edn, 1987).

—'Die deuteronomistische Redaktion des Amosbuches: Zu den theologischen Unterschieden zwischen dem Prophetenwort und seinem Sammler', *ZAW* 77 (1965), pp. 168-93.

—'Die prophetische "Grundgewissheit": Erwägungen zur Einheit prophetischer Verkündigung', in Neumann (ed.), *Das Prophetenverständnis*, pp. 537-64.

—' "Suchet den Herrn, so werdet ihr leben". Exegetische Notizen zum Thema "Gott suchen" in der Prophetie', in J. Bergman, K. Drynjeff and H. Ringgren (eds.), *Ex Orbe Religionum. Studia Geo Widengren XXIV mense Apr. MCMLXXII quo die lustra tredecim feliciter explevit oblata ab collegis, discipulis, amicis, collegae magistro amico congratulantibus*, I (Studies in the History of Religions, 21; Leiden: E.J. Brill, 1972), pp. 127-40.

—*Zukunftsgewissheit und Gegenwartskritik: Grundzüge prophetischer Verkündigung* (Biblische Studien, 64; Neukirchen–Vluyn: Neukirchener Verlag, 1973).

Schnutenhaus, F., 'Das Kommen und Erscheinen Gottes im Alten Testament', *ZAW* 76 (1964), pp. 1-22.

Schoville, K.N., 'A Note on the Oracles of Amos Against Gaza, Tyre, and Edom', in *Studies on Prophecy: A Collection of Twelve Papers* (VTSup, 26; Leiden: E.J. Brill, 1974), pp. 55-63.

—'The Sins of Aram in Amos 1', in Shinan (ed.), *Proceedings of the Sixth World Congress of Jewish Studies*, I, pp. 363-75.

328   *A Prophet in Debate*

Schunck, K.-D., 'בָּמָה', in *TDOT*, II, pp. 139-45.

Schwantes, M., *Das Land kann seine Worte nicht ertragen: Meditationen zu Amos* (trans. I. Kayser; Munich: Chr. Kaiser Verlag, 1991).

—*Das Recht der Armen* (BBET, 4; Frankfurt: Peter Lang, 1977).

Schwantes, S.J., 'Note on Amos 4 ₂ᵦ', *ZAW* 79 (1967), pp. 82-83.

Searle, J.R., *Expression and Meaning: Studies in the Theory of Speech Acts* (Cambridge: Cambridge University Press, 1979).

—*Speech Acts: An Essay in the Philosophy of Language* (Cambridge: Cambridge University Press, 1969).

Segert, S., 'Zur Bedeutung des Wortes *nōqēd*', in B. Hartmann *et al.* (eds.), *Hebräische Wortforschung: Festschrift zum 80. Geburtstag von Walter Baumgartner* (VTSup, 16; Leiden: E.J. Brill, 1967), pp. 279-83.

—'A Controlling Device for Copying Stereotype Passages? (Amos i 3–ii 8, vi 1-6)', *VT* 34 (1984), pp. 481-82.

Seierstad, I.P., 'Erlebnis und Gehorsam beim Propheten Amos', *ZAW* 52 (1934), pp. 22-41.

Seitz, C.R., 'The Changing Face of Old Testament Studies', in *idem*, *Word without End: The Old Testament as Abiding Theological Witness* (Grand Rapids: Eerdmans, 1998), pp. 75-82.

Selden, R., and P. Widdowson, *A Reader's Guide to Contemporary Literary Theory* (New York: Harvester Wheatsheaf, 3rd edn, 1993).

Sellin, E., *Einleitung in das Alte Testament* (Leipzig: Quelle & Meyer, 2nd rev. edn, 1914).

Selms, A. van, 'Amos' Geographic Horizon', in *Studies on the Books of Hosea and Amos* (OTWSA, 7/8; Potchefstroom: Pro Rege-Pers Beperk, 1966), pp. 166-69.

Seybold, K., 'Die Verwendung der Bildmotive in der Prophetie Zefanjas', in Weippert, Seybold and Weippert, *Beiträge zur prophetischen Bildsprache*, pp. 30-54.

Shapiro, D.S., 'The Seven Questions of Amos', *Tradition* 20 (1982), pp. 327-31.

Shaw, C.S., *The Speeches of Micah: A Rhetorical-Historical Analysis* (JSOTSup, 145; Sheffield: JSOT Press, 1993).

Shinan, A. (ed.), *Proceedings of the Sixth World Congress of Jewish Studies*, I (Jerusalem: World Union of Jewish Studies, 1977).

Shklovsky, V., 'Art as Technique', in L.T. Lemon and M.J. Reis (eds.), *Russian Formalist Criticism: Four Essays* (Lincoln: University of Nebraska Press, 1965), pp. 3-24.

Siegert, F., *Argumentation bei Paulus gezeigt an Röm 9–11* (WUNT, 34; Tübingen: J.C.B. Mohr [Paul Siebeck], 1985).

Simian-Yofre, H., and U. Dahmen, 'רחם, רַחֲמִים, רַחוּם, רַחֲמָנִי', in *ThWAT*, VII, pp. 460-77.

Sinclair, L.A., 'The Courtroom Motif in the Book of Amos', *JBL* 85 (1966), pp. 351-53.

Singer, K.H., *Die Metalle Gold, Silber, Bronze und Eisen im Alten Testament und ihre Symbolik* (FzB, 43; Würzburg: Echter Verlag, 1980).

Smalley, W.A., 'Recursion Patterns and the Sectioning of Amos', *BT* 30 (1979), pp. 118-27.

Smend, R., *Deutsche Alttestamentler in drei Jahrhunderten* (Göttingen: Vandenhoeck & Ruprecht, 1989).

—*Die Entstehung des Alten Testaments* (TW, 1; Stuttgart: W. Kohlhammer, 2nd rev. edn, 1978).

—'Das Nein des Amos', *EvT* 23 (1963), pp. 404-23.

Smith, G.V., 'Continuity and Discontinuity in Amos' Use of Tradition', *JETS* 34 (1991), pp. 33-42.

Smith, J.K.A., *The Fall of Interpretation: Philosophical Foundations for a Creational Hermeneutic* (Downers Grove, IL: IVP, 2000).

Snyman, S.D., 'Amos 6.1-7 as an Intensification of Amos 3.9-11', *In die Skriflig* 28 (1994), pp. 213-22.

Soden, W. von, 'Zu einigen Ortsbenennungen bei Amos und Micha', *ZAH* 3 (1990), pp. 214-20.

Soggin, J.A., 'Amos and Wisdom', in J. Day, R.P. Gordon and H.G.M. Williamson (eds.), *Wisdom in Ancient Israel: Essays in Honour of J.A. Emerton* (Cambridge: Cambridge University Press, 1995), pp. 119-23.

—'Amos VI.13-14 und I.3 auf dem Hintergrund der Beziehungen zwischen Israel und Damaskus im 9. und 8. Jahrhundert', in H. Goedicke (ed.), *Near Eastern Studies in Honor of W. F. Albright* (Baltimore: Johns Hopkins University Press, 1971), pp. 433-41.

—'Das Erdbeben von Amos 1 ₁ und die Chronologie der Könige Ussia und Jotham von Juda', *ZAW* 82 (1970), pp. 117-21.

Soper, B.K., 'For Three Transgressions and for Four: A New Interpretation of Amos 1.3, etc'., *ExpTim* 71 (1959–60), pp. 86-87.

Speier, S., 'Bemerkungen zu Amos', *VT* 3 (1953), pp. 305-10.

Staples, W.E., 'Epic Motifs in Amos', *JNES* 25 (1966), pp. 106-12.

Steck, O.H., *Exegese des Alten Testaments: Leitfaden der Methodik. Ein Arbeitsbuch für Proseminare, Seminare und Vorlesungen* (Neukirchen–Vluyn: Neukirchener Verlag, 12th edn, 1989).

—'Die Gesellschaftskritik der Propheten', in W. Lohff and B. Lohse (eds.), *Christentum und Gesellschaft* (Göttingen: Vandenhoeck & Ruprecht, 1969), pp. 46-62.

—*Old Testament Exegesis: A Guide to the Methodology* (trans. J.D. Nogalski; SBLRBS, 39; Atlanta: Scholars Press, 2nd edn, 1998).

Steiner, G., *After Babel: Aspects of Language and Translation* (Oxford: Oxford University Press, 3rd edn, 1998).

Steinmann, A.E., 'The Order of Amos's Oracles Against the Nations: 1.3–2.16', *JBL* 111 (1992), pp. 683-89.

Stendahl, K., 'The Bible as a Classic and the Bible as Holy Scripture', in House (ed.), *Beyond Form Criticism*, pp. 39-46.

Sternberg, M., *The Poetics of Biblical Narrative: Ideological Literature and the Drama of Reading* (Bloomington: Indiana University Press, 1987).

Steuernagel, C., *Lehrbuch der Einleitung in das Alte Testament* (Tübingen: J.C.B. Mohr, 1912).

Stoebe, H.J., 'Der Prophet Amos und sein bürgerlicher Beruf', *WuD* 5 (1957), pp. 160-81.

—'Noch einmal zu Amos vii 10-17', *VT* 39 (1989), pp. 341-54.

Stolz, F., 'אבל', in E. Jenni and C. Westermann (eds.), *Theological Lexicon of the Old Testament*, I (Peabody, MA: Hendrickson, 1997), pp. 21-23.

Stone, K., 'Gender and Homosexuality in Judges 19: Subject—Honor, Object—Shame?', *JSOT* 67 (1995), pp. 87-107.

Story, C.I.K., 'Amos—Prophet of Praise', *VT* 30 (1980), pp. 67-80.

Strijdom, P.D.F., 'What Tekoa Did to Amos', *OTE* 9 (1996), pp. 273-93.

Strong, J.T., 'Tyre's Isolationist Policies in the Early Sixth Century BCE: Evidence from the Prophets', *VT* 47 (1997), pp. 207-19.

Strydom, J.G., 'Sosiale geregtigheid by die profeet Amos: Die landsbelofte as vertrekpunt', *Hervormde Teologiese Studies* 52 (1996), pp. 431-48.

Sweeney, M.A., 'Formation and Form in the Prophetic Literature', in Mays, Petersen and Richards (eds.), *Old Testament Interpretation*, pp. 113-26.

—*Isaiah 1–39 with an Introduction to Prophetic Literature* (FOTL, 16; Grand Rapids: Eerdmans, 1996).

Swinburne, R., 'Review of Nicholas Wolterstorff's *Divine Discourse*', *Philosophy* 71 (1996), pp. 465-68.

Talstra, E., 'Text Grammar and Biblical Hebrew: The Viewpoint of Wolfgang Schneider', *JOTT* 5 (1992), pp. 269-97.

Terrien, S., 'Amos and Wisdom', in B.W. Anderson and W. Harrelson (eds.), *Israel's Prophetic Heritage: Essays in Honor of James Muilenburg* (New York: Harper, 1962), pp. 108-15.

Thiselton, A.C., 'Christology in Luke, Speech-Act Theory and the Problem of Dualism in Christology after Kant', in J.B. Green and M. Turner (eds.), *Jesus of Nazareth: Lord and Christ* (Grand Rapids: Eerdmans, 1994), pp. 453-72.

—*Interpreting God and the Postmodern Self: On Meaning, Manipulation and Promise* (Edinburgh: T. & T. Clark, 1995).

—*New Horizons in Hermeneutics: The Theory and Practice of Transforming Biblical Reading* (Grand Rapids: Zondervan, 1992).

—'The Parables as Language-Event: Some Comments on Fuchs's Hermeneutics in the Light of Linguistic Philosophy', *SJT* 23 (1970), pp. 437-68.

—'Speech-Act Theory and the Claim that God Speaks: Nicholas Wolterstorff's *Divine Discourse*', *SJT* 50 (1997), pp. 97-110.

—'The Supposed Power of Words in the Biblical Writings', *JTS* 25 (1974), pp. 283-99.

Thompson, J.A., *The Book of Jeremiah* (NICOT; Grand Rapids: Eerdmans, 1980).

—'The "Response" in Biblical and Non-Biblical Literature with Particular Reference to the Hebrew Prophets', in E.W. Conrad and E.G. Newing (eds.), *Perspectives on Language and Text: Essays and Poems in Honor of Francis I. Andersen's Sixtieth Birthday July 28, 1985* (Winona Lake, IN: Eisenbrauns, 1987), pp. 255-68.

Thompson, T.L., 'How Yahweh Became God: Exodus 3 and 6 and the Heart of the Pentateuch', *JSOT* 68 (1995), pp. 57-74.

Tillyard, E.M.W., *Milton* (London: Chatto & Windus, 1930).

Tillyard, E.M.W., and C.S. Lewis, *The Personal Heresy: A Controversy* (London: Oxford University Press, pbk edn, 1965).

Timm, S., *Die Dynastie Omri: Quellen und Untersuchungen zur Geschichte Israels im 9. Jahrhundert vor Christus* (FRLANT, 124; Göttingen: Vandenhoeck & Ruprecht, 1982).

Todorov, T., 'Viaggio nella critica americana', *Lettera* 4 (1978).

Toorn, K. van der, B. Becking and P.W. van der Horst (eds.), *Dictionary of Deities and Demons in the Bible* (Leiden: E.J. Brill, 2nd edn, 1999).

Toy, C.H., 'The Judgment of Foreign Peoples in Amos i. 3–ii. 3', *JBL* 25 (1906), pp. 25-28.

Trible, P., *God and the Rhetoric of Sexuality* (London: SCM Press, 1992).

—*Rhetorical Criticism: Context, Method, and the Book of Jonah* (GBS; Minneapolis: Fortress Press, 1994).

Tromp, N.J., 'Amos V 1-17. Towards a Stylistic and Rhetorical Analysis', in A.S. van der Woude (ed.), *Prophets, Worship and Theodicy: Studies in Prophetism, Biblical Theology and Structural and Rhetorical Analysis, and the Place of Music in Worship* (OTS, 23; Leiden: E.J. Brill, 1984), pp. 56-84.

Tsumura, D.T., ' "Inserted Bicolon", the AXYB Pattern, in Amos i 5 and Psalm ix 7', *VT* 38 (1988), pp. 234-36.

Tucker, G.M., 'Foreword', in Westermann, *Basic Forms of Prophetic Speech*, pp. ix-xvi.

—*Form Criticism of the Old Testament* (GBS; Philadelphia: Fortress Press, 1971).

—'Prophetic Authenticity: A Form-Critical Study of Amos 7.10-17', *Int* 27 (1973), pp. 423-34.

—'Prophetic Speech', *Int* 32 (1978), pp. 31-45.

—'Prophetic Superscriptions and the Growth of a Canon', in Coats and Long (eds.), *Canon and Authority*, pp. 56-70.

Ueding, G., *Klassische Rhetorik* (Munich: Beck, 2nd edn, 1996).

Uehlinger, C., 'Gab es eine joschijanische Kultreform?', in Gross (ed.), *Jeremia und die 'deuteronomistische Bewegung'*, pp. 57-89.

Ullmann, S., *Semantics: An Introduction to the Science of Meaning* (Oxford: Basil Blackwell, 1962).

Utzschneider, H., 'Die Amazjaerzählung (Am 7,10-17) zwischen Literatur und Historie', *BN* 41 (1988), pp. 76-101.

Vanhoozer, K.J., 'From Speech Acts to Scripture Acts: The Covenant of Discourse and the Discourse of the Covenant', in Bartholomew, Greene and Möller (eds.), *After Pentecost*, pp. 1-49.

—'God's Mighty Speech-Acts: The Doctrine of Scripture Today', in P.E. Satterthwaite and D.F. Wright (eds.), *A Pathway into the Holy Scripture* (Grand Rapids: Eerdmans, 1994), pp. 143-81.

—*Is There a Meaning in This Text? The Bible, the Reader, and the Morality of Literary Knowledge* (Grand Rapids: Zondervan, 1998).

Van Seters, J., *Abraham in History and Tradition* (New Haven: Yale University Press, 1975).

Vawter, B., 'Were the Prophets *nābî's*?', *Bib* 66 (1985), pp. 206-19.

Vermeylen, J., *Du prophète Isaïe à l'apocalyptique. Isaïe, I–XXXV, miroir d'un demi-millénaire d'expérience religieuse en Israël*, II (EBib; Paris: J. Gabalda, 1978).

Vesco, J.-L., 'Amos de Teqoa, défenseur de l'homme', *RB* 87 (1980), pp. 481-513.

Viberg, Å., 'Amos 7.14: A Case of Subtle Irony', *TynBul* 47 (1996), pp. 91-114.

Vickers, B. (ed.), *Rhetoric Revalued* (Medieval & Renaissance Texts and Studies, 19; Binghamton, NY: Center for Medieval & Renaissance Studies, 1982).

Vieweger, D., 'Zur Herkunft der Völkerworte im Amosbuch unter besonderer Berücksichtigung des Aramäerspruchs (Am 1,3-5)', in P. Mommer and W. Thiel (eds.), *Altes Testament— Forschung und Wirkung: Festschrift für Henning Graf Reventlow* (Frankfurt: Peter Lang, 1994), pp. 103-19.

Vollmer, J., *Geschichtliche Rückblicke und Motive in der Prophetie des Amos, Hosea und Jesaja* (BZAW, 119; Berlin: W. de Gruyter, 1971).

Vries, S.J. de, *From Old Revelation to New: A Tradition-Historical and Redaction-Critical Study of Temporal Transitions in Prophetic Prediction* (Grand Rapids: Eerdmans, 1995).

—*Yesterday, Today and Tomorrow: Time and History in the Old Testament* (London: SPCK, 1975).

Waard, J. de, 'The Chiastic Structure of Amos v 1-17', *VT* 27 (1977), pp. 170-77.

Wagner, A., *Sprechakte und Sprechaktanalyse im Alten Testament: Untersuchungen im biblischen Hebräisch an der Nahtstelle zwischen Handlungsebene und Grammatik* (BZAW, 253; Berlin: W. de Gruyter, 1997).

Wagner, S., 'Überlegungen zur Frage nach den Beziehungen des Propheten Amos zum Südreich', *TLZ* 96 (1971), pp. 653-70.

Wal, A. van der, 'The Structure of Amos', *JSOT* 26 (1983), pp. 107-13.

Waldow, H.-E. von, *Anlass und Hintergrund der Verkündigung des Deuterojesaja* (Bonn, 1953).

Walton, S., 'Rhetorical Criticism: An Introduction', *Themelios* 21.2 (1996), pp. 4-9.

Wanke, G., 'Zu Grundlagen und Absicht prophetischer Sozialkritik', *KD* 18 (1972), pp. 2-17.

—'Sprachliche Analyse', in Fohrer *et al.*, *Exegese des Alten Testaments*, pp. 58-83.

Warmuth, G., *Das Mahnwort: Seine Bedeutung für die Verkündigung der vorexilischen*

Propheten Amos, Hosea, Micha, Jesaja und Jeremia (BBET, 1; Frankfurt: Peter Lang, 1976).

Warner, M., 'Introduction', in *idem* (ed.), *Bible as Rhetoric*, pp. 1-25.

Warner, M. (ed.), *The Bible as Rhetoric: Studies in Biblical Persuasion and Credibility* (WSPL; London: Routledge, 1990)

Waschke, E.-J., 'Die fünfte Vision des Amosbuches (9,1-4)—Eine Nachinterpretation', *ZAW* 106 (1994), pp. 434-45.

Watson, D.F., 'Rhetorical Criticism', in *ISBE*, IV, pp. 181-82.

Watson, W.G.E., 'Chiastic Patterns in Biblical Hebrew Poetry', in Welch (ed.), *Chiasmus in Antiquity*, pp. 118-68.

Watts, J.D.W., 'A Critical Analysis of Amos 4.1ff', in McGaughy (ed.), *SBLASP* 108.2, pp. 489-500.

—'Images of Yahweh: God in the Prophets', in R.L. Hubbard, Jr and R.K. Johnston (eds.), *Studies in Old Testament Theology* (Dallas: Word Books, 1992), pp. 135-47.

—*Isaiah 1–33* (WBC, 24; Waco, TX: Word Books, 1985).

—*Isaiah 34–66* (WBC, 25; Waco, TX: Word Books, 1987).

—'An Old Hymn Preserved in the Book of Amos', *JNES* 15 (1956), pp. 33-39.

—*Vision and Prophecy in Amos* (Macon, GA: Mercer University Press, new edn, 1997).

Watts, J.W., 'Public Readings and Pentateuchal Law', *VT* 45 (1995), pp. 540-57.

—*Reading Law: The Rhetorical Shaping of the Pentateuch* (BibSem, 59; Sheffield: Sheffield Academic Press, 1999).

—'Rhetorical Strategy in the Composition of the Pentateuch', *JSOT* 68 (1995), pp. 3-22.

Watts, J.W., and P.R. House (eds.), *Forming Prophetic Literature: Essays on Isaiah and the Twelve in Honor of John D.W. Watts* (JSOTSup, 235; Sheffield: Sheffield Academic Press, 1996).

Weigl, M., 'Eine "unendliche Geschichte": אֶנָך (Am 7,7-8)', *Bib* 76 (1995), pp. 343-87.

Weimar, P., 'Der Schluss des Amos-Buches: Ein Beitrag zur Redaktionsgeschichte des Amos-Buches', *BN* 16 (1981), pp. 60-100.

Weinfeld, M., 'The Day of the Lord: Aspirations for the Kingdom of God in the Bible and Jewish Liturgy', in S. Japhet (ed.), *Studies in the Bible* (Scripta hierosolymitana, 31; Jerusalem: Magnes Press, 1986), pp. 341-72.

Weippert, H., 'Amos: Seine Bilder und ihr Millieu', in *idem*, Seybold and Weippert, *Beiträge zur prophetischen Bildsprache*, pp. 1-29.

Weippert, H., K. Seybold and M. Weippert, *Beiträge zur prophetischen Bildsprache in Israel und Assyrien* (OBO, 64; Freiburg: Universitätsverlag, 1985).

Weiser, A., 'Zu Amos 4 $_{6-13}$', *ZAW* 46 (1928), pp. 49-59.

—*Die Profetie des Amos* (BZAW, 53; Giessen: Alfred Töpelmann, 1929).

Weiss, M., *The Bible from Within: The Method of Total Interpretation* (Jerusalem: Magnes Press, 1984).

—'Die Methode der "Total-Interpretation": Von der Notwendigkeit der Struktur-Analyse für das Verständnis der biblischen Dichtung', in *Congress Volume, Uppsala 1971* (VTSup, 22; Leiden: E.J. Brill, 1972), pp. 88-112.

—'Methodologisches über die Behandlung der Metapher dargelegt an Am. 1,2', *TZ* 23 (1967), pp. 1-25.

—'The Origin of the "Day of the Lord"—Reconsidered', *HUCA* 37 (1966), pp. 29-60.

—'The Pattern of the "Execration Texts" in the Prophetic Literature', *IEJ* 19 (1969), pp. 150-57.

—'The Pattern of Numerical Sequence in Amos 1–2: A Re-Examination', *JBL* 86 (1967), pp. 416-23.

—'Wege der neuen Dichtungswissenschaft in ihrer Anwendung auf die Psalmenforschung: Methodologische Bemerkungen, dargelegt am Beispiel von Psalm XLVI', in P.H.A. Neumann (ed.), *Zur neueren Psalmenforschung* (WdF, 192; Darmstadt: Wissenschaftliche Buchgesellschaft, 1976), pp. 400-51.

Welch, J.W., 'Introduction', in *idem* (ed.), *Chiasmus in Antiquity*, pp. 9-16.

Welch, J.W. (ed.), *Chiasmus in Antiquity: Structures, Analyses, Exegesis* (Hildesheim: Gerstenberg, 1981).

Wellhausen, J., *Israelitische und jüdische Geschichte* (Berlin: W. de Gruyter, 9th edn, 1958).

Wendland, E.R., 'The Discourse Analysis of Hebrew Poetry: A Procedural Outline', in *idem* (ed.), *Discourse Perspectives on Hebrew Poetry in the Scriptures* (UBSMS, 7; Reading: United Bible Societies, 1994), pp. 1-27.

—'The "Word of the Lord" and the Organization of Amos: A Dramatic Message of Conflict and Crisis in the Confrontation Between the Prophet and the People of Yahweh', *OPTAT* 2.4 (1988), pp. 1-51.

Wenham, G.J., *The Book of Leviticus* (NICOT; Grand Rapids: Eerdmans, 1979).

—*Genesis 1–15* (WBC, 1; Dallas: Word Books, 1987).

—*Numbers* (OTG; Sheffield: Sheffield Academic Press, 1997).

Westermann, C., *Basic Forms of Prophetic Speech* (trans. H.C. White; London: Lutterworth, new edn, 1991).

—*Lob und Klage in den Psalmen* (Göttingen: Vandenhoeck & Ruprecht, 1977).

Westphal, M., 'Theology as Talking About a God Who Talks: Review of Nicholas Wolterstorff's *Divine Discourse*', *Modern Theology* 13 (1997), pp. 525-36.

Whedbee, J.W., *Isaiah and Wisdom* (Nashville: Abingdon Press, 1971).

White, H.C., 'Introduction: Speech Act Theory and Literary Criticism', in *idem* (ed.), *Speech Act Theory*, pp. 1-24.

—*Narration and Discourse in the Book of Genesis* (Cambridge: Cambridge University Press, 1991).

—'The Value of Speech Act Theory for Old Testament Hermeneutics', in *idem* (ed.), *Speech Act Theory*, pp. 41-63.

White, H.C. (ed.), *Speech Act Theory and Biblical Criticism* (Semeia, 41; Atlanta: Scholars Press, 1988).

Whybray, R.N., *The Intellectual Tradition in the Old Testament* (BZAW, 135; Berlin: W. de Gruyter, 1974).

—'Prophecy and Wisdom', in R.J. Coggins, A. Phillips and M. Knibb (eds.), *Israel's Prophetic Tradition: Essays in Honour of Peter R. Ackroyd* (Cambridge: Cambridge University Press, 1982), pp. 181-99.

Wicke, D.W., 'Two Perspectives (Amos 5.1-17)', *CurTM* 13 (1986), pp. 89-96.

Widbin, R.B., 'Center Structure in the Center Oracles of Amos', in J.E. Coleson and V.H. Matthews (eds.), *'Go to the Land I Will Show You': Studies in Honor of Dwight W. Young* (Winona Lake, IN: Eisenbrauns, 1996), pp. 177-92.

Wiener, H.M., *The Composition of Judges II 11 to 1 Kings II 46* (Leipzig: J.C. Hinrichs, 1929).

Wijngaards, J.N.M., *The Formulas of the Deuteronomic Creed* (Tilburg: Reijnen, 1963).

—'הוֹצִיא and הֶעֱלָה: A Twofold Approach to the Exodus', *VT* 15 (1965), pp. 91-102.

Wiklander, B., *Prophecy as Literature: A Text-Linguistic and Rhetorical Approach to Isaiah 2–4* (ConBOT, 22; Malmö: C.W.K. Gleerup, 1984).

Wildberger, H., *Jahwes Eigentumsvolk: Eine Studie zur Traditionsgeschichte und Theologie des Erwählungsgedankens* (ATANT, 37; Stuttgart: Zwingli, 1960).

—*Jahwewort und prophetische Rede bei Jeremia* (Theologische Dissertationen, 2; Zürich: Zwingli-Verlag, 1942).

Williams, A.J., 'A Further Suggestion about Amos iv 1-3', *VT* 29 (1979), pp. 206-11.

Williamson, H.G.M., 'The Prophet and the Plumb-Line: A Redaction-Critical Study of Amos vii', in A.S. van der Woude (ed.), *In Quest of the Past: Studies on Israelite Religion, Literature and Prophetism* (OTS, 26; Leiden: E.J. Brill, 1990), pp. 101-21.

—'A Response to A.G. Auld', *JSOT* 27 (1983), pp. 33-39.

Willi-Plein, I., *Vorformen der Schriftexegese innerhalb des Alten Testaments: Untersuchungen zum literarischen Werden der auf Amos, Hosea und Micha zurückgehenden Bücher im hebräischen Zwölfprophetenbuch* (BZAW, 123; Berlin: W. de Gruyter, 1971).

Wimsatt, W.K., 'Genesis: An Argument Resumed', in *idem, Day of the Leopards: Essays in Defense of Poems* (New Haven: Yale University Press, 1976), pp. 11-39.

—'Genesis: A Fallacy Revisisted', in P. Demetz, T. Green and L. Nelson, Jr (eds.), *The Disciplines of Criticism: Essays in Literary Theory, Interpretation, and History* (New Haven: Yale University Press, 1968), pp. 193-225.

Wimsatt, W.K., and M.C. Beardsley, 'The Intentional Fallacy', *Sewanee Review* 54 (1946), pp. 468-88.

Wittenberg, G.H., 'A Fresh Look at Amos and Wisdom', *OTE* 4 (1991), pp. 7-18.

Wolff, H.W., *Amos' geistige Heimat* (WMANT, 18; Neukirchen–Vluyn: Neukirchener Verlag, 1964).

—'Die Begründungen der prophetischen Heils- und Unheilssprüche', in *idem, Gesammelte Studien*, pp. 9-35.

—*Dodekapropheton. I. Hosea* (BKAT, 14.1; Neukirchen–Vluyn: Neukirchener Verlag, 4th edn, 1990).

—*Dodekapropheton. IV. Micha* (BKAT, 14.4; Neukirchen–Vluyn: Neukirchener Verlag, 1982).

—'Die eigentliche Botschaft der klassischen Propheten', in *idem, Studien zur Prophetie*, pp. 39-49.

—'Einführung in die klassische Prophetie', in *idem, Studien zur Prophetie*, pp. 9-24.

—'Das Ende des Heiligtums in Bethel', in *idem, Gesammelte Studien*, pp. 442-53.

—'Endzeitvorstellungen und Orientierungskrise in der alttestamentlichen Prophetie', in *idem, Studien zur Prophetie*, pp. 65-78.

—*Gesammelte Studien zum Alten Testament* (TBü, 22; Munich: Chr. Kaiser Verlag, 2nd edn, 1973).

—'Zur Gotteserfahrung der Propheten', in *idem, Studien zur Prophetie*, pp. 25-38.

—'Haggai literarhistorisch untersucht', in *idem, Studien zur Prophetie*, pp. 129-42.

—'Hauptprobleme alttestamentlicher Prophetie', in *idem, Gesammelte Studien*, pp. 206-31.

—'Prophet und Institution im Alten Testament', in *idem, Studien zur Prophetie*, pp. 50-64.

—*Studien zum Prophetie: Probleme und Erträge* (TBü, 76; Munich: Chr. Kaiser Verlag, 1987).

—*Die Stunde des Amos: Prophetie und Protest* (Munich: Chr. Kaiser Verlag, 1986).

—'Das Thema "Umkehr" in der alttestamentlichen Prophetie', in *idem, Gesammelte Studien*, pp. 130-50.

—'Das unwiderstehliche Wort: Amos und das verschuldete Ende', in *idem, Prophetische Alternativen: Entdeckungen des Neuen im Alten Testament* (Munich: Chr. Kaiser Verlag, 1982), pp. 9-23.

—'Das Zitat im Prophetenspruch: Eine Studie zur prophetischen Verkündigungsweise', in *idem, Gesammelte Studien*, pp. 36-129.

Wolff, H.W. (ed.), *Probleme biblischer Theologie. Gerhard von Rad zum 70. Geburtstag* (Munich: Chr. Kaiser Verlag, 1971).

Wolters, A., 'Cross-Gender Imagery in the Bible', *BBR* 8 (1998), pp. 217-28.

Wolterstorff, N., *Divine Discourse: Philosophical Reflections on the Claim that God Speaks* (Cambridge: Cambridge University Press, 1995).

Wright, C.J.H., *Living as the People of God: The Relevance of Old Testament Ethics* (Leicester: IVP, 1983).

Wright, N.T., *Jesus and the Victory of God* (Christian Origins and the Question of God, 2; London: SPCK, 1996).

Wright, T.J., 'Did Amos Inspect Livers?', *AusBR* 23 (1975), pp. 3-11.

Wuellner, W., 'Toposforschung und Torainterpretation bei Paulus und Jesus', *NTS* 24 (1978), pp. 463-83.

—'Where Is Rhetorical Criticism Taking Us?', *CBQ* 49 (1987), pp. 448-63.

Würthwein, E., 'Amos-Studien', *ZAW* 62 (1950), pp. 10-52.

—'Der Ursprung der prophetischen Gerichtsrede', in Neumann (ed.), *Das Prophetenverständnis*, pp. 361-79.

Yadin, Y., 'Hazor', in M. Avi-Yonah (ed.), *Encyclopedia of Archaeological Excavations in the Holy Land*, II (London: Oxford University Press, 1976), pp. 474-95.

Yadin, Y., *et al.*, *Hazor II: An Account of the Second Season of Excavations, 1956* (Jerusalem: Magnes Press, 1960).

Yamashita, T., 'Noqed', in L.R. Fisher (ed.), *Ras Shamra Parallels: The Texts from Ugarit and the Hebrew Bible*, II (AnOr, 50; Rome: Pontifical Biblical Institute, 1975), pp. 63-64.

Youngblood, R., 'לקראת in Amos 4.12', *JBL* 90 (1971), p. 98.

Zenger, E., 'Eigenart und Bedeutung der Prophetie Israels', in *idem et al.* (eds.), *Einleitung in das Alte Testament*, pp. 293-303.

—*A God of Vengeance? Understanding the Psalms of Divine Wrath* (trans. L.M. Maloney; Louisville, KY: Westminster/John Knox Press, 1996).

—'Das Zwölfprophetenbuch', in *idem et al.* (eds.), *Einleitung in das Alte Testament*, pp. 369-436.

Zenger, E., *et al.* (eds.), *Einleitung in das Alte Testament* (KST, 1.1; Stuttgart: W. Kohlhammer, 1995).

Zevit, Z., 'A Misunderstanding at Bethel: Amos vii 12-17', *VT* 25 (1975), pp. 781-90.

Zimmerli, W., *Ezechiel* (BKAT, 13.1, 2; 2 vols.; Neukirchen–Vluyn: Neukirchener Verlag, 2nd edn, 1979).

—*Grundriss der alttestamentlichen Theologie* (TW, 3.1; Stuttgart: W. Kohlhammer, 6th edn, 1989).

—'Wort Gottes im AT', in *RGG*, VI, pp. 1809-12.

Zobel, H.J., 'Prophet in Israel und Juda: Das Prophetenverständnis des Amos und Hosea', *ZTK* 82 (1985), pp. 281-99.

INDEXES

INDEX OF REFERENCES

OLD TESTAMENT

OTHER ANCIENT REFERENCES

JOURNAL FOR THE STUDY OF THE OLD TESTAMENT
SUPPLEMENT SERIES